Ethical Theory

The Problems of Normative and Critical Ethics

PRENTICE-HALL PHILOSOPHY SERIES
Arthur E. Murphy, Ph.D., Editor

ETHICAL THEORY

The Problems of Normative and Critical Ethics

RICHARD B. BRANDT

Professor of Philosophy
Swarthmore College

1959 | Prentice-Hall, Inc.   *Englewood Cliffs, N.J.*

PRINTED IN THE UNITED STATES OF AMERICA

29040

Preface

It is often supposed that the problems about the conduct and values that have occupied philosophers since the time of Socrates are of relatively minor importance for, or interest to, thoughtful laymen and students. This supposition, however, is profoundly mistaken. A great deal of practical decision making of the highest importance suffers from failure to make distinctions, or to embody clear and consistent policy, precisely on account of neglect of philosophical theory. Moreover, practically everyone has some thoughts about the problems that philosophers have debated, and is eager to learn about reasoning which can show that some particular theory of these matters is the most rational one. The study of ethical theory can clarify practical decisions in an important way, and can be an illuminating and liberating experience.

The problems of ethical theory are unfortunately not simple. The student who wishes to know where philosophical theory has really brought us must master a network of reasoning of some complexity. The aim of the present book has been to make this task possible, without avoiding or oversimplifying any serious problem, by a simple statement of the problems and theories.

There is more material in this book than can well be discussed in one semester's course. Some chapters can be omitted without serious effect on the understanding of later topics. For instance, Chapter 3 (except for the first part) and Chapter 4 are nonessential to a grasp of the rest. Furthermore, most students will be able to absorb the gist of Chapters 5 and 6 without much, or any, classroom discussion.

My experience has been that an exceedingly important part of a student's philosophical education comes from writing papers in which he is required to state, tentatively, his own reasoned view on important issues. For this reason I have included rather full lists of the literature which I think likely to be the most helpful for such projects, with the emphasis on original papers where the student will find serious reasoning of first-rate quality.

ACKNOWLEDGMENTS

A great many persons have had a share in the preparation of this book. I am much in their debt, and it is a pleasure at least to acknowledge by name those whose help has meant most. None of them, however, has seen the present book in its final form. If they had seen it, they doubtless would have raised more questions, ones that I might have perversely chosen to ignore, as I have ignored some of their actual queries. It is certain, however, that the finished product is a great deal more satisfactory than it would have been without their assistance.

My greatest debts are to William K. Frankena, of the University of Michigan, and to my colleague at Swarthmore College, Monroe C. Beardsley. Professor Frankena must have spent very many hours during the summer of 1958, reading the manuscript in its penultimate form. He examined it with most generous care and characteristic penetration, and provided innumerable critical comments and suggestions. Professor Beardsley read the manuscript not just once, but twice, at different stages. The reader should be especially grateful to him for simplifications in terminology and organization which have made the book substantially clearer without loss in content. Moreover, his commentaries, produced soon after each chapter was ready, were a source both of encouragement and of sustained critical re-examination.

Elizabeth Lane Beardsley, of Lincoln University, also read most of the manuscript, at an early stage, and joined with Monroe Beardsley in valuable critical comment and suggestion.

Several colleagues on the Swarthmore College faculty assisted me with individual chapters. S. E. Asch, William C. H. Prentice, and Henry Gleitman, all of the Department of Psychology, read and criticized all or part of the chapter on psychology. Indeed, Professor Asch examined it at several stages. Moreover, he, and on other occasions Peter Madison, collaborated with me in an interdepartmental seminar on values, from which the present volume has profited. Joseph W. Conard and William H. Brown, of the Department of Economics, gave me the benefit of their views about the reasoning in the chapter on distributive justice. J. Roland Pennock, of the Department of Political Science, commented learnedly on the chapter concerning human rights. William Hordern, a former colleague now on the faculty of the Garrett Bible Institute, challenged the cogency of my argument about the relation of theology and ethics, I hope to our mutual benefit. Several chapters have been subjected to the fire of departmental colloquia, where I have benefited from the suggestions of Jerome Shaffer, Michael Scriven, John M. Moore, P. L. Urban, and Gilmore Stott (who gave me a full-dress critical commentary on my pages about Immanuel Kant).

Patrick Suppes, of Stanford University, has given me expert advice on the parts of Chapters 12 and 13 which deal with problems of the comparison and measurement of values. Charles W. Hendel, of Yale University, made helpful comments on my discussions of Kant and human rights. Francis V. Raab, of the University of Minnesota, made useful suggestions about the content of the final three chapters—an area in which he is a specialist. Wilfrid S. Sellars, also of the University of Minnesota, has read and discussed with me both Chapter 14 and Chapter 15. These talks with him have helped me substantially in getting a clearer view of some difficult problems in this territory. Parts of Chapters 10 and 11 have been read to professional audiences, and I have had the benefit of numerous reactions to them. Of these I should single out the criticisms of Warner Wick, of the University of Chicago, and of my former colleague, Roderick Firth, now of Harvard University, who for many years has been a most constant source of ideas, criticism, and encouragement, in my thinking about the problems of ethical theory. Arthur E. Murphy, of the University of Texas, the editor of the Prentice-Hall series, has given me wise advice about several chapters of the book.

Two of my former students also deserve special mention: A. D. M. Speers, now a lawyer practising in Philadelphia, and John Brumbaugh, professor at the University of Maryland Law School. Both of them did yeoman service in calling my attention to important legal material, and in making my summary remarks about law, in Chapter 19, substantially more satisfactory to professionals in the legal field than they otherwise would have been. I wish it were possible to mention by name the many students at Swarthmore College, and graduate students at Princeton University whom I taught in 1956–57 and 1957–58, to whom I am indebted for their insistence on clarity and solid reasoning, their ingenious counterexamples, and their support of different ways of thinking.

Mrs. Karlene Madison never failed to produce, on time, a near perfect typescript. My daughter, Karen, in order to give me summer assistance where no professional typists were available, mastered the typewriter, and spent a large portion of her waking hours during an entire summer typing, when there were much better things for a young lady to do. She has also proved herself an efficient and meticulous proofreader. Finally, my wife Betty prepared the figures in the book, helped with a major portion of the proofs, relieved me of the most arduous part of the chore of preparing an index, has been an unfailing source of encouragement, and, like both my daughter and son Richard Jr., has borne my preoccupation with thinking and writing with patience and good humor.

In a book of this sort it would be improper to attempt to acknowledge the intellectual ancestry of all the ideas; and in any case I simply do not know, very often, who was the originator of a certain idea or argument. As far as I am aware, however, all articles to which I am indebted are listed among the readings at the end of the chapters. It is a fair, although not necessarily correct, assumption that my thinking has been influenced by these wherever my thought duplicates reasoning already expressed in them.

Swarthmore College   RICHARD B. BRANDT

Table of Contents

Chapter Ten

Chapter Eleven

Chapter Twelve

Chapter Thirteen

Chapter Fourteen

Chapter Twenty

Ethical Theory

The Problems of Normative and Critical Ethics

1

Ethical Theory: Its
Nature and Purpose

What is ethical theory about? Someone might propose as an answer: "Everybody knows what an ethical problem is; ethical theory must be about the solutions to such problems." Or again, someone might say: "Everybody knows what ethical opinions are; ethical theory must be about determining which ethical opinions are true."

These proposals are a good start, but do we really know precisely what an "ethical problem" is? Newspaper columns under this or a similar title are generally devoted to advice about proper behavior for young couples; however, this is not the only ethical problem. To be sure, there is agreement that some things involve ethical problems. For instance, it would be agreed that it is an ethical problem whether White children and Negro children should be taught in the same schoolroom—people would distinguish this problem from the legal problem of whether it is contrary to the Constitution of the United States for this not to be done. But in other matters there would be disagreement about whether the problem is ethical. "What is the proper wage for teachers?" and "Ought the automobile manufacturers to receive a smaller profit on their investment?" are regarded as ethical questions by many persons, but simply as economic questions, or as issues for bargaining, by others.

Similarly, there is agreement that certain opinions are "ethical opinions"; but there is a borderline class of opinions about which people are in disagreement as to whether they are properly classified as "ethical."

Nevertheless, something very like these proposals seems to be the best way, at least initially, of defining the content or concern of ethical theory. We shall begin with the concept of an "ethical statement"—roughly, the verbal expression of an ethical opinion. We shall then define "ethical

1

theory" roughly as a body of reflection answering, or intended to answer, certain questions about ethical statements.

1. WHAT IS AN ETHICAL STATEMENT?

There are various statements that we rather incline, if the matter is put to us, to classify as "ethical statements." For instance, it is natural to say it is an "ethical statement" if we say we feel an obligation to attend a lecture given by a friend. Or, if the proctor in a dormitory states that it is his duty to report to the deans that a certain student was grievously under the influence of alcohol last night. Or, if an editorial in a newspaper, commenting on a railroad accident, says that the engineer of the train was legally culpable but not morally so. Or, if we say that it was inexcusable and reprehensible for Professor Jones to have stood up after the lecture last night and declared that the speaker didn't know what he was talking about. All these statements, and any statements with *the same or similar predicates*, are ethical statements.

There are some further statements that most people would not readily call "ethical" (but perhaps, "value judgments") which it is convenient for our purpose to classify under this title, since they are closely connected with statements like the foregoing ones and present the same problems—for instance, statements like "It is a good thing to have a family," or "It is undesirable to work in the sun on a hot day."[1]

These examples, however, do not give us a precise rule for deciding whether a given statement is to be classified as "ethical." In order to have such a rule, we need a definition of the term "ethical" in the phrase "ethical statement." We shall now propose such a definition.

First, we shall call a statement an "ethical" one if it contains one of the following phrases used in the ordinary English sense (or any other phrase synonymous with one of them): "is a desirable thing that"; "is morally obligatory"; "is one's moral duty"; "is reprehensible"; "is morally admirable" (or "is morally praiseworthy"). Of course, a statement is an ethical statement if it *denies* that something is desirable, morally obligatory, and so on.

Second, we must broaden our specification so that statements will qualify as "ethical" even when they do not contain one of the phrases above or synonyms of them. So we shall say that a statement is ethical if it implies, entails, or contradicts any statement containing one of the phrases we have listed. (It is not necessary for the statement to be in English. We can per-

---

[1] We can mark a distinction between these two types of statement by calling the former ones "moral" statements. Such a distinction would correspond with the fact that we are inclined to say that statements of the first group express our "moral convictions"; whereas we should hardly say this of statements of the second group. However, we shall not have much occasion to make use of this distinction.

fectly well contradict an English statement by a remark in German.)[2]
There is one exception to this. We shall not call a statement ethical merely
because it contradicts a statement containing "is reprehensible" or "is
morally admirable" (or entails "is *not* reprehensible" or " is *not* morally
admirable"), but only if it implies or entails such a statement. The reader
need not be concerned about this exception; it is introduced only to exclude some sentences that the reader would never think of classifying as
ethical.[3]

Let us assume, now, that we have a reasonably clear definition, or rule
for the use, of "ethical statement." It is convenient to have at our disposal
another expression, "ethical word" or "ethical term" or "ethical predicate"—
all these phrases being used synonymously. What do we mean by these?
Let us take the words "desirable," "reprehensible," and the other expressions in our original listing. We shall call these "ethical terms." We shall
do the same for any word or expression that is crucial in making a statement in which it occurs an ethical statement. So, words like "right" and
"wrong," in many of their uses at least, will qualify as ethical terms.

So much, then, for the definitions of "ethical statement" and "ethical
term." We can define related expressions correspondingly. For example,
we can define an "ethical opinion" as an opinion that, if stated in words,
would be stated in an ethical statement.

One must admit that it is somewhat artificial, and perhaps in the end not
very satisfactory, to define "ethical statement" by referring to specific
English phrases. We would feel more nearly satisfied if we could pick out
some other property that the statements conveniently classified together as
"ethical" have in common, and define "ethical statement" by reference to
this common property. In fact, everyone who arrives at the end of his study
of ethics with a conviction that there is such a common property—and we
shall do so—can at that time formulate a less artificial definition than the
one above. But the definition we have suggested has a very important advantage: It enables us to mark out roughly the class of statements about
which we want to have a theory, without committing us in advance to

[2] There is, however, a puzzling problem concerning how we are to decide whether a
statement in one language implies or contradicts a statement in another language. For
instance, the Hopi language contains a term, *loloma,* which bilingual Hopi usually
translate by "good" or "pretty" or "nice." But one can well ask: How do we really
prove that to say something is "*loloma*" is to contradict a statement that it is "reprehensible"? We shall have to pass by this question here, although when we have come to
our final theory about the meaning of ethical statements, we shall be in a position to
answer it. Incidentally, in principle the question is the same as that of whether the
reader uses "is reprehensible" in the same way as Londoners do, or as his next-door
neighbor does.
[3] The reason for the exception is that, as we shall see in Chapter 18, "is reprehensible"
(and "is morally admirable") can be analyzed into two parts, so that it means "is P and
Q." It can therefore be contradicted by any statement that contradicts only *one* of
these parts. But we do not want to classify as "ethical" some statements that contradict
only one of these parts.

any particular theory about these statements. Most definitions do not have this advantage. For instance, suppose we defined an "ethical statement" as one which "cannot be true or false, or verified, but which expresses the feelings or attitudes of the speaker toward something." Then, we would have committed ourselves in advance to the view that ethical statements are neither true nor false, that what they do is express feelings—and whether or not this is the case is something that it seems unwise to decide by one's very definition of what is to count as an ethical statement. Our definition has the virtue of being neutral; it commits us neither to affirming that ethical statements may be true or false, nor to denying this. It is useful for getting the issues before us, but we need not end with it if we do not wish to.

It follows from our criterion for classifying a word in a concrete context as an "ethical term" that a good many words, on some occasions, can be counted as ethical terms. Among these are: "immoral," "wrong," "right," "shameful," "discreditable," "shocking," "excellent," "good," "bad," "wicked," "sinful," and "unjustifiable."

2. THE BRANCHES OF ETHICAL THEORY

We have suggested that ethical theory is a body of theory answering, or intended to answer, certain questions about ethical statements. But what questions?

There are two groups of questions, and, correspondingly, it has become customary in recent years to distinguish between two branches of ethical theory: *normative* ethical theory, and *critical* ethics or *metaethics*. Some philosophers write as if the two branches of ethics were entirely separate; but we shall see that, although the two branches are indeed in large part distinct, they also overlap.

Normative ethics. We may reasonably ask about ethical statements, "Which ethical statements are true or valid?" And "Why?" A person's answer to these questions may be called his "normative ethical theory." Everybody, of course, accepts some ethical statements, and will, when pressed, offer some kind of defense of them. To this degree, everybody has a "normative ethical theory" of a sort. A philosopher's normative ethical theory is thus essentially of the same nature as the opinions, on these points, of everyone.

Traditionally, ethical theory has, for obvious reasons, limited itself to a portion of the field of "normative ethics." In the first place, it has been concerned only with *general* ethical statements. It is an interesting question of normative ethics whether the British were justified in retaking the Suez Canal after it had been nationalized by Nasser. But this kind of question is not one with which ethical theory has been concerned—any more than physics is concerned with the size of the Rock of Gibraltar. What it is concerned with is general statements, such as whether *everything* of a certain kind (for example, every instance of pleasure) is worthwhile in itself.

However, ethical theory has not interested itself in all general ethical statements. It has not been concerned with statements like, "If one's wife asks one to go shopping, and it would be a pleasure for her to have one go, and if one has no other more pressing demands on one's time, then one ought to go shopping with her." Why has ethical theory not been concerned with such general statements? It is because it is not an important kind of statement, and one reason it is not important is that, if it is true, it is so because some more fundamental and abstract ethical statement is true—somewhat as Kepler's laws are true because Newton's laws and the principle of gravitational attraction are true, or as Euclid's theorems in geometry are implications of his basic axioms. What kind of ethical statement would be more "fundamental"? Consider this one: "A person ought to perform a certain act if and only if there is no other act that he could perform instead that would increase the net amount of happiness in the world more than this one would." This statement, which is a main thesis of the theory we shall call "hedonistic act-utilitarianism," is obviously more fundamental than the statement about taking one's wife shopping. What exactly is the difference? The answer is that the utilitarian thesis is more abstract, and therefore we may be able to show that the principle about shopping is implied by it; but obviously the utilitarian thesis is not implied by the more concrete principle. Ethical theory has been interested in finding a set of valid ethical principles, which is *complete* in the sense that all true ethical statements can be deduced from it (given an adequate stock of nonethical or factual premises), and which is also as *economical* as possible, in distinct concepts and principles. In other words, roughly what the philosopher is looking for is a set of general principles that have roughly the relation to the totality of valid ethical statements that Euclid's axioms and postulates have (or were intended to have) to his theorems.[4]

It is conjectural—we shall be able to decide later—whether a complete system of basic principles of ethics would necessarily be so complex as to defy formulation. If so, then we must be content with ascertaining important parts of it, samples of fundamental valid principles. Some philosophers have thought it unnecessary even to think of ethical statements as forming a geometry-like system at all; it is not required, for the solution of particular practical problems, to think of any such system—what is needed is simply sound "judgment" or "intuition." But the view of these philosophers is not well taken; we shall see later that clarity and certainty about concrete everyday matters can come only when we develop a sys-

---

[4] There is one difference. A geometrical system like Euclid's does not require any statements not contained among the axioms and postulates, in order to derive theorems. But ethics does. For instance, "Senator Smith ought to resign from the Senate" is an ethical statement that follows from the cited principle of utilitarianism, taken with the nonethical statement, "Senator Smith could increase the net amount of happiness most by resigning."

tem of basic principles. Normative ethics is like a ship without a compass if the ideal of a complete but economical set of general principles is given up or forgotten.

It may be helpful to mention a few other principles that at one time or another have been advocated as true basic principles in ethics: "An experience is desirable in itself if and only if it is pleasant"; "A person's act is reprehensible only if it was not done under coercion"; "If a person has promised to do something, he is thereby placed under a strong obligation to do it."

Normative ethical theory, however, has traditionally not been concerned only with basic ethical principles, or the axioms of ethics, for there are many nonbasic, less abstract ethical principles that it is highly important to assess. For instance: "There is an absolute right to freedom of speech." "Democracy is the best system of government." "The rulers in a democratic state have a moral right to the obedience of the citizens, which the rulers in a nondemocratic state have not." "The government has a right to punish citizens for disobedience of law." "Large incomes are justified." "In case of an accident, the responsible party should bear the expense." These issues are of the highest practical importance, and moral philosophers traditionally have been deeply concerned with them. We might call this branch of normative ethics the "criticism and justification of the major institutions of society" or the "examination of the ethical foundations" of these institutions.

It may appear that the answering of these questions is merely a process of deduction: one of starting with the fundamental valid principles of ethics, and, in view of true factual premises, deriving some theorems. If it is, then perhaps answering them is more properly the job of lawyers, psychologists, sociologists, and other specialists, rather than philosophers, since the specialists know the factual propositions we must know to apply the general principles accurately, and philosophers do not. Perhaps philosophers should confine themselves to discussing the fundamental axioms. Actually things are not as simple as this, however. For one thing, we cannot get a well-substantiated set of basic general ethical principles without looking into these more concrete problems, for we do not have sound reasons for adopting a proposed basic ethical principle until we have seen what it implies for these concrete questions. For instance, a principle of economic reward (say, the principle that one's rewards should correspond with the value of the services one has performed) may look very plausible until we see the difficulties of extracting definite implications for particular situations, or see how similar are the implications it does have to the implications of some other principles (like the principle of utilitarianism mentioned above). Thus, the moralist who wishes to discover the basic valid principles of ethics will find that the examination of these more concrete questions—the assessment of institutions—is a very rewarding enterprise.

Part of a person's normative ethics, we have said, is the *reasoning* or *defense* he gives of his ethical principles or statements. Obviously, just as a principle in physics must be supported by experimental evidence or otherwise, so the assertion of ethical principles must be supported. Providing this support is a part of normative ethics. We cannot discuss, at present, what kind of support this will be. Moreover, the general theory about how ethical principles are properly supported is a part of metaethics, not of normative ethics. However, it should be stressed that unsupported ethical statements are no better than unsupported physical theories. As a part of one's normative ethics, one will do *something* to support one's ethical assertions: perhaps deduce a given statement from more general and already well-supported principles, in some cases; perhaps something entirely different in other cases. To have a nomative ethics is to be prepared to do something—and the more forceful and systematic the defense one is prepared to give, the more developed his normative ethics.

Normative ethics, then, as a philosophical study, is an inquiry aiming to state and defend as valid or true a complete and economic set of general ethical principles, and also some less general principles that are important for what we may call "providing the ethical foundation" of the more important human institutions.

Critical ethics or metaethics. We have said that the aim of normative ethics is not only the formulation of valid ethical principles, whether very abstract and general or relatively concrete, but also a defense or justification of accepting these principles. But what kind of reasoning or evidence constitutes a valid "defense" or "justification" of ethical principles, and how can we show that some particular kind of reasoning is a valid defense or justification? Critical ethics or metaethics is mostly concerned with these questions, although it is also concerned with a closely related question: that of the *meaning* of ethical terms or predicates or statements. Metaethics thus has approximately the relation to normative ethics that the philosophy of science or epistemology or metascience has to science.

One might inquire whether there is any special problem here at all. Do not logicians discuss both inductive and deductive logic, and offer justifications for the use of these kinds of reasoning in science? Is there any reason for a special examination of the methods of justifying ethical statements?[5] Of course there isn't, if we can view the statements of ethics as essentially similar, in their logic, in their relation to their evidence, to the statements of logic (or mathematics) or of empirical science. But can we? It is not very plausible to say so. For instance, when two scientists disagree about the truth of some principle in science, they can often resolve their disagreement by devising a way to put the matter to experimental test. But

[5] It is an interesting but disturbing possibility that ethical statements may have to appear in the justification of the use of deductive or inductive logic. If so, there is an amusing problem, if critical ethics or metaethics makes use of inductive or deductive logic. This puzzle is worth the reader's reflection.

suppose two people are in disagreement about whether happiness—or, say, self-discipline—is the only thing desirable in itself. Can they, at least in theory, resolve their disagreement by some experimental test? Not very easily, if at all. Many people, on account of this sort of consideration, have thought that the role that empirical evidence has to play in ethics is quite different from that which it plays in empirical science; hence, they have concluded that it is fundamentally misleading to model ethical methodology after that of empirical science. If so, then there *is* a problem of how statements of ethics are to be justified, which is distinct from the problem of how the statements of empirical science are to be justified; and critical ethics or metaethics would be, in part, the theory of this special kind of justification of ethical statements.[6]

Let us assume for the present that this conclusion is correct, and hence that there is a special problem about the justification of the methods of normative ethics. *Critical ethics*, or *metaethics*, then, will serve as the name of a systematic inquiry, a major aim of which is to formulate precisely the correct method for justifying normative statements or opinions, and to show that this method is the correct method—to justify the method of justifying normative statements. We shall, however, exclude the theory of inductive and deductive logic from the scope of metaethics, however much we may make use of it.

We have suggested that metaethics is also concerned with the *meaning* of ethical terms or statements, and we have said that this question is closely related to the problem of justification of ethical statements. How is this?

The problem of how to justify a statement is very closely linked with what the statement means, or what it is doing or intended to do. Take, for instance: "He is angry." If what the speaker *means* by this statement is "He is livid and shouting and on the point of striking the person he is talking to," then the problem of justifying belief in the statement is very different from what it is if what he means is "He is experiencing an internal and, to us, unobservable sensation of a burning sort." Or again, suppose we receive an announcement from the president of our college to the effect that on a certain day "the faculty will appear on the platform in academic dress." Now, the president's statement may be merely a prediction; more likely it is a directive. How his statement will be justified depends, clearly, on which it is. If it is a prediction, we test its justification by looking to his

---

[6] The foregoing "proof" that the role of observation and experiment is essentially different in ethics from what it is in science is actually less effective than it at first appears. Many disagreements in science cannot be resolved by experiment (for example, conflicting accounts of the implications of the Heisenberg principle); whereas many disputes in ethics can be settled by experiment, at least in principle (for example, whether parents should administer corporal punishment for disobedience, a matter on which findings about long-range results of different methods of child-rearing may well be conclusive). Nevertheless, the writer believes the conclusion is correct, and the really good reasons for this conclusion—too complex for introduction at this stage—will make their appearance later.

evidence, as we should for a statement in an empirical science; but if it is a directive, we shall test it by looking to his reasons, his purposes—to acceptable ethical principles.

How it is proper to go about justifying ethical statements, then, depends on the kind of statements they are. Are they descriptions? predictions? explanations like those of atomic theory? directives? exclamations? or what? Many have held that ethical statements are not at all like the statements of science. Some hold that what ethical statements do, in large part, is give vent to the emotions of the speaker—like "Alas!" Others have held that they are tools for persuading people, rather subtle forms of a rap on the knuckles.

Writers who have tried to justify the methods of empirical science have asked themselves questions like: What is the job of these statements? What is the job of empirical science? And some of them have tried to justify the methods of science by proving that the job of empirical science could not possibly be done except by use of these methods. A similar argument can be used in ethics. (Of course, one may not be able to show that ethics has any particular "job," and then this argument does not work!)

The foregoing, then, illustrates why the problem of justifying and the problem of analyzing the meaning and function of ethical statements or language are so closely related. The first of these two is the primary and the more important; but it cannot be resolved without a theory about the second, which has interest in its own right. We shall use the terms "critical ethics" and "metaethics" indifferently, to refer to the inquiry aimed at solving either the whole of both or either of these problems, or any part of them.

These terms may be and often are used more broadly still, for there are certain tasks auxiliary to the main concern of ethical theory (normative or critical) as defined. "Critical ethics" may be extended to these tasks, or the results of performing them. For instance, there are certain words, not themselves ethical terms, frequently used in important types of ethical statements. For example: "What makes an act immoral is not its *consequences* but the *motives* of the agent." "A person is to blame for an act only if he *chose* to do it *freely*, or was acting *deliberately*." "*Happiness* is the only thing worthwhile in itself." People seldom trouble to define the italicized nonethical words. But, as soon as we begin a careful consideration of which ethical statements are acceptable, it is obvious that we need a fairly precise concept of what we are going to mean by these terms. Some of these statements may appeal to us only so long as the crucial terms remain vague. In view of this, preparing careful definitions of them is a necessary preliminary to a valid theory of normative ethics. Providing such definitions is often considered a part of critical ethics. We shall not attempt to describe others of the secondary tasks of critical ethics.

Obviously, it is necessary to answer the main questions of critical ethics before we have firm ground for constructing a system of normative ethics. Therefore, in this volume, critical ethics will come first, and will occupy the following ten chapters, except for two chapters in which we shall digress to summarize anthropological and psychological facts and theory relevant to our concerns. We shall consider the less plausible theories first. Only after we have come to some tentative conclusions about the main problems of metaethics shall we turn to normative ethics, and shall consider what general statements can validly be made about what is worthwhile or desirable for itself, about what our obligations are, about what kinds of action are reprehensible or admirable, about what things there are to which all human beings, as such, have rights. We shall then examine two more concrete problems in more detail: the ethical foundations of systems of distribution of economic goods, and the ethical foundations of the principles and practice of criminal justice. Finally, we shall consider whether, as some philosophers think, all or some of our tentative normative conclusions are overturned if human conduct is throughout determined by causal laws.

3. THE USE OF ETHICAL THEORY

Since everybody has to act and to decide, it may seem a very odd question to ask what is the use of the theory of justified policies of action or decision. Moreover, many if not most persons who have studied the problems of ethical theory are likely to be impatient with the question for a further reason. As in most branches of theory, once a person gets immersed in the problems, he wants to know the solutions for them, just for their own sake. To such a person, the question of utility is about as sensible as asking a chess enthusiast what is the use of knowing the solution to a certain chess problem, or asking a mountain climber what is the point of scaling Everest. So, in ethical theory as in all the branches of philosophy, we start by thinking it must be very simple to get the fundamental matters straightened out, but as we go on, puzzles keep developing in a tantalizing way. When they do, we have got to have the answers to them—and questions of utility seem inane and beside the point.

Nevertheless, it is not a waste of time to consider briefly some points at which the study of ethical theory is important; such a consideration may clarify our thinking in several directions.

Anyone who wishes to deny the utility of ethical theory is apt to do two things: to point out with derision that philosophers are still debating some questions (for example, whether pleasure is the only thing worthwhile) that agitated the early Greeks, with the implication that ethical theory has got nowhere; and to point out the lack of precision in some of the results, especially of normative ethics, which compare unfavorably, say, with the propositions of mechanics.

To the first of these claims, the correct reply is simply that the critic is mistaken about his facts. It is true that there are some central and difficult issues that the Greeks debated, and that are still debated today. But vast strides have been made, not entirely incomparable with advances in mathematics or even in the natural sciences, since the Greeks. If anyone doubts this, he should compare one of the major works of the present century (C. L. Stevenson's *Ethics and Language* or W. D. Ross' *Foundations of Ethics*) with Diogenes Laertius' description of the early philosophies of ethics, or even with that greatest single achievement in ethical theory, Aristotle's *Nicomachaean Ethics*. The gain in sophistication, in the elimination of confusions, in the distinguishing of separate issues, in the formulation of problems, is simply immense.

To the second of the critic's points, the best answer is to concede that the results of normative ethics are less precise than those of mechanics, but to quote from Aristotle:

> Our discussion will be adequate if it has as much clearness as the subject matter admits of, for precision is not to be sought for alike in all discussions, any more than in all the products of the crafts. Now fine and just actions, which political science investigates, admit of much variety and fluctuation of opinion, so that they may be thought to exist only by convention, and not by nature. And goods also give rise to similar fluctuation because they bring harm to many people; for before now men have been undone by reason of their wealth, and others by reason of their courage. We must be content, then, in speaking of such subjects and with such premises to indicate the truth roughly and in outline, and in speaking about things which are only for the most part true and with premises of the same kind to reach conclusions that are no better . . . for it is the mark of an educated man to look for precision in each class of things just so far as the nature of the subject admits. . . ."[7]

Ethical theory does not, for instance, use differential equations to make accurate predictions, nor does it have instruments that enable it to compare two courses of action, with respect to worth, down to three decimal places of some well-defined scale. But it does not follow that it is unable to give reliable answers to the important questions.

The moralist should concede to critics (we shall argue the point later) that the logical structure of *normative* ethics is different from that of empirical science. However, we should not infer that the results of normative ethics are unreliable relative to the purpose for which they are needed; they may not be as reliable as those of physics, but it would be extreme to say that they are less reliable than the theories of social psychology.

The methods of *critical* ethics are closer to those of empirical science, and at some points it is obvious there is no difference at all. Some aspects of critical ethics are mere descriptions of fact, and, thus, not different in principle from the descriptive aspects of empirical science. For instance,

[7] *Nicomachaean Ethics*, trans. by W. D. Ross (Oxford: Clarendon Press, 1925), Bk. I, chap. 3, p. 1094b. By permission.

descriptions of what people intend to ask (if anything) when they raise ethical questions are descriptions of fact, albeit of a subtle and elusive nature. This is also true for descriptions of what ethical deliberation ordinarily is.

Let us now consider why ethical theory is important for science and behavior. We begin with science. Various departments of the social sciences necessarily draw on ethical theory; they must build their theories on foundations that are the concern of the ethical theorist. This is perhaps obvious in the case of a branch of political science like political theory, or of works on economics that regard the task of economic theory as one of making valid proposals about the means to maximize welfare; these disciplines are essentially specialized continuations of that branch of normative ethics that consists of the critique and justification of institutions. But some branches of the more experimental social sciences also do, or should, draw on the concepts and distinctions that metaethics aims to criticize and clarify, particularly those parts of anthropology, sociology, and psychology that are concerned with values and attitudes and conscience (the "superego"). Some social scientists do make use of the results of critical ethics, but others do not, and perhaps the importance of metaethics for these branches of science is most easily made clear by mentioning some confusions of social scientists today that are a result of ignorance of ethical theory. (1) Some scientists have no criterion—at least, no satisfactory one—for distinguishing between ethical beliefs or judgments and nonethical ones. Hence, in their descriptive work they mix the two together indiscriminately, missing many opportunities for observations of theoretical importance. (2) Some social scientists do not distinguish the question of whether any ethical statements can be justified as correct for everybody, from the question of whether in fact now, as opinions stand (critized or uncriticized, informed or uninformed), people hold different views about ethical matters. They then proceed, from observations of variant ethical opinions among different peoples, to a wholly unjustified inference about the impossibility of making objective assessments as to whether progress has occurred or as to the comparative merits of different institutions and customs. Hence, they conclude with a dubious theory about the logical structure of the social sciences. (3) Some social scientists ignore the difference between beliefs about the good or desirable and beliefs about duty and obligation (and between corresponding attitudes), and thereby overlook the possibility that quite different accounts of the genesis of the two may be in order. And so on. Fortunately, in the past few years many of the leading figures in the various social sciences have come to recognize the necessity of familiarizing themselves with the main points of metaethical theory.

Is ethical theory also of serious practical importance, beyond what assistance it can offer in the solution of scientific and philosophical problems? It has often been called a "practical" science, but is it? The answer is

clearly affirmative. If the conclusions of normative ethics about the ultimately worthwhile, about duties and rights, and about the critique of institutions are well established, then ethical theory is of the highest practical
importance. Surely, if there is such a thing as a *best* kind of life, it is to our
advantage to know what it is. If, for instance, complete devotion to attaining business success and accumulating money can be shown not to be the
best way to live, we shall presumably want to know. Surely there is no
more sense in following childhood patterns on such matters than in the
case of scientific matters—provided, of course, that it can be shown that
childhood patterns are indefensible. Again, most people want to fulfill their
real obligations, and surely there is some point in seeing what these are, and
in seeing how much weight there is in the reasoning of those who have
held that our only obligation is to our own welfare or even pleasure. Moreover, most people are eager to secure for all persons whatever it is their
right to have; so it is of obvious importance to find out what can seriously
be claimed to be universal human rights. Again, we are all interested in having institutions that are just, and that serve the public welfare; we shall
hardly question, then, the worth of having information about which institutions have these qualities, and which ones do not, in certain respects.

Moreover, even if ethical theory is not in a position to give definite
answers to all ethical questions—and it never will be—there is much to be
learned from its disentangling of different but closely related and easily
confused questions. For instance, the individual who is considering whether
he should become a conscientious objector to military service will, if he
studies ethical theory, come to distinguish the following different questions (and perhaps further ones): (*a*) whether war is desirable as a means
of settling international disputes; (*b*) whether it is ever justifiable for a
nation to be the aggressor in a war, or to defend itself if attacked; (*c*)
whether it is right for a citizen to participate if his country unjustifiably is
engaged in a war; (*d*) whether it is right for an individual to refuse to
participate "as an example," even if he thinks his country justified in fighting a particular war; (*e*) whether an individual is morally to blame for refusing to do his share if he thinks his duty is to refuse; (*f*) what effect an
individual's motives have on the moral assessment of what he does in such a
situation. (C. D. Broad's brief *War Thoughts in Peace Time* and his essay
on this topic in his *Ethics and the History of Philosophy* are models of the
application of the results of ethical theory to a practical problem.) At the
very least, it is this kind of clarification of issues that we can expect from a
study of ethical theory.

Of course, a great deal of ethical theory is controversial, and study of
some parts of it raises more questions than it answers. Even so, there is
some good to be gained in being puzzled about things that are really complicated and debatable. In any case, it is worthwhile knowing where the

reflections of persons like Plato, Aristotle, Aquinas, Hume, Kant, and Russell have taken them, in the area of ethics.

There are some limitations to normative ethics. In practice, it can hardly be expected to ascertain and list *all* of even the basic ethical principles. Furthermore, it can hardly be expected to provide a list of basic ethical principles that will be acceptable to all persons; there is a sense in which, if a person wants a set of basic principles that suit his condition, he must think through the problems of ethics for himself. Furthermore, although ethical theory can be expected to consider some problems, or institutions, of major social importance thoroughly, it can hardly be expected to treat them all. As a result of these limitations, perhaps the most important thing we have to gain from the tradition of ethical theory is a *model* for an ethical system—what are the criteria for a tenable system of ethical beliefs. Then we must criticize our own system of ethical principles, for ourselves. Each individual must think out where *he* stands on the major issues of living, in the light of the model of the logical framework of a tenable system of principles. Most of us will probably not want more than this.

There is enrichment of personal insight to be gained from the study of normative ethics. Familiarity with the ethical tradition should make us see more features or aspects of problems of choice, aspects easy to overlook. Merely the explicit formulation of principles about obligations should make us more sensitive to those obligations. It should make us less liable to be deceived by selfish ethical reasoning in ourselves or others. It should make us more perceptive in our moral assessment of ourselves and our motivation.

People have often asked whether familiarity with ethical theory will make better men. Some moralists have thought that acceptance of false ethical theories could have a most deleterious effect; even recently it has been used as an argument for rejecting logical empiricism in ethics, that acceptance of its doctrines would undermine morality. There is some validity to this, especially in the case of normative ethics. Such astute persons as Socrates and Plato thought that if men only had knowledge of the good they would act accordingly, since everyone naturally seeks what he thinks is his own true good; and it is obviously true that a person is more likely to act rightly if he has correct ethical beliefs than if he has mistaken ones. However, the fact that a person knows clearly what he ought to do is no guarantee that he will do it; there are many other relevant facts besides knowledge, such as character—and this is, to a considerable extent, the result of early childhood training and innate dispositions. Critical ethics, of course, is not as closely related to conduct, and it is difficult to show that any particular normative conclusion is implied by some of the plausible theories in critical ethics. Perhaps the discovery that there is so much controversy in critical ethics may weaken someone's moral convictions. If so, the solution seems to be, not a cessation of thought about such matters, but more intensive thought, so as to arrive finally at the answers.

FURTHER READINGS

P. H. Nowell-Smith, *Ethics* (Baltimore: Penguin Books, 1954), chap. 1.
A. I. Melden, *Ethical Theories* (Englewood Cliffs, N.J.: Prentice-Hall, Inc., 1955), pp. 1–19.
E. F. Carritt, *Ethical and Political Thinking* (Oxford: Clarendon Press, 1947), chap. 1.
C. D. Broad, "Some of the Main Problems of Ethics," reprinted in H. Feigl and W. Sellars (eds.), *Readings in Philosophical Analysis* (New York: Appleton-Century-Crofts, Inc., 1949), pp. 547–63. A survey of some important theoretical problems in the field of ethics.
L. Garvin, *A Modern Introduction to Ethics* (New York: Houghton Mifflin Company, 1953), chap. 1.
P. Wheelwright, *A Critical Introduction to Ethics* (New York: Odyssey Press, 1949), chap. 1.

2

Two Tests of Ethical Principles:
Consistency and Generality

The basic task of critical ethics or metaethics, we have seen, is twofold. First, it must discover and state the properties an ethical statement or belief, or a system of these, must have in order to be acceptable or valid or tenable. (To state such properties is in effect to state what are good or justified methods of reasoning in support of ethical statements.) Second, it must *justify* its conclusion about what these properties are (or about what proper methods of ethical reasoning are), in some way or other.

We begin with this task. To begin here seems to be making a start at a point very far removed indeed from the practical problems of decision and evaluation. However, there is a decisive reason for beginning with these problems: If we have not faced them, we have no standard for our assessment of ethical principles. How are we to know what to look for, to determine whether a particular ethical principle is valid, until we have thought through the question of when, in principle, an ethical statement is justified? Our foundation would surely be unsteady if we were to recommend an ethical principle for various reasons, without having understood why these reasons are sufficient for thinking a principle to be adequate, correct, or justified.

In this chapter, we shall argue that there are two important tests that ethical statements or principles must pass in order to be tenable: consistency and generality. These are not the only tests, but if a person's statements or beliefs fail them, they are open to objection and a revision must be made.

1. CONSISTENCY

Inconsistency in an ethical statement or principle, or in a group of them, is a fatal defect. If someone uncovers an inconsistency in our ethical views,

16

we feel he has made a mortal thrust; something must then be changed. A person's ethical conviction or convictions, then, must be consistent. Indeed, this is one point on which perhaps everyone in the history of ethical theory has agreed.

Nevertheless, a curious person might ask: *Why* should this be? Fortunately, the answer to this question can be simple: Insofar as a person's principle or principles are inconsistent, he *has* no principle (or conviction) at all.

In order to see that this is so, it is helpful to look at some parallel cases. Suppose someone made this statement: "I have just had my house painted. Every bit of it is both white and yellow." What description has this person given us of the color of his house? What *is* it like? Obviously he has told us nothing at all about the color. Or suppose someone gives us an order: "Both open and don't open the door!" What *is* he directing us to do? What could we do that would constitute obedience to his order? It is not possible to answer. Or suppose a father with ten children read them a lesson on table behavior as follows: "Every one of you is to eat heartily at every meal; but never help yourself first—always help yourself only after one of your brothers and sisters!" What are the poor children to do?

Inconsistent ethical statements are like these. They do not set forth any definite statement about what kind of thing or conduct is desirable or right. Such statements can serve no purpose. Something must be changed if there is to be before us some intelligible proposal about what is justifiably desired, condemned, and so on.

It will be agreed, then, we assume, that a person's ethical views must be consistent.

This demand, however, may seem not to take us very far. This "test" for ethical convictions, one may think, is valid but rather toothless. Surely, only fools have had inconsistent principles! But *is* the test so toothless? If we consider it, we can see that it has some important lessons for us.

Consider the Ten Commandments. One of them reads: "Remember the Sabbath day, to keep it holy. . . . In it thou shalt not do any work." Another reads: "Honour thy father and thy mother." These rules, which we assume may be taken as ethical statements (for example, "It is always wrong not to honour your father and mother."), are doubtless rather vague. There is one point, though, on which they are not vague: It seems that there is something we are *always* to do. This fact leads to difficulties. Suppose my father calls me on the phone on a Sunday morning, tells me that a storm has blown off a piece of his roof the previous evening, and invites me to come and help him repair it before there is another rain. I seem not to be "honouring" my father if I refuse; I am breaking the rule about the Sabbath if I comply. (At least there will be some type of case for which this will be true, if the rules are definite.) As the rules stand, they make contradictory statements about what I am to do, if honouring my father requires that I work on Sunday. In order to be consistent, the Ten Commandments need a commentary-supplement, giving instructions about which rules have priority in case of conflict.

A difficulty like this is inherent in *any* set of moral rules of the form, "Always do. . . ." Any such set requires revision. We have suggested that such a set may be saved from inconsistency by a supplement, giving directives about priority in case of conflict. (Of course, then, the original principles must be modified to something like "Always do . . . except when some other principle takes priority, as hereinafter specified.") However, there are other ways in which consistency may be maintained. For instance, instead of having principles of the form "Always do . . . !" we might have moral rules of this form: "There is always a *strong obligation* to do. . . ." Then the rules themselves will not specify which rule is to have priority in case of conflict, leaving this decision to individual judgment. In this case, one's set of moral rules does not give specific instructions for all cases; it offers only signposts, as it were. We shall return to this matter later. Evidently, however, the requirement of consistency is more important than we might at first suppose.

Our examples of inconsistency have illustrated a special type of case: general principles that have clashing implications for possible cases.[1] Another type of inconsistency, doubtless one that seldom occurs in practice and causes few difficulties, is the failure of particular statements to agree with a person's general ones (for example, "This lie happens to be all right" does not agree with "Lies are always wrong"). There is a further type of inconsistency, however, that we are less likely to notice. This is the failure of comparative statements to have the property of "transitivity." For instance, suppose one's daughter says: "Angel food cake with white frosting is better than yellow cake with chocolate frosting. And yellow cake with chocolate frosting is better than devil's-food cake with butterscotch frosting. And devil's-food cake with butterscotch frosting is better than angel's food cake with white frosting." One thing is clear about these statements: they will never give her a clear directive about which one of the three kinds of cake to pick, if she has to make a choice among all three. Whichever she picks, there is always another piece that she says is better. Her statements are properly classified as inconsistent.

Our conclusion, then, is that ethical statements, to be acceptable, must be consistent (both *self*-consistent and consistent with all other statements one accepts). Although we conclude, however, that this requirement has some importance, we must concede that it does not take us very far, for there are many different ways of being consistent. Perhaps the Devil is perfectly consistent, but all his ethical principles are incorrect. All we

---

[1] Strictly, there is inconsistency only if we admit that some situations engage *both* principles. Thus, "Do *A* in situation *B*" and "Do *C* (something incompatible with *A*) in situation *D*" are inconsistent only if we add, "Some situations are both *B* and *D*."

can say is: *in*consistent ethical convictions cannot be accepted—at least, not all of them as they stand. On the other hand, a consistent set is not necessarily valid either; consistency is not enough.

Incidentally, a person can avoid inconsistency by confining his ethical beliefs to noncomparative statements about individual cases, such as "This action is right" and "That action is wrong." We shall argue in a moment that to stop with statements of this sort and refuse to go on to espouse general principles is also unacceptable. But it is unacceptable on grounds other than that of the requirement of consistency.

2. GENERALITY

The second test (by itself, again, not a sufficient or complete test) we shall call the test of "generality." It is a test that applies *only* to particular ethical statements, but it applies to particular ethical statements with all kinds of predicates (for example, "desirable," "wrong," "obligatory," and so on).

It can be understood most easily by considering a line of reasoning we all tend to adopt when we are confronted with some particular ethical statement with which we do not agree. Roughly, the line of reasoning consists in a demand for general ethical principles to support the particular judgment. Let us take an example. Suppose someone says, "Mrs. K. oughtn't to be seeking a divorce." We are doubtful, and ask, "Why not?" The reply is apt to be: "The children are too young and need both a father and a mother." If we are both pertinacious and unimaginative, we shall go on to ask, "Why is that fact relevant?" To this the speaker will reply, if he hopes to silence us, "Because parents should make at least modest personal sacrifices if these are required for the basic welfare of the children." The speaker has now taken us to a *general* ethical statement. It is evident that this general statement, if one combines it with some factual statements about the ages of the children and the effects of a divorce, will lead by a formal argument to the particular statement, "Mrs. K. shouldn't seek a divorce."

By a "general" ethical statement, we mean two things. First, it is universal, in the sense that it is a statement about *every* case of a certain sort, or about *everybody*. Thus, in our case the general statement is about what *all* parents should do. Second, it makes no reference to individuals, but is concerned only with properties. In our example, there is no mention of Mrs. K. or any other person; the statement is about those who have a certain property, that of being parents. One way of putting this that will be familiar to students of logic is to say that general ethical statements may contain only variables and the names of abstract properties—meaning by an "abstract property" the kind of property that might be contained in a scientific law, and the meaning of whose name could be explained without referring to any particular persons or things. Thus, the following statement is *not* general: "Anyone who is the son of Queen Elizabeth should receive special police protection." But a very similar statement *is* general: "Anyone who is in the direct line of succession to the throne of an important country should receive special police protection."

Any particular ethical statement that is valid *can be supported by a valid general principle* in the foregoing sense of "general." (To be "supported" by a general principle means that the general principle, combined with true statements of fact, logically implies the particular ethical statement.) This fact permits us to have a "test" of generality for a particular ethical statement. The test of generality, however, is not quite to demand that a particular ethical statement be supported by a valid general principle. The test is rather simply that one must be prepared to specify a supporting general statement on which one is ready to rest the validity of the particular statement. One's particular statement fails the test of generality if one cannot specify one's supporting general principle at all. The "test of generality" then is this: A particular ethical judgment is valid only if it can be supported by a general principle (and of course the principle must be valid, but this is another matter).

It does not follow from this "test" that a particular ethical statement is invalid unless someone can actually cite, at the time, a general statement which supports it. This is far from true. Very often we are convinced—and rightly, as it turns out in the end—that a particular ethical judgment is valid but, if the corresponding general principle is demanded, we are nonplussed and unable to specify it. There can very well be a valid general principle that supports a particular ethical statement, even if we are not able to formulate the general principle. Thus, a person is not conclusively refuted if he fails to meet our demand for a general statement supporting his particular one. Nevertheless, his failure is a weakness in his case. We can notice that people, when they are seriously in doubt about a particular judgment, do try to formulate the general principles supporting it. Also, if a person simply refuses to try to formulate such a principle and shows no interest in doing so when his particular statement is sincerely questioned, we have good reason to doubt his sincerity.

Most philosophers—and presumably the reader—are prepared to agree that the test of generality is a legitimate test of particular ethical statements, and that a statement which fails this test cannot be accepted. Not quite all philosophers are convinced of this, however, and perhaps the reader will be uncomfortable without further discussion. We shall therefore explain the reasons for setting up this "test." Unfortunately, the reasons are not quite simple, and the reader who is already convinced may prefer to skip the following argument.

The justification of the test of generality. That the test of generality is a legitimate test follows from the truth of the next statement, which, after some explanations, we shall expect to be conceded. The statement is: "If something has an ethical property (is wrong, is desirable, and so on), then anything else exactly like it in all other respects must have the same ethical property." One phrase in this statement requires discussion: "exactly like in all other respects," since some persons may suggest that two things cannot be *exactly* alike in all respects without being the same thing. The phrase "exactly alike," however, is being used here in the sense that two things can be exactly alike even if they do not have the same space-time locations; and it is being so used that two things *are* exactly alike if they are the same in respect of what we have above called "abstract properties." Roughly, then, what the principle means is that if one act *A* is said to have an ethical property (for example, is wrong), and another act *B* is said not to have it, then it must be that *A* and *B* differ in respect of some abstract property. This principle, we may note, is an interesting one, and certainly is not true of *all* properties; for example, it is certainly not true that if my house is red and yours is like it in respect of all other abstract properties, then your house is also red!

This principle leads directly to the requirement of generality. If it is true that whenever something has an ethical property *P*, then anything with the same abstract properties will also have *P*, we can conclude that whenever any particular ethical statement is true (namely, when something has an ethical property *P*), some supporting general statement is true, of the form, "Anything that has the abstract properties *A* ... *N* [the abstract properties of the thing having *P*] will be *P*." One objection to this might possibly be raised: The abstract properties of an object may be infinite in number, and we should hardly want to count as an "ethical principle" any statement that had to list an infinitely long list of abstract properties. Such a statement could not be written down. However, since we seem to know that some factors of particular situations are ethically irrelevant (for instance, the color of one's hair is seldom relevant to whether one should tell a lie), we may perhaps be allowed the assumption that if something has *P*, then anything that has certain ones of its properties *A* ... *N* (where the number of these properties is manageably finite) will also have *P*. This is the principle from which the test of generality is derived.[2]

The skeptical reader, however, may protest: "*Why* must I concede that if something has an ethical property, then anything exactly like it in all

[2] In the two paragraphs above, the term "ethical property" occurs frequently. The argument, however, does not assume that an ethical property is like the properties talked of in science. "Has some ethical property *P*" is essentially just a convenient scheme for suggesting that we may pick any ethical predicate we like, and the argument will still hold. For instance, wherever "has some ethical property *P*" occurs, we can substitute throughout "is wrong." The argument does not turn on the assumption that ethical predicates designate properties in some senses to be discussed later.

other ethically relevant respects must have the same ethical property?" This query must now be faced. We put forward the following points for consideration.

1. One must ask oneself this: "If it is right for me to do A in B circumstances, could it be wrong for anyone else to do A in the *same* circumstances?" If one thinks he wants to answer this question in the affirmative, then let him propose an example. If he still inclines to answer in the affirmative for the example, we then suggest that he scrutinize the example, to make sure the circumstances are the same in all respects. We feel confident the reader will conclude by answering the question with "No." Such an answer certainly coincides with our tendency to think that whether something is right or wrong, good or bad, depends on the *kind* of thing it is.

2. The reader may feel strongly inclined to answer the question stated in (1) with "No," but he may be inhibited by noticing that there do not really seem to be any observations or evidence requiring that he answer it one way or the other. If this is the reader's situation, then the following possibility is worth consideration.

The answer may be negative because of the *meaning* of ethical words like "wrong." Let us look at some parallels. Consider the principle: "If a person is a bachelor, then he is unmarried." In order to be justified in affirming this principle, we do not need to examine bachelors and determine whether they are married. It is a consequence of the rules for the correct use of "bachelor" in English, that all bachelors are unmarried—for if a person is married, it is simply incorrect to call him a bachelor. Or consider the principle: "If it is one's duty not to do x, then one oughtn't to do x." Why is this statement not open to question? Again, we do not need to look at examples of things it is our duty to avoid, and examine whether they are things we ought not to do. It is a consequence of the rules for correct use of these terms in English, that one ought to do one's duty—for if one oughtn't to do something, it is just incorrect to say it is one's duty to do it.

The question for us now is whether, in the same way, the rules for the correct use of all ethical terms in English are such that it is incorrect to say that one thing is wrong but that another thing exactly like it in respect of all abstract nonethical properties can be right. Possibly part of what we commit ourselves to when we say "That is wrong," is that nothing exactly like it in respect of abstract nonethical properties is right. Possibly the same is true for the names of other ethical properties.

What can be said in favor of such a view? The very fact that we cannot conceive of circumstances in which we should be prepared to say that our act is right, although an exactly similar act done by another was wrong, is testimony in favor of this proposal. Furthermore, if someone really maintained the opposite and held that the very same act could be right for you and wrong for me, we should be rather puzzled, perhaps, about what he meant, and might be inclined to think he must be using "right" and "wrong" in some special sense, or else that there had been misunderstanding in some way. Again, if we learned that in some other language an act could be properly called "*P*" if done by me, but the very same act could properly be called "*not-P*" if done by someone else, we should feel rather sure that "*P*" was not synonymous with "wrong," indeed was not an ethical term at all.

Considerations like these have convinced many philosophers that the "grammar" of ethical terms is such that the answer to the question in (1) must be negative. Whether or not we are entirely convinced, the argument is a forceful one.[3]

3. Before declining to insist that the requirement of generality must be met by ethical statements, or before answering the question in (1) with an affirmative, one should consider whether one can really accept the consequences. Two very serious consequences in particular should be examined.

First, suppose a person were not committed to any general principle by a particular ethical statement, or suppose he were allowed to refer to particular persons in his principles. Moral discussions would be exceedingly difficult. A person might assert moral principles that made an exception in favor of himself. Moreover, one natural and important way of proceeding in an ethical discussion is to get a person to state his relevant principles, and then to show him that he cannot really accept his principles in view of their implications—a procedure that has the effect of discrediting his initial particular judgment, at least until more satisfactory principles are unearthed. But if we do not insist on the requirement of generality, a person could simply question the necessity of stating any principles. It is hard to see how, in consistency, we could object to a man framing moral principles making favorable exceptions for himself, or merely refusing to state principles at all, if we do not accept the requirement of generality. We must ask ourselves if we are prepared to accept this consequence. (We need not suggest that ethical debate would be wholly impossible for one who declined to accept this principle.)

There is a second unpleasant consequence. It is plausible to say that part of what we are doing when we say an action is right (and similarly, for other ethical terms) is claiming or implying that a favorable attitude to it can be justified—that a favorable attitude toward it, a commendation of it, on the part of thoughtful persons will stand up when they know the relevant facts. We are urging that the act can stand a public airing, and that it will come through approved.

Now, we happen to know that if something can succeed in gaining the approval of reflective people, then anything exactly like it will also succeed

[3] Yet, possibly the evidence is accounted for just by the supposition that we do very strongly believe that the answer to the question in (1) is negative.

in gaining their approval. People's attitudes are such that if a certain argument or consideration will justify one thing to them, the same will work for a general policy—and hence for all similar cases. Likewise, an argument or consideration adduced to justify something will, in general, prove convincing only if it is devoid of essential reference to the personal or particular. People, in general, will not be moved by such considerations as "But *my* son was the one involved!" They will be moved only by a consideration that they might tend to use themselves, or that would move them if anybody used it. In particular, they will not be moved by obvious attempts to make an exception of oneself, or one's relatives and friends. In general, then, the considerations that will justify something to thoughtful people will be "abstract properties," properties devoid of reference to the particular.[4]

Now, if to say that something is right is to claim that it can be commended to thoughtful persons when they know the facts, and if thoughtful persons will approve of a particular action only if they are prepared to approve others like it in respect of abstract properties, then we must answer the question in (1) negatively, and accept the requirement of generality.[5]

How important is the test of generality? Some readers may not be wholly convinced by the arguments for the test of generality, but they need not be alarmed, however, for the requirement of generality will not play a significant role in our examination of the problems with which we shall be concerned for the most part. What we shall be doing later is assessing *general* ethical principles, with few exceptions. Obviously, when we are trying to decide among conflicting general principles, we are not much helped by knowing simply that particular ethical statements must be supported by general principles with no reference to particular individuals.

Indeed, the test of generality by itself will not even eliminate any particular ethical statement as invalid. It says that no particular judgment is valid unless it can be supported by a general principle. However, the test of generality does not by itself lay restrictions on the general principles which may be put forward. Thus, a person can always defend a particular judgment by citing *some* general principle that supports it. When this has been done, the person has met the test of generality, and if we wish to criticize we must show his general principle is invalid.

For instance, suppose someone advocates before the local school board that free education be provided Negroes in that town only through the eighth grade, but for White students through high school. We may then challenge his particular proposal. But suppose further he meets our chal-

---

[4] One might object that to justify something we need not commend it to human attitudes, but rather to human (or divine) standards or principles, but the same consequences would still follow.

[5] We shall wish to qualify some points in the foregoing reasoning in Chapters 10 and 11, but these changes will not affect the correctness of our conclusion.

lenge by citing the following principle: "In general, it is right to educate Negroes free only through the eighth grade, even though White children are educated free through high school." This principle is a general one, by our definition; it contains no reference to individuals, and it makes an assertion about all cases. Doubtless no one, faced by such facts as the existence of brilliant Negroes, the development of whose talents is socially important, would find plausible such a principle, which draws lines on a color basis alone, irrespective of capacities and social needs. Nevertheless, it is a general principle, and citing it so far meets the test of generality.

In this example, the test of generality actually serves an important purpose, that of forcing a person to defend a particular judgment by appeal to a general one that is manifestly implausible. The test is therefore not without practical value. We should notice, however, that a skillful debater would hardly have needed to defend this particular judgment by a general principle so blatantly untenable. He would choose, as it is open to him to do, some more plausible principle, of less scope. For instance, while conceding the desirability of equal opportunities as a general principle, he might defend his position on the local issue by a principle like this: "In communities where equal educational facilities would exacerbate racial tensions, it is right to educate Negroes only through the eighth grade . . ." and so on as before. This new principle is doubtless open to much question, but it is more guarded. The narrower the principle that is offered, the less one has to defend and still be able to meet the challenge of the generality test. Of course, one can go too far toward narrowness in selection of one's principle. One can go so far that it is obvious to everyone that one's principle is bogus, not a moral principle one seriously believes in at all, but one the advocate has manufactured tailor-cut to suit the particular point being defended. If one goes so far, one discredits one's own sincerity.

It would be a mistake to assume that moves of this sort are dishonest or rationalizing in all or most cases. Principles do need to be qualified; differences between different situations do need to be recognized. The only point we are making at present is that the requirement of generality is by itself a weak one.

It may then be asked: If the requirement is so weak, why make it seem so important? Why need we concern ourselves with it at all? (We could, of course, raise the same question about consistency with equal justice).

The answer to such questions is as follows. First, the fact that a test does not accomplish much by itself, does not show that it is not important when taken with other tests. A person may satisfy the generality test for a particular moral judgment by making certain moves, appealing to a general principle; but it is by no means necessarily the case that these moves will stand up when we bring in further tests. If his general principle turns out to be vulnerable, then we may have disposed of the particular judgment after all. A second point of great practical importance is this: People often have ethical opinions that they have not thought of as general principles at all, and when challenged to defend them as such, they are ready to retract. For instance, persons may vaguely think that Negro children should not have equal educational opportunities, but when the matter is explicitly put to them, they would not want to defend this as a general principle at all—but rather prefer to hang their case on a very different principle, for example, the principle that only children of promise should receive a free education beyond a certain point. (If this is the principle appealed to, their original contention is open to criticism on factual grounds.) The test of generality challenges us to formulate a consistent set of general principles devoid of reference to the particular; and when people seriously seek such a system, they often find that some principles they have been supporting in a vague and uncritical way have to surrender to other principles that on reflection appear more acceptable.

We may conclude with a warning about the use of the test of generality. A careless use of it may lead us to reject as invalid particular judgments that are perfectly tenable. Suppose a person is considering whether he ought to become a postman. He argues in this way: "Take the particular judgment 'It is right for me to become a postman.' If this judgment is valid, it must be that it can be supported by a general principle. This general principle must be 'It is right for anyone to become a postman.' But this general principle cannot possibly be valid, for if it is right for anyone to become a postman, it is right for everyone to become a postman. But if everyone were a postman, things would be chaotic. Therefore, my particular judgment must be invalid too, and hence I ought not to become a postman."

Something is wrong with this argument, for the same argument can be used to show that it is wrong for me *not* to become a postman, since if nobody became a postman, everything would again be chaotic, with no delivery of messages.

What is wrong with this reasoning? The test of generality does not commit us to defend *any* general principle that supports a particular judgment, if the particular judgment is to be valid. It asserts only that we must be prepared to defend some *one*—and this one need not be the one that we think of first, or happen to be appealing to. In the example at hand, it is not difficult to find a different general principle which is not implausible and which also supports the original particular judgment: "In case one wants to be a postman and is fitted to be a postman, and in case there is a need for postmen, then it is not wrong to become a postman." If one's own situation satisfies the conditions of this principle, the judgment that one ought to be a postman is supported by it—an apparently valid general principle—and there are no absurd results at all.

3. IMMANUEL KANT'S TEST FOR THE MORALITY OF ACTIONS

We have been suggesting that a person's ethical convictions are invalid or unsatisfactory insofar as they fail to satisfy two conditions: (*a*) mutual consistency, when taken with the person's factual beliefs; and (*b*) capacity of his particular ethical judgments to be supported by general principles that make no reference to individuals. There are further conditions that valid ethical convictions must satisfy, but failure to meet either of these two is sufficient ground for concluding that something is wrong with one's system of ethical beliefs.

These two conditions of validity were not first discovered in the twentieth century. One is inclined to say that some recognition of them (of course not explicit formulation) goes back as far as the earliest debate about ethical issues. Statements of principles roughly corresponding to them have occurred sporadically, since early times, in the writings of philosophers. However, one philosopher in particular, Immanuel Kant (1724–1804), had a good deal to say about a criterion for valid ethical judgments very similar to our two conditions. It will repay us to consider his theory.

There are several facts that make Kant's theory especially interesting, aside from its great historical influence. First, there are influential philosophers today who hold views very similar to his: for instance, H. J. Paton and R. M. Hare (whom we shall discuss in Chapter 9). Also, Kant's proposal is sufficiently different from what we have suggested that we should consider substituting it, or some variant of it, for our two conditions. Finally, Kant claimed that his test for a valid ethical judgment was a sufficient test by itself. It is worthwhile to examine this claim.

Kant's consideration of ethical problems is concentrated on one particular type of ethical statement, statements about duty or obligation. His most interesting thesis in fact is relevant only to this special case. This fact, however, hardly limits the interest of his reasoning, in view of the fact that the assessment of statements about obligation is perhaps the most important problem for ethical theory.

Let us now outline the main points of Kant's view. He begins his best-known work on ethics (*Grundlegung zur Metaphysik der Sitten*, first published in 1785),[6] by saying that there is only one thing that can be called worthwhile without any qualifications or conditions: a good character. He then asks himself: What is it that makes character good? His answer is that character is made good by just one thing, by being con-

---

[6] Translations by H. J. Paton, *The Moral Law* (London: Hutchinson's University Library, 1948); by L. W. Beck (ed.), *Critique of Practical Reason* (Chicago: University of Chicago Press, 1949); and by T. K. Abbott, in *Kant's Critique of Practical Reason and other Works on the Theory of Ethics* (London: Longmans, Green, and Co., 1909).

scientious, which is being ready to do one's duty as one sees it, and for no other reason than just that it is one's duty. On his view, generosity and sympathy have nothing to do with goodness of character. Kant thought that if we want to know whether a particular action was fine or praiseworthy, there is exactly one thing we have to know: whether the person performed the deed because he saw that it was required by duty. Otherwise, it was morally worthless and did not show forth a good character.

The reader may well think that some of these assertions are questionable. Let us not pursue this issue now, however; we shall deal with this topic in Chapter 18. The important thing now is what Kant proceeds to say about the concept of duty.

In order to understand Kant's view of duty, it is best to begin with his idea that every deed somehow involves a "maxim" (his term) or policy-directive. What he means is this. Whenever a person acts, at least whenever he is acting intelligently and not simply by reflex, he is aware of what the situation is, what are the probable consequences of various lines of action he might take, and of the relation of these consequences to the desires and needs of himself and others. He will be aware of these things to some degree at least. Furthermore, the fact that a person who is so aware acts in a certain way shows that he accepts, at least for the moment, a corresponding policy-directive relevant to his circumstances. He is accepting, for the moment, a general maxim or directive of the form, "In circumstances of the kind *FGH*, let me do *A!*" Of course, a person does not normally formulate such maxims when he acts, although in principle it seems he always could do so. Kant's view, then, is that in this sense every action or decision or resolve embodies a maxim like "Let me do *A* in circumstances of the kind *FGH!*" We should notice that there is a sense in which the maxim of an act is *subjective:* the "maxim" of an act represents the kind of act the agent *thinks* it is, and the kind of situation the agent *thinks* it is. Usually, of course, the real quality of the action, and of the situation, will actually be what the agent thinks, but it need not be. There will be some divergence, in all cases, between the subject's thought of his act and his situation, and the real character of his act and situation, for his act and situation will have many properties *in addition* to those the agent thinks of.

Kant believed that certain maxims in this sense are and can be shown to be *universalizable* in a sense to be explained in a moment. Furthermore, he held that if the maxim is universalizable, then it is morally permissible to perform the act of which we think in terms of that maxim; if it is not universalizable, then that act is not morally permissible (unless we contrive to think of the same act in terms of some other maxim that is universalizable). Furthermore, if it is not morally permissible to perform a certain act, it is one's *duty* not to perform that act. On Kant's view, then, if we can decide which maxims are universalizable, we have the key to deciding what is morally permissible and what is our duty.[7]

What is meant by saying that a maxim is *universalizable?* This is a central point of Kant's theory. What Kant has in mind is essentially very old but none the less impressive. *Roughly,* a maxim is universalizable if it accords with the Golden Rule: "Do unto others as you would have them do unto you." Or, more exactly but still only roughly: "A person's maxim is universalizable if, and only if, he can agree, as a matter of reflective policy, to everyone else also acting in accordance with it."

One might ask: "*Why* did Kant suppose that an action is morally permissible if and only if the maxim, in terms of which the agent thinks of it, is universalizable?" What Kant has to say about this is by no means as clear as one could wish, and what is clear is not very convincing. However, there are some simple considerations that undoubtedly influenced his thinking, and which we should not overlook. What do we think of a person who acts in a way in which he is well aware he does not want others to act? We think his act shows lack of respect for others; it is a selfish act. We think less of him on account of it. We tend to say that he did what he ought not to have done, that he did what it was his duty not to do. In contrast, if a person is always careful to act only in ways in which he would be willing to have others act, we are inclined to praise him. We think he has the most important part, at least, of a good character. We would be likely to say he does not fail to do his duty. Hence, Kant comes very naturally to his view about the relation of duty, or moral permissibility, and universalizability of maxim—although we shall see that his view is indefensible.

Let us now consider more carefully his view that it is one's duty to per-

---

[7] There are some puzzles here, to which Kant's answers are not clear. (1) Suppose the maxim in terms of which one thinks of an act is not universalizable, but some other maxim (say, a more specific one) in terms of which one could equally properly think of one's situation and act as they really are, is universalizable. Is it then morally permissible to perform the act? It seems that Kant ought to say that in one sense it is not (from the point of view of the actual agent and his thinking), but that in another sense it is (from the point of view, say, of a better informed or more thoughtful agent). Perhaps he could say: Subjectively it is not permissible, but objectively it is. But he does not make the distinction. (2) Suppose an agent's maxim is universalizable, but he is mistaken in his thoughts about what his situation is or his act would be. And suppose that a person more accurately informed would think of the situation and action in terms of a maxim that could not be universalized. Is the action permissible or not? Again, Kant ought to say that in a sense it is and in a sense it isn't.

Since an agent cannot get outside himself and think of an act otherwise than as he does think of it (except in being careful to get his facts as straight as he can), from the point of view of the agent the only thing that is important is how the situation looks to him. Kant can therefore be excused for neglecting the "objective" facts, from a practical point of view. Nevertheless, the distinction is important, particularly since two agents, in identical "objective" situations, might on Kant's theory have the duty of doing opposite things, if they were differently informed and thought of the situation in different ways.

We shall come back to these complications in Chapter 14.

form only morally permissible acts,[8] and that an act is morally permissible if and only if its maxim (as the agent thinks of it) is universalizable.

Duty demands, Kant says, that we act *only* on universalizable maxims. More explicitly, it demands the following: "Act *only* on that maxim on which you can will that everyone should act."[9] Kant has another way of putting it, which we may put in our own words as follows. Suppose it were true that, whenever we acted on a certain maxim, we should have a kind of hypnotic effect on other people, so that from then on they would always act on this same maxim. In this case, we should be very careful about our actions, knowing full well their effect on the actions of others toward us. With this (approximate) thought in mind, Kant says that duty makes the following demand on us: "Act as if the maxims of your action were to become through your choice a universal law of nature." So, one is failing in his duty if his action is not one he would perform if he knew this hypnotic effect would take place.

Does Kant mean that an act is morally permissible if and only if its maxim, as the agent thinks of it, *is in fact* universalizable, or if and only if the *agent thinks* it is universalizable? Kant seems to take the former stand, but we should notice that such a view raises questions. At least, if we think that it cannot be a person's duty to do something he cannot know is his duty, it would be odd to say it is his duty to avoid acting according to a maxim that cannot be universalized, if it so happens that the agent thinks it can be, and is not in a position to know that it cannot! But let us ignore this problem.

Let us now consider more carefully what it is for a maxim to be universalizable. Kant obviously meant to exclude altogether maxims that contain proper names. He seems to take for granted that we need consider, as candidates for the status of universalizable maxims, only those from which proper names can be eliminated—as we have required above that they be eliminated from "general" moral statements. What Kant is really saying, then, is that a maxim is universalizable if and only if it contains no proper names and its agent can choose . . . , and so on. Let us now examine, however, what he says explicitly about universalizability.

The question whether a maxim is universalizable is not quite as simple as it looks, as we shall see more fully when we consider some of Kant's

---

[8] Kant's view is not at all that it is our duty to perform *all* morally permissible acts, but only that we are enjoined *not* to perform ones that are not permissible. Thus, it may be morally permissible for me to invite Miss A to marry me; but there is not necessarily an obligation to do so.

[9] In his exact words, "Handle nur nach derjenigen Maxime, durch die du zugleich wollen kannst, dass sie ein allgemeines Gesetz werde." *Immanuel Kant's Werke,* edited by A. Buchenau and E. Cassirer (Berlin: Bruno Cassirer, 1922), vol. IV, 279.

The verb "will" in English seems to have no use corresponding to the German "wollen." A better translation would therefore be like one suggested earlier: "Act only on the maxim which you can agree, as a matter of reflective policy, to have made a guiding law for the action of everyone else."

examples. It has, in Kant's thinking, two distinct aspects or moments. First, a maxim is universalizable only if it is *possible* for *everyone* to act on it (or for it to be a universal law of nature). Thus, a maxim is disqualified if it is inconsistent. It is also disqualified if it is impossible for everyone to act on it, in the sense of "causal impossibility," that is, excluded from the range of possibility by the laws of nature. More fully, he thought that a maxim is universalizable only if it is possible (in the sense both of being logically consistent and compatible with the laws of nature) both for *one* person to follow it, and also for *everybody* to follow it. We may summarize all this by saying that one condition for the universalizability of a maxim, according to Kant, is the objective possibility of everybody acting according to it. There is a second condition, however. A maxim is universalizable only if it is *possible for the agent to choose*, as a matter of reflective policy, that everyone follow it. We might say, then, that a second condition for a maxim being universalizable is that its being universally followed is subjectively acceptable to the agent. Kant thought that some maxims will satisfy the first condition but not the second. He wrote:

> Some actions are of such a nature that their maxims cannot even be conceived as universal laws of nature without contradiction, far from it being possible that one should choose that they be so. With others there is not this inherent impossibility, but it is still impossible to choose that their maxims be elevated to the status of universal laws of nature, since such a choice would contradict itself [weil ein solcher Wille sich selbst widersprechen würde].[10]

The second of Kant's two conditions is more puzzling than may appear at first glance. Isn't it possible that one person might be willing for a certain maxim to be universally followed, but a second person not? In this case, it would seem that the first person could say, correctly, "Action on this maxim is permissible," although the second person could also say, correctly, "Action on this maxim is not permissible." Many will think that any such result shows that something has gone seriously wrong—although perhaps not justly, for we shall see that "ethical relativists" insist that this very outcome is unavoidable (and, up to a point, we shall hold this ourselves). It seems that Kant himself was convinced that this difficulty would not arise (or at least was not aware of the fact it might arise), perhaps because of a further point, in his second test, that we have not yet emphasized. It appears that Kant intended to say not merely that it must be possible for the agent to choose that everyone act on a maxim, but that it must be possible for him so to choose "without contradicting" himself, that is, without this choice falling into conflict with stronger or more important wants or desires in himself. (This supplement to the concept of universalization is a complication, however. Now, in order to decide whether a maxim is moral, we have to ask

[10] Cassirer, IV, 282; Abbott translation, pp. 41–42.

not merely whether we can accept its being made universal law, but whether we can choose *without internal disharmony* that it be made a universal law—a much more complex matter, so that perhaps we can seldom be quite sure whether we can or cannot.) Even with Kant's test so amended, however, it is not obvious that the original puzzle is avoided. Perhaps some people are so constructed that they can choose, without internal disharmony, that a certain maxim become a universal law of nature, whereas other people are so constructed that they cannot. Kant might deny that they are or can be so constructed, but he certainly gives no reason for thinking they are not. We need not say that this is a serious difficulty for his view, but we should be aware of the fact that his view leads to this result.

Let us now look at his examples. Kant gives separate examples to illustrate the two different parts of universalizability, two for the first part, and two for the second. Let us begin with the first part, the *possibility* (logical or causal) of everyone conforming to the maxim.[11]

Kant considers the following maxim: "When I think myself in need of money, I shall borrow and promise to repay, although I know that I can never do so." Kant argues that this maxim is not universalizable.

> How would it be if my maxim were universal law? Then I see at once that it could never hold as a universal law of nature, but would necessarily contradict itself. For supposing it to be a universal law that everyone when he thinks himself in a difficulty should be able to promise whatever he pleases, with the purpose of not keeping his promise, the promise itself would become impossible, as well as the end that one might have in view in it, since no one would consider that anything was promised to him, but would ridicule all such statements as vain pretences.[12]

It is well to notice right away that Kant's argument does not prove what he thinks it does; it does not prove that it is *impossible* for everyone to act on the maxim. What it is plausible to argue is that, were everyone to feel free to borrow money with false promises, then soon very few would lend money in response to such pleas, and the desire that usually motivates attempts to borrow would in most cases be frustrated. Such considerations perhaps do show that no intelligent person would be willing to agree to a universal policy of following the maxim; hence, Kant could fairly say that he shows the maxim does not satisfy the second condition in his test. However, he has not shown it does not satisfy the first condition; he has not shown it is *impossible* for all to adopt the maxim. It is *possible* for everyone to adopt the maxim and follow it, for everyone can perfectly well resolve

[11] When a maxim is disqualified by this test, Kant says we have a "perfect" obligation not to perform the corresponding act. By saying the obligation is "perfect," Kant apparently meant that it is proper to enforce it by law, and that its force can never be overridden by conflicting obligations. See H. J. Paton, *The Categorical Imperative* (London: Hutchinson's University Library, 1953), pp. 147 f.

[12] T. K. Abbott (translator), *Kant's Critique of Practical Reason and other Works on the Theory of Ethics* (London: Longmans, Green, and Co., 1909), p. 40. By permission. Cassirer edn., IV, 280.

that, *if and when* some gullible person is willing to lend money on the strength of a promise to repay, one may borrow from him, knowing full well one can never repay. True, such gullible souls may rarely turn up if everyone adopts this maxim, but they may occasionally, and the maxim directs how to handle them when they do.

One would like to know if there is *any* maxim that an individual could follow (in the sense that it would not be impossible for him to follow it) but that could not be followed by everyone. Kant evidently thought there are many such, but he did not succeed in showing that there are. It would be rash, however, to say that there are none. For instance, a couple might plan to have a baby born in the following year, its arrival being timed so that it would be the one baby born first that year, but not *every* couple could successfully execute such plans. If this example is well taken, then Kant's condition of possibility of universal acceptance does disqualify at least one maxim, but it is not yet clear that it disqualifies any that are of serious moral interest.

Let us now look at Kant's illustration of the second part of his test for universalizability: the subjective acceptability of a universal law. This time he is attacking a refusal to give to charity. He says:

> A fourth [man], who is in prosperity, while he sees that others have to contend with great wretchedness and that he could help them, thinks: What concern is it of mine? Let everyone be as happy as Heaven pleases, or as he can make himself; I will take nothing from him nor even envy him, only I do not wish to contribute anything to his welfare or to his assistance in distress. Now no doubt if such a mode of thinking were a universal law, the human race might very well subsist. . . . But . . . it is impossible to *will* that such a principle should have the universal validity of a law of nature. For a will which resolved this would contradict itself, inasmuch as many cases might occur in which one would have need of the love and sympathy of others, and in which, by such a law of nature, sprung from his own will, he would deprive himself of all hope of the aid he desires.[13]

This second part of Kant's test clearly does what the first does not: it disqualifies many maxims, some of them important. At least, presumably the reader will be able to think of many maxims he would not be able consistently to accept as universal laws. It is more questionable whether it disqualifies many important maxims *for all agents*, in view of the "relativistic" implications pointed out above. Take, for instance, his example of charitable giving. Doubtless every prudent person would hesitate at least briefly before supporting the selfish rule. However, if one's investments are well chosen, and if one also takes an optimistic view of the future of capitalist society, perhaps he could choose the selfish maxim without internal disharmony. Probably some could choose it, and some could not. This result of the application of Kant's test will go far to discredit it in the eyes of anyone who is convinced either (1) that charitable giving is the duty of everyone who can

13 T. K. Abbott (translator), *Kant's Critique of Practical Reason and other Works on the Theory of Ethics* (London: Longmans, Green, and Co., 1909), p. 41. By permission. Cassirer edn., IV, p. 281.

afford it, or (2) that if charitable giving is the duty of anyone it is the duty of everyone in the same situation.

Let us look at two further difficulties in Kant's test for universalizability.

Consider an example. Suppose a student has borrowed $9.81 from his roommate, and is considering whether he should repay it. He finds it impossible to universalize the maxim, "When you have borrowed money, don't repay." But there are somewhat more specific maxims, which he can equally well regard as the maxims of his act. He happens upon this one: "Whenever one student in a small coeducational college borrows exactly $9.81 from another student who is his roommate, and on the day of the loan the borrower is exactly —— years old (corresponding to his own age), and the creditor is exactly —— years old, and the borrower's weight is exactly —— and his height exactly ——, and the creditor's weight is exactly —— and his height exactly ——, and if the borrower finds it very inconvenient to repay, then let him not repay the money." The student finds himself heartily in favor of universalizing this maxim. Hence, he concludes it is morally permissible to ignore the debt.

On Kant's theory this reasoning is perfectly legitimate. The maxim obviously fits the student's situation; he believes about it all the things mentioned in the maxim. Similar reasoning could be produced in support of any action one cared to justify. Therefore, although the second part of Kant's test will disqualify many important *maxims*, it is clear that a suitable choice of maxims will allow one to conclude properly that any *action* that one may wish to show is morally permissible, is morally permissible.

The final difficulty with the test is that its implications do not agree with what anybody can seriously believe about what is morally permissible. Consider another example. Suppose there were a slave-owner, perfectly secure in his power, and, further, that he pondered over the following maxim: "Let a slave-owner put a slave to death with torture, if it pleases his fancy." The reader will presumably agree that no such rule is acceptable, and that action in accordance with it would be immoral. But can it not survive Kant's test? It is not easy to see why it *cannot* be made a rule for everybody; indeed, very possibly there have been times in the history of the world when all slave-owners have in fact accepted it. Moreover, the slave-owner could *accept* such a maxim as universal law without suffering internal disharmony. Doubtless sensitive, thoughtful people would wish no such thing made a universal law, or rather would want no such thing to occur at all, but, it seems, some persons might.

One is inclined to suggest that two complications of Kant's proposal are called for, at the very least. First, it would be more plausible if Kant said a maxim is universalizable if the agent could accept it as universal law *even if he did not believe that he would be in some favored position, or if he were an impartial and sympathetic person.* Presumably no slave-owner who met these qualifications could accept the maxim as universal law; hence, it would not qualify as universalizable. Second, it would be more plausible if Kant said a maxim is universalizable only if the agent would accept it as universal law if he had *perfectly vivid and correct beliefs about what it would be like to have it made universal law.* This further condition would disqualify many maxims that we should agree ought to be disqualified. Conceivably, some Kantian scholars may maintain that the theory Kant in fact held already includes these amendments. We shall not attempt to decide on this point. We can agree, however, that his theory would be much more plausible than the theory we have attributed to him, if it did.

We now understand what Kant meant when he said that it is a person's duty to avoid any action that is not morally permissible, and that an act is morally permissible if and only if the maxim in terms of which the agent thinks of it is universalizable, that is, if and only if it is both objectively (causally and logically) possible, and subjectively acceptable to the agent, for everybody to adopt the maxim as a guiding rule for conduct. We can also now understand why his proposal is unacceptable at least as it stands. (1) Highly immoral maxims can be both objectively possible and subjectively acceptable to the agent, if the agent is a calloused person and is in a favorable position. (2) To many it will be a serious objection that his theory leaves open the possibility that a maxim will be universalizable for one person, but not for another. Many people think, for strong reasons, that if an act is right at all, it is right for everybody in the same circumstances. (3) If an agent wishes to justify an act, he can choose to think of it in terms of a maxim so specific that he need have no qualms about embracing it as a guiding rule for conduct for everybody. According to Kant's theory, anybody who is eager to justify his action to himself can always succeed in doing so. There are also subtler difficulties in his theory, which the reader will be able to appreciate after reading Chapter 14.

Everything considered, it seems quite clear that it is a mistake to think that Kant's criterion is an accurate test for deciding when an action is our duty, or when it is morally permissible. Could Kant's criterion be made satisfactory, by minor improvements? Perhaps. We shall see in Chapter 9 how some improvements could be made; and the "test" we shall argue for in Chapter 10 will be similar to Kant's in various ways.

FURTHER READINGS

On the Requirement of Generality:
R. M. Hare, "Universalizability," *Proceedings*, The Aristotelian Society, 1954–55, pp. 295–312.
M. G. Singer, "Generalization in Ethics," *Mind*, LXIV (1955), 361–75.
A. C. Ewing, "What Would Happen if Everybody Acted Like Me?" *Philosophy*, XXVIII (1953), 16–29.
C. D. Broad, "On the Function of False Hypotheses in Ethics," *Ethics*, XXVI (1916), 377–97.

E. A. Gellner, "Ethics and Logic," *Proceedings,* The Aristotelian Society, 1954–55, pp. 157–78. ———"Morality and *Je Ne Sais Quoi* Concepts," *Analysis,* XVI (1956), 97–103.

J. Harrison, "When is a Principle a Moral Principle?" The Aristotelian Society, Supplementary volume XXVIII (1954), pp. 111–34.

On Kant:

I. Kant, *The Groundwork of Morals:*
　H. J. Paton (trans.), *The Moral Law* (London: Hutchinson's University Library, 1948).
　L. W. Beck (ed.), *Critique of Practical Reason and Other Writings in Moral Philosophy* (Chicago: University of Chicago Press, 1949).
　T. K. Abbott, Kant's *Theory of Ethics* (London: Longmans, Green & Co., Inc., 1899).

The introductions to these translations may be consulted with profit.

H. J. Paton, *The Categorical Imperative* (London: Hutchinson's University Library, 1953). A full, careful, detailed analysis and commentary.

W. D. Ross, *Kant's Ethical Theory* (Oxford: Clarendon Press, 1954).

C. D. Broad, *Five Types of Ethical Theory* (New York: Harcourt, Brace & Co., 1934), chap. 5.

S. Körner, *Kant* (Baltimore: Penguin Books, 1955), chap. 6.

J. Harrison, "Kant's Examples of the First Formulation of the Categorical Imperative," *Philosophical Quarterly,* VII (1957), 50–62.

3

Can Science Solve All
Ethical Problems?

There is little temptation to believe that all consistent sets of ethical statements are valid or justified, or that all general sets are valid or justified
—or even that consistency and generality together are enough to secure
the validity of any system of beliefs that has these properties. Practically
any set of beliefs could pass these tests. The analogue of natural science is
a reminder; it is generally recognized that the principles of science must
not only be consistent but also—and this is crucial—conform with observation. If the principles of science needed only to be consistent, the world-
systems of ingenious cranks would be true. Something more is needed for
reliable knowledge in science, namely, experiment and observation, and
conformity with them.

It seems plausible to assume that a similar property is sufficient to insure
the validity of a system of ethics: conformity with observation and with
the content of empirical science, if we mean by "content of empirical science" the sum total of statements rationally inferrable from observation and
experiment.

This is an important possibility to be explored. Indeed, there can be
no question as to whether observation and scientific knowledge are relevant
for determining the answers to ethical questions. Obviously they are. The
only question is exactly how they are relevant, and whether they are, when
taken with consistency and generality, a sufficient test for the validity of
an ethical statement, or set of ethical statements. In a sense, of course, such
facts *must* constitute all the *information* we need for the solution of ethical
problems, if we hold, as most philosophers today do hold (not rationalists
and not some theologians, as we shall see), that there is no other information
available. It is also tempting to maintain that we can solve all our ethical
problems by a rather simple appeal to science because in some way this is

how we *do* solve many of them at least. For instance, if we wish to know whether we should discipline our child for disobedience, we may go to a psychologist, and we consider our question answered in the negative if he says something like this: "If you discipline him, you're sowing the seeds of unhappiness in his later life; his present disobedience is a normal symptom at his age and it will pass."

Let us consider, then, the role that science can and should play in the resolution of ethical problems. In doing so, we shall try to give more solid underpinning to the claim made earlier (pp. 7–8) that there is a "special" problem of justifying ethical statements, different from that of justifying the statements of the empirical sciences.

1. MUST ETHICAL REASONING START WITH ETHICAL PREMISES?

We have just said there is some temptation to think that an appeal to science can answer ethical questions, and that scientific knowledge, in conjunction with the requirements of consistency and generality, provides a sufficient test for the validity of ethical statements. However, there is also quite a temptation, when we look at some other facts, to come to the opposite conclusion, that science does not establish any ethical propositions at all, that there is a great gulf between scientific statements and ethical statements, so that scientific knowledge gets us nowhere in our attempt to establish ethical propositions.

A good many social scientists today, along with many philosophers, hold this second view. The results of science, they say, do not imply or require any propositions of ethics. Usually, although not always, this leads them to say that ethical propositions cannot be rationally supported at all. "Science," they say, "has to do with facts; but ethics is a matter of personal opinion"—a view doubtless familiar to the reader.

This second view is, up to a point, certainly correct. We must examine why, and, as a result, we shall begin to be convinced, if we are not convinced already, that there is a "special" problem of justifying ethical statements. What, essentially, is the point of these scientists and philosophers? Why is there a special problem of justifying ethical statements?

First of all, one cannot formally *deduce* an ethical statement from a set of premises that does not contain any ethical statements. To understand this, let us look at a sample of deductive reasoning that is valid—a simple example of syllogistic reasoning, which for our purposes can be taken as representative of deductive reasoning in general.

PREMISE 1: Any act that maximizes happiness for all affected, among those open to an agent, is *right*.

PREMISE 2: Under circumstances Z (specified), telling a (specified) lie to Mr. A will maximize happiness for all concerned.

CONCLUSION: Therefore, telling a lie (as specified) to Mr. A under circumstances Z is *right*.

The point to notice about this example of valid reasoning is that the term "right" could not have appeared validly in the conclusion unless it—or at least some term synonymous with it—had occurred in the premises. We can generalize this: *no* ethical term (remember our criterion for an ethical term on p. 3) can appear in the conclusion of an example of valid reasoning, unless it—or some term synonymous with it—appeared in the premises. Therefore, unless the premises in an argument contain an ethical statement, the conclusion cannot be an ethical statement. So, *if* we assume that the content of science does not already contain ethical statements, then use of the results of science as a set of premises will never yield an ethical statement as a conclusion.

Deductive reasoning is only one kind of reasoning; there is also inductive reasoning. However, unless there are already some ethical statements among the premises, a process of *inductive* reasoning will also never give an ethical statement as a valid result. To understand why, let us first look at a very simple inductive inference.

> PREMISE: This is a piece of *copper,* and it *conducts electricity*.
> CONCLUSION: It is *more* probable, in view of this fact, that *all copper conducts electricity*.

The conclusion here is obviously a justified inference from the premise. Similarly, we would be justified in the following ethical inference:

> PREMISE: That act was one of *telling a lie,* and it was *wrong*.
> CONCLUSION: It is more probable, in view of this fact, that *all lies* are *wrong*.

In each of the inferences above, the conclusion asserts a greater probability, in view of the fact cited in the premise, of a statement that is merely a generalization of the situation alleged in the premise. In other words, from "This is f and g," it is inferred "It is more probable, in view of the fact that this is f and g, that all things f are g." As a result, we can see that if, in the second case, the predicate of the premise had not been an ethical term, the predicate of the generalization said to be more probable, by the conclusion, could not have been an ethical term. Thus, we can conclude that *if* the empirical reports of science do not already contain ethical statements, then by inductive inferences we shall not reach an ethical conclusion.

This reasoning leads us to an apparently drastic conclusion. Who would want to say that the premises of inductive reasoning in science—the reports of experiment or observation—are ethical premises? If they aren't, however, then the laws, the generalizations of science, will not contain any ethical statements (for these laws are derived from the reports of experiment or observation by inductive inference). This means science contains no ethical statements at all, and if so, no chain of *deductive* reasoning from scientific premises can validly yield ethical conclusions, for there will be no ethical premises from which it can start—at least not any established by inductive science. So, it seems, observation and science can yield no valid inferences for ethical conclusions at all.

Is there any way in which we can admit that neither deductive nor inductive reasoning can yield valid ethical statements as a conclusion unless it starts with ethical premises, and at the same time avoid the drastic conclusion that ethical statements cannot be validly justified at all? Or must we at least concede that science and observation can play an important role in establishing ethical theorems only if the fundamental premises of ethics are justified in some manner which makes no use of observation?[1] It seems that there is a way to avoid such conclusions; in fact, there are at least three ways, although we do not say three *plausible* ways.

1. We might argue that a false dichotomy has been made between ethical statements and the content of science or of reports of observation. We might argue this on the basis of a theory of what ethical statements *mean*. For instance, we might claim that what it *means* to say "*x* is worthwhile in itself" is to say "*x* is a pleasant experience." Hence if, as would be agreed, "This is a pleasant experience" is the report of an observation and can be taken as a premise for inductive inference in science, we could—if this proposal about meanings is correct—hold that "This is worthwhile in itself" is the report of an observation and can be taken as a premise for inductive inference. In this case, science itself contains value statements—ethical premises—at many points. So, we can conclude, although it is true that no ethical conclusions follow, either deductively or inductively, from nonethical premises, the fact is that science itself does contain many ethical premises—an obvious point, as soon as we grant the proposal about what ethical statements mean. People who take this position as a way of showing how science can establish ethical statements, we shall call "naturalists," and we shall discuss their view extensively in Chapter 7.

2. We might agree that neither inductive nor deductive reasoning can draw ethical conclusions from nonethical premises (reports of observations, or statements drawn from empirical science), but hold that there are *other valid modes of inference* that can do so. We shall consider this suggestion in detail in Chapter 10.

3. There is a third possible position. It rejects both (1) and (2) as solutions to the problem: It denies that the meaning of ethical terms is such that reports of observations can themselves be ethical statements, and it does not hold that there is a third possible "valid mode of inference." Positively, it asserts both that nonethical premises cannot validly yield ethical conclusions, and also that there *is no ethical premise that in principle cannot be assessed*—justified as valid or invalid—by observation and the methods of science. How is this possible? One can say that the whole puzzle has arisen from our tendency to look at ethical problems too much in the abstract. If

---

[1] We shall see in Chapter 8 that "rationalists" hold that the fundamental premises of ethics can be justified by appeal to "intuition" in some sense.

we looked at them *in context*, noting when and under what conditions practical problems arise, we would notice that we *always do have ethical premises available* for the assessment of any ethical principle about which we may have serious question—perhaps not premises that everyone else would accept, and not premises that are infallible, but at least premises sufficient for the purposes of the one who has the problem. (The student of epistemology or the philosophy of science will recognize this view as the analogue in ethics of epistemological views of pragmatists like C. S. Peirce or of philosophers of science like Karl Popper.)

We must examine all these three possibilities, and we shall begin with the third, since it is the simplest and initially looks more plausible than the other two. What we must do is work out the details of this possible position, and support it with some examples. We can then proceed to assess it, in more critical vein.

It is convenient to have a name for this possible theory about how ethical statements can be justified, how science can play a central role in establishing ethical propositions. We shall call it "contextualism"—with apologies to all who may have used this term in other senses—on account of its central claim that in the context of actual ethical problems, ethical premises are always available, and that philosophical difficulties arise only when we view ethical problems or questions, and try to answer them, outside of concrete, practical contexts.

2. A PROPOSAL: IN CONTEXT ANY ETHICAL STATEMENT CAN BE ASSESSED BY OBSERVATION AND SCIENTIFIC METHOD.

In order to explain our "contextualist" proposal further, let us look at a typical ethical problem.

Let us suppose a parent cannot decide whether he should punish his child for disobedience. In the past, we assume, this parent has been operating on the (ethical) principle: "When children disobey their parents, they should be punished." Recently, however, this parent has noticed that punishment has seemed to affect unfavorably the affectionate relationship between him and his child, and has seemed to produce a rebellious attitude rather than the result intended. Consequently, he has come to doubt the principle and wants to know what kind of principle should govern his behavior in this area. Can science tell him? The proposal we are considering says it can. It maintains that, given the parent's undoubted ethical principles, and the set of facts that science can establish (in principle, whether or not it has them already), a relevant principle can be reached by deductive reasoning. In particular, we may assume that psychological research can determine whether punishment probably will affect the personal relations of parent and child unfavorably, or whether such relations are so firmly fixed in early life that they can be considered safe. Again, we may suppose that psychological research can predict the probable results of entrusting the child's decisions to himself. Again, science may tell whether the current tendencies toward rebelliousness are a phase to be expected at a certain stage of development, or whether they constitute a danger sign.

The proposal is that if we combine these results of science with some ethical principles that the parent certainly does not question, at least at present, his problem is resolved. What might be some of the unquestioned ethical premises of the parent? Presumably something like these: "Children should be brought up so that they will not be frustrated, unhappy adults." "Children should be brought up so that they will be responsible husbands or wives, and responsible members of the community." "Children should be brought up so that they will be able to use their talents and energies to the maximum extent." Doubtless every parent will find, if he reflects, that he accepts some principles of this sort. Assuming, then, that all these principles, when combined with the scientific facts, point in the same way, the parent will find himself guided to a new principle governing conduct in this area, and will properly consider his problem resolved.

Furthermore, one might make essentially the same points, on the subject of how to resolve ethical disputes. Parties to the dispute are to turn to science in the way our parent is supposed to. In this case, however, the ethical premises that are to play a role in the solution do not consist of those principles that one *or* the other of the disputants at the moment finds unquestionable; the premises to be used for the purpose of the resolution of the disagreement will consist of those principles that *both* of them accept, and are willing to use as a basis for the solution of the problem. Given these mutually acceptable ethical premises, and the facts ascertainable by science, a solution of their problem can be discovered, at least in principle.[2]

Now, whatever one may say in criticism of this proposal, there is something we must concede. Very often we *do* solve our ethical problems in the way contextualism suggests; and we often *do* try to reach an understanding with a friend along the lines suggested for interpersonal disputes. Perhaps, indeed, this sort of procedure is the most common one.

Someone might ask: Does a person always have a store of relevant unquestioned premises? We might answer: Of course, he can't help but have them. A person doesn't have a *problem* unless he has some standards, values, or ideals that are somehow being threatened in the situation. If our parent, for instance, did not think *both* that disobedience is somehow a bad thing, with probably bad consequences for the future, and *also* that an affectionate

---

[2] The foregoing formulation is somewhat rigid. If the sets of ethical premises are different, then A's ethical premises, taken with one set of scientific data, may lead to the *same* principle to be used for the problem at hand, as will B's different ethical premises, taken with a slightly different set of the scientific data (the scientific statements being used thus remaining different although mutually consistent—different parts of what is known).

relationship between parent and child is a good thing, he would not be worrying. Why else would he concern himself? One might reply: He doesn't have to have any *ethical principles;* he can worry merely because the situation threatens something he *wants.* This is possible, but very unlikely, for usually, when we want something, we are assuming that having it is a desirable thing, at least from our own point of view, so that we do have an ethical principle after all. (Later we shall see that there *is* a question of how to identify a person's "unquestioned ethical principles," but our discussion will not affect the present point.) It is hard to imagine a problem situation in which a person would not have *some* relevant unquestioned ethical principles.

The availability of unquestioned ethical principles in every actual problem situation has been emphasized by various writers of contextualist leanings. For instance, Sidney Hook, writing about John Dewey's theory, remarks:

> But still, one asks, aren't there certain standards or values which we must use in order to determine whether the consequences of acting on our ends . . . are satisfactory? Certainly there are. A whole host of them like friendship, wisdom, beauty, courage, health, security, adventure. Yet note: although these goods are assumed to be immediately valid, none of them is taken as finally good. None . . . above the necessity of pointing to consequent goods in case its own presumptive validity is threatened.[3]

Or again, Abraham Kaplan, commenting on the ethical theories of Rudolf Carnap and Hans Reichenbach:

> To be sure, no proposition about future experiences can be deduced from the value judgment [being assessed] *alone;* but we *can* make such deductions if we are given also propositions about the values already operative in the context in which the judgment is made. . . . Every judgment, as a concrete utterance, is made in a context in which some ends are given. Only when the judgment is analyzed in abstraction from its context can the end which it enjoins be regarded as categorical. . . . But not everything is problematic at once; were this so, nothing would be capable of validation for lack of data, of givens, on the basis of which validation could be arrived at. . . . We remain at *every* step with a certain set of moral premises. . . .[4]

The contextualist makes a point of insisting that the principles unquestioned in one context can themselves be doubted in another context. No principles are fixed, in principle exempt from liability to doubt. (He would say the same of principles of science.) He is also not committed to saying that all such principles necessarily will be questioned. His view is that none is in principle exempt from questioning in every context, and that when *any*

[3] Sidney Hook, *John Dewey: An Intellectual Portrait* (New York: John Day Company, Inc., 1939), p. 132.
[4] Abraham Kaplan, "Logical Empiricism and Value Judgments," to appear in the forthcoming volume in THE LIBRARY OF LIVING PHILOSOPHERS, *The Philosophy of Rudolf Carnap*, edited by Paul Arthur Schilpp, and to be published shortly by Tudor Publishing Company, New York. Quoted by permission of author and editor.

principle is called in question its status is to be settled in the manner outlined, by appeal to science in conjunction with ethical principles that at *that* time are unquestioned.

Incidentally, the answers of science are not fixed for all future time, and when modifications occur, we shall naturally reopen ethical questions to which the changes are relevant. Many parents will recall the frequency with which they have changed their methods of disciplining, or even of feeding, young children, on account of changing medical advice about the probable effects of using different methods.

A critic of contextualism might say: "A given individual may indeed have unquestioned ethical premises relevant to his problem, but will two or more individuals have common unquestioned principles that they can use to solve an ethical dispute?" To this the contextualist might reply: "At any rate, there is no rational solution to your problem if such premises are *not* available. You will then have to resort to force (or propaganda methods, and so forth), unless you have a common premise that the use of force is worse than compromising."[5]

The contextualist may, however, offer a different answer. He might say: "This is a question of fact, a question for sociologists and anthropologists. What they tell us is that there are in fact many ethical principles fairly well agreed on by all mankind." As examples of some principles that have found universal acceptance, he might suggest the following: "One ought not to cause pain for sentient creatures (except where some other ethical principle demands it—a qualification of all the principles here listed)." "We should make for happiness where we can." "It is wrong for one person to treat others in a way in which he would regard it as unjustified for others to treat him." "People have no obligation to perform acts beyond their mental or physical capacities." "Members of a family have a responsibility for each other's welfare that goes beyond what they owe, normally, to others." "People should not take their pledged word lightly."

The contextualist naturally will not claim that, in all cases, there will be factual information sufficient to solve ethical problems, even given the context of ethical assumptions. In some cases we may have to act blindly, using whatever clues we have, but without assurance that our decisions are really correct. This fact is, of course, no objection to the contextualist thesis (it is true on any theory). The thesis is that, in principle, if scientific knowledge of a certain sort *were* available, the problem would be resolved, given the ethical assumptions actually available in the context.

Notice that the contextualist does not claim that this method is capable of establishing general ethical principles, outside actual concrete problem situations. He is merely saying that his method establishes them for the

---

[5] We should not forget that it has certainly not yet been *shown* that no other "rational" method is possible. One cannot show this except by examining the alternatives in detail.

problem situations. He makes a point of emphasizing that the unquestioned premises present in a problem situation *are suitable* for resolving the problem of *that* situation—because *it is these premises that set the problem.* The individual's problem is set by not knowing what to do, in relation to his own ethical or value judgments. The solution to *his* problem, therefore, properly proceeds within the framework of *his* unquestioned premises that are responsible for the problem.

We might summarize the "contextualist" proposal as follows: (1) In every problem situation the individual has some unquestioned ethical premises—for these premises set the problem, and there would be no problem but for them. (2) These ethical premises, when conjoined with nonethical statements from common experience or science, support logically ethical principles that are suitable for use as guides in the problem situation. At least they *may* do so, and *in principle* can do so. (3) The premises unquestioned in one context may be questioned in another. No ethical premise is essentially infallible, although there may be some that never will be questioned. (4) Disputes may be solved rationally, along parallel lines, by the use of premises common to the disputants (or sometimes by different premises that nevertheless, conjoined with different results of science, will lead to the same ethical conclusion).

We have stated this proposal in a general way, so that it applies to all the various different types of ethical questions. We can state it much more simply if we consider only a special type of case that is, after all, the most familiar one. Suppose we are in doubt what it is *desirable to do, or aim for,* in a given situation. Our "contextualist" proposal, then, in effect comes to this: Let science tell us the *means* by which various possible aims or ends would have to be reached; and let it tell us the *consequences* of reaching each of the several possible goals by these available means. Then, the proposal runs, *if one's examination of this sort is thorough enough,* one will find that the problem has solved itself, for when he considers a number of goals *in conjunction* with the necessary means and the inevitable consequences, he will find that there is no longer any doubt about which goal is best aimed at. Although, given the value judgments one does not seriously question, he may not be able to choose between several possible ends *taken abstractly* and not in connection with means and consequences, nevertheless his unquestioned value judgments will decide, will make clear what is best done, when he considers the several ends in a context with their means and consequences. (The importance of considering goals *in connection* with means and consequences suggests a further meaning to be carried by the term "contextualism.")

When we put the matter in this specific way, we have a theory of the proper role of science in ethical reflection that is quite similar to, if not identical with, the theory of John Dewey and other "instrumentalists."

3. A PROBLEM: DOES CONTEXTUALISTIC REASONING REALLY JUSTIFY?

The contextualist proposal about how to use science to solve ethical problems is certainly well taken. Hardly anyone today would question the suggestion that no ethical principle is absolutely infallible and known to be valid in its present form. Again, the suggestion has pointed out the manner in which science may be used in ethics: by showing the necessary means to and inevitable consequences of certain goals for action, or, more generally, by showing how certain ethical principles commit us in unexpected directions because of natural laws. We must use science in ethical thinking; if we set great value on our son's being an unfrustrated adult, for instance, we must see that this commits us to courses of action we do not like and would not choose just for themselves.

Yet, is contextualism a proposal that solves our problem about how to assess ethical beliefs? Does it show us a general method for testing ethical beliefs, applicable to all types of situation? Does it show us that every ethical belief that has passed this test is valid or justified? There are two main difficulties with the proposal. The first, and more important, of these is simply that it does not show us why we should regard any ethical belief as *justified* at all. Why?

Let us first note a distinction. Everybody will agree that if premises, *known* to be true, entail a certain conclusion, then the conclusion is true. This fact, we may suppose, tends to make us think that the contextualist method will give us true conclusions in ethics. But the theory is not suggesting that we can start from *known*, or necessarily even true, premises; it proposes that we start merely from *undoubted* premises, from *our* premises. By no means does it follow that, if premises, that we do not doubt, entail a certain conclusion, the entailed conclusion will be justified. All that follows is that we shall be inconsistent if we do not accept the entailed conclusion. Our conclusions are no better than our premises.

Certainly when we are thinking of someone else's ethical reasoning we do not think his conclusion is "justified" because he arrived at it by the use of science, taking his unquestioned ethical beliefs as premises. Suppose the officers of the Ford Motor Company, starting from their unquestioned (perhaps conservative Republican) ethical premises, arrive by rigorous use of logic and scientific method at the conclusion that wages should be reduced. Will the union leader be impressed? Will he be inclined to say their conclusion is "justified"? Not at all. The contextualist will, of course, and perhaps properly, protest that to say this is unfair, possibly on the ground that we say a conclusion is "justified" only if it can be arrived at, in the specified manner, from premises *we* do not question.

In order to make the point more penetrating, then, let us suppose that we are officials of the Ford Motor Company, and that we think back over the process of arriving at our conclusion about wages from our "unquestioned" premises. Suppose further that we are made aware of the fact that our unquestioned premises are not true by definition, and that they are not inductively supportable by observation in the manner in which the statements of empirical science are so supportable. Shall we not become puzzled? Shall we not start asking ourselves whether our unquestioned premises oughtn't to be questioned? We shall, it seems, *start* questioning *all* our ethical premises, doubtless not knowing quite what we should count as a satisfactory basis for ethical beliefs. So, once distinctions are made, we *don't have unquestioned premises* at all.

Let us put the matter in still another way. If we had good reason to regard our ethical premises in any given context as themselves valid or warranted, we could feel that the "contextualist" mode of reflection would give only valid or warranted conclusions. But this is not so. It is true that the proposal suggests that we may always go back and make further inquiry about any premises that we seriously doubt. However, the difficulty is that for this further inquiry we need more premises, and if we are to trust these more remote premises, we need still more, and so on without end. The proposal is, in effect, that we arrange to support ourselves by tying ourselves to the end of a chain, without assuring ourselves that the chain is itself supported. The advice of the theory is, in case we doubt that the support is sound, to look to the link to which we are tied and see if it is well supported by another link. If we are still doubtful, then it tells us to continue to look at some more links. However, what we want to do is get to the top, to have a view of a support that is not just another link in the chain. This kind of assurance the method of contextualism rules out in principle. So, we conclude, the contextualist proposal needs to be supplemented in some fashion.

This reasoning is worthy of careful assessment, for if it is true that the contextualist proposal is not enough, we are faced with some rather unpalatable alternatives—especially the two that we described earlier (p. 40). Thus, we had better look assiduously for a flaw in the reasoning we have been using. Perhaps contextualism does do what is wanted, after all. What could be said in defense?

1. It may be replied that what we are recommending is that one be dissatisfied with, doubtful of, every belief until one has shown a strict logical connection with other beliefs already somehow certified. We are recommending wholesale doubt until some ideal of certification has been met. But in fact, it is said, such wholesale doubting is impossible; the demand is artificial and even philosophers who profess adherence to this ideal of certification do not really succeed in withholding belief until it is met. There is the example of Descartes, who talked as if he doubted all common-sense beliefs, although he did not really doubt any of them—and, as might have been expected, after elaborate philosophical maneuvering, he managed to show to his own satisfaction that he was, after all, quite well justified in

believing the things he probably did not doubt in the first place. Indeed, it may be said, we must not forget that Descartes would not have rested content with his theory unless it had succeeded in showing that these very common-sense beliefs were justified. Aren't we in the same position as Descartes? Aren't there ethical propositions we can't seriously doubt? Isn't this inability to doubt shown by the fact that we would not rest satisfied with any ethical theory that did not succeed in justifying what we do not doubt anyway?

Will this answer satisfy? The critic of contextualism is likely to go on as follows. Certainly, he will say, we do have beliefs that we find it hard to lay aside, but belief is not evidence. If we cannot find the evidence on which these beliefs are based, ought we not to call them merely "fundamental prejudices"? Moreover, he will continue, is this "wholesale doubting" impossible, or a purely artificial enterprise? Have not various people at least wondered seriously whether they owe anything to anybody, whether they should not simply look out for themselves? Have people not even thought seriously that perhaps they should not bother to be concerned about their own futures, but rather to let the joys of the present be the fundamental concern? Obviously, they have. Indeed, can one not wonder whether it would be as well to drop "ought" and "wrong" and "is desirable" altogether, and confine ourselves to thoughts of what we want and like? Such questions are perhaps especially appealing to young persons, in whom, possibly, the conflict between impulse and norm is apt to be felt most strongly. Perhaps those who think that the assumption of unquestioned principles is satisfactory are mostly well-disciplined old men, firmly established in their conformity to social norms. Surely, if we are to feel that our standards are justified, some systematic account of our whole system of ethical beliefs—all of them together—must be given.

2. The contextualist has a second point. The method of moral inquiry as outlined, he will say, is the very same, in principle, as the method used by empirical science. Note how a physicist, when he is working on some physical problem, does not assume that he knows nothing, that he must start from the beginning. On the contrary, he assumes there is a mass of well documented knowledge that he feels free to use—even though he concedes that every principle in science is open to question, fallible, possibly requiring modification. Now, the contextualist will say, surely we cannot wish for more in morals than we have in empirical science. In both we are justified in starting with an unquestioned base, even though we recognize that other problems may arise that will require revisions.

The contextualist raises large issues when he makes this claim about the methods of science. Since he has raised them, though, we must consider them as best we can. The critic's answer must be: *Is* the parallel with empirical science quite exact? It is true, of course, that the working scientist is not always starting from the very beginning but is assuming the truth of a great mass of propositions. Nevertheless, there is much more to be said. He does, after all, make *observations*, and there are many statements he is justified in believing, because they simply report what he observes, or what he remembers he did observe. Doubtless even the reports of observations are fallible, but these reports are still based on a direct touch with fact. So, the scientist *could, if he wanted to take the time*, start with observations and recollections of observations, with evidence and not just belief—he could start with these, and justify the main beliefs of science by showing that such principles are necessary in order to account plausibly for his basic evidence. To use a technical term, we can say that the scientist can work out a *logical reconstruction* of his scientific beliefs, based on his direct observations. Now, the critic will say: Can the moralist do the same for his ethical principles? Perhaps, but at any rate contextualism is not proposing to do it; in principle, it is not attempting this task. The contextualist is ignoring a crucial question for the theory of ethics: whether there can be a logical reconstruction of ethical belief essentially comparable to what is possible for science. He claims that the logic of science is parallel with the logic of ethics, but he fails to see a crucial difference: that the rules of inductive inference permit us to pass directly from observation reports to the statements of empirical science—but not to any ethical statements.[6]

3. A further point might be made by the contextualist: If what is wanted is a wholesale justification of *all ethical beliefs at once*, it must be realized that no such justification of ethical statements *can* be given. Those who insist on such a justification are doomed to end up as skeptics. This warning is one we should remember. It is, of course, only a prediction, and if we are optimistic, we will want to investigate further, before reducing our critical demands.

4. Another line of defense for contextualism may consist in an appeal to more general pragmatic conceptions of when a belief is warranted, true, or justified. It may be said that what we *mean* (at least if our concepts are sharply defined and our terms are employed in a useful way) when we say that any belief is *warranted* or *justified* is that it is the outcome of a process of resolution, through the use of scientific method, of the problem that

[6] The contextualist might take the position that ethical statements are presupposed in science, or in the justification of scientific reasoning. If this can be demonstrated, there would be more difficulties in contrasting the logical basis of scientific beliefs with that of ethical beliefs.

It has recently been suggested by an important philosopher of science that what it *means* to say "The hypothesis H is confirmed (or rendered more probable) by the observation O" is something like "A person who observed O *ought* to place more confidence in H than if he had not observed O." If this "ought" is an ethical "ought," ethics and empirical science are certainly tangled.

The writer must confess that he is supposing that a logical justification of the beliefs of empirical science can be given, which does not presuppose or involve ethical propositions in this way.

instituted the inquiry. For instance, we had the problem of what to do about disciplining our son. Using the methods of science, we found out something about means and consequences. This led to an outcome: a new preference for, say, "no disciplining, with its consequences" over "disciplining, with its consequences" (both as envisaged after the investigation). There is no longer a problem, because our unquestioned value judgments are now clearly on the side of no discipline. The problem has been solved by appeal to the methods of science; our puzzlement has been banished by scientific inquiry. Why should we not say that our new belief is "warranted" or "justified"? If this is not justified, then what does it mean to have a "justified" belief? So, if we question whether ethical beliefs attested in the contextualist manner are "justified," we are really contradicting ourselves, exposing our lack of awareness of what, after all, we do (or should) mean by "justified."[7]

This defense is certainly interesting. However, *is* this what we do (or should) mean by "justified ethical belief"? Unfortunately, this issue is a large one, with which we are not yet properly equipped to deal. But the critic of contextualism may point out some things that will be seeds of doubt. First, he will point out that dictionaries do not offer definitions of "justified" along this line, and one has only to ask one's roommate in order to find that people do not include such definitions in their standard mental equipment. Moreover, the definition of "justified" may be a very complicated matter—remember, we say "His anger was quite justified," and there we obviously mean something quite different from what the contextualist is here proposing. These two points are not conclusive, but the contextualist has to keep in mind that there are other proposals for defining "justified." We shall suggest one such alternative proposal later (p. 268). There are also more radical proposals, such as that "The belief in *p* is justified" means roughly "Do believe in *p!*" Contextualists have certainly not shown that their definition is to be preferred to these others. (We shall be discussing what is required for a satisfactory definition in Chapter 7.) Again, one might argue that if there are no objections to defining "justified" as here suggested, there can be no objections to defining the ethical terms, such as "desirable," themselves. Then naturalism (p. 40) is open to us, a much simpler view. It is certainly far from obvious that this definition of "justified," among those we might consider, is the correct one.

[7] We could put the process of "resolving" our problem differently by saying that our unquestioned premises are: "The happiness of our son is something to be achieved unless there are strong contrary considerations," and "The development of a responsible character in my son is. . . ." and "The maintenance of a warm relation of affection between my son and me is. . . ." Now, suppose science tells us that continued punishment will prevent achieving these ends, and will serve no other purpose. Then, if we have another premise, such as "We ought to do what will realize important goals," it seems to follow we ought to stop disciplining our child. This is a new ethical conclusion arrived at by scientific method.

The contextualist may argue that, even if we do not mean by "justified" what his definition suggests, it would be *better* if we did. However, the logic of his argument is made more complicated still by such a proposal, since to say one usage is "better" seems itself to be making an ethical statement.

4. A SECOND PROBLEM: CAN APPEAL TO SCIENCE JUSTIFY NOVEL PRINCIPLES?

If our suggestion is well taken, that the contextualist proposal fails because inferences starting from unquestioned but not necessarily valid premises need not lead us to valid conclusions, we know already that the contextualist mode of reasoning cannot really justify *any* ethical principle— and therefore we need not concern ourselves especially with whether it can justify novel principles. For the sake of examining some further interesting points, however, let us tentatively forget our first criticism and start afresh.

Let us now ask ourselves this. Suppose I am a hedonist in ethics; that is, suppose I hold that something is worthwhile in itself only if—and to the degree that—it is a pleasant experience. This means that I reject such propositions as: Thinking true thoughts is better in itself than thinking false ones —a proposition many people have been convinced of. The question that comes up, then, is: *Could* contextualistic reasoning ever show that this second proposition is true and that my original belief is therefore, at least partly, false? Can any appeal to science ever establish a novel ethical principle of this kind?

Our suggestion is that the answer to this question is "No," and if correct, this seems to be an objection to the theory. It does seem that somehow we do and must adjudicate proposals of such novel principles. Perhaps we do so only by bad reasoning. (We must later consider and assess what seems to be a more satisfactory alternative account of justification, and, until we have done this, the possibility remains that the contextualistic reasoning is the only valid type of reasoning in ethics.) Nevertheless, pending further discussions, it does seem that if contextualistic reasoning cannot adjudicate novel principles, there is something wrong, and we have less than what we are looking for.

On what grounds might one say that contextualistic reasoning cannot adjudicate novel principles of the kind mentioned? Let us look at an example.

Suppose I want to assess the proposition, "Thinking true thoughts is better in itself than thinking false ones"—or, for short, "Knowledge is worthwhile in itself." How might a contextualist try to judge this? Let us assume he has one undoubted ethical premise—the hedonist premise. In order to assess whether knowledge is worthwhile, he therefore appeals to observation and science, to see if knowledge is apt to bring worthwhile experiences. That is, he will attempt to use an argument like this:

PREMISE: Something is worthwhile in itself if and only if it is a pleasant experience.

PREMISE (from science): Having knowledge is apt to produce pleasant experience in such-and-such ways.

CONCLUSION: Having knowledge is apt to produce what is worthwhile in itself.

FURTHER CONCLUSION: Having knowledge is instrumentally worthwhile, that is, worth seeking in view of its probable effects.

The appeal to science is in establishing the second premise. To be sure, in this case there is not an appeal to "science" in any very elaborate sense. Rather, the contextualist will point to simple and obvious facts, such as that knowledge (for example, psychological) will help in self-understanding and, hence, help to avoid frustration, or that knowledge of the principles of aesthetics is likely to help one enjoy novels or pictorial art more fully, and so on. Doubtless all of us could point out a good many ways in which having knowledge adds, or is likely to add, to the enjoyment of life.

However, note that what this argument shows is that having knowledge is instrumentally worthwhile, worth seeking in view of its probable effects, and *not* that it is worthwhile in itself, that is, worthwhile when we disregard its effects. What we set out to establish was that knowledge is, or is not, worthwhile *in itself*. The reasoning along contextualist lines has not done this, nor can it do so. If one starts out with the premise that pleasure is worthwhile in itself, one can never, by adducing nonethical premises, establish that knowledge is worthwhile in itself.[8] The premises can only show that having knowledge usually results in pleasure, in one way or another, and therefore that knowledge usually is worth choosing on account of its consequences.

The argument can be put in more general terms. Suppose we start with an ethical premise, "Being *P*, by itself, makes something more *G* than it otherwise would have been" (where "*G*" designates some ethical property). Now suppose we say that, for this context, a derived ethical principle is a *novel* one only if (1) it has the form, "Being *R*, by itself, makes anything more *G* than it would otherwise have been" and (2) being *R* does not logically necessitate being *P*. It is then clear that we shall never, by adding nonethical premises to our ethical premise, demonstrate that a *novel* ethical principle must be accepted. Premises drawn from science and observation might help show that something which is *R* would, on account of the consequences of being *R*, be more *G* than it would otherwise have been—but not that it would be because of *R by itself*. Nonethical premises could lead to this latter conclusion (when taken with the given ethical premise) only if they could show that being *R* logically entailed or necessitated being *P*,

---

[8] It cannot be established unless one asserts that knowledge is a *species* of pleasure. But this is not true, as we shall see later (p. 334). Even if it were, one's original premise, "Pleasure is worthwhile in itself," would not need amplification. It would not be as if something different from pleasure had been shown to be worthwhile in itself.

for instance by showing that what it is to be R is to be P and something else, say Q. But then the conclusion still is not novel, since it now fails to have the second property of "novel" principles.

The contextualist will presumably reply by admitting the inferences but adding that there is no particular reason why we should be interested in establishing "novel" principles, in the sense above. In particular, he may profess disinterest in knowing what is *worthwhile in itself*. The practical question, he will say, is merely knowing what is worthwhile or best. We want to know whether knowledge is worthwhile; contextualist reasoning can establish this, starting from such a premise as the one that states that enjoyment is worthwhile. The question whether something is worthwhile in itself is an artificial philosopher's problem, with no relevance to the practical problems of conduct.

This contextualist reply is not very satisfactory. First, and less important, is the fact that even if these questions—whether "novel" principles can be established, or whether things besides pleasure (or whatever the initial premise is about) are worthwhile in themselves—had little or no importance for practical decisions and are philosophers' questions, they are none the less interesting for that. We do want to be able to decide such questions, and we seem to be able to do so. (Theologians will want to know, because many of them will find a theistic metaphysics less compelling, if the only thing worthwhile in itself is pleasure.) But second, these issues are *not* irrelevant to practical decisions. Let us see how this is.

Suppose two men are arguing about how monetary income should be distributed to workers. There are only two general ethical principles they can agree on: that people ought to promote the good, and that one thing worthwhile in itself is pleasure or enjoyment. One of them, however, holds a further ethical principle: that equality of welfare is important in itself. Now, the question is: If they argue *solely* on the basis of the agreed principles, but use as many facts drawn from science as possible, will they come to the same conclusions, about how money should be distributed, to which they would come if they also agreed about the value of equality of welfare? The answer is that they will *not*. What, in particular, will be the difference in practical outcome? For one thing, we shall see (in Chapter 16) that argument on the fewer principles will not enable them to justify compensating workers for the relative unpleasantness or risk or onerousness of their jobs; such reasoning will not allow us to justify (certainly if we decline to use a type of reasoning which many do not accept) the view that everyone should be paid a "living wage" or that there should be a "floor" of welfare below which society should allow no one to fall. Surely these consequences are serious matters. If they are not "practical," then what is?

In asserting, as we do, that use of contextualist reasoning cannot establish any novel ethical principles, there are some things we must be careful not to deny. Of course, such principles as this can be established: "Knowledge is usually worthwhile on account of its probable contribution to enjoyment" (if we are starting with a premise about the worthwhileness of enjoyment). This is a "novel" principle of a sort (although not in the sense explained above). Moreover, we must be careful not to deny that, as a consequence of the occurrence of contextualist reasoning, people *may come to accept as unquestioned* some principles that initially they had not accepted. What is to be counted as one's stock of "unquestioned" principles can vary from time to time; and surveying the facts of science may well result in this stock being narrowed or widened. As a result of reflecting on the contributions of knowledge to enjoyment, a person might come to accept, as an unquestioned principle, that knowledge is worthwhile in itself. Note, however, that this result, if it occurs, is only a *psychological effect* of the reasoning; it is not *logically established* by the contextualist method. Theoretically, the method must ignore the adoption of new principles in the course of reflection—because, in principle, it cannot assess novel principles.

Our conclusion is that contextualist reasoning—starting from a base of unquestioned ethical principles, and drawing on the results of science to move by logic to other statements, theorems that happen to be of interest to us—is incompetent to assess some ethical principles that are philosophically interesting and practically important to assess. There is a good reason, then, for looking around carefully for a more satisfactory theory of valid ethical reasoning than contextualism.

Incidentally, contextualism is by no means as sharply defined a theory as appears at first, and some contextualists would perhaps be given pause if they explored some of its vague spots. For instance, how do we identify an "unquestioned principle," and how do we explore the scope of a person's stock of "unquestioned principles"? Are these the principles he would cite firmly as being true and relevant to a given problem, or at least those he vaguely has in mind when a certain problem is raised? Or those he would assent to confidently if they were suggested to him? Or are we to count the fact that, *if* a situation of a certain sort arose, he *would* think or feel very decidedly about the matter? Or suppose a person asserts *contradictory* principles very firmly. Shall we say, perhaps, that his unquestioned principles are those he would espouse if he settled these contradictions— and perhaps settled the conflict between them and the particular judgments he would make if he were placed in certain situations (for example, if he were put in a position where he could see what race-discrimination is like in the concrete)? It would be extremely interesting to have answers to these questions.

The critic of contextualism ought not to question the thesis that we do often argue in the manner the contextualist describes. Of course, we do. The only thing he should doubt is the exclusive feature of the theory: the proposal that reasoning of the contextualist type is the only sort of reasoning in ethics that is valid reasoning. This he should deny, or at least question. Reasoning of the contextualist type is proper, valid, and important; it cannot be left out of any adequate theory of what constitutes proper ethical reflection and criticism. However, the critic will say, and we agree: It is only part of the story.

FURTHER READINGS

John Dewey, *Essays in Experimental Logic* (Chicago: University of Chicago Press, 1916), chap. 14.

————, *The Quest for Certainty* (New York: Minton, Balch, and Co., 1929), chap. 10.

————, *Theory of Valuation*, in *International Encyclopedia of Unified Science* (Chicago: University of Chicago Press, 1939), vol. II, No. 4.

————, *Human Nature and Conduct* (New York: Carlton House, 1922), Part III.

————, and J. H. Tufts, *Ethics* (New York: Henry Holt & Company, Inc., 1938), chaps. 10 and 11.

Joseph Ratner (ed.), *Intelligence in the Modern World: John Dewey's Philosophy* (New York: Modern Library, 1939), chap. 14.

Sidney Hook, *John Dewey: an Intellectual Portrait* (New York: John Day Company, Inc., 1939), chap 7.

————, "The Desirable and Emotive in Dewey's Ethics," in Sidney Hook (ed.), *Philosopher of Science and Freedom* (New York, Dial Press, Inc., 1950).

A. Edel, *Ethical Judgment: The Use of Science in Ethics* (Glencoe, Ill.: Free Press, 1955).

————, "Naturalism and Ethical Theory" in Y. H. Krikorian (ed.), *Naturalism and the Human Spirit* (New York: Columbia University Press, 1944).

M. C. Beardsley, *Aesthetics: Problems in the Philosophy of Criticism* (New York: Harcourt, Brace & Company, 1958), pp. 524–43, 555.

4

The Use of Authority in Ethics

The requirements of consistency and generality, we have seen, are not by themselves adequate tests for the validity of a set of ethical principles. Conformity with observation and the substantiated results of science is another requirement we may fairly make of ethical principles. But is this enough? In the preceding chapter we decided that it is not, *provided* a naturalistic theory about the meaning of ethical terms is indefensible, and *provided* there is not a "third mode of inference," neither inductive nor deductive, which permits us to draw ethical conclusions from nonethical premises. Since we have not yet discussed these provisos, we have not quite finished with the question of whether coherence with observation and the results of science conjoined with consistency and generality, in the sense already discussed, is not a sufficient test for the validity of ethical beliefs. Since we are not yet ready for these issues, however, it is better to postpone discussion of them.

Instead, let us consider now another test for valid ethical principles, that of conformity with some "authority," whether religious, institutional, or otherwise. Many people have supposed that appeal to an authority—for instance, a comparison of one's own ethical views with those of Jesus or Buddha—is a proper test of one's ethical views; and undoubtedly, awareness of the ethical principles of such "authorities" has greatly influenced the moral thinking of conscientious people. We must examine with care the question of whether, or to what extent, such appeals to authority are justified, whether they are a good and accurate test of the validity of ethical statements.

It is convenient to formulate three different assertions that may be made about an "authority," whether religious, institutional, or any other. (1) It might be said that whenever the authority "says" (in some sense) that something is right, or desirable (and so on, for all ethical predicates), then that thing *is* right or desirable *usually*, or for the most part. Anyone who asserts this might be said to think that an authority is *importantly relevant* in ethics. This is the mildest of the claims that can properly be called an "authoritarian" view. (2) It might be said that whenever the authority "says" (in some sense) that something is right, then that thing *always* is right. Anyone who asserts this may be said to hold that an authority is *infallible* in matters of ethics. A person who takes this view is committed to holding that whenever there is a conflict between ethical opinions, however tested otherwise, and the authority, the authority must always be deferred to. But he need not deny that there can be reliable ethical knowledge got otherwise than by consulting the pronouncements of the authority. (3) A more extreme view is to hold that there can be *no* reliable ethical knowledge without appeal to the authority. More specifically, it may be held that any valid justification of an ethical belief must include a correct statement about the view or pronouncement of the authority, so that, in order to be justified in believing any ethical statement, one would first have to be justified in believing a statement about the view or pronouncement of the authority. Let us call this view the *authoritarian theory of justification*.

It will be convenient and clarifying to keep these three possible authoritarian claims separate for the various types of authority we must consider. In each case, it will be simplest to begin by assessing the first and weakest claim, then to examine the third claim, and finally to consider the second claim.

Historically, such claims have been made principally on behalf of two types of "authority": first, public opinion or institutions and customs; and second, religious teachers or supernatural beings such as God. We shall begin with the former.

1. PUBLIC OPINION OR INSTITUTIONS AS AN AUTHORITY

Practically everyone is inclined, in case of doubt whether something is desirable or right, to follow generally-accepted ethical views, if there are any and if their character is known—particularly views common in the social group to which one wishes to belong and with which one wishes to be classified. We could also say that in case of doubt one is inclined to follow the "institutions" or "customs" of one's social group. What we want to assess is the justification for this common—perhaps we should say, all *too* common—inclination.

In order to assess this inclination, let us examine the three types of view we have said might be taken about public opinion as an authority—or other kinds of authority. Let us ask (1) whether public opinion is always an importantly relevant fact to take into account in deciding what is right. Let us ask (2) whether public opinion is infallible in matters of morals. And let us ask (3) whether it is reasonable to say we can have no reliable knowledge in ethics, except as we know about public opinion. We shall, however, postpone the second question to the end.

Is public opinion importantly relevant? There are many cases in which we do think that one person should take very seriously into consideration the views or advice of some other person, in deciding what he should do. Consider, for instance, the case of a twelve-year-old boy who is strongly tempted to decline an invitation to a dance-party by a girl he does not particularly like. Most of us would agree that in this, as in most other matters, he should follow the advice of his parents. Why? His parents' advice in this case is based, we may suppose, on the desirability of his having an opportunity to learn some of the social graces, or of his learning habits of courtesy and politeness toward persons with whom he is apt to associate in later life and with whom a friendly relationship will be ultimately pleasant. These considerations may make little appeal to a twelve-year-old boy; he is not apt to think of them at all, and even if he does he has not had enough experience to be able to visualize the alternatives adequately, or to assess their relative desirability from his own point of view. Usually, when a child's view about what is desirable or right differs from that of his parents, his view is comparatively indefensible, for some reasons of this sort.

Something similar may be said of an individual's relation to group ethical convictions. Such convictions, we may assume, have been subject to and have withstood criticism over the years, especially by those who may have suffered from them; hence, the main moral convictions of the group may be expected to have strong reason on their side. If a person differs with these convictions, very often it will be because he has not thought of various important supporting considerations; or if he has, he may not be able to visualize them clearly—or impartially, if his own personal interests happen to collide with them.

In general, then, there is a presumption that any generally accepted moral conviction has some validity to it. Probably no one would question that this is so. Although conformity is often derided, much can be said in defense of it, up to a certain point. The accepted moral convictions of one's group are certainly *importantly relevant;* they are likely to be sufficiently defensible so that serious consideration should be given them.

Must we know public opinion in order to get at ethical truth? We now turn to a much more radical proposal. Why should anyone think that we cannot *possibly* have a justified ethical opinion about something unless we already know what public opinion is? Some maintain the position that we cannot for a reason that, incidentally, also proves (if it is correct at all) that public opinion is infallible in matters of ethics. Their reason is that "*x* is right" *means* only that "public opinion is in favor of *x*" (and similarly for the other ethical terms), or something of this sort. Obviously, if this is correct we have to know what public opinion is in order to know what is right.

This seems an extreme view, and one may wonder whether anyone really believes it. It is true that one rarely sees it in print, but it seems likely that many modern parents think that morality is not distinguishable from the fact of group approval—doubtless without seeing the full implications of their view. This view, however, has sometimes been advocated by substantial figures in the social sciences, for instance, by the French sociologist Emile Durkheim, and early in the present century a Yale sociologist, W. G. Sumner, wrote that

> We shall find proof that "immoral" never means anything but contrary to the mores of the time and place. . . .
> For the people of a time and place, their own mores are always good, or rather . . . for them there can be no question of the goodness or badness of their mores. . . .
> The "right" way is the way which the ancestors used and which has been handed down.[1]

We should notice that according to Sumner's view, what it means to say that an act is immoral is not that it is contrary to the customs or public opinion of *our* present society and age, but to those of the society and time in which the act occurred.

But does "immoral" or any other ethical term *mean the same* as some statement about the public opinion of the time and society in which an act occurred? It is easy to show that the answer is negative. For instance, suppose a New Yorker and an Alabaman are engaged in an argument about whether it was right for a certain jury in Mississippi to bring in a verdict of "not guilty" in the case of the trial of a White man for the murder of a Negro, in the face of overwhelming testimony of eye-witnesses about what occurred. If Sumner's theory were correct, it would seem the two are arguing about whether most people in the state of Mississippi approve of the act. But this is an absurd proposal. The New Yorker might concede, for the sake of the argument, that most Mississippians did approve, but regard this matter as quite irrelevant to the dispute. Can one seriously urge that he *is* arguing only about whether most Mississippians approve, despite the fact that he thinks he is arguing about something quite different? Nor is it any more impressive to say that he is, rather, making a claim about what "most Americans" think. The Alabaman might be quite ready to agree that there are more Northerners than Southerners, and hence might willingly concede that most Americans would disagree with the verdict, but he might still go

[1] *Folkways* (Boston: Ginn and Company, 1934), pp. 418, 58, 28. Sumner, however, is a very loose writer, and it is doubtful if he seriously intended to say what he in fact says. He is quite willing to criticize mores for their adaptiveness. Indeed, he says that if anybody criticizes a feature of the mores, this shows they are on the way to a new adjustment! From this one might infer from one's own doubt, that the doubted folkway must be mistaken and due for a change.

on to defend it. According to the theory in question, the statement "The verdict was immoral" means "The verdict was contrary to the mores of the time and place." In other words, according to it, the New Yorker, if he says, "The verdict was not contrary to the mores of the time and place but it was still immoral," is saying something as self-contradictory as if he said, "The man has been married, but he is still a bachelor" (if we assume that part of the meaning of "bachelor" is "never has been married").

In a later chapter (Chapter 7), we shall examine more extensively how we must go about deciding what a word means, but we do not need the benefit of this discussion to be quite clear that, whatever ethical terms may mean, ethical statements are not just comments about the public opinion of the times. We are not contradicting ourselves when we say that it was wrong to practice child exposure in Greece, or duelling in France, or capital punishment for the theft of twopence in England, however much we acknowledge that these actions were approved and accepted at the time.

Is public opinion infallible in ethics? If we adopted the view of Sumner about the meaning of ethical terms, then public opinion could not be mistaken (except when it condemns acts in another age or society!), for all it means to say something is right is to say that the public opinion of the relevant society approves. But one can renounce Sumner's untenable thesis and still think that public opinion is infallible in ethics. Writers like G. W. F. Hegel, F. H. Bradley, and Edmund Burke have thought that when an individual's private opinion about a moral issue clashes with accepted moral beliefs or institutions, the individual at least almost always does well to defer to the accepted. They have thought that the social forces that produce institutions and widespread beliefs are such as almost to guarantee that these are best for the situation. There is an "unconscious reason" in the development of institutions that practically assures that the *status quo* is the ethically most defensible arrangement for society.

We need not enter upon the details of the views of these writers about the dynamics of social institutions, in order to assess their view. We may agree with them—and with most sociologists today—that all institutions and customs are socially beneficial *in some respect or other*, but this is by no means to say that it would always be better if generally accepted ethical convictions were followed in preference to some less generally accepted convictions. We can sometimes know that the prevailing institution is worse than some alternative that could be adopted, and we can see clearly how the social forces that operated in its adoption were such that a better alternative was necessarily passed by. Take for instance the divorce laws in Nevada as compared with those in New York State. The advocate of the infallibility of institutions must argue that conditions in Nevada are such that a lenient law is best there, whereas conditions in New York are such that a very strict law is in order there. Nothing could be more absurd; it is quite clear that the conditions in the two states warrant no such difference, but rather that the laws in one state (maybe both) are in need of overhaul-ing. However, it is not surprising to us that there are these disparities, for we know that laws are often the work of pressure groups, or of well-organized minorities. The activity of a few ardent anti-vivisectionists, or of a religious group desirous of having its traditional views about marriage made into law, or of ardent proponents of race purity, or of a few men fearful of foreign entanglements and convinced of international programs suitable only for the nineteenth century—such activity and its success are well known, and it would be a rash person who would say that such successes are always for the best. Or consider the influence of small pressure groups. Should the petroleum industry be subject to price regulation by the federal government? Congressmen from consuming areas tend to say "Yes"; congressmen from producing areas tend to say "No." Can we seriously suppose that what this process produces will always be in the best interests of the nation? Much the same can be said of the birth and life of institutions generally—and for the prevalence of moral beliefs. We need not agree with the Marxist view that the social "superstructure" of institutions and moral beliefs always reflects class interests and the play of economic forces, but we ignore plain fact if we deny that sometimes moral beliefs and institutions enjoy their status through ignorance, inertia, or group-interest.

2. RELIGIOUS TEACHERS OR GOD AS ETHICAL AUTHORITIES

A question very similar to the one we have been considering is: "What is the reasonable attitude for us to take toward the moral teaching of religious leaders like Jesus or Buddha, or commandments ascribed to God?" The attempt to answer it, however, is much complicated by the fact that we cannot know by observation whether there is a God who issues commandments, much less what such commandments are; and by the fact that it is often held that some religious teacher speaks for God, or he himself in some sense *is* God.

It is convenient to divide this question into three different but related questions, parallel to those we have just examined in connection with the thesis that public opinion should be one's ethical authority.

First Question: Are the ethical recommendations of religious teachers deserving of serious consideration?

In considering the first question, we shall tentatively set aside the view that a religious teacher is or speaks for God; if that is true, doubtless the teacher deserves more than "serious consideration." For the present, let us consider what may be said if we make no such assumption.

Many people have reported that they have found great religious litera-ture, in some cases Buddhist and in others Jewish or Christian, a source of ethical insight. Moreover, religious leaders have undoubtedly made considerable contributions to the ethical tradition of mankind. For instance, if we look at the impact of the Jewish prophets and of Jesus on the Judaeo-Christian tradition, and then compare the whole of this tradition with Greek ethical thinking, we shall probably conclude that these religious men have taught Western thinking much on such matters as justice for the poor and the enslaved, the ideal nature of marriage and the family, the proper position of woman in society, and the propriety of helpfulness and sympathy for the sick and aged.

These reflections alone should convince us that we do well to familiarize ourselves with the work of the great religious teachers, as a means of enriching our ethical thinking and sharing as fully as possible in the Western tradition of ethical thought. However, in order to get the logic of the situation as simple as possible, let us consider the following as a justification for looking seriously to, say, the teachings of Jesus, when perplexed by an ethical problem:

A person might say: "I have read a good deal of the teaching of Jesus. I can see that, on what are clearly subtle moral matters but ones on which I have myself reflected very carefully, the teaching of Jesus is accurate, indicative of profound insight. Therefore, I am justified in turning to his teaching for guidance on matters on which I have myself not reflected deeply, or about which I may well be biased by personal interest; for probably his teaching will be right." Of course, a given person's evaluation of the teaching of any particular religious figure may not be as favorable as is here suggested. For instance, in the case of Jesus one might feel that the teaching about divorce is so rigid as to be unrealistic; or one might criticize Jesus' act in sending demons into a herd of swine that belonged to somebody else (Luke 8: 32–33). But the reasoning is formally sound, being an inductive argument generalizing from past experience to probable future experience, of the kind familiar in science.

This type of reasoning can be applied more widely than just to the case of religious leaders; a similar argument will justify similar conclusions about anyone who has shown subtle moral insight in the past. Perhaps many persons are superior in moral insight, and the great religious figures are rather like the tallest peaks in a range rising gradually from a plateau. The argument may justify us in giving special thought to the ethical reflections of our next-door neighbor!

We may conclude, then, if we accept the premises of this reasoning, that it is justified to regard the ethical teaching of some religious figures as importantly relevant, worth serious consideration in moments of ethical perplexity. This, of course, is *not* yet to say that we should always accept the teaching of any religious figure, irrespective of the extent and care of our own moral reflections. Further, the reasoning does not, of course, justify accepting the ethical pronouncements of a religious teacher if he has not demonstrated his ethical insight in areas of ethics where we are in a position to judge ethical penetration.

We should notice, however, that one cannot consistently use this reasoning if one is or thinks oneself devoid of independent ethical knowledge. In order to be able to assert the conclusion of a valid argument, we must be in a position to know that the premises are true. In this case, the premise is an assertion that the ethical teachings of a religious leader are "accurate, indicative of profound insight"—something one cannot know unless one has ethical knowledge independently of the authority of the religious teacher, since one is justified in relying on his teachings (at least, as a consequence of this argument) only after the premises are established.

Second Question: Is knowledge of religious teaching essential to the justification of ethical beliefs?

We come now to a much more complex issue: whether we can ever be justified in accepting any ethical principle except as we know it was taught by some religious leader, or perhaps a religious book, such as the Bible. This issue is certainly an important one: Our conclusions about it will decide whether we can reasonably expect to find a way to determine the validity of an ethical statement short of elaborate theological inquiries, or to determine, without such inquiries, what are the important valid ethical principles.

Why should anyone think that ethical knowledge depends on acquaintance with the ethical doctrines of some religious teacher? A double reason is commonly given: (1) It is thought that one cannot know that an ethical principle is true unless one knows some *theological* proposition, for example, a proposition about God's will or commands—meaning by a "theological proposition" any statement about a God in the sense of a self-conscious, powerful, and supernatural being. (2) It is thought that the theological propositions relevant for ethics can be known, not by ordinary human reflection, but only through revelation, that is, through some person who, being God or being somehow "inspired" by God, is competent to speak accurately, at least for the most part, about God.

The more important of these two reasons, and the one with which we shall concern ourselves for the present, is the former one: that we are justified in believing an ethical statement only if we are justified in believing some theological proposition.

In order to avoid unfortunate misunderstandings, let us begin by formulating two points that are not here in dispute, and that are a matter of general agreement and beyond controversy.

First, it is agreed that there are *some* ethical statements or principles for the justification of which theological knowledge is essential. Consider, for example: "One should worship God," or "One should not take the name of God in vain," or "One should rest on the Sabbath day, to keep it holy." It is rather obvious that, in order to justify these statements or injunctions, one must have some reason for believing that there is a God, and that it is God's desire or command that no one should work on the Sabbath day. Moreover, if there is to be an obligation to do God's will on the matter of the Sabbath observance, it is surely relevant whether God has created, preserved, and redeemed man, and whether, therefore, there may be obligations of gratitude to God in view of these benefits to us—in accordance with the general ethical principle that "one ought to express one's gratitude to those who have conferred a benefit on one." Obviously, in the case of ethical statements that refer especially to God, or that are statements about religious duties, theological propositions must form part of the justification. The question before us now, however, is whether they must form part of the justification for every ethical statement.

In the second place, it is agreed that an answer to the question of whether theological knowledge is needed as a foundation for ethical knowledge does *not* commit us, necessarily, on the question whether moral propositions can somehow lead, logically, to theological propositions. Suppose that we hold —as we shall—that theological statements are *not*, in general, an essential part of ethical justifications. It is still open to us to say that ethics somehow commits us to a theology; at least whether it does is still a question to be argued on its own merits. Some writers have held that we cannot *explain* how there are ethical facts at all unless there is a divine mind that somehow sustains or underlies such facts; it has also been argued that no area of facts can be independent of the divine nature, and hence that all facts must somehow point to God. We need not dispute this. What is here being discussed is what is required in order to know that an ethical statement is true, as distinct from what follows, if some ethical statement is, or is known to be, true. To use technical terms, we are discussing an "epistemological" as distinct from a "metaphysical" point, and our epistemological conclusions need not rule out a theological metaphysics. The distinction we are making is common, and sharply made by various Catholic writers; one of them has put it as follows:

> Morality as such essentially presupposes God's existence. . . . We want to say that moral values only possess the ultimate reality which justifies the gravity of the moral order, of its majestic obligation, if they are ultimately rooted and embodied in the Absolute Person of God. . . . This does not mean, however, that we must have a knowledge of God's existence, either by Revelation or by rational demonstration [for the purposes of ethics].
> . . . The notion of a personal God is not indissolubly connected with the experience of moral values, nor does the voice of conscience presuppose the knowledge of a personal God.[2]

Some views of religious writers on the second question. The most widely held view among Christian theologians has been that ethical knowledge does *not* in general require knowledge of theological propositions. Hence,

[2] D. von Hildebrand, *Christian Ethics* (New York: David McKay Company, Inc., 1953), pp. 455–56.

it has been admitted that atheists and pagans can have moral knowledge of at least limited scope.[3]

St. Paul, for example, wrote in the Epistle to the Romans: "When Gentiles who have not the law do by nature what the law requires, they are a law to themselves, even though they do not have the law. They show that what the law requires is written on their hearts." Professor Reinhold Niebuhr, the eminent contemporary Protestant theologian, has commented on this: "Following St. Paul, Christian thought has consistently maintained that the law must be regarded, not simply as something which is given man either by revelation, or for that matter by the authority of society, but as written in the heart. This can only mean that the requirements of action, dictated by man's essential nature, are a part of his real self."[4] It is possible, of course, that both St. Paul and Professor Niebuhr hold only that men have irrational moral *convictions* irrespective of theological knowledge, but that a *justification* of these convictions would necessarily involve theological propositions; but there seems no reason for making this interpretation—although in the case of St. Paul it is probably a mistake to suppose that he has a definite theory of ethical justification or knowledge at all.

The main tradition of Catholic thought, similarly, has denied the dependence of ethical knowledge on theological knowledge of any sort; the basic principles of ethics, it is usually said, are rationally self-evident. V. J. Bourke, an influential contemporary Catholic writer, quotes with approval the following passage from St. Thomas Aquinas:

> The precepts of the law of nature [moral law] are related to practical reason [moral reason], as the first principles of demonstration are to speculative reason, for both are self-evident principles. . . . It is necessary that every act of reasoning proceed from some knowledge which possesses a certain uniformity and stability. This [knowledge] does not come about by discursive investigation; rather, it is presented all at once to the intellect. For, just as reason in speculative matters goes deductively from some self-evident principles, the habitus of which is called understanding, so also must the practical reason make its deductions from some self-evident principles (for example, that evil should not be done, that the precepts of God will have to be obeyed, and others such); and, the habitus of these is synderesis. . . . If any error could befall these, no certainty would be found in the entire consequent knowledge. . . . So, we concede that in it [synderesis] there could not be sin."[5]

St. Thomas Aquinas goes on to say that "No one can know the eternal law as it is in itself, except God and the blessed who see God in His essence. But every rational creature knows it according to some reflection, greater

---

[3] The most reasonable discussion by a Protestant theologian is in Hastings Rashdall's *Conscience and Christ* (London: Gerald Duckworth & Co., Ltd., 1933). Catholic readers might well consult the article "Ethics" in the *Catholic Encyclopedia*.

[4] Reinhold Niebuhr, *The Nature and Destiny of Man* (New York: Charles Scribner's Sons, 1941), I, p. 275.

[5] V. J. Bourke, *Ethics* (New York: The Macmillan Company, copyright 1951), pp. 188–93. Used by permission of The Macmillan Company.

or less. For every knowledge of truth is a kind of reflection and participation of the eternal law. . . . Now all men know the truth to a certain extent, at least as to the common principles of the natural law [moral law]." Hence, he infers, "The natural law is common to all nations." In the case of complex moral problems, he says, matters are not so obvious and there are differences of opinion. Further, moral knowledge may be corrupted by bad habits, to some extent. "Thus at one time theft, although it is expressly contrary to natural law, was not considered wrong among the Germans, as Julius Caesar relates." Aquinas regards the basic moral principles, however, as essentially knowable independent of revelation, or of any theological knowledge whatsoever.[6]

Nevertheless we do encounter contrary views, and we should look at these. Among earlier theologians, William of Ockham and possibly some passages in the work of Duns Scotus[7] propose that the basic propositions of ethics are true only because of an arbitary divine act, and therefore, presumably, we could not know that these ethical propositions are true if we did not somehow know of this divine act.

Again, the contemporary Anglican theologian, R. C. Mortimer, Bishop of Exeter, writes:

> God made us and all the world. Because of that he has an absolute claim on our obedience. We do not exist in our own right, but only as His creatures, who ought therefore to do and be what He desires. . . . From the doctrine of God as the Creator and source of all that is, it follows that a thing is not right simply because we think it is, still less because it seems to be expedient. It is right because God commands it. . . . There is a real and objective difference between right and wrong which is rooted in the will of God.

It sounds very much as if Mortimer holds that one can justify a claim that something is right only if one is in a position to show that this is consistent with God's will, that is, if one knows a theological proposition.[8]

The neo-orthodox Protestant theologian, Emil Brunner, has stated a rather similar view:

> The Good has its basis and its existence solely in the will of God. An idea like that in the religion of Zarathustra: that God became Lord because He chose the Good, the idea of a law which is even higher than God Himself, is

---

[6] *Summa Theologica* first part of the second part, q. 93, art. 2; q. 94, arts. 2, 4.

[7] But the eminent Catholic historian of philosophy, Frederick Copleston, S.J., holds that the view of Scotus was that the content of moral law, at least as regards first principles, is independent of the divine will, and necessarily true. See his *History of Philosophy*, II (London: Burns, Oates & Washbourne, Ltd., 1954), chap. 50.

[8] R. C. Mortimer, *Christian Ethics* (London: Hutchinson's University Library, 1950), pp. 7–8. But Mortimer is far from consistent. For instance, in the passage cited, Mortimer says that since God created us, we "ought" to do his will. Is *this* fact constituted merely by God's wanting us to do his will? It would be circular to argue that we ought to do God's will because he so wills it. Moreover it certainly does not *follow*, at least logically, from the proposition that God has created us, that God's commands fix what is right and wrong.

unthinkable in the Old Testament. God is not merely the guardian of the Moral Law and of the moral ordinances, but their Creator. . . . There is no Good save obedient behaviour, save the obedient will. But this obedience is rendered not to a law or a principle which can be known beforehand, but only to the free, sovereign will of God. The Good consists in always doing what God wills at any particular moment. . . . Every theme of dogmatics is also inevitably a theme of ethics. Dogmatics does not exist independently, nor does ethics, but dogmatic knowledge as such always aims at existential, that is, ethical thought, and ethical knowledge is rooted in knowledge of dogmatics. . . . There is no such thing as an "intrinsic Good." The hypostatization of a human conception of the Good as the "Idea of the Good" is not only an abstraction in the logical sense; it is due to the fact that man has been severed from his Origin . . . that is, that man makes himself God. . . . Therefore of ourselves we cannot know the Good or the Will of God. . . . Even human nature, the human spirit, and its innermost sanctuary, the conscience, does not know God's will. . . . Man of himself knows God's Law, it is true, but not His Command, and because he does not know the Law as His Command, he does not rightly know the meaning of the Law, which is love. . . . God wills our true happiness; but He wills it, and He wills it in such a way that no one else knows what His will is. It remains outside our disposal, and indeed we do not know it. We never know what is right for us, nor what is best for the other person. We go astray when we think that we can deduce this from some principle or another, or from some experience, and we distort the thought of the divine love if we think that we know what He ought to do for us in accordance with his love.[9]

The same belief is to be found in some fundamentalist groups; and as an example of this, we may cite the contemporary theologian, E. J. Carnell. According to him, "There is no morality without metaphysics. What the Christian thinks of God controls what he thinks of the . . . good, . . . for God gives . . . content to the good. . . . The good is what God rewards and the bad what he punishes." He goes on to say:

The universe, with all of the evil in it, is the best possible of all worlds, for the very reason that God, the standard of good, has called it good. . . . God's nature, then, is one which expresses itself in making this kind of a world where some men go to heaven for obedience and some go to hell for disobedience. . . . Since God's standards *are* good, it is well that we point out exactly what the element of univocity is in the propositions, "What God does is good" and "What a properly ordered society does is good." . . . The solution to the problem is this. The univocal element . . . in both usages of the term "good" is, "approbated by the will of the Almighty." . . . Both are reflections of the one will of God. The ten commandments are good, and damning those to hell who trample under foot the Son of God is good, solely and only because God approves of such acts. . . . God's laws, then, define the duty for man.[10]

[9] Emil Brunner, *The Divine Imperative* (Philadelphia: The Westminster Press, 1947), pp. 53, 83, 84, 114–15, 120. See also Paul Ramsey, *Basic Christian Ethics* (New York: Charles Scribner's Sons, 1952), pp. 6, 10, 14, 73, 84, 88.

[10] E. J. Carnell, *An Introduction to Christian Apologetics* (Grand Rapids: W.B. Eerdmans Publishing Company, 1950), pp. 300, 303, 312, 329.

Carnell cites (pp. 305–06) a large number of divine acts or judgments, and various acts of Jesus, which he concedes sensitive persons now would regard as unjust and immoral. That there is this conflict between divine act and human moral judgment he regards as simply a reflection on the latter, defending his view by Calvin's remark that "the will of God is the highest rule of justice; so that what He wills must be considered just, for this very reason, because He wills it."

It is difficult to be sure that our interpretation of these writers, as holding that ethical statements can never be justified unless we have knowledge of the will of God (hence, theological knowledge), is entirely just. All of them also say, at some point or another, that man can know his duty independently of his theological beliefs. But the serious question is whether this view—irrespective of whether it is consistently advocated by these or other writers—is a tenable one.

Difficulties for the view that theology is necessary for ethics. The proposal that theological knowledge is required for a complete justification of *any* ethical conviction must face some very serious objections.

First, it implies that no atheist or religious skeptic can have a justification for any ethical beliefs, for if a person doubts or disbelieves a certain proposition, it follows that he does not *know* that this proposition is true—for to *know* something means, in part, to believe it with utmost conviction. Therefore, religious skeptics and atheists do not know any theological proposition to be true. Thus, if knowing a theological proposition is required for a complete justification of an ethical conviction, no religious skeptic or atheist can possibly justify his belief in any ethical proposition. This is to say that a religious skeptic or atheist cannot possibly justify the judgments universally made about murder, theft, and qualities of character like kindness, sympathy, and generosity. This is a startling conception. Indeed, something even more startling also follows from the view. Does a person really *know* any theological propositions unless he has scrutinized the rational proofs (or verified the credentials of a teacher who claims to reveal divine truth) and seen that the theological propositions in question are logically inescapable? Who has done this—if indeed anybody has—except a few theologians? It follows, then, that the only persons who can justify their ethical views are those who *know* theological propositions, that is, a few theologians. This is difficult to believe.

Second, if it is true that theological knowledge is required for a complete justification of any ethical conviction, then some major proofs for the existence of God as a personal being are guilty of circularity. The moral arguments, which explicitly use ethical statements as premises, are obviously circular if one cannot know that an ethical statement is true until one knows there is a God. The same thing is also true of the teleological argument. It is essential for the movement of this argument to show that the kind of universe we actually have is one of the few possible types of universe that are worthwhile or valuable; so that if the statement that this universe is worthwhile cannot be known to be true except as we already know that some theological propositions are true, the argument contains a circularity.[11] Incidentally, a good many people have based their estimate of the person of Jesus on the subtle perceptiveness of his moral teaching and his moral stature as a man. It is not easy to see how this line of reasoning escapes circularity if ethical justification depends on theological knowledge—and the circle is plain if the theological propositions are defended as being declarations of Jesus, whose own authority is justified by his moral stature.

A third difficulty, which we must discuss at more length, is the fact that it is pointless to hold that theological knowledge is necessary for ethical knowledge, if one cannot show that theological propositions *can* justify ethical propositions. One only talks oneself into skepticism if he argues that we cannot know a certain statement S except somehow through knowing S', and then fails to show how knowing S' enables us to know S. In the following pages we shall explore the prospects for justifying ethical propositions by appeal to theological propositions; our tentative conclusion will be that the only known plausible way of doing this is *inconsistent* with holding that reliance on religious authorities (revelations of God's will), or, indeed, knowledge of any specifically theological propositions whatever, is *necessary* for the justification of ethical beliefs.

Before turning to this task, it is well to note that no one has demonstrated that a nontheological justification of ethical principles is impossible. It is hard to imagine how such a demonstration could be given. Demonstrations that a certain proposition cannot be justified without certain premises are in general very difficult—in part because it is not very sharply defined what counts as a "justification." At any rate, we can rest assured that no such proof has been forthcoming. Theologians who argue in this direction often try to show that without theological premises one is reduced to a relativistic position (according to which no single set of directives can be established as the one justifiable set of moral principles). But they have not proved this; nor have they proved that a moderate form of relativism is unpalatable or implausible; nor have they shown how we are saved from relativism even if we have some theological premises.

Can theological premises justify ethical conclusions? In order to assess the point of the claim that theological knowledge is essential for the justification of ethical propositions, we have to consider how—and whether —theological knowledge can serve to justify ethical propositions. Of course, as we have already pointed out, it can serve to show, and is indispensable in showing, the justification of ethical propositions specifically involving God, for example, ones about religious duties. In such special cases, how-

---

[11] The circularity may be avoided, in this instance, by one who holds that knowledge only about what is right, ought to be done, is morally good, and so forth, depends on theological knowledge, but not knowledge about what is desirable or worthwhile. Such a position has sometimes been occupied.

ever, we assume ethical premises. For instance, we prove that we ought to be grateful to God from the theological premise that God has given us things of great value, conjoined with the ethical premise that we ought to be grateful to all benefactors. The question before us, however, is whether our basic ethical premises can somehow be justified from theological knowledge, without the help of further ethical premises.

This question is parallel to the question of whether ethical conclusions can be justified by appeal to empirical premises, premises drawn from observation or the content of empirical science. Therefore, we can use our analysis of the preceding chapter as a guide for investigating the present issue, and can take as already established that we cannot derive, by formal deduction, any ethical conclusions from premises that contain no ethical terms. In other words, no ethical propositions follow *formally* from such propositions as "God loves all men equally" or "God disapproves of divorce"—statements in which no ethical terms occur.

If a person were asked how theological premises tend to show that certain ethical propositions are valid, he would probably offer the following deductive arguments:

PREMISE: God loves all men as children.
PREMISE: All men should love with sibling-love anyone whom God loves as a child.
CONCLUSION: All men should love all other men as brothers.

Or again:

PREMISE: God disapproves of remarriage after divorce.
PREMISE: Anything God disapproves is wrong.
CONCLUSION: Remarriage after divorce is wrong.

Both these arguments are formally impeccable, but the second premise in each case is an ethical premise, and the question remains how this premise is to be established by theological reasoning. Unless it can be, we do not have a purely theological justification of the conclusion. How then is the theological moralist to proceed?[12]

He may follow the lines suggested in the previous chapter; and if so, he

----

[12] It may be suggested that there is a simple way to remove the difficulties: We first show that God is omniscient. If he is omniscient, then he knows all true moral propositions, and disbelieves all false ones (by definition of "omniscient"). He will also approve what he knows to be good or right, and disapprove what he knows to be bad or wrong (although the justification of this assumption doubtless needs scrutiny). So, once having proved omniscience, we can make use of God's judgments of right or wrong, and his approval or disapproval, as guides for our own judgments—assuming, of course, that we are able to learn what God judges or approves.

This proposal, however, only pushes the difficulties to another point, for now we have to prove that true moral propositions are among the various things of which God has knowledge. How are we going to do this? Of course, if one has a blanket proof of omniscience, all is well, but have we any such thing—especially in view of the fact that we are prevented, on grounds of circularity, from using teleological or moral proofs?

This line of argument also ignores the question of what kind of evidence establishes ethical propositions—how God can have evidence for them. So, it illuminates nothing.

will consider three possible ways of extricating himself from the difficulty.

First, he may take a view parallel to contextualism, urging that in practical contexts there are always available ethical premises, relating ethical predicates with theological predicates, as in the second premises of the arguments above. As far as the writer knows, no advocate of theological justifications of ethics has taken this line; and if he did he would face the very same objections that seemed to us conclusive objections to scientific contextualism. This mode of escape from difficulties, then, can be disregarded.

Second, he may agree that neither inductive nor deductive reasoning can draw ethical conclusions from theological premises, but hold that there are other *valid modes of inference* that can do so. This suggestion, in the case of science, we said might not turn out to be as unpromising as it looks at first; and it will be developed at a later stage. Why, then, cannot a comparable claim be made for some type of theological justification? The answer to this question seems to be: Nobody has ever worked out such a line of argument. It has not been demonstrated either that such a justification can be given or that it cannot be given. At a later stage, we shall speak about the specific direction such a theory might take, and about its plausibility. For the present, however, we shall ignore this possibility, while continuing to bear it in mind.

Third, a person may argue that ethical conclusions can be logically derived (not *formally*, except with an extra premise stating the identity of certain meanings) from theological premises because ethical statements really *are* theological statements, when we consider their *meaning*. For instance, one might say that "*x* is wrong" *means exactly the same as* "God disapproves of *x*." So, if we know that God disapproves of *x*, we thereby automatically know that *x* is wrong. A theory of this sort, about the meaning of ethical terms, thus is parallel to the naturalistic theory of the meaning and justification of ethical statements (p. 40). We may call it the *supernaturalist* theory.[13] Everyone must agree that, if ethical terms can be adequately *defined* by theological terms, then theological propositions can imply ethical ones. If ethical supernaturalism is true, it is reasonable to hold that ethical knowledge is required for the justification of ethical propositions.[14]

What are we to say to this third theory—one apparently held by some of

---

[13] We must be careful to distinguish ethical supernaturalism, a theory about the meaning of ethical terms, from other views that may broadly be termed "supernaturalism," that is, any views according to which theological propositions are necessary or sufficient for the justification of all ethical propositions.

[14] We should notice a special form of theory for the case of "obligation." One might say, "*x* is morally obligatory" means "if one does not do *x*, one will be severely punished." Then, a theory of divine commands and punishments may be introduced, in order to show that, by virtue of these prospective punishments, something is obligatory. The objection to this view is that what we mean by "morally obligatory" is certainly not what the theory supposes. Historically this theory has been popular.

the theological writers we have quoted, including E. J. Carnell? To begin with, we must grant that the supernaturalist view is not a satisfactory account of the meanings of ethical terms, as used by *some people*. There are some persons who definitely either disbelieve in the existence of God, or are quite doubtful about this, but who on the other hand have very decided ethical convictions. It would be most implausible to suppose that what these people mean, when they say that murder is wrong, is that there is a God who disapproves of murder. Moreover, surely there are a great many people who think that it is at least a rather debatable issue whether there is a God, but who regard certain ethical propositions as true beyond the shadow of a doubt. A supernaturalist account of the meaning of ethical terms is not suitable for them, either.

If supernaturalism is to be saved, then, it must be conceded that it is a true account of the meanings of ethical terms as used by *some* people only, and not by all. Any person who holds that all persons use ethical terms in substantially the same way (and surely there is much to be said for this, in view of the fact that we rarely hold that ethical disputes arise from a real misunderstanding of ethical terms, as used by one or another party to a dispute) must admit at once that supernaturalism cannot be a true theory.

Yet, there is something to be said for the view that people use ethical terms with different meanings. Perhaps a child means by "*x* is wrong" merely something like "whoever does *x* will be punished." Similarly, there may be some who mean by "*x* is wrong" just "*x* is forbidden by God, on pain of punishment." At any rate, various intelligent persons have *thought* they meant something like this by ethical terms—for instance, Emil Brunner and E. J. Carnell. If the reader wishes to determine whether some form of supernaturalist definition is an accurate account of *his* use of ethical terms,[15] he must ask himself whether he would assert, deny, or be doubtful about the applicability of some ethical term (for example, "morally right") to any act or situation (actual or only hypothetical) if and only if he would assert, deny, or be doubtful about the application of the supposedly corresponding theological expression (for example, "not disapproved by God"). If there is not a perfect correspondence, then the supernaturalist definition must be rejected as an accurate rendering of what he means by ethical words.

The plausibility of the supernaturalist thesis to some people probably derives from their failure to raise a certain question, a question about what they *mean* by the term "God." Traditionally, we may suppose, what has been meant by saying "God disapproves of *x*" is something like this: "There is one and only one being who is creator of the universe, immaterial, not composite, infinite, omnipresent, omnipotent, omniscient, perfect, immutable, loving . . . and this being disapproves of *x*." (There are some puzzles here, for some theologians appear to hold that *no* human concepts apply

---

15 We shall discuss the criteria for deciding what a person means by a given term at some length in Chapter 7.

to God; in this case it seems that a logical consequence of their view is that the word "God" has no meaning. If one combines this consequence with the supernaturalist theory of ethical terms, there is the further implication that ethical terms, too, have no meaning. In view of this, it is proper to ignore these theologians here, and to follow the less agnostic view about the meaning of "God.")[16] Now, if this is what is meant by "God disapproves of *x*," the proponent of the supernaturalist theory of ethical terms should ask himself whether he really wants to hold that quite all this is *meant* by ethical terms. Does the use of an ethical term really assert the existence of some infinite or omnipotent being? Or, is it not rather the case that at least some of the defining attributes of God are *not* included in the meaning of ethical terms? Is the extent of God's power, or his infinity, really involved in the fact that something is wrong? It would seem not. Then we should ask the correlative question: Which of God's attributes *are* involved in its being the case that something is wrong?

The reader may feel, perhaps with reason, that there is somehow something in the supernaturalist definition, and that we are making a mistake if we just flatly say that it is indefensible. Perhaps we can discover the sources of one's feelings about this matter by considering another definition of ethical terms, in many ways similar to supernaturalist definitions but also significantly different—a definition which, however, has the effect that it is plausible to say that God's approval would, if we knew when it is given, be a guide to what is right or good. This new definition asserts that "*x* is wrong" means the same as "*x* would be disapproved by any person who knew all the relevant facts, could visualize them perfectly, and who loved all sentient beings strongly and equally."[17]

This proposal differs from the "God disapproves of *x*" definition in several important ways. First, it implies that only certain attributes of God are relevant to the truth of an ethical statement: his knowledge and his equal love for all. This seems plausible; it does seem that God's power is irrelevant to his infallibility as a moral judge, whereas his love and knowledge are not. Second, a person who asserts ethical propositions is not committed, by this definition, to asserting the *existence* of God, for, on this view, to say "*x* is wrong" is only to say that *x would* be disapproved by such-and-such a being *if* there *were* one. Hence, an atheist or skeptic may perfectly well be using ethical terms in the way this definition suggests, and therefore the theory has more plausibility as an account of the meanings of ethical terms as used by everybody. Third, the definition is more properly

[16] Some theologians would apparently not be unwilling to accept these implications, and to adopt the view that neither theological nor ethical statements have cognitive meaning in the sense in which scientific statements do. We shall deal with the merits of "noncognitive" theories of ethical terms in Chapter 9.

[17] We shall discuss a definition of this type more fully later (p. 173 ff.). A proposal of this sort has been worked out in considerable detail by Roderick Firth in "Ethical Absolutism and the Ideal Observer," *Philosophy and Phenomenological Research*, XII (1952), 317–45.

viewed as a naturalist rather than as a supernaturalist one. This will be clearer when it is discussed again as a form of naturalism; but for now it will be enough to suggest that it is a naturalistic definition because in principle we can determine by observation (in part by extrapolation of what we find ourselves approving) what a fully informed (and so forth) being would probably approve—just as we can determine how a gas will behave at a temperature of absolute zero, although no gas has ever been observed at that temperature, by extrapolating its behavior as its temperature becomes very low and approaches absolute zero. We need not regard it as a supernaturalist definition, partly because we do not need revelation in order to determine what such a being would approve, and partly because in order to know what such a being would approve of we do not need to know what a being with the specific attributes traditionally ascribed to God—simplicity, immateriality, and so forth—would approve of.

A person might ask why this new definition is regarded as plausible by anyone. To this it may be replied that a person who loves all sentient beings strongly and equally, is fully informed on the relevant facts and able to visualize the facts perfectly, is the kind of person whom we tend to regard as an ideal moral judge. Should we not incline to think something was right if we knew such a being approved of it, even if we personally—with our less adequate knowledge, and so forth—did not?[18] It is not suggested by us that this definition is correct, but only that it has *more* plausibility than a strict supernaturalist definition, and probably comes close to what many who have urged theological definitions would want to propose but have not proposed because they have not been aware of the possibility of this type of definition.[19]

[18] Yet there is difficulty here; perhaps we are leaving out certain necessary characteristics. Perhaps, to represent our meaning accurately, the being must be *human*, in a *normal* frame of mind. This is certainly a possibility to be considered.

If additions like these have to be made, then the definition is more decidedly different from the theological ones, for the main reason why this definition is like the theological ones, is that God appears to fit the description in the definition—to be, according to traditional ideas, perfectly loving and omniscient. For this reason, God's approving of something is some reason for thinking it is right, according to the defintion. However, if we have to add to it such further properties as "human" and "in a normal (human) state of mind," then it is by no means clear that God's approving of something is good reason for thinking that this is right.

[19] A reply should be made to one type of criticism of all definitions in terms of "approval," including theological definitions, popular from the time of Socrates down to the present. It is said that such definitions are necessarily circular, for the reason that approval of something necessarily implies prior knowledge that it is good or right. Approval, it may be said, is merely being in favor of something because one thinks it right. Hence, the definition of "*x* is right" turns out to be "*y* is favorable to *x* because *y* thinks *x* right"—and since "right" appears in the definiens, the definition is circular.

But this objection can be met. It is true, possibly, that it is incorrect to say "I approve" unless one would also be willing to say, "It is right." But what has to be proved is that writers who have held the approval theory have *meant* by "approval" a psychological state that cannot be defined except by ethical terms. Surely they have not done so; and surely there *is* such a thing as being in favor of something, admiring it, and so forth, without any prior ethical judgment.

If this definition is correct as an account of the meaning of "right," then, with one proviso, we can infer that something is right from theological knowledge, that is, from knowledge that God approves it. Assuming it is agreed that God is loving and omniscient, it logically follows from the fact that God approves of something that *one* being who is loving (and so on) approves. It does not logically follow that *any* such being, or *all* such beings would, although the definition requires that *all* such beings should approve, in order to say that the thing is right. The proviso, then, is the assumption that if *one* being qualified in the way stated approves, then *all* will do so. This proviso may seem one that is obviously acceptable, but later we shall see that there are questions to be raised about it. Granted this, however, then information about what God approves of (assuming this definition of "right") can tell us that something is right, or not right.

But equally, if this definition is correct, we can know whether something is right *without* knowing about God's attitudes, for what we have to know is whether a being with certain qualities would approve of something. This is a kind of knowledge—being a psychological point—that in principle can be ascertained by observation and the methods of science. So, if this definition is correct, although it is true that theological propositions can imply ethical propositions, it is *not* true that we *need* theological propositions, much less revelation, in order to evaluate the truth of ethical propositions.[20]

Let us now summarize this rather long discussion of our second question. We have concluded, first, that theological premises will justify ethical propositions only (ignoring the possible "third mode of inference" theory) if ethical statements, in view of their meaning, must be construed as theological statements. Is this view of the meaning of ethical statements plausible? We decided that it is definitely unsatisfactory for the usage of some people, although conceivably accurate for the usage of others. But the definition has uncomfortable implications for proofs of the existence of God, and we doubted that ethical terms really mean anything quite as complicated and elaborate as any concept including the traditional concept of God. We then suggested that a closely related definition might prove acceptable to writers who espouse supernaturalist definitions, if they considered it; and this definition has various attractions. According to it, however, although it is true that theological propositions (with one proviso) do imply ethical propositions, theological knowledge, nevertheless (much

---

[20] Many religious people have thought they *can* ascertain what is right or wrong independently of revealed knowledge of God's will. For this reason many have concluded that assertions made about God in the Old Testament cannot really, many of them, be accepted as correct, because a moral being could never have behaved as God is there asserted to behave. Take, for instance, the order allegedly issued by God, in *I Samuel 15:* "Go and smite Amalek, and utterly destroy all that they have, and spare them not; but slay both man and woman, infant and suckling, ox and sheep, camel and ass." Liberal Protestants, at any rate, would not accept this statement as an accurate account of the will of God.

less knowledge obtainable only through revelation by some inspired religious teacher), is not *necessary* for the justification of ethical statements. So, if we accept this alternative definition, our second question, about whether such knowledge is essential for ethical knowledge, is answered in the negative.

One crucial question we have not answered: whether some strictly supernaturalist definition of ethical terms is correct, as far as the *reader's* usage is concerned. We strongly suspect that the answer to this question is negative; and if so, then unless the alternative definition expresses his usage satisfactorily, he cannot assert that theological propositions imply ethical propositions. In that case, he cannot say that theological knowledge is essential for ethical knowledge, without becoming an ethical skeptic. (If he accepts the alternative near-theological definition, he still cannot say that knowledge strictly about God, much less revealed propositions about God, are necessary for ethics.) But if the answer is affirmative, if a strictly supernaturalist definition does suit the reader's use of ethical terms, then theological knowledge will imply ethical propositions, and theological knowledge will be essential in the justification of any ethical principle.

Third Question: Is the ethical teaching of some religious leaders infallible?

In answering our first question, we decided that the ethical doctrine of some religious teachers may well be importantly relevant for our ethical reflection. The question remained open whether there is reason to think that the teaching of some individual can be known to be infallible—whether we should always be more likely to be right if we adopted his principles than if we didn't, irrespective of the extent to which reflection and evidence seemed to point in a contrary direction. We must now examine this issue.

The question is one of first importance for anyone who thinks that ethical statements can be justified only by theological knowledge, for example, knowledge of the will of God. For a person who claims that ethical knowledge is so dependent on theological knowledge must rely on some revelation for pertinent information, for example, about the divine will. This might be denied, on the supposition that the will of God can be known by reason, in either of two ways. It is worthwhile seeing why this supposition is incorrect.

First, one way in which it may be said we can learn of God's will (without relying on moral convictions, which on this view are to be appraised by comparison with the content of God's will) is by observing nature, from which we can infer some intentions of God.[21] For instance, it may be argued that God must have intended that man propagate, else God would not have given man the sexual organs that are the means to propagation. Unfortunately, inferences of this sort are without foundation. They founder

---

[21] John Locke, for instance, in the *Two Treatises of Civil Government*, first published in 1690, argued in this way in establishing the basic principles of natural law and rights. See Part II, chap. 2.

on the fact that *all* the possibilities that are considered for action are based on, or reflect, natural capacities (no matter how bad), and hence can be said to be intended by God. Should man commit suicide? No, it will be argued, because God has given man an instinct of self-preservation. But God has also given man a dislike for pain, and an intelligence that can assess the prospects of future pains and enjoyments, and the means for taking a painless exit from this life. So, we can argue equally well that God has intended that man commit suicide when prospects for the future become grim and unbearable. Nor can it be argued that the generally accepted ethical convictions of mankind must have been intended by God and are therefore correct, for we can as well argue that since there are skeptics in ethics, God must have intended skepticism. Even if we could infer that God intended that man have certain ethical convictions, we have not yet shown that these convictions are true, for it may have pleased God that we believe false ethical propositions for some reason or other. It may be protested that such things cannot be true because God is good; but the protest is unavailing, for we are not in a position to say what things a good God would permit, until we have found what things are good, and this, *ex hypothesi*, we do not know until we have discovered the will of God.

Second, it may be argued that we can learn God's will without appeal to the "supernatural" argument, by a careful appeal to what we approve of ourselves—since our minds are examples of what a loving, informed being will approve, and we can, by extrapolation, infer what God will approve of. (It was suggested above that we do in fact often draw inferences about what God might or might not have commanded in just this way.) But we should notice that this argument draws God after our own image. The more a theologian argues for the difference between God and man, for the incomprehensibility of God in human categories, the infection of the human will by sinfulness, the more he in effect condemns the logic of such an argument. What our evidence shows is what a finite mind, with relatively full information in a certain matter but by no means omniscient, with human passions and attachments and childhood conditioning, will approve of in a certain situation. Can we really draw inferences from this about how a timeless being, exempt from all childhood conditioning and punishment and parental admonitions, devoid of human needs and wants and suffering, infinite, immutable, bodiless, and so forth, would feel? In order to have good grounds for doing so, we must know that certain characteristics of God—the very ones that differentiate him from man and make him God—are causally irrelevant to ethical approval. Do we really have such information? Not if we have no antecedent ethical knowledge, about what merits approval or disapproval.

It seems, then, that if we really need to know what *God* approves of in order to know what is right and good, we shall have to be able to identify, by reasoning that does not make use of the assumption of any moral knowledge, some special source of information.[22] If there is not any such identifiable source of information about the divine will or approval, the person who holds that theological knowledge is essential for ethical justification is reduced to skepticism in ethics.[23] Is there such a source of information?

There are two types of argument by which we might attempt to show that there is, and to identify such a source of information: an empirical argument and a supernatural argument.

The "empirical" argument is simply an extension of the argument formulated above (p. 62), to the effect that a teacher's record for accuracy of moral insight, on matters where we think we are in a position to judge, may be so impressive that it is reasonable to take his view seriously on matters about which we are in doubt. The "extension" of the argument consists in this: We might hold that his record for accuracy of insight on many matters is so impressive that it is reasonable to defer to his view even on matters about which our inclination, even after careful reflection, is to decide very differently. Is such an extension reasonable?

It is *not* reasonable, if what is meant is that we are always justified in deferring to the teacher's principles, irrespective of the strength of our own convictions and the care with which we have reflected. After all, our justification for accepting the teacher as an authority is, according to this line of argument, simply his accordance with our own past insights; if these can confirm his authority, insights that are discrepant with his principles can also invalidate it. There is a close analogue with scientific theories. Conformity with experiment can so impressively establish a scentific theory that we would keep the theory despite results that did not clearly support it and despite even a few experiments that were clearly discrepant with it, preferring to view these discordant results as a consequence of unknown experimental error. However, there is certainly a point at which carefully conducted experiments will be accepted as fact even when they are discrepant with a well-established theory, and emendation of the theory will be required in order to conform with them. If a theory in science is confirmed by experiment, it can be invalidated by more experiment; no scientific theory is infallible. Similar reasoning is applicable in our present problem. If a reputation for moral perceptiveness is established by conformity with the results of our own most careful ethical thinking in the past, this reputation may justify us in deferring to this teacher in some cases where

22 Strictly, we do not need an *infallible* source of information about God's will; if we even knew that some source of information represented the will of God most of the time, it would seem that the best chance of doing what is right would be to follow the directions of this source of information—on the assumptions of the theory under consideration.

23 Plato represents Socrates as raising this very sort of difficulty for a supernaturalist ethics, in the *Euthyphro*.

we would adopt a different view but for knowledge of his principles; but the teacher's reputation cannot be infallibly established, so that we should reasonably defer to his ethical principles in future, no matter what. The "empirical" argument will not prove infallibility.

The "supernatural" argument, in contrast, does not rely at all on our moral perceptiveness as evidence of the moral infallibility of a certain person or book. Rather, the infallibility of a teacher is proved by arguing that either he is, in some sense, God, or that his ethical pronouncements are directed by God in such a way that they can be viewed as the statements of God.

This kind of argument *must* be used by any person who thinks that a moral belief is justified only insofar as it can be derived from theological knowledge, such as knowledge about the will of God. On this view, if we are to know our duty, we must first know the will of God, and in order to identify a spokesman for the will of God, we cannot assume—as the "empirical" argument does—that we already have a moral perceptiveness on which we can rely to decide that his moral insights identify him as a spokesman for God. If it is assumed we have no moral knowledge until we know the will of God, we cannot presume to rely on our own moral judgment to identify what is the will of God.

But, more specifically, what kind of argument does prove, or can prove, that someone is God or speaks for God? We know that different people with different religious commitments make conflicting claims about which person or book really speaks for God: whether the *Koran*, the Old Testament law as formulated in *Exodus* and *Leviticus*, the sayings of Jesus, the New Testament as a whole, the entire Christian tradition including the decisions of church councils and the statements of the popes on matters of morals. Which, if any, of these claims is defensible? And how is any such claim to be supported?

There has been a great deal of discussion of this question, and the interested reader must pursue the details elsewhere. We must limit our comments to one historically popular line of reasoning: the argument from miracles. Roughly this argument asserts as fact that God has occasionally suspended the order of nature in such a way as to provide a sign that some individual spoke for him; for example, it is said that God, by empowering some men to perform miracles, has set his seal upon their words, and that therefore we should believe them.

But this type of reasoning faces grave difficulties. First, there is a special problem for those who wish to identify Jesus as the spokesman for God by appeal to his miracles, set by the fact that Jesus himself declared, when asked by the Pharisees to identify his teaching by a sign from heaven, that he would give no sign—an episode which shows that critics in his own day thought no authenticating miracles had been performed, and that Jesus possibly did not claim otherwise.[24] More important, however, is a logical difficulty. In order to know that natural law has been suspended, we have to know what the natural laws are. For example, in the present day of psychosomatic medicine, influence on bodily ailments by the mind is by no means necessarily evidence of any suspension of natural law. Reports of alleged miracles may be reports of suspensions of what the observers *took* to be natural law, but in fact is not natural law at all. Furthermore, it is well known that the human mind has a serious tendency to invent or magnify interesting stories—especially when the truth of the story would support a cause to which one is committed. There is more than ground for doubt whether the miracles alleged to authenticate the teaching or person of any religious figure have been reported by individuals with a sufficiently scientific and critical turn of mind to place their testimony above serious question.

The argument from miracles to the conclusion that Jesus (or some other religious teacher) is God or spoke with divine direction does not, everything considered, seem coercive. Other reasons of a supernatural kind, aimed to establish the same result, are no stronger. More convincing as an argument for the inspiration of Jesus or the Bible is the ethical content, but of course a person who thinks ethical knowledge must be founded on theological knowledge cannot use such reasoning without circularity.

Suppose, however, some reasoning could establish that Jesus spoke infallibly about God's will; suppose further that it were somehow shown that ethical statements could be inferred from information about God's will. Or more simply, suppose merely it is shown somehow that the ethical statements of Jesus were wholly true. Would his teaching furnish an adequate foundation for normative ethics? It is doubtful, at the least.

We shall be able to appreciate the difficulties fully only at a much later stage. The trouble is that, if we really assume that we have no reliable source of ethical knowledge other than a given set of doctrines, the given doctrines must be adequate to furnish guidance for all the problems that may arise. Unfortunately, there are few types of theory that can provide any such set of doctrines in a compact form. We shall see later that hedonistic utilitarianism—roughly, the theory that a person always ought to do what will enhance happiness most—is one such, but Jesus did not subscribe to this theory. Other theories, we shall see, require a complex and perhaps unlimited set of principles. Did Jesus leave any such set of principles? Did he

24 *Mark* 8: 11–12: "And the Pharisees came forth, and began to question with him, seeking of him a sign from heaven, tempting him. And he sighed deeply in his spirit, and saith, Why doth this generation seek after a sign? Verily I say unto you, There shall no sign be given unto this generation." *Matthew 12*, in relating a similar episode, quotes Jesus as saying that there will be one exception, that Jesus would be buried three nights and days before the Resurrection; but there is every reason to think Mark's version more reliable. We must remember that the New Testament concedes that many people have the power to "cast out devils," and the capacity to do so is not claimed to be a unique mark of authority for Jesus.

leave principles that enable us to decide, without appeal to any other source of ethical information, whether, say, corporate income taxes are unfair? Does his teaching tell us whether a woman, who has promised to marry a man, but has discovered that he is suffering from a psychological problem that will in all probability make married life miserable for her, is bound to keep her promise? If we examine the general principles expressed by Jesus, the "Do unto others . . ." rule and the "Love your neighbor" rule, we do not seem to have clear directives for such cases. Moreover, the more specific ethical teachings of Jesus were addressed to fairly specific situations, and there is not much indication of how much allowance, if any, is to be made for this in the case of different situations. For instance, does his rigorous teaching on divorce and remarriage apply to conditions in the United States today? Why? We should notice that the teaching about divorce does not appear to follow from the general principles. Indeed, the general rule would seem to permit divorce by mutual consent, at least if there are no children. The job of scholars is to try to reconstruct the ethical principles of Jesus in the same objective scholarly way in which Plato's teaching has been reconstructed. However, it appears as if anything that can seriously be established as the ethical view of Jesus will fall far short of providing the kind of set of principles needed for the solution of practical ethical problems.

The outcome of our total thinking about the appeal to religious authority in ethics, then, is this. First, the ethical teaching of religious leaders may be importantly relevant—established as such by the congruity of such teaching with our own most careful ethical reflection. Second, the infallibility of such teaching cannot be established by an "empirical" argument; nor does it seem capable of being established by a "supernatural" line of reasoning—and even if it were, it is highly doubtful whether the ethical doctrines of any religious teacher actually comprise a sufficiently rich and complex system to furnish directives for all the practical problems of ethics. Finally, the thesis that theological propositions must play an essential role in justifying ethical convictions—that we must know, say, the will of God in order to ascertain what is right or good—proves to be patently invalid. This is so, partly because the supernaturalist theory of the meaning of ethical terms is probably untenable, except possibly in such a form as is inconsistent with the general thesis itself; but partly also because, if we assume the thesis to be true, we cannot consistently identify an authentic source of information about the divine will: "supernatural" arguments are not coercive and the use of the "empirical" or moral arguments is inconsistent with the assumption. Further, we cannot determine the content of the divine will by any rational inference from nature. The thesis, worked out consistently, leads to ethical skepticism.

If we are to justify any ethical principles as valid at all, then, we must be able to justify at least some of them independently of any theological premises. The question of how to do this still remains, however, for we have already seen that conformity with empirical science and observation, and the requirements of consistency and generality, are not enough to identify a valid set of ethical principles. There is still room for hope, however, for we have not yet considered the theories of major importance today.

Before we turn to these theories, however, we must make an excursus. For in order to be able to appreciate the force of these theories, and their difficulties, we must familiarize ourselves with certain theories and facts of observation that have strongly influenced modern thinking about ethics, among both philosophers and social scientists—and have inclined many toward a theory we shall call "ethical relativism." In the next two chapters, then, we shall review some facts and theories in psychology and anthropology that may be relevant to our concern.

FURTHER READINGS

On theology, religion, and ethics:

Plato, *Euthyphro*

Hastings Rashdall, *Conscience and Christ* (London: Gerald Duckworth & Co., Ltd., 1933). An excellent evaluation of the reasonable place of Christ's teaching in the ethical thinking of a Christian.

Paul Ramsey, *Basic Christian Ethics* (New York: Charles Scribner's Sons, 1952). An analysis by a theologian.

Emil Brunner, *The Divine Imperative* (Philadelphia: Westminster Press, 1947). The view of a neo-orthodox theologian.

R. C. Mortimer, *Christian Ethics* (London: Hutchinson's University Library, 1950). An elementary discussion by an English bishop.

Catholic Encyclopedia (New York: Robert Appleton Co., 1909), "Ethics."

V. J. Bourke, *Ethics* (New York: The Macmillan Company, 1951). A Catholic statement.

Dietrich von Hildebrand, *Christian Ethics* (New York: David McKay Company, Inc., 1953). The work of a well-known Catholic philosopher.

L. Garvin, *A Modern Introduction to Ethics* (New York: Houghton Mifflin Co., 1953), pp. 429–40.

F. C. Sharp, *Good Will and Ill Will* (Chicago: University of Chicago Press, 1950), chap. 8. An empirical study of the role of authority of various kinds in actual ethical thinking.

5

Ethical Standards in Different Cultures and Their Development

Since the earliest times, men have found the customs, laws, and moral standards of different social groups an intriguing topic. In the last hundred years, anthropologists have begun a serious scientific investigation of these cultural forms, and in the past fifteen years, the values and ethical standards of different peoples have been the object of especial attention and of field activity of considerable scope.[1]

In the present chapter we shall consider only one segment of the results of these inquiries by the anthropologists: the facts and theories relevant to *critical* ethics.

Before beginning, however, we should note two points of very great importance that have often been overlooked with unfortunate results.

The first is that it is one thing for a person to have a certain ethical opinion or ethical conviction, and another thing for that ethical opinion to be correct. I may think that euthanasia is morally permissible, but in fact it may not be. It is because of this contrast between the opinions we hold and those we ought to hold (the ones we would hold if our opinions were correct) that there is such a subject as normative ethics (the theory of what principles are correct) or critical ethics (as the theory of valid inference to correct moral principles). Since there is this difference, a social scientist might, in principle, know what, in fact, are the ethical opinions of everyone, but be completely unaware of which opinions are correct or justified. Therefore we cannot infer, certainly without much more discussion, from the fact that different individuals or groups have had conflicting views

[1] See, for instance, the many articles and monographs resulting from the "Rimrock Values Study" at Harvard University, a list of which is printed in the *Papers of the Peabody Museum of American Archaeology and Ethnology*, Harvard University, Cambridge, XLI (1954), No. 2, pp. viii-x.

about what is right or wrong, good or bad, with respect to many or even all topics, that there is more than one valid or justifiable answer to any ethical question. It does not follow directly from the fact that the Romans approved of infanticide and we do not, that infanticide was really right for them and really wrong for us or that it is neither right nor wrong for everybody.

The second point is that it is one thing to have a scientific theory, in the sense of a *causal understanding*, of an individual's or group's belief that some conduct is right or wrong; it is quite another thing to have a normative ethical theory which shows that some conduct really is right or wrong. Knowing the causes why a man believes something is right not only is not yet knowledge that it *is* right, but may not even be knowledge relevant to whether it is right, any more than knowing that a person rejects the theory of evolution because of his religious commitments is relevant to knowing whether this theory is a satisfactory theory of the development of species. So, we may know that a man rejects a given ethical belief because his father holds it and because rejection symbolizes total independence of his father's hated domination; knowing this has no obvious bearing on whether his ethical belief is valid or true. In general, then, we cannot draw inferences about the validity of ethical principles, at least in any simple way, from a scientific causal theory of the development of ethical standards, individual or cultural.

Once these distinctions are realized, one is apt to move to the opposite extreme and say: "The anthropologist's facts and theories about ethical standards can have no bearing on the philosophical problems of ethics." But this would be going much too far. Let us consider why this is so.

We can best explain how the anthropologist's material is relevant to the philosophical problems of ethical theory by reviewing some specific inferences which philosophers have made on the basis of this material with at least some plausibility. And first, as an interesting historical sidelight, we should notice a line of reasoning (but one the logic of which is dubious) familiar to Plato, and which Plato put into the mouth of Callicles:

> The makers of laws are the majority who are weak; and they make laws and distribute praises and censures with a view to themselves, and to their own interests; and they terrify the stronger sort of men . . . in order that they may not get the better of them; and they say, that dishonesty is shameful and unjust; meaning, by the word injustice, the desire of a man to have more than his neighbours; for knowing their own inferiority, I suspect that they are too glad of equality. And therefore the endeavour to have more than the many, is conventionally said to be shameful and unjust, and is called injustice, whereas nature herself intimates that it is just for the better to have more than the worse, the more powerful than the weaker. . . . But if there were a man who had sufficient force . . . he would trample under foot . . . all our laws which are against nature . . . and the light of natural justice would shine forth. And this I take to be the sentiment of Pindar,

when he says in his poem, that "Law is the king of all, of mortals as well as of immortals"; this, as he says, "Makes might to be right. . . ."[2]

Callicles is arguing that ordinary moral standards are a device used by the inferior masses to achieve by indirection what is to their interest; inferiors satisfy their interests by "might" of law, praise, and censure. The strong man, in contrast, serves his interest more directly, using his strength to get what he wants. We need not concern ourselves with the details of Callicles' reasoning by which he was led to conclude that might makes right. The point of interest to us is that he was using a theory about the *motivation* of moral standards and discourse to support a fundamental ethical principle, and to discredit ethical reasoning in its conventional forms.

Many writers today, like Callicles but with more careful logic, employ anthropologists' facts and theories about moral systems to support views about the philosophical problems of ethics. The types of reasoning by which they move from anthropological material to conclusions about ethical theory are described below; there are five of them. Such arguments may, of course, come to grief at either of two points: their premises may be incorrect in asserting that anthropological material shows something to be the case; or it may be that the inference drawn would not follow anyway, even if the premises were correct. The reader who is doubtful whether *anything* about ethical theory can reasonably be inferred from *any* proposition which anthropological research might possibly show to be true, will be primarily concerned to examine whether the arguments below come to grief in the second of these ways. Unfortunately it would be repetitious to examine each of the following arguments in detail at present; each will be assessed carefully at a later stage (primarily in Chapters 8, 10, and 11). It may be a helpful forecast for the reader, however, to state now that later we shall raise questions about the third and fifth of these arguments on the *second* count; the other three are not defective in their reasoning, although we shall have some questions, in some cases, about their premises.

(1) First, then, it has been argued by some (particularly social psychologists) that all human beings, at least when not subjected to unusual pressures, are in agreement about the *basic* principles of ethics. This is their anthropological premise. The inference is that all ethical disputes can be settled rationally; for since ethical disagreements do not result from disagreements about basic ethical principle, they must arise from misunderstandings about nonethical facts. Therefore, when we have arrived, as we can do, at agreement about the nonethical facts by using scientific method, we shall have ethical unanimity. (2) Some writers, starting from the anthropological premise that there is much variation of beliefs about what is right and wrong conduct, in different societies, have inferred that there cannot be "intuitive" knowledge of what is right or wrong conduct. (3)

[2] Plato, *Gorgias* (Jowett translation), pp. 483–84 (in standard pagination of Plato's works). It is interesting to compare this with Nietzsche's *Genealogy of Morals*, Essay I.

Some have asserted, as a premise drawn from anthropology, that there are much wider differences of opinion about ethics than there are about non-ethical facts. They have inferred from this that there is ground for thinking that an "ethical opinion" essentially *is* merely the having of an emotional attitude or at least that it involves such an attitude in an important way. (4) Some writers assert that people, at least when they are serious, argue ethical questions in a uniform manner and offer only one type of reason (or a standard few) in defense of institutions or ethical standards. They then infer that this manner of arguing ethical questions is the only justified or correct one; or sometimes it is proposed that ethical terms must therefore be viewed as correctly definable in such a way that the standard type of reason offered is really a conclusive reason for the ethical statements it is used to support. (5) It is sometimes supposed that social science can tell us that the "function" of moral systems, conscience, and ethical discourse is so-and-so—perhaps to serve as an informal means of social control, or to provide rules for adjudicating conflicts of interest. Writers then go on to infer that ethical norms are valid if and only if they are suited to accomplish these ends; for instance, it is inferred that a rule is valid if and only if its acceptance would enhance the general welfare in the long run.

But let us turn now to the concrete material.

1. **THERE ARE ETHICAL STANDARDS IN EVERY SOCIETY.**

The anthropologist Meyer Fortes remarked, while writing about the Tallensi,

> To study Tale kinship institutions apart from the religious and moral ideas and values of the natives would be as one-sided as to leave out the facts of sex and procreation. . . . Every social system presupposes such basic moral axioms. They are implicit in the categories of values and of behavior which we sum up in concepts such as rights, duties, justice, amity, respect, wrong, sin. Such concepts occur in every known human society, though the kind of behaviour and the content of the values covered by them vary enormously.[3]

Such a statement is typical of those made by students of culture today: The members of every society have ethical standards of one sort or another, just as in every society people marry and participate in games.[4] Yet, to say that ethical standards are universal may be as misleading as to say that religion is universal, for it may well be that the structure present in

---

[3] *The Web of Kinship among the Tallensi* (London: Oxford University Press, 1949), p. 346.
[4] Of course, just as not everybody marries, and not everybody participates in games, at least in the same ones or to the same extent, so not everyone in a given cultural group necessarily has the same ethical standards, and some individuals in a group may have few moral standards of any kind, although a person can hardly be without values of any sort.

all societies is very simple. In what sense, then, can we say that "ethical standards" are universal?

Anthropologists tell us that everywhere language enables one to distinguish between the desired and the desirable, the wanted and the good or right. So, we can infer that everywhere there is some sort of distinction between momentary impulse or personal desire, and what is good, desirable, right, or justifiable in some sense or other. Professor Raymond Firth has in effect gone further, suggesting that it is of the essence of moral standards (and these he thinks are required by every social system) that they are regarded as "external, non-personal in their origin" and "invested with a special authority" that "demands that they be obeyed."[5]

Can we also say that the several ethical concepts—of the desirable, of duty and moral obligation, of the reprehensible and the morally admirable—are present in all societies, even if not sharply distinguished? We can draw inferences about this question from general considerations about the conditions of living, especially social living. First, recollections of unpleasant consequences must force upon human beings everywhere some contrast between the wanted and the preferable—the justifiably wanted, chosen, or preferred. Second, in view of the inevitable clashes of interest typical of social coexistence, and in view of the necessity of predictability of behavior in enterprises that require the cooperation of various persons (such as family life), the great utility of rules regulating what is to be done in types of recurrent situation is obvious. (In the following section we shall consider the importance of moral rules more at length.) The importance of such rules for social living will lead us to expect that surviving societies will have some kind of authoritative rules of this sort, and hence, some concept like "it is legally obligatory to" or, for more informal rules, "it is morally obligatory to," or both.

Third, if there are rules, and concepts of preferable behavior, in a society, there can hardly fail to be classification of persons and behavior as conforming or failing to conform with these rules and standards, since human beings are observant, classifying beings, with some personal stake in the behavior of other persons. Human beings are given to judging other human beings, and we will expect that where there are standards and rules for conduct, people will be judged in relation to these, their characters classified favorably or unfavorably, as being "conscientious" or "cooperative" or "thoughtful," and the like. Presumably, also, the attitudes that people will take toward persons so classified will vary somewhat accordingly. If so, then all societies must develop ideas that approximate to the concepts of the reprehensible and the morally admirable.

The conclusions of our a priori reasoning appear to conform with fact. As far as the writer knows, no societies have been reported that are without some authoritative rules for behavior in some sorts of recurrent social situ-

[5] *Elements of Social Organization* (London: Watts & Co., 1952), pp. 186 and 197.

ations; nor have societies been reported in which criticism and praise of conduct do not occur. So it appears there is ground for thinking that in at least most societies there is an approximation, at least, to the principal distinct concepts that we have urged are definitive of ethical discourse.

Yet, some qualifications and reservations are necessary. In the first place, the writer was not able to find any Hopi terms that exactly correspond to "It's his *duty* to . . ." or "He has a *moral obligation* to. . . ." What the Hopi can say is, "It is bad (*kahopi* or *kaloloma*) not to . . ." or "It's *part of your job* (*ayawat*) [as chief, daughter, and so on] to. . . ." The second of these expressions comes very close to "It's your duty to . . . ," but it is doubtful whether Hopi contains any words that exactly parallel the English expressions. Thus, in saying that all or most languages "approximate" to the principal ethical concepts in English, we must be careful not to imply by this that most or all languages contain expressions exactly parallel to the English ethical expressions. The most we can say is that probably every language contains expressions that, in particular contexts, can get the same idea across, accomplish much the same effect, given the assumptions and attitudes of participants in ethical discourse.

There is another reservation. Some of the attitudes typical of Western moral experience may not be duplicated everywhere. For instance, in Western societies people frequently feel guilty or remorseful about their deeds even when they know their actions are safe from discovery and will never make them an object of criticism or ridicule; people feel constrained to live up to their moral standards and to be a certain sort of person, to some extent independent of pressure by the thoughts and attitudes of others. But is this universally the case? It need not be, since what is important for society is that people direct their conduct in accordance with certain rules; it is not important to society whether conformity is motivated by a concern for duty and personal ideals on their own account, or merely by a highly developed sensitivity to public opinion. Societies can have the benefits of rule-guided behavior and institutions even though their members do not develop consciences like ours, with our feelings of guilt and remorse, with our concern to behave in certain ways and to have certain qualities of character irrespective of pressure from other persons. Many anthropologists believe, moreover, that in fact the members of some societies do not develop consciences like ours. Societies in which a conscience like ours is typical they call "guilt societies" and societies in which sensitivity to public opinion is the predominant motivation for obedience to moral rules are called "shame societies." (It is generally allowed that guilt phenomena will occur among some individuals in shame societies, just as obviously shame phenomena are extremely important in guilt societies like our own; the difference is a matter of frequency of the phenomenon, or its degree of development in the average individual.) It may be a mistake, then, to think that all societies are guilt societies, or to think that in all societies the thoughtful individual would agree that traits of good character, such as conscientiousness, are worthwhile in themselves.

2. THE REASON FOR ETHICAL STANDARDS

When we say that a group has "ethical standards," at least part of what we mean is that its average member has beliefs about what is justifiably chosen or preferred, regards some rules for conduct as authoritative and justified, sometimes criticizes persons and their conduct for the breach of moral rules, and is motivated to some degree to choose the preferable and to conform with moral rules either for this in itself or on account of an interest in the approval of others.

We have suggested in the previous section that probably all societies have ethical standards in this sense.

If this suggestion is correct—and let us assume it is—then we are tempted to inquire further: What is the reason for ethical standards and why are they universal? This question, however, like the title for the present section, is ambiguous. It may mean: What is the *causal explanation* of ethical standards, of their pervasiveness? Or: What *benefit justifies* the having of ethical standards of some kind or other? We shall say something about both these questions, but note that the second is an ethical question, and we shall be using our own ethical beliefs in answering it.

First, then, what is the causal explanation of there being ethical standards at all, or of their pervasiveness? In large part we must plead ignorance on this matter. There are no observations of the beginning of ethical standards in any society; in our own cultural tradition, standards antedated the development of writing. How they came into being, then, must be a matter for speculative reconstruction. Furthermore, unfortunately, the development must have been complex, for it involves not only the appearance of certain attitudes but of certain concepts and presumably the appearance of certain words (like "duty") corresponding to these concepts. Also, we have no right to assume that all cultural units necessarily reached the same result by identical routes. In view of the difficulties, we shall confine our remarks about the first question to two points. First, it is reasonable to assume that the development of ethical systems involved causal processes of the type that today observably keep ethical systems in being; we shall have something to say of this toward the end of the present chapter and in the following one. Second, the utility of ethical systems, which we shall discuss more fully in a moment, must have played a considerable role. This point needs to be enlarged.

In the first place, it is plausible to suggest that many or most moral rules would not have occurred at all if our world had been like paradise. Imagine a world in which there were food and drink aplenty, where somehow there was no motivation for personal jealousy or slanderous attack. In this world there would be no property claims as far as food is concerned (any more than there is in ours about oxygen), for more would always be within easy reach. So, there could be no such thing as theft, and it would make no sense to have a moral rule forbidding it. Many moral rules forbid the doing of something that someone may well be tempted to do and that would be injurious to someone else. In a paradise, to some extent neither of these conditions would occur, and to this extent there would be no moral rules. In other words, it is plausible to say that a prerequisite for the occurrence of some moral rules is the existence of such conditions as would make them useful. We must be cautious, however. Some moral rules may well develop without a function. For instance, if it becomes customary to perform certain actions in private, then, perhaps as a result of associations, even in our paradise there might be criticism if one performed these actions in public. Furthermore, all the argument shows is that some moral rules would probably not have occurred if certain conditions had not been given; but it by no means follows that the occurrence of these conditions is the whole causal explanation. In assuming that it is, a necessary condition for the existence of something would be confused with the sufficient conditions for the occurrence of that thing.

Second, a "survival of the fittest" argument has some plausibility. It is known that in the primitive conditions at the beginning of human society, survival was a most precarious matter. At that time, any advantage of one primitive band over another might well mean the difference between survival for the one and destruction for the other. So, it may be argued, the introduction of ethical standards would be a decided stabilizing advantage for any primitive group; and it is believable that groups that failed to develop standards simply disappeared. The universality of ethical standards is thereby accounted for—and essentially by their utility for survival. This argument, however, does not explain the *appearance* of ethical standards— just as the theory that the fittest species will survive does not by itself explain how some species came to be more fit. So, although it is rather plausible as an account of why there are few if any societies without ethical standards, by itself it does not explain why there are ethical standards at all.

Third, the "survival of the fittest" argument may be supplemented by appeal to psychology. It may be said that psychology tells us that individuals tend to drop behavior patterns that are punishing (or thought to be disadvantageous) and that they maintain behavior patterns that are rewarding (or thought to be advantageous). So, if we think of the having of ethical standards as a behavior pattern, it follows from the utility (rewardingness) of having ethical standards that they would tend to develop at least in many social groups. It seems, then, that we have a simple explanation of the universal development of ethical systems; but again we must be cautious. At best, the principle predicts adoption of a form of behavior if it is useful for the individual (and not just for the group), whereas the utility of many moral rules for the individual is often not obvious. Indeed, some moral rules, such as sexual prohibitions, may be primarily restrictive, as far as the individual is concerned. Too, the development of ethical standards requires the formation of certain concepts (of the desirable, of wrong and duty), whereas it is not clear that the simple principle about the consequences of the rewarding effects of behavior patterns explains this at all plausibly.

Despite the grounds for caution, however, it is reasonable to think that the utility, in some sense, of ethical standards has played a large causal role in the development of standards and in their being as pervasive in human societies as they are.

Let us turn now to our second question: What are the benefits or utilities that help justify having ethical standards?

In the first place, to have ethical beliefs is to have a system of recipes for action, for analyses of alternative actions in terms of favorable or unfavorable points. If we had no beliefs like "Knowledge is a good thing" or "One should tell the truth except . . ." as guides, we would either act blindly or else have to expend large amounts of time reflecting on each separate occasion. To have no ethical beliefs of any kind or no tendency to be guided by such beliefs, would be like having no general beliefs at all, or having no habits. Having some standards is, therefore, an essential economy measure for the individual—although it is true that having some standards might be worse than none at all.

Furthermore, if life is to be tolerable it must provide some measure of security, protection from personal violence or other attack on the fundamental conditions of one's existence. There must be peace and order within a social group, despite the fact that clashes of interest are inevitable within every actual society. To provide security, then, there must be authoritative rules. Such rules might be purely legal, but it is much more efficient if there is an informal and automatic enforcement device that will work quickly and without excessive cost. Moral standards provide this sort of mechanism. Ideally, an individual's own sense of obligation will induce him to conform his conduct to the rules. If this guide falters, then other people will criticize, so that, since everyone has some interest in enjoying the esteem of his fellows, one is further motivated by the prospect of communal approval, in the direction of conformity. Ethical standards—feelings of obligation, the prickings of conscience, criticism, and disapproval—then, are an informal analogue of the system of criminal law.

Ethical standards are useful, however, not merely as an efficient means of providing security but also as an efficient system of guides for cooperative living, like the laws of the road. Institutions, like the family, marriage, and others, are needed for social living—not necessarily the institutions that we may have, such as monogamy, but at any rate some institutions. And such institutions consist, in part, of ethical standards, of recognized rights and responsibilities. Ethical standards prescribe, for many contexts, the part that given individuals are to play in institutional behavior. Of course, such performance could be prescribed as a matter of law. Ethical standards, however, are more efficient than legal standards.

Of course, ethical standards also have their unfavorable aspect. People may be overly conscientious, ridden by guilt feelings, so anxious to do what is right that they lose the power to make unpopular decisions that are justifiable and demanded by their own welfare. Ethical criticism may be idle chatter; worse, it sometimes does serious and lasting damage, and quite unjustly. Moral rules may be chains not easily cast off, especially when they work hardship only on some special group, or when, despite being out of accord with experience, they have tradition behind them and can challenge alternative rules as untried and dangerous. Still, by and large, the moral system is unquestionably of tremendous advantage to men, directly or indirectly.

It is well to repeat that these last remarks (about how ethical standards are a *good thing*) are normative statements and belong to normative ethics. There is no harm in making them now, since we shall not use them to establish any normative principles; and we shall argue for the relevant principles later.

3. HOW SIMILAR ARE THE ETHICAL PRINCIPLES OF DIFFERENT SO-
CIETIES?

We have concluded that there are ethical standards of some sort in every society. We could have gone further and said that there are probably everywhere ethical prohibitions and requirements relevant to the major areas where clash of interest seems inevitable in social life: sex and marriage, the family, property and income, the security of life and limb and reputation, contracts and promises, the care of the aged or sick or needy, and so on.

The exact content of these prohibitions and requirements, however, and the major conceptions of what is worthwhile or bad in life, appear at least on the surface to differ from one group to another—just as it seems to, to some extent, from one person to another in our own society. We must look at this, particularly on account of its implications for "ethical relativism," a theory to be examined in Chapter 11.

We must begin, however, with some preliminary points. The first is that the working ethical principles of individuals and groups ordinarily form rather complex systems. Philosophers and religious teachers have sometimes offered simple ethical systems containing just one or two principles, supposed to cover everything. For instance: "Love God with all your heart, and your neighbor as yourself." "It is always right to do whatever will maximize the happiness of all concerned." "Do to others as you would have them do to you." "Always act so as to express a trait of character that is midway between extremes." Such comprehensive principles, however, do not sum up adequately the actual ethical thinking of most individuals. To see this, let us consider an example. Suppose A and B are the principal competitors for a fellowship, for which applications must be filed in a certain office by noon on June 1. Then, suppose A meets B on May 31, and A happens to remark that he intends to file his application *next week*, revealing that, unless someone informs him otherwise, his application will be filed too late to be considered. What should B do? Let us ask ourselves what points B will consider in order to make up his mind. Probably, B will consider as relevant such points as: that everyone has some obligation to prevent such awards going to anyone but the ablest man; that A is his friend, and that it would be inconsistent with the spirit of their friendship for B not to inform A of the facts; that A has performed various services for B in the past; that it is a person's responsibility to look out for his own welfare, and that a person has no right to count on his competitors' looking out for this; that A needs the money more (or less) than B; that to fail to note A's error is in effect to misinform him, since A has explicitly stated a dangerous and mistaken premise in B's presence, so that B in a sense attests to the truth of this premise by failing to question it; and so on. B has many principles, then. Normally a person's ethical thinking does not go on in terms of such abstract and general principles as we have listed above.

There is a sense in which we could say, if we wished, that people's ethical beliefs—though explicitly couched in relatively concrete terms—really are capable of summary by one of the listed abstract principles. *If* one could *deduce* all the explicit working ethical principles of an individual or a group from one of the more general principles like those listed (in conjunction, of course, with factual statements believed by the individual or group), it would do no harm to say that this general principle is the basic principle of the person's (or group's) ethical thinking, even if this general principle had never occurred to the person himself (or to the group). Thus, one might say that the basic principle of a society is "Never do what is dangerous for you or your family."[6] Of course, one must always state clearly whether or not the basic principle really plays a fundamental role in the conscious reflection of the group, whether a member of the group would subscribe to it if the matter were put to him, and so on.

Let us confine our attention to those ethical principles of groups that actually play a role in their conscious thinking.

In order to answer our question of how similar these systems are, we should consider a further preliminary point: In what ways *can* the ethical principles of an individual or group differ from those of another individual or group? To this question we can answer as follows. First, A's principles

---

[6] See John Ladd's characterization of the Navaho code, in his *The Structure of a Moral Code* (Cambridge: Harvard University Press, 1957), chap. 16.

may declare some kinds of action or state of affairs to be obligatory or worthwhile, which B's principles do not mention at all. Second, A's principles may prescribe what B's principles permit or prohibit. Third, A's principles may prohibit or prescribe some things the same as B's, but *more strongly*. Strictly speaking, difference of strength may not be a new dimension of difference between systems of principles, however, but merely a development of the second dimension of difference, for the following reason. Our judgment that A's principle about something is a stronger prohibition than B's is necessarily based largely on the exceptions that will be permitted. For example, A's principle might say: "Never tell a lie even if someone's life depends on it," whereas B's might say only: "Never tell a lie unless it is rather advantageous to do so." Nevertheless, it is convenient to count the *intensity* or *strength* of an ethical rule as a third dimension for comparisons. Finally, some principle of A may differ from a corresponding one of B in that it is a *basic* ethical principle, whereas B's is not. That is, it may be that some principle is one of A's ethical *premises*, that he does not hold it *because* he believes some other ethical principle (or at least not wholly for this reason), so that if we were to represent by a deductive system the dependencies in A's ethical thinking, we should list this particular principle as a premise, whereas in B's thinking it would appear as a theorem. For instance, A might believe "Don't lie except . . ." as a kind of ultimate commitment, whereas B might believe the same thing, but as a consequence of his thinking that lies normally cause suffering and of his prior ethical principle that we ought not to cause suffering.

There are other ways in which an individual's or group's ethical principles may differ from those of another individual or group, but the foregoing are the most important for our purposes.[7]

There are difficulties of principle about how to justify making comparative statements of some of the kinds mentioned, especially judgments of comparative intensity; and the problems are much greater still if one hopes to justify comparative judgments on the basis of the existing literature about the ethical standards of various peoples, which happens to be our present job. Let us, however, consider what inferences the evidence justifies about our main question of how similar are the ethical standards of various social groups.

If we consult one of the great compendia of the ethical standards of different social groups, such as Sumner's or Westermarck's,[8] we find that there is a good deal of difference on almost every topic. Take, for instance, views that have been held about parricide, the killing of one's father or mother. In many societies this seems to be considered the most heinous of

---

[7] For a discussion of further points, see Clyde Kluckhohn, "Values and Value-Orientations in the Theory of Action," in Talcott Parsons and E. A. Shils (eds.), *Toward a General Theory of Action* (Cambridge: Harvard University Press, 1951).

[8] On many topics there is elaborate information in the Human Relations Files at Yale University and other universities.

all crimes. Plato remarks in the *Laws* that a person who commits this crime should be punished with death many times. In Rome, according to Westermarck, such a person "was sewn up in a leathern sack with a cur, a cock, a viper, and an ape, and, when cooped up in this fearful prison, was hurled into the sea. . . ."[9] But in other groups it is customary for the aged to be abandoned or killed. Sometimes the children customarily stab an aged parent to death; in the South Pacific, parents were sometimes buried alive by their children. Sometimes such deeds are performed only when the food supply is short and a choice has to be made between the aged and the young and healthy; sometimes they are done to put an end to misery, or, in migrant tribes, when the aged cannot endure a journey. The aged sometimes themselves insist upon such an end, as their right. It is not clear whether such deeds are sometimes performed, and approved, in the entire absence of such circumstances as we should think give some justification.[10]

On most topics there is a comparable degree of variation in the ethical thinking of different social groups.

But there are also points of general agreement. For instance, there is no group that thinks it right to kill an adult, healthy member of the society who has committed no crime and whose death is not required by the welfare of the group. There is no group in which marriage or sexual intercourse is approved between members of the immediate family, with the possible exception of some royal families and with the further exception of some important ritual occasions. There is no society in which kindliness, sympathy, hospitality, or regard for others and their rights is disapproved. In all these cases, of course, there may well be difference in *degree* of disapproval of violations.

The picture we gain from such surveys, of great variety among ethical systems, is apt to be misleading in at least two ways. First, the surveys ignore the fact that the life conditions of these peoples differ greatly, and even when in fact the conditions do not differ, the peoples may think they do. This fact means that some variations of ethical belief are properly regarded as simply applications of identical basic principles in the light of different assumptions about the facts.[11] It is no great surprise if atheists and theists differ about whether we have religious duties. The sur-

[9] Edward Westermarck, *The Origin and Development of the Moral Ideas* (New York: The Macmillan Company, 1906), vol. I, p. 384.

[10] For a general survey on the treatment of the aged, see Leo Simmons, *The Role of the Aged in Primitive Societies* (New Haven: Yale University Press, 1945).

[11] For example, in the Middle Ages it was considered immoral to practice "usury," that is, to take interest on money lent. With the rise of capitalism, this practice gradually became accepted. Does this show the emergence of a new and different basic principle? Not necessarily, for in early times loans were used mostly for personal consumption; in a capitalistic society they are used mostly for investment, hence for gain. Thus, in the capitalistic system, the collection of interest can be viewed simply as collecting a share in the profits arising from use of one's money. See Karl Duncker, "Ethical Relativity," *Mind*, XLVIII (1939), 40–41. He discusses a number of such historical examples.

veys blur this point. Second, a total survey properly presents a picture of no world-wide agreement on anything (or almost anything), despite the fact that no social group surveyed differs from any other, in moral standards, on more than a few points. The survey is therefore apt to mislead us into thinking that, if one were parachuted from a plane into the midst of some primitive people, their modes of thinking would seem so different that one would hardly think them human.

In order to counterbalance the impact of world-wide surveys like Westermarck's, let us take a brief look at the *total* ethical system of one people, in the context of their life situation: the Hopi Indians of Arizona.[12] Now, it is true that the Hopi may not be the best possible example, if we want to know just how different from ourselves other people can be, for there are other groups with a vastly simpler mode of existence: the Australian bushmen, or pygmy groups in the Philippines or in South Africa. However, we know far less about how life looks from their point of view than we do in the case of other tribes, especially North American Indian groups, and, if we are to choose among groups about which there is quite substantial information, the Hopi tribe seems as good as any.

If a traveller found himself among the Hopi, and had occasion to engage in an ethical discussion (with the services of a good interpreter) about the proper charge for a certain service, or about the defensibility of the policies of the government or its local agent or of a local chief, he would feel himself right at home—for he could argue in exactly the same way as at home, with his points having a normal impact, and he would find himself being countered with arguments he might well have expected. All this is true although the historical sources of the Hopi tradition are entirely different from our own (except for their brief contact with the Spaniards in the late sixteenth and seventeenth centuries, and with White teachers and government officials since the beginning of the present century).[13] If the traveller stayed longer, he would find some points of difference. For instance, if he urged a young Hopi to consider marriage with his pretty cousin (his mother's sister's daughter), with whom he seems so congenial, the traveller would find his suggestion viewed as shocking, and for no good reason as far as he might see. But let us take a closer look at what the traveller might discover.

Suppose he asked his Hopi guide what he thinks important in life, either good or bad. What would he likely mention? Things like this: having a good harvest; having money; having amicable relations with other people, being liked by them and not criticized by them; having health and strength, and not dying before one's time; having a family and children; having well-

<hr>

[12] The Hopi are selected because of the writer's firsthand experience with them. The facts to be reported are drawn from his *Hopi Ethics: A Theoretical Analysis* (Chicago: University of Chicago Press, 1954). By permission of the University of Chicago Press.

[13] The young Hopi have had much more extensive contacts, for instance, through service in the army. The writer's facts, however, were gathered in 1945–47, and attention was concentrated on the older Hopi.

behaved children of whom one can be proud; having tasty food; having an attractive wife who is loyal; belonging to a large and respectable family group; being able to do well things that other Hopi admire, such as weaving or running. All of this sounds familiar enough; we would say comparable things ourselves. Who would disagree with these desires—except perhaps for not caring about the size of one's family group?

To be sure, when we get down to the fine details, we find some things that strike us as odd. For example, a Hopi might say that one of their cere-monial dances is "the finest spectacle in the world." But on second thought this remark is not surprising, when we consider that the speaker has never been outside Arizona, and has never seen the Grand Canyon. The Hopi might also show a surprisingly emotional concern about his neighbors' attitudes toward him. However, this seems not so unjustified, when we con-sider that, unlike an apartment-house dweller, he has to live his whole life with his neighbors. Again, the Hopi might likely surprise us by his advice on the importance of being cheerful, of not being envious of others, of not worrying about oneself or grieving about events that can't be changed. But when he goes on to explain to us his view about how cheerfulness is essential for health and for a good harvest, we shall probably conclude that his attitute would be justified enough, if his assumptions were correct.

Much the same is true if we look at a different side of Hopi ethical think-ing: his views about what kind of personality or character one should have. Again we find a familiar note. The Hopi will tell us that people should be cheerful, keep their tempers, be prudent, reliable, industrious, manly, brave, cordial, friendly, cooperative, persistent, kindly, gentle, sympathetic, generous, thrifty, truthful, and hospitable. He disapproves of a person being envious, vengeful, excitable, boastful, lazy, argumentative, snobbish or conceited, or a gossip. Hopi disagree among themselves about whether one should be *hamaana*, that is, bashful or shy. Even this disagreement makes some sense to us, however, when we find some who disapprove saying that this sort of attitude "doesn't get you anywhere," whereas some who approve say that people of this sort "pay attention to their own business." The same also applies to being *nuvö*, that is, a young person preoccupied with sex (but with the implication of not being very successful); for some who approve say that "this is human nature," whereas some who disapprove say that such a person is "liable to get into trouble; that's all he thinks of." On the other hand, we also find subtle points of difference from ourselves, differences in judgment about what is more important. And some differ-ences are marked. To take perhaps the most striking example, the Hopi approve of a person who habitually hides his light under a bushel. They have no sympathy for a person who aspires to a position of political power or leadership, or indeed to be outstanding in any respect. Some Hopi who are well enough educated to read the New Testament depiction of the humility of Jesus find themselves very responsive to the fact that although

Jesus is said to have had power, he never showed that he had, and permitted himself to be humiliated and tortured. The ideal Hopi is on the submissive side; he would not think of violence or even fighting back verbally if criticized—even standing up for his rights. The quiet, unobtrusive person, the follower who takes a subordinate position, the man who never bothers anybody else but rather lets himself be pushed around—this seems to be one of the Hopi ideals for human personality. We shall probably find this a too frightened attitude toward one's social environment. There are also further differences between the Hopi ideal for man and the Western ideal, because of the fact the Hopi seem not to have framed any concepts of certain traits: dignity, self-control, impartiality, conscientiousness, tolerance, and self-confidence, for example.[14]

On the other hand, what prescriptions and prohibitions for conduct, the specific Do's and Don'ts, are typical of the Hopi? As we might have expected, the Hopi disapprove of murder and personal violence of all sorts (even verbal aggression); incestuous marriage or sexual relations, and indeed all sexual intercourse outside of marriage, with the exception of couples seriously intending marriage; desertion; getting drunk and particularly operating a car while drunk; gambling; divorce; and suicide. As for positive prescriptions, the Hopi say one should help others where one can. One should care for one's children and for one's parents. (The Hopi reckon close relationship along lines rather different from those of the Western world; and naturally there are correspondingly different views about obligations.) One should keep one's promises and agreements. One should make a suitable gift in case a service is performed for one, especially if the service is dangerous or requires special talents. (The Hopi traditionally make generous gifts in return for the services of "doctors.") One should be truthful. One should respect the property of others. One should deal equally with one's children except in special situations, such as when one child has been especially helpful over the years. All this seems familiar enough.

There are also some differences. Although the average Hopi disapproves of suicide, there are many Hopi who see nothing wrong in it, provided a person has no one dependent on him. (The Hopi do not view human life as a gift from God, for which man is responsible to God.) On matters of sexual relations, the Hopi are in general more permissive. Many Hopi see nothing wrong at all in sexual intercourse outside of marriage between unattached unrelated persons, and regard rape as a peccadillo. Adultery is frowned upon, but we may have doubts about how serious disapproval is, considering reports of its frequency. On the other hand, there is strong disapproval of any incestuous relationship, and "incest" is counted to include any sexual relation between persons whose blood relationship can be

---

[14] E. M. Albert's description of the values of the Navaho society makes an interesting comparison. See "The Classification of Values: A Method and Illustration," *American Anthropologist*, LVIII (1956), 221–48.

traced through women. (Relatives on the father's side hardly count, in this connection.) Again, the Hopi permit a good deal of maltreatment of small animals, especially on the part of children. There is no sadistic cruelty, but rather a carelessnesss about pain to cats, dogs, and small birds.

Many Hopi ethical beliefs that are deeply immersed in their distinctive way of life do not permit any simple comparison with corresponding ethical beliefs among ourselves: for instance, the view that it is a good thing for participants in religious ceremonies to concentrate on "wishing for rain"; or the obligation of a woman to entertain her brother and his friends with a feast on the occasion of religious "dances."

On the whole, it would not be difficult for one of us to feel at home in the Hopi ethical system, if we shared their life situation, and especially if we could follow them in their beliefs about the supernatural. Indeed, we could probably find people in any Western city whose ethical views diverge from ours at least as much as do those of the average Hopi. Of course, our picture of the Hopi has been rough. If we examined their beliefs minutely —if, for example, we tried to run down the details of their view of situations in which lies are permissible or even definitely called for—we would probably find a great many disagreements we have not mentioned. But, on the other hand, if we looked closely, we would probably find a great many disagreements with our next-door neighbor, too. Of the Hopi one could hardly say what John Locke said of the Tououpinambos and the Turks:

> The virtues whereby the Tououpinambos believed they merited Paradise, were revenge and eating abundance of their enemies. The saints who are canonized amongst the Turks, lead lives which one cannot with modesty relate.[15]

4. ARE THERE ULTIMATE DISAGREEMENTS ABOUT ETHICAL PRINCIPLE?

No one seriously doubts that there are differences of ethical principle of the sort we have been describing. However, there is a question about these differences, and its answer is controversial. In order to mark this question, let us use the phrase "*ultimate* difference of ethical principle," and let us then ask ourselves whether some of the differences we have been describing can be considered ultimate differences of principle.

What is meant by an "ultimate" difference of principle? Consider first an example of conflicting evaluations of a particular action. Suppose Smith gives his father an overdose of sleeping pills, resulting in death. Suppose further that Jones hears of this event, but thinks no worse of Smith for this reason, because he knows that Smith's father was dying from cancer and in a very painful condition, and he believes Smith's act was done as an act of mercy. We might say he thinks Smith's act was right, because it was of

---

[15] John Locke, *Essay Concerning Human Understanding*, Bk. I, chap. 3, para. 9.

the kind *ABC*. Suppose, now, that Brown also learns of Smith's act, but, unlike Jones, he thinks it was wrong. Brown knows that Smith's father was wealthy and that Smith was penniless, and he believes Smith's act was done to expedite the transfer of his father's property to him. Brown, then, thinks Smith's act was wrong, since he assumes that it was of the kind *ADE*. Brown and Jones, then, differ in their appraisal of the act, but possibly they do not differ at all in their ethical principles, but only in their factual beliefs about the properties of the act. It may well be that Brown and Jones both agree that all acts of the kind *ABC* are right, and that all acts of the kind *ADE* are wrong. In this case, we do not wish to say there was any *ultimate* disagreement between them.

Let us now turn to disagreements about ethical principles. We said that the Romans decidedly did not think it right to put one's parents to death. In some of the Eskimo groups, however, this is thought proper. One observer has told of an Eskimo who was getting ready to move camp, and was concerned about what to do with his blind and aged father, who was a burden to the family. One day the old man expressed a desire to go seal-hunting again, something he had not done for many years. His son readily assented to this suggestion, and the old man was dressed warmly and given his weapons. He was then led out to the seal grounds and was walked into a hole in the ice, into which he disappeared.[16] The Romans, we may expect, would have been shocked at this deed. The Eskimos think it right, in general, to drown a parent who is old and a burden; the Romans, we guess, think this is wrong. The Romans, we may say, think that all acts of the kind *ABC* are wrong; the Eskimos deny this.

But may it not be that the Eskimos and the Romans in some sense have different acts in mind? Suppose that Eskimos, through their experience with the hardships of living, think of parricide as being normally the merciful cutting short of a miserable, worthless, painful old age. And suppose the Romans think of parricide as being normally the getting rid of a burden, or a getting one's hands on the parent's money—an ungrateful, selfishly motivated aggression against one whose care and sacrifices years ago have made the child's life a rich experience. The Eskimos are more-or-less unconsciously taking for granted that putting a parent to death is euthanasia under extreme circumstances; the Romans are more-or-less unconsciously taking for granted that putting a parent to death is murder for gain. In this case, although the Romans and the Eskimos may use the very same words to describe a certain sort of act—and then may express conflicting ethical appraisals of it—actually in some sense they have in mind quite different things. The Eskimos, perhaps, are accepting something of the kind *ABCD;* the Romans are condemning something of the kind *ABFG*. In this situation, we do not want to say there is necessarily any ultimate disagreement of principle between them.

[16] G. de Poncins, *Kabloona* (New York: Reynal & Hitchcock, 1941).

When, then, do we want to say there is ultimate disagreement about ethical principles? Let us suppose that A thinks that anything of the kind *FGH* is wrong; and let us suppose that B denies this. But now, let us suppose further that there is some property *P* that A is more-or-less consciously supposing that everything has, if it is of the kind *FGH*, whereas B does *not* more-or-less consciously suppose that everything of the kind *FGH* has *P*. Furthermore, let us suppose that if A ceased to believe that things that are *FGH* are also *P*, he would *cease* to believe that they are wrong; and also that if B began to believe that things that are *FGH* are also *P*, he would *begin* to believe that they are wrong. In this case, we shall say there is *not ultimate* disagreement, in respect of the ethical principle about things that are *FGH*. But if, as far as conscious beliefs are concerned, A thinks all things of a certain kind right, and B denies this, and there is no more-or-less conscious belief having the status described, then we shall say there *is* ultimate disagreement of principle between A and B.

It is theoretically quite important whether there is ultimate disagreement about ethical principles. It is important for critical ethics because, if there is *no* ultimate disagreement, then all ethical disputes are in principle capable of solution by the methods of science; for all we should have to do, to resolve a dispute, is first to find the ethical principles common to both parties, and then to use observation to determine how these principles apply to the case at hand.[17] But the matter is equally important for psychology. Many psychologists have assumed that we must so conceive the process of learning beliefs and attitudes that it can happen that people arrive at ethical convictions between which there is an ultimate clash; whereas other psychologists do not believe this is the case, thinking rather that conflicting ethical assessments are always a consequence of different cognitive fields, of different apprehensions of or beliefs about the properties of the thing being assessed.

It is not easy to answer the question whether there is ultimate disagreement on ethical principles between different groups. Most of the comparative material assembled, for instance by Westermarck, is of little value for this purpose, for in large part what it tells us is simply whether various peoples approve or condemn lying, suicide, industry, cleanliness, adultery, homosexuality, cannibalism, and so on. But this is not enough. We need, for our purpose, to know how various peoples *conceive* of these things. Do they eat human flesh because they like its taste, and do they kill slaves

---

[17] By no means all the problems of critical ethics would be solved, however, although there would probably be decidedly less interest in them. For instance, whether or not there are disagreements, there is still the question of the sense in which ethical statements can be justified, or in which there is evidence for them. One can still be puzzled about what one could do to settle an ethical dispute, if one *did* arise.

Even if there is ultimate disagreement, however, all ethical disputes are still in principle capable of solution by the methods of science, if some form of naturalism is true.

merely for the sake of a feast? Or do they eat flesh because they think this is necessary for tribal fertility, or because they think they will then participate in the manliness of the person eaten? Perhaps those who condemn cannibalism would not do so if they thought that eating the flesh of an enemy is necessary for the survival of the group. If we are to estimate whether there is ultimate disagreement of ethical principle, we must have information about this, about the beliefs, more or less conscious, of various peoples about what they do. However, the comparative surveys seldom give us this.

In view of the total evidence, then, is it more plausible to say that there is ultimate disagreement of ethical principle, or not? Or don't we really have good grounds for making a judgment on this crucial issue?

First of all, we must report that no anthropologists, as far as the writer knows, today deny that there is ultimate disagreement—although doubtless many of them have not posed the question in exactly the above form. (*Almost* no philosophers deny it either.) This seems a matter of importance, because, even if they have not explicitly argued the matter out, their intuitive impression based on long familiarity with some non-Western society should carry considerable weight. However, we must concede that no anthropologist has offered what we should regard as really an adequate account of a single case, clearly showing there is ultimate disagreement in ethical principle. Of course, we must remember that this lack of information is just as serious for any claim that there is world-wide *agreement* on some principle.

Nevertheless, the writer inclines to think there is ultimate ethical disagreement, and that it is well established. Maybe it is not very important, or very pervasive; but there is some. Let us look at the matter of causing suffering to animals. It is notorious that many peoples seem quite indifferent to the suffering of animals. We are informed that very often, in Latin America, a chicken is *plucked alive*, with the thought it will be more succulent on the table. The reader is invited to ask himself whether he would consider it justified to pluck a chicken alive, for this purpose. Or again, take the "game" played by Indians of the Southwest (but learned from the Spaniards, apparently), called the "chicken pull." In this "game," a chicken is buried in the sand, up to its neck. The contestants ride by on horseback, trying to grab the chicken by the neck and yank it from the sand. When someone succeeds in this, the idea is then for the other contestants to take away from him as much of the chicken as they can. The "winner" is the one who ends up with the most chicken. The reader is invited to ask himself whether he approves of this sport. The writer had the decided impression that the Hopi disapproval of causing pain to animals is much milder than he would suppose typical in suburban Philadelphia—certainly much milder than he would feel himself. For instance, children often catch birds and make "pets" of them. A string is tied to their legs, and they are then "played" with. The birds seldom survive this "play" for long: their legs are broken, their wings pulled off, and so on. One informant put it: "Sometimes they get tired and die. Nobody objects to this." Another informant said: "My boy sometimes brings in birds, but there is nothing to feed them, and they die."[18] Would the reader approve of this, or permit his children to do this sort of thing?

Of course, these people might believe that animals are unconscious automata, or that they are destined to be rewarded many times in the afterlife if they suffer martyrdom on this earth. Then we should feel that our ethical principles were, after all, in agreement with those of these individuals. But they believe no such thing. The writer took all means he could think of to discover some such belief in the Hopi subconscious, but he found none. So probably—we must admit the case is not definitively closed —there is at least one ultimate difference of ethical principle. How many more there are, or how important, we do not say at present.

Possibly we need not go as far afield as Latin America or the Hopi to establish the point. The reader *may* have argued some ethical point with a friend until he found that, as far as he could tell, there were just some matters of principle on which they disagreed, which themselves could not be debated on the basis of any further common ground. In this case, the conclusion is the same. Note, however, that we say only "may have argued." Some people say they cannot remember ever having had such an experience; and perhaps the reader has not. In this case, we do need to go afield.

It is obvious that if there is *ultimate* disagreement of ethical opinion between two persons or groups, there is also disagreement in *basic* principles—if we mean by "basic ethical principle" what we suggested earlier (p. 94), the principles we should have to take as a person's ethical premises, if we represented his ethical views as a deductive system. We have so defined "ultimate disagreement" that a difference in the ethical theorems of two persons or groups does not count as being "ultimate" if it can be explained as a consequence of identical ethical premises but different factual assumptions of the two parties. Since ultimate ethical disagreements, then, cannot be a consequence of the factual assumptions of the parties, it must be a consequence of their ethical premises. Hence, there is also disagreement in "basic" principles. Our conclusion from our total evidence, then, is that different persons or groups sometimes have, in fact, conflicting basic ethical principles.

The significance of this conclusion for "ethical relativism" we shall assess at a later stage.

[18] See the writer's *Hopi Ethics, op. cit.,* pp. 213–15, 245–46, 373; and Wayne Dennis, *The Hopi Child* (New York: Appleton-Century-Crofts, Inc., 1940).

5. THE SCIENTIFIC THEORY OF THE ETHICAL STANDARDS OF SOCIAL GROUPS

The question of whether there are ultimate disagreements of ethical opinion is of sufficient interest that it is worthwhile asking not only "Is there empirical evidence strongly supporting the position that there are (or are not) such disagreements?" but also the question, "Is there theoretical reason of any sort for thinking that there probably are?" The methodological difficulties of deciding the question about observation—and much more if we ask (as we shall later want to do) *how widespread* ultimate disagreements are—are such that it would be most welcome to be able to cite the support of theory for any conclusion. It seems worthwhile, then, to survey existing theory in this area. There is point in doing so, over and beyond the interest in the existence and extent of ultimate disagreement, for we shall have occasion to support our conclusions in later chapters by referring to this material.

We should emphasize at the start, however, that the "theory" of the ethical standards of social groups is in its infancy. There are some observations, some generalizations, some correlations, some common-sense inferences, some interpretations in terms of psychological theory. But in this area there is nothing worth calling "theory" at all, if the kind of thing we mean by "theory" is the atomic theory in physics, or even the Darwinian theory of the origin of species.

Theories of the ethical standards of social groups may conveniently be classified into two types: those intended to explain why there is a certain complex in one or more societies, or why there is a certain geographical distribution of ethical standards (in other words, theories intended to explain static facts), and those intended to explain changes or developments in ethical standards (those intended to explain dynamic facts). Some of these theories "explain" only in the sense of stating that a certain kind of phenomenon always or usually happens. The former type of theory will be discussed first.

We may begin with a very simple common-sense kind of explanation, which consists in pointing out that, considering that people are rational and intelligent to some extent, we may expect them to accept the logical implications of their own premises. For instance, suppose a society is committed to the premise, "It is wrong to disobey God." Suppose further the society recognizes a certain book as containing a revelation of God's will, and in this book it is stated that God has forbidden suicide. We shall naturally expect that the society will draw the inference and believe that it is wrong to commit suicide. Very often, and probably usually (there have not been systematic studies of the point), this expectation will be correct. The pattern of a society's beliefs, then, is in part explained by its own rational coherence.

A special and important type of explanation of this sort is that in which the connection between two ethical beliefs is affected by one or more cause-effect beliefs. Consider the following "reasoning" of the Hopi.

> PREMISE: It is wrong to do what will seriously harm the Hopi.
> PREMISE: Failure of rainfall will cause such harm.
> PREMISE: If a participant in a religious ceremony gives way to angry thoughts, there will be no rain.
> CONCLUSION: It is wrong for a participant in a religious ceremony to give way to angry thoughts.

In this case, we have excellent reason for thinking that acceptance of the conclusion is an effect of (is explained by) acceptance of the premises, for some Hopi who no longer accept the third premise have, rationally enough, ceased to subscribe to the conclusion.

But other, less common-sense, explanations of ethical standards and values have been of more interest to social scientists.

Let us begin with an example. In a recent series of lectures, Professor Robert Redfield urged[19] that, in substantial measure, peasant populations all over the world have the same view of life and the same values. If a peasant, he says, from among Hesiod's Boeotians of the sixth century B.C., from the Maya Indians of Yucatan, or from Surrey "could have been transported by some convenient genie to [the home of] any one of the others and equipped with a knowledge of the language . . ., he would very quickly come to feel at home. And this would be because the fundamental orientations of life would be unchanged. The compass of his career would continue to point to the same moral north." One gets the impression from literature about peasantry, he says, that "the circumstances of peasantry tend to bring about in such peoples views of life that have some similarity. . . ." Similarity in what respects? There is "an intimate and reverent attitude toward the land; the idea that agricultural work is good and commerce not so good; and an emphasis on productive industry as a prime virtue . . . the acceptance of arduous labor, yet with great enjoyment of its surcease." Moreover, in their "scheme of values sobriety is the chosen mode. The peasant values decorem and decency. Passion is not to be exhibited. A man does not flaunt his appetites, or make a show of his emotions." As a result, "there is little room for sexual exploit as a sport or for bravado." They minimize "sexual experience as a good in itself or as a sport of manly achievement." Further, there is a "distaste for violence, a disfavor of prowess in any form of conspicuous aggressiveness." Thus, there is a syndrome of values or ethical standards in peasant societies.

Why is there such a syndrome? Redfield does not speculate on the details of the way in which the life experience of the peasant has molded his tra-

[19] *Peasant Society and Culture.* Copyright (1956) by The University of Chicago. All quotations are from chap. 4.

dition of values, but his view is that the essential form of the agriculturalist life, along with the complex relation to the city and gentry to whom he feels inferior, is the main responsible fact.

During the last century, W. E. H. Lecky, composing a history of European morals, had come to much the same conclusion about the influence of a mode of life on ethical values. He wrote:

> To the observations I have already made concerning the moral effects of the industrial life, I shall at present add but two. The first is that an industrial spirit creates two wholly different types of character—a thrifty character and a speculating character. Both types grow out of a strong sense of the value and a strong desire for the attainment of material comforts, but they are profoundly different both in their virtues and their vices. The chief characteristic of the one type is caution, that of the other enterprise. Thriftiness is one of the best regulators of life. It produces order, sobriety, moderation, self-restraint, patient industry, and all that cast of virtues which is designated by the term respectability. . . . In an industrial civilisation, prudent forethought is regarded not simply as lawful, but as a duty, and a duty of the very highest order. A good man of the industrial type deems it a duty not to marry till he has ensured the maintenance of a possible family. . . .

Lecky held that the mode of life not only tends to produce people with certain virtues, but people with corresponding ethical principles.

> The morals of men are more governed by their pursuits than by their opinions. A type of virtue is first formed by circumstances, and men afterwards make it the model upon which their theories are framed. Thus geographical or other circumstances, that make one nation military and another industrial, will produce in each a realised type of excellence, and corresponding conceptions about the relative importance of different virtues widely different from those which are produced in the other.[20]

Lecky was bolder than Redfield in suggesting details about the influence of ethical values by mode of life.

There are other and somewhat more developed theories, intended to explain either the framework of standards of a particular social group, or statistics about the incidence of a particular standard in different cultural structures of a given type. One of the earliest of these—which however had its roots in the work of still earlier writers, including O. Spengler—was Ruth Benedict's suggestion that a group can somehow acquire a basic value-attitude, or dominant purpose, and that the acceptance or rejection of more specific standards or values will take place so as to be compatible with the basic attitude. For instance, Benedict proposed that among the Zuñi Indians sobriety, a love of measure, and a dislike of disruptive psychological states are fundamental, and that these provide the key to an understanding of such

[20] W. E. H. Lecky, *History of European Morals* (3rd ed., rev.; New York: Appleton and Company, 1887), vol. I, pp. 140 f., 150 f.

apparently disconnected items as their attitudes toward alcohol, their treatment of sex, their control of emotions, their seeking relationship to the supernatural only through group ceremonies, the disapproval of violence, and so on.

In recent years, a good deal of work has been done to ascertain the value systems of different societies by the use of various tests and the analysis of dreams and biographical material; and theories in experimental psychology and psychoanalysis have been drawn upon to provide theoretical explanations of the relations between these facts and the life experiences of the typical individual. For instance, Abram Kardiner, a psychoanalyst who has collaborated with the anthropologists Ralph Linton and Cora DuBois, has studied the influence of childhood experiences on basic personality type, and on the expression of this, again, in adult culture patterns, including value standards. He has proposed that psychoanalytic theory would lead us to expect[21] that a child reared in Alor, given the patterns of child-rearing, would feel hatred, distrust, and isolation, and would lack self-confidence, interest in the outer world, and enterprise. This constellation in turn, he thinks, explains such facts about typical Alorese adults as: a low interest in developing skills, low aesthetic sensitivity, a strong concern about prestige, and more broadly a weak superego development—a weak personal concern with moral standards or ideals for the self.[22]

Others have interpreted cultural facts by appeal to principles of experimental psychology. For instance, G. P. Murdock recently proposed an explanation of the variations in rules about incest in various cultures, by using the learning-theory concept of stimulus-generalization. His proposal was essentially that the prohibition of marriage and sexual relations between members of the basic family—a rule present in all societies—tends to generalize to those individuals who are most like (socially in a position similar to) the ones already included in the prohibition for a given person. Thus, in a society where mother's sister's children have the same social relation to one, approximately, as one's own siblings, the prohibition may be expected to generalize to them. Murdock's theory has some support in the statistics of the extension of the incest rule over several hundred societies. Others have suggested explanations of social ethical norms by appeal to the learning-theory principle that rewarded types of behavior tend to become established. Much the same point is made by others who urge that the culture pattern of a social group must serve the basic needs of its members; those of its elements that are rewarding in this way will tend to be retained;

[21] But, in the present state of psychoanalysis, we cannot be confident that other psychoanalysts would think that psychoanalytic theory leads us to expect the same things! Many psychoanalysts are critical of Kardiner's whole enterprise.
[22] See Cora DuBois, *The People of Alor* (Minneapolis: University of Minnesota Press, 1944); Abram Kardiner, *The Psychological Frontiers of Society* (New York: Columbia University Press, 1948).

those that stand in the way of gratification will tend to be extinguished; and every society will find some way to meet its basic needs.[23]

The theory of the changes or dynamics of systems of ethical standards is distinct from the theory of the statics of such systems, although of course not entirely so. (Linton and Kardiner, for instance, have used their theory to explain changes in the Tanala value system, consequent upon alterations in their basic living conditions.) As in the case of the theory of the statics of value systems, the theory of changes is only in its infancy, and research studies on the problem are only beginning to accumulate.[24]

It is convenient to divide our discussion into two parts: first, the theory of changes that involve intercultural contact in an important way; second, the theory of internal dynamic processes leading to change.

When two social systems are in contact in one way or another (through intermarriage, missionaries, traders, government agents, immigration), one group often adopts a standard from the other or else makes some alteration of its standards at least partly as a consequence of knowing about the standards of the other group. This phenomenon has its humble analogue in our relations with our next-door neighbor: For instance, we observe him fertilizing his trees by digging deep holes and then pouring fertilizer in the holes; being taken with the probable efficacy of his method, we go and do likewise. Of course, the adoption of values is somewhat different from the imitation of a technique; we do not so readily become enthusiastic about tree-fertilizing because our neighbor is.

There obviously are cases of the transmission of ethical standards by intercultural contact. The history of successful missions is a case in point; or of the development of democratic systems of government in backward areas. Even in cases where no historical data are available, we must surmise that transmission by contact has taken place. If, for instance, we compare Hopi values with those of the neighboring Navaho, and then both with those of more distant tribes, it is clear that somehow diffusion has taken place between Hopi and Navaho, in one direction or the other. The two groups could hardly have arrived at such similar results along causally independent lines of development.

The interesting question about diffusion by intercultural contact is not

---

[23] F. Engels and others have preached an elementary form of reward theory in their view that moral systems are essentially class moralities which either justify (rationalize) "the domination and the interests of the ruling class" or else "the revolt against this domination and the future interest of the oppressed." *Handbook of Marxism* (New York: International Publishers Co., 1935), pp. 248–49.

Robert Lowie has used the concept of association in interpretation of standards. *Primitive Society* (New York: Liveright, 1920), p. 245. See also Raymond Firth, "The Study of Values by Social Anthropologists," *Man*, LIII (1953), 152; and A. L. Kroeber, *Anthropology* (New York: Harcourt, Brace & Company, 1948), pp. 316 ff.

[24] An excellent example of these is E. Z. Vogt, "Navaho Veterans: a Study of Changing Values," *Papers of the Peabody Museum of American Archaeology and Ethnology*, Harvard University Press, vol. XLI, No. 1, 1951.

whether it occurs, but when it will occur, or by what laws its occurrence is governed. About this there are various generalizations that seem to be reasonably well established. (1) Diffusion will occur more easily in the case of standards whose existence is easily observable. Thus, E. Z. Vogt could report that the Navaho are tending to drop mother-in-law avoidance rules because it is so obvious to them that White people do not have such rules. As he remarks, "It is quite likely that the mother-in-law taboo has been the first important element to change in the Navaho system, largely because it does differ so obviously from the White pattern. The most frequently mentioned sanction for not following the taboo is that 'White people don't do it and they don't go blind.' "[25] (2) If a new standard can be subsumed under or otherwise supported by standards already in currency, its acceptance is made easier. (3) Prestige factors make a difference. When two societies are in contact, one may have the reputation with the other of being more clever or advanced. Thus, the writer met Hopi who regarded White Americans as "more civilized" as a group. In this case there is apt to be a generally receptive attitude toward the culture system of the group with prestige. The prestige of individuals who initiate a change (and their having extensive family ties) is also important. If the person who is baptized and espouses Christian values is an African chief, the influence may be considerable. (4) The anthropologist H. G. Barnett has suggested, as a result of field studies, that acceptance of the values of another group may be accelerated if some individuals in the recipient group are frustrated and, hence, motivated to attach themselves to another group. Thus, a person who is disgraced with his own group is under strong psychological pressure to identify himself with another group, adopting its values and proclaiming himself superior on that account. One of the writer's Hopi informants, who was poor and lazy and hence frustrated by the demands of the Hopi wedding ritual, developed a view that the White ceremony is "just as good." After the Second World War, E. Z. Vogt made a study of the values of Navaho veterans, and compared the situations of those whose values had apparently changed little, with those of persons whose values had altered most markedly. The following factors are among those he found to be relevant to a tendency to adopt White values: the extent of connections with older and more conservative relatives and particularly with leaders in the family group; whether the family-group leaders were White-oriented or conservative; the orientation of one's own father; the extent of contact with White people, and one's success in this relationship; the understanding of the White world, its friendliness toward Indians and its values of democracy and equality; whether a traditional value or belief (for instance, belief in witchcraft) had some utility in resolving psycho-

[25] *Op. cit.*, p. 114. The last statement illustrates the complexity of such processes. Part of the reason for adopting the White pattern is that one of the basic Navaho reasons for following the rule is undermined by observations of White people to the effect that there are no evil consequences of not following it.

logical tensions. Vogt's conclusions, in general, support Barnett's proposal about the critical role of personal conflicts in cultural change.

Most of the changes of ethical beliefs with which the reader will be familiar, however, will be results of internal dynamisms, not of contact with other cultures. The reader might amuse himself by reflecting on all the modifications wrought in the ethical thinking of Americans by the introduction of the motor car. Often, of course, such chains of development are initiated by some borrowing from another society. For example, Thurnwald points out that the introduction of money into Africa by Europeans set in motion a chain of repercussions: a widespread desire for monetary gain, hitherto unknown competitive situations, even changes in the institution of marriage.[26] The effects of the introduction of the horse among American Plains Indians had similar far-flung results. Among the north Asian Chukchi, the introduction of domesticated reindeer seems to have resulted in the adoption of polygyny among reindeer-breeding groups; and this same fact may be the reason why among this group, where the old men enjoy great prestige as property-owners, there is not the practice of the killing of the aged that obtains among the maritime Chukchi, who make a precarious livelihood by fishing and hunting seal. In none of these cases, we should note, was there copying of an antecedent pattern from a group with prestige.

There are doubtless various patterns into which such internal developments may fall. We shall mention two. (1) Sometimes a new situation will furnish strong motivation (or reduced aversion) to deviate from the accepted norm, with the effect that the standard itself is modified to permit the new behavior. (The standard may remain fixed, however, if the reasons for it are clear.) As Llewellyn and Hoebel put it in another context, "What comes to be in the way of practice produces in due course its flavor of felt rightness among its practitioners. This takes no planning, no preaching, no thinking; it just happens. Change of practice changes the base line of standard."[27] For instance, old Hopi strongly disapprove of drinking any kind of alcoholic beverage, whereas young Hopi men who have spent time in the army or off the reservation, appear to feel differently, and indeed think that a drink (sometimes, getting drunk) is a good thing. Why? Probably during the young men's temporary absence from the reservation, there were social pressures to drink, enjoyment of these occasions, and therefore repetitions; moreover, during these absences the social constraints exercised by the older Hopi at home were inoperative. (The young men were probably affected further by the behavior and values of White people, and also by personal experience with alcohol that indicated that the dangers of its use

---

[26] Richard Thurnwald, "The Psychology of Acculturation," *American Anthropologist*, XXXIV (1932), 557–69.

[27] K. N. Llewellyn and E. A. Hoebel. *The Cheyenne Way* (Norman, Okla.: University of Oklahoma Press, 1941), p. 280. This remark is similar to what was suggested by Lecky above (p. 106), and by Lowie on association (p. 108).

had been exaggerated by the old Hopi.) (2) The second pattern consists in modification of factual beliefs about some form of behavior, quality of mind, or state of affairs. For instance, many Hopi do not now condemn, in any way comparable to what would have been the case many years ago, a person's introducing some change into one of the religious dances. The reason for this is the obvious one: the young men do not have as much credence in the traditional supernaturalist view of the dance. Therefore, they do not regard innovation as fraught with serious consequences for the group, since rainfall and livelihood are not thought to depend on letter-perfect performance according to the traditional pattern. In this case, the alteration in factual belief about the act concerned its *consequences* for the group. But other kinds of change in belief can have similar effects. For instance, we may change our views about the propriety of punishment of certain types of criminals if we get a certain picture of the psychological or social conditions responsible for their particular kind of offense.

Many other types of process are probably important; we need to know more about the effects of revolutions, of religious developments, and of what Kroeber has called "cultural fatigue."[28]

What inferences may be drawn, from these theories of the dynamics of value systems, about whether there are ultimate disagreements of ethical principle among different social groups? If it is true that temptation to violate an established norm, or the prestige of a culture system, or personal conflicts and pressures to identify with another group do lead to changes of moral standard, we do have good ground for expecting that there are "ultimate" disagreements of ethical principle. The same is true of some theories of the statics of ethical standards: probably that of Benedict and of the theories within the psychoanalytic tradition, and certainly of proposals that make use of conceptions drawn from behavioristic learning theory (or the principle of association). In all of these cases, the theory implies that a change might take place without a corresponding change in relevant factual beliefs of the group involved. Whatever weight these theories carry—and we should re-emphasize that they are rather speculative —must be added to the thesis that there are ultimate differences of ethical standard, when different social groups are compared.

We might get the impression from the foregoing, considering the multiple factors that influence ethical standards, that the changes in ethical systems are and may be expected to be chaotic, with no trend or direction. This, however, is not wholly the case—and we should not expect it to be the case when we reflect that the factual beliefs that affect moral standards tend to become more correct as time goes on.

A. L. Kroeber has called attention to three types of cultural movements that appear to be nonreversible steps of a progressive kind, and that carry

[28] A. L. Kroeber, *Anthropology* (New York: Harcourt, Brace & Company, 1948), chap. 10.

important implications. The first two of these concern knowledge of cause-effect relations. One is the growth of science and technology; the other is the decline of magic and superstition. There has been a nonreversible decline in the "bestowal of social rewards for the inability to distinguish subjective experiences from objective phenomena, or for the deliberate inversion of the two." Societies do not revert to esteem for shamanism, visions, or magical devices. There has been a third, more directly ethical, trend. Societies do not revert to practices that involve "what strikes us as the gratuitous obtrusion into public recognition and the social order of physiological happenings, including blood and death and decay, which we tend to regard as matters best kept private and unemphasized, and their public obtrusion as unpleasant and useless." Such practices include deformations of the body, blood sacrifices, puberty rites, preoccupation with the dead body, and cannibalism. Kroeber goes on:

> All in all, retarded cultures seem infantile both in their unabashed preoccupation with the bodily functions and in their disregard of other human lives as compared with the gratifications of the ego. In this sense, advanced cultures may be described as psychologically more adult. Hence their . . . concern about humaneness. The latter is manifest also in trends like those of opposition to slavery, torture as a judicial procedure, beatings as legal punishment, execution with torture, slaughter of prisoners of war.[29]

The anthropologist Robert Redfield, commenting on the foregoing passage from Kroeber, remarks further that

> . . . along with the growing disgust with blood and decay and violence toward the human body goes a growing concern for the welfare and dignity of others. . . . The moral canon tends to mature. . . . I cannot prove to you that man should act more decently and humanely. I follow Kroeber in saying that on the whole he has come to.[30]

FURTHER READINGS

Monographs on primitive peoples, with information on ethical standards:

D. Jenness, "The Life of the Copper River Eskimo," *Report of the Canadian Arctic Expedition 1913–18* (Ottawa: F. A. Acland, 1922).

K. Rasmussen, *The Netsilik Eskimos* (Copenhagen: Gyldendal, 1931).

R. B. Brandt, *Hopi Ethics: A Theoretical Analysis* (Chicago: University of Chicago Press, 1954).

J. Ladd, *The Structure of a Moral Code* (Cambridge: Harvard University Press, 1957).

R. F. Barton, *The Kalingas, Their Institutions and Custom Law* (Chicago: University of Chicago Press, 1949).

H. A. Stayt, *The Bavenda* (Oxford: Oxford University Press, 1931).

R. Firth, *We, The Tikopia* (New York: American Book Co., 1936).

[29] *Op. cit.*, p. 301.
[30] *The Primitive World and its Transformations* (Ithaca: Cornell University Press, 1953), pp. 162–64.

R. F. Fortune, *Sorcerers of Dobu* (New York: E. P. Dutton & Co., Inc., 1932).

R. H. Lowie, *The Crow Indians* (New York: Farrar and Rinehart, Inc., 1935).

E. A. Hoebel and K. N. Llewellyn, *The Cheyenne Way* (Norman, Okla.: University of Oklahoma Press, 1941).

G. B. Grinnell, *The Cheyenne Indians* (New Haven: Yale University Press, 1923).

Cora DuBois, *The People of Alor* (Minneapolis: University of Minnesota Press, 1944).

A. MacBeath, *Experiments in Living* (London: Macmillan & Co., Ltd., 1952). A summary of several groups.

Theoretical and general discussions by anthropologists:

R. Firth, *Elements of Social Organization* (London: Watts & Co., 1951), chap. 6.

E. Westermarck, *Origin and Development of the Moral Ideas*, 2 vols. (New York: The Macmillan Company, 1906). A world-wide survey by topics.

E. Z. Vogt, "Navaho Veterans: A Study of Changing Values," *Papers of the Peabody Museum of American Archaeology and Ethnology*, Harvard University, XLI, No. 1.

R. Benedict, *Patterns of Culture* (New York: Penguin Books, Inc., 1934).

———, "Configurations of Culture in North America," *American Anthropologist*, XXXIV (1932), 1–27. A theory of patterning.

M. E. Opler, "Themes as Dynamic Forces in Culture," *American Journal of Sociology*, LI (1945), 198–206.

———, "An Application of the Theory of Themes in Culture," *Journal of the Washington Academy of Sciences*, XXXVI (1946), 137–66. Another proposal about patterning.

A. Kardiner, *The Individual and His Society* (New York: Columbia University Press, 1946).

———, *The Psychological Frontiers of Society* (New York: Columbia University Press, 1945). Interesting speculations by a psychoanalyst on the dynamics of cultures.

C. Kluckhohn, in F. S. C. Northrop, *Ideological Differences and World Order* (New Haven: Yale University Press, 1949), chap. 17.

H. G. Barnett, "Personal Conflicts and Culture Change," *Social Forces*, XX, 160–71. Dynamic forces in culture change.

R. Thurnwald, "The Psychology of Acculturation," *American Anthropologist*, XXXIV (1932), 557–69.

R. Redfield, *The Primitive World and its Transformations* (Ithaca: Cornell University Press, 1953).

———, *Peasant Society and Culture* (Chicago: University of Chicago Press, 1956).

6

The Development of Ethical Values in the Individual

Questions about the ethical values of individual persons can be raised that are parallel to those we have asked about the standards of social groups. "Does everyone have ethical values?" "Is there ultimate disagreement between the values of different people?" "When and why do values change?" "Are values influenced by other qualities of one's personality, and how?" For an answer to such questions we turn to psychology.

Psychological theory and research are of importance for us on points other than those to be considered in this chapter: for instance, on the question of whether everyone's motivation is always purely selfish. Such matters we shall consider in later chapters.

In the present chapter, we shall concentrate our discussion around a central question: How do individuals come to have the ethical standards and ethical "experience" they do have? First, however, let us ask ourselves, as we did in the preceding chapter: What is answering this question going to do for our problems? Will answering it show that some method for justifying ethical principles or convictions is the right one?

Let us commence answering these questions by repeating a warning we sounded in the previous chapter: There is a difference between a person's values[1] (in the sense of his beliefs about what is valuable, his preference judgments, and so forth) and in fact being that things or actions worthwhile, right, praiseworthy, and so on; and there is a difference between having an understanding of the causes and genesis of a person's values, and knowing whether his values or standards are justifiable. These differences are analogous to the fact that it is one thing to know that Darwin's beliefs about the origin of species would have been different if his personality, his

[1] We shall give more precise meaning to "a person's values" shortly.

114

values, and his religious beliefs had been other than they were, and it is another thing to know whether or not his theory is correct.

Partly in view of this distinction, philosophers have been chary, in recent years, of affirming *any* positive bearing on ethical theory of psychological theories of ethical values. Nevertheless, there is some bearing, which we may roughly summarize as follows:

1. Psychological theories about individual values may give us ground for feeling more secure about any conclusions we may have reached about whether there are ultimate disagreements in ethics, by showing how in principle such disagreements can (or cannot) be produced in the individual —just as the theory of group standards, discussed in the preceding chapter, can give support to such conclusions.

2. More important, theories in critical ethics about the meaning and justification of ethical statements all have *some* commitments about observable facts. For instance, most of them have commitments about what people actually do when they find it necessary to review or reconsider their values, or to justify them to other people. Or again, if a metaethical theory holds that ethical knowing is essentially like knowing in empirical science or like knowing in mathematics, it must be able to explain apparently contrary facts, for example, why there is so much disagreement in ethics, or why ethical beliefs are so easily changed by "prestige suggestion." (This is like the fact that a theory of perception must be compatible with the existence of illusions.) So, in general, there are unquestionably facts of observation that metaethical theories must explain—indeed, a metaethical thesis must look largely if not wholly to such facts for its evidential basis. The serious question is whether psychological experiments, correlations, generalizations, and theories relevant to the genesis of values are among the facts of substantial significance for metaethical theory. On this point, three things seem obvious. The first is that facts about genesis are a problem for some metaethical theories: For instance, it is awkward to say that ethical insight into what is fitting in particular situations is somehow an "intuitive apprehension of an objective fact," and at the same time to admit that some psychologists are right in supposing that one's particular "insights" derive from the values of one's father and are a result of "identification" with him (and would have been quite different if one's father's values had happened to be different). The second is that some metaethical theories assert that the use of ethical words can produce important conditioned effects. Such theories obviously must come to terms with psychological theory and experiment. Third, and perhaps most important, the central concepts and assumptions of one's metaethical theory should have good standing or at least not bad standing, in psychological theory. If, for instance, it utilizes a concept of "experience of obligation," its concept must broadly make sense in terms of what psychological knowledge we have,

and things must not be said about it that psychological theory and experiments render dubious. How much of a restriction this point is, we shall not try to estimate just now; in any case, since theories about ethical values are far from being in a mature state at the present time, the restriction may come to mean more in future years than it does at present.

3. The third point is more practical. At present, a certain amount of information about psychological findings or theories relevant to ethical values is quite widespread. Furthermore, inferences are undoubtedly drawn from this information, whether justly or unjustly, about questions both of metaethics and normative ethics. What sorts of inference are these? Of most importance are inferences leading to skeptical conclusions: inferences that, since ethical values are absorbed from one's parents and one's social group, it is foolish to suppose that one person's ethical principles—at least, his fundamental ones—are any more solidly grounded than any other person's, or that there is such a thing as ethical *knowledge* at all. As a result, it seems worthwhile at present to attempt an accurate survey of what really has been proved by experiment, and what psychological theories really say, relevant to ethical values. We shall then be in a position to examine the major metaethical theories, and discard those that really are in conflict with soundly-based psychological theory. We shall also be in a position to estimate the force of skeptical inferences.

1. THE PROBLEM FOR PSYCHOLOGY

The question we are going to discuss is: "How do individuals come by their ethical standards or ethical 'experience'?" Or, in other words, "How do individuals come by their ethical values?"

The first thing we have to do is assign a fairly specific meaning to this question. Let us begin by considering an example of an actual ethical experience. Presumably the reader can recall comparable experiences of his own.

On one occasion several years ago, the writer had spent the day working in the library of Stanford University. His wife met him near the library building at an agreed time, to drive him home for dinner. The drive home required traversing about a mile of campus road, on which there was heavy traffic, but near which there were no buildings. While moving along this road, we noticed a car pulled off to the side of the road, with a man in it slumped over the wheel—as if asleep, or ill. The question at once was raised: "Should we stop and see if that man is ill and in need of help?" (The writer's father died of a heart attack, and the writer is thus inclined toward heart-attack diagnoses of such behavior.) There were strong motivations not to stop: disinclination to make oneself look foolish by waking someone out of a comfortable afternoon nap, disinclination to be involved in handling an emergency case in an unfamiliar city, a feeling that the problem could be handled very well by local residents whose cars were streaming by, or certainly by a police patrol car that could be expected in a few minutes—not to mention the facts of being tired and hungry. At any rate, the discussion of whether to stop lasted so long that the writer's car got onto a clover-leaf where it was not possible to stop. So, with many glances backward, to see whether perhaps some other more public-minded citizen would stop (none did), the writer drove on out of sight and resolved to put the matter out of mind. This, however, was not so easy. The writer felt uncomfortable at intervals; his thoughts returned to the incident; he reproached himself for having been so hesitant. Fortunately, the local paper of the following day did not mention any untoward event having taken place on the stretch of road in question—as it surely would have done had someone been taken seriously ill. After perusing this paper, the writer felt relieved and had no further difficulty putting the incident out of mind. Let us refer to this episode as the "parked-car" episode.

It is obvious that not everyone would have reacted to the situation as the writer and his wife did. It might not have occurred to some that the man might be ill; or if it did, it might not have occurred to them that they had any obligation to do anything about it, and they might have felt little or no impulse to stop. On the other hand, some public-spirited people might have stopped and made inquiries without hesitation. Furthermore, the same people who would feel no impulse to stop would presumably not have the incident on their minds thereafter, and would not reproach themselves or feel any guilt. In view of these differences, we might say that people may differ in their *ethical responses* to situations, or in their *readiness* to make ethical responses of a certain sort to certain types of situation.

But what were the main features of the episode?

1. There was verbalizing. It was not in fact about ethical principles, but about the likelihood of aid being needed and the possibility that someone better qualified to give it would stop. Note, however, that here, as in any situation we are tempted to call "ethical," there was readiness to make general statements about features of the situation that bear one way or the other on how one ought to act; "principles" are always at our fingertips.

2. There was actually an impulse to stop. Indeed, the writer let up on the accelerator, pulled over into the right-hand lane, and proceeded at a reduced rate of speed before the discussion about what to do was more than barely under way. Moreover, all the looking back, and the discomforts and reproaches later on, are testimony to the fact that there was motivation to stop that was partially successful in controlling behavior.

There are some interesting things to be noticed about this motivation. Perhaps most important is the fact that the writer in a sense did not *want* to stop, certainly not in the way in which he wanted his dinner. In such cases, we normally say that we did not want to do a certain thing, but did it because we thought we ought. The writer was, in this case, not considering stopping in order to terminate some organic discomfort, as he might be doing if he saw a restaurant. Nor did he consider stopping in order to get or do something for himself, as he might be doing if he stopped at a postbox to mail a letter. Rather, the impulse to stop derived from confrontation with the probable needs of another person, and of course doubt whether anyone else was likely to meet those needs. Some psychologists, at least partly in order to give recognition to the distinctiveness of the motivation, have suggested calling this sort of experience an "experience of requiredness"; but this term has come to carry a good many associations of which the writer wishes to be free. We shall not use this terminology, then. Also, there is no reason why we should not use an ordinary mode of speech to cover it: "I felt an obligation to. . . ."[2]

3. Now let us point out something that did not actually occur, but that clearly would have occurred if the situation had been different. Suppose there had been a third party in the car, and he had taken the writer to task for his behavior. Suppose he had said: "Why do you think you have to get excited about whether somebody else is sick? Can't you learn to enjoy life? What did your mother do to you when you were a baby?" These questions would have stimulated the writer to lengthy verbalizing, justifying his principles and motivation. We need not now go into the question just what form this defense would have taken, but we may observe that different people would offer different defenses. For instance, it would not naturally occur to the writer to defend his principles by citing the parable of the Good Samaritan (unless he happened to know that this point would tell with his critic), but presumably for many this would be a natural move to make. The point is, however, that everybody, or practically everybody, will make some defensive verbal moves; and practically everybody is convinced that some such move *could* be made successfully, even if in the particular situation he happens to be unable to make it.

So much for a description of the parked-car episode. How typical is it as an exhibit of the operation of ethical standards and the nature of ethical experiences? In some ways it is not quite representative. (1) It was a face-

---

2 It may be true that to "feel an obligation to . . ." is not to experience any localized thrill or twinge; it may not even be like a thrill of joy, which seems associated with the chest area. Writers who speak of an "experience of requiredness" may be right if they insist that no element of the experience is within the confines of the experienced body, in the way in which toothaches, itches, tinglings, and thrills are experienced as within the body. Remorse feelings, however, are experienced as within the body, and can be, at least roughly, localized.

On the other hand, we do speak of "shrinking" at the thought of being responsible for a certain event, and there is such a thing as a felt impulse to do a certain thing; indeed, in our episode, the writer actually began stopping.

to-face interaction of human beings, and one in which rather basic ethical principles and motivations were directly engaged. If, on the other hand, one is Secretary of State and considering how to react to a "peace proposal" from a power whose intentions are suspect, things are not so simple. Here one has to remind oneself (presumably) what one's ethical principles are, and then work out, by reasoning, their implications for the problem at hand. (2) Sometimes there is difference of quite another sort: Our relation to the sheer welfare of others is not the crucial thing. Our feeling of obligation derives from the fact that we made a promise, or injured someone, or because the other party is a son of ours or a long-time friend. (3) Again, sometimes welfare is scarcely involved at all. For instance, people feel obligated to abstain from certain forms of sexual behavior even when they do not think there is apt to be any unfavorable effect on the welfare of anyone else; or they may feel they ought not to commit suicide, even if such an act would harm no one—and might be a relief to many. (3) The parked-car episode is primarily an "agent" situation. However, there are also "spectator" situations, where we observe how someone else meets a problem like the ones we have been sketching—and we criticize, feel shock or indignation or annoyance or admiration, and classify him as a certain kind of person. (4) Finally, there is something rather different: decisions about actions that we make, for ourselves or families or business firms, for example, in connection with which we do not feel, or think of, obligations at all. They are rather decisions about doing what we "think best." There is thought about alternative plans, and about what things it is "good to do" or "have," and about the relation to these of plans being considered. There are conflicting inclinations. Also, as in the case of the parked-car episode, there are *post mortems:* strong regrets about one's decision and consequent action, self-reproaches if a mistaken decision resulted from personal faults of one kind or another. But in most cases, these decisions seem very different from the parked-car episode, since we feel that we are primarily deciding what is for our own welfare, or at least the welfare of our family or firm, which we think of as being "ours" as much as our personal welfare.

For better or for worse, we shall very largely have to group these experiences together indiscriminately in our psychological discussion, but not entirely: We shall concentrate attention very strongly on the kinds of experience listed earlier, to the exclusion of the last one, although many of the points we shall be making appear to be valid for *all* the types of experience listed. It is unfortunate that the available evidence does not permit more discrimination. One's instinctive feelings suggest that somewhat different genetic accounts ought perhaps to be given for some of these different types of case. However, there simply is not sufficiently abundant experimental material. Indeed, experimental data do not enable us to discuss separately the verbal as distinct from the motivational aspects of these experiences.

We need a simple term to refer to a person's disposition or readiness to have responses like those described in the case of the parked-car episode (dispositions, we have noted, that can vary considerably from person to person), and to refer to dispositions to have ethical responses in the other types of case we have listed. We shall use the term "values" for this purpose; and we shall use "moral values" to refer to readiness to have experiences or responses of the kind that occur in all the types of situations we have listed *except* the last. This usage may at first seem odd, but actually it diverges little if at all from some ordinary uses of these terms, and is consistent with usage in vogue among some psychologists and social scientists (who count a tendency to feel obligated not to do a certain thing as a "moral value" of the person in question).[3] Consider, for instance, a remark we might make of our neighbor: "What peculiar values he has!" What would we say we were talking about, if we had to explain? Perhaps we mean that he is devoted to Westerns on television and will watch nothing else; perhaps that he is greatly disturbed by the discovery that his daughter smokes, but jokes about cheating the newsboy himself. It is not just what he says, or thinks to himself; it is also what he does, is motivated to do, feels strongly about—the kinds of things we have listed.

There are some difficult questions we might be asked. "What is the difference between values, in this sense, and *manners?*" "Are a person's *aesthetic* values just a subdivision of his values in this sense?" "What is the relevance of economic value?" "What should we say about an Englishman's feelings about things no 'gentleman' would do? Are these his values, or his moral values?" "How would we classify the anxieties of a child in transgressing parental prohibitions?" In answer to these questions, we are simply going to say that we already have enough to do discussing ethical values. We certainly do not mean to suggest that there is any sharp division, psychologically, between these various things and what we are going to talk about. But to describe typical experiences having to do with manners, or aesthetic values, and so forth, and to contrast them carefully with the experiences we have described, would be a lengthy job, and to do this would serve little purpose, since the psychological material we are about to describe is quite unrefined, and the introduction of such subtle distinctions might mislead us into thinking it is not. These comparisons and distinctions, then, we must leave to others.

[3] It may be helpful to social science students to mention a somewhat different use of "values" that has been influential in empirical research. Professor Clyde Kluckhorn has proposed the following definition of "value": "A value is a conception, explicit or implicit, distinctive of an individual or characteristic of a group, of the desirable which influences the selection from available modes, means, and ends of action." In T. Parsons and E. A. Shils (eds.), *Toward a General Theory of Action* (Cambridge: Harvard University Press, 1954), p. 395.

Our initial question, then, can be restated thus: "How do people come to have the values they do have—especially the moral values they do have?"

In answering this question, we shall do two things. First, in the following section, we shall list a number of factors that, on statistical grounds or otherwise, may reasonably be supposed to affect a person's values to some extent. We shall describe, as far as we can, just what kind of effect they have. Second, we shall describe some important types of more speculative theories—behavioristic, Freudian, and Gestalt—theories that try to arrive at the basic laws of human development. These theories, just because they are trying to get down to fundamentals and to formulate basic laws, tend to classify values with other types of human phenomena—for instance, as a subclass of conditioned responses—and they classify the various causes of value development so as to fit in with their fundamental ideas about what types of things influence human behavior and development. These theories are speculative and controversial, and some psychologists would advise us to confine ourselves to observable facts. However, such theories broaden our thinking and give us perspective on our material. Moreover, theory is a necessary guide for the interpretation of information about correlations and causal connections; unless we are content with a host of correlations, we shall want to identify the more fundamental causal relationships, and there is no way to do this except by trying to fit experimental material together in the framework of a comprehensive theory.

2. OBSERVATIONS ABOUT THE GENESIS OF VALUES, ESPECIALLY MORAL VALUES

Let us now consider what appear to be major factors that influence the values of the individual. Some of the anthropological observations already recounted are equally weighty, for ascertaining such factors, as are statistical observational studies. Some points, incidentally, are so obvious from ordinary experience that they do not really need any more elaborate proof.

Home influences. It is obvious that, in one way or another, the child's experiences in his home have a great deal to do with both the content of his moral values and their importance for him (that is, the extent to which they succeed in controlling his behavior in spite of his personal wishes.) As we should expect, studies show that the views of siblings about issues that involve ethical questions are correlated well above chance, and the same is true for the views of children and their parents. Even on a topic like justice in the punishment of children, about which children have had experience of their own and also have ideas of their own that differ from those of their parents, there have been found to be marked differences between socioeconomic groups (in London) that must be ascribed to the home environment.[4] Nor is the influence of the home confined merely to the verbal level; one study, for instance, showed that a child's cheating at school had no correlation with attendance at Sunday School, but a substantial one with some features of the family background. The interesting question, however, is not simply whether the total home experiences have an important influence on the development of values, but, rather, precisely which ones of these experiences are the important ones.

A plausible proposal is that the child initially accepts what his parents tell him about what is good or right or justifiable. Since the child is unfamiliar with any alternatives, has good reason to regard his parents as sound sources of information, and has no reason to suppose that there are special epistemological puzzles about ethical questions, why should he not accept the statements of his parents? There has not, however, been any careful substantiation of this hypothesis, perhaps because it is regarded as just obviously true. Children have been shown, as we should expect, *not* always to agree with their parents on certain matters where they have experience of their own, for example, the justice of parental rules about when and where to go swimming. But this fact hardly reduces the plausibility of the proposal about the source of a major portion of the child's earliest thoughts on ethics. A difficulty of the proposal is the inability of adults to remember many such preachments by adults (and adults will be able to think of many points on which they now think their parents' views were just mistaken); but there is evidence that such parent-child communications can be effective and then be forgotten (we do not remember being taught English, either!)—as was shown by a study of Southern attitudes to Negroes, when older children could not recall directive comments by parents, although younger children could.[5] Of course, direct parent-child transmissions need not be regarded as the sole source of parent-child agreements in ethical views; parents and children have common institutional attachments, such as church and club membership, common experiences,

[4] M. R. Harrower, "Social Status and the Moral Development of the Child," *British Journal of Educational Psychology*, IV (1934), 75–95. This study raised questions about generalizations from an earlier investigation by Jean Piaget, who had proposed that there is a typical early stage of moral belief, in which moral rules are looked on as eternal and independent of social function, in which degree of blameworthiness depends not on intent but on the seriousness of the effects of an offense (so that unintentional breaking of an expensive dish is morally worse than deliberate smashing of an inexpensive one), in which punishment is called for with a severity comparable to the seriousness of the offense, and in which it is expected that moral offenses will result in some sort of "punishing" mishap, even if no one finds out about them. This set of ideas is sometimes called "moral realism" and it is sometimes found among adults in primitive societies. Harrower's results suggest that the occurrence of this set of ideas is a culture-generated and therefore variable phenomenon, not an essential stage in the moral development of every child, as Piaget had supposed it was.

[5] E. L. Horowitz and Ruth E. Horowitz, "Development of Social Attitudes in Children," *Sociometry*, I (1938), 301–38.

common sources of information, for instance books and magazines in the home—and all of these things may play an important role.

The child does not, however, merely learn about what is good or right like any other piece of information. He incorporates at least some of the parental preachments into his motivation: He comes to give up certain things he wants, or to undergo experiences he would like to avoid (for example, the unpleasant consequences of telling the truth), and he comes to experience guilt and remorse. How is this? There are several things to be noted. (1) Parents do not merely speak well or ill of certain types of behavior; they *enforce* preferred modes of behavior by punishments. (2) Children come to develop an interest in how other persons, including their parents, *rate them as persons.* Why and how they come to develop such an interest is a complex story, but the fact is that they do—and that it is obvious to them that their own behavior and their expressed values make a difference to other persons' ratings of them as persons. (These points we take to be too obvious to require further observational support.) (3) There is evidence that a relation of affection within a family group is important for the motivational development here being considered. For instance, one survey showed that delinquent children express a relatively high preference for turning to friends rather than to parents in time of trouble. An extensive study of school children in an Illinois town showed that children from families rated high for affectional relations scored comparatively very well in a variety of tests for honesty, moral courage, friendliness, loyalty, and responsibility. One writer, commenting on the relative ineffectiveness of physical punishment for the development of moral values, has remarked:

> [The] early establishment of a strong positive relationship between parent and child may lead directly to a strong superego and also permit reliance upon techniques of punishment which are effective only in the presence of a strong positive relationship.[6]

(4) It is widely believed that there is a set of further mechanisms—which we shall group together under the term "identification"—that cause the child to incorporate the values of his parents or persons who have to him roughly the sort of relation that parents have (maybe one's employer, in later life). Recent discussions of this topic have been more theoretically than experimentally oriented, however, so that this topic is better discussed at a later point, in connection with Freud. However, we should notice here that there has been recently a convergence of opinion to the effect that there is a correlation between a motivationally well-developed value system in the child and the use of psychological, "love-oriented" sanctions

[6] I. L. Child, in Gardner Lindzey (ed.), *Handbook of Social Psychology*, (Cambridge: Addison-Wesley Publishing Co., 1954), p. 684. See A. W. Brown, Joan Morrison, and G. B. Couch, "Influence of Affectional Family Relationships on Character Development," *Journal of Abnormal and Social Psychology*, XLII (1947), 422–28.

rather than physical punishment. "Love-oriented" punishment consists in withholding expressions of affection and regard for the child, thereby arousing anxiety in him about parental love and regard, while at the same time supporting, or at least not interfering with, the child's desire for parental regard and affection.[7] At a later age, parents presumably are less important objects of "identification." At least, when children were asked to write an essay on "The Person I Would Like to Be Like," the very young children quite frequently chose a parent or other near relative, whereas the older children chose with greater frequency, some "composite or imaginary" figure.[8]

Other prestige figures. It has been suggested above that the influence of the parents might be wielded by other persons, if they happened to stand in a position psychologically comparable to that of the parents. As the child grows older, the parents' reputation for omniscience tends to decline; so perhaps the views of scientists, philosophers, and others—or, more likely, the opinions of the child's peer group, or the opinions he attributes to the community or nation—will tend to be accepted as authoritative. Again, the child's interest in respect and affection turns more and more toward persons outside his family. He takes the affection of his family for granted, and his efforts are directed to winning a place for himself in a wider group, especially of persons in his own age group. So, we might anticipate that other figures will assume the role of the parents as the child grows older.

We must be careful, however. Many writers think that a person's basic values are already firmly fixed for life by the time he is ten years old. Moreover, we must remember that value statements of parents to very young children fall on virgin soil, where there are no frameworks of ideas to offer competition. A person's intellectual life is much richer when he emerges onto the wider scene, and our *a priori* reflections on what is probable may lead us astray. What evidence is there?

There have been many studies of "prestige" effects on the opinions of adults. Some of these have been in the area of ethical opinions. Essentially, these studies show that college students exhibit more sympathy with certain statements of social and ethical aims (or rate the merit of art objects more highly) after being informed that these statements are subscribed to by

---

[7] See the discussion by J. W. M. Whiting and I. L. Child, *Child Training and Personality* (New Haven: Yale University Press, 1953), pp. 240–46; also the summary of studies by Child in the article cited in the preceding footnote. Also R. R. Sears, E. E. Maccoby, and H. Levin, *Patterns of Child Rearing* (Evanston, Ill., Row, Peterson & Company, 1957), chap. 10, especially pp. 386–90.

[8] A good many children, in the middle group especially, picked "glamorous" adults such as movie stars or athletes; but the investigators' statistics convinced them that anyone over fifteen who chooses such a person as an ideal is "immature." Teachers were seldom chosen; and substantial figures in history, like Lincoln, were mentioned much less frequently than appears to have been the case in earlier studies. R. J. Havighurst, M. Z. Robinson, and Mildred Dorr, "The Development of the Ideal Self in Childhood and Adolescence," *Journal of Educational Research*, XL (1946), 241–57.

some prestigeful individuals or groups. The students were first asked to express favorable or unfavorable attitudes on various ethical statements about social issues; they were retested later, after part of the group had been told that certain eminent persons held certain views on these issues, or that the majority vote had been in a certain direction in the first test. On the retest, a substantial shift of opinion was registered in the direction of agreement either with the eminent persons or with the majority.[9] This result agrees with many investigations showing the influence of beliefs about the opinions of others on a person's own beliefs and attitudes, on a wide variety of subjects—even on judgments about the relative lengths of lines that the subjects could actually see.[10] In general, the extent of "prestige" effects has been found to vary with many factors: the relationship of the individual to the group, the personality of the prestigeful person, the conformity of the suggested opinions with the interests of the person being tested and with the frame of other beliefs already accepted by him, and his familiarity with the relevant evidence and the clarity of the import of such evidence.

What is proved by the tests that are specifically relevant to ethical values? They show that learning about the opinions of prestigeful persons has *some* influence. However, the issues were complex ones, on which two opinions were quite possible. It does not follow from the fact that a person's opinion on such matters is changed by information about the views of others that a person can be induced, by such information, to approve of murder or dishonesty or of any behavior whose social undesirability is obvious. Indeed, it is consistent with all the experimental data to hold that the effect of the report about the opinions of others was not at all to change any basic ethical opinions but simply to change their application. Perhaps the students were simply stimulated to review the facts, or to notice certain aspects of the situation that they had been overlooking. No check was made to determine whether this possibility was in fact the case. Moreover, no attempt was made to show that ethical judgments can be moved in either of opposite directions with equal facility. What was shown was that students can be moved in what is objectively a more "liberal" direction by certain means. Could they be moved equally well in

[9] C. E. Arnett, H. Davidson, and H. N. Lewis, "Prestige as a Factor in Attitude Changes," *Sociology and Sociological Research*, XVI (1931–32), 49–55; and D. Wheeler and H. Jordan, "The Change of Individual Opinion to Accord with Group Opinion," *Journal of Abnormal and Social Psychology*, XXIV (1929–30), 203–06; H. T. Moore, "The Comparative Influence of Majority and Expert Opinion," *American Journal of Psychology*, XXXII (1921), 16–20.

[10] See M. Sherif and H. Cantril, "The Psychology of 'Attitudes,'" *Psychological Review*, LII (1945), 295–319, and LIII (1946), 1–24; T. E. Coffin, *Some Conditions of Suggestion and Suggestibility*, *Psychological Monographs*, LIII, No. 4, 1941; and especially S. E. Asch, *Social Psychology* (Englewood Cliffs, N.J.: Prentice-Hall, Inc., 1952), beginning with chapter 14.

the opposite direction? Still, ethical judgments about *complex problems* were modified to *some* extent, *somehow*.

One piece of experimental work, done by M. Sherif, deserves mention here because of its wide influence on thinking about standards, especially among sociologists.

Sherif introduced subjects into a dark room where they could see nothing but a point of light, which was actually motionless. Such a light will appear to move, to all persons, after a time (the "autokinetic" effect). Sherif's subjects, who did not know that the light was actually motionless, were asked to give reports on when and how far the light moved. This they did, and each established a rather fixed range of distance judgments. Later, subjects were tested in groups, in which each was permitted to hear the reports of the others. In this situation, the previous typical range of distance judgment was modified in the direction of the judgments of others, and a common range established. The group ranges were found to hold over for later situations of individual testing. Sherif and others have taken the results of this experiment to be illustrative of the basic psychological processes involved in the formation of norms of all kinds. As one writer put it, "There is evidently something about expressing judgments to others and hearing others expressing their judgments that affects a person's standards of judgment."[11]

If this experiment can safely be taken as relevant to the formation of values (the similarity between the cases, however, is rather slight), what is shown is that knowing the value judgments of others will function, *somehow*, to produce a measure of conformity with average group evaluations. The power of the experiment lies in its illustrating this fact in a simple and graphic way; it does not add to the experimental data already cited except to show that similar effects can be produced for simple perceptual judgments. In particular, it should be noted that the experiment did not show *how* information about the judgments of others functioned to produce the effect. Any conclusion that the experiment shows that people have an automatic tendency to move toward agreement with the expressed views of others, no matter what they are, reaches beyond the evidence.[12]

11 T. M. Newcomb, *Social Psychology* (New York: Dryden Press, 1950), p. 265. For Sherif's work, see M. Sherif, *The Psychology of Social Norms* (New York: Harper & Bros., 1936), Chap. 6.

12 The subjects of the experiment believed the motion was objective, and we may suppose they assumed from previous experience that the distance judgments of others were likely to be as accurate as their own. Thus, when they heard the conflicting reports of others they were faced with a logical problem that they had somehow to resolve. Sherif did not report detailed subjects' descriptions of their thought processes. His data leave open the possibility that his subjects were behaving in a highly rational way: that they were busy forming hypotheses about the situation that would account for the discrepancies, and that the changes in their judgment range reflected a reasonable hypothesis about the total situation. This interpretation is supported by the experimental findings of H. G. Sperling, reported by S. E. Asch, *op. cit.*, pp. 487 ff.

Light is thrown on the details of real-life processes by a study, by T. M. Newcomb, of the social and political attitudes of students at Bennington College, although here again the report is about opinions on complex problems and not fundamental ethical principles. Newcomb found, as one might expect, that the college student's "liberalism" increases during his four college years. But he also found some other things that were by no means obvious. First, he noted that students associated a "liberal" view on social issues with the Bennington faculty and with "leading" groups of students there; the college community as a whole was stamped as "liberal" in student thought. Second, the tendency of the students to be receptive toward this prevailing cast of opinion was influenced by the individual student's relationship to the community—by success at college, including acceptance by classmates and feelings of security and of being respected; by the existence (or nonexistence) of strong family ties motivating them to cling to family social attitudes rather than to those of the college community; by motivation to achieve prestige and position in the college community; by intellectual energies that enabled them to be aware of the situation and to participate actively in nonacademic thinking and activities. The most favorable conditions for acceptance of the community ideology were awareness of what the ideology was, feelings of security and acceptance and success at the college, absence of dependence on one's family or other individuals outside the college, and a desire to make a place for oneself in the life of the college.[13] These findings, incidentally, are closely parallel to anthropological reports already cited (pp. 109–10) about conditions facilitating group changes in ethical standard.

Our conclusion must be that ethical values, *but possibly not one's fundamental ones* (p. 94), are influenced to some degree in adult years by awareness of the values of other persons. The degree of such influence appears to depend on various factors, such as one's position in a group (for example, one's feeling that one has or hasn't freedom to express disagreement), the strength of the attachment to a group or to others outside it, one's familiarity with evidence relevant to particular values, the structure of one's values that are already relatively secure from question, and the structure of one's personal interests.

We should emphasize that the evidence specifically about ethical judgments is rather fragmentary.

Information, consistency, and personal experience. One might infer from what has been said that a person's ethical opinions are very largely plagiarisms of the views of others. But a little recollection by the reader—on the topic of the sources of his present views about things like whether Red China should be admitted to the U.N., euthanasia, sex mores, the satisfactoriness of "honors systems" for dealing with cheating in examinations, the

[13] See T. M. Newcomb, *Personality and Social Change* (New York: Dryden Press, 1943); also the critical summary by Asch, *op. cit.,* pp. 594–601.

justice of high corporate income taxes, and the desirability of a "core curriculum" of liberal arts subjects in programs of higher education—will probably be conclusive evidence that copying of the ethical values of others is by no means the entire answer to the sources of our ethical values. In order to fix our minds on other factors, let us look at an excerpt from a statement sent by a student to his draft board, explaining the background of his conscientious objection to military service.

> My social conscience was awakened from attending a Unitarian work camp about four years ago. I learned for the first time with real understanding that peace comes from working together and trying to understand one another. Religion began to have real social implications, rather than being a set of morals learned in Sunday School. I also learned of the dangers of making the nation come before God, and "patriotism" a religion.
>
> In my two years at —— University the most profound thing I learned was the literal translation of the words of the angels at the birth of Christ: "Glory to God in the highest and peace on earth among men of good will." . . . It is quite obvious, though usually overlooked, that you just don't have peace unless there is good will. This basic message is found elaborated and applied in the Quaker Report on Russo-American relations.
>
> Of the tragedy of war I learned directly from the death of my brother-in-law . . . , and indirectly from reading, movies, and conversation with acquaintances, who had been to Europe and elsewhere and seen the suffering, poverty, and moral degradation caused by war.
>
> From authoritative reports I learned of the moral indefensibility of the bombing of Hiroshima and Nagasaki; from Greek tragedy I learned of the self-destruction wrought by the blind pride of an individual or nation; and from Gandhi, that non-violent techniques are practical. . . .
>
> Last year I became acquainted with Mr. and Mrs. ——, two very active Quakers, and learned to respect, if not completely accept, the pacifist approach. With the outbreak of the war in Korea I realized I might soon have to take a definite stand. I could not and cannot see any middle way in the event of war, between the supporters of non-violent techniques and those favoring the use of arms. After discussing the problem with ——, a pacifist, and after reading A. J. Muste's *Not by Might*, my personal religious convictions were crystallized.

It is easy to see that the writer's thinking has brought a mass of experience and established ethical convictions to support a conclusion about conscientious objection to bearing arms. We might recast his reasoning as follows.

1. War has evil consequences (premise partly ethical, partly factual).
2. We ought to avoid supporting what has evil results (unexpressed moral premise, which, incidentally, is not unqualifiedly true).
3. Nonviolent techniques are practical, an effective way to achieve those ends that people often try to achieve by war.
4. There is no third possibility in addition to supporting nonviolent techniques and supporting war.
5. Peace cannot come except through the development of good will; nonviolence promotes good will and hence is a means to peace.

6. Good will and nonviolence as paths to peace are a central tenet of the Christian faith.
7. It cannot be argued that *our* military ventures should be viewed as morally justified exceptions to the condemnation of war, for our bombing of Hiroshima was indefensible; we must beware of being blinded by pride to our own faults.
8. Nor can it be argued that refusal to fight is morally indefensible disloyalty; there are more stringent obligations than those of patriotism.
9. Therefore, everything considered, one ought to support nonviolent techniques by refusing to fight.

The foregoing reasoning is clearly not the sole reason for the student's acceptance of his ethical conclusion. There were such things as home influence, motivation deriving from knowledge of the implications of his decision for his personal future, a desire to be able to identify himself with the pacifist group, which he regarded as a very intelligent group of people sharing a fine religious tradition, and so on.

But it would be arbitrary and foolish to say that his assembling of facts and ethical premises in a fairly coherent framework had *nothing* to do with his conclusion. The reader perhaps can find some flaws in the reasoning, a failure to make important distinctions, but he can hardly fail to feel that it has some force, or to see that it might prove strongly convincing to some people.

It has not been shown, of course, that reasoning like this does (or doesn't) affect our basic moral principles, but the simplest introspection places beyond question that such reasoning is sometimes causally important for some ethical beliefs. Moreover, we have seen evidence that comparable reasoning has played a role in the change of the ethical values of primitive societies.[14] Abundant evidence is available on all sides of the influence of such thinking in the genesis of views on social issues.[15]

We can distinguish, if we analyze influences of this sort on value formation, the roles of the drive toward rational consistency, of factual information, and of personal experience. Let us look at these separately.

First, consistency. Everybody has *many* factual beliefs and *many* ethical convictions. These beliefs have logical relations to one another. If a person notices a logical incoherence—if he notices that he believes P and Q and R, and that P and Q together imply that R is false—there is a tendency for some belief of his to be changed, a tendency that seems to vary in strength from one person to another. (Some people will avoid the difficulty by forgetting that it exists.) Conversely, there is resistance to giving up a belief if its logical relations are such that rejecting it would require a mass of

---

[14] See above, p. 111, and Vogt's remark cited on p. 109; also the writer's *Hopi Ethics*, pp. 277–81.

[15] See, for example, Brewster Smith, Jerome Bruner, and R. H. White, *Opinions and Personality* (New York: John Wiley & Sons, Inc., 1956), especially chap. 10. This book is a study of the thinking of ten men about how the U.S. should behave toward Russia.

other beliefs to be discarded. So much, it appears, is established by direct observation.

Second, let us look at information about facts, whether firsthand or secondhand.[16] In the example of ethical reasoning we have been considering, it is clear that factual beliefs about the effects of war were founded on reading, movies, testimony of individuals about their experiences, and observation. The student also reported the effects of attending a work camp where he said he learned "that peace comes from working together and trying to understand one another"—doubtless a substantial extrapolation from his observations of interpersonal relations at the work camp, but no less effective for that. It looks as if this student's ethical conclusions were influenced by his factual information. We have repeatedly seen evidence, moreover, that factual beliefs play an important role in ethical thinking—that a person's total ethical beliefs must agree with his total factual beliefs.

But do "personal experiences" in some further sense play a role? Let us consider an example.

A student wrote an essay for the writer in which she asserted that she had been brought up to believe that White people should not associate freely with Negroes. However, in high school she formed a close and satisfying friendship with a Negro girl. When her parents discovered this, they reprimanded her severely and forbade further association. The girl made an initial effort to carry out her parents' orders, but when she saw how cruelly her conduct hurt her Negro friend and when she noticed how keenly she herself felt the loss of this friendship, she decided that her parents' views, with all the arguments used to buttress them, were mistaken. She renewed her friendship, and since that time has felt strongly that one has a right to choose one's friends on the basis of personal qualities only, and without regard to any general rules—in particular, rules about the separation of races.

What exactly was the effect of this experience? Partly, it was simply informative; it enriched her concept of a Negro. Furthermore, the frustration caused her to review very critically her parents' arguments, which objectively were very likely feeble. But was this all? We are speculating when we say so; but it does not seem likely that it was. It seems likely, at least, that her sympathetic response to the suffering caused by her own conduct, and her own unhappiness arising from the loss of valued companionship, operated positively and directly to make her both want to renew the friendship and to "feel an obligation" to do so. Why do we say this?

---

[16] It is helpful to distinguish "personal experience" from firsthand information, even firsthand information that is impressive because of a dramatic situation or emotional involvement. In speaking of the influence of "personal experience" we shall *exclude* influence that occurs entirely or almost entirely because of the acquisition of factual information, however dramatic. What is to be included will appear below.

The existence of such direct influence of personal experience on moral values has not been documented by experiments or questionnaires, but it stares us in the face. That is, there are occasions when, without reasoning out what is morally required on the basis of already accepted ethical principles and factual premises, we find ourselves feeling obligated to do something, or moved to condemn or admire some deed or person (and at the same time disposed to say, correspondingly, "I am obligated to do this" and so on), even though these reactions cannot be viewed as expressions of some value of long standing—or rather, even when they conflict with what have been our values. For instance, the reproachful glance of a friend may make us feel differently about loyalty; seeing the results of a thoughtless exaggeration may make us feel quite differently about minor trifling with the truth. Perhaps such influences never come alone; perhaps any event resulting in novel feelings of obligation and so forth, always also makes the facts look differently, at least shows them in a new light. Perhaps, too, any corresponding judgment is always capable of support by appeal to ethical principles we have been holding all along, so that the ultimate result in the total structure of our ethical commitments is rather a restructuring than a complete novelty. Nevertheless, whatever the qualifications, it looks as if personal interaction with situations or behavior—being made to suffer or being given joy by it, being emotionally moved by it—can result in novel ethical responses and corresponding ethical judgments that are new departures for us. When such novel "feelings of obligation" and judgments occur, our structure of values tends to be altered to make room for them—just as our structure of scientific beliefs may be modified in order to accommodate a novel observation.[17]

In general, then, we suggest that the values of adults are influenced by factual information, by "personal experiences," and by the intellectual necessity for having a coherent structure of beliefs.

Personal interests, needs, temperament. Our frequent talk of "rationalizing" expresses the common belief that ethical judgments are often much affected by personal interests, however much people may proceed to defend their judgments by considerations of principle. At least on complex matters—such as whether there should be price supports for farmers, or whether the price of natural gas at the wellheads should be subject to regulation by a certain principle, or whether divorces should be obtainable on certain grounds—observation suggests a correlation between judgment and personal interest. Statistical evidence is scanty and poorly documented on

---

[17] An interesting Ph.D. (Cornell University, 1949) dissertation by R. L. Egbert, *The Effect of Some Childhood and Adolescent Experiences on the Emergence of Values,* suggests various ways in which "personal experience" might affect nonmoral values. His statistics, for instance, indicate that unsatisfactory relations with both teachers and peers, and at home, tend to increase one's valuations of intellectual things and of privacy. Perhaps punishment in some areas produces higher interest in nonpunishing areas or in areas in which some achievement and recognition are possible. Egbert's autobiographical material is rich in such suggestions.

this point, as far as what we tend to call "moral principles" are concerned. But if we consider the whole area of social and political attitudes (about "what ought to be done"), the statistical support becomes very substantial. In fact, social scientists at present no longer question whether personal interest plays a role in such thinking, and are interested rather in the more specific issue of the particular conditions under which it does so. It would of course be a gross mistake to suppose that people can believe just anything they would like to believe, in ethics any more than elsewhere. For instance, a survey of penitentiary inmates showed that, with the exception of some sex criminals, inmates' views of the morality of the offense for which they were in prison did not differ significantly from that of the general population. Moreover, it appears that information and intelligence often play a larger role in producing nonconformist social views than do considerations of personal interest, at least if the latter are not obvious and of substantial magnitude. But personal interest undoubtedly plays a role.[18]

The interests, of course, need not be economic. Let us quote from a résumé of influences found to underlie the views of ten men about how to deal with Russia:

> As we have noted, a man's interests come to include certain highly specific modes of activity which yield him personal satisfaction. Rock, for example, found great satisfaction in the activity of visiting the poor; if this function were taken from him by state intervention, his own life would be emotionally impoverished. Similarly, Osgood's participation in private civic activities and Chatwell's delight in argumentative court procedures represented sources of emotional income with which it would be difficult to dispense. Perhaps the most interesting example is that of Daniel, who strongly favored a number of the Communist economic goals but who with equal vehemence preferred the means of attaining them (collective bargaining between unions and management) that had brought him personal success. Several of our men thus exhibited a *vested interest in a particular mode of activity* which, for reasons not always even remotely economic, had come to play a vital part in their lives.[19]

One might ask *how* interests could have this effect. We need not attempt to answer this question fully, but it is generally agreed that part of the answer is that interests induce a person to avoid meeting unfavorable evidence, to forget such evidence (or such arguments) when he has met it, or to provide a framework of interpretation that takes the sting out of the facts.

One type of personal interest that merits special mention is the interest in favorable relations with other persons, especially with persons with

---

[18] See G. Murphy and R. Likert, *Public Opinion and the Individual* (New York: Harper & Brothers, 1938); M. Sherif and H. Cantril, "The Psychology of 'Attitudes,'" *Psychological Review*, LIII (1946), 17; R. M. Simpson, "Attitudes of Teachers and Prisoners toward the Seriousness of Criminal Acts," *Journal of Criminal Law and Criminology*, XXV (1934–35), 76–83.

[19] Reprinted with permission from Brewster Smith, Jerome Bruner, and R. H. White, *Opinions and Personality*, copyright 1956, John Wiley & Sons, Inc., p. 263.

whom one wishes to have close association. We may be faced with the fact that our parents will no longer accept us if we take an antisegregation stand, or that we shall not be elected to the club of our choice if we advocate socialized medicine, and so on. This kind of interest, and its important role, has in effect already been discussed in connection with the influence of parents on the values of children, and of "prestige figures" on the values of their admirers.

Sometimes, of course, there is an interest or need that moves in a direction just the opposite of the usual case: For example, an adolescent may feel the necessity of staking out some views of his own that are different from those of his parents.

More speculative is the possibility that certain types of personality are congenial to certain kinds of value. There is some reason for claiming a correlation between values and bodily type: On the Allport-Vernon values test,[20] endomorphs score high on social values (values of affiliation), ectomorphs on theoretical values, and mesomorphs on political values. We have already described A. Kardiner's theory that some values of the Alorese (and other primitive groups) derive indirectly from the methods of child-rearing to which they have been exposed, because of the effect these methods have on the adolescent and adult personality. Smith, Bruner, and White have proposed interpretations, for some of the ten men they studied, along a somewhat similar line: For example, a person of sanguine disposition will expect good things from everybody, including the Russians. Such expectations inevitably influence one's judgments about what ought to be done.[21]

Sympathy. Some of the most perceptive of the great philosophers (David Hume and Adam Smith, for example) regarded people's moral values as almost entirely a matter of sympathetic responses, and moral judgments as almost entirely derived from these. These men have gone too far, but they did point to an extremely important factor.

The term "sympathetic response" covers such phenomena as the impulse to relieve a person or animal perceived to be in distress, being shaken emotionally by perception of a pain or distress situation, and experience of a thrill of joy at seeing another transported by joy on account of some good that has come to him. (The experience of drama consists in good part of sympathetic emotions.) There is difference of opinion among psychologists about how these phenomena should be described and about their genesis, but it seems certain that they occur early in childhood and that their occurrence is not wholly derived from the learning of values from

[20] T. E. Coffin, "A Three Component Theory of Leadership," *Journal of Abnormal and Social Psychology*, XXXIX (1944), 63–83; H. C. Smith, "Psychometric Checks on Hypotheses Derived from Sheldon's Work on Physique and Temperament," *Journal of Personality*, XVII (1949), 310–20.

[21] Smith, Bruner, and White, *op. cit.*, p. 258.

parents, and so forth; to some extent, such reactions are found among the higher animals.[22]

The important point for us here is that sympathetic responses may clash with accepted forms of behavior or ethical thinking; we have already described a possible example of this sort (p. 130). Again, sympathetic enjoyment of the happiness of others can serve to confirm approval of a rule of behavior just as well as can the favorable effect of such a rule on our personal welfare. The exact scope of sympathetic reactions and the details of their repercussions on values need more investigation, but there seems little room for doubt that they do occur and do affect an individual's value system.

We shall now broaden our perspectives by taking a brief look at three general theories of behavior: one type of stimulus-response theory of learning, Freudian psychoanalytic theory, and Gestalt theory.

3. A STIMULUS-RESPONSE THEORY OF LEARNING: CLARK HULL

We begin with a theory of learning that we shall attribute to Clark Hull, even though some of the ideas to be formulated are rather the work of some of his associates. There are various other similar theories of learning we could discuss instead of Hull's, but his has been the most fully developed and the most widely discussed.

Hull's theory consists of a complicated set of laws connecting stimulus fields, drives like hunger or thirst or for achievement (innate or learned), responses, the success of past responses in reducing drives or the stimuli from drives (for example, the pangs of hunger), and various other factors both observable and unobservable. These laws are so framed that, given certain information, we can predict behavior. For instance, if we know how a rat (and the theory is based almost entirely on experimental work with rats) has behaved in certain situations in the past, and know something about his present drives (for example, how hungry he is—assuming this depends on the time interval since the last feeding), Hull's laws will imply predictions about what the rat will be likely to do in a given situation.

Hull's laws about responses and response tendencies are of interest to us, since ethical verbalizing, incipient movements toward assisting someone,

---

[22] Charles Darwin discussed sympathetic reactions at some length in *The Descent of Man*, chap. 4. Elaborate observations of children's sympathetic responses are reported in L. B. Murphy, *Social Behavior and Child Personality* (New York: Columbia University Press, 1937). They are discussed at length by Adam Smith in *The Theory of Moral Sentiments* (1759), and more recently by W. McDougall, *Social Psychology* (London: Methuen & Co., Ltd., 1948), pp. 61 ff., and Gardner Murphy, *Personality* (New York: Harper & Brothers, 1947). Their influence on mature ethical values has been emphasized recently by J. G. Flugel, a writer in the psychoanalytic tradition, in *Man, Morals, and Society* (New York: International Universities Press, 1947); and by James Gibson in "The Implications of Learning Theory for Social Psychology," in J. G. Miller (ed.), *Experiments in Social Process* (New York: McGraw-Hill Book Company, Inc., 1950), pp. 149–67.

and feelings of guilt can be counted—or at least *are* counted, by some of Hull's associates—as behavioral responses to which Hull's "laws" about the learning of response habits apply. More important, we are interested in his theory of learned ("secondary") drives, since motivation to help someone in need, aversion to breaking a promise, interests in knowledge or qualities of character or in having equal opportunities for all—all these can be and are viewed as drives, and presumably as learned "secondary" drives.

Hull's proposal about the learning of response tendencies is roughly this: A response *R* will tend to occur in connection with a stimulus *S* (providing there are drives that are present along with *S*), if and only if a response similar to *R* has occurred in temporal proximity to a stimulus like *S* on occasions when a drive reduction, or satiation (or reduction in drive stimulus, that is, reduction in thirst or hunger pangs caused by bodily need, for example), has occurred nearby in time. Thus, roughly, if I happen to raise my hand while I am hearing a bell, and immediately afterward someone gives me a chocolate, which I eat and enjoy, I shall acquire a slight tendency to raise my hand whenever I hear a bell; and if I am so happily rewarded on many occasions when raising my hand coincides with the ringing of a bell, I shall acquire a strong habit of raising my hand when I hear a bell ring. (More realistically, the same reasoning explains why I put the chocolates in my mouth.) Hull's equations are such that it makes a difference how *close* the drive stimulus reduction was to the bell-hearing and hand-raising, how *close* together in time these latter were, how much *work* it is to raise my hand (effort required for a response tends to inhibit it), how *similar* the earlier stimulus (bell-ringing) is to the present stimulus, and so on.

Learning occurs, then, when there is a reduction of drive or drive-stimulus; this reduction serves to reinforce, or stamp in, a tendency for any responses made to be repeated, when given a similar stimulus. What are these "drives" or "drive-stimuli" whose reduction has this effect? A drive-stimulus (like thirst) is a representation in experience of an internal state of need, just as sounds or visual appearances are representations in experience of external objects. The drives are of two kinds. Some are organic needs, which Hull called *primary*. The need for water is an example. The theory is not committed to any particular list of primary drives; identification of them is properly left to experiment. Some drives, however, are not organic needs, and are learned. Hull called them *secondary*. They are of special interest to us, because it seems likely that the motivation to give aid to someone in distress, described above in connection with the parked-car episode, should be classified as a secondary drive. How, according to the theory, are such drives acquired?

What Hull says about this phenomenon is puzzling, and in part contradictory. But if we follow the most influential interpretation or development of the theory, we shall construe his proposal as being essentially as follows. If a stimulus has been associated with the evocation and reduction of drive-stimuli, its occurrence will in future tend to produce these same drive-stimuli on its own account. For instance, suppose a child visits the office of a dentist. The sight of the office occurs in a context in which pain-caused drive stimuli of fear are evoked by the activities of the dentist with his drill, and are reduced when the dentist finally ceases his drilling. According to Hull's theory, as a result, the very sight of the dentist's office will thereafter tend to arouse the drive stimuli of fear (anxiety).[23]

Let us now return to our parked-car episode, and consider how Hull's theory would interpret this event and explain the various "response tendencies" of the writer that were manifest in it. We recall that the writer, at the visual stimulus of a man slumped over the wheel of a parked car, was partially motivated to stop, verbalized about stopping, and later suffered from guilt feelings. Let us ignore the verbal behavior for the moment, and concentrate on the motivation and subsequent guilt feelings. What might Hull say about these? He *could* say that the motivation was the manifestation of an innate "sympathy" drive, but, in fact, theorists like Miller and Dollard, who have worked with adaptation of this type of theory to more complex human situations, have viewed it as a secondary drive. Their reconstruction of the genesis of this secondary drive would be somewhat as follows. We may suppose that, when the writer was young, he was once in a position to give aid to someone in distress, but failed to do so. Because he failed, he was reprimanded or punished in one way or another; and this event caused pain. The pain, in turn, produced anxiety responses at the time, since anxiety is an innate response to pain. But anxiety is a drive stimulus (we try to get rid of it), and therefore when the punishment stopped, there was a reduction of drive stimuli—the sort of event that, according to the general theory, reinforces or stamps in an association between the responses occurring at the time and the stimuli at the time. Among the responses occurring at the time were the anxiety responses themselves, however; and among the stimuli occurring at the time were verbal rehearsals by the parent of the fact that the writer failed to give help, and recollections by the writer that he did not. The effect of the reduction of the anxiety response, then, was the stamping in of an association between the anxiety response and the stimulus or idea of failing to give help to someone in need.

---

[23] For further discussion of the theory see E. R. Hilgard, *Theories of Learning* (New York: Appleton-Century-Crofts, Inc., 1956), chap. 5, especially, for "secondary drives," pp. 123–24, 128–30, 148–49, 177; C. E. Osgood, *Method and Theory in Experimental Psychology* (New York: Oxford University Press, 1953), chaps. 8–10, and especially pp. 428–43. Also C. L. Hull, *Principles of Behavior* (New Haven: Yale University Press, 1952); and for a simpler account, his chapter in *The Psychology of Learning*, Natl. Soc. Stud. Educ., 41st Yearbook, Part II, 61–95; also C. L. Hull, "Value, Valuation, and Natural-Science Methodology," *Philosophy of Science*, XI (1944), 125–41; J. M. W. Whiting, *Becoming a Kwoma* (New Haven: Yale University Press, 1941), chap. 7; Neal Miller and John Dollard, *Social Learning and Imitation* (New Haven: Yale University Press, 1941); and John Dollard and Neal Miller, *Personality and Psychotherapy* (New York: McGraw–Hill Book Company, Inc., 1950), pp. 25–94.

Presumably, the recurrence of similar punishment situations further built up in the writer a tendency to have anxiety responses at the perception, or thought, of a person's needing help and of the writer's failing to give it. We can understand, then, why the writer experienced guilt feelings after the parked-car episode, when he recalled the fact that someone had been in distress and that he had failed to give aid: the feelings of guilt are conditioned anxiety responses. Moreover, we can also understand why the writer was *motivated* to give aid at the time. Anxiety is innately motivating; we want to get rid of it. In the course of time, subsequent to the first forming of an association between the stimulus of being in a situation where someone in distress required aid but was not given it by the writer, and anxiety responses, the writer presumably learned to give aid, as a way of ridding himself of anxiety responses. That is, the response of giving aid was reinforced by a reduction of drive stimuli—in this case the anxiety responses themselves. The writer had then learned to make the response of giving aid, in situations where someone required it and he was in a position to give it.

The foregoing suggestion is one possible account of the writer's motivation in the parked-car situation, in terms of Hull's theory of learning. There are other somewhat different explanations possible within the framework of Hull's theory. We shall sketch an alternative "identification theory" account of the learning of the aiding-the-distressed motive at a later point.

Similar explanations could obviously be given of motivation to keep our promises, recompense those we have injured, abstain from unacceptable sexual behavior, and so on.

Hull's theory of this matter is impressive because of the extent to which it is consistent with, and explains or predicts, many of the very facts we have described in the preceding section. His theory accords to praise, reward, blame, and punishment something of the influence we are already inclined to give them, on the basis of information about the influence of the home on moral standards and behavior. It is not difficult to see how his theory can give a role in the development of personal values to one's peers (for example, in the school period), or of prestige figures—when we remember how rewarding or punishing our peers' attitudes toward us were during our most formative years. Again, his theory predicts that "personal experiences" may work to establish ethical values, quite independently of rewards or punishments by parents or other human beings; for interaction with certain objects or situations can be intrinsically rewarding or punishing. Further, the theory is consistent with an effect on one's ethical values of one's personal interests, since the frustration of them will be punishing, the promotion of them rewarding. To a considerable extent, then, Hull's theory in a loose way explains why a person's ethical values (at least on the motivational side) are influenced, as they seem to be, by parents, by other "prestige" figures, by personal experiences with relevant objects, and so on; and fundamentally, according to Hull, the reason is that all of these persons or experiences are in some way rewarding (or punishing).

So far we have said nothing about the application of Hull's theory to the *verbal* part of ethical experience: the talking and thinking in terms of principles and their application, and the readiness to defend one's ethical principles along various lines. Hull and his immediate associates have had relatively little to say on this topic, although, obviously, language responses must be treated as learned responses along the lines of the general theory (in good part as responses to the self-stimulation of one's own previous remarks), as they have been treated recently by writers less closely related to Hull.[24] One point of emphasis by Hull, however, has been the possibility that words can, like the smiles or frowns of one's parents, function as "secondary" reinforcements to behavior. The following remark of Hull's may be of interest:

> . . . Certain signs such as frowns and other kinds of threatening movements, as well as certain words (overt threats) through their association with attack, acquire the power of evoking flight reactions. . . . Thus words acquire a certain real power to punish, and so to deter, transgressors. And since the statement that a person has transgressed in a certain way is associated with punishment, and since such a statement is a moral judgment, it comes about that the overt passing of an adverse moral judgment becomes a deterrent to forbidden acts. In a similar manner, the passing of a favorable moral judgment becomes a secondary reinforcing agent fostering desirable action.[25]

One is inclined to say that Hull's theory implies that there can be the widest sorts of differences between the ethical values of different people; for, if only the rewards are properly arranged, it would seem that ethical values can be formed in any conceivable way. Theoretically, such an inference about his view is correct, but there are two considerations to be kept in mind. First, it is an empirical question what kinds of response tend, without conditioning, to be aroused by certain kinds of stimulus. Hull's theory in principle has no commitment on this, whatever may be the predilections of its supporters, because his theory is a theory of *learning*, not a theory about unlearned tendencies. More important, perhaps, is a second fact: that in the situation in which the learning of the child principally takes place, in the home, rewards and punishments will be dealt out in considerable part with an eye to conserving human welfare. Parents, we may assume, will not encourage the smashing of furniture, the mistreatment of baby sisters, and so on; for they themselves (as Hull's theory predicts) will have learned to take a protective position on such matters. Since the teachers of ethical

---

[24] See B. F. Skinner, *Verbal Behavior* (New York: Appleton-Century-Crofts, Inc., 1957); and C. E. Osgood, *Method and Theory in Experimental Psychology* (New York: Oxford University Press, 1953), chap. 16, and *The Measurement of Meaning* (Urbana: University of Illinois Press, 1957).

[25] C. L. Hull, "Value, Valuation, and Natural-Science Methodology," *op. cit.*, p. 137.

values are themselves motivated to conserve some things—and this motivation is by no means wholly dependent on their own early ethical training—children's values will be respectful of these things.

How seriously ought we to take Hull's theory, as at least an approximation to the truth, about the topics of interest to us? We can answer that Hull's theory is of great interest, as probably the most carefully developed theory in all of psychology, and perhaps as the psychological theory that has been most discussed in recent years. However, there has been a vast amount of experimental work—for example, by E. C. Tolman, James Olds, P. T. Young, H. F. Harlow, and David McClelland—that has shown that Hull's theory is at least overly simple. It appears that his "laws" of learning are just not correct, and that, in particular, "rewards" do not play as significant a role in learning as his theory proposes.[26] Moreover, we shall see when we come to Gestalt theory that it appears there are more unlearned tendencies or directions in the human mind than Hull allowed; and possibly one would be right if he suggested that sympathetic responses or unfavorable attitudes toward injustice are innate. We must remember, too, that Hull's theory of moral phenomena is speculative; the observational or experimental material specifically relevant to values is as we have summarized it in the preceding section. Some of the criticisms of Hull's theory, however, may be of only relatively minor importance for us; if values are a result of training and could have been entirely different if the training process has been different, it makes little difference, from the point of view of moral philosophy, whether Hull's theory or some other theory is exactly right about the details of the laws governing the process.

4. FREUDIAN PSYCHOANALYTIC THEORY

Hull's stimulus-response theory, we have seen, views the acquisition of ethical attitudes as being like the acquisition of a conditioned reflex, or more exactly, like the acquisition of conditioned anxiety. In contrast to this, the Freudian model for the acquisition of ethical values is that of eating one's father—or, in more complicated terminology, the "oral cannibalistic incorporation" of one's father. We might as well add, while we are thinking in terms of simple models, that the Gestalt model implies that having ethical values is like having the stars in the heavens fall into groups —constellations—or like having insight into the validity of a piece of reasoning. Conditioned anxiety, eating one's father, and the perceptual grouping of stars into constellations—these are the ways in which the major theories think of ethical values and their development.

These models of "eating" and "star-grouping" are not very meaningful to us as yet, but it may be helpful to say in advance that there is no neces-

[26] The student should consult critical works like David McClelland, *Personality* (New York: William Sloane Associates, 1951), or D. O. Hebb, *The Organization of Behavior* (New York: John Wiley & Sons, Inc., 1949).

sary opposition between Hull's and the Freudian concept. Developing an ethical value may be *both* getting a conditioned anxiety (or at least some conditioned drive) *and* "eating one's father." In fact, the recent tendency of stimulus-response and psychoanalytic camps has been to merge. However, stimulus-response concepts and Gestalt concepts are completely incompatible—and roughly the same is true of Freudian and Gestalt concepts. Between Gestalt theory and the other two there can be little compromise or common ground.

What exactly is the Freudian conceptual scheme, insofar as it is relevant to our topic? Freudian ideas, unlike Hull's, are not a tight theoretical system aimed at predicting controlled experimental data; they are a rather loosely organized set of ideas that approved themselves to Freud by their success and illumination in the treatment of neurotic patients. The central theme is this. The problem of every human being is that of satisfying its instinctive drives (hunger, thirst, sex, and so forth), within the framework of possibilities offered by its world, *and* within the framework of rules and ideals of its own conscience or superego. The problem is a difficult one, but it must be faced; the self suffers acutely when it fails. Or at least the self *may* suffer acutely; sometimes, in order to avoid such suffering, the self makes moves of avoidance that may involve it even more deeply in failure: moves that psychoanalysts have classified as "repression," "reaction formation," "sublimation," "projection," and "regression." These diagnoses of the unrealistic moves of a suffering self are the clinically important ideas of psychoanalysis. The theory also, however, contains proposals about the nature and development of conscience or the "superego." This last element of the theory is the point of primary interest to us, although the major neurotic "mechanisms" obviously are relevant to the values of the patient.[27]

Like the stimulus-response theory, Freud viewed conscience as a social product, the result of interaction with other persons; and he supposed that reward and punishments, whether physical or psychological, play a role in its development. But his accent was elsewhere, on a process he called "identification": the (supposed) tendency of a person, under certain emotional conditions, to imitate, consciously or unconsciously, the whole personality of another—including behavior, attitudes, and values. Normally, in childhood the main object of a child's identification will be the parent of the same sex. Freud says: "A little boy will exhibit a special interest in his father; he would like to grow like him and be like him, and take his place everywhere. We may say simply that he takes his father as his ideal."[28] More fully, he wrote:

> The role, which the super-ego undertakes later in life, is at first played by an external power, by parental authority. The influence of the parents

[27] See, for instance, C. R. Rogers and R. F. Dymond, *Psychotherapy and Personality Change* (Chicago: University of Chicago Press, 1954).

[28] S. Freud, *Group Psychology and the Analysis of the Ego* (New York: Liveright Publishing Corporation, 1949), p. 60.

dominates the child by granting proofs of affection and by threats of punishment, which, to the child, mean loss of love, and which must also be feared on that account. This objective anxiety is the forerunner of the later moral anxiety; so long as the former is dominant one need not speak of super-ego or of conscience. It is only later that the secondary situation arises . . . ; the external restrictions are introjected, so that the super-ego takes the place of the parental function, and thenceforward observes, guides and threatens the ego in just the same way as the parents acted to the child before. . . . The basis of the process is what we call an identification, that is to say, that one ego becomes like another . . . ; it imitates it, and as it were takes it into itself. This identification has not been inappropriately compared with the oral cannibalistic incorporation of another person.[29]

A child's parents, however, are not the only "models" for his conscience; as Freud put it, a person is a "component part of numerous groups, he is bound by ties of identification in many directions, and he has built up his ego ideal upon the most various models." Elsewhere he says: "As a child grows up, the office of father is carried on by masters and by others in authority."

We have, then, the novel proposal that the development of conscience is part of a wholesale incorporation of the qualities of other persons, primarily the parent of the same sex. But just how does this work? One need not accept Freud's suggestions about this.[30] One can adopt an account like Hull's instead, and this is what is often done. Thus, it may be held that the "wholesale incorporation" comes from the child's *practicing* the role of the parent, either overtly or in fantasy, and being rewarded for this. In doing so, the child "takes on the [parental] role itself, at least momentarily, with all the feelings, attitudes, values, and actions that he attributes to the person who actually occupies the role." How is such behavior thought to be motivated, and how is it rewarded? One important idea is that behaving like the mother will be pleasant (rewarding) because it reminds the child of the loving, gratifying behavior of the parent. Again, if

[29] S. Freud, *New Introductory Lectures on Psycho-analysis* (New York: W. W. Norton & Company, Inc., 1933), pp. 89–90.

[30] Freud thought that identification with the parent of the same sex is an outgrowth of an Oedipus complex. In the case of the male, this results in fear of drastic retaliation by the father (castration). Partly as a defense against this painful situation the boy identifies with the father. Identification with the father also inflates the ego of the child, enabling him to feel that he has all the power and status of the father.

Some modern writers manage to incorporate a form of such concepts in their theory, for example, R. R. Sears, E. E. Maccoby, and H. Levin, *Patterns of Child Rearing* (Evanston, Ill.: Row, Peterson & Company, 1957), pp. 373–74. See the criticism by S. M. Stoke, "An Inquiry into the Concept of Identification," *Journal of Genetic Psychology*, LXXVI (1950), 163–89.

Observations raise a question whether values are as sex-typed as Freud's theory would lead us to believe. See, for example, A. J. Brodbeck, "Oedipal Motivation as a Determinant of Conscious Development," *Journal of Genetic Psychology*, LXXXIV (1954), 219–27. If this criticism is correct, we must give up the emphasis on identification with the parent of the *same sex*.

one is worried about parental love, or if one feels deprived because of one's mother's absence or lack of attention, imitation of the mother will reduce one's tensions. For this imitation can include affectionate behavior toward oneself, which will be reassuring. There are further forces, along the same line, supporting role imitation, either of father or mother.[31] The main point, however, is that one can adopt a theory like Hull's—or still other theories—about the mechanism of identification.

It would be misleading to suggest that there is controversy only about how identification works in detail. On the contrary, there is disagreement about whether any such process plays a major role in the development of conscience. Observational material still fails, by far, to settle this issue beyond a doubt.[32]

Psychoanalytic concepts are sometimes used to account for particular ethical values. For example, present beliefs about the punishment of criminals, with their emphasis on proportion between crime and punishment, tend to persist, according to some psychoanalysts, because many people feel a need for punishment when they have done wrong—on account of the fact that the anger of parents abates only when they have punished the child, so that the child too comes to be unable to feel relief until after punishment. Again, Freud attributed (in mythological form) strong revulsion against sexual relations between a boy and his mother to the conflict between Oedipal wishes to possess one's mother (and murder one's father) and love and admiration for one's father. Further, certain moral feelings are regarded as defense measures, operating to assist in the repression of tendencies banned by parents. In this connection, F. Alexander writes:

> Although repression is an unconscious process, it leaves certain emotional phenomena of a defensive nature on the surface of consciousness. In the place of coprophilic tendencies, *disgust* appears. The desire to play with excrement disappears from consciousness, leaving a feeling of disgust. *Pity* is a similar overprotective countercharge (counter-cathexis) against original tendencies toward cruelty. The most primitive *sense of justice* is also a protective countercharge against the child's desire to have everything for himself, expressed in the envy of siblings.[33]

---

[31] See Sears, Maccoby, and Levin, *op. cit.*, pp. 368–76, which the foregoing suggestion has followed; also Stoke, *op. cit.*; and L. M. Lazowick, "On the Nature of Identification," *Journal of Abnormal and Social Psychology*, LI (1955), 175–83. G. H. Seward, "Some Cultural Aspects of Identification," *Journal of Genetic Psychology*, LXXXIV (1954), 228–36; this article has emphasized the use of identification models drawn from outside the family.

[32] See *supra*, pp. 121–24; also Sears, Maccoby, and Levin, *op. cit.*, chap. 10; Whiting and Child, *op. cit.*; Helen Faigin, *Child-rearing in the Rimrock Community*, Harvard Ph.D. dissertation, 1952; Eleanor Hollenberg, *Child Training among the Zeepi*, Harvard Ph.D. dissertation, 1952.

[33] Franz Alexander, *Fundamentals of Psychoanalysis* (New York: W. W. Norton & Company, Inc., 1948), pp. 98–99. See also Flugel, *op. cit.*, pp. 146 ff.

The foregoing comments descriptive of psychoanalytic ideas have been limited to theory of the "superego." If we inquired what psychoanalysts have to say about preferences and motivation in general, and the changes of these, we should have to bring in much more than we have done. Certainly, many psychoanalysts would feel that one of the major results of psychoanalytic treatment is modifications in the patient's system of preferences or values in some sense or other.

Psychoanalytic theory, like Hull's stimulus-response theory, favors the possibility of ultimate differences of ethical opinion, for the reason that there is no inherent limit to the kind of value that can be "introjected" from the parents by identification. Theoretically, the standards of the child might become practically anything. Yet, as we pointed out in the case of Hull's theory, there is in fact much restriction on the kind of value that can develop. For instance, as we have just remarked, Freud viewed it as no accident that there is disapproval of incestuous sexual relations, stemming from the conflict of natural Oedipus desires with natural love for the father figure; and non-Freudians would add that this disapproval is required for any social order in which the basic units are small family groups, at least if these groups are to be tolerably well ordered and free of strain and conflict.

Psychoanalytic theory certainly does not provide the complete answer for the psychology of ethical values, for it contains no theory of the extinction of ethical values. It has nothing to say about changes in ethical standards during adult years, as a result of information and reflection. It provides us with no tools for understanding the modifications in ethical values in a social group. Nor does it explain why there should be intercultural universal values, such as the universal disapproval of violence against one's neighbors. However, it is a widely supported theory, which many clinicians think has brought illumination to their experiences with patients, and which doubtless is at least close to part of the truth.

5. GESTALT THEORY

Each of the general theories here being considered consists in an incorporation of ethical values within a framework of ideas found successful in dealing with some different area of facts. Hull's theory was developed as a theory of the behavior of rats, essentially of rats learning to run mazes: hence the model of the conditioned reflex or conditioned anxiety. Freud's theory developed as a system of ideas useful for treating neurotic patients, among whom regression to patterns of childhood response is important: hence the emphasis on ethical values as simply an incorporation of the values of important childhood figures. Gestalt theory began as a theory of perception, and its theory of values is an extension or application of general ideas successful there.

In order to clarify the main ideas, let us return to our parked-car episode. We may pass over the point of the verbal behavior; Gestalt psychologists have had little to say about ethical discourse. We saw, however, that there was motivation to do something for someone else—a motivation not deriving from any organic discomfort of the writer, nor as a means of reaching what we would say were the writer's own goals. The motivation apparently derived from confrontation with the needs of another person—a total stranger. The motivation conflicted with what the writer personally *wanted to do*. It was reflected in later guilt feelings. Finally, we said that the writer would have offered some argument in justification of this motivation, had the occasion called for it.

The Gestaltists recognize, indeed insist, that there are experiences like this, and that psychological theory must have a place for them.[34] They have argued, further, that this motivation is importantly similar to experiences we do not call ethical: the motivation to stop a car when a policeman holds up his hand, the motivation to leave some pleasant occupation to return to one's study when one remembers an important job that must be finished, the motivation to straighten a picture, the motivation to inscribe a big question mark in the margin if we come across a grossly defective argument in a book. (Incidentally, they point out that we sometimes experience motivation for someone *else* to do something, for example, make a certain move in chess, necessary in order to avoid a trap.) How are we to understand experiences like these?

At this point, the Gestalt psychologists look to perceptual phenomena, and theories of these, for a clue. Take for instance the following dots:

...   .

Everyone will see these as three groups: one of three, one of two, and the third of five dots. Or think of the constellations of stars. We think of the Big Dipper, and see it, as a distinct group of stars. The grouping of the dots seems to be as fundamental a fact as the appearance of the dots themselves. Why is this? The Gestaltist says, the simplest explanation compatible with the experimental facts is just to hold that there are general laws of perceptual organization, just as fundamental as laws that describe the seeing of the dots; and Gestaltists have set out to state these laws. Their statement of them has been the major Gestalt contribution to psychology. (Some Gestaltists think of these laws of perceptual organization as themselves explicable by reference to laws of physics, laws about the flow of electric currents in certain conditions—since they think of the perceptual facts as representations of brain facts, electrochemical events in the brain tissue.) This

---

[34] See, for example, W. Köhler, *The Place of Value in a World of Facts* (New York: Liveright Publishing Corporation, 1938), chap. 3; and the description in M. H. Mandelbaum (a philosopher much influenced by Gestalt conceptions), *The Phenomenology of Moral Experience* (Glencoe, Ill.: Free Press, 1955), pp. 51–59.

mode of thinking about the matter has enabled the Gestaltists to explain a multitude of particular facts about perception.

Perhaps this same mode of thinking can explain some of the motivations of interest to us. Köhler begins with a simple example. Take the following two figures:

The figure on the right, Köhler suggests, will be experienced as having something "wrong" with it that needs to be changed. Why is this? The thought is that it is just a fundamental fact about perceptual processes that, in a total context of this sort, there is "rejection" of the flat segment of the curve on the right.[35] There is experimental reason for thinking that there are such "corrective" forces operative in perception, since figures are seen, appear in consciousness, in a form that diverges somewhat from the form of the corresponding retinal image.

How far will this sort of thinking take us? Is there any reason for thinking that such processes are important for more complex experiences? One is at once struck by the possibilities for an understanding of preferences for certain visual forms in art, generally. Again, why might they not be the reason why young infants—human or chimpanzee—react to a hideous or scowling face with fright, but respond happily to a smile? Moreover, emotions seem to arise universally in the presence of certain meanings, goals, and tensions—in the presence of a characteristic *structure* of experience.[36] Perhaps such processes can explain this fact, and also the fundamental sympathy behavior, of which we have already spoken (p. 133)? S. E. Asch has remarked: "The understanding of the situation of another . . . can arouse in us tensions and goals that can be removed only by acting in a way relevant to the other's needs."[37] Perhaps this phenomenon is best viewed in the way in which perceptual organization is conceived, and not as a result of conditioning.

At any rate, the Gestalt psychologists are unimpressed by the Hullian

[35] Köhler, *op. cit.*, pp. 348–50; also pp. 351–57. Köhler thinks that there is a brain-physiology explanation of this fact: The electrochemistry of the brain-correlate of the perceived curve is such that forces in the direction of changing the curve are brought into being. The above figures are drawn from Köhler, *op. cit.*, p. 348, by permission of Liveright Publishing Corporation.

[36] See the treatment of anger by T. Dembo, "Der Ärger als dynamisches Problem," *Psychologische Forschung*, XV (1931), 1–144; also the topological analysis of anxiety by D. W. MacKinnon, "A Topological Analysis of Anxiety," *Character and Personality*, XII (1944), 163–76; and W. McDougall's discussion of the emotions in *Outline of Psychology* (New York: Charles Scribner's Sons, 1923), pp. 334–41.

[37] S. E. Asch, *Social Psychology*. (Englewood Cliffs, N.J.: Prentice-Hall, Inc., 1952), p. 357.

and Freudian explanations of these phenomena. Asch does not believe the typical experience described in the parked-car episode can be viewed as a case of conditioned anxiety or conditioned fear.

> It is understandable that rewards and punishments produce desire and fear, but there is no way of seeing how they can produce the experience of "should." Habit can produce strong connections; it can give rise to a feeling of familiarity and even to a sense of necessity; but there is no known way for an habitual connection to produce the specific experience of obligation. . . . When we admire an act of courage or when we are shaken by deceit and treachery, when we are determined to tell the truth even if it is painful or when we dismiss a plan we consider unworthy, we are granting recognition to certain properties of action that are not described in the current categories of habit and desire. The reductionist interpretations fail us at the start; they cannot tell us by what alchemy the phenomena of which they speak give rise to the generic fact of value.[38]

We recall that a central idea in the Hull interpretation of "identification" is role practice. It was said that the child imitates the parental role, "with all the feelings, attitudes, values, and actions . . ." (p. 141). The Gestaltist will raise some questions here. True, the child can imitate what the parent does and what he says, perhaps even his gestures and facial expressions. But how can he *imitate* the "feelings, attitudes, values?" Can he *see* these? Is imitation of these under his motor control? Something seems missing here. But perhaps the Gestaltists have not quite done justice to the possibility of conditioned anxiety as a source of the learning of the motivation of interest to us (pp. 136–37).

Suppose we agree to follow along with the Gestaltists, in terms of their model. The grouping of dots has been found to follow certain definite laws (assumed to be derivative from the electrochemistry of brain tissue); emotions have been found to occur in certain conditions of structuring in experience. Then, we might say, should not our ethical motivations or values follow certain laws (ultimately dependent on the electrochemistry of the brain, of course entirely speculative in cases of complex ethical values)? And if so, what are some of these laws? The Gestaltists are ready to give some examples. When a queue has formed, Asch says, one "ought" to go to the end of the line. There "ought" not to be arbitrary inequalities. A person "ought" to be punished only if he is guilty. Wertheimer[39] has suggested other cases: One "ought" not to snatch food from a hungry child. If one has a brick and a piece of bread, and is facing a hungry man and a man building a house, one "ought" to give the bread to the hungry man, the brick to the house-builder. Nor is this a matter of personal preference: One may dislike the hungry man and still see the rightness of giving him the

---

[38] Asch, *op. cit.*, p. 356. See also Peter Bertocci, "A Reinterpretation of Moral Obligation," *Philosophy and Phenomenological Research*, VI (1945–46), 270–82.

[39] Max Wertheimer, "Some Problems in the Theory of Ethics," *Social Research*, II (1935), 353–67.

bread, just as one can add up one's bank balance and get a result very different from what one would like.

But, one is inclined to ask, if there are these laws, why aren't ethical values the same the world over? To this the Gestaltist replies: "Are you really sure they aren't?" The Gestaltists point out that many people have thought there are gross differences in ethical values in different cultures, because they failed to make a crucial distinction: between psychological and stimulus (physical or sociological) situations.[40] This distinction is best seen in a case of aesthetic appreciation. Two persons look at a picture and have opposite reactions. Why? The difference in reaction may not imply different aesthetic preferences at all; it may be that the same physical picture has caused different *experiences* because of differences in what the two persons bring to the situation. The picture may be seen as rich with meaning by one person, as pointless lines by the other. Each reacts to the picture as it is in *his experience* (corresponding to the neural process in *his brain*); and it may be that each would make the *same* evaluation if the two persons had the *same experience* of the picture. The same is true for ethical values. As we have noted above (p. 99), one person may disapprove of a man's killing his father because he sees the act as one of murder for gain, whereas another may approve of the same act if he sees it as an act of mercy. In other words, one man may approve of an act that, as a physical or sociological event—an act of violence resulting in the death of the agent's father—is the very same act of which another disapproves. Psychologically, however, the acts are different for the two persons. So, the Gestaltists suggest, possibly acts that are psychologically the same always receive the same ethical appraisal; perhaps *basic* ethical values are everywhere the same, so that there is no *ultimate* disagreement anywhere.

The Gestaltists make use of this same distinction in their thinking about changes of ethical standards or values. Perhaps, they suggest, basic ethical values *never* change; perhaps what changes is just the meaning or psychological character of the situation being appraised. What does "prestige suggestion" do? Finding that an intelligent person holds a view opposite to our own may be a refreshing experience, causing us to review the situation and notice points we had not seen before. The object may get a new psychological "face," and our appraisal will therefore change. The influence of personal interests and needs may be interpreted in the same way. What these factors do is cause review of the facts, or cause us to ignore some facts, or to emphasize certain elements of a situation. Furthermore, the Gestaltist is most cogent when we come to matters like the sympathy phenomena and the influence on ethical thinking of information, or the demand for consistency. The importance of just such things is what he would have expected. Whether the theory does as well in explaining all phases of the

---

[40] This was the point of the article, "Ethical Relativity?" by K. Duncker in *Mind*, XLVIII (1939), 39–57.

effects of interactions with the objects of one's ethical appraisals is another matter.

The Gestaltist is not committed to holding that every case of "feeling obligated to . . ." is correct. It would be more plausible to suggest that the theory is committed to holding that every "feeling of obligation" is correct, for the situation *as the person understands* it. But Köhler would apparently hesitate to go so far.[41] And Koffka has suggested[42] that the evaluation of an aesthetic object can be wrong if a person brings *too much* with him to the experience of seeing or hearing it; that is, he may bring awareness of conventional standards, so that the object is made to appear strange and is not judged on its merits. Again, Asch suggests that special subject conditions may prevent the "normal" occurrence of tensions or "oughts." Strong needs, he says, may "desensitize" us to the situation before us, prevent us not only from seeing but also from feeling what we see. "Interest, fear, and ambition," he says, "are capable of deforming the operation of principles to which we give general adherence. . . . Custom blunts our sensitivity and renders us callous to indefensible practices."[43]

Evidently, the Gestaltists are not prepared to argue that ethical values are quite as simple a matter as perceptual grouping. The laws of values or "feelings of obligation" do not connect "feelings of obligation" simply with conscious experiences of objects or situations; ethical responses must be viewed as dependent in part on past experiences, associations, or needs that are not represented in present consciousness.[44] As a result, the gap between Gestalt and the other theories of values is somewhat narrowed, both requiring that the understanding of values necessitates reference to personal needs and the results of (traces left in the brain by) past experiences. The Gestaltist will insist, however, that there are structures or directions in human values that, however laws about them must refer to unconscious facts about the self and however they may presuppose some learning, cannot be viewed simply as results of conditioning.

Is there any possibility that we can avoid simply making a choice between these warring theories? There is an obvious possibility to be considered: Future experimentation may show that there are some rather fixed

---

[41] Köhler, *op. cit.*, pp. 97, 339.

[42] K. Koffka, *Principles of Gestalt Psychology* (New York: Harcourt, Brace & Company, 1935), pp. 347 ff.

[43] Asch, *op. cit.*, pp. 603 and 362.

Wayne Dennis has remarked, about Hopi indifference to the fate of small animals, that "These observations would tend to show that generally speaking no sympathy for animals develops when there is an absence of training in that direction. We would suggest as an important factor in this failure to develop sympathy the fact that pets are given to children when they are so young that their manual habits are entirely inappropriate to the handling of small live animals. It may be that rough handling, established at an early age, tends to prevent the later development of sympathy for its victims." *The Hopi Child* (New York: Appleton-Century-Crofts, Inc., 1945), p. 112.

[44] See also Köhler, *op. cit.*, p. 339.

and apparently unlearned structures important for values (perhaps tendencies to have sympathetic responses), and also that past experience and training have a great deal to do with some values. It may be, then, that future observation will show that both modes of thinking are justified, but that neither model fits the case of values exactly. Such an expectation seems the most reasonable one at present, but only the future can tell the precise ground that can be held, or must be yielded, by the two theories.

Perhaps the reader will think that we cannot rest with any compromise solution, that if we are Gestaltists then there can be a discipline of normative ethics, and otherwise not. But such inferences would be mistaken. We shall see as we go on that it is possible to hold that there is *ethical knowledge*—and that certain normative theories can be shown to be true, or false —whichever one of these psychological theories we espouse. It is true that if we are Gestaltists we shall feel less necessity to be "ethical relativists"; but we shall see later that the doctrine of ethical relativism, insofar as it is defensible, is not ruinous for normative ethics, but only makes things somewhat more complex. The reader may wonder how it is possible to take an extreme Hullian view of ethical values, and at the same time to hold that there is ethical knowledge; but, since the matter is not a simple one, the explanation of this is better postponed for a later chapter.

From now on we shall try to avoid asserting anything in conflict with the major psychological theories or, especially, with the empirical evidence reviewed earlier in the chapter. We shall feel free to regard it as a decisive objection to other philosophical theories of ethics if they are in conflict with the empirical evidence, and as a difficulty of weight if they make assertions in conflict with the major psychological theories.

FURTHER READING

J. W. M. Whiting and I. L. Child, *Child Training and Personality* (New Haven: Yale University Press, 1953), chaps. 2, 7, 11. A behavioristically oriented psychologist and an anthropologist survey the evidence.

James Gibson, "The Implications of Learning Theory for Social Psychology," in J. G. Miller (ed.), *Experiments in Social Process* (New York: McGraw-Hill Book Company, Inc., 1950). A discussion in terms of Hull-like learning theory, with comments on sympathy.

R. R. Sears, E. E. Maccoby, and H. Levin, *Patterns of Child Rearing* (Evanston, Ill.: Row, Peterson & Company, 1957), chap. 10. An experimental study, with a behaviorist and psychoanalytic point of view.

S. Freud, *The Ego and the Id* (London: Hogarth Press, 1949), chap. 3.

———, *Group Psychology and the Analysis of the Ego* (New York: Liveright Publishing Corporation, 1949), chap. 7.

———, *New Introductory Lectures in Psychoanalysis* (New York: W. W. Norton & Company, Inc., 1933), pp. 82–98.

F. Alexander, *Fundamentals of Psychoanalysis* (New York: W. W. Norton & Company, Inc., 1948), chap. 5.

J. G. Flugel, *Man, Morals, and Society* (New York: International Universities Press, 1947), chaps. 3–5.

S. M. Stoke, "An Inquiry into the Concept of Identification," *Journal of Genetic Psychology*, LXXVI (1950), 163–89.

S. E. Asch, *Social Psychology* (Englewood Cliffs, N.J.: Prentice-Hall, Inc., 1952), chaps. 11–14, pp. 289–321. Statement of Gestalt theory.

M. Wertheimer, "Some Problems in the Theory of Ethics," *Social Research*, II (1935), 353–67. Another Gestalt formulation.

W. Köhler, *The Place of Value in a World of Facts* (New York: Liveright Publishing Corporation, 1938) chaps. 1–3, and pp. 194–96, 329–40, and 363–68. A classic statement of the Gestalt point of view.

W. F. Dukes, "Psychological Studies of Values," *Psychological Bulletin*, LII (1955), 24–50. A survey of the literature.

David Hume, *Inquiry into the Principles of Morals*, sects. 1, 2, 5. A classic statement of the sympathy view of moral judgments.

Adam Smith, *Theory of the Moral Sentiments*, in A. Selby-Bigge, *British Moralists* (Oxford: Clarendon Press, 1897), I, pp. 257–336. Another statement of the sympathy theory.

T. M. Newcomb, *Personality and Social Change* (New York: Dryden Press, 1943). An empirical study of the formation of social attitudes.

7

Ethical Naturalism

We must now return to the main task of critical ethics: to state the conditions under which an ethical statement is tenable, valid, or adequately supported, and to justify our conclusions about what these conditions are.

Thus far we have not made much headway with this; what we have mostly succeeded in doing is showing that certain proposals are not satisfactory. We have, of course, argued that a valid set of ethical opinions must be self-consistent, and that any particular judgment in ethics, to be tenable, must be supportable by a valid general principle. These points, we think, form solid ground, but they do not take us far. When we scrutinized certain larger proposals, claimed by some to supply us with the objects of our quest, we found them wanting. Kant's proposal that an ethical principle is valid if it is universalizable, the program of the contextualist, the invitations to rely on the ethical advice of authorities either social or religious—all of these proved to be unsatisfactory.

But we have deliberately postponed until now the theories that have been most widely supported and discussed in recent times. In the next four chapters we shall concern ourselves with these.

The central ideas of three of these theories are simple, and it may be helpful to summarize them now, in order to have an over-all view of the field onto which we shall be moving. (The contentions of the fourth theory, however, cannot well be formulated at this stage.) None of these three "theories" is quite just one single theory; they are rather types of theory, clusters of somewhat different proposals, with central tenets held in common. We shall sketch out some of the major specific theories within these theory types, in the course of our discussion, as far as space permits; but for the present let us look merely at the common elements in these theory types.

The first theory is *ethical naturalism*, which we have already mentioned

151

briefly (p. 40). The essential thesis of naturalism is the proposal that ethical statements can, after all, be confirmed, ethical questions answered, by observation and inductive reasoning of the very sort that we use to confirm statements in the empirical sciences—and for a reason that the other theories overlook or do not take seriously: because of what ethical statements *mean*. In other words, it is held that on reflection we can see that the *meaning* of ethical statements is such that we can verify them just like the statements of psychology or chemistry. Perhaps this seems surprising, and we may ask: What is their view, then, of the meaning of ethical statements? The answers to this question differ, however, from naturalist to naturalist. One example must suffice for the moment. It has been suggested that "is desirable" means just "is desired by somebody." If this proposal is right, then, of course, observation can tell us what is desirable.

The second theory is *nonnaturalism*. Nonnaturalists agree with naturalists that ethical statements are like the statements of science up to a point. At least they are statements about facts and are true or false according as they describe these facts correctly or incorrectly; and we do have knowledge that some ethical statements are true. But the nonnaturalist cannot agree with the naturalist's proposal about the meaning of ethical statements; and consequently, he cannot accept the naturalist's belief in verifiability by observation. The nonnaturalist thinks we can, indeed, know that ethical statements are true; but the way we know this is not by observation but by something special, "intuition" or "rational insight"—concepts that we must explain.

The third theory is *noncognitivism*. The noncognitivist objects to the nonnaturalist view that ethical knowledge can be had by "intuition" or "rational insight"; like the naturalist, he finds talk of such special kinds of awareness quite mysterious. On the other hand, like the nonnaturalist, he is convinced that ethical statements cannot be construed as scientific statements, as confirmable by observation and inductive reasoning. What then can he hold? What he does is to reject the thesis held in common by both naturalism and nonnaturalism; he thinks that we miss the nature of ethical statements entirely if we treat them as statements of fact, as if their primary job were to convey information. If we are to understand ethical thinking and discourse, he says, we must notice that ethical sentences are used primarily to perform non-fact-stating jobs (just as sentences may be used to ask questions, or to express wishes, and so forth). Just what job, then, are ethical sentences used to perform? Here noncognitivists differ among themselves. Some say they are used to express moral attitudes; some say they declare the speaker's policy; others say they are used to issue commands. Still others say they are prescriptions; they are used to tell people what to do. At any rate, they are not used primarily to tell us *that* something is the case, as scientific statements are.

We begin with naturalism. But before doing so, we shall digress to explain some words that are frequently used in classifying not only naturalist but also nonnaturalist, supernaturalist, and in some cases noncognitive theories. It is useful to be familiar with these terms, not only because they are in frequent use in literature dealing with ethics but because familiarity with them emphasizes the affinities of certain types of theory, which we might overlook if we classified metaethical theories as simply naturalist, nonnaturalist, supernaturalist, and noncognitivist.

Unfortunately, the use of some of these terms has been by no means uniform, and sometimes it has been vague or confused. Therefore, to some extent the following definitions are less representative of accepted usages among philosophers than recommendations for clear and helpful usages. We shall introduce these terms as pairs of contradictories.

Realism—Mentalism. Let us say that a metaethical theory is *mentalist* if and only if its view of ethical terms is such that every ethical statement logically implies something about minds—either that there is at least one mind, or that it is true of minds that they do behave in some way or would behave in a certain way if there were any. Contrariwise, a metaethical theory is *realist* if its view of ethical terms is such that no such implication follows from ethical statements.

Supernaturalist theories, and most naturalist ones, are mentalist. The supernaturalist says that "*x* is good" means something like "God approves of *x*." Therefore, ethical statements imply the existence of God, and, assuming God is a mind, they imply that there exists at least one mind.

Nonnaturalist theories are always realist. It is true that nonnaturalists often hold that nothing is in fact desirable in itself except states of minds or acts of minds (and the same for the other ethical terms), but this fact does not make their view mentalist in our sense. Some naturalistic theories, also, are realist. For instance, one can define ethical terms by means of biological concepts; thus Herbert Spencer suggested that "good conduct" is "relatively more evolved conduct."

Objectivism—Subjectivism. These terms have been used more vaguely, confusedly, and in more different senses than the others we are considering. We suggest as a convenient usage, however, that a theory be called subjectivist if and only if, according to it, any ethical assertion implies that somebody does, or somebody of a certain sort under certain conditions would, take *some specified attitude* toward something. A theory may be called objectivist if this consequence does not follow. A theory may be subjectivist with respect to some ethical terms, and objectivist with respect to others.

Supernaturalism is thus a subjectivist theory, since it holds that "*x* is wrong" means "God disapproves of *x*," and disapproval is clearly the taking of an attitude. All the naturalist theories we shall discuss in this chapter are subjectivist, but a naturalist theory need not be subjectivist. For instance, we saw that Herbert Spencer's theory is realist, and *a fortiori* it is objectivist. Similarly, W. H. Sheldon held that the "value" of an object is its "helping to complete or fulfill some tendency already present." Various writers have said that being "intrinsically worthwhile" means approximately being "a pleasant experience"; whether such theories are subjectivist depends on whether being pleasant involves something's having an attitude —a question to be discussed later.

Nonnaturalism, being realist, is necessarily objectivist. A mentalist often is, but need not be, a subjectivist.

Relativism—Absolutism. A theory of ethical terms is relativist if, according to it, it is logically possible for two persons to accept verbally conflicting ethical statements without at least one of them being mistaken.[1] A theory is absolutist if it does not permit this.

Nonnaturalism, at least in its historically important forms, is an absolutist theory. Supernaturalism is also absolutist: God either approves or not, and there cannot be two conflicting but correct opinions about this. (In the *Euthyphro,* Plato poses the puzzling possibility that there might be several gods, some of whom approve and some of whom disapprove. But, if so, then what is sometimes true, if "is right" means "is approved by all the gods," is not that sometimes conflicting ethical statements are both true, but that sometimes neither of two contradictory ethical statements is true.) Many forms of naturalism are absolutist, but some are not. For instance, as we shall see, Edward Westermarck held that "x is morally wrong" means essentially "I [the speaker] have a tendency to disapprove of x." On his view, sometimes one speaker can correctly say that something is morally wrong, whereas another speaker can correctly deny this of the very same thing. The Ideal Observer theory, we shall see, can take either an absolutist or a relativist form.

A subjectivist, clearly, can be either an absolutist or a relativist. An objectivist, not so obviously, also may be either. It might seem he would always be an absolutist, but "x is wrong" may be taken to mean, "x is contrary to the institutions or customs of my society." This theory is objectivist, unless "contrary to the institutions . . ." is thought to refer implicitly to attitudes; but the theory is relativist.

It may be helpful to classify theories we have discussed, or shall be discussing, in a table:

NONNATURALISM	SUPERNATURALISM	E. Westermarck	NATURALISM R. B. Perry	Ideal Observer
realist	mentalist	mentalist	mentalist	mentalist
objectivist	subjectivist	subjectivist	subjectivist	subjectivist
absolutist	absolutist	relativist	absolutist	absolutist in some forms; relativist in others.

1 We shall discuss relativism at length in Chapter 11. But there we shall define "relativism" in such a way that it is not merely a thesis about the meaning of ethical terms, although it has implications for the meaning of ethical terms, excluding some theories about this. The foregoing, however, is a useful way to use "relativist" as a classification of proposals about the meaning of ethical words.

1. THE CENTRAL IDEA OF ETHICAL NATURALISM

Ethical Naturalism, which is a theory with a long tradition going back to the Greeks, including Aristotle (although they did not formulate it as sharply as we are able to do today), asserts that ethical statements can be confirmed or verified in a way parallel to that in which the statements of the empirical sciences can be confirmed. Ethical beliefs, like scientific beliefs, can be supported by observation; they are generalizations, extrapolations, and so forth, of empirical evidence.

Naturalism, then, is a view quite different from the theory we called "contextualism." The contextualist, too, holds that, in principle, the questions of ethics can be answered by the methods of the empirical sciences. But in his case there is an important proviso. That is, the contextualist asserts that the questions of ethics can be answered by the methods of science *if* we can assume some ethical premises as given, as reasonable assumptions not needing to be questioned, for the purposes of the problem at hand. The naturalist theory does not include any such proviso: It holds that the methods of science can support ethical statements *without* the assumption of any ethical premises. Indeed, naturalism holds there is really no difference at all between an ethical statement and a statement in science; ethics *is* a department of empirical science.

Naturalism is not, however, merely the thesis that ethical statements can be confirmed like those of empirical science. It is a theory about the *meaning* of ethical statements. Naturalists hold that an ethical statement—that is, a statement with words like "wrong" or "undesirable"—is exactly identical in meaning with some other statement in which ethical words do not occur, and which everyone will recognize as a statement that can be confirmed or tested by the methods of science, by appeal to experience. Or, in other words, naturalists hold that any ethical statement can be translated, without any change of meaning, into a statement in the language of empirical science.[2]

Let us look at some examples. Aristotle says that the good is "that at which all things aim" or "that for whose sake everything else is done." Aquinas follows Aristotle, saying, "Goodness is what all desire." Spinoza said: "By *good* I here mean every kind of pleasure, and all that conduces thereto, especially that which satisfies our longings, whatsoever they may be. By evil, I mean every kind of pain, especially that which frustrates our

[2] A technically more satisfactory definition of "naturalism" is to say that it is the theory that all ethical statements can be translated, without loss of meaning, into an "empirical language," where "empirical language" is explained by reference to the details of its construction, beginning with logical terms and observation predicates. The reader should consult C. G. Hempel, "Problems and Changes in the Empiricist Criterion of Meaning," *Revue Internationale de Philosophie*, No. 11 (January, 1950), pp. 41–63, especially pp. 50–57; also Hempel, "Fundamentals of Concept Formation in Empirical Science," *International Encyclopedia of Unified Science* (Chicago: University of Chicago Press, 1952), vol. II, No. 7.

longings. . . . The knowledge of good and evil is nothing else but the emotions of pleasure or pain, in so far as we are conscious of them." John Stuart Mill wrote (although this statement is not representative of his more considered thought) that "to think of an object as desirable (unless for the sake of its consequences), and to think of it as pleasant, are one and the same thing." Among contemporary writers, we may cite Ralph Barton Perry, who says: "An object is *good* in the generic sense when it is the object of a positive interest; it is *morally good* in the special sense when the interest which makes it good satisfies the requirement of harmony, that is, innocence and cooperation." More recently still, A. C. Garnett proposed: " 'X is good' means 'X is an object toward which enlightened understanding tends to develop a favorable attitude.' "

Naturalistic definitions of ethical terms are not, of course, confined simply to "good" and "desirable"; comparable definitions are proposed for "right," "wrong," "morally obligatory," "duty," and others. Ralph Barton Perry, for instance, says " 'right' means conduciveness to moral good." "When it is said that an act 'ought' to be performed, it is meant that the act is called for by some good to which the act is conducive." Edward Westermarck says (roughly; we shall look at his view more carefully below) that to say an act is wrong is to say that we have a tendency to feel moral disapproval of it.

These proposals about the meaning of ethical terms are not necessarily the most plausible suggestions that have been made. However, they give us a general idea of the sort of thing that has been claimed by naturalists, and it is quite obvious that, if any such proposal is correct, then ethical statements can be confirmed like the statements of science.

There is an ambiguity about what the naturalist intends, a question we must now resolve. It is clear that the naturalist so construes the meaning of ethical statements that these statements can be confirmed by observation (or this plus reasoning), like the statements of the empirical sciences. But one might ask this: When we say the naturalists "construe" the meaning of ethical statements to be a certain thing, which of the following do we mean? (1) One possibility is that naturalists are merely announcing that they personally are proposing to use words like "wrong" and "desirable" in a certain way in their books. They may be saying merely that, as they propose to use these terms, ethical statements turn out to be confirmable by observation. (2) A second possibility is that they are both proposing to use these terms in a certain way themselves, and for various reasons also recommending that others do the same. They may be arguing that it would be *better* if everybody used words like "wrong" and "desirable" in a certain way. They may be pointing out that, if everybody did use them in this way, then what would be meant by ethical statements would be confirmable by observation. If what they are doing is the first of these things, we had better say, following customary terminology, that what they are doing is offering *stipulative* definitions of ethical words; if what they are doing is the second of these, let us say that what they are doing is offering *reforming* definitions. (3) But they may be doing something different still. They may be saying that ethical terms are *actually* so used by persons who understand the language, that the definitions offered correctly represent their actual meaning—just as dictionaries do. They may be saying that these actual meanings are such that ethical statements are confirmable by the methods of science. In this case, let us say that the definitions are claimed to be, purport to be, *reportive* definitions.

Which of these three things, then, is the naturalist doing? Should we view his definitions of ethical terms as stipulative, as reforming, or as at least intended to be correct reportive definitions? When the naturalist says that ethical statements can be confirmed by the methods of science, is he talking about the statements he makes with ethical words as he personally uses them; or is he talking about the statements everybody would make with ethical words if they used them as they ought to (in his opinion); or is he talking about the statements people actually make with ethical words as they actually use them?

Doubtless historical figures ordinarily classified as naturalists were sometimes not clear in their own minds what they were doing. Moreover, ethical language is a bit vague and imprecise and perhaps confusing, so that, in supplying precise definitions, naturalists to some extent must deviate from ordinary meanings. Nevertheless, it seems clear that historical naturalists have thought that their definitions did justice to the substantial content of the ethical questions people actually raise. So, despite the fact that naturalists have in effect sometimes proposed clarifying emendations of ethical language, they supposed that their definitions were correct *reportive* definitions,[3] in the sense that they reported the essential content of actual ethical statements, and that their definitions did justice to the essential puzzles or problems to which people give expression when they raise ethical questions. What they are doing, then, doubtless often somewhat confusedly, is the *third* of the possible things we have listed. Accordingly, we shall *define* "naturalism" as the view that the *actual* meaning of ethical statements, as made by intelligent people who understand the language, is such that ethical statements can be confirmed by the methods of science.[4]

---

[3] This has been denied. See P. B. Rice, *On the Knowledge of Good and Evil* (New York: Random House, 1955), chap. 5.

[4] A naturalist may, however, be offering a reforming definition in the following sense. He may propose, on the basis of a broad view of the human situation and the problems of social living, that there are good and sufficient reasons why there should be words in the language that enable us to raise precisely the questions ethical sentences do raise, and why there should be words that enable us to state precisely the things ethical sentences do state. A naturalist may, then, have a theory about the "functions" of ethical language, and assert that ethical language performs these functions beautifully as it stands, or approximately as it stands. In other words, the naturalist may be offering a kind of stationary reforming definition; he thinks there are good reasons why ethical language should not be different, but just as it is; and he is also purporting to offer a correct reportive definition.

One might ask: If all the naturalist is doing is framing a definition of the actual meanings of ethical terms, and pointing out that ethical sentences using these words with these ordinary meanings are confirmable by the methods of science, what possible service can he be rendering? Is he not inflating the obvious into a grand theory? Are dictionaries not sufficient for telling people the meaning of ethical words, in case they do not understand the language?

These questions are important, because they point to a fact of great significance: We sometimes understand a language and know quite well how to use the words in it, but are led into puzzles and confusions because we are not clearly aware of just how we are using certain words. Take the word "I" as it occurs in phrases like "I think" or "I did." All of us use this word all the time, and we should hardly be accused of ignorance of English on account of failure to use it correctly. But as soon as we begin to ask ourselves what it refers to, we become puzzled. It does not seem to refer to our bodies. Some philosophers have thought it refers to an invisible soul, and that the supposition that it does is necessary for making sense of many things we say that obviously are intelligible. It would be quite a contribution to clarification if we had a clear account of the meaning of this word. Much the same can be said for ethical words. In some sense we understand them well enough; we use them all the time without mistakes identifiable as mistakes in English. But we do not have ideas about their meaning clear enough for it to be obvious to us how ethical questions in principle should be answered. We should all have made substantial progress, presumably, if our ethical questions could be rephrased so that they became clearer and the method for answering them more patent. If the naturalist does this for us, he has performed a signal service.

2. HOW SHALL WE DECIDE WHAT OUR WORDS MEAN?

Naturalists, then, offer us definitions of ethical terms—some, one definition, others, different definitions. These definitions, they suppose, are correct reportive definitions, in the sense that the defining expression *means the same* (or substantially the same) as the ethical term it is intended to define. All of the defining expressions are such (if they were not, we should not call the definitions "naturalist") that, if we substituted them for the original ethical term in an ethical sentence, we should have left a statement obviously confirmable by the methods of the sciences.

Two related questions must be answered if we are to assess the various naturalistic theories we shall describe: Do any naturalistic definitions really reproduce accurately the meanings of ethical words? If so, which ones? (They cannot *all* be correct, for they are incompatible with each other.)

Incidentally, it is widely agreed today that *some* correct reportive definition can be given for most if not all ethical terms. It is obvious that, almost always, a sentence with an ethical term in it can be rephrased so that we have a different sentence, with the original ethical term missing, but one with exactly the same meaning. For instance, "*x* is my duty" is perhaps synonymous with, "I am morally obligated to do *x*, everything considered." Or, "*x* is better than *y*" may be said to mean "It is fitting or justifiable to prefer *x* to *y*." These rephrasings are to some extent helpful and clarifying. However, they are not naturalistic definitions in the sense that they replace *all* ethical terms with different expressions, with the result that we end with a statement that obviously is confirmable by the methods of the sciences.

Correct reportive definitions of many ethical terms, at least, then, can be given—but definitions that are of limited clarifying force. The question is still open whether correct reportive *naturalistic* definitions can be given.

Let us continue, then, with our questions: whether any naturalistic definition is correct in the sense of rendering the actual meaning of ethical terms, and if so, which one or ones.

Answering these questions looks like an easy task, for if there is any question we ought to be able to answer without stirring from our chairs, it is whether two words or expressions, as we use them generally or in some special context, *mean the same*. Surely we all know what it is for two expressions to mean the same, and surely we all know how to decide whether or not they do. Can't we tell without difficulty whether Locke was right that "is good" means "is apt to cause or increase pleasure, or diminish pain, in us"?

Unfortunately, deciding what we mean is not so simple in all cases. It *is* easy in some cases. The definitions of some words are practically on the tips of our tongues, and when a definition is proposed, we instantly say "Yes" or "No"—and obviously are right in what we say. Take for instance kinship terms, like "brother" and "uncle." Any child of five can tell you that to be one's uncle is to be the brother of one's father or one's mother. Just *why* it is so easy to decide (correctly) about the meanings of these words is an interesting question in itself. Possibly the reason is that these words were *taught* us not just by example, but by the use of explanatory definitions.

There are some other expressions, however—"belief," "statement," "I," "number," "probable," "means the same," "reason"—that in the end are plausibly viewed as correctly defined by certain phrases. But, in their case, we seem not to be equipped with an infallible internal signal that marks proposed definitions as correct or incorrect (much less an infallible internal preceptor that advises us, on call, of the correct definition of any such term we wish to define). The discrimination of good definitions, in such cases, is less an intuitive matter than a matter for discursive demonstration and confirmation. Then, if ethical words are like these words, it will not be a matter of simple intuition to decide which definitions are correct and which ones are not.

How, then, *shall we decide* whether a reportive definition is correct (whether the proposed defining term really means the same as the term defined)?

Let us narrow this question slightly. Let us simply ask ourselves how to decide whether two *property-referring expressions* mean the same. This limitation is a convenient simplification. Of course, terms like "is right" and "is desirable" do seem to be property-referring expressions, in the sense that "That act is right" does seem to affirm that the act being talked of has the property of being right.[5]

When, then, do two property-referring expressions *mean the same?* Roughly, we might say, when we apply the terms to the same objects, and when we decide whether to apply them by the same criteria. Let us spell this out a bit more explicitly. The proposal is, then, that, for the speech habits of a particular person, two property-referring expressions mean the same if and only if they satisfy the two following conditions:[6] (1) For every actual thing or situation, the speaker must, if called upon to judge, be willing either to apply both expressions, to reject both, or must be in doubt about both. Thus, if "square" and "rectangle with equal sides" mean the same, it must be that, for every thing he is asked to judge, he will either apply both, or reject both, or be doubtful about both. (A person may be mistaken about what he would do, if he were in an actual situation and called upon to judge; we are interested in what he *would* say, if called upon to make a serious judgment, not in what he *thinks* he would say.) (2) The first test is not quite adequate, for it would permit us to say that "unicorn" and "centaur" mean the same. In order to avoid this difficulty, we must consider the speech responses of a person to things or situations that are not actual. For instance, we may present a person with drawings, and ask him whether the words of our interest apply to the thing there depicted. Or we may *describe* things or situations for him (not, however, by use of the terms whose meaning is being tested, but by reference to more specific properties), *not* necessarily limiting ourselves to things or situations that are causally possible in nature. If two terms mean the same for a certain person, he will apply both, reject both, or be doubtful of both, for all such

---

[5] It may be objected that it is a mistake to view ethical terms as property-referring. (The view that they are not will be formulated and examined in detail in Chapter 9.) But there can be no harm in a preliminary assumption that they are property-referring. If they are not, presumably we shall be unsuccessful in finding which property they refer to. Indeed, a failure in the quest to find expressions in the language of empirical science that mean the same as ethical expressions would constitute stronger evidence than any other that ethical terms are not property-referring.

[6] See, for instance, Rudolf Carnap, "Meaning and Synonymy in Natural Languages," *Philosophical Studies*, VI (1955), 33–47. Some writers believe the second condition is unnecessary, or that it cannot be clearly stated and so must be discarded. Other writers think that further conditions must be met, usually some concerning the "intentions" of the speaker. For some complications that cannot be discussed here, see C. I. Lewis, *Analysis of Knowledge and Valuation* (LaSalle, Ill.: Open Court Publishing Co., 1946), pp. 85 ff.

depicted or described situations, whatever they may be, if he is called upon to make a serious judgment. Thus, if "unicorn" and "centaur" do not mean the same for me, then, if I am shown an ample series of animal drawings, and asked to classify them in terms of the applicability of these expressions, I shall find some to which I readily apply the one, and to which I am unwilling to apply the other.

We can illustrate these tests with an example. Suppose we wish to find a correct reportive definition of the verb "assert."[7] We consult a dictionary and find the following definition: "to utter a declarative sentence in a manner conventionally indicative of belief in what one says, and having such firm conviction as to be indifferent to any contrary evidence that might be offered."

Is this definition a good and correct one? The proposals of the dictionary raise several questions. Can a person "assert" something if he is just talking to himself, with no audience? Must a person actually speak in order to "assert," or is a nod, or a statement in writing, sufficient? Must a person believe what he says in order to "assert" it—or may one "assert" when one is deliberately lying? Can a person "assert" something if he is drunk, or if he is talking in his sleep? Or, is it true that, if a person "asserts" something, he will refuse to retract irrespective of any evidence that may be drawn to his attention? These questions all raise issues about what is to be incorporated in the definition. How may our two criteria be applied to decide about them?

If we really want to know what is the correct definition, say, for our own usage of "assert," perhaps the simplest thing, if we have the money, is to engage someone to follow us with a camera with sound track. In the course of time, our cameraman will catch us in a good many uses of "assert." For instance, he might catch us saying that Mr. X had asserted something on a certain occasion, even when we knew perfectly well that Mr. X had retracted five minutes later, after having been faced with evidence. In case this happened, it is clear we would have to withdraw from our definition any clause requiring that a person who "asserts" be "indifferent to evidence," for in this instance, we actually *said* that a man asserted, and on the other hand it is clear that we definitely believed, and would have said, if asked, that the man was not indifferent to evidence.

We can supplement this "real-life" technique with the second, "hypothetical cases," procedure. For instance, we might run off a film made from Disney drawings, and have ourselves asked questions about the action while it is occurring. (Since the film makes the situation rather realistic, we are

[7] For the moment we omit complications that arise from the fact that a word often has several associated senses. The word "assert," for instance, means one thing in the expression "asserted that . . ." and quite another thing in such combinations as "asserted himself" or "asserted his rights." It is sometimes not easy to decide whether a word is used vaguely, or whether it has several closely related senses.

more apt to get what we should say if we really were commenting spontaneously in a situation, and not merely what we think we should say.) Of course, in the case of the word "assert," we do not need to use hypothetical cases for the reason we need them for terms like "unicorn"—that there are no actual unicorns. Presumably, real-life situations can illustrate how we use "assert," clearly enough for the purpose, say, of dictionary-making.[8]

These, then, are our criteria for deciding whether two property-referring expressions mean the same. It is a question of whether the person will apply both, refuse to apply both, or be doubtful about both, for every object or situation, actual or not, that is in some way presented or described to him.

Correspondingly, the proper procedure for showing that a definition is mistaken is to pose a "counterexample"—an example, actual or possible, to which all or most people would apply the one term but not the other. Clear counterexamples definitely prove that a definition is mistaken—except for words sometimes used in one sense and sometimes in another.

Once we think about it, we can see that it is much easier to disprove a definition than it is to establish that one is correct, for a disproof (except where there are several senses) requires only a single counterexample. But how can we establish a definition? The answer is that in general we cannot *prove;* we can only do our best to make sure no types of counterexamples have been overlooked. Of course, sometimes we justifiably feel confident of this, for we are familiar with our own speech habits.

Sometimes, to be sure, there is something further that we can do. Sometimes we can find some fact that for some reason cannot be explained unless

[8] Is there any way in which our criteria can be formulated so as to provide a test for whether a given definition renders what was meant by a particular definiendum, as used on a particular occasion? This is of special interest to us, because most words are used in various senses, and it is often important to be able to identify the sense in which a word was used in a given context.

We can use a variation of our second criterion for this purpose. Suppose we said a certain event or thing A was P, and we want to know whether P, as used in that context, meant the same as Q. The first thing to do is ask ourselves whether we might also have said that A was Q; if the answer is negative, then obviously P did not mean the same as Q. The simplest next thing to do is ask ourselves whether we should have been content to have said "A is Q" instead of what we did say; and if not, why not—what was different about what we would then have been saying? If we can pick out a difference, then obviously the terms did not mean the same. If we think we would have been content to say the one as well as the other, there is still some question. To be certain, we can think of A as being varied in certain ways, different from what it was, including (if the problem is a serious one) even variations that could not occur in nature. Then, for each variation we can ask ourselves whether we would still have said "A is P" and also "A is Q." If we find, after persistent reflection, that in all cases we ~~Some writers appear to feel that matters are much simpler, that all we have to do is~~ certain as we can be that we used P to mean the same as Q.

Some writers appear to feel that matters are much simpler, that all we have to do is ask ourselves about our intentions—what we intended someone else to learn from what we said. But how are we supposed to find what our intention was, except by noticing what we would have been content to say instead of what we did say—except, perhaps, in specially simple cases?

two expressions do, or do not, mean the same. For instance, we may know that a person is in doubt whether something is *P*; and therefore *P* cannot mean the same as *Q*, if it is clear that he knows quite well whether the thing is *Q* and could not truly be in doubt about it.

3. OVERT AND COVERT SYNONYMY

It will be helpful to make one further distinction. On reflection it will be obvious that our two criteria can be satisfied by two expressions that do not *obviously* mean the same, in the way in which "is my male child" and "is my son" obviously mean the same. Because of this, our criteria permit us to say that definitions may be given for "reason," "believes," and "is a cause of," whereas probably *no* reportive definitions of these terms can be claimed to be correct if we demand that the defining phrase *obviously* mean the same as the definiendum.

It is useful to mark a difference between the case of two expressions satisfying our criteria and also obviously meaning the same, and the case of expressions satisfying our criteria but *not* obviously meaning the same. In the former case, we shall say they *overtly* mean the same, or are *overtly* synonymous; in the latter case we may say they only *covertly* mean the same, or are *covertly* synonymous. If we just say that two terms "mean the same," we shall be asserting only that one or the other of these relationships is the case, without specifying which.

There is not a great deal of difference between overt synonymy and covert synonymy. In both cases the synonymous pairs have several properties. (*a*) Obviously—as a consequence of satisfying our criteria—synonymous terms apply to the same things or situations, and fail to apply to the same things or situations. (*b*) If *P* and *Q* are synonymous for a given person's usage, he will not be able to find any property that a thing has when it is *P*, as distinct from what it has when it is *Q*, and vice versa. Consequently, he will not be able to specify any difference between asking "Is this *P*?" and asking "Is this *Q*?" (*c*) Such a person will confirm or verify that something is *P* in the same way in which he will confirm that it is *Q*.

The only difference between the two types of synonymy is this: Terms that are overtly synonymous not only satisfy our criteria; it is also true that the person, for whose usage they are overtly synonymous, thinks after the briefest reflection (if the question is put to him) that the two terms are merely different verbal devices for saying the same thing; he recognizes them intuitively as alternate, freely interchangeable expressions—perhaps because he has been taught the meaning of the one by reference to the other. This is not true if two terms are only covertly synonymous.

Incidentally, when a person becomes convinced, from observing his own verbal usage, that two expressions are covertly synonymous (as he uses them), he is apt to start having the experiences typical of overt synonymy.

That is, the expressions begin to seem to him, intuitively, like alternate, freely interchangeable expressions.

Overt and covert synonymy, then, are not very different, and there is no sharp line between them. It will be useful to keep the two concepts distinct, however. We may as well remark in advance that in our opinion *no naturalistic definition* of any ethical term can plausibly be claimed to mean the same, *overtly*, as the ethical term of which it is intended to be a good reportive definition—except possibly for the usage of some naturalistic philosophers who have been living with the idea that the definition is a good one. To our mind, the only serious question is whether any naturalistic definition really qualifies as being covertly synonymous with some ethical term.

Before turning to the statement and examination of some typical and influential naturalistic theories, there is a preliminary item to be disposed of. In 1903, a book on ethics was published by G. E. Moore[9] which has had enormous influence. In it certain ideas were put forward about how to decide whether two expressions mean the same. Moore thought that as a result of these ideas all naturalistic definitions of ethical terms can be conclusively shown to be mistaken. He did not recognize any distinction between overt and covert synonymy; and we have to bear this fact in mind, in considering what he said.

Moore's most important suggestion was the proposal of what has been called the "open question" test or criterion for sameness of meaning. This test is approximately as follows. Suppose you have two terms, P and Q, and it has been suggested that they mean the same. Now, Moore said, a way to test whether they really do mean the same is this. Compose a question of this form: "Is everything P also Q?" (or the reverse). Then ask yourself whether this question is "intelligible" or "significant" or whether you understand what it means to doubt that the answer is affirmative. If the question *is* intelligible and significant, Moore said, then the terms do *not* mean the same, for if they did, the question would be no more intelligible or significant than would be the question: "Is everything P also P?" This latter question, Moore suggested, is neither intelligible nor significant; nor can we understand what it would mean to doubt it. Moore thought that no naturalistic definitions pass this test. Certainly "desirable" and "is desired by somebody" do not, for "Is everything that is desired by somebody also desirable?" seems to be an intelligible and significant question.

In one important respect, Moore's test is not as clear as we could wish. It is essential that we understand how to decide whether a sentence is "intelligible" or "significant." What does Moore mean by these terms? Clearly there is one ordinary sense in which "Is everything P something that is P?" is an intelligible question, for we *understand* it, and the answer to it is "Yes." Presumably, then, Moore means by "intelligible" something

---

[9] *Principia Ethica* (Cambridge, Eng.: Cambridge University Press).

like "can be raised with some point." But how do we tell whether a question is raised with some point?[10] Of course, we can know this of "Is everything *P* also *Q?*" if we happen to know that *P* does *not* mean the same as *Q;* but this is not helpful, for we are trying to devise a test to decide, for doubtful cases, whether *P* means the same as *Q.* Similarly, we can know this of "Is everything *P* also *Q?*" if we happen to know that it is logically possible for something to be *P* but not *Q* (or the reverse); but this again is not helpful, for if there is doubt whether *P* means the same as *Q* there is exactly the same doubt whether it is logically possible for something to be *P* but not *Q.* (It is not logically possible for something to be *P* but not *Q* merely because *P* and *Q* are different words.) What can Moore mean, then, when he says that, in doubtful cases, we are to ask ourselves whether his question is intelligible, an "open" question? *Perhaps* what he means is simply this: that *P* and *Q* do not mean the same for a person if, when he asks himself "Is everything *P* also *Q?*" he is *doubtful* of the answer, or the answer does not *seem to him obviously affirmative.*

But if this is what Moore meant, then it appears he was mistaken at least for covert synonymy, for it might well be the case that two terms do covertly mean the same, as a given person uses them, so that he could never correctly deny that everything that is *P* is also *Q,* but, if the person were not clearly aware of his use of terms, he might remain doubtful, and the answer might seem to him not obviously affirmative. Consider the question: "Is every male over fourteen who has never been married a bachelor?" A person who had frequently been caught overlooking subtle points about the meanings of words (for example, by Professor Moore!) might not feel sure whether to say "Yes" or "No." In other words, the two expressions might well mean the same, as the person uses the terms, although it would not seem obvious to him whether the correct answer to the question was affirmative or negative. Furthermore, two terms might pass Moore's test even if they didn't mean the same. Take "bachelor" and "unmarried male," which do not mean the same (presumably in the usage of anyone who speaks English). Moore would decide whether they mean the same for a certain person by asking him, "Is every unmarried male a bachelor?" Unwary persons might very well answer "Yes," and say that the answer is *not* doubtful, just because they do not remember that they do not apply "bachelor" to divorced males or widowers. Moreover, when we are inquiring about the correct definitions of puzzling terms like "statement," "myself," and "probable," it just seems too optimistic to expect Moore's test to be reliable.

The "open question" test is possibly a good test for overt sameness of

---

[10] There is also no point in raising a question if everybody already knows the answer. If we are walking in a pouring rain, there is no point in asking "Is it raining?" except as a joke.

meaning, but—unless we have misinterpreted it—it seems to be too strong a test, or generally a questionable test, for sameness of meaning in general.

Nevertheless, although it is justified to use our two criteria as the only clear tests for sameness of meaning, we should be alert to the following possibility. Suppose that, by our criteria, two expressions mean the same, for example, "scab" and "man who takes the place of a striker." But suppose further that we find that people sometimes say, "That fellow taking a striker's place is a scab!" as if they were making a useful and important statement. If this happened, we should want to consider whether one or the other of the terms was functioning not merely to refer to a property, but in some other way as well. Speech can do other things besides give information (for example, "Get out of here!"), and words, even adjectives or descriptive phrases, may do something else besides refer to some property. There may be other dimensions to language, and we may have to take these into account in order to explain why people use a sentence like the one above, and think it is a significant statement. Perhaps we also have to take other such dimensions into account in order to understand ethical language thoroughly.

4. FIRST EXAMPLE OF NATURALISM: EDWARD WESTERMARCK

We shall now describe three examples of naturalism that seem representative of the most plausible and interesting types of naturalistic theory. The first writer we shall consider was an extraordinarily learned man (but a careless writer), primarily an anthropologist, whose work was published in the first four decades of the present century.

Westermarck's theory concentrates on certain moral terms: primarily on "reprehensible" ("morally bad," "wrong"), "praiseworthy" ("morally admirable," "meritorious"), and "duty" ("ought"). He has little or nothing to say about terms like "desirable." We shall concentrate on his theory of "reprehensible"; his view of the other ethical terms is substantially the same as his view of this one.[11]

To say that an action is reprehensible, according to Westermarck, is essentially to say: "I have a tendency to feel moral disapproval toward the agents of all acts like this one." Moral disapproval, he says, is a hostile attitude of mind toward someone, but one that is, or at least is assumed to be, disinterested or impartial in the sense of being uninfluenced by any personal relationship with the individual toward whom the emotion is directed (such as being the victim of his act). We may, therefore, expand our definition of "*x* is reprehensible" so that we get: "I have a tendency to feel

---

11 Westermarck's major works are *The Origin and Development of the Moral Ideas* (2 vols.; New York: The Macmillan Company, 1906); and *Ethical Relativity* (New York: Harcourt, Brace & Company, 1932).

angry resentment at the agent of any act like *x*, and this tendency is dis-interested and impartial."[12]

Westermarck did not claim that his definition of this moral term would appeal to our language sense as an obviously correct account of its meaning. On the contrary, he explicitly acknowledged that it would not.[13] His defi-nition is claimed only to give the meaning but not the *overt* meaning of ethical terms.

Let us cite a representative statement from Westermarck (which illus-trates the provoking indecisiveness of his writing):

> I maintain . . . that the qualities assigned to the subjects of moral judgments really are generalizations derived from approval or disapproval felt with regard to certain modes of conduct, that they are tendencies to feel one or the other of these emotions interpreted as qualities, as dynamic tendencies, in the phenomena which gave rise to the emotion. A similar translation of emotional states into terms of qualities assigned to external phenomena is found in many other cases: something is "fearful" because people fear it, "admirable" because people admire it. When we call an act good or bad, we do not *state* the existence of any emotional tendencies, any more than, when we call a landscape beautiful, we state any characteristics of beauty: we refer the subject of the judgment to a class of phenomena which we are used to call good or bad. But we are used to call them so because they have evoked moral approval or disapproval in ourselves or in other per-sons from whom we have learned the use of those words. . . . A judgment which contains such a concept may be said to be true if the person who pronounces it actually has a tendency to feel the emotion in question with reference to the subject of the judgment. . . . If I say that it is wrong to resist evil, and yet resistance of evil has no tendency whatever to call forth in me an emotion of moral disapproval, then my judgment is false.[14]

Like all naturalisms, Westermarck's theory implies that the truth of ethical statements can be determined by observation; my ethical statement is true if I have a corresponding tendency to feel emotion, which is impar-tial and disinterested. However, he was a relativist; he was concerned to emphasize that there is no such thing as absolute truth in morals in the sense of there being moral statements that everyone must accept *independently of how he feels*. We cannot establish the statement, say, "Homosexuality is a bad thing." We can show that it is correct for you to say this, or for me, depending on our feelings; but if someone comes along who does not get excited about homosexuality, then he would be mistaken if he said it is wrong. On account of Westermarck's relativism some writers decline to call him a naturalist at all; but of course he must be classified as a natural-ist, given our definition of "naturalist."

---

[12] See *Ethical Relativity*, pp. 90–93, 100, 205–06.
[13] See *Ethical Relativity*, p. 116; also pp. 50–51, 144–49.
[14] *Ethical Relativity*, pp. 114–15, 141–42; and *The Origin and Development of the Moral Ideas*, I, pp. 17–18.

Why did Westermarck think that his definition correctly represents the meaning of "reprehensible"? We can distinguish several reasons. Part of his reason, of course, was the fact that he felt the alternative theories were implausible; we confine ourselves to his more positive reasoning.

1. On introspective grounds he thought that when we judge seriously that something is reprehensible, it is always true that we have a tendency to feel unfavorable emotions about the act, or at least think we do. 2. If ethical terms did not refer to some subjective property such as the speaker's emotional tendencies, but referred either to some logical relation or to some nonsubjective phenomenon, it would be hard to understand why there is as much apparently ineluctable difference of opinion in morals as there is, and why there is so little sign of progress toward universal agreement. 3. Westermarck thought that certain historical changes in moral views (for example, about the treatment of foreigners, and the rights of animals) were correlated with, and were a result of, widespread changes in emotional attitudes, especially a widening of altruistic or sympathetic interests. This is most simply explained if moral judgments are construed as assertions about the emotional attitude of the speaker.

These reasons are by no means foolish. The factual claims embodied in them appear to be at least nearly true: We do usually have tendencies to feel moral approval or disapproval when we praise or condemn actions; there are basic differences of opinion about ethics; and Westermarck's theory of the changes of certain moral beliefs, from one age to another, is a plausible one. But do these points *require* Westermarck's explanation?

They do *not* require his theory, because, as we shall shortly see, they are equally well explained by other (for example, noncognitive) theories. It may be, however, that an ethical theory must be rather similar to Westermarck's if it is to be able to take account of these facts.

In the years subsequent to the appearance of Westermarck's books, many philosophers have essayed to prove that Westermarck's theory is mistaken. However, so many of these "proofs" have failed that it requires some temerity to argue that he was definitely wrong. Nevertheless, one might say that Westermarck's theory is unacceptable. (1) There are some minor ways in which his theory should be tidied up, as is shown by the following frequently-used argument. Westermarck, it is said, could not allow that I can say truly, "It *was* wrong for Nero to . . ." because Nero's activities occurred before my birth, and at that time I was not there to have any moral attitudes at all, favorable or unfavorable. But surely, the criticism goes on, it is absurd to hold a theory that implies that my condemnation of any event before my birth is incorrect! But does his theory have this consequence? It doesn't; but Westermarck could have put the matter more clearly. He should have explained that to say "Nero *was* wrong in . . ." means "Nero *did* . . . and I *now* have a tendency to feel. . . ." If the use of the past tense (and correspondingly for the future tense) in ethical statements is interpreted in this way, the alleged difficulty for his theory does not arise. (2) On Westermarck's theory, if I now have a tendency to feel disapproval, of a disinterested sort, of acts like *x*, and if I know that I do, I cannot have any doubt about whether *x* is wrong, for in knowing that I have the tendency, I also know that the act is wrong. But is this true? It seems not. For instance, suppose a person approves of permitting abortions for social and economic reasons, and even feels disinterested indignation at persons who stand in the way of such measures. Now, if a person is *actually feeling* such indignation and has good reason for thinking his feeling is impartial (if the parties concerned are unrelated to him, and so on), then he can certainly *know* that he has a tendency to feel disapproval of this act and of acts like it. On the other hand, this particular ethical issue is a complicated matter, and it seems likely that this same person, if he is reasonable, will admit that he *could* be mistaken, that possibly it is wrong to permit abortions for other than medical reasons. (3) According to the Westermarck theory, the only reasonable ground for doubt about a moral issue is whatever ground there is for doubting that I now do have a tendency to feel disapproval, or for doubting that my tendency to disapprove is impartial. It is plain, however, that there are other grounds for doubt. I can properly feel doubt if I think my disapproval may be based on misinformation about, or an inadequate analysis of, the facts. I may also properly feel doubt if I find difficulty in formulating the general principle involved. (4) If Westermarck's definition is correct, then each of us can assert truly the following proposition: "Something is wrong if and only if I have an impartial tendency to disapprove of it." Furthermore, according to him, if I say "*x* is wrong," I am not contradicting anyone who says "*x* is right," although of course we may not be aware of this on account of misunderstanding of our own meanings. These results are implausible enough to raise some question whether Westermarck's definition can be correct.

5. SECOND EXAMPLE OF NATURALISM: RALPH BARTON PERRY

Ralph Barton Perry, whose theory[15] is similar to many ethical theories both historical and contemporary, takes "desirable" or "good" as basic terms in ethics and explains "duty" and "right" in terms of them.

Perry begins by defining "desirable" in the sense of "desirable in some respect."[16] To be desirable in this sense, he says, is to be the *object of a*

---

[15] We follow the account of his most recent book, *Realms of Value* (Cambridge: Harvard University Press, 1954), but supplement this on occasion from his earlier *General Theory of Value* (New York: Longmans, Green & Co., Inc., 1926).

[16] Perry would rather say he is defining " 'good' in the generic sense." I believe my terminology is more satisfactory, however. Further, I substitute the phrase, "desirable, everything considered" for his "morally good." The expression I use seems to come closer to what he had in mind than "morally good." Perry does not seem to have been very sensitive to English usage at this point.

pro attitude, or a favorable interest, on the part of somebody. What is a "favorable interest"? If one is willing to act (expend energy) in a certain direction whenever so doing is expected to result in a certain event, the event expected is said to be the object of a favorable interest. For example, eating a steak or passing time conversing with one's mother might be objects of favorable interest. (Something is an object of unfavorable interest if anticipations of it motivate avoidance behavior.) Feelings or emotions can be clues to the presence of an interest: for instance, pleasure at the sight of a good steak, or a thrill at being reunited with one's long absent mother. Perry does not say how many interests a person normally has, or what they are, or what is their normal intensity, or what are the causes for interests of different kinds; these issues he leaves to psychology.

Perry next defines "desirable, all things considered." This phrase means the same as "is the object of an interest when the interest . . . satisfies the requirement of harmony." When is an interest said to "satisfy the requirement of harmony"? There are two cases to be considered. First, there is the case in which only one person is affected by whether the interest is satisfied, the person who has the interest. In this case, the interest is "harmonious" if, roughly, satisfying it does not conflict inordinately with the satisfaction of the person's other interests. More exactly, the interest is harmonious if satisfaction of it is included in a plan or schedule that the individual freely adopts after informed reflection on all his interests, their mutual conflicts, and possible ways of satisfying different sets of them. Second, there is the case in which the satisfaction of an interest affects several persons. In this case, the interest is "harmonious" if its satisfaction is included in a collective schedule that is acceptable to *all* parties concerned, when each has a benevolent interest in the satisfaction of all, and has reflected (ideally with full information) on the possible schedules that might be adopted. (This last sentence formulates Perry's view of the ideal of democratic decisions, and his conviction of their importance.) A life lived according to such schedules Perry calls one of "harmonious happiness."

To say that an act is "right," according to Perry, is to say that no other act can contribute more to the harmonious happiness of the group. One is "morally obligated" to perform a certain act, if its performance "is called for by the end of the moral good, that is, by harmonious happiness." As Perry says:

> Duty is a stronger term . . . since it is associated with an implied promise by which the agent has bound himself. When it is said that every right [here in the substantive sense, like "the right to freedom of speech"] has its associated duty, it is meant that in claiming his benefit as a moral right he has committed himself to allotting some equivalent benefit on the other party. If he does not fulfill his part, not only as beneficiary but as benefactor, he

incurs the charge of inconsistency, as well as the justifiable resentment of the other beneficiary."[17]

Perry's definitions, unlike Westermarck's, are absolutist. If an event is desirable at all, or if an act is right or wrong at all, it can be correctly said to be so by everybody. Whether an event is desirable, or an act right or wrong, does not depend on who is speaking.

Why did Perry think these definitions represent the meaning of these ethical terms? Perry is generally not very lucid on this point. In fact, some passages in his last book sound more as if he thinks it would be a good thing for the world at large if people used the familiar ethical terms in line with his definitions, than as if he thinks they actually do. These passages suggest he is offering a "reforming" definition. However, we propose to interpret Perry in the light of those passages that appear to argue that his definitions are reportive, a correct representation of the actual meaning of ethical terms.[18] If we proceed on this basis, we note that Perry offers two major arguments. (1) He first points out that there is much agreement among educated and reflective people about the things to which moral predicates ("right," "desirable," and so forth) apply: those things mentioned in "generally accepted maxims, precepts, and virtues," including such virtues as "courage, temperance, wisdom, and justice." But now, he argues, *if* people were following his definitions of these terms, and using the methods of science to determine the applicability of these terms accordingly, they *would* come to apply moral predicates, at least approximately, to those things to which they do in fact apply them. This is some reason for thinking the definitions represent what people actually mean by ethical predicates. (2) Perry then argues in effect that what we accept as evidence, in a common-sense way, for a course of action being right (and so on), is exactly what his definitions prescribe that we should accept as evidence. "When men differ as to the specific applications of moral opinion it is to the standard of harmonious happiness that they look for common ground. And it is by this standard that men criticize and justify their major social institutions—conscience itself, polity, law, economy. . . ." In other words, Perry appears to think that in real situations of moral puzzlement, a person finds his doubt resolved, finds himself willing to say "That's the right thing to do" (and so on), only when he believes the act in question is related to the ideal of harmonious happiness in the way specified by Perry's definitions.

These are powerful arguments if the premises are correct. But are they? Consider the premise of his first argument, that people in fact believe those things to be desirable or right that we might expect them to, if they meant

[17] *Realms of Value*, p. 109.
[18] The reader interested in arriving at an accurate and balanced judgment about what Perry believed should read chap. 8 of *Realms of Value*.

by "desirable" and "right" what Perry suggests they do. But is such correspondence universal? There are facts that raise doubts. One of the most widespread moral rules is the prohibition of marriage not only between members of the same family, but between more distantly related persons (the precise prohibition differing widely from one group to another). Is the extension of this rule beyond the nuclear family a result Perry's view would lead us to expect? Again, Christian thinking has traditionally been opposed to suicide, and, partly as a result, suicide or euthanasia with the aim of avoiding severe pain during a terminal illness is contrary to law in the United States. Does Perry's theory predict such view?[19] Or consider his second argument. Is it really true that men solve their moral puzzles by appeal to the standard of harmonious happiness? We of course must agree with Perry that men normally do take this standard into account when they are puzzled about a moral problem. But do they consider nothing else? Surely some men have considered what they thought were signs of the will of God, as revealed by some spokesman or by the "obvious intent" of nature. Surely others have looked within, at the promptings of conscience, and have found there instructions about an ideal of equality, or about obligations to which we are subject because of promises made or benefits received. We must recall, too, facts we noted about the psychology of ethical deliberation, which made it look less tidy and systematic than Perry's theory suggests it is. Actual moral thinking does not conform to any simple pattern.

There are further difficulties for Perry's theory of the meaning of ethical terms. Take his definition of "desirable in some respect." *Do* we say something is desirable in some respect when we know it is the object of somebody's interest, no matter what? For instance, do we think a man's painful death desirable in some respect when we know a sadistic enemy wishes for it? Or suppose a crazed bomb-thrower destroys a library. Would we say this event was desirable in any sense? Or suppose we know a piece of music or a painting is not an object of interest to anyone. Does this prove it worthless—if we have some reason to suspect that someone who understood it *would* take an interest in it?

Moreover, if we mean by "right" and "desirable, everything considered" what Perry says we mean, we are committed by our meanings to a sophisticated form of utilitarian theory. We are committed to believing that an act is morally right if and only if it will, or probably will, be more conducive to the harmonious happiness of mankind than any other act we might perform instead. But we shall see later that people are not prepared (whatever they may think at first) to accept a utilitarian theory about what is right, as a result of the meaning of their terms or for any other reason. Again, there must be something wrong with Perry's definitions.

---

[19] If our discussion of the causation of moral standards and their changes is substantially correct, we should not expect the correlations that Perry's theory predicts.

6. THIRD EXAMPLE OF NATURALISM: THE IDEAL OBSERVER THEORY

The third theory to be considered also has its roots in the past, since the central ideas are to be found in Adam Smith, and, on possible interpretations, in David Hume and Frances Hutcheson.[20] We shall describe a variant of a form of the theory recently proposed by Roderick Firth.[21]

The main idea is that ethical terms should be defined after the pattern of the following example: "*x* is better than *y*" means "If anyone were, in respect of *x* and *y*, fully informed and vividly imaginative, impartial, in a calm frame of mind and otherwise normal, he would *prefer x* to *y*." For the definition of other ethical terms, the last clause would be modified so as to refer to a different kind of attitude. For instance, in the case of "is reprehensible," the last clause might take the form, "would have an unfavorable [for example, indignant] attitude toward the agent of *x*." Or, for "*x* is morally obligated to do *y*," it might take some such form as "would take an unfavorable attitude toward *x* if he omitted doing *y*" or "would *feel obligated* to do *y* if he were *x*, and would feel like demanding that *x* perform *y* if he were not."[22] In other words, the theory supposes that ethical statements assert about their subject-term that any person who fulfilled certain qualifications at the time would experience a certain reaction toward the subject-term. It is obvious why the theory is referred to as the "ideal observer" theory, although the term is rather misleading since it suggests "*moral* observer," whereas this is not in the least intended.

The theory resembles Westermarck's in that it proposes that ethical statements should be construed as statements about attitudes or feelings or desires. As stated above, however, it escapes the objections to the Westermarck theory. Unlike Westermarck's view, the theory is absolutist. It can, however, be given a relativist form, by substituting "I" (the speaker) for "anyone" in the above pattern, thus getting, for the definition of "*x* is better than *y*," something like "If I were, at the time . . . , I would prefer *x* to *y*." This version, however, has difficulties at one of the points at

---

[20] Hutcheson wrote, for example: "When we say one is obliged to an Action, we either mean, 1. That . . . : Or, 2. That every Spectator, or he himself upon Reflection, must approve his Action, and disapprove his omitting it, if he considers fully all its Circumstances." The suggestion is that "to be obligated" means "to be the case that one would disapprove omitting the act, if one were reflective and fully informed of the circumstances." From *An Essay on the Nature and Conduct of the Passions, with Illustrations upon the Moral Sense*, 1728, reprinted in L. A. Selby-Bigge (ed.), *British Moralists* (Oxford: Clarendon Press, 1897), vol. I, p. 408.

[21] In "Ethical Absolutism and the Ideal Observer," *Philosophy and Phenomenological Research*, XII (1952), 317–45. See his discussion with R. Brandt, the same journal, XV (1955), 407–23; and remarks by Jonathan Harrison, the same journal, XVII (1956), 256–62. My exposition of the theory, however, gives a more exclusive place to feelings, emotions, or desires (on the part of an "ideal observer") than did Firth's.

[22] Perhaps in the sense described above, pp. 117 f.

which Westermarck's theory is open to objection. We shall discuss the theory in its absolutist form.[23]

We must explain further the properties of the "ideal observer." (1) A person is "fully informed and vividly imaginative" if he has all true non-ethical beliefs and lacks all false nonethical beliefs that would affect his reaction of feeling or desire; and if he has these beliefs in mind as vividly as if he were perceiving the facts believed. (2) A person is "impartial" with respect to a particular reaction if the reaction is not influenced by the fact that some special individuals or groups are involved in the situation to which he is reacting; his reaction, in other words, would have been the same no matter what other individuals or groups were involved, so long as they had the same abstract properties (p. 19) as those actually in question. ("Impartial" connotes many things to different people, for example, "un-biased." The theory means by "impartial" just what is here stated, *noth-ing more.*) (3) What is it to be "in a calm frame of mind and otherwise normal"? It is not possible to be entirely precise here. To be "calm" means that one's reaction is not influenced by prior states of anger, depression, fear, grief, and so on. To be "otherwise normal" implies, first of all, that one is a human being, reared in society and beyond the stage of childhood, that one is not insane, debilitated by fatigue, seriously ill, and so forth. In neither case is it possible to specify exactly what is required, but it is felt there will be agreement, at least for extreme cases, about when the conditions are satisfied and when they are not.

One may ask why this theory is classified as "naturalist." Is it really true that this theory so construes ethical statements that ethical questions can be answered by the methods of science? One may say that it is not clear how observation will answer ethical questions on this view, for are there any "ideal observers" whose reactions we can inquire about?[24] To this query it may be replied that we often have excellent reason for thinking that we ourselves are impartial, in a calm frame of mind, and otherwise normal; and we can observe ourselves reacting in this condition. Sometimes we seem to have comparable information about other people. But do we ever know that we have "full information"? Probably we *sometimes* do. Suppose a surgeon asks us whether it is preferable for him to perform an

23 The writer defended a relativist form of the theory in the discussion with Firth referred to above (pp. 408–09), and suggested one in *Hopi Ethics,* pp. 108–09. In reply to the fourth objection to Westermarck, p. 169, one can say that although conflicting statements made by different people strictly do not contradict each other on this theory, we can easily see why they occasionally debate. The statements will be defenses of clashing courses of action; and further, people are so much alike that if one person can truly make an ethical assertion, it is very unlikely that another person can truly make one that conflicts with it.

In the writer's opinion, the relativist form is the more plausible form of the theory, but many do not share this view.

24 A similar question may be raised about Perry's definition of "desirable, all things considered."

amputation with or without anaesthetic. After having made inquiries about what possible reasons there could be for dispensing with anaesthetic, it would be fanciful to suppose facts might turn up that would make us feel unfavorably inclined toward the anaesthetic. Perhaps we cannot have certainty; but the probability is surely very high. In other cases (for example, when we want to know how strong an obligation is created by a certain kind of promise), it is doubtless more hazardous to suppose we are reacting on the basis of "full information," much less on the basis of "vivid imagination" of all of it; and this implies that the probability that our reactions are a reliable guide to a "qualified reaction" is so much the lower. But this is what we should expect; a definition of ethical terms would be dubious if it implied that we could have certainty about complex moral issues! It might be asked how we can infer from the fact that *we* feel in a certain way in the "ideal" conditions, that everyone else, irrespective of his background and training, will feel the same way. Clearly, such an inference is precarious; and we shall see in a moment that basic differences of such a sort between people—if there really are any—are a problem for the theory.

Why have philosophers thought this sort of definition represents accurately the meaning of ethical terms? (1) Some philosophers have felt that they cannot remember a case of judging something wrong (and so on) and at the same time definitely disbelieving that an "ideal observer" would disapprove; and vice versa. It is also thought, on introspective grounds, that when we are puzzled about whether something is right or wrong we do decide by relying on our feelings or attitudes, as corrected in the way the theory suggests. (2) The theory implies that moral opinions are subject to criticism and are correct or incorrect. In this respect, the theory corresponds much better with our intuitions about what we mean than does a relativist theory like Westermarck's. (3) The theory is consistent with the facts that we saw could be offered in favor of Westermarck's theory. A person's judgment about how an "ideal observer" would feel must be very largely based on how he feels himself; so it is only to be expected that there should be differences of opinion in ethics, and that historical changes in ethical views should correlate with changes in emotional attitudes, just as Westermarck says.

But there are some serious objections to the theory. (1) A good many people today—a substantial percentage of college students and an even greater percentage of graduate students—have come to the conclusion, doubtless partly on the basis of psychological and anthropological literature, that "ideal observers" as defined above may not always have the *same* reaction to the same event. How a person will react morally, they will say, will depend on his conditioning, his early training, his life experiences. It strikes them as quite natural that the Hopi, for instance, should have no kind feelings for animals. Now, this leads to the following problem for the present theory: If a person believes that *not* everyone who is an "ideal ob-

server" would disapprove of cruelty to animals, and at the same time is ready
to affirm that cruelty to animals is wrong, it cannot be that what he *means*
by "is wrong" is that *all* "ideal observers" would disapprove. If people
both think that something is wrong (and so on), *and also* think that "ideal
observers" do or might differ in their reactions about this thing, the
present theory must be mistaken about the meaning of "is wrong."[25] One
might meet this difficulty by adopting the relativist version of the "ideal
observer" theory, but we saw (p. 173) that there are some objections to
this version. (2) Very possibly the theory, in one of its forms, fits the
usage of ethical terms by some people. Indeed, of all the historic forms of
naturalism, it seems the most plausible. Certainly it may well give the correct definition of the reader's ethical terms. Nevertheless, it seems a bit
implausible to urge that it fits the usage of *everybody*, for there seem to be
people who think an ethical issue is decided if and only if they know the
"revealed word of God" on the point—people who distrust their own consciences as being another work of human pride. Also, there seem to be
people who think an ethical issue is decided if and only if its implications
for human happiness have been shown to be favorable or unfavorable. And
so on for others. So, perhaps we must say that the meanings of ethical terms
vary from one set of persons to another, correspondingly. (We say only
"perhaps"; at a later point we shall suggest that a uniform definition *can*
be given after all.)

7. CONCLUDING REMARKS ABOUT NATURALISM

None of the three naturalistic definitions we have considered is entirely
convincing. The Ideal Observer theory is the most plausible of the three,
but it has difficulties of detail. It is not easy to be convinced that it is a correct account of the meaning of ethical terms as used by some people, for
example, those who identify being desirable with conformity with the will
of God. So, even if the Ideal Observer theory correctly represents the
meaning of ethical terms as employed by some people, it will not do as a
dictionary definition, as an account of the meanings of everyone who uses
the language correctly.

Will any other naturalistic definition do better? We postpone an answer

---

[25] Suppose it were simply the *fact* that "ideal observers" sometimes differ in reactions
—leaving out of consideration whether people believe they do. What would be the
consequence for the theory? According to the theory, "is wrong" means roughly, "all
ideal observers would disapprove"; and "is right" means roughly, "no ideal observers
would disapprove." Now, if some, in fact, might approve and some might not, what are
we to say? We cannot say the act is *either* wrong *or* right. And yet, *as we use these
terms*, it seems that every act must be either wrong or right; if it is not wrong, then it
is certainly right (although not necessarily praiseworthy).

One may escape this difficulty by arguing that it has not yet been proved, beyond a
shadow of a doubt, that "ideal observers" can disagree. Whether this escape is plausible,
we shall not try to decide.

to this question to Chapter 10, where we shall be ready for still another type of naturalistic definition, one which seems to us more convincing.

There are several considerations that often sway people either for or against the abandonment of naturalism, in addition to those points of detailed objection to the several theories that we have already discussed. It is worthwhile to consider some of these.

1. A person might say: "As for myself, *my* ethical words mean exactly what the Ideal Observer theory [or Perry, or Westermarck] says they do. It may be there are other people who use terms differently—who perhaps use 'is desirable' to mean 'conforms with the will of God.' How other people use ethical words does not concern me. I am fully occupied with my own puzzles; let other people worry about theirs. As for me, the Ideal Observer [or some other] theory clarifies my usage, makes explicit to me meanings that formerly were unconscious. So this theory is right for me."

This is a possible position, and perhaps in the end it is the kind we have to settle for. It is disquieting, however. Most people will be motivated to look farther.

One might attack the suggested view, on the ground that we *know* that usages or meanings do not vary in this way, and that if a definition of ethical terms is clearly correct for me, it will be correct for everybody. This is true, it may be said, because ethical discussions do not reveal the kind of misunderstanding typical of situations in which people are really using words in different senses—such as occur when people have different native tongues, or are using technical terms in differing senses.

But is this reasoning effective? We must recall that, even if people were using terms in different senses, they might understand each other well enough for practical purposes, and have little occasion to notice a difference of meaning. Someone who used ethical words in the supernaturalist sense could get on very well discussing ethics with R. B. Perry, provided the former thought (as he likely would) that God's will for men is that they act so as to promote harmonious happiness. Disagreement about meanings would be masked unless evidence were unearthed, showing unmistakably that God commands suppression of personal desires, self-sacrifice where there is no reason for it, or human misery for the glory of God. If such evidence came to light, then we should see who is a supernaturalist; otherwise very likely we would not. Much the same can be said about the Ideal Observer theory. If a person used ethical terms as this theory says one does, the fact of disagreement with Perry's definitions would not be obvious if the person thought that an "ideal observer" would always favor acts promoting harmonious happiness.

Indeed, quite different ethical usages could result in certain key ethical propositions all being true by definition. Take, for instance, "It is wrong to cause intense pain to anyone except to serve some important good of conscious beings." Perry's definitions obviously imply the truth of this proposition. But so may a supernaturalist's, for he might not be willing to call a being "God" unless he disapproved of suffering for no reason. Or again, a person whose ethical usages follow the Ideal Observer formula might be unwilling to say that a person is "normal" unless he disapproved of cruelty. And so on.

Perhaps, then, it is not so obvious after all that, if some naturalistic definition is correct for ethical terms as used by you, the same one is correct for ethical terms as used by me.

2. One may think that naturalist definitions have the important consequence of enabling us to justify (or criticize) a person's basic ethical principles and the methods by which he reaches his ethical beliefs; and this may attract one toward naturalism.

To think this, however, may very easily be to think something that is not quite true, for the suggestion is that we can, armed with our naturalistic definitions, go to someone with whose ethical views we disagree, and say (correctly), "See here. Your ethical views are mistaken. We can prove this by showing what you *mean* by ethical words." Let us see why the suggestion that we can do this is misleading.

The reason why all problems of ethics can be solved by the methods of science, if naturalism is true, is that the naturalist's definitions (like every definition) enable him to assert that some fundamental ethical statements are true by definition—statements he can use as the basic premises of his system of normative ethics.[26] For instance, Perry's definitions enable us to say, "Any act is right if and only if it will contribute more to harmonious happiness than anything else the agent could do instead." The Ideal Observer definitions permit us to assert, as true by definition, "Anything is desirable if and only if an informed (and so on) person would want it to occur." In general, a definition will permit us to say something of the form, "Anything is E [ethical term] if and only if it is a *PQR*." Then, since science presumably can tell us what will contribute most to the harmonious happiness, or what an informed person would want, and so forth, it will carry us to conclusions about what is right or good.

Suppose, however, someone questions the basic premises. Can we show that he is mistaken by pointing to his meanings, as we can show a child that 6 x 7 is 42 by explaining that "6 x 7" just *means* "the sum of six 7's"?

No, we cannot. Suppose we find a person who acknowledges that something is PQR, but does *not* think the thing is E. Or at least, he genuinely doubts whether it is E. What can we do for him, on the basis of our naturalistic definitions? Nothing at all. The reason for this is that the naturalist does not really *derive* the premises from the definitions; he *starts* with the premises. It is their status, their use (the willingness to apply E if and only

---

26 As far as normative ethics is concerned, the outcome would be the same if *somehow* we could justify accepting these basic premises; there is no gain for normative ethics in holding that they are true by definition.

if *PQR* applies), that is the naturalist's ground for his conclusion about the person's meanings. If a person learns that doing a certain thing will maximize the harmonious happiness of mankind but remains in doubt whether doing that thing is right or desirable, the implication is not that the person is mistaken, but that Perry's definition is mistaken.

In other words, *if* a person is ready to call something *E* if and only if it is *PQR*, the naturalist can point out this fact and help him with any temporary confusion, and he can further point out that the methods of science can now show him what is *E*, since they can show him what is *PQR*. But *if* the person doubts whether something that is *PQR* is *E*, the naturalist not only cannot help him; the naturalist is *mistaken* in his view about what people in general mean by *E*. So, if a person really doubts whether some act is right when he has reflected fully on the fact that it will make the greatest possible contribution to harmonious happiness, the naturalist misunderstands the logic of his own position if he thinks he can force the person to retract, by logic and appeal to the meaning of his ethical terms.

The naturalist's definitions are tenable only if this latter situation does not arise. They are sound only if a person's doubt about basic ethical propositions (those made true by definition if the given form of naturalism is correct) does not reach far enough to place in jeopardy the naturalist's thesis about his meanings.

3. Many philosophers at present are dubious about naturalism for a further reason, which does not, however, appear to be a good reason. The argument is this: Ethical statements have *moving* effects on auditors that naturalism overlooks; and they perform jobs or functions that naturalism not only overlooks but that ethical sentences could not perform if they meant what the naturalist says they mean.

In Chapter 9 we shall discuss the theory that these philosophers would put in the place of naturalism. For the present we shall make just two points.

First, suppose a young lady looks at her watch and observes to her escort, "Why, it is twelve o'clock!" Her statement is a "moving" one. Not only may her escort well be motivated to depart, if he believes that what she says is true—at least if he has to catch a bus at quarter past twelve. He may also be emotionally excited—perhaps because he thinks he may miss his bus, but perhaps also merely because the fact that she says it (particularly if she says it while stifling a yawn) shows him something about her and her lack of interest in him.

Almost any statement can, in context, be moving in one way or another. This is true even, it has been pointed out, of the statements of arithmetic —if one's instructor shouts, "Six times seven is forty-two!" The same is true, of course, about ethical statements.

An utterance, then, is not shown not to be a statement, or to be unconfirmable by the methods of science, just because it is moving. If someone shouts at us, "You are an immoral scoundrel," his remark is not demonstrated to have no meaning of the sort contemplated by naturalists, just because the remark shows our critic to be so angry that it frightens us half to death; nor because the remark results in our immediate backing down.

Perhaps naturalists have devoted inadequate attention to these aspects, but it is not obvious that their existence is good reason for doubting the truth of naturalism's view of ethical statements. Why should it be—any more than it is for doubting a naturalist view of "It's twelve o'clock"?

Second, sometimes the argument is put in a different way. Ethical language, it is said, has the job of answering practical questions, of the form "What shall I do?" But a *statement* of *any* kind cannot do this; statements tell us what is the case, but they do not advise us what to do. So, since we know that ethical sentences do function to advise us what to do, they cannot be fact-statements.

But is it so obvious that fact-statements cannot function to answer practical questions? It depends on what our problem is. If we wish to know whether we must go in order to get our bus, the statement "It's twelve o'clock" may resolve our problem perfectly well. And if we want to do what's best—in the sense of what a person would choose to do if he were fully informed, impartial, and in a calm and normal frame of mind—it is not clear why our practical problem is not answered by the statement that the Ideal Observer theory claims we make when we say "It's best to . . ." So, even if we do agree that the basic job of ethical sentences is to answer practical questions, it is not clear that naturalism is mistaken.

Nevertheless, despite the fact that reasoning like this does not show naturalism to be mistaken, it may very well be that we have to pay more attention to other dimensions or functions of language besides the property-referring and the fact-stating than does naturalism as it has here been defined, if we are to understand ethical language adequately. We shall return to this possibility in Chapters 9 and 10.

4. Some further dubious criticisms of naturalism have been provided by philosophers who are or were nonnaturalists. Bertrand Russell, for instance, at one time argued that all naturalistic definitions must be incorrect, because there have been so many different naturalistic definitions. People do not, he wrote, debate about alternative and conflicting definitions of "square." The very fact there is so much debate shows no such definition is correct. The naturalist, of course, will reply to this that it just happens that the matter is complicated and it is not obvious what is the correct definition. He may also inquire whether Russell would be willing to take the same position for all other terms about whose correct definition there has been much controversy.

Nonnaturalists have also argued (A. C. Ewing says this is one of the two "fatal" objections to naturalism) that naturalistic definitions cannot be accepted, because, if they were, something would be true which in fact we know is false. What? Simply the fact that questions of ethics could be settled by the methods of the empirical sciences. We know, it is said, that we cannot settle questions of ethics by the methods we use to settle questions in physics or psychology. It follows from this that naturalistic definitions must be mistaken.

Is this reasoning correct? We should want to agree that questions of right and wrong cannot be decided in the physics laboratory, or by looking at a test tube, or by a sociological survey, but naturalistic definitions do not necessarily imply that ethical questions can be answered in such simple ways. Take, for instance, the Ideal Observer definition. On this theory, the answer to ethical questions must be got, as we have suggested (p. 174), by noting what we approve of when we are in a calm and impartial frame of mind, and when we have the most adequate information possible, by making inquiries about what others approve of when they are in such a state of mind, and by extrapolating this information in a way suitable to cover any question under examination. This is very different from looking through a microscope or circulating questionnaires. Nor is it obvious that this procedure is different from the procedure we think proper for answering questions of ethics.[27]

FURTHER READINGS

G. C. Field, "The Place of Definition in Ethics," *Proceedings*, The Aristotelian Society, 1931–32, pp. 79–94.
———, *Moral Theory* (New York: E. P. Dutton & Co., Inc., 1921), chap. 11. A naturalist who discusses the role of naturalist definitions and offers one.
R. B. Perry, *Realms of Value* (Cambridge: Harvard University Press, 1954), chaps. 1–3, 6–8, 12. A leading naturalist summarizes his views.
Aristotle, *Nicomachaean Ethics*, Book I. A classic naturalism.
B. de Spinoza, *Ethics*, Bk. I, appendix; Bk. III, Prop. 9, Note. Another classic statement.
C. I. Lewis, *An Analysis of Knowledge and Valuation* (La Salle, Ill.: Open Court Publishing Co., 1946), chaps. 12, 13, 16, 17. A hedonist analysis of "desirable."
———, *The Ground and Nature of the Right* (New York: Columbia University Press, 1955).
E. Westermarck, *Ethical Relativity* (New York: Harcourt, Brace & Company, 1932), chap. 5. A relativistic subjectivist.
R. Firth, "Ethical Absolutism and the Ideal Observer," *Philosophy and Phenomenological Research*, XII (1952), 317–45.
———, "Discussion: Reply to Professor Brandt," *ibid.*, XV (1955), 414–421. Excellent statement of the ideal observer theory.
F. C. Sharp, *Good Will and Ill Will* (Chicago: University of Chicago Press, 1950), pp. 156–62.
———, "Voluntarism and Objectivity in Ethics," *Philosophical Review*, L (1941), 253–67. Another form of ideal observer theory.

[27] For a discussion of other arguments of this type, see Jonathan Harrison, "Empiricism in Ethics," *Philosophical Quarterly*, II (1952), 289–306.

F. C. Sharp, "Hume's Ethical Theory and its Critics," *Mind*, XXX (1921), 40–56, 151–171. Analysis of Hume as being an adherent of ideal observer theory.

G. E. Moore, *Principia Ethica* (Cambridge, Eng.: Cambridge University Press, 1929), pp. 1–21. A famous and highly influential criticism of naturalism.

——, *Ethics* (Oxford: Oxford University Press, 1912), chaps. 3 and 4. A criticism of relativistic subjectivism.

A. C. Ewing, *The Definition of Good* (New York: The Macmillan Company, 1947), chaps. 1 and 2. A survey of criticisms of types of naturalism.

——, *Ethics* (London: English Universities Press, 1953), chap. 6. A more elementary survey of criticism.

——, "Subjectivism and Naturalism in Ethics," reprinted in W. Sellars and J. Hospers, *Readings in Ethical Theory* (New York: Appleton-Century-Crofts, Inc., 1952).

B. Russell, *The Elements of Ethics*, reprinted in Sellars and Hospers, *Readings in Ethical Theory*, pp. 1–17. Criticism of naturalisms.

——, *Human Society in Ethics and Politics*. (London: George Allen and Unwin, Ltd., 1954), Pt. I, especially chap. 9.

W. D. Ross, *Foundations of Ethics* (Oxford: Clarendon Press, 1939), chaps. 2 and 11. Another criticism of naturalism.

R. M. Hare, *The Language of Morals* (Oxford: Clarendon Press, 1952), chap. 5. Criticism of naturalism from noncognitivist point of view.

J. Harrison, "Empiricism in Ethics," *Philosophical Quarterly*, II (1952), 289–306. A reply to the standard criticisms of naturalism.

W. K. Frankena, "The Naturalistic Fallacy," reprinted in Sellars and Hospers, *Readings in Ethical Theory*. An examination of Moore's argument.

R. B. Brandt, "The Status of Empirical Assertion Theories in Ethics," *Mind*, LXI (1952), 458–79. A reply to some recent criticisms of naturalism.

Paul Edwards, *The Logic of Moral Discourse* (Glencoe, Ill.: Free Press, 1955), chap. 2. A criticism of some types of subjectivism, especially Westermarck's.

C. L. Stevenson, "Moore's Arguments against Certain Forms of Ethical Naturalism," in P. Schilpp (ed.), *The Philosophy of G. E. Moore* (Evanston, Ill.: Northwestern University Press, 1942). A defense of subjectivist theories.

8

Nonnatural Properties

Of the other major theories about the meaning and justification of ethical statements, the only one comparable with naturalism in length of tradition and number of historical advocates is *nonnaturalism*. So, here we shall begin our quest for a more convincing theory.

The theory was first clearly and fully stated by Richard Price in 1758, but its roots go back much further, for the theories of many much earlier figures resemble nonnaturalism more closely than they resemble any of the other major theories. Plato, for instance, seems close to nonnaturalism when, in the *Republic*, he describes the vision of the Good. In the present century, nonnaturalism has been very popular; in the 1930's, it was probably the prevailing view in the leading universities, although since midcentury its influence has been on the wane, and today it is probably the least widely accepted of the major theories.

1. THE CARDINAL TENETS OF NONNATURALISM

Nonnaturalists usually begin their books with a criticism of naturalism and supernaturalism. It is not surprising that they employ this strategy, for they share with naturalism and supernaturalism the view that ethical utterances make statements that are either true or false. What they wish to do is merely to quarrel with the particular account of *what* ethical utterances mean, offered by naturalists and supernaturalists; and then to offer us nonnaturalism as the alternative. Let us formulate the outline of the nonnaturalist argument.

The nonnaturalist begins, we have suggested, as we have done. He examines the supernaturalist and the naturalist proposals about the meaning of ethical terms. He concludes, as we have done, and on account of arguments substantially like those mentioned, that these proposals are unsatisfactory. We should notice, incidentally, that his conclusion on this implies that ethical words cannot refer to *observable* properties; thus "desirable" and "right" are not like "red" or "loud." Why? If they did, we could observe directly whether ethical statements are true or false; then naturalism would be true (since naturalism merely asserts that the meaning or reference of ethical terms is such that the truth of ethical statements can be assessed by direct observation or the methods of scientific inference).

At this point, the nonnaturalist makes a generalization. He says: *No definition of ethical terms, unless the defining phrase itself contains ethical terms (as in " 'x is my duty' means 'I am morally obligated, everything considered, to do x' "), is a correct reportive definition.*[1] This generalization has some weight, for the nonnaturalist has examined numerous proposed definitions and found them wanting. "Is it likely," he says in effect, "that others will be better when these have failed?" His generalization, of course, is not strictly *proved*, and all one need do to overturn it is to produce a definition that is a good one.

Still, proved or unproved, this is the *first thesis* of nonnaturalism: that ethical terms can be defined, if at all, only by phrases that themselves contain ethical terms, and that therefore they do not refer to observable properties. We shall be able to amplify this thesis further in a moment.

The *second thesis* of nonnaturalism is one that it shares, roughly, with naturalism: that ethical terms refer to properties. The nonnaturalist holds that most adults in most societies in some way understand, or are familiar with, ethical properties, just as adults who are not color-blind are familiar with the property *Red*. Moreover, just as most languages contain words that adults use to refer to *Red*, so most languages contain words that adults use to refer to ethical properties. Thus, we have "red," "rot," and "rouge," all referring to *Red* (or used to say that something is red); and we have "good," "gut," and "bon," all referring to *Good*. Nonnaturalists do *not* say that *all* languages have such terms. Moreover, children and primitive people may not be familiar with ethical properties and, hence, may not use words to refer to them, just as some people are color-blind and not familiar with *Red* and do not use "red" to refer to it, and just as others have never grasped the concept of an infinite number or a second derivative.

Why do nonnaturalists believe this second thesis? Historically, when nonnaturalism began as a theory, no one had thought to question it, at least not in an influential way. The competitors of nonnaturalism, historically, were naturalism and supernaturalism, which shared the thesis. At a later stage, when the thesis had been emphatically questioned by noncognitivists, the nonnaturalists rose vigorously to its defense. Also, it is a natural view to take that ethical terms refer to properties. At least, people do ordinarily think of ethical statements as being correct or incorrect; they think of ethical questions as having right answers.

---

[1] As we shall see in a moment, he actually goes further still, saying that some ethical terms cannot be defined *at all*. However, he offers no *argument* for this last statement.

Having stated this second thesis, we can now amplify the first one. Nonnaturalists say not only that ethical terms cannot be defined accurately except by phrases that contain other ethical terms; they hold that *some* ethical terms cannot be *defined at all*, because the property to which they refer is *simple and unanalyzable*. They think that some ethical terms designate properties unlike *Square* (which can be analyzed as being a plane figure bounded by four straight lines of equal length, meeting at right angles) but like *Yellow* (which cannot be analyzed in a comparable way). Like *Yellow*, they think, the property designated by some ethical terms is simple. Hence, although there may be synonyms for such ethical words—for example, "good" is a synonym of "valuable" and "desirable"—these words cannot be defined in the sense that there is some more analytic, more explicative phrase that means the same—as there is in the case of "square." Now, *other* ethical terms, they think, *can* be defined, as "square" can be. But when they can, one of the indefinable ethical terms must appear in the definition. Thus, for example, it may be said that "right" can be defined roughly as "will produce the most *good*," just as it may be said that "square" can be defined if one has the term "straight line" to begin with, but "straight line" cannot itself be defined. Thus, it is argued that the word "right" can be defined, if one has "good" to start with. Nonnaturalists disagree among themselves about *which* term is absolutely indefinable: Some say "good," others "obligatory" or "right," still others "fitting." They also differ as to whether only one, or more than one, ethical term is absolutely indefinable. What is common, however, is the complex thesis that (1) at least one ethical term is absolutely indefinable, (2) that a correct analytic definition of any other ethical term must contain one of these absolutely indefinable terms (at least if it is complete), and (3) ethical terms do not refer to observable properties. Such is the *amplified* first thesis of the nonnaturalist.

This nonnaturalist thesis, including the proposal that at least one ethical term is absolutely indefinable, does not *follow* from the proposition that all definitions of ethical terms are unsatisfactory unless the defining phrase contains an ethical term and that ethical terms do not designate observable properties. (The latter, incidentally, is all that is supported by the criticisms of naturalism.) But if one grants this proposition, and the view that ethical terms are property-referring, the amplified thesis has at least plausibility.

Surprisingly enough, it is consistent to assert both the two theses of nonnaturalism, as stated, but to deny that anything in fact has the properties referred to by ethical terms. So, we must add, as a *third thesis* of nonnaturalism, that some things *do* have these properties, and that at least sometimes *we know that they do*. Some philosophers have accepted the first two theses of nonnaturalism, but have rejected the third. Richard Robinson, a philosopher at Oxford, has done just that; he has proposed that the nonnaturalist is right in thinking that ethical terms are indefinable and refer to unobservable properties. But, he says, it just so happens that nothing ever has such properties. His theory is that ethical terms

> name unanalysable qualities belonging to certain acts or objects in complete independence of all human feelings and thoughts. [But] . . . In this descriptive use the ethical words involve an error, because nothing has such an unanalyzable independent attribute as they name.[2]

The following three theses, then, are the common core of nonnaturalism: (1) that ethical terms are indefinable (etc.) as stated; (2) that they refer to properties; and (3) that some things have these properties, and are known to have them.

In the previous chapter nonnaturalism was classified as *realist, objectivist,* and *absolutist* in certain specified senses. We can now see why. Since the nonnaturalist thinks that the basic ethical terms are absolutely indefinable, he cannot hold that ethical statements containing them logically imply anything about minds. Hence, his view of these basic statements is not mentalist. Theoretically, his definition of the nonbasic ethical terms could be such that ethical statements containing them are construed as implying something about minds; but in fact this is not the case.[3] So, the nonnaturalist view is realist; and as such, *a fortiori* it is objectivist. Nor is a nonnaturalist a relativist—certainly not about the basic ethical terms—for if two individuals are both talking about an absolutely indefinable property, and one asserts that an act or situation has the property, and the other denies this, how could more than one of them be correct? The matter could be different with ethical terms that are not basic; but in fact there are no relativistic forms of nonnaturalism.

The nonnaturalist theory is easy to state. Unfortunately, when we begin trying to identify these simple properties, it is less easy to believe. Perhaps the central difficulty is this: The nonnaturalist denies that ethical properties can be *observed* in the way in which we can observe sense qualities like *Yellow*. This fact raises two questions: (1) How do we ever get the concepts of these simple unobservable properties? Ordinarily, we suppose, people get their concepts of properties either through definitions or being

---

[2] "The Emotive Theory of Ethics," Aristotelian Society, Supplementary volume XXII (1948), 83–84.

Robinson later goes on to argue, apparently, for a further thesis that raises amusing logical questions. He says (*ibid.,* p. 87), "we use it [an ethical term] to mean an attribute entirely independent of minds, but *there is no such attribute.*" (Italics mine.)

In these words Mr. Robinson argues, as it were, not only that there are no perfect circles (although we use "perfect circle" to refer to Perfect Circularity), but that there is no such thing even as Perfect Circularity. Some logicians would balk at this, saying that if we use "perfectly circular" with meaning, there must be such an attribute as Perfect Circularity, even if there are no perfect circles.

[3] In the case of some nonnaturalists, there might seem to be an exception to this. For example, A. C. Ewing defines "good" as meaning approximately "a fitting object of a pro-attitude on the part of someone." But a careful examination of the definition of "mentalist" (p. 153) will reveal that this definition does not qualify as mentalist.

shown samples. But these ethical properties are simple (cannot be explained by definitions); and they cannot be observed. Isn't it as absurd to say that we have such concepts as to say that we have the concept of some color that human beings are incapable of seeing—having it just as we have the concept of *Yellow?* (2) What reason can we ever have for believing an ethical statement? for saying we know something has an ethical property? Since ethical facts are unobservable, we cannot be aware of them by inspection, as we can be aware of a sunset. Further, since ethical terms are not definable naturalistically, ethical statements cannot be supported logically by any statements drawn from observation or science (pp. 38–40).

Nonnaturalists must face these questions. However, there is no common nonnaturalist answer to them. There are two major types of proposal, which we shall call respectively the "Rational Insight" theory and the "Intuition" theory. It is possible to combine the two answers in various ways. Moreover, some nonnaturalists do not appear to distinguish the theories as clearly as they should and can hardly be said to have any definite theory on the point at all.

Rational Insight. The first theory offers no *explanation* how we come to have ethical concepts. It simply says that we do have them, and that we must recognize that the human mind just does have the capacity to acquire concepts in ways other than by being shown samples or by being given definitions. However, ethical concepts, it is asserted, are not the only ones that show that we have this power. There are others (although one might question whether they really are concepts of simple unobservable properties or relations): for instance, concepts of the possible and the impossible, causal necessity, geometrical points or lines, and physical "thingness."

In answer to the question of how we can know the truth of ethical statements, the theory first asserts that the fundamental principles of ethics are *necessarily* true. They are, it is said, like the principles of logic or mathematics. Or, more exactly, they are like the propositions that space has three dimensions, that a cube has twelve edges, that anything that is red is colored, that anything that is red has spatial extension, that events in nature are related by natural law to preceding events, and so on. All these propositions, it is said, are not only true; unlike the proposition that the diameter of the Earth is less than 20,000 miles, they *could not* be false. Now, the theory goes on, in the case of necessary propositions it is possible for a rational person to see, once the meaning of the proposition has been fully grasped, that the proposition cannot be false. Once one sees what "red" means and what "colored" means, one sees that any red thing *must* be colored. Perhaps we cannot *explain* how or why the mind has such a capacity; but it does have it. The same is true for ethical knowledge. It is a necessary truth that a state of knowledge is preferable to a state of ignorance, other things being the same. It is a necessary truth that others have no more of an obligation to take an interest in my welfare, than I have to take an interest in theirs.

Once rational minds have understood these propositions, they can see them to be true. Knowledge is possible. We cannot explain this further, but to deny it would be absurd.

Of course, ethical knowledge often does not involve formulating any general proposition. We do not say to ourselves: "Clearly it is universally and necessarily true that lies are wrong; therefore this lie is wrong." But, although we do not formulate the general proposition, we see that the property of this act, that of being a lie, *involves* its being wrong. This act, we see, *as being a lie*, must be wrong. There is insight into the necessary presence of ethical properties, in particular situations, even when no universal truths are formulated.

Intuition. Many nonnaturalists, however, regard the rational insight theory as overly intellectualistic. Very often, they say, when we are most sure of ethical truth—for example, when we are quite clear what our own obligation is—we not only do not and cannot formulate any applicable general principle, but we also are not clear *exactly why* our obligation is what it is. We know that we have an obligation, but we do not have rational insight into its deriving from certain particular aspects of the situation. Moreover, sensitive feelings appear to be an indispensable part or precondition of our awareness of the ethical facts. It is symptomatic that we talk of "feeling that we have an obligation" or that we talk of "moral sensitivity." Ethical awareness is more like sensing or perceiving or feeling.

Writers of this persuasion speak of ethical knowing as "nonperceptual intuition" or "emotional intuition," that is, direct awareness of particular ethical facts that differs from sensory awareness in the absence of a sensory presentation like a color patch or a sound. When we *see* a dog, we have perceptual intuition, in the sense that we see that there is a dog *via* sensory presentation, a visual appearance. In nonperceptual intuition, there is awareness of particular facts ("That lie was wrong") but without any sensory presentation, although there is an analogue to this in the emotional experience that ordinarily accompanies ethical experience.

The doctrine that there is nonperceptual intuition of ethical facts doubtless sounds mysterious, but intuitionists urge that ethical intuition is by no means unique. It is asserted that we have comparable intuitive awareness of facts in the past, of the inner experiences of other persons (which of course we do not see), of an object's causal efficacy when a flying stone makes a window shatter. So, it is said, we have nonperceptual intuition with us all the time. There are many things in nature that cannot be seen with the eyes, but can be with the "mind's eye."

Nonnaturalists of either variety do not claim infallibility. They are apt to say that some moral points are crystal clear (and we should all tend to agree with this); but other matters they concede are very murky. One of the most eminent nonnaturalists has remarked that, in complex situations, whether we apprehend our duty aright is very largely a matter of good fortune.

Nonnaturalism, then, is a theory consisting in the three theses cited earlier, plus one or the other (or some combination of both) of these two views, either the Rational Insight theory or Intuitionism.

2. PUZZLES FOR NONNATURALISTS

It is not hard to see what motivates belief in the nonnaturalist theory. People are convinced that ethical statements are property-affirming, and that we know such statements to be true. Furthermore, they are convinced that naturalistic definitions have not been made to work. The theory is a structure elaborated to explain how these facts can all be true.

However, although it is easy to see the *motivation* of nonnaturalists, it is difficult to see how they can believe the theory as a whole. *Do* we actually have any concept of a simple unobservable ethical property? *Do* we have intuitive knowledge that things have it? *Do* we see the necessity of an ethical truth in whatever way we see that anything red is necessarily colored? For our part, the answer to all these questions is simply: Definitely not. And perhaps that is reason enough for dismissing the nonnaturalist theory.

Needless to say, however, these reflections will not convince nonnaturalists. They, too, have thought about these questions and, surprising though it may be, have decided that the answer to them (or to at least two of the three) is affirmative. They concede, of course, that the issue is not a simple one and that first impressions are apt to be unfavorable to their view. If we are to convince nonnaturalists, then, we must produce some arguments, some difficulties that cannot be so easily ignored.

There is one "argument" of which we shall not avail ourselves. Some philosophers would dismiss nonnaturalism at once because it contradicts the basic principles of "empiricism": the principles that no statement is meaningful if it cannot be translated into the language of the empirical sciences, and that no statement can be known to be true unless it is true by definition or confirmable by observation after the manner of confirmation in the empirical sciences. The reason we shall not use this "argument" is that the nonnaturalist is quite deliberately challenging the principles of empiricism; he knows that his doctrine is nonempiricist and he questions the truth of the empiricist principles. We would beg the question if we dismissed nonnaturalism because it is in conflict with these principles—unless, of course, empiricist philosophers have (as they do not) a demonstration of their theory, using agreed premises as a basis.

But there is one point, related to the contentions of empiricism, that we wish to make. Nonnaturalists say that adults in civilized societies have "concepts" of unobservable, simple ethical properties. One would like, however, to have them explain *in what sense* there are concepts of these properties. We do not have concepts of these properties, of course, in the sense of ability to conjure up an *image* of them, as we can in the case of colors or shapes. Is it, then, that we know what experience will be like, if something has an ethical property—as we know what experience will be like, if there is a crash of thunder? No. Nor do we have concepts of them in the sense in which we have concepts of scientific properties like being malleable or a conductor of electricity; nor in the sense in which we have concepts of electrons, unconscious processes, and comparable "theoretical constructs." The alleged concept of a nonnatural property is not connected with experience, does not function to guide expectations, is not part of a theoretical system with consequences predictive of observation, in the way in which this is true of the concepts of empirical science.[4] So, we repeat, although admitting that there are ethical *words*, we ask the nonnaturalist: *In what sense* are there concepts of nonnatural properties corresponding to these words? We doubt whether any such sense can be identified.

The most vulnerable point of nonnaturalist doctrine, however, is the epistemology, the theory of how we know or are justified in believing ethical statements. We shall devote the remainder of this chapter to the profusion of nonnaturalist difficulties on this score. We shall deal with the alternative theories separately, beginning with Intuition.

Intuition. We have seen that some nonnaturalists believe that ethical statements are confirmable by appeal to intuition in the sense of nonperceptual awareness of particular ethical facts, rather like perceptual awareness that there is a dog at the gate, but without any analogous sensory presentation. This view suffers from four types of major difficulties.

1. The theory postulates a *direct* awareness of ethical fact, but there are numerous facts suggesting that any awareness of ethical fact somehow must be *indirect*.

Let us begin with the decisions, acts, and states of mind of *other* persons. Do we have intuitions of their ethical properties? We do not *perceive* these things; if we know about them it is because we can draw inferences from behavior that we do perceive. Since we do not preceive the decisions, acts, or events themselves, it is odd to say that we are directly aware of their qualities. We concede that it is not contradictory. But there is a further point: It is quite plain that our moral estimates of the deeds or mental states of others are based on our *beliefs* about the nature of these deeds or mental states. If A and B are estimating the morality of an act by C, and A thinks C's act was motivated in one way whereas B thinks it was motivated in another, the estimates vary correspondingly. The estimates

[4] Cf. C. G. Hempel, *Fundamentals of Concept Formation in Empirical Science,* International Encyclopedia of Unified Science, vol. II, No. 7 (Chicago: University of Chicago Press, 1952); also H. H. Price, *Thinking and Experience* (London: Hutchinson's University Library, 1953); B. F. Skinner, *Verbal Behavior* (New York: Appleton-Century-Crofts, Inc., 1957).

do not suggest a direct awareness of the moral qualities of C's act, independent of *beliefs* about the act's nonethical nature.

It is more plausible to claim intuitive awareness of the ethical qualities of our *own* acts or states of mind; at least, in this case we do have inspective awareness of the acts and states of mind. But it is dubious whether we have a right to make a sharp distinction between awareness of ethical properties in our own case and that in the case of others; for we do not *seem* to have more direct awareness of the ethical qualities of our own acts. Moreover, there is still ground for doubt about the directness of awareness; our estimates even in our own case seem to be based on our beliefs about the nonethical qualities of our acts or states of mind. If we think our act was unselfishly motivated, our moral estimate is high; when we see later that our motivation was really selfish, we reverse the moral estimate. Or we may value a state of mind, thinking it a state of knowledge; later we see that our state of mind was one of unfounded and erroneous belief, and again we reverse the estimate. We should not expect this dependence, this error arising from erroneous factual belief, if there were direct awareness of the real ethical properties of a state of mind.

Even less plausible is a claim that we have direct awareness of our *duty*. How much easier it would be to find what our duty is if all that were required were an inward inspection! Everyone knows that ascertaining one's duty is often a complicated matter, involving scrutiny of the probable results of various courses of action, and review of various aspects of the situation, such as promises made, benefactions accepted, and so forth. Why should this be, if the direct awareness theory is correct? It may be replied that at least we can have direct awareness of our several obligations (for example, to keep our promises, show gratitude, and so forth) even if not of our over-all duty in a complex situation. Even so, we obviously know the nature and direction of our obligations not directly or, as it were, out of nowhere, but only from awareness of the situation. For instance, if we know that we have an obligation to pay $5 to A, it is because we know we have borrowed $5; we do not just suddenly become aware of an obligation to pay someone $5!

2. Let us recall the ethical problem of the parked-car episode (p. 117). Then, let us ask ourselves at what point, if any, in this episode there was an intuition. Was it when an impulse to stop was first felt, and was the intuition going on as long as the motivation to stop was manifesting itself, including the guilt feelings later? Or was it rather when the writer decided he really, everything considered, ought to stop? Are there intuitions when one is debating a general issue as an onlooker (for example, U.S. foreign policy), or only when one is faced with making a personal decision? If there is direct awareness of ethical properties, one might expect that there would be moments in moral deliberation when it seems as if a curtain is withdrawn and one sees the facts directly. But this is absurd; there is no

such moment, and we do not know how to answer any question about when one's intuitions occurred.

The serious consequences of this inability to identify intuitive experiences should not be overlooked. It is crucial to the intuition theory to say we are *familiar* with ethical properties; for it is this familiarity with them that explains how ethical words can refer to them. But if we cannot remember incidents of "seeing" the properties, how can we say we *are* familiar with them? If we could not remember what a red thing looks like, we would not say we were familiar with the property *Red;* and if we cannot remember what it is like to be aware of reprehensibility, how can we say that we are familiar with the property *Moral Badness?*[5]

3. The theory that there is intuitive ethical knowledge, nonperceptual awareness of particular ethical facts, has trouble with the obvious fact that equally conscientious people have conflicting convictions about what one's duty is, what one's obligations are, and what is intrinsically worthwhile.

If there are such differences, the intuitionist must answer two queries. First, how is it possible for there to be such conflicts, if conscientious, civilized adults have direct awareness of real ethical qualities and relations? Second, if there are such conflicts and the intuition theory is true, it must be that there are pseudo intuitions that may easily be mistaken for real intuitions. Is there any way of identifying a real intuition, so that we may found our moral thinking on knowledge and not on error?

The intuitionist may question whether there is a problem here, on the ground that it has not yet been clearly established that there are *basic* conflicts of opinion in ethics. But is this objection to the point? Mr. A, an Eskimo, drops his aged father through a hole in the ice. Mr. B, a British bystander, is horrified. Mr. A thinks his action right; Mr. B thinks it unjustified. If there is really direct awareness of right and wrong in particular cases, how is this possible? It is not relevant that Mr. B may not fully appreciate Mr. A's economic predicament, the difficulty of transporting an aged father across the ice for long distances, the monotony of the father's helpless existence. If there is right and wrong there that is open to direct inspection, as the theory says there is, the differences in understanding the situation should make no difference.

But let us waive this point, conceding it to the intuitionist. Let us agree that there are problems only if there are "basic" conflicts of opinion about ethics, and let us confine our attention to these. So far we have claimed only one point of basic disagreement as clearly decided by the evidence—about the morality of causing animals pain. But if we ask ourselves whether the preponderance of evidence suggests basic difference *only* on this point, we must answer that the *preponderance* of the evidence suggests no such

[5] See the critique by P. F. Strawson, "Ethical Intuitionism," *Philosophy,* XXIV (1949), reprinted in Sellars and Hospers, *Readings in Ethical Theory* (New York: Appleton-Century-Crofts, Inc., 1952), pp. 250–59.

thing. Quite the contrary, for it is as hard to demonstrate identity of opinion about basic principles as it is to demonstrate difference. Furthermore, there are only a few types of case for which the rough evidence strongly suggests identity of basic ethical principle throughout the world: such as the prohibition of sexual relations within the primary family; or the prohibition of killing or assaulting adults who are members of one's own society, who are sane, healthy, and guilty of no crime, and whose continued life is not in conflict with the needs of society. On other matters, there seems prima facie to be disagreement: about the morality of suicide, about the precise conditions in which a promise may be broken, about what is owed to the aged and infirm, about to what extent criminals should be treated kindly and when it is permissible to put a criminal to death, about when it is a moral obligation to render assistance to strangers in need. Now, it is *possible* that much more evidence would show that, in many or even all of these areas, the apparent differences of ethical opinion are not basic differences of opinion at all. At present, however, we certainly do not have the evidence to give serious support to such an interpretation. The available evidence suggests that there are more than a few basic differences.

Let us assume, then, that the intuitionist must concede that there are fairly numerous cases of such differences.[6] In fact, it is doubtful whether any nonnaturalist actually denies this. Then we must press our questions.

The first was: How are these differences possible, if there is direct awareness of ethical properties and relations? In order to answer the question, the intuitionist must and does rely on analogies with other "faculties." The organ of intuition, it is said, may be defective, just as the eye is defective in the color-blind. Or, the organ of intuition is undeveloped, just as the capacity for abstract thought is underdeveloped in primitive societies where there is no stimulus to think abstractly. Or, it is suggested, similarity to past occasions when there was real intuition may lead us, through association, to think mistakenly that we are having an intuition now.

Thus, the intuitionist can answer our first question. Ethical intuition is a function *both* of the real ethical qualities and relations of events and also of the state of the intuitive "organ"—just as the appearance of a physical thing is a function of its qualities, and also a function of the brain and nervous system of the perceiver. What we are aware of, then, is "ethical qualities as they appear to us," not ethical qualities as they are. This is what we might expect, on an intuitive theory.[7]

Now we must face our second question. How, in principle, are we to identify *correct, veridical* intuitions?

[6] The evidence is discussed more fully later (pp. 285–87).

[7] This is an odd situation, however, for the intuition theory holds that there *is* no appearance, no "look of things," no sensory presentation, in the case of ethical intuition. Does it make *sense*, then, to say that what we are aware of is "ethical qualities as they appear to us"?

Let us first make a distinction. We do not for a moment wish to question that our ethical experiences—our qualms of conscience, our "feelings of obligation," our preferences—somehow function as a source of ethical knowledge. We believe (and in Chapter 10 shall try to show) that it is possible to distinguish the justified among these from the unjustified. What we question is a very special claim.

The nonnaturalist thinks that in order to know our duty (and so on) we must find out whether certain events have certain unobservable properties. How? Sometimes we have, the intuitionist nonnaturalist says, direct awareness of them; but he concedes that there are sometimes illusory, pseudo intuitions, just as there are illusory sense appearances and hallucinations. The nonnaturalist is, therefore, faced with the job of determining which things have the unobservable properties on the basis of a collection of "ostensible intuitions," some of them certainly mistaken. What he must do, apparently, is show by deductive or inductive reasoning, or otherwise (presumably in a fashion similar to what is possible for the case of sense perception), what the real ethical facts are, and thereby identify some ostensible intuitions as veridical. Now, given this formulation of the task, can the job be done?[8]

Unfortunately nonnaturalists have not, at least in their published work, given the matter serious attention. There is discussion enough of how differences of opinion about ethics could arise, even if *some* ethical intuitions are veridical, on account of various defects of the intuitive organ. But how, if we know only that many ostensible intuitions are illusory but do not know *which ones*, we are to identify the veridical ones and base ethical knowledge thereupon, is a topic that has received little attention. Usually it is simply assumed that somehow we know that *our* ethical beliefs, or at least the consistent ones among them, or at the very least, the ethical beliefs common to the men who are best and wisest (how do we identify these?) in the Western tradition, are veridical; and a start is made from there. But how is this assumption, this procedure, to be justified?

It is a fact that no nonnaturalist *has* given a substantial theory of how one might move logically from ostensible intuitions (given we are informed how to identify these) to an identification of veridical intuitions or

---

[8] The intuitionist might say that he will do exactly what we advocate doing in Chapter 10, except that he will write "intuition" wherever we write "attitude" or "feeling." But it is one thing to try to show that some human attitudes are justified, and another thing to show that some ostensible intuitions are really views of a nonnatural fact. Reasons that can be adduced in favor of a certain procedure for picking out justified human attitudes cannot be offered in favor of regarding certain ostensible intuitions as veridical awareness of nonnatural facts.

Since we have restricted our attention to cases where there is "basic" disagreement, namely, cases where differences of "intuition" cannot be traced to different understandings of the facts of the case, it will not be possible to identify the pseudo intuition simply by enlarging or refining the person's view of the facts about the particular situation being assessed morally.

to objective ethical knowledge. But *could* such a theory be given? This is a teasing question.

It may be said that we can determine which intuitions are illusory much as we determine which visual appearances are illusions and which are veridical appearances of physical things as they are. Can we? Take for instance the Müller-Lyer illusion, in which two straight lines of equal length look to be of markedly different lengths. How do we decide they are really the same? Well, we measure both; or we fold the paper so that one line is superimposed on the other. This is not like comparing our intuitions with the intuitions of the "wisest and best," because everyone will see the same illusion. However, it may be said it is like comparing one intuition with the total mass of our intuitions and seeing that the illusory one is inconsistent with the vast majority. Isn't it a matter of checking one visual appearance for consistency with other visual appearances? If so, then isn't the logic of determining which one is illusory the same for visual appearances as for ethical intuitions?

If the logic of the two cases is the same, then we should be able to convince a man with a (supposed) moral "illusion" that he is suffering from an illusion, in at least roughly the same way as we can convince him that the Müller-Lyer illusion is an illusion. Can we? Suppose someone insists that the Müller-Lyer illusion is not an illusion, that the lengths of the two lines are really different. There are several things we may do to convince him. (1) We can point out that if they are different, then he must say either that a ruler changes its length while being moved, or he is having an illusion when he thinks the ends of the line coincide with certain points on the ruler. If he seriously supports either of these hypotheses, he can be faced with numerous objections. (2) We can cover up the arrowpoints at the ends of the lines, and as a result the lines will look the same in length. Will he maintain that they change their lengths when we remove the covers? If he does, he is defending a principle in physics that will be hard to support. (3) We can show him many examples of the influence of the context of the stimulus object on appearances, and we can tell him of some interesting theories of the physiology of perception that seem to be steps in the direction of an explanation. It is hard to imagine that our argument will be ineffective.

Now let us consider, as a parallel case, a disagreement of "intuitions" in ethics, on a point of basic principle. Let us suppose Mrs. A, who is very unhappy with her husband and is planning a suit for divorce, is discussing the matter with her sister, who is familiar with the problem, so that there is no disagreement between them about the facts of the case. But the sister thinks the contemplated suit for divorce would be wrong, that Mrs. A is obligated to stay with her husband—for the reason of principle that promises are sacred, that the marriage vow was a solemn vow "until death do us part." It seems that there are different "intuitions" about the obligations of a person who has taken a marriage vow, and whose reasons for breaking it are those Mrs. A has. How will the sister show that Mrs. A's "intuitions" are only pseudo intuitions? Can she produce conclusive reasoning, parallel to that available in the case of the Müller-Lyer illusion?

We cannot *demonstrate* that *no* such reasoning can be produced. But we can say that no nonnaturalist has proposed a description of such possible reasoning up to now, and we are unable to think of a way in which it could be done. Thus, until some nonnaturalist shows how pseudo intuitions can be identified, what marks them as such, his theory does not show how ethical knowledge can be distinguished from mere belief.

4. The intuitionist view is incompatible with all the major *theories* of psychology. Let us revert to our parked-car episode. Presumably the intuitionist will say that at some point during this episode there was an intuition of an objective ethical fact. *Something* in the experience is presumably to be *explained* by this—just as the psychological fact that I see a typewriter now is explained by the fact that there is a typewriter in front of me, and by the fact that my sense organs are in good condition and my eyes wide open. So the intuitionist will say: The explanation of the conviction that there was an obligation to do a certain thing is that it *is* obligatory to do that thing, and that one's intuitive organs are in good condition. Now, what would the psychologist say to this? Hull's theory makes use of no such assumption; he supposes that the perception of the parked-car situation activated a secondary drive, itself a result of conditioning, to give aid to a person believed possibly to need assistance. What would Freud say? His theory, too, makes no use of intuitions. His proposal is doubtless not too clear, but substantially he would say that perception of the parked-car situation aroused values or censuring attitudes, which have been learned by identification from one's father (and so forth). Nor is the Gestaltist much more sympathetic. It is true that the Gestaltist will say that a person experiences "vectors," "demands" or "requiredness," seeming to come from the situation and not from personal need. But if one asks the Gestaltists *why* there are these vectors, his reply is not that there *are* requirednesses with which our intuitive faculties acquaint us, but instead that there are electrochemical forces in the brain that are represented in consciousness in these experiences. The experience of obligation is no more "objective" than are the constellations of the stars, which we know are a result of visual grouping that has nothing to do with spatial proximity of the stars themselves.

The intuitionist may perhaps best reply: All this is only speculative theory; my view is sounder.

Suppose we grant, for the moment, that psychological "theories" of the genesis of values are speculative. But can intuitionism stand up even against the simplest observations, the simplest empirically-founded generalizations, related to the genesis of ethical convictions?

What is the intuitionist's explanation of the correlation between the ethical opinions of parents and those of their children? or of the influence of prestige suggestion? We do not know; intuitionists have not concerned themselves with such matters. Again, the evidence seems to show that thinking (trying to order one's facts and ethical opinions in a coherent logical system), personal interests and needs, and sympathetic reactions affect our ethical beliefs and judgments. What will the intuitionist say to this? We do not know. The theory does not tell us how to identify an ostensible intuition, so that we are at a loss how to decide whether the psychologist's evidence is to be taken as a fact about influences on intuitions or about something else. The intuitionist might say that ethical opinions like those tested in these empirical inquiries are the mere periphery of ethical experience, whereas intuitions are quite another matter. These inquiries investigated opinions about large impersonal issues, whereas intuitions occur only in connection with real personal decisions. We grant that this distinction is possible. However, one must doubt the wisdom of such a separation, for convictions about large issues like racial integration are not insulated from personal decisions about how to vote, whether to patronize a local barber who practices discrimination, or how to advise our daughter what to do if someone from another race invites her to dance. It *looks*, then, as if the many different factors described somehow influence the center of our moral thinking. Shall we say they influence "intuitions"; and if so, how are we to conceive of this? Or, if not, are we not suggesting that "intuitions" have an incredibly insulated place in moral experience?

Rational Insight. The second nonnaturalist view of ethical knowing likens ethical insight to mathematical knowledge, or better, to "seeing" that anything red will be colored or spread out spatially, or that anything spread out spatially will have some shape. Such propositions, according to the nonnaturalist, are like substantive ethical propositions, not true by definition alone; but neither do we know them just by observation and inductive generalization, as we do statements of the empirical sciences. Rather we have insight into necessity; we can just see, when we reflect, that something red could not fail to be colored or extended spatially; or that something spread out spatially could not fail to have some shape. The same capacity for insight is important in ethics.

The Rational Insight theory, then, unlike Intuitionism, does not assume perception-like awareness of particular ethical facts.[9] It differs from Intuitionism in another way that is likely to be overlooked. It is natural to interpret the intuitionist as holding that intuition is a highly frequent affair in human experience; possibly he thinks we have intuitions whenever we face an ethical problem seriously. But with the Rational Insight theory this

[9] The two theories can be combined. Just as (it is held) we can *observe* that red things are spread out spatially, and also can see that they could not fail to be spread out spatially, so it may be held that, say, there is intuitive awareness of the fact that this lie or that one is wrong, and also rational insight that it could not be otherwise.

may not be so. A proponent of this theory *may* say that we have rational ethical insights all the time, that whenever we "see" what our obligation is in a complex situation, we are having one. But he need not. He may hold merely that one *can* see the truth of the basic principles of ethics if one takes the trouble. He may hold—as Sidgwick did—that the ethical truths into which we can have insight are highly abstract, far removed from ordinary reflection.

Is the Rational Insight theory plausible?

1. When we reflect on ethical statements, we do not have an experience similar to the plausible cases of "insight into necessity" that we have listed.

Perhaps it is not *ever* plausible to say that we have "insight into the necessity" of some proposition. But let us not debate this; the issue is a large one. Let us rather simply consider one proposition: "If anything is red, it is spread out in space." (It is simpler to interpret this as referring to phenomenal or apparent color, and to phenomenal extension.) Let us concede, for the sake of the argument, that we have "insight into the necessity" of this proposition. What we want to know, then, is whether we can seriously claim that ethical reflection is like this "insight."

There are obvious differences. It is not possible to conceive what it would be like for something to be red but not be in any way spread out in space. Nobody contends it is. But is this true for ethical statements? We shall see that hedonists deny that knowledge is intrinsically worthwhile; but they do not say that nonhedonists are unable to conceive of what it would be like for knowledge to be intrinsically worthwhile.

Furthermore, there are in fact no serious disagreements about whether red things ever fail to be spatially spread out. In ethics, the contrary is the case.

Again, the proposition that all red things are spread out in space is concerned with two properties that are observable: being red, and being spatially spread out. Nonnaturalism holds this is not the case in ethics; no ethical properties are observable.

Our conclusion is that it is plausible to concede that there is "insight into necessity" in the case of the proposition that all red things are spread out spatially, and to refuse to classify ethical reflection as such "insight." The dissimilarities are substantial.

2. There is a more crucial difference between ethical reflection and the insight that red things must be spatially spread out.

Let us first observe that whenever something's having one property P requires that it have another property Q, then the general statement is true, "Anything that is P is Q." Conversely, if even a single thing that is P is not Q, evidently having the property P does *not* require having the property Q.

The nonnaturalist supposes that one or more natural properties of some-

thing require the ethical property, and that it is insight into this requirement that occurs in ethical reflection.

Now the first thing to notice is that *some* ethical properties, at least, are
totiresultant properties, that is, are dependent in some way not just on some
one or two nonethical properties of the event or action, but on an indefinite
number—whatever about the event or action is "ethically relevant." (If it
could be shown that only one sort of property is ethically relevant, of
course, this contention would be pointless.) Among these totiresultant
properties are those of being on balance *desirable*, and of being on balance
one's *duty* or *obligation*.

In the case of these totiresultant properties, it is not possible to pick out
some property or properties and say that the occurrence of the totiresultant
property was required by them. Clearly it was not: for they could have
been present, along with some further ethically relevant property, and
the totality might well not have been "desirable" or someone's "duty."
What requires that a whole event is on balance desirable is not any single
natural property of the event or even any complex of natural properties—
but only these *and the fact that no other ethically relevant properties were
present*. Thus, we cannot say, "Anything that is PQR is desirable"; the
most we can say is, "If anything is PQR and has no other ethically relevant
properties, then it is desirable." This is a very different thing indeed. To
this extent, there is a great dissimilarity between the insight into "Anything
red is extended" and these totiresultant properties, for sometimes, when
PQR is present the event will be desirable; but sometimes it will not be—
when some counteracting property is also present. How can it be said,
then, that we have insight into the natural properties of a thing necessitating
the ethical properties?

However, some ethical predicates are not totiresultant. At least, it has
often been argued that sometimes a single fact about a situation (for example, having made a promise) will establish *some obligation* to do a certain thing. It has often been argued, too, that sometimes a single fact about
a situation is at least *favorable* to its being desirable—is what has been called
a "good-making" element. Perhaps we can plausibly say that there is rational insight into the necessity of some propositions about such facts.

But there is a further difficulty. Such ethical principles are seldom simple. Consider promises, for instance. Is it really the case that *every* promise creates *some* obligation to fulfill it? Well, consider promises made under
duress, or promises made on the basis of a deliberate misrepresentation of
the facts by the person to whom the promise has been made. Obviously
such promises create no obligation. Take enjoyment as another example.
Is every kind of enjoyment good-making? Is sadistic pleasure so? This is
at least debatable. Or, take knowledge. It is often said that a state of knowledge is good-making. But is this true of *every* kind of knowledge? Is it
good-making to know the intimate details of the lives of others? Or, are

there no facts so insignificant that knowing them is not good-making at all?

Now perhaps we can formulate some plausible universal propositions here. Perhaps we can specify just exactly which kinds of promise create some obligation, and which ones not, and the same about which kinds of knowledge or pleasure are good-making. We shall not deny this, although it is doubtful whether we are currently in a position to state such propositions accurately.

But even if we can, the kind of reflection by which we arrive at them is wholly different from the kind of reflection by which we arrive at "If anything is red, it is spread out spatially." How do we decide what kind of promise really does create some obligation? We start out in reflection, with the simple statement that *all* promises do. Then we look for exception-types. We consult law books to find when contracts are regarded as null and void, when courts will refuse to enforce a contract. We try to remember cases when we made a promise and then felt no compunction about breaking it. Then, after deciding which cases strike us as real exceptions, we form a general statement with the proper qualifications. But we do not feel sure we have included all possible exceptions, or even, perhaps, that the exceptions allowed are really universally exceptions.

Now is this anything at all like the case of the spatial extension of red, except in one respect—that, in the end, after reflection, we have come to believe a universal proposition? It does not seem so. If the experience of "insight" in the color case is the paradigm that explains what it means to have "rational insight into necessity," it seems we should *not* say there is rational insight into necessity in the case of ethics—even for these properties that are not totiresultant.[10]

3. According to the Rational Insight theory, the source of ethical knowledge is rational insight. It is not necessarily claimed that ordinary mortals are having rational insights with every moral problem, or even that every mortal being has at least one sometime. The point is that intelligent people, who will be patient and think carefully, *can* see the necessity of ethical propositions.

But, in ethics, even the doctors disagree. Some say that character is an

---

[10] There is another objection along this line that is obviously fatal, if it is allowed. Suppose the Rational Insight philosopher says that what we can know by insight is the truth of statements like this: "If x has promised to do y, x is under *more* of an obligation to do y than he otherwise would have been." Now, P. F. Strawson (*op. cit.*, p. 256) has suggested in effect that we must construe this statement as follows: "If x has promised to do y, then x will more *frequently* be duty-bound to do y than he would otherwise have been," or perhaps "*Most* persons who make promises are duty-bound to keep them." Nobody would say that these statements can be known to be true by rational insight; they are not necessary statements at all. The nonnaturalist is caught, then, if he can be forced to concede that Strawson's proposals correctly explicate the meaning of the statement he says is necessary and can be known to be true by rational insight. But it is by no means obvious that the nonnaturalist need, or should, make such a concession.

intrinsic good; others deny it. Some say that a solemn promise creates some obligation irrespective of the effects of a breach of it on human welfare; others question this. Some say that no act is reprehensible if in all details it was causally determined by events or states of affairs in existence before it took place; others are quite unconvinced by such considerations.

It seems, then, that we must say that, if there are rational insights in ethics, there are also erroneous, pseudo insights. If so, the difficulties, then, of identifying veridical insights appear to be the same as those considered in connection with the Intuition theory. Knowing as we do that there are erroneous, pseudo insights, how shall we justify to ourselves our believing what we do believe, without some general theory enabling us to distinguish the veridical from the pseudo insights? Needless to say, no such general theory has been produced. The kind of advice usually offered us is this: "Be consistent" (but *which* of the inconsistent propositions shall we reject?) and "Agree with the consensus of the best people" (but who are they, and are they necessarily correct?). Surely this is not enough.

Perhaps the issue can be put in a simple question: Can the Rational Insight philosopher tell us how to distinguish between merely *believing a proposition strongly* and *having rational insight into its necessity?* Surely there must be a clear distinction if this theory of ethics is worth our time. But what exactly the difference is, these philosophers have never troubled to explain.

The fact that there is disagreement in ethics does *not* imply that there is not ethical knowledge. Far from it. The trouble arises in combining this fact with the Rational Insight theory, from the claim that the basis of ethical knowledge is rational insights into the necessary connection between unobservable simple ethical properties and nonethical properties, simple or complex. If it must be conceded that some or many of these elusive insights are mistaken, then we build our ethical knowledge on an unsound foundation, unless we have a justifiable method, consistent with our nonnaturalistic assumptions, for deciding which insights are veridical.

FURTHER READINGS

Richard Price, *Review of the Principal Questions of Morals*, partly reprinted in A. Selby-Bigge, *British Moralists* (Oxford: Clarendon Press, 1897), II, 105–84. A clear-headed classic figure.

Thomas Reid, *Essays on the Powers of the Human Mind* (Edinburgh: Bell and Bradfute, 1808), Essays on the Active Powers, III, Part III, chaps. 5 and 6; Essay V, chap. 1. Another important classical statement.

Plato, *Republic*, Bks. IV–VII.

G. E. Moore, *Philosophical Studies* (London: Routledge and Kegan Paul, Ltd., 1948), chap. 8.

———, in Paul Schilpp (ed.), *The Philosophy of G. E. Moore* (Evanston, Ill.: Northwestern University Press, 1942), pp. 535–611.

W. D. Ross, *The Right and the Good* (Oxford: Clarendon Press, 1930), pp. 39–41, 114–32.

——, *Foundations of Ethics* (Oxford: Clarendon Press, 1939), chaps. 1, 8, and 11.

C. D. Broad, *Examination of McTaggart's Philosophy*, vol. I (Cambridge, Eng.: Cambridge University Press, 1933), pp. 46–53.

——, *Five Types of Ethical Theory* (New York: Harcourt, Brace & Co., 1934), pp. 266–73.

——, "Is 'goodness' a name of a simple non-natural quality?" *Proceedings*, The Aristotelian Society, 1933–34, pp. 249–68.

——, "Some Reflections on Moral-Sense Theories in Ethics," *Proceedings*, The Aristotelian Society, 1944–45, pp. 131–66.

N. Hartmann, *Ethics*, vol. I (New York: The Macmillan Company, 1932), chaps. 14 and 16. The concept of emotional intuition.

A. C. Ewing, *The Definition of Good* (New York: The Macmillan Company, 1947), chap. 5. A contrast of types of nonnaturalist theory.

Paul Edwards, *The Logic of Moral Discourse* (Glencoe, Ill.: Free Press, Inc., 1955), chaps. 4, 9, and 10. A criticism.

Philip Rice, *On the Knowledge of Good and Evil* (New York: Random House, 1955), chap. 2. A summary and critique.

P. Nowell-Smith, *Ethics* (Baltimore: Penguin Books, Inc., 1954), chaps. 2–4. A criticism.

P. F. Strawson, "Ethical Intuitionism," reprinted in W. Sellars and J. Hospers, *Readings in Ethical Theory* (New York: Appleton-Century-Crofts, Inc., 1952). A terse penetrating criticism.

S. E. Toulmin, *An Examination of the Place of Reason in Ethics* (Cambridge, Eng.: Cambridge University Press, 1950), chap. 2. A criticism.

A. MacBeath, *Experiments in Living* (London: Macmillan & Co. Ltd., 1952), chaps. 13 and 14. A criticism on the basis of anthropological evidence.

E. W. Hall, *What is Value?* (New York: Humanities Press Inc., 1952), chaps. 2–4. An analysis of nonnaturalist concepts and problems.

9

Noncognitivism: The Job of Ethical Sentences Is Not to State Facts

We seem to be at something of an impasse. Naturalism, at least of the varieties we have considered, is not wholly convincing; nonnaturalism is even less so.

Whenever thought seems to be at an impasse, it is a good idea to consider whether the problem has been wrongly formulated, whether perhaps the assumptions that structure the problem can be questioned. In our case, there is an assumption common to both naturalism and nonnaturalism, which we can question—although whether in the end we can avoid returning to it, or something close to it, is another matter. The assumption is this: We have been supposing that ethical terms refer to properties, and that ethical statements are either true or false—in the sense of correctly or incorrectly representing some facts—in the way in which scientific statements are true or false. We have also been assuming that there is knowledge in ethics, knowledge like that of the empirical sciences (as naturalism holds) or like knowledge of the basic postulates of logic (as nonnaturalism says). Now, if we discarded these assumptions we should be out of our impasse, our impasse about the identity of the property referred to by ethical terms (for we should be saying they don't refer to *any*), and also our impasse about the theory of ethical knowledge (since we should no longer be claiming ethical knowledge).

Of course, one has no metaethical theory at all if he merely says that ethical terms are *not* property-referring and that ethical statements *cannot* be known to be true or false. No theory can consist simply of denials. If one is going to give an account of the nature and function of ethical statements, he must at least tell us positively what ethical utterances are, why they occur at all, and what role they have in discourse. Where might we find suggestions for such a positive account?

A wise thing to do, if one is looking for a radically different view of ethical statements, is to turn to grammar, which has long recognized forms of speech that are not fact-stating: commands, questions, exclamations, optatives, and others. Take: "Confound it!" "Are you going to be in town?" "Please close the door." These sentences illustrate forms of speech that play an important role in living, but nobody would say that any of them states a fact, or is true or false.

In the past twenty-five years, many philosophers who were looking for a theory of ethical statements have gone to grammar, borrowed some of the grammarians' ideas, and have said: Why not regard ethical utterances as disguised commands, or disguised exclamations, and so forth—"disguised" because they occur in misleading statement-like form. Rudolf Carnap, for instance, has proposed that ethical statements are disguised commands; and A. J. Ayer has suggested that ethical predicates are like exclamation points of a special kind, that "Stealing is wrong!" is a misleading way of putting "Stealing!!!" where the triple exclamation point is taken to express horror or indignation. (Grammarians often say that exclamations "express strong or sudden feeling.")

One might question whether it can be helpful to think of ethical utterances as being something different from fact statements, on the ground that to *be* a fact statement is just to have a certain verbal form: that of a declarative sentence. And ethical sentences obviously have this form. "His act was unjustified" is just like "His act was illegal" or "His act cost the company a million dollars." Imperatives, one might say, are formally different: in English an imperative starts with the verb in a special form "Do . . . !" The same is true for questions, which start with an interrogative word or a special part of the verb, and have a rising inflection. And so on, for the others.

The objection is sensible, but it is easily answered. Of course, ethical sentences are declarative, but we must distinguish between the job or function of a sentence and its form. There is normally a correspondence between the job and the form, but this is not always so. Grammarians themselves recognize a dual basis for classifying sentences: in terms of their form, and in terms of their function. There is the job of fact-stating (usually done by declarative sentences), the job of asking questions, the job of issuing commands or orders (usually performed by imperatives), the job of expressing feelings (usually, perhaps, done by exclamations). There are these various jobs or functions, and one of them is not *necessarily* always done by a sentence of a certain *form*. For instance, one can issue an order with a declarative sentence: "The faculty will wear academic dress at the convocation."

Grammarians, unfortunately, have not developed functional thinking about language very far. From a functional, and not purely formal, point of view, what exactly is a statement, a question, an exclamation, a command, the expression of a wish (if this is what optatives normally do), and so on?

Grammarians do not say much about this. Moreover, one would like to know whether, if we are going to classify speech acts functionally and not formally, we have got *all* the proper headings. The headings we have got were suggested by formal differences; but perhaps there are important headings that do not correspond to grammatical forms. In fact we know there *are* others. For instance, "I bet you a dollar!" or "I christen thee 'Queen Mary'!" Neither of these sentences makes a statement, asks a question, or fits into the other classifications we have mentioned. J. L. Austin, who first noticed their peculiarity and proposed a classification for them, has called them "performatory" expressions.

We can see, then, that there are interesting possibilities that may be worth exploring, if we are dissatisfied with both naturalism and nonnaturalism and wish to question whether ethical statements are like the statements of science. Moreover, this set of possibilities is the one that *noncognitivists* have been considering, and from which they have drawn some interesting suggestions.

Many kinds of noncognitive theory have been proposed, and we shall examine the most important general types. We shall call a theory "noncognitivist" if it (1) asserts that ethical utterances are best understood, in point of meaning and function, by assimilating them or likening them to commands or exclamations or sentences of some other functional speech-type different from fact statements (or perhaps to several of these, the particular one depending on the context), and (2) denies that ethical terms are property-referring and that ethical sentences state facts and that there is knowledge of ethical truths—or at least holds that, insofar as ethical terms in some sense are property-referring, and so on, this fact is of secondary importance for understanding ethical discourse and for the methods of criticism in ethics.

1. THE EMOTIVE THEORY

It is convenient to begin with what we shall call the "emotive theory." Although it had been thought of long before, the emotive theory became a recognized major type of metaethical theory only in the third and fourth decades of the present century. It is a painful reminder that important ideas often are not appreciated in the time of their authors, when we recall that some parts of this theory were anticipated in a brief passage in a book by Bishop George Berkeley that appeared in 1710. Furthermore, its major outlines were at least suggested in books by Francis Hutcheson, published in 1725 and 1728, and in a work by David Hume, brought out in 1738.[1]

[1] George Berkeley, para. 20 of the Introduction of *A Treatise Concerning the Principles of Human Knowledge*. Francis Hutcheson, *An Inquiry into the Original of our Ideas of Beauty and Virtue*, 1725, and *An Essay on the Nature and Conduct of the Passions, with Illustrations upon the Moral Sense*, 1728. David Hume, *Treatise of Human Nature*, 1738. See also W. K. Frankena, "Hutcheson's Moral Sense Theory," *Journal of the History of Ideas*, XVI (1955), 356–75.

The development of the emotive theory in the present century has been in considerable part the work of C. L. Stevenson,[2] but the earliest suggestions of the theory in the present century seem to have been made by W. H. F. Barnes and A. Duncan-Jones.

The theory consists in the following contentions.

1. *People have attitudes that often clash.* The theory begins by noting some obvious facts. First, people have *attitudes* toward various things. We need not try to define "attitude" formally, but to say someone has an attitude toward something is to say that he is for or against it, or that he wants or seeks it, or that he dislikes or avoids it, or that he is emotionally concerned about it, or the like. Thus, a person may have attitudes toward tobacco, his mother-in-law, the Reciprocal Trade Agreements Act, the Republican party, and so on. Attitudes are either favorable or unfavorable (for or against).

The theory also observes that there is a distinctive subclass of attitudes: attitudes toward forms of behavior and persons on account of their behavior—dispositions to be indignant with others if they behave in a certain way, and to feel obligated to behave in certain ways oneself and to feel guilty and remorseful if one does not. The subclass of attitudes may be called "specifically moral attitudes."

The attitudes of one person may conflict with those of another; what one is for, the other is against. Sometimes a person does not care whether the attitudes of someone else agree with his or not; one may not mind whether his neighbor is a pacifist. But sometimes it makes a great deal of difference, for instance, if you are in favor of a wage increase and your employer is against it. In this case, you may take an interest in changing the attitudes of your employer. This interest often leads to ethical discourse. The several attitudes of an individual may also clash with one another; when they do, action may be paralyzed, and deliberation ensue; in this case, there may be ethical questioning, and ethical deliberation.

2. *To have an ethical conviction or opinion is to have an attitude.* The relation of attitudes to ethical discourse is much more intimate, however, than simply the fact that conflict of attitude or interest is apt to lead to ethical discourse and reasoning. According to the theory, to have an ethical "opinion" or "conviction" about a thing (for example, to the effect that it is desirable) *is* in major part, to have an attitude toward it; and to have a "conviction" of the kind we should ordinarily express by sentences with terms like "reprehensible" and "duty" *is*, primarily, to have an attitude of the specifically moral sort. Thus, Mr. A and Mr. B can properly be said to "disagree" in ethics if and only if their attitudes conflict.

[2] In *Ethics and Language* (New Haven: Yale University Press, 1944); and "The Emotive Meaning of Ethical Terms," *Mind*, XLVI (1937), 14–31; "The Emotive Conception of Ethics and its Cognitive Implications," *Philosophical Review*, LIX (1950), 291–304; and "Brandt's Questions about Emotive Ethics," *Philosophical Review*, LIX (1950), 528–34.

Naturally, the emotivist's view of ethical "opinion" and "disagreement" is connected with his theory about the meaning and function of ethical language. Let us consider why. Obviously, to have an "opinion" is to be ready to *say* something; and to disagree with somebody is to stand ready to deny what he says on a certain topic. Moreover, to have an ethical opinion is to be ready to say such things as "That is a desirable thing"; and for two persons to disagree in ethics is for one of them to stand ready to say something like "That is a desirable thing" and for the other to stand ready to deny this. Now, if a person who stands ready to say "That is a desirable thing" must have an *attitude* (as we have just seen the emotive theory says), and if one person will stand ready to deny an ethical utterance that the other makes if and only if they have clashing attitudes, there must be something peculiar about ethical talk. At any rate, it is very different from statements like "That's malleable," for surely, in order to stand ready to make *this* statement, or any other scientific statement, we don't have to have an attitude; nor can two people properly be said to disagree on a matter of science if and only if they have conflicting attitudes. Of course, this is exactly what the emotive theory holds: that ethical utterances *are* peculiar, different from scientific ones.

What is the emotive theory about the meaning and function of ethical statements? The proposal is best considered in two parts.

3. *Ethical sentences have a magnetic effect on attitudes.* Consider how "Attention!" may cause well-trained soldiers to leap, as it were instinctively, to a certain stance; or how the ringing of a bell caused Pavlov's dogs to salivate. In roughly the same way, according to proponents of the theory, hearing "is a good thing" will magnetically attract an auditor's favorable attitude toward whatever is designated by the subject of such predication; and hearing "is a bad thing" will magnetically repel favorable attitudes from what is designated by the subject. The term "magnetically attract" is appropriate, because it is supposed that the effect is a result of conditioning to the ethical words, and independent of the meaning of the words, or of what use of them may show about the attitudes of the speaker. In Clark Hull's terms, ethical words have acquired the property of being "secondary reinforcers" of behavior (p. 138). One might wonder how ethical words have acquired such magical powers, how they have become a device for easy access to the favors of one's audience. The answer, according to this theory, lies in conditioning by childhood experiences. "That's good" or "Good boy, Charlie" have been heard on occasions when one's mother accompanied them with a smile and a hug, and all the signs of admiration, not to mention more solid rewards.[3]

We can now see why the emotive theory can say that to have an ethical "opinion" is, at least in part, to have an attitude, for to have an ethical

---

[3] Some of the details, however, are not easy to work out. See R. Brandt, "The Emotive Theory of Ethics," *Philosophical Review*, LIX (1950), 305–18.

"opinion" is to stand ready to make an ethical statement like "A wage increase would be a *good thing.*" Since "good thing" has magnetic power, to stand ready to make this statement is to stand ready to *encourage* a wage increase. But a person will be ready to encourage a wage increase only if he *wants* a wage increase, that is, if he has a *favorable attitude* to a boost in wages. So, his "opinion" will be that a wage increase is good only if he has a favorable attitude in that direction.

4. *Ethical utterances express the speaker's attitudes, and as a consequence are moving.* The next thesis of the theory is, up to a point, simply an observation of fact (like the first thesis of the theory). It is that ethical utterances express the attitudes of speakers, and as a result have a moving influence on the attitudes of hearers.

Everyone must agree with this to the following extent: It is generally believed, and doubtless true, that ethical statements *usually* are signs of a corresponding attitude in the speaker. If a man earnestly protests that a certain course of action would be "wicked," we need little imagination to make the inference that he is against it; and normally he is. If he says that "it would be a fine thing to send Mr. Blank to Congress," we assume he is for Mr. Blank and shall be surprised if he votes for someone else; and normally we shall be right in this. So, when a person makes an ethical statement, we have fairly reliable reason for inferences about his attitudes; and normally we draw such inferences automatically. In this sense, ethical statements "express" the speaker's attitudes. Of course, there are exceptions. People can pretend, and we can be misled. Sometimes "is good" is said in a sarcastic way that instructs us to draw conclusions opposite to the normal ones.

Furthermore, everyone must agree that we tend to be moved to agree with a speaker, if he addresses an ethical statement to us, under certain conditions, for example, if he is a man whose opinion we respect, and the issue is a complex one. Just how much we are apt to be moved in a particular situation will be a function of many factors (p. 125). In general, however, we must agree that there is *some* tendency to move toward agreement with the expressed views of people we respect.

There are two points, then, with which all must agree: that ethical statements "express" attitudes in the sense that they are grounds for inferences about attitudes, and that we draw such inferences automatically; and that ethical statements by respected persons tend (by "prestige suggestion" or on more rational grounds) to elicit our agreement.

There is a further point that emotive theorists sometimes have in mind, which we need not question: that ethical language is sometimes a more effective, more living presentation of our attitudes than any description of them, just as a sign or a gesture may be a more vivid depiction of a state of mind than a verbal description. "That was a reprehensible thing to do!" *may* be more vivid than "I'm much annoyed at what you've done!" (which one would hardly say if one *were* much annoyed).

However, the emotive theory goes beyond this: According to it, the fact that ethical terms express the speaker's attitudes is a built-in feature. Ethical statements convey the speaker's attitudes, according to the emotive theory, not because they *say* the speaker has a certain attitude (like "I'm for it")[4] and because we infer that he must have the attitude (else he would not say so); nor do they express the speaker's attitudes in the way a child's continuous commentary on the weather may betray his fear of an approaching storm (because we know from experience that children talk this way only when they are afraid of something). No, ethical sentences convey the attitudes of the speaker because that is their particular job. They are speech forms that have been learned to this very end; children so learn language that these speech forms become associated with certain attitudes, with the result that ethical terms are employed if and only if the speaker has the attitude—unless he is deliberately trying to deceive. They are somewhat like groans, if we assume that groans do not occur in private but are used to communicate, to express pain, without explicitly saying that one is in pain. Ethical words are put in sentences as if they referred to properties of objects, but we have learned to use them if and only if we have certain attitudes to those objects (and wish others to share these attitudes). Perhaps the closest analogue to ethical terms in speech is phrases like "*Would that I had been there!*" or "*If only I had been there!*" These phrases do not *say* "I wish," but they express the wish (in the sense just described). The learning process gives them this one job, which, incidentally, they perform more vividly and effectively than "I wish that . . ." does it. None of these phrases is learned merely as an automatic ejaculation, like "Ouch!" when one whacks one's thumb with the hammer. They are devices used deliberately to communicate our attitudes, and to invite others, in a subtle way, to share them. As such, they might be said to function as *declarations* or *announcements* of our attitudes, and perhaps as *invitations* to share them. Some emotive theorists believe that ethical terms have some other jobs besides this one; but they think that this one, along with "magnetic influence," is the important feature of ethical words.[5]

5. *To support an ethical statement by a "reason" is to mention a fact that will influence the corresponding attitude.* The emotive theory does

---

[4] Some emotive theorists, however, for example, C. L. Stevenson, do think it plausible to construe ethical statements as making this statement. Others do not.

[5] If a person adopts the proposal of Chapter 7 about a criterion for determining "the same meaning as," he will well wonder why it is not proper to suppose, on this account, that ethical statements actually mean, "I approve. . . ." Emotive theorists who deny this, and at the same time think ethical terms work in the way described, must be using "the same meaning as" in the sense of "the same *overt* meaning as" (p. 163).

We should notice that ethical terms do not "express" pro attitudes or con attitudes in the sense in which a person may "express regret," since to say that someone expressed regret is to say that he *actually said* he regretted, or was sorry, or used other words with similar meaning. A person does not "express regret" by dropping a tear, being sympathetic, or by other indirections. The same is true for expressing fear, hope, uncertainty, and so on.

not suggest that in a practical debate—for instance when union and company bargainers are gathered around a table—all that is done in the way of persuasion is for the various parties to make ethical statements to each other, making use of the "magnetic" effect or expressive force of ethical terms. The use of ethical statements is acknowledged to be only a small part of ethical discourse. What people do, when they disagree practically, is in some sense to "reason" with one another. The emotive theory provides an account of this.

The emotive theory's proposal is that ethical "reasoning" is utterly different from ideal reasoning in science, because facts of observation cannot support ethical convictions in the way in which they do the theories of science. However, ethical "reasoning" is just as important in its own way. It consists in drawing attention to facts, awareness of which by hearers will (or is expected to) influence their attitudes to move in a direction the speaker wishes.

Attitudes, the emotive theory notes, have causal relations among themselves. For instance, a businessman is strongly concerned about the welfare of his business. He comes to believe that the operation of a certain act by Congress will be damaging to his business. The result is opposition to the act. Obviously, if he had believed the effects of the act were different, or if he had not cared about his own business, his attitude to the act probably would have been other than what it was.

Ethical debate, according to the theory, is in good part an exploitation of this fact, that one attitude can be brought in as support for another attitude through the mediation of suitable beliefs. Thus, if I want someone to become more favorable to a certain act, I shall attack the view that it is really damaging to his business (assuming that he takes an interest in his business). To do this is to give a "reason" against his conviction that the act is bad, in the sense that I cite a fact that (if he believes it) tends to change his attitude.

The same reason may not always "prove" the same thing. If I show that the act will damage Mr. A's business, he will presumably tend to disfavor it; the reason has been a reason against the bill. However, if I make the same point to Mr. B, who dislikes Mr. A and would like to see him fail, Mr. B will tend on that account to favor the act; the reason has been a reason for the bill.

According to the theory, whether a given reason is *relevant* to a given issue depends on the attitudes of the disputants. A reason may be relevant, relative to one person; not so, relative to some other. In fact, however, certain types of reason are almost universally effective. Most people have certain attitudes: most have some public spirit, love their children, dislike seeing other people unhappy and dislike being the cause of another's unhappiness, do not wish to tell lies, approve of "fair play," and so on. As a result, reasoning will often resolve ethical disagreements. But whether reasoning, when indefinitely prolonged, could resolve *all* ethical disagreements, the emotive theory does not say. It might or it might not. It depends on what fundamental attitudes people have.

The "logic" of ethical reasoning, then, is thought to be quite different from that of reasoning in science or mathematics. Indeed, there is no "logic" at all. Anything goes that works. It is as if we recognized any argument in science that *persuades* a person, as being as valid, objectively, as any other argument.

6. *The use of ethical sentences in self-exhortation is parallel to interpersonal persuasion; personal "reasoning" about ethics is similar to interpersonal debate.* The emotive theory takes note of the fact—and it surely is a fact—that sometimes we have conflicting attitudes, cannot make up our minds what to do, or cannot wholeheartedly either support or oppose something. Perhaps part of us very much wants to do something that at the same time the rest of us will feel guilty about doing. In this case, part of us may try to convince the other part, or we may reflect and reason, or we may ask the opinions of others. Whichever we do, the emotive theory has a distinctive proposal about what is going on.

If one part is trying to convince the other part by using ethical language, for example, if we exhort ourselves, the theory proposes that we are making use of the magnetic force of ethical words, just as if we were trying to persuade someone else.

If we reason or deliberate, what we are doing, according to the theory, is reviewing the facts or noting connections, with the hope that something will come to light that will enable us to make up our minds, to support something wholeheartedly. We think, or rehearse facts, in order to achieve harmony among our own attitudes.

What are we doing if we raise a question? Are we asking for information? Not at all, according to the theory. We are requesting influence, assistance in making up our minds. Perhaps we are asking for information in a sense: information that will be "relevant" to, and will help to settle, our practical problem.

7. *Ethical sentences do not state facts, although in some contexts they give information; or else they state facts, but their doing so is of only secondary importance.* Proponents of the theory differ about the extent to which ethical statements in some way state facts. Let us look at several views.

The simplest proposal is to the effect that they state no facts at all, that their sole force in communication is magnetic and expressive.[6] Even if this

---

[6] We can still call ethical statements "true" or "false," meaning that we agree or disagree with them, thereby expressing our own attitudes. If we like, we can also, in an appropriate sense, say that one ethical statement "contradicts" another.

is true, however, making an ethical statement may communicate some of the speaker's beliefs about the object judged, and to this extent it may be factually informative. For instance, if Jeremy Bentham says that a certain piece of legislation would be a good thing, we can at once infer, *knowing his utilitarian principles*, that he believes passage of the bill would augment human happiness. For *him* to make the ethical statement is tantamount to saying (implies that he thinks) the act will have this effect. Other persons have different values. If a wealthy woman with known conservative views says that her daughter's suitor is a "very fine young man," that it would be a good thing for the two to marry, we can properly draw many inferences. Her statement is almost as informative as if she had said he dresses well, shares her conservative opinions, and so on.

Some emotive theorists find it natural and convenient to say that ethical statements *assert* facts of these sorts. The conservative lady is asserting, functionally if not in so many words, that the young man is a man of means, has solid values, and so forth. It is natural to say she is asserting such facts, it is argued, because if we ask her, "What do you *mean* by saying 'He is a fine young man'?" she will probably say, "I mean, a young man of means, who has solid values. . . ." Furthermore, these philosophers think it helpful to say that what any sentence means is identical with the set of statements that might be offered in support of it, were it challenged. In our case, if anyone did challenge the proposal that "he is a fine young man," the lady would retort by making these points—just as Bentham would retort, if his ethical judgment were questioned, by pointing to the effects of the bill on human happiness. Doubtless the passage, in the minds of some, from an ethical statement to these supporting reasons is so natural and rapid, that there is some further similarity to the conditions we have identified as the criteria for sameness of meaning (Chapter 7). Thus, these philosophers say that ethical statements should be construed as asserting the very facts that would be adduced in their support by the person who makes them. Of course, this view has the result that people with different ethical standards will *mean* different things by ethical terms, and that the same person may mean different things when talking of different subjects—if the facts he would adduce in support of one ethical judgment are different in kind from those he would adduce in support of another judgment.[7]

Some proponents of the emotive theory go further still; they suggest that, in some groups where values are stable, ethical words may well have as definite a property-reference, perhaps of the sort suggested by naturalists, as expressions like "is square."

One might ask: "If one goes as far as this, has one not essentially returned to naturalism?" This would be denied. It would be urged that to say these things is not at all to discard the view that to have an ethical opinion is, in

---

[7] We shall shortly offer our objections to this manner of speaking (pp. 230–31).

major part, to take an attitude, or that ethical disputes are basically disagreements in attitude. Why not? Why not construe the logic of ethics as exactly like the logic of science, if ethical sentences state facts in principle capable of observation? The answer is this: The magnetic and expressive properties of ethical terms, it is said, remain *fundamental*, whatever property-reference it may be correct to ascribe to ethical terms as used by somebody. What I am basically doing when I say something is "desirable" is expressing my favorable attitude and encouraging (by its magnetic force and otherwise) the favorable attitudes of others. For this reason, there will never be reason to construe my ethical terms as referring to a certain property unless I have favorable attitudes (if favorable terms are used) to whatever has this property; for I shall apply "desirable" only to things I favor, and I shall cite, in support of my judgment that something is desirable, only facts that I judge are likely to elicit favorable attitudes. So, one will never have reason (from the objects to which I apply the term, or from the supporting evidence I adduce) to construe "is right" as meaning "contributes to human happiness" unless I approve of something whenever I think it contributes to human happiness. This fact has an important methodological consequence: It remains true that, in order to refute a person's ethical conviction you have to change his *attitudes*, and nothing else. One might question this, arguing that if what a person *means* by "is right" is "contributes to human happiness," then the questions of ethics can be settled by the methods of science, just as naturalists have said they can be. The emotive theorists reply that this is not the case. Suppose a situation arises such that I have an *unfavorable* attitude to a certain act, but concede that it will contribute to human happiness. Has it then been *proved* to me that the act is right? Not at all, because, to avoid this consequence, all I need do is *change* my meaning for "right," introducing some qualifications and exceptions of a kind to exclude the type of action toward which I have an unfavorable attitude. (Or, we could put it another way. We could say that the very fact that I refuse to apply "right" to this action, despite full information about its character, shows that it was *mistaken* to suppose that I mean just "contributes to human happiness" by "right.") Furthermore, such a modification would be only a minor change in speech habits, since my fundamental use of "is right" has been, all along, just an expressive and attitude-moving one;[8] and this is not modified by alteration of the property-reference. As a consequence, the fact that we choose to say that ethical terms "designate" certain properties—something that may be very convenient in a society where values are stable and largely matters of agreement—does not alter the methodology of ethics and convert ethics into an empirical science. It remains true that "ethical convictions" are essentially

---

[8] Perhaps "right" has also meant "approved by me."

the having of attitudes, and that ethical language is fundamentally magnetic and expressive.[9]

2. WHY BELIEVE THE EMOTIVE THEORY?

The emotive theory is attractive. It frees us from talk of nonnatural
properties, intuitions, and rational insights. It does not ask us to believe that
an ethical term means the same as some expression in the language of science (or of theology), when we are not clear that it does mean the same.

Still, there are many grounds for doubt, which we shall review shortly.
Some of the objections we shall see are not easy to surmount; so, even if the
mere statement of the emotive theory is enough to recommend it to the
reader, it will not be valueless to present, in as systematic a way as possible,
reasoning that has been offered in support of the theory.

It will be convenient to arrange our discussion of the evidence in two
parts: first, evidence supporting the emotive view of the function of ethical language—the theses that ethical words have "magnetic effect" on attitudes, and that they are dedicated to expressing attitudes in the way in
which "Would that . . ." is dedicated to expressing wishes—and second,
evidence supporting the view that to have an ethical conviction is essentially to take an attitude pro or con (so that to "reason" for an ethical conviction is primarily to draw attention to facts that fortify an attitude). We
begin with arguments supporting the emotive theory of ethical language.

Emotive theorists believe that Moore's "open-question" argument (pp.
164–66) shows that no form of naturalism is tenable, or at least that ethical terms have some further important function or meaning in addition to
any reference they may have to observable properties. Moreover, for one
reason or another, nonnaturalism is thought objectionable. Ethical terms,
then, must have some function other than stating facts. What can this be?
One thing we know: that ethical sentences sometimes do sway the attitudes
of hearers, and further they "express" the attitudes of the speaker in one
sense—that people normally and properly draw inferences about such attitudes on the basis of ethical statements made. Would it not be a simple, and

---

[9] See, for example, Stevenson, *Ethics and Language*, pp. 222–239.

The foregoing theory is complicated and not very plausible. It assumes that somehow we know that the *basic* use of ethical terms in some sense is expressive and directive
of attitudes, and that the property-referring use is secondary. It is difficult to imagine
on what facts an emotive theorist might base such speculations. Sometimes the
emotivist disdains any facts and makes it a matter of *definition*, saying that unless the
expressive and attitude-moving features of an ethical term are fundamental on a given
occasion, then the utterance does not qualify as an ethical or normative utterance on
that occasion. There is no reason, however, why a critic of the emotive theory should
be compelled to concede that the emotive theory is true by definition. What we want
to know is the meaning and function of terms like "desirable" or "obligation" in contexts where their use is intuitively identifiable as a serious assertion. Whether, on such
occasions, they are primarily property-referring or primarily expressive and attitude-
moving is a matter for observation to decide, not a matter of definition.

therefore plausible, view of ethical words, then, to say that they are "expressive" in the sense in which "Would that . . ." expresses wishes, and that they have "magnetic power?" Such a theory explains all the facts economically.[10]

This reasoning has some force. However, we must notice that even if we felt compelled, by the difficulties of naturalism and nonnaturalism, to hold that ethical language has some emotive job—arousing or expressing attitudes—we might still think that in some sense ethical statements *make claims* about facts. We might say that this other feature of ethical statements is of importance for understanding ethical discourse equal to that of their "emotive" features. The reasoning stated does not support a straight emotive theory any more than such a combination theory. Does the argument really force us, though, to adopt precisely the emotive theory of ethical language, as stated, at all? Suppose it does prove that ethical terms are not primarily fact-stating, but do *some* other job. Need this other job be exactly the one stated? Perhaps what ethical language does is advise, urge, praise, or exhort, and does not have exactly "magnetic influence" in the sense described. Or perhaps *part* of what the emotive theory says is true, but not all of it; perhaps we should adopt the emotive view that ethical terms are "expressive" but not the proposal that they have "magnetic influence"; or the reverse. Evidently this first argument does not establish the whole theory of ethical language.[11]

The first argument is sometimes buttressed with a second, aimed primarily to support the view that ethical terms have "magnetic influence." The second argument is an appeal to analogy with "poetic" language. It is said that it is a well-established thesis that some words are rich in "emotive charge." For instance, "steed" and "charger" are emotionally fitted for poetic writing, in a way in which "horse" is not. We must admit, then, that some words have special emotive charge. The emotive theory of ethics is simply the proposal that ethical words have a feature that we already know some words to have.

Just how similar can we plausibly say is the working of "desirable" to that of "charger"? We should first note that the emotive theorists themselves are urging a marked difference: They are claiming that ethical words have "magnetic influence" in the sense of attracting the hearer's favorable

---

[10] One need not hold exactly the "magnetic influence" view. One could equally well say that everybody associates some factual properties with ethical terms. That is, each will associate "wrong" with sorts of thing *he* disfavors, for example, with hurting somebody. When he hears someone else say that something is wrong, this property will be suggested to him. Then, if he does have an unfavorable attitude to this property, the statement that suggests that something will have this property may tend to arouse an unfavorable reaction to whatever it is about. Different people will associate different things with ethical terms, but the typical effect on attitudes of a given ethical statement will be standard.

[11] Later we shall describe some quite different theories, all of which are consistent with the premises stated above.

attitudes toward whatever is designated by the subject term of the sentence in which the ethical word occurs. No one claims this for "charger," whose appearance in a sentence will have only slight and rather diffuse emotional effects, their precise character depending on the context. If "desirable" works only like "charger,"it is hard to see how it can do the job the emotive theory sets it. In the second place, the emotive force of "charger" is not—as the emotive theory tends to claim it is for "desirable"—an external attachment (by conditioning) quite independent of the property-reference of the term. What makes "charger" a poetic term is what it *means*. What child cannot tell you the difference between a charger and a horse? A charger is strong and dashing; he is handsome; he is usually arrayed in shining armor and astride him sits a knight. What vivid images the name arouses! And these do have emotive repercussions. "Charger" is a useful word for poetry, but is so, apparently, precisely because it is rich with meaning, not, as emotive theorists tend to hold for ethical terms, empty of it. Indeed, we do not contradict anything that is really known today if we say that discourse *never* moves our attitudes or feelings in any substantial way except by making us believe something, perceive something, think something, or imagine something—never just by the naked force of words alone.

The supposed analogue to "poetic" language, then, provides little support for the emotive theory.

There is a third argument for the theory's view about ethical language. Suppose there were independent reason for identifying "ethical convictions" with having attitudes. Then we could infer that at least a part of the peculiar job of ethical language is that of expressing attitudes, in a sense at least close to the emotive theory's sense of "express." No one will deny that ethical statements do function to express the speaker's ethical convictions; it is obvious that they are dedicated to this job—just as obviously as that the language of science is dedicated to describing and explaining facts. Thus, if ethical convictions *are* identical with attitudes, it is plausible to identify the job of ethical language with that of expressing attitudes. However, *is* the primary supposition sound? One must concede the reasoning if one concedes the premise.

Let us turn, then, to the reasons one can muster in support of the other major thesis of the theory—that to have an ethical conviction is to take an attitude. These are much stronger. In fact, even if they are not conclusive, they are illuminating and worth our most careful study. We shall consider four lines of thought.

1. *The Argument from Disagreements in Ethics*. The first line of reasoning is this. Either ethical convictions are primarily *beliefs* that something has a certain property, or they are primarily having *attitudes*. (For the sake of the argument, let us not deny that this disjunction is exhaustive.) If they are primarily beliefs, then—assuming nonnaturalism is indefensible—they

must be beliefs somewhat like the beliefs of science. Why, if they are, is there not the agreement in ethics, or at least the steady progress toward agreement, that we find in science? But the very disagreement that is a stumbling block for the traditional theories is what we should expect according to the emotive theory, because attitudes cannot be coerced by evidence, and we may expect them to vary, as a result of rewards, identifications, personality type, and so on. The emotive theory, then, is consistent with diversities of ethical standard, whereas the other theories are not.[12]

This reasoning is probably the weakest of the arguments we shall consider. Various types of naturalism (not to mention other views to be considered) can explain diversity in ethical opinion with equal ease. Take, for instance, the Ideal Observer theory. On this view, the observation of one's own attitudes must play an important part in the confirmation of ethical beliefs, and therefore we must expect the very difficulties in reaching agreement to which the emotive theory points. Or, consider Perry's theory. Modern science has not yet seen fit to tell us exactly what means will lead to "harmonious happiness"; there can be many opinions on this matter. Can we really say that the diversity of ethical opinions is greater than we need expect if Perry's theory were a correct account of what we mean by "right" and "wrong"?

2. *The Emotive Theory Explains Motivation to Do What We Think Right*. Proponents of the emotive theory point out that whenever a person is honestly convinced that he *ought* to do a certain thing (and similarly for the other ethical terms) he is almost always more inclined to do that thing than he otherwise would have been. The emotive theory, they say, explains this—since it asserts that to have an honest conviction *is* to have an attitude. No other theories offer an explanation. For instance, suppose we become convinced that something ought to be done in Perry's sense, that doing it will contribute to harmonious happiness. Shall we then be more inclined to do this thing? Well, *only* if we happen to be interested in harmonious happiness. Or, take the nonnaturalist theory. If we become convinced that we stand in a certain nonnatural relation, why should we be inclined to act in a certain way? There is no puzzle, however, for the emotive theory.

Emotivists assert that there is a closely related fact that supports their identification of ethical conviction with attitude. Ask yourself when you think a person "really believes" a moral principle or has a moral conviction, and you will find that you think "actions speak louder than words." We judge by whether he shows motivation to *live by* his conviction, by whether at least symptoms of inner conflict or remorse are visible when he doesn't live by it. Our criteria for "having a moral conviction" are motivational. This is as it should be if the emotive theory is true.

---

[12] The emotive theory can also cite the other arguments of Westermarck.

This reasoning has weight. It shows, at least, that there is a *close connection* between having ethical beliefs and having attitudes. But does it show more? Not conclusively. The critic of the emotive theory can explain this close connection without *identifying* ethical opinion with taking an attitude. He may suggest that most people have simply been *trained* to do whatever they think right or best; this training, then, provides the bridge between opinion and behavior. Or, he may suggest that most or even all people have at least some public spirit, some altruism; and this will motivate them favorably when they think—to follow Perry's analysis—that some action is right in the sense that it will contribute to harmonious happiness. In either case, it will be possible normally to use behavioral criteria as a clue to what a person really thinks he ought to do.

The critic may also suggest that possibly sometimes moral training does not "take," and hence that a person may sometimes have a genuine ethical belief without the corresponding motivation. *If* there are such cases, the emotive theory is in trouble, for, on the emotive view, such discrepancies are logically impossible.

3. *The Aim of Ethical Argument Is Obviously to Change Attitudes.* Ethical arguments, the emotivist continues, are practical, not intellectual. When we argue an ethical point, we are aiming to affect what our opponent will do, or be inclined to do, or at least how he tends to feel. If we don't accomplish this, we think our argument has failed. We don't think we have got a man to agree with us ethically, unless his motivation is won over. Just notice at what point you feel that you have *won* an ethical argument, at what point you feel satisfied not to argue further. It is when the other party agrees with you in feeling and motivation. The emotive theory is right, therefore, in identifying having an ethical conviction with having a corresponding attitude.

But we must be careful to make a distinction, a very common-sense one: between what a person thinks he *ought* to do, and what he *wants* to or *does* or *decides* to do. We all know that a person can want to do what he thinks he ought not; he can also decide to do, and do, what he thinks he ought not. When he does what he thinks he ought not, we often say he has "yielded to temptation." Now, correspondingly, we must distinguish two types of argument. First, we may try to convince someone that he *ought* not to do something. Second, if he is already convinced that he ought not, we may argue in the hope of dissuading him from doing it. These two aims are obviously quite different. It is also clear that, when we speak of an argument about an "ethical" point, what we are speaking of is a debate of the *first* sort, about what is right or worthwhile, and so on. Thus, if we have got a person to agree with us about what he ought to do, we have won the ethical debate. Any argument dissuading him from doing what he ought not ("You'll be sure to be caught!") is an entirely different matter. Ethical arguments, then, are *not* "practical" in the sense of being aimed to affect the *conduct* of another person, or his motivation, directly. To this extent it is not obviously intended to change attitudes.

Sometimes the emotivist uses a slightly different argument. He may say: "If we are not trying essentially to mold a person's attitudes, why do we use the emotionally charged, expressive, non-fact-stating language of ethics—words like 'duty'—in an ethical debate?"

This argument is circular, however. The doubter to whom the argument is addressed presumably is not yet convinced that ethical language *is* essentially emotionally charged, expressive, non-fact-stating language. To assume that it is, is to beg the question. Moreover, one may ask, *do* we actually make much use of ethical language in a debate? Our opponent must not be very subtle if he is moved by our repeating, "But it *is* your duty." Finally, if ethical language is the only language we have for stating our ethical views succinctly, it is not surprising that we use it to state our views—and the fact that we do would be no evidence of an aim to influence attitudes, even if it were "moving."

Still another type of emotivist argument, to show that the aim of ethical reasoning is to redirect attitudes, is this. If you will notice, it is said, what facts are considered *relevant* to an ethical discussion, you will see that they are just the ones that are thought likely to influence the other person's attitudes. For instance, suppose Mr. A asserts, "Colleges should accept direct grants-in-aid from government." Mr. B is opposed. Now, what arguments will Mr. A consider relevant in arguing his case with Mr. B? They are the ones that Mr. A thinks, in the light of all he knows about Mr. B's attitudes, will be likely to move him. Thus, it is said, clearly what ethical arguments are expected to do is influence attitudes. This is precisely what we should anticipate, if, after all, to *have* an ethical conviction is to have an attitude.

However, the emotivist is mistaken about his facts. We do *not* consider an argument relevant or well-taken *just* because it is successful in influencing attitudes. If Mr. B is a legislator and Mr. A wants to influence his vote, there are various "arguments" he might use that no one would think ethically relevant. Mr. A might say: "Your alma mater will surely go bankrupt unless this bill is passed." Or, perhaps better, he might say, "Your daughter will be admitted to —— College, if you vote for this bill; otherwise she won't be." These arguments may be of wonderful effect in changing Mr. B's attitudes, but they are not ethically relevant. On the contrary, suppose Mr. A argues about the importance of having independent educational institutions, where absolutely uncensored thinking and discussion can occur. In this case, Mr. A will have argued relevantly, irrespective of whether Mr. B is interested.

4. *The Goal of Ethical Deliberation Is Resolution of Conflict among*

Attitudes. The emotivist says that what we do when we deliberate about what is right or best is quite different from what we do when solving a theoretical problem. We are not thinking about proofs or evidence. When we are first faced with an ethical problem, we think over all its aspects, registering a reaction to them. At the end, we seem to sum it up, to see how we feel about the thing as a whole. If it isn't clear how we feel, or if we have conflicting impulses, and don't know what we want to support, we re-examine the facts, trying to see more facts or relationships that will release the indecision or remove the conflict. As Stevenson says, it is as if one were trying "to make up his mind whether to approve or disapprove something. . . . And only when he has resolved his conflict, making his attitudes, at least in greater degree, speak with one voice, will he have made his decision. . . . As we commonly put it, he is making up his mind about 'what he really approves of.' " Ethical deliberation seems to aim at a state of mind in which we know where we stand, where our attitudes speak with one voice. To come to an ethical conclusion, then, is for one's attitudes to be clearly formed and harmonized. This is what we should expect, if the emotive theory is correct.

Now, the emotivist's proposal certainly has much resemblance to the facts, but it is oversimplified in some respects. For example, if we are trying to decide what we (or someone else) ought to do, what our (or someone's) moral obligations are, it is clearly *not* the case that we are simply asking what we *want* to do. Very often we conclude, after moral reasoning, that what we most insistently want to do must simply be set aside (or at least that it *ought* to be). Even when we are considering some action that would affect no one but ourselves, what we *want* to do is not the only thing people typically consider. In what sense, then, can one say that ethical deliberation aims at getting our attitudes to speak harmoniously?

The emotive theory may perhaps meet this point by proposing that when we are deliberating about ethical questions, we are trying to make our specifically *moral* or else our *impersonal* attitudes "speak with one voice." Such a proposal could be made, because some advocates of the theory do distinguish such attitudes from attitudes in general.[13] In fact, such a view was held by earlier writers, such as Francis Hutcheson and David Hume, and a modified form of it is now espoused by W. K. Frankena. Possibilities of this sort, however, have not been emphasized by the leading spirits of the

---

[13] Such a change would necessitate complications in their account of moral deliberation. Deliberation, then, would not only consist in getting attitudes to be harmonious, but in making sure that it is the *moral* attitudes that are speaking. C. L. Stevenson suggested defining "moral" attitudes by reference to specific feelings; moral attitudes are ones that issue in feelings of shock, indignation, and remorse. Given his definition, it will not be easy to decide whether it is "moral" attitudes that are engaged in coming to a harmonious commitment.

emotive theory. The emotive theory, then, as it is generally formulated today, is not supported by a fair analysis of ethical deliberation, which cannot be viewed as just an attempt to get *all* our attitudes (selfish and otherwise) into harmonious accord.[14]

3. A REVISION: R. M. HARE

If one reviews the reasoning in support of the emotive theory, he is apt to feel that the "magnetic influence" thesis is a less well supported view, one with much less right claimed to describe an important feature of ethical language, than is the "expressive" thesis. Moreover, it seems clear that, to be plausible, the emotive theory must say that ethical convictions are to be identified not with the having of personal attitudes or wishes but perhaps with impersonal or "moral" attitudes—and that these are what is given expression by ethical language.

A recent book by R. M. Hare has proposed a view, otherwise very similar to the emotive theory, with modifications precisely in these two areas.[15] Hare's essential points were these:

First, he proposed that ethical statements should be viewed as a species of "prescribing," which is something, he says, that is done in common by commands, requests, orders, and cookbooks—but not by fact-stating sentences. The cookbook, for example, says, "Take two eggs . . . ," which is not like saying, "Using two eggs will produce a tasty cake." Requests and orders do not tell us that something is the case, as statements do. Prescribing, in general, *tells us to do* something, in contrast to statements, which tell us *that* a certain thing is the case. For every prescription we can find a corresponding fact statement, a statement of what would be the case if the prescription were fulfilled. For instance, to the prescription "Please close the door" there corresponds the fact statement "The door is closed." Hare finds it convenient to write these in a standard form, in order to mark the difference: "The door being closed, please" for the prescription and "The door being closed, yes" for the fact statement.

---

[14] The suggestion has been made that the emotive theory has been less an attempt to give a careful descriptive account of what ethical deliberation and debate are like, than an attempt to think through what ethics—and the methodology of ethics—would be, if we just assumed that ethical words are essentially emotive words, their job primarily that of "magnetic" influence and the expression of attitudes. This suggestion is doubtless not quite fair. Nevertheless, it is true enough to be illuminating when reading the work of emotive theorists. The suggestion, however, is far from implying that the task emotive theorists have set themselves is an unimportant one. Viewing ethical deliberation and argument in this light has been extremely fruitful.

[15] *The Language of Morals* (Oxford: Clarendon Press, 1952).
Whether or not one says Hare's theory is a "form" of the emotive theory is a question of personal preference in terminology. At first glance Hare's view appears quite radically different from the emotive theory; but some of the apparently novel features are more terminological than substantial.

To prescribe, Hare insists, is a very different thing from having emotional impact, from influencing a hearer's attitudes. Prescribing may, in certain circumstances, have influence on attitudes; but one prescribes successfully whether or not this result occurs. One has prescribed if he has told someone to do something and that person has understood; it makes no difference whether the prescription influences his conduct. Thus, Hare's proposal about the meaning and function of ethical language is quite dissimilar to the "magnetic influence" theory. In fact, at first, it seems to be different from the "expressive" thesis too, for it does not seem that to prescribe is to express an attitude. The first impression here is a bit misleading, however, because, Hare points out, one difference between statements and prescriptions is that to express agreement with a statement is to express belief in what the statement says, whereas to express agreement to a prescription, to accept it, is to *express one's resolve* or decision to carry it out. Now, as we shall see, to issue an *ethical* prescription is also to express acceptance of the prescription for oneself, so that issuance of a *moral* prescription is in effect, at least in part, to declare one's own resolve or decision. It is not easy to see the difference between this and *expressing one's attitude,* in the sense in which "Would that . . ." expresses a wish. In this way, Hare, although rejecting the "magnetic influence" thesis, accepts the "expression" thesis of the emotive theory.[16]

Hare's second major proposal is that general ethical statements (for example, "Promises ought to be kept") are a distinctive variety of prescriptions: They are *universal* prescriptions. "Don't smoke here!" is a prescription, but very different from "It is wrong to smoke." The difference is this: "It is wrong to smoke" means approximately the same as "No smoking *anywhere* at *any* time by *anyone*, please." The moral prescription, then, is directed to everyone at every time, past and future. As such, it is directed at the speaker himself, too; it is *reflexive.* Moreover, since the issuance of a reflexive prescription includes its acceptance, an ethical statement can be construed both as the issuance of a universal "order" or

---

[16] Hare distinguishes sharply between prescriptions and statements, but this may be questioned. When we "command" someone to do something, the success of our effort depends on two things: first, that the person commanded understand that he is being notified that we want him to do something; and second, that he understand that if he does not do this thing, he will be considered guilty of insubordination, with whatever unpleasant consequences this may entail. Therefore, it is natural to propose that "Close the door" is identical in meaning with the statement "I wish the door closed," or the statement "If you don't close the door, something unpleasant will happen to you," or both together. Of course, the imperative does not say this in so many words; but functionally it comes to the same thing.

Hare, however, insists vigorously that the two are quite different. But on what grounds? A distinction is plausible, if, in general, we make the intention of the speaker very important for the classification of utterances. We shall discuss this below (p. 233).

A subtle discussion of prescriptions is to be found in John Ladd, *The Structure of a Moral Code* (Cambridge: Harvard University Press, 1957).

"directive" and at the same time as an announcement, or expression, of one's acceptance of it for oneself, which one might otherwise express by "Let me not smoke!" There is, however, a second feature of a "universal" prescription. It is not only a prescription directed at all and sundry persons, but it is a prescription that can be formulated without the use of proper names, or in other words, by use of abstract terms alone. Thus, "Everyone at all times doing whatever will make *me* happiest, please!" does *not* qualify as a universal command, whereas "Everyone at all times doing whatever will maximize happiness in general, please!" does so qualify.

One can scarcely take particular ethical statements ("You oughtn't to break that promise to Smith!") to be universal prescriptions in this sense. Hare proposes that these be construed, roughly, as "If you do a certain thing [for example, break that promise to Smith], you will be infringing a universal prescription to which I hereby subscribe." Hare's proposal thus has the effect of recognizing what we earlier (Chapter 2) called the "requirement of generality" and of incorporating it explicitly into the analysis of ethical language.

Are these proposals really marked advances on the emotive theory?

Our suggestion has been that the first one is an improvement in that it eliminates an element of doubtful value, but that in principle it is not different from the emotive theorist's view that ethical statements' essential job is to *express* the speaker's attitudes.[17]

The second of Hare's proposals is a marked improvement over the emotive theory. On the one hand, it quite properly asserts that it is a gross error to confuse an ethical statement with an expression of a mere personal wish, as if "I want that milkshake" necessarily implied "It is desirable [or a moral right] for me to have that milkshake." On the other hand, as a consequence, Hare can say that a reason supporting an ethical statement is "relevant" only if it cites a fact that may or will influence a person's *universal* wish or policy. This proposal has the effect of classifying as "relevant reasons" a class of reasons much more nearly identical with the ones we should ordinarily take to be relevant reasons in ethics, than is the class

[17] Conceivably, it is not fair to Hare to fail to acknowledge some further contribution of value in his proposal that ethical statements are prescriptions. Unfortunately, it is not clear what "prescribing" is supposed to be, beyond expressing one's attitude as pro or con toward some form of behavior, for evidently moral statements do not issue orders, or make requests, or give commands. It may be suggested that "prescribing" is not any one of these, but something they have in common. But what could this common element be? Or, it might be said that ethical prescribing is *like* these three things but different; but like in what respect? Perhaps the most plausible thing to say is that the common element is that of *recommending*, and that ethical statements are essentially general recommendations. But what exactly is it to make a general recommendation? Would it not be to *express oneself as being in favor* of doing a certain thing? Very well, but this again is not to differ substantially from the emotive theory view that ethical statements "express" attitudes in the way in which "Would that . . ." expresses a wish.

of reasons that most proponents of the emotive theory (for example, Stevenson) call "ethically relevant."[18]

Hare's second proposal is reminiscent of Kant's view that an act is morally permissible if and only if the maxim in terms of which the agent thinks of it could possibly serve as a universal rule of conduct, and the agent is prepared to accept it as such. Hare is saying that if (and only if) one is in favor of a universal prescription one may say "People ought to do a certain thing"; and one can say a particular action is wrong if it infringes such a prescription. Hare's theory is also an improvement over Kant's. First, Hare's theory (apart from the obscurities of "prescription") is a clearer proposal (not necessarily more correct) about what an ethical statement is. On Hare's theory, an ethical statement simply *is* the issuance of a universal prescription, and, as such, the expression of a universal preference or wish and the announcement of a resolution to abide by the content of it. Moreover, Hare's view makes clear the relation of the criterion or test for an action being one's duty or morally permissible, for it follows from his theory that the statement "Mr. X can say honestly that everyone ought . . . if and only if he prescribes that everyone in all conditions . . ." is true by *definition*, on account of the meaning or use of "ought." Second, Hare sees clearly, and explicitly accepts, the relativistic consequence that we noted in the case of Kant (pp. 31–35). Different people may correctly (in the sense, "without misusing ethical terms") make ethical statements that are contradictory. One person may say, "Promises should be forgotten after two years"; and someone else may say, "Promises should be held sacred, no matter how long ago they may have been made." If one person really wishes the one thing universally done, he may properly express the fact by saying the one thing; and if the other wishes a contrary thing universally done, he may properly express this fact by saying the other thing. Kant's theory, we saw, leads to this consequence; but Kant did not embrace it. Hare does. And it is always an improvement to admit and assert openly what your theory implies!

There is another advantage Hare's theory has over Kant's, which is more important. At an earlier stage, we remarked that Kant's "universalizability test" for maxims of conduct is satisfied by a great many maxims that ought not to satisfy any such test. One of these was this: "Let a slave-

---

[18] Hare does not, however, distinguish "People are morally obligated to keep their promises" from "It is desirable for people to keep their promises." He combines judgments of obligation together indiscriminately with judgments of worth or value. This, as we shall see later, is a mistake.

Incidentally, it is much more plausible to view "You ought to . . ." as a prescription than so to view judgments of worth. Suppose I say, "Considering all the suffering he had in the last few months, it is a *good thing* that his life is ended." Or, "His act of sacrifice was *admirable.*" What is being prescribed, and to whom? Hare has been subject to just criticism on this point. See J. Harrison, "When is a Principle a Moral Principle?" The Aristotelian Society, Supplementary vol. XXVIII (1954), 134; C. Johnson, "Commending and Choosing," *Mind*, LXVI (1957), 63–74, and S. Zink, "Objectivism and Mr. Hare's *Language of Morals*," *Mind*, LXVI (1957), 79–87.

owner put his slave to death with torture, if it pleases his fancy." We proposed that a slave-owner, who knew that neither he nor anyone he cared about would be a slave, and who was a cruel and callous person, might well be prepared to see the corresponding maxim made universal law. Now, Hare's theory does not permit this, because of his understanding of "universal wish." Hare says a man does not wish an imperative (maxim) for conduct made universal unless he wants such a system for every *possible* situation including those that he knows will never come about in fact, and in particular for the situation in which *he himself* has the role of slave. One does not want something universally unless he wants it for all *logically possible* cases, including the ones in which roles are reversed so that he is the patient, not the agent. Since a slave-owner, no matter how cruel, may be expected not to wish to have somebody else put him to death with torture, the statement "it is right for the owner to put a slave to death with torture, if it pleases him" cannot properly be made, since it *purports* to express the fact that something is the universal will of the speaker, when actually it is not. Possibly Kant meant to say this; in this case, he is excused from the difficulties mentioned.[19]

4. DOUBTS ABOUT THE EMOTIVE THEORY, REVISED OR UNREVISED

Although the emotive theory has been, in many ways, a fruitful theory, there are, nevertheless, objections to it, which taken together seem conclusive. They are as follows:

1. Ethical utterances are not obviously the kind of thing the emotive theory says they are, and prima facie, at least, should be viewed as fact statements. There are several reasons for saying this.

First, the emotive theory has no explanation for the facts that people have so often tried to explain ethical language as fact-stating, and that other proposals have waited for the twentieth century. There has not been a comparable tendency to treat other utterances as fact-stating: Grammarians have never tried to construe "Would that . . ." utterances as fact statements. Nor can the persistent efforts at naturalistic definitions of ethical terms be attributed simply to the fact that ethical statements are cast in declarative form. Nobody has ever seriously proposed that "The faculty will wear academic dress at the coming convocation" (when issued from

---

[19] One might feel there is a difficulty here, since one cannot have a wish in the sense of a serious aim, plan, or purpose to realize what he knows is impossible, and therefore he can have no serious plan for encouraging his master to put him to death with torture. Still, one can ask himself whether he wishes that, were he to be a slave, his master would put him to death with torture. He might even wish both to be a slave and to be put to death with torture—or the reverse.

To have such a wish for a hypothetical situation is quite distinct from its being the case that, *if* one *were* in the position of being a slave, he *would* want his master to execute him with torture if it pleased the master.

the office of the president) is a fact statement; it has been unhesitatingly recognized for what it is—a polite directive.

Second, people *think* that ethical statements are true or false, statements of true ideals, say, to which choices or conduct or attitudes should conform. They do *not* think that, when an ethical statement is made, the speaker is merely voicing his personal feeling or attitude.

Third, when people change their ethical views, they do not regard their earlier stand as just different; they regard it as mistaken. This contrasts sharply with what happens when they change what obviously is just an attitude. Suppose, for instance, as a child a person disliked eating peas. When he recalls this as an adult he is amused and notes how preferences change with age. He does not say, however, that his former attitude was *mistaken.* If, on the other hand, he remembers regarding irreligion or divorce as wicked, and now does not, he regards his former view as erroneous and unfounded.

One may, of course, concede that ethical utterances are not obviously emotive, that prima facie they should be viewed as fact statements, but still conclude that in fact they really are just "magnetic" and expressive, that our first impressions are just mistaken. Very well, this may be so, but our first point simply is: Ethical statements do not look like the kind of thing the emotive theory says they are.[20]

2. Let us now turn to the "magnetic influence" thesis, and let us state this broadly. Let us say that this thesis is that ethical terms, somehow, but roughly as a consequence of conditioning, have special directive influence on the feelings and attitudes of others—directive influence in the sense that "*x* is wrong" tends to make a person behave much as he would behave if he were obeying the order "Don't do *x!*"[21]

Is it plausible to suppose that "magnetic influence" is an important, or the principal, point or function of ethical terms? If it is, then it is very puzzling why we make some of the ethical statements we do make. For instance, I say to my wife, "The action of the Senate on foreign aid policy was morally unjustified." Further, suppose I already know my wife agrees with this. On the magnetic influence theory, what was I trying to do with this sentence? Whom was I trying to influence? Or, I say to myself, "I certainly should

---

[20] For some further points along the same line, see H. D. Aiken, "Emotive 'Meanings' and Ethical Terms," *Journal of Philosophy,* XLI (1944), 456–70, especially p. 463; and "The Authority of Moral Judgments," *Philosophy and Phenomenological Research,* XII (1952), 513–25, especially p. 516.

[21] On account of this analogy, some people tend to speak of the magnetic influence as "imperative import." But the parallel with imperatives is misleading. The force of a command derives from the fact that (a) the command form announces that the addressee is hereby officially notified that the speaker wishes a certain thing done by him, and (b) warns him that he is subject to charges of insubordination if he neglects to perform the action specified. The force of commands, then, is entirely different from what is envisaged by the "magnetic influence" theory—and obviously different from the force of ethical statements.

not have done that." Again, what was the point of this remark? Or, suppose I am writing a biography of Nero. Toward the end of the book, I feel it proper to make a final estimate of his character; I discuss whether his acts must be condemned as utter callousness, or whether there were misunder-standings or extenuating circumstances that might make our condemnation less complete. Now, what I must be doing, in good part, on the "magnetic influence" theory, must be preaching to my readers in a subtle way. (And the same for testimonials.) This may be the case, but surely the biographer would be horrified if he thought he was doing this. Take still another case. Suppose we say, "*If* the policy is morally wrong, then that settles the mat-ter," or "It *must* be right or wrong—so let's think it through and find out which."[22] In these sentences, "wrong" seems to be functioning in the normal way. But it obviously cannot be acting directively; much less is it intended to do so. One may retort that these are not normal uses. *Is* there a difference, though, between the meaning of the term in these uses and the meaning in "That *is* wrong"? Isn't it only that the latter expression asserts that some-thing is wrong, whereas the other sentences make only conditional assertion to this effect?

The most convincing type of case, in support of the "magnetic influence" theory, is one where, say, a mother says to her child, "That's naughty," hoping thereby to dissuade him from doing whatever he is up to. Such language, it may be said, is just like shouting "No!" to a dog. Its job is to stop behavior, and it is uttered for no other purpose. But is this so? There is a complexity here, of course, for "naughty" may *not* be functioning here as an ethical term at all; a child of three very likely has no ethical concepts. However, let us assume he does—that the mother's remark to him can be construed just as if it had been addressed to her husband. Now, is "That's naughty" just like "Stop that!"? It seems not to be. Perhaps the total moti-vation of the mother is to control conduct, but, by using "That's naughty!" she is doing so in a special way, an indirect way. She is doing it by calling the child's attention to a certain status of his action, and relying on his "inner-directedness" to motivate him to refrain from doing what he is doing. (Certainly this is what she is doing if she is addressing her husband.) In other words, although her *larger* goal may be control of conduct, in using this particular device, her route to that goal becomes a devious one; she pro-poses to reach a subgoal first, one that she thinks will lead naturally to the other. The subgoal is to get the child to see that the act is naughty. If the child retorts, "So what?" or "Why should I care?" it is evident that the subgoal was reached, but not the ulterior goal. In other words, although one may concede, for the sake of the argument, that "That's naughty" was said in order to control behavior, it also seems that the *peculiar* job of "That's naughty" is done if the child understands that (and perhaps best, why) that is naughty—whether or not he changes his conduct.

[22] See P. T. Geach, "Imperative and Deontic Logic," *Analysis*, XVIII (1958), 54*n*.

In *most* cases—and, except in addressing children, we very rarely are so blunt as to use ethical phrases in a way that looks at all like the way in which imperatives are used—we have no *intent* to influence the attitudes of hearers. If the peculiar function of ethical words, then, is merely to do this, we must be using them very badly.

3. The "expressive" thesis—the view that what ethical utterances do is express some motivational fact about the speaker, much as "Would that . . ." expresses a wish—is more convincing. There are words and forms that have an expressive job (for example, word order and rising or falling inflection for expressing questioning and asserting); perhaps ethical words do this sort of thing. Further, on this view we do not have to suppose that condemning Nero is trying to reform somebody; it makes some sense to say that condemning him is expressing an over-all, unfavorable attitude of our own.

Nevertheless, the moment we begin to ask ourselves *what* attitudes or motivational facts are expressed by ethical language, we run into puzzling difficulties. An early form of the emotive theory has generally been abandoned for this very reason. It had been supposed that ethical sentences express *actual emotions*, like indignation and horror. This view was discarded because, on reflection, it was seen to be obvious that on many occasions when ethical terms are used normally the speaker has no such identifiable emotions, and hearers are not led by his speech to suppose he has.

Let us survey some possible views.

One might suggest that ethical sentences express the speaker's over-all motivation, as pro or con. Thus, "It would be wrong (or undesirable) for me to do this" gives expression to my decision, my over-all inclination, not to do this. But this proposal is not satisfactory, because sometimes, when we think and say that something is wrong or undesirable, we clearly are not completely opposed, for actually we do the thing. Sometimes we call this "succumbing to temptation." (If one doubts this, one should ask oneself whether he can remember an occasion on which he did something that at the time he clearly thought was wrong. Almost everyone can. Do we cheat in examinations only when we think we ought? Do we always give as much to charity as we think we should?) Nor is this surprising from a common-sense standpoint. The ordinary view is that, when we make such statements, we are expressing our views about what is standard or ideal, and our actual conduct may conform or not.

Confronted by this difficulty, it is natural to suggest that ethical sentences express only *some* attitude or inclination, not necessarily the over-all balance of one's attitudes. According to this, then, to say something is wrong is to express some tendency to disfavor, some tendency to be shocked, and so on. But surely this is not quite right. It is not a proper use of English to use ethical language merely because we have *some* inclination in a certain direction. For instance, I may have *some* inclination to hasten the demise of my grandmother, knowing I am mentioned in her will. But surely it would be a gross mistake to think I can then correctly say, "It is desirable to hasten grandmother's demise" much less "I have an obligation to. . . ." What we properly can say is, "I'm *tempted* to murder grandmother." Moreover, on most issues we have some inclination toward and some inclination against. If the view in question were correct, it would be normal usage to say, of both *x* and non-*x*, that it is right or wrong or desirable, as the case may be. However, this is not how we use these words.

The most plausible suggestion, it seems, is to say that ethical language expresses a *special kind* of *over-all* attitude, say, of an impersonal or unselfish kind. "Is desirable," then, would express an over-all, impersonal kind of favoring; "is an obligation" would express an over-all, impersonal sense of obligation (as in our parked-car episode) or an over-all, impersonal inclination to demand that a certain thing be done. Again, "There is some obligation to . . . on account of your promise" would express an over-all, impersonal inclination to demand doing a certain thing when the aspect of breaking the promise is the only one in view.[23]

Such a view is very close to naturalism. It does not permit us to say that ethical utterances are true or false in the sense of science, but it does permit us to say they are misleading, for if a person uses an ethical sentence, which is the proper vehicle for expressing impersonal attitudes, when he has no such impersonal attitude, his statement is misleading. If a hearer is fully aware of this process, a proper retort from him might be something like this: "You say I have an obligation to do a certain thing but what you really mean is that you want me to."[24]

But is the proposal defensible? One somewhat implausible point about it (and related proposals) is that it is not clear that an attitude of any sort, impartial or otherwise, is expressed by all ethical statements. Suppose someone, whom you meet by chance on a train, asks your advice about the selection of a college for his daughter. You may give careful thought to his description of the problem, and conclude by saying, "I think she ought to apply at Pembroke College, at least among other places." But do you really care where she goes? Or does your hearer suppose you care? Consider another case. Suppose a fundamentalist is reading the Biblical account of the—apparently pointless—execution of someone (say, all men, women, and children among the Amalekites) at the behest, allegedly, of God. He says to himself, "That's strange. But it must have been right; otherwise God would not have ordered it." This use of "right " appears to be a normal one.

[23] This is much like Hare's proposal, but it is simpler in construing particular and universal judgments in a very similar way. The difference is that, whereas Hare proposes that ethical language expresses a universal wish or preference, the foregoing suggestion is that ethical language expresses impartial or disinterested attitudes.
[24] Such a view is defended by W. K. Frankena; see his review in *Review of Metaphysics*, X (1957), especially pp. 468 ff., and his "Hutcheson's Moral Sense Theory," *Journal of the History of Ideas*, XVI (1955), 356–75.

But is it a use that expresses the speaker's over-all, impartial preferences? No, rather the statement as a whole functions to *direct* his preferences. He *thinks* it can be *proved* that whatever God wills must be right; therefore he infers that this act was right and feels he must accept it.

4. There is a further objection to the "expression" thesis *unless* it is combined with the view that ethical statements *also* make a claim or assertion. It cannot explain the possibility of certain types of ethical doubt. Let us consider an example. Suppose a person thinks abortions should be permitted for social and economic reasons, in addition to the medical reasons currently approved by law and medical practitioners. Suppose there is no personal involvement, so that the attitude is a definitely impartial one: The individual simply thinks the present practice causes needless suffering and anxiety. The person's attitude is also definite; if he had the decision to make, he would sanction such abortions, and defend such action as being right.

Yet such a person might wonder and feel a lingering doubt. He might know that his view could be attacked on certain lines—for example, that in consistency he should permit infanticide and even murder. He is convinced that this attack will not be successful—but one cannot be sure of this, just as one may not be sure that a flaw in a mathematical proof cannot be detected.

If the emotive theory is true, how could there be such doubt? His impersonal attitudes are harmonious, speak "with one voice." (And, in this case, there is no conflict with personal desire.) Further, since, according to this view, there is no external standard beyond actual attitudes, by which attitudes can be measured, ought he not express his attitudes with conviction, without doubt?

If the theory that ethical language expresses some motivational state (not belief state) of the speaker breaks down, it is equally unacceptable to say that an ethical "conviction" just *is* the taking of an attitude—or that disagreement in attitude is a necessary and sufficient condition of ethical disagreement. For to have an ethical "opinion," obviously, is to have the sort of mental state to which an ethical sentence gives expression.

5. A final point about the emotive theory requires brief comment. We have seen that some emotive theorists have supposed that ethical statements make no assertion. Others have suggested that they do, and think that this suggestion removes an air of paradox from the theory. *What* ethical statements mean, according to this proposal, may differ from person to person and from case to case; the meaning comprises whatever fact statements the speaker would offer in support of his original ethical statement, if it were challenged. So, "That was wrong" might in one case be taken to assert "That was a breach of promise"; elsewhere it might mean "It caused unnecessary injury to other persons." In general, people who have different values or ethical principles will be making different assertions when they use ethical language; and the same person will be making different assertions

by the same word when the ethical principles he thinks relevant are different for the several contexts.[25]

Now, we are prepared to agree that ethical statements make assertions. We cannot agree, however, that what they assert, if anything, is identical with what this proposal suggests. Why should these things be said to constitute the *meaning* of the statement? Surely to say this is systematically to confuse the meaning of a statement with the *evidence* for it. Ordinarily, we distinguish the two quite clearly. "A is the murderer of B" is one statement, and "Blood was found on A's coat" is another statement by no means included in the first, although the truth of the second statement may be strong evidence for the first. This distinction cannot be abandoned without extraordinary confusion. Moreover, the proposal leads to numerous awkward consequences. Suppose I say something is wrong, on the basis of a general survey of the situation, without thinking *why* it is wrong (and sometimes saying why is a difficult matter). Shall we then say that at first my statement had *no* propositional content, and that a later repetition of the statement, after I had figured out my reasons, meant something different? This is implausible. It is also implausible to say we are using "wrong" in one sense when we support it by one kind of reason, and in a different one when we support it by another kind of reason. (This is like holding that "It is cold outside" *means* something different depending on whether I support my statement by saying I have just come in, or by pointing to an outdoor thermometer, or by pointing to a patch of ice on the sidewalk.) We would not think two persons were making different assertions if both said something was wrong, even if their reasons were quite different. Again, we do not think a child has failed to learn the meaning of "wrong," or to learn the word in the sense in which we use it, until he has come to agree with our moral principles. It is one thing to teach a child the meaning of the term, quite another to teach him the principles of ethics. It *is* true that words like "bad" have several senses; "bad egg" is different from "bad thing to do." But this kind of difference, which *is* a difference of meaning (although some philosophers dispute this), is unlike uses of "wrong" for different reasons—uses that may be the same in meaning.

5. MORE JOBS FOR ETHICAL LANGUAGE: MULTIFUNCTIONALISM

We have seen that there are many things we can do with words, such as make statements, express our feelings, give commands, issue invitations,

---

[25] See Hare, *op. cit.*, chap. 7; also C. L. Stevenson, *Ethics and Language* (New Haven: Yale University Press, 1944), chaps. 9 and 10.

Some of these writers are of the opinion that some ethical statements would not be supported by *any* further judgment, for example, "Enjoyment is a good thing." These statements, they say, therefore have no propositional content. See, for instance, Paul Edwards, *The Logic of Moral Discourse* (Glencoe, Ill.: The Free Press), pp. 182 ff.

make promises, christen ships, declare a resolution, and so on. The thought may well occur to us, then, that there are other jobs which we have not yet considered—different from stating facts, expressing attitudes, or having magnetic influence—which are done by ethical terms. Moreover, a second thought may occur to us: that perhaps a single ethical word may not always do the same job, on all occasions, even when being used in its ordinary ethical sense; and it may do more than one job on one occasion. Maybe there are many jobs that are done by ethical words, but most or all of them noncognitive jobs. Perhaps we should agree with P. Nowell-Smith, a British writer, when he says:

> They [ethical terms] are used to express tastes and preferences, to express decisions and choices, to criticize, grade, and evaluate, to advise, admonish, warn, persuade and dissuade, to praise, encourage and reprove, to promulgate and draw attention to rules; and doubtless for other purposes also. . . . What a person is doing with a particular value-word at a particular time can only be discovered by examining what he says in its context, but it would be just as absurd to suppose that there is no connection between these activities as to suppose that the same expression can only be used to do one job.[26]

There is one sense in which this proposal is unquestionably true, but not very important. That is, if what is meant is that the wider purposes that motivate ethical speech are quite numerous and that they differ from one occasion to another, what is said is certainly the case. Sometimes we use ethical language to extract a contribution, sometimes to prevent someone from doing something foolish, sometimes just to try out our opinion and see if it is defensible, and so on, almost endlessly.

The proposal can be an important one and worth serious examination as a theory of the nature and function of ethical terms, however, if we draw a distinction between *direct* and *consequential* jobs. Just as one might say the direct job of a hammer is to drive in nails (and that there is only one), but that it has many consequential uses (such as joining boards, building houses, and so on), so one might say that the direct job of ethical language is to do a certain thing (for example, make statements, express attitudes), and that the consequential jobs are things like praising, encouraging, urging, and so on. In this case, to make a statement about the plurality of direct jobs of ethical language, and the variety of these jobs from case to case, would be to make an important statement with which a naturalist and an emotive theorist must disagree; whereas the plurality of consequential jobs is a matter of little interest. We must look at this, for the distinction in question will throw more light on the difference between statements, commands,

---

[26] P. H. Nowell-Smith, *Ethics* (Baltimore: Penguin Books, Inc., 1954), p. 98. See also J. O. Urmson, "On Grading," *Mind*, LIX (1950), 145–69; H. D. Aiken, "A Pluralistic Analysis of the Ethical 'Ought,'" *Journal of Philosophy*, XLVIII (1951), 497–505, and "The Levels of Moral Discourse," *Ethics*, LXII (1951), 235–48.

invitations, and so forth, and accordingly on the difference between various theories of ethical speech.[27]

The difference between the direct job of an utterance, and its consequential job may best be explained by an example. Suppose you notice that someone is depressed and you wish to cheer him up. You can do this, often, by complimenting him, by remarking that he has done an exceptionally fine piece of work. You might say: "Your paper was the clearest, most penetrating, most delightfully written philosophical essay I have seen for several years." By saying this, you have done several things: you have (a) made a statement about his paper, (b) complimented him on his work, and (c) perhaps cheered him up. Your over-all guiding aim in making the statement was, of course, to cheer him up. But you chose a special way of doing this. The utterance of your sentence reached the remoter goal in the end by means of accomplishing something else first: conveying to your auditor that unless you are lying you have a certain belief about his paper, to the effect that it ranks first, on several counts, among many papers you have read. This result was something you intended to achieve by using the words you did. Moreover, this result is one thing you can achieve (if your auditor understands English) by your speech behavior alone. In contrast, whether your utterance cheers the man up depends on further factors, in particular on the causes of his depression, and on whether or not he is interested in excellence in philosophy. We need not decide whether complimenting him is done by your words alone; but it is worth noticing that if your auditor is Bertrand Russell and you are a housewife who has skimmed his book while doing the ironing, it is doubtful whether your words will compliment.

In the above instance, let us say that making a statement and having it understood was a *direct* job of the speech-act, whereas cheering up was a *consequential* job. In general, we may speak of an effect of a speech-act as a *direct* effect, job, aim, or function of the act (a) if, for the type of context in which it occurs, the effect is accomplished by the speech-act alone, without benefit of favorable circumstances other than the auditors' familiarity with the language,[28] (b) if it was intended,[29] and (c) if its accomplish-

---

[27] Some of my points and examples have been suggested by the Ph.D. dissertation of Dr. George Pitcher, entitled "Illocutionary Acts," 1957, deposited in the Widener Library at Harvard University. The content of this dissertation was in its turn to some extent suggested by lectures, classes, and remarks by Professor J. L. Austin. I do not suggest that anything I say would necessarily be approved either by Dr. Pitcher or Professor Austin.

[28] It is not clear how much we should include in "familiarity with the language." Is a soldier's response to "Attention!" a result solely of his familiarity with (army) language? Such details require further examination. "Speech-act" must include intonation, some facial expressions, and possibly still other things.

[29] Not necessarily in the sense of any preceding conscious plan, but only in the sense in which putting my hand in my pocket to get matches, while engaged in a conversation, is intended to produce matches. For a discussion of this point, and illuminating remarks on other puzzles pertinent to the present context, see H. P. Grice, "Meaning," *Philosophical Review*, LXVI (1957), 377–88.

ment is not causally dependent on other effects of the same speech-act with properties (a) and (b). Other intended effects of a speech-act which lack either property (a) or (c) may be called "consequential" jobs, effects, or functions. The direct job of a speech-act may have distinguishable components, for instance, if I both urge and advise a person with one and the same utterance.[30]

If one can show that ethical words are used to do numerous *direct* jobs— some of them over and above making statements (naturalism), expressing attitudes, exercising "magnetic influence" (emotive theory)—the result is an important one. The same is true if one can show that an ethical word does different direct jobs depending on the context. In contrast, everyone can agree that consequential jobs are numerous, and variable from case to case.

Take as an example an ethical sentence that was, or might have been, used (in its Greek translation) by Socrates, when his friends urged him to take advantage of their arrangements for a flight from prison and escape from death. Suppose he said: "It is *wrong* to avoid a sentence duly imposed by the courts of the land," in a firm voice. There are many things that, in the context, Socrates has done. In effect, he has announced a negative decision; he has expressed an unfavorable evaluation of the offer; he has gently reproved those who would help him; he has declared a moral conviction. But are these jobs of his sentence direct or consequential? It makes a great deal of difference: A naturalist will agree that all these things are done, but will suggest that the direct job was that of making a certain statement of fact. And the same is true, *mutatis mutandis*, for the emotive theory. The naturalist—and any "monist" about the direct jobs of ethical words—is not refuted until it has been shown that the direct jobs done by ethical words are numerous and variable from case to case.

How shall we decide the matter? We cannot criticize any specific proposals about various things that ethical words may do directly, by posing counterexamples. The thesis we are considering is *not* that there are certain direct jobs that ethical sentences are used to do on *every* occasion. It is held only that in *some* contexts ethical words do one job, whereas in other contexts they do another job. Obviously, we do not show that ethical words

---

[30] Notice that the direct aim of a command-making utterance is different from that of a statement-making utterance. Take "Close the door!" as compared with "The door is closed." The latter has the direct aim of getting across to the auditor that the speaker, unless he is lying, believes that the door is closed. The former has the direct aim of getting across to the auditor that he is being notified of the speaker's wish that the door be closed, and that the speaker may hold him guilty of insubordination if he fails to close the door. (If it is obvious that the speaker is not in a position to hold the auditor guilty of insubordination, the effect will be different—and we shall construe the whole procedure as an impolite request.) In many contexts "The door is closed" may function as a request or as a command; but we must construe these as consequential, since inferences by the auditor, with premises about human nature or customs or manners, are necessary in order for the effect to occur.

never do a certain job, simply by showing that they do not do it in one type of context.

What we can do is give sympathetic attention to individual cases that look prima facie like plausible examples of the new thesis, and examine what we somehow know about them. Ideally we should consider many examples, but we must content ourselves with one. One example, however, can serve to establish a number of important points.

Let us, then, take a homely example, and examine what we can fairly say are the direct jobs of the ethical language used. Suppose a father and his son have been discussing rules for the son's use of the family car. Suppose further the discussion becomes mildly heated, and the son passes a somewhat uncomplimentary remark about his father's attitudes and values. And suppose finally the mother intervenes and says to the son: "You *ought* to apologize to your father for that remark." This sentence seems a typical example of an ethical remark.

What has the mother done? What was the direct aim of her remark? The naturalist will say that it was to make a fact statement and have it understood; the emotive theorist will say that it was to influence her son to apologize by the "magnetism" of the ethical words, and to express her attitude. But there are many other possibilities: that she was advising, urging, commanding, requesting, entreating, exhorting, and so on.

We may concede, for the sake of the argument, that the over-all guiding aim of the mother was simply to extract an apology—just as we suggested, above, that the over-all aim of a compliment was to cheer someone up. But this was not the direct aim of her remark. What then was it? Let us eliminate some possible proposals.

She was not commanding or ordering: In order to command one must make clear not only what he wants done, but in the context it must be apparent that the addressee may be held guilty of insubordination if he fails to do what is wanted. The mother is not saying something like: "Apologize to your father, or you'll not use the car for a month!" Nor is she requesting. She is not making a wish known, and making it a matter of politeness to her that the wish be fulfilled. She is not saying something like: "Would you mind apologizing, John?" Nor is she entreating. She is not making a wish known and making clear that it means a great deal to her whether the act is done. She is not saying something like: "I beg of you, John, please for my sake apologize to your dear father!" She has not done any of these things.

On the other hand, one can say that the mother has (and doubtless with intent to do so) urged, expressed a preference, advised, and exhorted her son to make an apology. Can we say, then, that urging or advising and so forth is the direct job of her remark?

Not quite, for none of these listed jobs[31] is exactly identical with what has

---

[31] We ignore "exhorting" since this term, according to Webster, refers to "strong urging by words or advice."

been done. If her direct aim had been just to advise, clearly it could have been achieved as well by saying "I advise you to apologize." But saying this would have left open the question whether she thought he ought (in the moral sense); sometimes we advise when we don't think a person ought in this sense, and there are many good grounds for advising a person to do something, other than the fact that we think he morally ought. Parallel reasoning leads to the conclusion that she was not just urging, for she obviously would have left open the question whether she thought he ought in the moral sense, if she had said merely "I urge you to apologize." Similarly, she was not just expressing a preference, since, again, "I should prefer that you apologize" leaves open questions which "You ought to apologize" does not. In other words, if the direct aim of the actual remark had been identical with the suggestions listed, the mother could have made the same point by an alternative locution. But it is clear that none of these alternative locutions does just the same thing as the original statement.

If we have to choose, it seems more plausible to say that the direct job of the mother's utterance was to make a statement to the effect that disapproval of failing to make an apology can be objectively justified—provided, of course, we can give a further explanation of what "objective justification" is, of a kind to escape the objections to naturalism. If one took this view, the urging, advising (and other) jobs of her statement would be consequential, causally dependent on the fact that she affirmed this proposition with conviction and feeling.

But there is another alternative that has some plausibility. Although it is clear that the direct aim of "You ought to apologize" is different from that of "I advise you to apologize" (and so on), it is possible that the direct job of "You ought to apologize" is identical with some *special kind* of advising, urging, and so forth. Such is the proposal of P. Nowell-Smith. Ethical language, unlike "I advise" language, can be properly used only when certain recognized conditions are fulfilled; and because this is the case, use of ethical language has special *contextual implications* in the sense that it authorizes certain inferences (variable according to the context). There are certain things, then, that ethical sentences cannot be said to assert or state, but that their use implies in the context. When the mother says "You ought to . . ." in this context, she authorizes inferences she would not have authorized had she said "I advise you to . . ." or "I urge you to. . . ."[32]

What inferences might be said to be authorized by ethical language, such as to distinguish it from ordinary advising language? Nowell-Smith has sug-

---

[32] Nowell-Smith discusses "contextual implication" in *Ethics, op. cit.,* pp. 80 ff. According to his account, inferences are authorized in the sense that people will naturally draw them—because they know that ethical language is *normally* used only if certain conditions are fulfilled—and since everyone knows that they will, one is deliberately permitting them to be drawn unless one does something to prevent it.

gested several. First, use of ethical language implies that competent persons would agree with one's advising or urging; one may not, without misleading, use "ought" for advice known to be peculiar, unless one explicitly points out the fact. Next, ethical language implies that the speaker would give the same advice in all similar situations. Third, use of "ought" in its moral sense implies that the speaker's advice is based on reasons, that it is in conformity with the relevant recognized moral rules or with the speaker's moral principles.[33]

Some other writers have made somewhat different suggestions. They have said that the *special* force of ethical language—over and above the job it shares with other language, of advising, expressing attitudes, expressing preferences, and so on—is to make some sort of *claim*. What sort of claim? One proposal[34] has been that a moral statement claims that the attitude expressed demands priority in the direction of behavior, and that this demand can be justified in an appropriate way. Another suggestion[35] is that ethical statements claim that the attitude declared "will commend itself to anyone who considers the facts and allows them to register on his moral sensibility" and that it has "survived and will survive the impact of criticism." Still again, it is suggested[36] that the attitude declared is "unbiassed," that it is "based on adequate knowledge of the nature and effects" of the kind of thing toward which it is directed, and that "it will be shared by others who are also unbiassed and knowledgeable."[37]

If we combine these suggestions with the view we have been describing, the total proposal is this: Ethical utterances sometimes have one direct job (usually or always noncognitive) such as advising, expressing a preference, urging, and so on, and sometimes another; there is not just one direct job that ethical utterances always have, but several different ones; and the direct jobs of ethical sentences, although similar to those that can be done by non-ethical sentences, are special jobs, because of the claims made and

---

[33] See Nowell-Smith, *op. cit.*, pp. 186–92, 268, 306 ff.

[34] John Ladd, *The Structure of a Moral Code* (Cambridge: Harvard University Press, 1957), chap. 5, especially pp. 85, 101–07.

[35] W. H. F. Barnes, "Ethics without Propositions," Supplementary volume XXII, the Aristotelian Society, 1948, pp. 27–28. See also, W. K. Frankena, *op. cit.*

It is not suggested that the writers whose "suggestions" we are now recording necessarily hold the view stated above, that there are many different direct jobs of ethical terms, and that a term does one or more of these in one context, others in another. Some of them hold monistic theories, for example, the emotive theory, that ethical terms always express attitudes and that this is always the whole or the major part of their direct job. These "suggestions," then, are ones that *may* be combined with the thesis here under discussion.

[36] Jonathan Harrison, "When is a Principle a Moral Principle?" Supplementary volume XXVIII, the Aristotelian Society, 1954, p. 133.

[37] A somewhat similar view is expressed by J. N. Findlay, "Morality by Convention," *Mind*, LIII (1944), 142–69.

the inferences authorized. Let us, for convenience, call this proposal "multi-functionalism."[38]

Is the multifunctionalist theory an improvement over the emotive theory? One major point of difference is that this theory asserts that ethical statements have many and different direct jobs, whereas the emotive theory thinks that magnetic influence and expression of attitude are the features of all ethical statements important for understanding them. The mutifunctional thesis is helpful because it encourages us to notice the details of the use of ethical terms in various contexts. On the other hand, the emotive theory is helpful because of its challenging generality. Moreover, it may be that the multifunctionalists' talk of advising, urging, and so on is capable of further analysis.

A second major point of difference between the theories is in the assertions made about the implications or claims of ethical statements. The emotive theory, except in its simplest form, does not deny that ethical statements imply, suggest, or even assert propositions. However, unlike multifunctionalism, the emotive theory does not say that such implications or claims are what is *distinctive* of ethical language, or suggest that there are *standard* implications that distinguish ethical language. And because the multifunctionalist does say these things, it is open to him to say that ethical utterances are sometimes *misleading* or *improper*—thereby approaching close to the naturalist and nonnaturalist view that ethical utterances are true or false. These proposals are promising, and may justify saying that the multifunctional theory is an important advance over the emotive theory.

Can we say that the multifunctionalist theory is good enough? One difficulty is that the theory, as we have stated it, is an amorphous thing; it is a collection of theories, or a pattern for theories. As we have stated it, the theory leaves several questions open. One is: *Exactly what* descriptions should be given of the direct aims or jobs of this or that ethical statement? Obviously, the proposal of the theory might be right, that there are many and that they differ from case to case; but particular descriptions of the process may be quite erroneous. The correctness of the pattern does not guarantee the accuracy of its application. Another and more important question is: *Exactly what* are we to say constitutes the implications and claims of ethical statements, which distinguish the ethical from other types of language? It is possible to concede that there are some, but to say there are some is not to state correctly what they are. A multifunctionalist is not saved, by his theory, from giving a hopelessly unsatisfactory account of these. To say that the distinctive thing about ethical language is its implica-

[38] The example we have used—the mother urging an apology—is not representative of other contexts. Take a comment, after perusing a book on Roman history: "What Nero did was wrong." Here, no advice is being given; no one is being urged. What we are doing is (it might be said) condemning Nero, expressing an unfavorable moral attitude toward Nero. Of course, as in the other case, this is being done in a special way, with claims or authorizing of inferences.

tions that one's advice is not peculiar, that one can provide some reasons, and that one's advice is in conformity with generally recognized moral rules may in fact not do justice to the specific claim or implications of ethical terms.

The pattern of the theory, then, may be correct, but the pattern is not enough. We need an accurate filling of the pattern, and for this many suggestions have been made. We may choose between these; or we may make novel suggestions of our own. Obviously we must pursue this question somewhat further. We shall approach it from a new direction in the succeeding chapter; at its close we shall suggest the most convincing form a noncognitivist theory can take.

FURTHER READINGS

A. J. Ayer, *Language, Truth and Logic* (London: Victor Gollancz Ltd., 1948), chap. 6 and pp. 20–22. A vigorous statement of the emotive theory.

——, *Philosophical Essays* (London: Macmillan & Co. Ltd., 1954), chap. 10.

R. Carnap, *Philosophy and Logical Syntax* (London: Kegan Paul, Trench, Trubner & Co., Ltd., 1935), sects. 1, 2, 4.

B. Russell, *Religion and Science* (New York: Henry Holt & Company, Inc., 1935), chap. 9.

C. L. Stevenson, *Ethics and Language* (New Haven: Yale University Press, 1944), chaps. 1, 2, 4–7, 9. The most important statement of the emotive theory.

——, "The Emotive Meaning of Ethical Terms," *Mind*, XLVI (1937), 14–31.

——, "The Emotive Conception of Ethics and its Cognitive Implications," *Philosophical Review*, LIX (1950), 291–304.

——, "Brandt's Questions about Emotive Ethics," *Philosophical Review*, LIX (1950), 528–34.

A. I. Melden, "On the Method of Ethics," *Journal of Philosophy*, XLV (1948), 169–81.

J. E. Ledden, "On the Logical Status of Value," *Philosophical Review*, LIX (1950), 354–69.

R. Robinson, "The Emotive Theory of Ethics," The Aristotelian Society, Supplementary volume XXII (1948), 79–106.

Philip Rice, *On the Knowledge of Good and Evil* (New York: Random House, 1955), chap. 3.

J. Harrison, "Can Ethics Do Without Propositions?" *Mind*, LIX (1950), 358–71. Lucid summary and critique.

E. F. Carritt, *Ethical and Political Thinking* (Oxford: Clarendon Press, 1947), chap. 3. Criticism.

A. C. Ewing, *Ethics* (London: English Universities Press, 1953), chap. 7. Criticism.

S. E. Toulmin, *An Examination of the Place of Reason in Ethics* (Cambridge, Eng.: Cambridge University Press, 1950), chapters 3 and 4. More criticism.

V. Tomas, "Ethical Disagreements and the Emotive Theory of Values," *Mind*, LX (1951), 205–22. Criticism.

Henry Aiken, "Emotive 'Meanings' and Ethical Terms," *Journal of Philosophy*, XLI (1944), 456–70. A criticism.

John Ladd, "Value Judgments, Emotive Meaning and Attitudes," *Journal of Philosophy*, XLVI (1949), 119–29. Criticism.

John Dewey, "Ethical Subject-Matter and Language," *Journal of Philosophy*, XLII (1945), 701–11. Criticism.

H. J. Paton and R. C. Cross, "The Emotive Theory of Ethics," The Aristotelian Society, Supplementary volume XXII (1948), 107–140. Critical articles.

R. B. Brandt, "The Emotive Theory of Ethics," *Philosophical Review*, LIX (1950), 305–18.

——, "Stevenson's Defense of the Emotive Theory," *ibid.*, 535–40.

——, "Some Puzzles for Attitude Theories of Value," in R. Lepley (ed.), *The Language of Value* (New York: Columbia University Press, 1957). See also the reply by C. L. Stevenson, in Lepley, pp. 317–23. All critical.

E. Vivas, *The Moral Life and the Ethical Life* (Chicago: University of Chicago Press, 1950), chap. 10.

R. M. Hare, *The Language of Morals* (Oxford: Clarendon Press, 1952). A "prescriptivist" theory properly regarded as a variation of the emotive theory.

W. K. Frankena, "Hutcheson's Moral Sense Theory," *Journal of the History of Ideas*, XVI (1955), 356–75.

——, "Ethical Naturalism Renovated," *Review of Metaphysics*, X (1957), 459–73. Suggestions for a more satisfactory revision of the emotive theory.

W. H. F. Barnes, "Ethics without Propositions," The Aristotelian Society, Supplementary volume XXII (1948), 1–30. Suggestions for revising the emotive theory.

Paul Edwards, *The Logic of Moral Discourse* (Glencoe, Ill.: Free Press, 1955), chaps. 5–8. A well-written defense of a form of the emotive theory.

W. D. Falk, "Guiding and Goading," *Mind*, LXII (1953), 145–69. A criticism.

H. Feigl, "Validation and Vindication," in W. Sellars and J. Hospers, *Readings in Ethical Theory* (New York: Appleton-Century-Crofts, Inc., 1952). A form of emotive theory.

H. J. N. Horsburgh, "Criteria of Assent to a Moral Rule," *Mind*, LXIII (1954), 345–68.

A. Kaplan, "Are Moral Judgments Assertions?" *Philosophical Review*, LI (1942), 280–303. A form of emotive theory.

P. Nowell-Smith, *Ethics* (Baltimore: Penguin Books, Inc., 1954). A multifunctionalist theory.

J. O. Urmson, "On Grading," *Mind*, LIX (1950), 145–69.

10

The Justification of Ethical Beliefs

Despite the arguments back and forth, there are vigorous and intelligent representatives of contextualism, supernaturalism, naturalism, nonnaturalism, and noncognitivism at the present time. Evidently, none of these groups is yet willing to concede that it is wrong. But we have seen that all of these theories, at least in the forms in which they have been stated, are open to strong or even conclusive objections, although the conclusiveness of the objections varies from case to case. Of the five theories, naturalism and noncognitivism show by far the most promise of formulation in some way that might be satisfying.

In recent years, however, various writers have rejected all of these theories, and have surveyed the problems from a new point of view. On the one hand, they have opposed naturalism: they have urged that ethical statements are in important ways quite different from the statements of the sciences, certainly from simple scientific statements like "Copper conducts electricity." On the other hand, they have also opposed nonnaturalism: they have said there are no nonnatural facts, that there is no intuition or rational insight, and that the only facts to which we properly appeal in assessing ethical statements (or convictions) are natural facts, among which human attitudes have a paramount place. But noncognitivism has also been criticized, at least in many of its forms. It has been claimed that there are *correct* procedures for answering ethical questions and assessing ethical statements; it is not true that just any procedure, as long as it convinces someone, is as proper as any other. Further, when the proper procedure is applied, some ethical statements stand up as justified, whereas others are shown to be indefensible. It has also been suggested that it is not misleading to say that ethical statements are correct, valid, true, or known; at least, it would be more misleading to deny these things.[1]

[1] Among the writers I have in mind are Kurt Baier, W. D. Falk, J. N. Findlay, Jonathan Harrison, John Rawls, Israel Scheffler, S. E. Toulmin, and Morton White.

241

The contentions listed do not by themselves constitute a complete meta-ethical theory: the framework must be filled in. In particular, as stated they do not identify the "correct method" for resolving ethical questions or explain why it is correct. They include, furthermore, no positive theory about the meaning and function of ethical statements. But perhaps they are enough to give us hints that types of theory have been proposed, or could be proposed—perhaps to some extent developments or modifications of some theory already discussed—that might escape the objections to the views we have examined.

In the present chapter we shall develop a theory along these lines and explain the reasons that support it. We shall not attempt to summarize the total views or reasoning of the writers who have advocated the theses we have cited; their theories are too different and too complex. What we shall do is pose in our own way a form of theory, of this general type, that strikes us as most convincing.

1. A PARALLEL WITH THE LOGIC OF SCIENCE

There are problems about the justification for believing laws or theories in science that are very similar to the problems about the justification of ethical beliefs. We can ask, in the case of ethics, when or in what conditions a person is warranted or justified in having an ethical conviction; and we can ask, in the case of empirical science, when or in what conditions a person is warranted or justified in believing a scientific law or theory. The one belief is practical, the other theoretical; but there is a problem of justification in both cases.

It is not merely that there are similar questions in the two fields; the things that can be said in answer to them are also rather similar. Indeed, the more we think of it, the more we shall see that the parallel is extensive, and that reflection on it is clarifying. Let us begin by noting two similarities of considerable importance, the second of which we shall develop in some detail. In the course of our discussion, further and more detailed parallels will be pointed out.

First, it seems plausible to suppose that ethical statements are correct or incorrect, but at the same time it does not seem that any evidence of observation actually entails or requires any ethical belief. But scientific laws and theories are in the same case: None of these is entailed or required by observational evidence alone. It may be argued, however, that the parallel breaks down at an important point if the evidence of observation can at least refute or require the rejection of a scientific law or theory (whereas such evidence does not seem sufficient to falsify an ethical belief); but to this one can reply at least that one or even many observations do not strictly and unconditionally falsify a scientific theory—since one can always question whether they were carefully made, and so on.

There is a second parallel which is more important for us. All of us will agree that, even if some factual statement—law, theory, or prediction—is not entailed by observational evidence, we may be justified in believing it on the basis of observation. We think that, given certain kinds of observational evidence in certain circumstances, we can assert a corresponding statement with reason. There is no accepted general statement, applicable to all types of scientific statement, about the circumstances and the kind of observational evidence which warrant a given degree of confidence in a statement supported by observation. But some writers have formulated, for an especially simple kind of case, a rule prescribing that statements be accepted in the presence of a certain type of observational evidence—what is sometimes called "a rule of induction." An example of such a rule will be helpful for our purposes. Suppose we are considering a simple prediction of the form: "The next observed A will be B." All of us agree that we have observational evidence of some weight for this prediction if we have observed a large number of A's in the past and all, or almost all, of them have been B. We might then formulate a general directive, for predictive statements of this type, which embodies our belief about the force, as evidence, of past observations. We might propose the following general sort of directive: "If m/n of the observed A's have been B, then believe that the next A will be B with a degree of confidence $m/n+1$!" We might accept this rule, as a good rule directing or licensing beliefs in predictive statements; and this rule might give expression to our view that a certain degree of confidence in a predictive statement is warranted on the basis of observational evidence of the kind specified.[2]

Suppose someone questioned such a directive. What could we say in support of it? One thing we might say is that, although it is not true by definition or confirmable by observation, still practically all thoughtful people accept it (or something very like it), or at least act as if they did. Perhaps not all; perhaps mystics do not, and some people act as if they do not, when the generalization affects matters close to personal concerns. Second, some reasons can be given for following the directive. What sort of reasons? There is much controversy about this. One possible type of reason is: we need a policy for predicting the future, and it can be proved by deductive logic that this policy will be successful in the long run if any systematic policy will be.

Is there a close parallel to this in ethics? Is there some relation between ethical judgments or principles and "evidence" of some kind, so that it is justified or warranted to assert an ethical proposition if it stands in this relation to the evidence? If so, then we can frame a rule or directive like the

---

[2] Some philosophers rephrase the consequent clause so as to read "then it is probable to the degree $m/n + 1$ that the next A will be a B" and urge that the whole statement is true by virtue of the definition of the word "probable."

above, tellling us when ethical propositions may be accepted. And it might be quite general in form, like the directive formulated above.

Furthermore, it is possible that, if we had such a rule before us, we could support it by considerations similar to those which support the above "rule of induction." On the one hand, we might be able to say that practically all persons accept the rule, that they are prepared to assert an ethical statement, or say it is justified or warranted, if and only if it conforms to this rule. Perhaps not *everybody*; perhaps some people think in different ways. Moreover, we might be able to give reasons for accepting the rule, reasons that do not demonstrate but which are still convincing reasons, in view of what ethical convictions are, what purposes they serve, and so on.

The question of whether there is a rule or directive about the acceptance of ethical propositions that has this kind of status, is one we must investigate through most of the present chapter.

2. THE QUALIFIED ATTITUDE METHOD AS THE "STANDARD" METHOD

Is there, then, a general rule or directive that has the same status, in ethics, as a rule of induction has for empirical science?

In order to answer this question, we must first examine whether any such rule or directive is embodied in the practice of reflective people when they consider whether an ethical statement is justified, whether it is warranted or defensible. If there is, then it would have an initial force comparable to that which a rule of induction enjoys if it is shown to give formal expression to the practice of working scientists, to their practice of placing confidence in theories that have a certain relation to the evidence.

But is there anything at all of this sort that can be said about a "standard practice" of thoughtful people? Is there any consensus at all? One might think not, but we must not forget that we must answer homely questions of ethics nearly every day, and that we are not absolutely paralyzed by the problems set before us. Suppose your roommate asks your advice about whether to invite a certain young lady to the junior prom; he wants to know what is the "best thing" to do. Or a college is offered a gift of a million dollars by an alumnus, provided the college will agree to a complex form of transaction that will result in the entire gift being deductible from the alumnus' income tax; the college president asks himself whether accepting the gift would be immoral. Surely we are often faced with such questions —and have some procedure for getting an answer for them. Perhaps we do not *think* we have a standard procedure, simply because we do not pay attention to the methods we use.

Let us then ask ourselves: What *is* our method or practice in assessing ethical opinions when, for the sake of *our own* decisions, we are motivated to undertake a *full-dress* review? And is there a consensus, an agreement, on the proper method?

In order to see whether we have a "standard" practice in ethical reflection, comparable to the consensus of working scientists about when confidence should be placed in a hypothesis, let us look at a real-life example. The example we choose does not concern a matter of importance, but it has some illuminating features. It concerns a question of obligation, but there is no reason to think that other ethical questions (for example, about what is worthwhile or admirable) are not answered in similar fashion.

A Hopi Indian once asked the writer for an opinion about the following problem. He (Don) had owned a colt. About a year previously, a neighbor of his, named John, who also owned a colt, had come to him and proposed a trade. Both colts were of similar age, and, as Don thought (so he said), of about equal promise. Don agreed, and the exchange was effected. During the ensuing year, however, John's newly-acquired colt (the one that had belonged to Don) developed lameness. John therefore went to Don and proposed to re-exchange, offering Don's former colt and $10, in return for the animal he originally had. Don would not agree to this. John then insisted that Don *must* re-trade, on moral grounds. Don was adamant. The issue put to the writer was: Is Don bound morally to a re-exchange? .

Doubtless everyone will agree with the answer the writer gave—that Don's refusal was well within his moral rights.

What happened in the course of reflection that led to the writer's venturing this opinion? Two things. On the one hand, in the course of listening to the story he *formed an initial attitude*. There was nothing in the situation as depicted that moved the writer to *favor* Don's returning the horse, much less to *favor asking or demanding* that he do so. Nor could the writer imagine he would feel obligated to return the horse in similar circumstances. Quite on the contrary, he did favor John's desisting from putting pressure on Don, and would have approved someone's telling him to do so.

However, there was a second element in the writer's reflection. We saw in Chapter 2 that a particular moral judgment must be supported by a general principle. Thus, while listening to the story, the writer was wondering whether there was any tenable moral principle that would require that Don return the horse. In fact, as the story came to its conclusion, it seemed to the writer there was none. Actually, what kind of principle could have such a consequence? Such a principle, it would seem, must be roughly this: "Whenever two persons have made a trade, each is obligated to call it off, even as much as a year later and no matter how (within some limits) the situation has changed, if the other party requests it and has good reason to be disappointed with the deal." But (the writer thought) such a principle would be unworkable, and no one would advocate it seriously. If such a principle were universally adopted, the consequences would be chaotic—and very likely the amount of trading would be greatly reduced.

Nevertheless, before feeling quite satisfied with our conclusion, there are some questions which we should want to ask. For instance, is it quite clear that Don did not know in advance of the defects of his colt, that he did not misrepresent its condition, that he did not really instigate or at least encourage the trade with the colt's defects in mind? If these things were true, we should be more inclined to say he must return the horse. Again, was there any understanding, at the time of the trade, about a right to a re-exchange in case there was not satisfaction, and if so, exactly what was the understanding?

Why do we raise these questions? It is because our reflection on the situation brings to mind certain, doubtless vague, principles that we accept. So, we put these questions, with the thought of extracting further relevant information that might lead to an opposite judgment on the issue. When the answers to the questions are satisfactory (as they were), we are reinforced (as the writer was) in our original conclusion.

We test our tentative conclusion by appeal to principles, then: both by a review in terms of principles we do accept, and by considering whether we could accept the kind of principle that would lead to a contrary decision. Then, if this review by appeal to principles leads to a conclusion coinciding with the attitude we have formed, the issue is normally thought decided. In most cases, doubtless, no further procedures are required or used.

It might be thought that in our description of a "standard" method we should give primary weight to appeal to principles, particularly principles also acknowledged by the community to which we belong—and so we should. However, it would be a mistake to think that appealing to such principles is all we do, or all that we need to do. In many instances the other aspect—the forming of an attitude, a preference, an impulse, a "feeling of obligation" or "requiredness-experience," a feeling of remorse or indignation or admiration—is indispensable. It is for this reason that historical moral philosophers have emphasized "particular intuitions" as much as they have. We must see why.

It is possible to think of an adult person's mind or conscience as rather like a living telephone book, stocked with moral principles of the Ten Commandments type, but more numerous and more complex. The principles might be like the ones indicated above, but including others like "Don't take the property of someone else without his permission"; "If you have promised to do something, you must do it"; and "Never injure another person." We might think of our mind as a kind of IBM machine: It is fed a description of a particular situation and then searches for the appropriate rule or rules, which then appear suddenly in our conscious thoughts.

Doubtless things are this simple for many, perhaps most, cases in daily life. On the other hand, it is easy to see that they are not always so simple —for three main reasons.

First, sometimes the relevant principles result in conflicting directives.

For instance, one makes a promise to meet a friend at the shore for a fishing trip and cannot reach him in order to obtain a release from the promise; but one's wife falls ill, and one feels obligated to remain at home. What is one to do? One principle, we may suppose, directs that one keep his promises, and hence tells him to meet his friend. Another principle, however, directs one to care for members of his family who need his care, and hence tells him to stay at home. There is no superprinciple, in one's head in the way in which these principles are, to give direction. It may be suggested that there is such a superprinciple, to the effect that obligations to care for one's family always take precedence over promises to others (or the reverse); but certainly this is not true—what we should do surely depends on the detailed nature of the promise and the circumstances and the situation in one's home. It has been suggested that there is a rule for all such situations of conflict, to the effect that we should do whatever is likely to maximize the welfare of everyone involved; but this proposal seems oversimplified as an account of any "standard" practice of resolving conflict among moral principles. The moral principles we have explicitly in mind, then, seem to need supplement for purposes of practice.

Second, the rules we have in mind are imprecise. Indeed, it is doubtful whether anyone has ever written down a moral principle with all the qualifications and exceptions that we should want written into it if we are to take it seriously. Take, for instance, the preceding statement about keeping promises. Hardly anybody would demand adherence to this principle as it stands, for there are promises we are not bound to keep, for example, ones made under duress or on the basis of deliberate misrepresentation by the person extracting the promise. For application to particular cases, then, principles as we have them in mind must often be filled in, specified, or somehow supplemented.

Third, obviously sometimes we find it necessary to correct or abandon some principle as hitherto formulated. We may, for instance, have been operating on a parental principle, "Always form your friendships with members of your own race." We may now find it necessary to reject such a principle altogether. There is, of course, no sharp line between the need to correct or abandon a principle and the need to fill it out or specify it.

Something beyond an appeal to our stock of already accepted principles, then, is sometimes necessary in ethical thinking. This conclusion does not, of course, disparage the importance of explicit principles. One must agree that, for most situations of daily life, they are sufficient, and in every case they function to direct attention, at least, to relevant aspects of a situation. Moreover, they have presumptive force. Thus, if I have made a promise, the rule, "Keep your promises," stands, simple as it is, until rebutted—until it is shown that there is a stronger counterobligation, or that there are special circumstances.

When something more is called for, some supplement to our stock of principles, however, what *can* we do and what *do* we do? The answer to this question is not easy, and our suggestion will doubtless be too simple in some respects. For one thing, it would be surprising, considering the role of analogy in legal thinking, if appeal to analogy were absent in moral thinking. Again, problems at this level may just be overwhelming to many people, so that "solutions" are got in a rather random way; to this extent, people do not have a "standard" practice. Nevertheless, there are some things that can be said.

One thing that we can do, when a supplement to principles is required, is to accept the *promptings of the attitudes* we find persisting in ourselves, with certain important restrictions and reservations to be noted.[3] We *can* do this, and it seems that sometimes we do. For instance, we may have been operating on the principle, "Thou shalt not bear false witness." Suppose, then, we are thrust into a situation where truth would cost an innocent man his life—say, in a concentration camp. Very likely in this case there will also be another principle that we accept and is relevant to the case, perhaps "Give help to anyone in dire need." How do we decide what we ought to do, since we may very well not have any superprinciple that gives direction for this contingency? In this situation we may very well *feel a strong obligation* (in the sense explained on p. 118) to lie, and be sure that we shall never forgive ourselves if we do not. If so, we shall then feel compelled to modify the first of the foregoing two principles: either considering it as no longer a matter of absolute obligation, or introducing specific types of exception.[4] It seems, then, that we sometimes "correct" our principles by appeal to attitudes, probably (we shall discuss this at more length later) by appeal to *preferences* in the case of principles about what is desirable, *to feelings of obligation and inclinations to make demands on others* in the case of principles we would express by speaking of "obligations," to *feelings of remorse or indignation* (and so forth) in the case of principles about acts or persons being morally reprehensible or admirable; and so on. For a real-life example of this sort of process, we may recall the case of the girl who rebelled against her parents' views on race relations, described earlier (pp. 130–31).

There is point in comparing the role of feelings or attitudes in ethics with

---

[3] There is not as sharp a distinction as we might suppose, between following the direction of an attitude and appealing to a principle. Take the principle that we should keep our promises except those made because of deliberate misrepresentations by the other party. We do not carry this principle around with us explicitly in a quotable form. Rather, we notice we are influenced in our inclinations to judge cases by certain features, and we think, on reflection, that these features are of general weight. Hence, we form in words a rough corresponding principle, and say we "accept" it. Such a principle is, however, more like having an attitude than are the moral slogans we have been taught from early childhood.

[4] Very likely the feelings or attitudes we have are often a consequence of believing the principles we do. But this is not always the case. If it were, we should not be able to correct our principles by appeal to our attitudes.

the role of observation in science. Every scientist accepts a host of theories and laws about the subject matter with which he works, just as all of us have principles in ethics. But these beliefs are subject to continuous revision in the face of experience; theory must conform with observation. "Standard" thinking in ethics is similar: we revise our principles to conform with our persistent attitudes (feelings, impulses, emotions), with some qualifications to be mentioned.[5] There are further parallels. For instance, in empirical science, observations do not determine exactly how principles are to be revised; often there are various possibilities and a choice between them must be made. Again, sometimes an observation may conflict with scientific theory so sharply, and in such an isolated way, that it is simplest to discount it as illusory, or as a result of an undetected defect in one's experimental arrangements, or even to lay it aside as just "unfinished business." Perhaps the same situation exists in ethics.

There is a final complication. We suggested that, when a supplement to principles is called for, we accept the promptings of our attitudes, with some *restrictions and reservations*. What are these? Well, just as we rely on observations in science only if they are carefully made and in some sense public and repeatable, and otherwise discount them, so in ethical reflection there are some attitudes we discount.

1. We discount an attitude if we think it not *impartial*. For instance, in our horse-trading example, the writer would have discounted his attitude, would not have thought he was taking a "moral" attitude, if he had supposed his attitude about returning the horse was a result of his friendship with Don, and would have been different had the positions been reversed. What is it to be "impartial"? It is to take an attitude that would not be changed if positions of individuals involved were reversed, or if the individuals were different from whom they are. One recent writer (Kurt Baier) has called substantially this the condition of "reversibility."

We may test a person's impartiality by the "requirement of generality" discussed in Chapter 2. That is, we inquire whether a person is willing to advocate a general principle corresponding to his attitude; if he is not, we question his impartiality. Strictly, however, impartiality is not adequately tested by this device, for, as we saw in Chapter 2, the *letter* of the requirement of generality can be met by a general principle carefully

[5] There is one difference. Physical theory, taken with a description of the experimental setup, may logically imply "The ammeter will point to 30" and we can observe whether or not this is the case. Whereas, although in ethics we may reject "There is no obligation to do *x*" by appeal to the fact that we feel a strong obligation to do *x* (if some further qualifications are met), we cannot say that ethical principles entail anything about how we shall feel—at least not in any direct way. All we are saying is that, just as we *test* physical theory by observations about ammeters, so we *test* ethical principles by appeal to observations or feelings of obligation. We do not suggest that the relation of physical theory to statements reporting observation is *exactly* the same as that of ethical principles to statements reporting observations.

framed so as to permit for some persons behavior that the author of the principle would not really want for all.

2. We discount an attitude if we think it *uninformed*. An attitude is uninformed if, were the person impartial, it would not have occurred as it did if he had acquired true beliefs or been disabused of false beliefs, or if his true beliefs had been more vivid, like what they would have been if he had observed the facts. An attitude is informed, in brief, if it would stand up in the face of a vivid awareness of relevant facts, if the person were impartial.

3. An attitude is discounted if it is a consequence of an *abnormal* state of mind. The criterion for normalcy is inevitably somewhat vague. It is not a matter of statistical averages. Rather we have a concept of a healthy state of mind: alert, responsive to the facts, free of repressive burdens. We contrast it with states of illness, insanity, fatigue, anger, grief, and depression.

4. An attitude—or some one of a set of attitudes—is discounted if accepting its prompting would be incompatible with having a system of principles both consistent and general in the sense explained in Chapter 2.

Or rather we should say that an attitude is discounted if accepting its prompting would be incompatible with having a system of consistent general principles which is *not excessively complex*. This last condition is vague. We should certainly not reject an attitude because keeping it might require an ethical system to contain a dozen principles in contrast to an alternative system with only two or three, if the attitude in question were quite decided. We do, however, demand that guiding attitudes lead to principles which are simple enough to permit explicit statement. And we do demand that the system of principles be simple enough so that it can be understood by interested persons of reasonable intelligence, and serve as a guide for conduct.

In summary, our proposal about the "standard" method of ethical thinking is this. (1) We decide particular problems both by appeal to principles that we already have more or less explicitly in mind and by appeal to our preferences, feelings of obligations, and so forth (which kind of attitude depending on whether the question is one about what is desirable, or what is obligatory, and so on). (2) We correct our principles if they are incompatible with our criticized (undiscounted) attitudes (feelings of obligation, and so forth); and we rely on our criticized attitudes in filling out and weighing our principles. (3) Judgments, as noted in Chapter 2, must be consistent, and particular ones must be generalizable. (4) Attitudes are discounted if they are not impartial, informed, the product of a normal state of mind, or compatible with having a consistent set of general principles not excessively complex. Ethical thinking, then, is a complex interplay of attitudes, principles, formal requirements for principles, and rules for discounting. None of these can be submerged in the other three. Perhaps there are complications we ought to add.

Whether or not in fact the foregoing is a correct account of the "standard" method of testing ethical judgments, obviously the method described *could* be the standard method. Let us call the possible method for testing ethical judgments that we have described, the *Qualified Attitude Method.* Our supposition is that the Qualified Attitude Method represents the practice of many or most thoughtful people in testing ethical judgments. Accordingly, we can now put forward for consideration a general principle about when an ethical statement is to be asserted, comparable to a rule of induction. The principle is this: "Assert an ethical proposition if and only if it satisfies the conditions of the Qualified Attitude Method!"

A natural question for the reader to be asking at this juncture is what is our *evidence* for thinking that the Qualified Attitude Method *is* the standard method. We should be clear about this. In the first place, then, there have not been empirical inquiries directly on this issue. Moreover, the introspective reports that philosophers have offered from time to time differ, to some extent, from what has been suggested.[6] The chief reason for the reader to accept our proposal must be that he himself *recognizes* the method as the one he uses. (We do not expect everyone to recognize this, for we do not suppose that everybody uses the method all the time.) Of course, some parts of the method will hardly be queried, for example, that we have statable principles and do appeal to them in particular situations requiring moral decision or advice. What is most likely to be questioned is whether we rely on the guidance of our attitudes in correcting and weighing principles, and whether we "discount" them for the reasons stated.

The reader who is doubtful whether he uses the method we have described, in "correcting" his principles, should not overlook the fact that we sometimes offer, as a point relevant to someone's ethical statement, "You wouldn't feel this way if you were completely impartial about it." Or, "You'd approve of this if you knew all the facts." Or, "You might feel differently about it if you were yourself." The fact that we do is some reason for thinking that we do discount moral attitudes or feelings for the reasons stated. Furthermore, the fact that we do suggests that we think that such feelings and attitudes play a guiding role in moral judgment— what we would expect if we all appeal to attitudes in weighing, filling out, and correcting our principles.

Our contention is, however, not only that the Method (and the cor-

---

[6] See S. E. Toulmin, *An Examination of the Place of Reason in Ethics* (Cambridge, Eng.: Cambridge University Press, 1950), chap. 11; C. L. Stevenson, *Ethics and Language* (New Haven: Yale University Press, 1944), chaps. 5–7; C. D. Broad, "Some Reflections on Moral-Sense Theories in Ethics," *Proceedings, The Aristotelian Society,* 1944–45, p. 166; W. F. R. Hardie, "Naturalistic Ethics," *Proceedings of the British Academy,* XXXIII (1947), pp. 18 ff.; W. H. F. Barnes, "Ethics without Propositions," *The Aristotelian Society,* Supplementary volume XXII, 1948, pp. 23 ff.

responding rule) represents our practice in moral reflection (just as inductive methods and the rule of induction represent the practice of working scientists), but also that there are good reasons for using the method, for accepting and following the rule. We shall now consider these.

3. IS THERE AN ACCEPTABLE ALTERNATIVE?

Are there any good reasons why people should accept this rule and test ethical statements by the Qualified Attitude Method?

We shall have one good reason if it turns out that there is no systematic alternative not subject to serious objection. Therefore, we must now examine some other possibilities. We cannot hope to assess all possible methods, but we can review the ones most likely to be convincing.

1. *A theological rule.* A theologian might suggest, as an alternative, that ethical judgments are justified if they coincide with the *will of God.* Unlike the supernaturalist who *defines* "right" as something like "approved by God," this theologian merely says there are good and sufficient reasons for adopting the rule, "An attitude is justified if there is good reason to think God approves of it." It might be argued that Christians accept this rule, or indeed, that the basic commitment of the Christian is just to accept this rule.

Unfortunately, although a position of this sort is possible and doubtless worth working out, in fact no one has defended such a view at any length. Nor is the present a proper place to attempt to develop such a theory. We shall, therefore, offer only cursory comment.

There is one major difference between the Qualified Attitude Method and any test by appeal to the will of God. The Qualified Attitude Method is a definite account of how exactly we do or should go about answering ethical questions. The theological method is not: It does not tell us how to ascertain the will of God, whether we are to do this by exegesis of revealed documents, by consulting "insights" after or during prayer, or perhaps by using the Qualified Attitude Method. We have already reviewed the limitations inherent in a resort to revelation as a source of knowledge about divine approval. Until some further explanations are provided, then, the theological method of ascertaining one's duty is not an alternative method at all, for it does not tell us what to do in order to answer ethical questions. This objection is conclusive.

It may be that we are misreading some theologians if we think they wish to advocate an ethical method different from the Qualified Attitude Method. Certainly, some theologians have meant by "God" just "the moral law" or "those principles to which we ought to give our ultimate allegiance." Other theologians regard it as gross anthropomorphism to suppose that God "approves" or "has a will" in any sense substantially similar to that in which human beings approve or have aims or policies; in fact, they tend to say that God is altogether incomprehensible to human beings. If so, possibly the injunction to follow the will of God is intended quite metaphorically. It may be, then, that the aim of some theologians is not so much to provide an alternative method for answering ethical questions, as to add a supernatural dimension to the result. They may be saying: "True, we must answer our ethical questions by the kind of reflection you describe. But one must not think that your conclusions are a mere reflection of human attitudes. Justified ethical convictions are also ones that in some sense enjoy cosmic support. And this gives them a new significance." With such a view, of course, we need have no quarrel, as students of metaethics; whether, as students of theology, we should object is a question we need not pursue.

2. *The appeal to nature.* Another alternative to the Qualified Attitude Method for answering ethical questions is simply advice to find out what is "natural." So, it may be said: "An ethical proposition is to be asserted if it prescribes what is *natural*." Or, "approval of *x* is justified if *x* is natural."

Unfortunately for such proposals, *whatever happens* is "natural" at least in the sense of being in accord with natural law. Whereas these writers have intended, at least, to infer by their method that some things that happen are not right. In order to make the distinction they want to make, the distinction between right and wrong acts or desirable and undesirable events, it is necessary to suppose that some things that occur and are in accordance with natural law (in the sense in which science talks of "natural law") can be out of conformity with "ideal nature." The question then becomes, how do we decide what is "ideal nature"? Or, in other words, how do we decide what *ought to be*, is *desirable*, in nature? But this question is precisely the duplicate of the question we were wanting to answer in the first place. If there are any problems we have been trying to solve, in order to determine what is right or good, all of them are repeated in the question, what kinds of events are good or desirable in nature, or what is "ideal nature"? Attempts to solve our problem by appeals to what is "natural" are nests of confusion.

3. *The utilitarian method.* The method (and corresponding rule) for answering ethical questions that is most likely to seem convincing today, as an alternative to the Qualified Attitude Method, is the Utilitarian. We shall conclude our discussion with this Method. Unfortunately there is not just one method properly classified as utilitarian. In order to do the possibilities as much justice as we can, we shall discuss briefly a form that is today more widely influential, and more convincing, than any other. It is conveniently called "Rule-Utilitarianism."

The theory consists primarily of the proposal of a method for determining what acts are right.[7] Roughly the method is as follows: (*a*) A particular act is permissible if it is not prohibited, in one way or another, by the

---

[7] The method is described more fully in Chapter 15.

ideal rules of the society in which it is performed. (*b*) The ideal rules for a given society are to be ascertained as follows. First, they must have certain formal characteristics: They must be general prescriptions or prohibitions that contain no proper names; they contain all necessary qualifications and reservations; they may include second-order rules prescribing what is to be done in case the first-order rules give conflicting directions. Among all possible sets of rules having the formal properties mentioned, the set that is correct for a given society is the one that has this characteristic: that a conscientious effort to conform to it, by everyone in the group, would *maximize the welfare* of sentient beings (taking into account the results of possible planning on the expectation of such conformity), as compared with a comparable effort to conform with any other of the possible sets of rules.

The Rule-Utilitarian Method for answering ethical questions is quite similar, in many ways, to the Qualified Attitude Method. The formal requirements, for principles of obligation, for instance, are much (not exactly) the same. It is quite possible that an application of the Rule-Utilitarian method would lead to the very set of principles of obligation to which the Qualified Attitude Method would lead. But it need not. The Qualified Attitude Method leaves open the possibility that utilitarianism, even when interpreted broadly, is not quite true; whereas Rule-Utilitarianism does not.

There are three reasons for preferring the Qualified Attitude Method to Rule-Utilitarianism. (*a*) Application of the Rule-Utilitarian method presumes our ability to compare different sets of rules in point of their welfare-producing capacities, and therefore ability to compare, in respect of relative welfare, different hypothetical social systems. But how are we supposed to decide whether one social system contains more "welfare" than another? As we shall see more fully in Chapter XV, there is no plausible alternative to appeal just to preferences—and presumably not just to anybody's ill-considered preferences, but to the preferences of an informed, impartial, consistent person in a normal frame of mind—the same kind of person presumed for the Qualified Attitude Method. If so, the Rule-Utilitarian Method is bound to use the Qualified Attitude Method for deciding what social system will yield maximum welfare. Now, if we are going to use this method anyway for making comparisons of welfare, it is *simpler* to use it also for answering questions about obligations, about right and wrong. The fact that it is simpler to do this is a reason for doing so, unless there is some special reason to the contrary. (2) There may be things which should be taken into account in determining what behavior is right or wrong, in addition to the welfare of sentient beings. The Rule-Utilitarian Method necessarily rules such things out of consideration. The Qualified Attitude Method leaves the issue open. The fact that it does is a point in favor of the Qualified Attitude Method. Perhaps the point is not an important one if in fact we have no reason to think the two methods would yield conflicting prescriptions. But we should reflect about whether, if it came down to a choice, we could still accept the prescriptions of Rule-Utilitarianism, if they conflicted with those of the Qualified Attitude Method. It is doubtful whether we would; and this doubt is supported by historical fact—that earlier and simpler forms of utilitarian method were supplanted by the Rule-Utilitarian theory very largely because the implications of these views were seen to be sharply at variance with "intuition" or "common sense"—or, as it seems to us, with what the philosopher in question supposed would be supported by the Qualified Attitude Method. (3) But we can also say something much stronger. The objection to Rule-Utilitarianism is not simply that theoretically it might rule out some consideration of importance for deciding what conduct is right or wrong. In fact it does rule out something important. For we shall see in Chapter 16 that some facts which we can summarize under the term *"equality* of welfare" are important for whether something is right or wrong. Our prediction is that the reader, when he sees what acceptance of the Rule-Utilitarian Method would commit him to on this point, will be strongly disinclined to adopt this method in contrast to the Qualified Attitude Method.

The functional argument. The Rule-Utilitarian Method has recently been supported in an interesting and novel fashion, in a book by Professor S. E. Toulmin.[8] The importance of his reasoning transcends the particular issue of the Rule-Utilitarian method, however, for the type of argument used raises a general question: whether an analysis of the *function* of ethical language, of conscience, of ethical reasoning—of the whole cultural complex which we can call "moral systems"—can successfully be used as the premise of a demonstration that some method of ethical thinking is correct. Toulmin thinks it can.

Toulmin begins by suggesting that the function "of ethics" is to "correlate our feelings and behaviour in such a way as to make the fulfillment of everyone's aims and desires as far as possible compatible." From this view of the function of ethical thinking and discourse, and of the "purpose" of the activity of which they are a part, he infers that the Rule-Utilitarian method is correct. But how *exactly* does the conclusion follow from the premise? Toulmin's discussion is far from explicit on this point, and we must simply do our best to reconstruct his line of thinking. We shall begin with the last stage of his reasoning, and attempt to work back from there.

Toulmin's thinking appears to be as follows: If the *one and only thing that justifies* engaging in a certain activity is its achieving a certain effect, then one ought to engage in this activity if and only if doing so will achieve this effect, and in such a way as to achieve this result. (We must agree.)

---

[8] *An Examination of the Place of Reason in Ethics* (Cambridge: Cambridge University Press, 1950). For comments on the "function" of ethics see pp. 84, 130, 137, 142, 170, 223–24.

Now, the one and only thing that justifies engaging in ethical reflection or discourse is the end of correlating the behavior of all, by general rules, so as to maximize the welfare of one's society. (This has to be proved.) Therefore, one ought to engage in this activity (saying "That's wrong," giving and being convinced by reasons for ethical conclusions, and so on) in such a way that this will result in correlating the behavior of all by general rules. Hence, one will properly say of a particular act, "That's wrong" (thereby discouraging such behavior) if and only if it infringes the general moral code of the group (for this is the system of general rules that are to correlate behavior); and one will properly advocate amendment of the code (perhaps by saying, "It's really wrong to do that, although most people in this society think it right") if and only if the code is in a relevant respect falling short of its function of providing rules that will, if followed, maximize the welfare of the group.

There is much force in this reasoning if one is convinced of the important premise that the one and only thing that justifies the activity of saying or thinking "That's wrong" (and so on), or reasoning about rightness and wrongness, is correlation of the behavior of all, by general rules, for maximizing the welfare of the group. But how is one to show this? This is puzzling; for to say that "the one and only fact that justifies" doing something is a certain thing appears to be making an *ethical* statement. If Toulmin's argument is based essentially on the *assumption* of an important ethical premise, his argument is fruitless.

Toulmin thinks, however, that we can *infer*, from the fact that the "function" of ethical reasoning is a certain thing, that the one and only justifying reason for it is that certain thing. This suggestion is worth our examination. We shall, however, examine the proposal with the assumption that "function" means the sort of thing many social scientists mean by it, and not with the assumption that "function" means "purpose of those who judge and reason ethically," the sense in which Toulmin seems to use the term. The thesis, interpreted in this way, is of considerable inherent interest, and in any case the outcome of our examination will be substantially the same as it would be if we interpreted the thesis in what seems to be Toulmin's sense.[9]

[9] But Toulmin also argues in another way. Sometimes he says we can ascertain the "function" of ethical judgment and reasoning by a procedure no more complex than simply noticing what kind of decision we *call* "ethical"; in his words, we must notice how "reasoning must be designed to influence behavior if it is to be called 'ethical.'" *Op. cit.*, pp. 131, 144. Thus, the argument seems to be simply that we refuse to call judgments and reasoning "ethical" except insofar as they are controlled by the aim of directing behavior, by general rules, so as to maximize welfare. In other words, argument and reasoning are called "ethical" if and only if their purpose or intent is that of directing behavior, by general rules, so as to maximize welfare.

It then appears to be argued that, since the purpose of "ethical" argument and reasoning is (by definition) that of directing behavior (and so forth), therefore the one and only thing that *justifies* engaging in ethical discourse is the end of correlating the

In order to assess the validity of such inferences, we must know what is meant by "function." This term is seldom defined by social scientists, but their practice (so far as it is clear) permits us to view its meaning as not different from the one it obviously has in the following sentence: "The function of the heart is to pump blood." The meaning of "function" in this statement may be inferred from the kind of explanation that ordinarily would be given of the statement: that blood would not circulate but for the pumping activity of the heart; and that the organism would die if the blood did not circulate. So, it seems we may fairly say that "the function of x is F" means approximately the same as, "There is some system S that would disintegrate (or become maladjusted) except for F, and x is necessary for the maintenance of F." The proposal about the function of ethics might, accordingly, be explained as follows. The system S may be identified as the social group, and the form its maladjustment might take is the frustration or nonfulfillment of its members. It might then further be said that this system would be maladjusted without the presence of an effective method for correlating behavior by general rules (F). Finally, it might be said that ethical reasoning and judgments are a necessary condition of

---

behavior of all, by general rules, so as to maximize the welfare of one's society—the premise questioned in the text.

There are various difficulties with this reasoning. (1) It is implausible to suggest that the *overt meaning* of either "ethical reasoning" or "moral reasoning" is what Toulmin suggests it might be. It is not true that, if we inquire of anyone what he means by these terms, he will reply by referring to the controlling purpose of the reasoning or judgment, much less that he will specify that this controlling purpose is what Toulmin suggests it is. (2) His proposal about "ethical reasoning"—which is parallel to naturalistic definitions of terms like "desirable" and "wrong"—is faced by serious counterexamples. For instance, in Chapters 15 and 16 we shall suggest some reasons for thinking rule-utilitarianism is mistaken. This reasoning seems to us clearly "ethical" reasoning, but it is not reasoning controlled by the end of maximizing the welfare of society—since the aim of the reasoning is to show that maximizing the welfare of society is not precisely what we ought to aim at. The same is true of many historically important ethical discussions, for example, Butler's and Kant's. (3) It seems that more discussion is needed, in order to pass from the proposition, "The *purpose* of all ethical reasoning is to correlate the behavior of all . . ." (which is a statement about the factual intent of persons who reason or judge "ethically"), to the proposition, "The one and only thing that *justifies* engaging in ethical reflection or discourse is. . . ." The former seems to be a factual and nonethical statement, the latter an ethical one. (4) We cannot too often insist on the importance of the point made in the course of criticizing naturalism (pp. 178–79), that one cannot coerce a person's basic ethical judgments (here about what kind of activity and reasoning is "justified") by facing him with the *meaning* of his words (here "ethical"). In the present case, if someone persists in thinking that nonutilitarian considerations are good reasons for accepting or rejecting ethical judgments, this fact shows that his critic has simply given the *wrong* definition of "ethical reasoning," at least for the usage of this nonutilitarian thinker. Another way of putting much the same point is to say that the nonutilitarian thinker can answer his critic's argument simply by saying, "From now on I am using the phrases 'ethical reasoning' and 'ethical judgment' in a way different from what you suggest, namely as follows. . . ." To this retort the critic (and Toulmin) can give no answer.

See the review of Toulmin's book by R. M. Hare, *Philosophical Quarterly*, I (1951), 372–75; also G. Nakhnikian, "An Examination of Toulmin's Analytic Ethics," *Philosophical Quarterly* IX (1959), 59–79.

having such an effective system. "The function of ethical judgments and reasoning is the correlation of the behavior of all by general rules . . ." may be taken to mean, "The social group would become seriously maladjusted (its members not having self-fulfillment) but for some effective system for correlating the behavior of all by general rules, and ethical judgments and reasoning are a necessary part of such a system."

We must agree that if the meaning of "the function of ethical judgments . . ." is as suggested, then whether the function of ethics is as stated can be decided by empirical inquiry. But a "function" statement is then a *causal* statement; and it clearly does not follow from *any* causal statement (any more than it follows from a factual statement about somebody's *purpose* in doing something) that the one and only thing that *justifies* doing something is some stated particular thing. One who does not think that "self-fulfillment" is the only proper aim of conduct will question whether the fact that something helps secure it is a conclusive point in favor of that thing (perhaps securing equitable distribution is another ultimate aim of conduct); at any rate, the issue is an ethical one.[10]

The difficulty is a general one, infecting all attempts to extract, from analysis of the "function" of ethical thinking or moral systems in society, either rules about what kinds of reasoning in ethics are "good reasons" or rules specifying when ethical judgments are justified. We have ourselves agreed (pp. 89 ff.) that in all probability ethical reasoning would not exist but for certain typical problem situations in society (temptations to steal, murder, and so on), that the capacity of moral systems (conscience, ethical language, ethical reasoning, criticism of others, and so on) to solve these problems to some degree is the explanation of their existence in human culture, and that moral systems are essential for tolerable social life. What conclusion, however, with respect to ethical principles or rules for "valid" ethical reasoning, *strictly follows* from such considerations? None whatever; at least none *without the addition of ethical premises or naturalistic definitions* of "valid reasoning," "good reasons," "justified attitude," "justified thinking," and so forth.

Nevertheless, such matters are not irrelevant. Logically they do not prove, but they can persuade. What does not logically entail a proposition can in its own way be "good reason" for it. So, a survey of the role of ethical principles, conscience, and ethical reflection in social life may *incline us to endorse* ethical judgments that have certain properties, to affirm ethical propositions only when certain conditions are met. The functions of ethical reasoning, then, might properly *incline* us to accept the Rule-Utilitarian Method, or, equally well, the Qualified Attitude Method.

[10] Some of the foregoing remarks are indebted to a paper by C. G. Hempel, read on April 18, 1958, and to Ernest Nagel, "Problems of Concept and Theory Formation in the Social Sciences," *Proceedings of the American Philosophical Association* (Eastern Division), I (1952), 43–64.

4. POSITIVE SUPPORT FOR THE QUALIFIED ATTITUDE METHOD

Let us suppose many people *do* accept, think warranted, an ethical proposition if and only if they think it is indicated by the Qualified Attitude Method. Is there any reason they could give for their doing so, if someone chose to raise a question? They might of course reply, as we have been doing, "What is your alternative?" But we have by no means shown there is *no* substitution for this method. We have only cast serious doubt on some methods that might well appear attractive substitutes. Is there any support, of a more positive kind, that the disciple of the Qualified Attitude Method might call on, in answering the charges of some skeptic?

The question is a difficult one. If we accepted the Ideal Observer form of naturalism, we could defend the method by appeal to what ethical statements *mean*. According to this view, all ethical statements assert that a fully informed, vividly imaginative, and impartial person, in a normal frame of mind, would take a certain attitude toward something; and use of the Qualified Attitude Method certainly tends to establish, indeed is the only way to establish, that this is so. But we have questioned this theory, so that justification of our method simply by reference to the meaning of ethical statements is ruled out for us. We might try to defend the method by appeal to the meaning, not of ethical words themselves, but of phrases like "justified ethical opinion" or "rational moral conviction," thereby trying to show that it is true by definition that an ethical opinion is "justified" or "rational" if and only if it satisfies our method. But we have already seen (pp. 178, 257) that a person cannot be coerced into agreeing that an ethical opinion is "justified" if and only if a certain condition is satisfied, by appealing to his (supposed) meaning for "justified." The very fact that he asserts persistently that some ethical opinion is justified that is not justified, according to a given proposal about his meaning for "justified," is good evidence that the proposal about his meaning for "justified" is a mistaken one. Again, we have questioned whether any method can be supported by a straightforward argument based on conclusions about the *function* of ethical statements; we cannot say "Because their job is this particular thing, therefore it follows that they must be tested in this particular way." Furthermore, it is obvious that our reasoning would be circular if we endeavored to support the Qualified Attitude Method by an *ethical* argument, say, by trying to show that it would be the *best thing* for everybody if we acted on the basis of principles sanctioned by the method. What we are considering, after all, is the logical foundation of any and all ethical statements.

There is one thing we can do consistently and without circularity. We can make some points that in fact will *dispose* all intelligent people who have thought through the difficulties of other methods, *to feel satisfied* with accepting ethical propositions if and only if they meet the requirements of the Qualified Attitude Method. A proper appeal to the functions of moral systems may be incorporated in an argument of this sort.

At first thought it may seem that an argument in support of the Qualified Attitude Method is not very helpful, is not impressively rigorous or coercive, if all it does is *dispose* people to favor or feel satisfied with doing something. Such an argument will seem more impressive, however, when we recall that it is in all respects on a par logically with the kind of argument that can be given in support of central points of scientific method, such as the license to generalize on the basis of observations.

It may be objected that an argument of such a type, in support of an ethical method, can never get us anywhere. For one consideration that will dispose a person for or against a given method will always be whether this method will endorse his firmly-held ethical convictions; if a person sees that a given method is incompatible with a cherished ethical belief, he will to some extent be disposed not to accept the method. Therefore, it may be said, an argument of this sort for an ethical method can never succeed in recommending a method which will require a person to change his ethical views, and in that sense use of it will never get us anywhere. But such criticism overlooks two important points. We must concede that the incompatibility of an ethical method with deeply-entrenched ethical beliefs will dispose a person not to accept the method. But something comparable is true for recommendations of scientific method. Recommendations of scientific method would also fail if a person saw that acceptance of the method would require him to deny that he had a mother or that he lived on the surface of the earth. If it is no objection to a line of reasoning in support of scientific method that no one would accept it if so doing would commit one to wholly absurd factual beliefs, then it is no objection to a line of reasoning in support of a method for ethics that no one would accept it if it led to wholly absurd ethical conclusions. There is a second reply. This is that it will be difficult for a person to find a systematic method for ethics which will just fit his particular set of ethical commitments, which will permit him to believe just the ethical propositions he already accepts. One can find an ethical method which will support some or even many of one's ethical convictions. But *whichever* systematic method one picks, one will probably find it is incompatible with *some* of one's ethical beliefs. Thus, it is an exaggeration to say that an argument of the type we are considering, in support of an ethical method, can get us nowhere; for the adoption of practically any systematic method for ethical reflection will be incompatible with some ethical beliefs and hence may get us somewhere.

A second objection may be raised. "How," it may be asked, "is one to make points which will dispose people to feel satisfied with accepting ethical statements if and only if certain conditions are satisfied, *before* one has decided what ethical statements mean? Does one not *first* have to come to some conclusion—naturalist, nonnaturalist, or noncognitivist—about what ethical statements mean or do, before one can sensibly consider reasons for accepting them if and only if certain conditions are met?" To this question the answer is that, certainly, we are in a *better* position to consider reasons for accepting ethical statements *after* we are clear what they mean or do. But we can also say that we are in a *good* position to do this as things stand, before we have decided about one of these theories. There are many things we already know about ethical statements, and what acceptance of one commits us to. We are familiar with the use of ethical language before we have an explicit formulation of what it means and does; and this familiarity will help us judge intelligently whether a good reason has been given for accepting an ethical statement if and only if it meets certain conditions. For instance, we all know that to say "It is right to do so-and-so" is to sanction doing so-and-so on the part of anybody and everybody; it is to say that there is no reasonable and serious objection from the point of view of society, to so-and-so being done. To say that something is right may be to do much more than this; but at least it does do this. It seems, then, that we may not have to come to agreement about the precise meaning of ethical terms in order to reflect intelligently on whether there are convincing reasons for using the Qualified Attitude Method.

Are there really any reasons, which will be convincing to all intelligent persons who have been disabused of factual mistakes, in support of use of the Qualified Attitude Method? Let us turn to this.

First of all, which are the points of the Method for which a defense is most likely to be demanded? Perhaps these: (1) that the weighing and filling out of ethical principles is to be guided by one's corresponding attitudes, except where there is reason to discount the attitude; (2) that attitudes are to be discounted if they are uninformed; (3) that attitudes are to be discounted if they are products of an abnormal frame of mind; (4) that ethical principles must be general (in the sense we have given this term), and that (much but not exactly the same thing) attitudes are to be discounted if they are not impartial. Let us now see what may be said that will dispose an intelligent person to accept these aspects of the Qualified Attitude Method.

1. Why should we follow our attitudes in filling out ethical principles and weighing the force of conflicting principles? Part of the answer to this question is that it is difficult to think of an alternative, if we wish a general procedure for all types of ethical principles. Logical considerations are not sufficient; what we need is something to which we can appeal in much the way in which empirical science can appeal to sense experiences for filling out principles and deciding between conflicting principles. Attitudes or feelings can do this job, and it is not clear that there is anything else that will. We can agree with John Stuart Mill when he said—albeit with too little qualification—that "the sole evidence it is possible to produce that

anything is desirable, is that people actually do desire it."[11] Moreover, I think we may take it as uncontested that attitudes are at least relevant guides, reliable at some points. Take the case of desires and the desirable. Will anybody in fact deny that a certain kind of thing is desirable, if in fact everybody would desire it in all circumstances? Or will anybody in fact deny that a thing is not desirable, if nobody would desire it under any circumstances whatever? We may doubt whether anybody would in fact deny either of these things. So there is prima facie plausibility in the proposal that desire of some sort, or under some conditions, is a test of the desirable. But how about other types of ethical principle? How shall we show that we should frame principles about moral obligation to conform with our (discounted) feelings of obligation and our (discounted) impulses to make demands on the behavior of others, or our principles about the morally reprehensible or admirable to conform with our (discounted) feeling of pride, remorse, indignation, and admiration? About these principles we can say something exactly parallel to what we have just said about reliance on criticized desires as a test for the desirable.

2. Why are attitudes to be discounted—ignored in the framing and correcting of corresponding principles—when they are uninformed? The answer is this. Suppose we want to know whether some action—the acceptance of a certain job, for example—is desirable. If we do, we want to know whether the *whole* situation as it is or will be is desirable, not merely part of it. If a position is such that we shall be underpaid, or that our health will be undermined, we do not want merely to know whether the course of accepting it is desirable aside from these unfavorable points. We want to know whether the total situation, everything considered, is desirable. Now, if in order to make this decision we must rely on whether we want to take the position—whether the thought of it elicits our desire, strikes us as attractive—we shall obviously want *all* aspects of the situation before our minds, certainly not just aspects of it different from the unfavorable points mentioned. Our estimate will be incorrect, probably, if all the aspects which would attract or repel us are not represented in our thought of the object, vividly before us. We shall hesitate, then, to follow the guidance of an attitude if we think it is uninformed, and we shall prefer to follow the guidance of the better informed as compared with the worse informed, when we know one attitude is better informed than another.

3. Much the same can be said in favor of discounting attitudes expressive of an abnormal state of mind, in favor of those expressive of alert, discriminating states of mind, free of emotion and repressive burdens. For abnormal states are states in which we react to situations not fully as we know them to be, but as schematic outlines; thus if we are angry with a person, we are apt to forget his good points. Abnormal states are states of reduced sensitivity, states when aspects of an object that would normally attract

11 *Utilitarianism*, Chap. 4.

or repel us do not affect us, because parts of us are silenced. Normal states of mind do justice to the nature of the object, to subtler tendencies to react on the part of the subject. They are more adequate clues for an evaluation of an object as it really is. Moreover, normal states of mind give us representative responses to situations; they yield responses which we shall be able to endorse when we are in another mood or time. This is not true of abnormal frames of mind. Hence, if we want an ethical principle we can stick with, we had best correct our principles by our attitudes in normal frames of mind.

4. But why should we require that ethical principles be general (of universal form, and with no proper names), and why should we discount attitudes that are not impartial? This question is an important one. (*a*) The first thing we can say is that if these requirements were not made, nobody could ever be forced by facts and logic to embrace any ethical principle or application that he personally did not like. Everyone could insist on formulating ethical principles so as to permit exceptions for himself and friends. This, of course, would be fatal to the hope that ethical thinking can provide a reasonable adjudication of conflicts of interest— "reasonable" adjudication in the sense of being made by appeal to principles suited to command respect from all parties to a dispute. A principle, in order to fill the office of principle suited to adjudicate conflicts of interest, must avoid arbitrary selection of personalities as ones to be favored, and prescribe a solution for conflicts by reference to features of the objective situation. A general principle, supported by or guided by impartial attitudes, is fitted in just this way, and can command the respect of reasonable men. If ethical principles are general and impartial principles in this sense, then and only then are they fitted to the social task ethical principles are ordinarily expected to perform. (*b*) Suppose it were in our power to choose whether a country should be governed by general laws (with no proper names in them), passed by disinterested legislators, or whether the opposite system is to obtain. Knowing what we do about human beings, we know that the chances of general benefit will be greater, under the impartial-legislator system, than under the alternative. Now, moral systems are an informal analogue of public law, with the difference that each person has the responsibility of deciding for himself what set of laws he will follow in his conduct and advocate for others. In this informal analogue, it is as obvious as in the case of public law that the general interest will be served better if the "legislators" confine their rules to general laws following impartial attitudes than if the opposite is the case. On this account, a benevolent person will be inclined to favor that kind of "legislation." But so will a prudent person, if he considers what kind of "legislation" he prefers as general practice, for he will see that his chances, on the average, of living well under a system of impartial legislation will be better than they would be with an opposite arrangement.

The preference of rational persons, then, must favor impartial attitudes as the guides of moral legislations, and laws that are general in form.[12]

The reader must decide whether these considerations—especially in the light of other methods—constitute a recommendation for the Qualified Attitude Method that will have universal appeal. We think they do, and we therefore conclude that human beings have a common basis on which the solution of ethical questions can rest—although not a guarantee that everyone must give identical answers to such questions, as we shall shortly see.

5. THE MEANING AND FUNCTION OF ETHICAL TERMS AGAIN

Many or most people, we have suggested, will assert an ethical statement, view it as justified, if and only if they think it meets the conditions of the Qualified Attitude Method. We have also said, they can defend their doing so by pointing to the fact that other tests that are likely to be seriously advocated today suffer by some failing or other, and by citing good reasons —not inferior to the kind we might expect to be available in a matter of this sort—in favor of their view.

One might stop at this point. One might say that the important thing for ethical theory is to find the correct method for solving ethical problems, for answering ethical questions. One might say that if we can count on agreement about this, we need not worry too much about the meaning of ethical statements—especially since in some sense everybody who speaks a language knows this well enough.

Nevertheless, we certainly do not have a complete theory if we stop here. There still is the question: What is the meaning or function of ethical terms? We do want an answer to this question, and we particularly wish to know what answers to it are consonant with what we have just decided about the existence of a justified method in ethics.

Let us survey some proposals which have plausibility.

1. *The Ideal Observer form of naturalism.* It might be argued that what we have said about the Qualified Attitude Method being the "standard" method, and its being a defensible method, is so much reason for accepting the Ideal Observer theory of the meaning of ethical terms, discussed and questioned in Chapter 7. It might be said we ought to reconsider this theory.

We have noted that anyone who accepted the Ideal Observer theory of the meaning of ethical terms would be committed to use of the Qualified Attitude Method, as the one method that would show what attitude toward something would be the attitude of a fully informed, vividly imaginative, impartial person, in a normal frame of mind. But is a converse inference

12 See Kurt Baier, *The Moral Point of View* (Ithaca: Cornell University Press, 1958), pp. 308–15 and chap. 8. Essentially this point was made by Thomas Hobbes, as Baier points out. Hobbes argued that it is to the advantage of every citizen to choose an absolute sovereign who will have no motivation to be otherwise than just.

valid? If our argument is correct that the Qualified Attitude Method is the "standard" method for criticizing ethical judgments, and if there are good reasons for using it, may we then infer that, after all, the Ideal Observer definition is a correct reportive definition of ethical terms?

No, we cannot draw this inference, for we have not argued that *everyone* is convinced of the Qualified Attitude rule, or makes use of it in practice. We concede—at least this is plausible—that some people really use a theological rule in their moral thinking; others a utilitarian rule; and so on. We cannot argue, therefore, that what they *mean* by ethical terms—in the sense we took as basic, much less in the sense of *overt* meaning—is what the Ideal Observer theory says they mean.

One might, of course, urge that the Ideal Observer definition is correct as an account of the meaning of those persons who already criticize their ethical thinking by standards of the Qualified Attitude Method. One would then say that some people mean one thing by ethical terms, other people another thing. This is a possible view.

From one point of view the outcome of future chapters in this book would be the same if we advocated the Ideal Observer definition. The reason for this is that we shall use the Qualified Attitude Method for testing ethical beliefs; and of course this is the very method we would use if we held that the Ideal Observer definition was correct. At some points in future chapters, however, we shall find it necessary to discuss the *meaning* of particular ethical terms. At those points what we shall say will differ from the implications of the Ideal Observer theory.

2. *A quasi-naturalist definition.* In view of the conclusions of the earlier parts of the present chapter, it seems worthwhile to consider a novel form of naturalistic definition. This definition, however, is so markedly different from other naturalistic definitions that we call it "quasi-naturalist." We shall explain the definition first.

Let us first agree to speak of a "corresponding attitude" for every ethical term. To "preferable" the attitude of preference will correspond; to "obligation" something like "feeling obligated" for the case of agents and "inclined to demand" for observers; and so on. Roughly what we mean by a "corresponding" attitude is the attitude someone justifiably has if some ethical statement is properly asserted by him. There can be further discussion, obviously, of the question of what attitude corresponds, in this sense, to any ethical term in which one happens to be interested.

The quasi-naturalist definition proposes that "x is E" (where E is some ethical term) means the same as "The E-corresponding attitude [which will be determined once we have specified the ethical term] to x satisfies all the conditions that would be set, as a general policy, for the endorsement of attitudes governing or appraising choices or actions, by anyone who was intelligent and factually informed and had thought through the problems of the possible different general policies for the endorsement of such attitudes." For example, "*x* is preferable to *y*" would mean "Preferring *x* to *y* satisfies all the conditions that would be set. . . ."[13]

This definition is properly classified as naturalist, because whether an "*E*-corresponding attitude" satisfies "all the conditions" can in the end be decided in principle by observation and the methods of science. In other words, the definition can be translated into the language of empirical science (p. 155). But it is also properly distinguished as "quasi-naturalist" in order to mark two important points. Some naturalist definitions, like the proposal that "*x* is worthwhile in itself" means "*x* is pleasant," have the consequence that important substantive ethical principles are true by definition (in this case "Something is worthwhile in itself if and only if it is pleasant"). The quasi-naturalist definition has no such implication. Second, other naturalist definitions, like the Ideal Observer theory, have the consequence that it is true by definition that a certain method must be used if true or valid ethical propositions are to be discovered. The quasi-naturalist definition, again, has no such implication, for in order to determine what ethical method will lead to valid ethical statements, it implies we must first ascertain what conditions would be set by an intelligent, informed person for the endorsement of attitudes of a certain kind.

It is no objection to this definition, as it is an objection to the Ideal Observer definition, that some people do not use the Qualified Attitude Method, but, rather, a theological or utilitarian method. The reason for this is that someone's use of a theological method, for instance, may simply show that he believes that "all the conditions that would be set" include some condition having to do with the will of God.

These distinctive features of the quasi-naturalist definition are strong recommendations of it. Everyone is under the impression that whatever he is saying, when he makes an ethical statement, it is something which is correct or incorrect, valid or invalid. The quasi-naturalist definition has the desirable implication that this impression is correct. On the other hand, the definition is framed so as not to exclude, as necessarily irrelevant, any of the arguments actually used about particular ethical principles, or any of the debates about ethical method which strike us as seriously relevant.

Of course this definition must be able to survive criticisms of the kind that have been leveled at traditional naturalist definitions, in order to be acceptable as a reportive definition of ethical terms. It must also be able to stand up against the reasons that have been offered for the emotive theory (pp. 214–20). It is not clear, however, that any of these points is a serious objection to it. Of all the naturalistic definitions it seems decidedly the least open to objection.

---

[13] There is a point of vagueness in this definition, corresponding to one in the Qualified Attitude Method, which we shall discuss in the following chapter. There are also particular phrases in the definition that are vague. For example, when has one "thought through" the problems mentioned? But such vagueness is not necessarily an objection.

3. *A noncognitive theory.* One may think, however, that the quasi-naturalist definition is too remote from our overt meanings to qualify as what we *mean* when we use ethical terms. It is, therefore, worthwhile to consider whether some form of noncognitive analysis of ethical language might be more satisfactory. Let us explore this.

First of all, however, we should remind ourselves that a noncognitivist need not deny that the Qualified Attitude Method is the "standard" method of evaluating ethical statements, or that good reasons can be given for following it, of the kind we offered. This is obvious, when we remind ourselves of the definition of "noncognitivism" (p 205); this theory asserts only that ethical statements are best understood by likening them to some speech form different from fact statements, and that ethical terms are not property-referring at all—or at least that, if they do refer to properties, the fact is of secondary import for understanding ethical discourse. The noncognitivist's theory commits him in consistency only to saying that ethical statements certified by the Qualified Attitude Method need not be viewed as confirmed by evidence in the way in which the statements of the empirical sciences are confirmed, either in view of the meaning and function of ethical terms or in view of any other facts. Let us, for the sake of the argument, not contest this point.

There is a more questionable assertion that the noncognitivist may make, although he need not. This is that, even if most people are prepared to make an ethical statement only if they think it meets the conditions of the Qualified Attitude Method, and even if there are convincing reasons in support of so doing, the fact is unimportant and can be ignored—because whether people accept the Qualified Attitude Method as a standard for ethical reasoning and whether they are convinced by reasons that support its use is in the end a matter of their attitudes and not of sheer logic. This point, however, is mistaken. It leads the noncognitivist who accepts it to an insupportable neutrality in his own appraisal of methods in ethics—to the view that one is just as good as another. It leads him to overlook the fact that there are conclusive reasons for preferring one method of ethical deliberation to another. It leads him to overlook the fact that ethical thinking and debate are very similar to inductive reasoning—reasoning according to a "standard" form which can be supported by good reasons and to which there is no serious alternative.

Let us now suppose that the noncognitivist agrees that in the sense explained the Qualified Attitude Method is the "standard" method of ethical reflection, that following it can be supported by strong reason, and that on this account some ethical judgments—those which satisfy the conditions of the Method—have a correspondingly approved status. But will this affect his account of the *meaning and function* of ethical terms? Let us see how we can or must reconstruct his theory so as to allow for agreeing to these various things.

First, the noncognitivist can continue, without change, to say that the primary job of ethical language is noncognitive. He may say that the primary job is to advise, or to urge, or to express attitudes, or to express over-all moral or impartial attitudes in the sense described in the preceding chapter (p. 229), or some combination of these things. Perhaps he will say that there are different noncognitive jobs done by the same ethical words on different occasions. So much for the noncognitive side of ethical language.

We have seen that there is reason to recognize another aspect of ethical language. Toward the end of the preceding chapter we saw that many noncognitivists suggest that ethical language does not do *merely* a noncognitive job, or at least that it does such a job in a special way. It has been proposed that the use of ethical language has certain "contextual implications" or makes certain claims. What is *distinctive* of ethical language, it has been held, is the making of certain claims or the having of contextual implications of a special sort. But there were differences of opinion among noncognitivists about just what these claims or implications are.

On the basis of our argument so far, we are now in a position to make a proposal about an important one of these claims or implications. Our suggestion is *not* that ethical statements claim that the attitude (etc.) they express satisfies the conditions of the Qualified Attitude Method; it is not this, because we agree that some persons do not use this Method, and have not thought of the reasons which support it. Our suggestion is rather a weaker one; it is that ethical language *claims, of the attitude* (etc.) *which it expresses*, that it satisfies all the conditions which would be set, as a general policy for the endorsement of attitudes governing or appraising choices or actions, by anyone who was intelligent and factually informed and had thought through the problems of the possible different general policies for the endorsement of such attitudes. In other words, we suggest a noncognitivist should say that the use of ethical language makes a claim about the attitude it expresses, which is identical with part of what the quasi-naturalist definition says ethical terms assert. For instance, "It is desirable to do *x*" may be construed as (1) the expression of an over-all impartial preference (or, perhaps, as equivalent to "I advise you to do *x*"), and (2) as claiming or at least implying that favoring *x* is *justified* in the sense that it satisfies the conditions which would be set by intelligent persons, and so forth. Ethical statements, then, may be construed as both doing something and making a validity-claim of this sort.[14]

14 We should notice that a philosopher might propose theories, like the three just formulated, not of ethical terms themselves, but of the term "justified." He might refuse to analyze ethical terms themselves, saying that we understand them well enough, but might propose any one of them for the term "justified" as applied to ethical statements.

Such a view is not very satisfactory. For we shall still want some view about ethical terms themselves. Moreover, there is no reason to think that such analyses of "justified" are any better established than corresponding analyses of ethical language itself.

In order to distinguish the foregoing analysis clearly from the quasi-naturalist one, we must, of course, be clear about just what it is for a statement to make an assertion, and what are the criteria for deciding the content asserted by a given statement. Similarly, we must be clear what it is for a statement to express something, or to make a claim; and we must know what the criteria are for deciding what is expressed or claimed. Let us assume that the problems involving in clarifying all those things can be satisfactorily overcome.

Is there anything to choose between the quasi-naturalist analysis of ethical terms, and this noncognitivist account? Despite some reservations (particularly about whether such a noncognitivist can consistently say the noncognition function is *primary*), we prefer to say there is nothing to choose. On the contrary, we do assert that there is no insuperable objection to either one, and that one or the other of them is correct. For our future purposes, however, it is simpler to adopt the quasi-naturalist definition. We shall, therefore, in the future, talk as if this definition should be given preference. But, whenever we use it, it would be possible to make the same point by using the noncognitive theory just suggested. We believe there is no sound objection to the quasi-naturalist definition, but we have no quarrel with one who prefers the above noncognitive analysis instead.

FURTHER READINGS

S. E. Toulmin, *An Examination of the Place of Reason in Ethics* (Cambridge, Eng.: Cambridge University Press, 1950), pp. 67–72, 82–85, chaps. 9–11.

———, "Principles of Morality," *Philosophy*, XXXI (1956), 142–53.

S. Hampshire, "Fallacies in Moral Philosophy," *Mind*, LVIII (1949), 566–82.

K. Baier, *The Moral Point of View* (Ithaca: Cornell University Press, 1958).

———, "Good Reasons," *Philosophical Studies*, IV (1953), 1–15.

———, "Proving a Moral Judgment," *Philosophical Studies*, IV (1953), 33–44.

J. N. Findlay, "Morality by Convention," *Mind*, LIII (1944), 142–69.

———, "The Justification of Attitudes," *Mind*, LXIII (1954), 145–61.

J. Harrison, "When is a Principle a Moral Principle?" The Aristotelian Society, Supplementary volume XXVIII (1954), 111–34.

W. Kneale, "Objectivity in Morals," reprinted in W. Sellars and J. Hospers, *Readings in Ethical Theory* (New York: Appleton-Century-Crofts, Inc., 1952).

I. Scheffler, "Justification and Commitment," *Journal of Philosophy*, LI (1954), 180–90.

M. White, *Towards Reunion in Philosophy* (Cambridge: Harvard University Press. 1956), chaps. 14, 16.

J. Rawls, "Outline of a Decision Procedure for Ethics," *Philosophical Review*, LX (1951), 177–97.

A. Edel, "Ethical Reasoning," *Proceedings of the American Philosophical Association* (Eastern Division), II (1953), 127–42.

E. Hall, "Practical Reasons and the Deadlock in Ethics," *Mind*, LXIV (1955), 319–32.

W. K. Frankena, "Obligation and Motivation," in A. I. Melden (ed.), *Essays in Moral Philosophy* (Seattle: University of Washington Press, 1958).

N. Kretzmann, "Desire as a Proof of Desirability," *Philosophical Quarterly*, VIII (1958), 246–58.

C. A. Baylis, "Grading, Values, and Choice," *Mind*, LXVII (1958), 485–501.

II

Ethical Relativism

A Greek philosopher who lived in the fifth century B.C., named Protagoras, seems to have believed two things: first, that moral principles cannot be shown to be valid for everybody; and second, that people ought to follow the conventions of their own group.[1] Something like this combination of propositions probably had been thought of before his time. Primitive people are well aware that different social groups have different standards, and at least sometimes doubt whether one set of standards can really be shown to be superior to others. Moreover, probably in many groups it has been thought that a person who conforms conscientiously to the standards of his own group deserves respect.

Views roughly similar to those of Protagoras may be classified as forms of *ethical relativism*. The term "ethical relativism", however, is used in different senses, and one should be wary when one comes across it. Sometimes one is said to be a relativist if he thinks that an action that is wrong in one place might not be in another, so that one is declared a relativist if he thinks it wrong for a group of Eskimos to strip a man of his clothing twenty miles from home on January 1, but not wrong for a tribe at the equator. If "relativism" is used in this sense, then practically everyone is a relativist, for practically everyone believes that particular circumstances make a difference to the morality of an act—that, for instance, it is right to lie in some circumstances but wrong in others. Again, one is sometimes said to be a relativist if he asserts a pair of causal propositions: that different social groups sometimes have different values (ethical opinions) as a result of historical developments; and that an individual's values are near-replicas of the tradition of his group, however strongly he may feel that they are "his own" or that they are "valid" and can be supported by convincing

[1] For Protagoras' view, see Plato, *Theaetetus*, pp. 166 ff.; and F. J. Copleston, *A History of Philosophy*, I (London: Burns Oates & Washbourne Ltd., 1956), pp. 87–90.

271

reasons. We shall not use "ethical relativism" for either of these views, but reserve it for a theory at least fairly close to that of Protagoras.[2]

1. THE QUESTION: "ARE CONFLICTING ETHICAL OPINIONS EQUALLY VALID?"

The position of Protagoras, however, is somewhat vague, and if we are to assess it, we must sharpen it. It is also convenient to deal separately with its two parts. We shall begin with a restatement of the first part of his theory, and then assess it at some length; only then shall we consider the second half of his position. As we go on, we shall see that the first part of his theory is theoretically more interesting and important than the second. For this reason, we shall apply the term "ethical relativism" to any theory that agrees with our sharpened form of Protagoras' first point, irrespective of its attitude toward the second.

It is clarifying to substitute, in place of our initial statement of Protagoras' view, the following, as a brief formulation of the relativist thesis in ethics: "*There are conflicting ethical opinions that are equally valid.*" But this formulation requires discussion in order to be clear.

The first thing to notice—although the fact will not be obvious until we have explained the phrase "equally valid"—is that the statement is *about* ethical opinions or statements, but is not an ethical statement itself. It is not like saying, "Nothing is right or wrong!" or "Some things are both right and wrong!" It is a metaethical theory.

Next, the statement is cautious. It does not say that no ethical opinions are valid for everybody. It says only that some ethical opinions are not more valid than some other ethical opinions that conflict with them.

Third, our relativist thesis is not merely the claim that different individuals sometimes in fact have conflicting ethical opinions. It does assert this, but it goes further. It holds that the conflicting ethical opinions are *equally valid.* We do not establish this merely by showing that people disagree. Nor do we establish it by showing that individuals' ethical opinions are at least to some extent dependent on the cultural stream within which they stand. Everyone must agree to this— although everyone must also admit that somehow societies often spawn their own moral critics. Nor do we establish it by showing that the standards of a given society

2 It is useful to compare Protagoras' relativism with the special theory of relativity in physics. One implication of this theory is that measurements of certain physical quantities, like the temporal distance between two events, will come out differently for different frames of reference (one "frame of reference" being the set of observers having the same relative rectilinear motion). All the careful observations in *one* frame will give the *same* result; and in this sense there is a "right" answer for this frame. But different frames will have different "right" answers, and there is in principle no way of showing that one of these is the "really right" answer. However, certain quantities (like the spatio-temporal distance between two events) are absolutes, in the sense that careful measurements will give one right answer for everybody.

have their causes. Of course they do; and so do the scientific opinions in a given society, although we hardly think this necessarily impugns their universal validity.

Fourth, what do we mean by "conflicting ethical opinions"? We mean, of course, by an "opinion" the readiness to make a sincere statement. Thus, a person has an "ethical opinion" to the effect that a particular thing is right or wrong if he could, when asked, make without deception an ethical statement to the effect that that thing is right or wrong. (We explained how to identify an "ethical" statement in Chapter 1.) Now, suppose Mr. A makes an ethical statement, and Mr. B makes a different ethical statement. How shall we tell whether the two statements "conflict"? A sufficient condition of conflict is this: that both statements are about the *same subject* (we explain this in a moment), and the one applies to this subject an ethical predicate P, and the other applies to it the same ethical predicate prefaced by the English "not" or something that means or entails the same. For instance, one may say "is morally right" and the other may say "is not morally right," of the very same subject. But now, when do two ethical statements have the *same subject*? This is a more awkward question. We cannot test this just by observing the verbal forms. For instance, Thomas Jefferson said, approximately, "A revolution every few years is a fine thing." But suppose Karl Marx also said, "A revolution every few years is a fine thing." Could we assume that these two men were necessarily saying the same thing? Of course not. Or again, suppose Mr. A, a resident of the South Pacific, says it is right to bury one's father alive on his sixtieth birthday, irrespective of his state of health; and suppose I say this is not right. Are we talking about the same thing? Not necessarily. The kind of situation Mr. A has in mind is likely to be very different from the kind of situation I have in mind. Perhaps he is assuming that the body one will have in the next world will be exactly like the kind one has just before departing this life (and hence, may think it advisable to depart before feebleness sets in); whereas I may think one has no further existence at all after one's earthly demise. He is talking about burying alive a father who will exist in the next world in a certain kind of body; and I am not. In this situation, it is only confusing to say that our ethical opinions "conflict." Let us say that two people are *talking about the same subject* only in the following situation. Let us suppose A and B make conflicting ethical predications about something or some kind of thing, ostensibly the same for both. But suppose further there is some property P that A more or less consciously believes this thing or kind of thing has, whereas B does *not* believe this. Further, let us suppose that if A *ceased* to believe this, he would cease to have the same ethical opinion about it but agree with B; and let us suppose that if B *began* to believe this (other things being equal), he would change his ethical opinion and agree with A. In this case, let us say that A and B are *not* appraising the same subject. But if there is no more-or-less conscious belief having the status described, then we shall say that they *are* talking about the same subject, and that their ethical opinions are conflicting.

But now, finally, what is the meaning of the phrase "equally valid"? In order to clarify this, let us draw a parallel with language we use in appraising scientific theories. Suppose we have two conflicting theories about natural phenomena. Each of these theories might explain a large part of the known facts, but not all of them, at least not very well. We might then say, "In the light of presently known facts, the two theories are equally plausible." On the other hand, we might make a more radical supposition. Suppose, when thinking about these theories, we make the daring forecast about future evidence, that when scientific investigation has been indefinitely prolonged and all possible experimental data are in, both of these theories will explain all the facts, and there will be no ground for a rational preference of one to the other, although parts of the two theories do contradict each other. In this case, we might say, although this sounds startling, "Although these theories are mutually contradictory in some respects, they are both *valid*." What a person who made such a statement would be saying is that the use of a refined inductive logic, on a complete set of experimental data, would support as strongly confirmed *both* of two conflicting theories. We need not argue whether in fact this case ever does or even could arise, but we can understand the possibility, and the important thing is the parallel with ethics. Now, the ethical relativist is not merely making the uninteresting claim, when he says two conflicting ethical statements are equally valid, that the two statements are equally plausible in the light of the facts known at present. He is saying something much more radical, about what would happen if one were testing these statements by the best possible ethical methodology, and in the light of a complete system of factual or nonethical knowledge. In other words, he is saying that the application of a "rational" method in ethics would support, equally, two conflicting ethical statements even if there were available a complete system of factual knowledge—or else that there is no "rational" method in ethics comparable to an ideal inductive method for empirical science.

I have used the phrase "rational method in ethics" as designating something roughly parallel in ethics to inductive logic in empirical science. This idea will be familiar to us from the preceding chapter, where we argued that the Qualified Attitude Method has this status.

We can now explain exactly what it means to say that two conflicting ethical statements are "equally valid." What it means to say this, is that *either* there is *no* unique rational or justified method in ethics, *or* that the use of the unique rational method in ethics, in the presence of an ideally complete system of factual knowledge, would still not enable us to make a distinction between the ethical statements being considered.

The ethical relativist asserts that there are at least *some* instances of conflicting ethical opinions that are equally valid in this sense.

There are more, and less, radical relativists. The more radical kind of relativist asserts that there are conflicting ethical opinions and that there is *no unique rational method in ethics.* To mark this, let us call him a "methodological relativist" or an "ethical skeptic." The less radical relativist does not say there is no unique rational method, but says that there are still some instances of conflicting ethical opinions that are equally valid. Let us call him a "nonmethodological relativist." We must look at the logic of, and the evidence supporting, these two kinds of relativism separately.

2. METHODOLOGICAL RELATIVISM

It would perhaps be better to call a "methodological" relativist a "skeptic" and not a relativist at all.[3] Nevertheless, it is established usage to classify various writers, especially anthropologists, as "relativists," although they are methodological relativists in our sense. In order to avoid confusion, we shall follow this terminology.

In order to assess the truth of the theory, the first thing to decide is whether there *are* conflicting opinions about the *same* subject at all. It has been denied that there are. Karl Duncker, in an article in *Mind,* in 1939, questioned whether any anthropological evidence establishes that there are—and suggested that anthropologists had overlooked the fact that when different societies ostensibly advocate different moral principles (for example, the U.S.A., monogamy; Moslems, polygamy), they actually have different situations in mind. However, we have already assessed the evidence on this point (pp. 99–103), and concluded that there are conflicting ethical judgments even when speakers have the same situation in mind. So far, then, methodological relativism stands up.

But is the theory correct in its assertion that there is no unique rational method in ethics? Obviously it is not, if the argument of the preceding chapter is sound. We need not go over this ground again. The reader will by now have made up his mind whether or not this is the case.[4]

If the reader found the preceding chapter convincing, he may be puzzled by the fact that there are methodological relativists among social scientists.

---

[3] Certainly this position is different from "relativism" in physics. In relativity physics, there are *correct* judgments for each frame of reference; only, it is impossible to say that one of these judgments (correct for its frame of reference) is really correct for everybody.

[4] Notice, however, that the acceptance of the quasi-naturalist definition leaves open the question of methodological relativism, for it might be that intelligent (and so on) persons would set *no* conditions for the endorsement of attitudes governing choices in community living. In this case, *every* attitude would pass, and there would be no ground for preferring one of two conflicting ethical statements to the other. The same is true for the noncognitive analysis we discussed.

The reason is simple: the kind of theory we are suggesting is of a species that has only recently been proposed, and social scientists are unfamiliar with it.[5] (Neither, for the most part, are they familiar with sophisticated forms of naturalism.) When they say that one ethical statement cannot be shown "objectively" to be more valid than another, what they mean, and all that they mean, is that one cannot show that ethical statements are confirmed or refuted by observation in *exactly the same way* as are hypotheses in science. They rightly see that "is desirable" must be tested in a way different from "is desired," and they conclude that ethical statements cannot be evaluated at all—overlooking the fact that tests appropriate for assessing ethical judgments may be somewhat distinctive, but none the less defensible, given their subject matter.

Moreover, many social scientists simply do not realize that their acceptance of inductive logic is no more "rational," in the sense of no more supportable by the canons of deductive logic, than is the "standard" method of ethical thinking. Yet, without qualms they make use of inductive logic—but at the same time condemn as "subjective" the appraisal of ethical statements, although in fact the "standard" method is warranted by reasons equally as good as those that can be adduced to support inductive reasoning in science. Presumably, as time goes on (and scientists become more familiar with the results of contemporary thinking about inductive logic and ethics), social scientists will cease making this irrational distinction.

The reader need not, incidentally, feel that he has to choose between what we have called the "standard" method, and methodological relativism. We might be mistaken about what the "standard" method is. It might very well be that there is one and only one method that would be used to resolve ethical issues by intelligent (and so on) people, but that it is somewhat different from the method we have described. The "methodological relativist" (as we have defined this term) is making a strong statement: he is saying that there is *no* method that is a "rational" method in the sense of being the one unique method that would be used to resolve ethical issues by intelligent (and so on) people. But there might well be such a method, even if it is not the one we have described.

Of the theories we have been considering in previous chapters, which ones are forms of methodological relativism and which are not? Clearly naturalism is not, for naturalists so construe the meaning of ethical statements that ethical statements have the same capacity to be confirmed by

---

[5] A contributing factor is that some social scientists do not distinguish "relativism" in the sense of methodological or nonmethodological relativism as defined above from other senses of "relativism" (described on p. 271). Hence, they think that the truth of one can be inferred from the truth of the other. Since relativism in the senses described on p. 271 is doubtless true, one who does not make the proper distinctions naturally concludes that relativism in one or the other of the two senses now under consideration is also true. Such an inference is, of course, entirely unwarranted.

observation as do the statements of empirical science. There is one "unique rational method" for assessing ethical statements, and it is simply the method of inductive logic. Some of the naturalists, on the other hand, are nonmethodological relativists, for instance, Westermarck.[6]

The emotive theory, on the other hand, *as it is usually worked out*, belongs to the methodological relativist species. The whole concept of validity in ethics is banned. The theory does not recognize any unique rational method of ethical deliberation; on the contrary, anything is allowed that is effective, that wins harmony of attitudes either interpersonally or intrapersonally. Indeed, ineffective reasoning is all right too, according to this theory; it merely *is* ineffective. As a result, there is no way in which any ethical conviction can be "objectively" criticized as being defective, incorrect, or erroneous.

On the other hand, the emotive theory *need* not be a species of methodological relativism. For instance, if it is held that ethical statements are expressions of over-all, impersonal attitudes, then an ethical statement may be "mistaken" if the speaker does not have the over-all, impersonal attitude he purports to have. Much the same is true if it is supposed that the use of ethical language has certain "contextual implications" or makes certain "claims," for then we can say that ethical statements are at least "misleading" if not "incorrect"—if the "contextual implications" or "claims" distinctive of ethical language are not satisfied.[7]

If the argument of the preceding chapter is correct, we have said, the methodological relativist is mistaken because there *is* a unique rational method in ethics. Worse still, it *may* be that he is *contradicting* himself if he both affirms methodological relativism *and* makes ethical statements (which the relativist presumably, like other men, will often do). Whether he is contradicting himself depends on what he means by his ethical statements. He certainly is contradicting himself if he means what the Ideal Observer form of naturalism (in its absolutist form) says ethical statements mean (p. 173).

The relativist of this variety need not, however, renounce engaging in ethical debate, or stop thinking that such debate is fruitful. Indeed, he may think that the major questions of normative ethics can be answered—not

---

[6] Different "unique rational methods" vary in the extent to which they can succeed in resolving ethical disputes. There could well be a "method"—and it might well be the only method we could claim to be a "rational" method—that marked a few ethical judgments as definitely untenable, but gave us no help on the serious issues. In fact, this is the case with Westermarck's view. The unique rational method is the method of empirical science. But if ethical statements mean what Westermarck says they do (p. 166), the method can show that some ethical statements are unwarranted and false, but will not in all cases resolve ethical disputes in the sense of showing that only one of two conflicting statements, made by different people, is correct.

[7] The reader should examine R. M. Hare, *The Language of Morals* (Oxford: Clarendon Press, 1952), p. 69, and P. H. Nowell-Smith (Baltimore: Penguin Books, 1954), p. 319.

in the sense of finding a "right" answer for them, but in the sense that *agreement* is attainable. He can hold, as many social scientists do, that there are points of ethics about which there is universal agreement, common ground on the basis of which discussion and adjudication can fruitfully proceed. He may think there is a wide basis of agreement that can be extended further, by pointing out the implications—in view of known scientific facts—of commitments already made. For instance, agreement on a program of economic reform might be reached, starting from agreement that suffering is evil and to be avoided—by showing that these economic reforms are necessary means for avoiding suffering. Indeed, the methodological relativist can, in general, espouse ethical reasoning of the form licensed by "contextualism"; but no more than that.

3. NONMETHODOLOGICAL RELATIVISM: RELATIVISM "PROPER"

The second and less radical form of relativism agrees with the first form that there are conflicting ethical judgments about the same subjects; but it differs by holding that there is a unique rational method for answering ethical questions. It then goes on to assert that when we apply this method even to an ideally complete set of data, it sometimes happens that it is impossible to decide between conflicting ethical judgments. Practically, it is an important question how often and where this "sometimes" is; but we postpone this question for the moment. Is methodological relativism true or tenable?

We have already conceded the thesis it shares with the more radical view: that there are conflicting ethical judgments about the same subjects. But, where there are such conflicting judgments, are the judgments ever *equally valid?* This question is a difficult one. Indeed, it may be *inconsistent* to suppose that they ever are. We must consider this.

There are *some* metaethical theories that are consistent with nonmethodological relativism, with saying that conflicting judgments are sometimes equally valid. Take, for instance, the view of Westermarck. He is a naturalist and therefore thinks that the rational method for answering the questions of ethics is the method of science. On the other hand, he thinks that "*x* is wrong" means "I have a tendency to feel impartial resentment toward people who do things like *x*." Given his premises, is it consistent to be a relativist? That is, is it consistent to say that conflicting ethical statements are sometimes both "valid" in the sense permitted by his theory? Yes, for we can describe conditions in which conflicting statements would both be "valid." Suppose Jones and Smith are debating whether it is right to pluck a chicken alive, in order to secure a somewhat tastier dish. Jones says it is; Smith says it isn't. Now suppose Jones has been so conditioned that he really would tend to feel impartial resentment toward anyone who did this sort of thing. Further, suppose Smith, who was reared in South America, would not; he simply cannot get excited about whether chickens are plucked before or after they are killed, and in any case he is very fond of the taste of succulent chicken. In this situation, according to Westermarck's analysis, it really would be true and correct for Jones to say, "That is not wrong," and for Smith to say, "That is wrong." Perhaps this outcome suggests something wrong with Westermarck's analysis; but this is what his analysis implies, and there is nothing inconsistent about the reasoning or conclusion.

But it is inconsistent to assert nonmethodological relativism and also certain other metaethical theories: e.g., nonnaturalism, Perry's theory, the absolutist form of Ideal Observer theory.

The intriguing question for us is whether the thesis developed in the preceding chapter leads to the same conclusion.

The main burden of our previous chapter was this: (1) The Qualified Attitude Method is the "standard" method for evaluating ethical statements and can be defended by good reasons. (2) Ethical statements either assert or claim or imply that a corresponding attitude (for instance, preference in the case of judgments about what is preferable) meets all the conditions which would be set by informed, reflective people for the endorsement of attitudes governing choices in community living. Is the thesis of nonmethodological relativism inconsistent with either of these assertions? Let us consider them in order.

(1) Nonmethodological relativism is consistent with our conclusions about the Qualified Attitude Method if and only if it is logically possible for two conflicting ethical judgments both to satisfy the conditions of this Method. *Is* this logically possible? When we think of it we can see that in one respect our description of the Qualified Attitude Method was incomplete. It told us how each of us is to proceed in order to decide whether a given ethical judgment is valid—that it must jibe with our corresponding attitudes in so far as they need not be "discounted," and so on. But it did not make perfectly clear whether a person's ethical judgment is valid if it satisfies the tests as made by him but *not the tests as made by other persons.* One could make it a part of the Qualified Attitude Method that a judgment is satisfactory only if it meets the prescribed tests as performed by everyone. If, on the other hand, it is enough for the validity of a judgment made by a particular person, that it satisfy the tests as performed by him, then it is logically possible that conflicting judgments both be valid.

How shall we decide this matter? It is not easy to say what is "standard" practice. It is at least very infrequently that we think our judgment meets the conditions we have enumerated as parts of the Qualified Attitude Method, and at the same time think that a conflicting judgment by someone else meets the same conditions, as tested by him. So it is not easy to say whether, if we did think these things, we should feel free to assert our own ethical proposition. Nevertheless, we have observed above (p.

175) that there are persons who think there are great variations in moral beliefs and who do not think it likely that *everybody's* judgments, however corrected or qualified, will necessarily agree on many issues. Still they are quite prepared to go ahead and make moral assertions as required by consonance with their own criticized attitudes. They think that a person can say, like Martin Luther, "Here *I* stand; I can do no other," irrespective of information about the attitudes of others. So a formulation of the Qualified Attitude Method consistent with relativism has some support in ordinary thinking. Moreover, there are reasons for *recommending* such a formulation—reasons to the effect that adherence to an absolutist formulation would paralyze moral judgment by making it impossible to claim either a pro- or a con- judgment as justified in far too many cases. Therefore we shall not regard it as part of the Qualified Attitude Method that one's ethical judgment be found compatible with the discounted attitudes of *everybody;* what is required is only that it be compatible with the judge's *own* discounted attitudes. So far, then, it is consistent for us to assert that the Qualified Attitude Method is the proper test of ethical judgments, and also to assert the thesis of nonmethodological relativism.

(2) We stumble into a logical difficulty, however, when with this conclusion in mind we consider the consistency of nonmethodological relativism with our proposal that ethical statements assert or claim that a corresponding attitude meets all the conditions that would be set (and so on). The difficulty is as follows. Suppose Mr. A makes careful use of the Qualified Attitude Method, and as a result says, "*x* is desirable." And suppose Mr. B, after the same process, says, "*x* is undesirable." The view of the nonmethodological relativist is that this situation can really arise, that both parties really can have applied whatever unique rational method is available. But how can one person say *x* is desirable, and the other correctly deny this, *if our proposal about the meanings is correct?* At least, how can it be if what Mr. A is saying is, "Desiring *x, on the part of everybody*, meets the conditions . . ."? Surely this cannot be asserted if Mr. B's desiring of *x* does *not* meet the appropriate conditions at least as tested by Mr. B.

Evidently, if we are to be consistent relativists, we must not only have a specific understanding of the Qualified Attitude Method (as suggested above), but also a particular understanding of the quasi-naturalist definition. We must specify this definition in a relativist direction, just as the Ideal Observer theory has a relativist form (p. 173). We can say, to take "desirable" as an example, that "*x* is desirable" means "Desire for *x on my part* satisfies all the conditions that would be set . . ." (and so on), with the understanding that the "set conditions" may be such that desire for *x* on the part of one person may meet them, and desire for non-*x* on the part of some other person may also meet them. With this emendation, the quasi-naturalist definition is brought even closer to the noncognitivist counterpart described at the end of Chapter 10—the view that to say that "*x* is desirable" is (1) to express a desire for *x*, perhaps an overall impartial one, and (2) to claim or imply that the desire expressed satisfies all the conditions (and so on, as before).

If we are not prepared to understand the quasi-naturalist definition in some such manner, we must in consistency reject relativism.

It makes little difference, for the topics we have to discuss beyond the present chapter, whether we make these specifications and adopt relativism, or do not make them and accept absolutism. The reasons for relativism are fairly weighty, but we shall see that the issue hardly arises in later contexts. In particular, it will not be necessary to distinguish relativist from absolutist forms of the quasi-naturalist definition in later discussions. We shall feel free to ignore the difference partly because nothing will turn on it, and because the relativistically-minded reader can supply the emendations without difficulty (except perhaps in Chapter 14, where the changes must be slightly more complex).

In order to continue the argument, let us assume that we are now agreed that it is *consistent* to adopt certain metaethical theories (and in particular approximately the one outlined in Chapter 10), and at the same time to be a nonmethodological relativist. Nevertheless, it may still be that nonmethodological relativism is just plain *false*. We must now consider this possibility. How shall we decide this? Again, it depends on our metaethics. Take Westermarck's view. If the attitudes of all impartial persons were in agreement, then one person could never truly say, "I have an impartial tendency to feel resentment against the agent of acts like *x*," and at the same time someone else correctly say, of the same *x*, "I do *not* have an impartial tendency to feel resentment against the agent of acts like *x*." Then, according to Westermarck's definitions, one person could not truly say, "*x* is wrong," when another one could truly say, "*x* is not wrong." Hence, conflicting ethical statements would in fact never be "equally valid." Relativism would be false.

Similar reasoning must be used to decide whether relativism is true or false, if we adopt the view that the "rational" method in ethics is the Qualified Attitude Method. Essentially the issue is this: If one informed (and so on) attitude in fact never clashes with another attitude that is equally qualified, both of course being directed at the same act or thing, then one person can never correctly claim, "*x* is wrong," when someone else can correctly say, "*x* is not wrong." *Valid* ethical statements would then never conflict, and relativism would be false.

Relativism is right, then, according to our theory (and Westermarck's), essentially if "qualified" (in the sense of not requiring to be "discounted") attitudes toward the same act or event can be conflicting.

Well, can they, or can they not? Or what should we believe?

The simplest way to answer these questions, of course, is just to find two individuals, both qualified in the relevant ways, and observe whether in fact one wants, abhors, feels obligated to do, demands from others, feels indignant or disgusted at, admires, or prefers things, actions, or events to which the other individual takes an opposite attitude. It is difficult, though, ever to be certain that such individuals are before us. How can we be sure that all the relevant facts are believed by both, and that neither needs to be disabused of false beliefs? How can we be sure that all the relevant considerations are present to the minds of both, with requisite vividness? Perhaps, of course, individuals on occasion may with reason be said to approximate to these conditions. It seems preferable, however, not to rest one's argument on such possible cases.

There is an indirect method for answering our question. Consider a parallel: that we feel free to make statements about how gases *would* behave at an absolute-zero temperature, although we have not actually observed gases in this state. Why? We draw inferences from relevant causal laws. The same is true in our case. If we have good reason to believe causal laws, to the effect that a person's attitudes are not a function solely of his information (or its vividness) and his state of personal needs or wishes (at the time) and his normalcy, then we have so much reason to think that "qualified" attitudes occasionally vary. If we happen to know precisely the nature of these laws, we may be able to specify the conditions under which such variation will occur. Psychological theory and experiment, then, are the most obvious source for an answer to our question.

Unfortunately, psychological theories do not provide a uniform answer to our question. Gestalt theory would lead us to believe that attitudes ("ought" experiences) to a situation will be identical, if the situation is identically understood, and personal needs and interests do not play a distorting or blinding role. Psychoanalytic theory and Hullian learning theory, however, provide a different answer. According to these theories, two attitudes, equally "qualified" in the sense of occurring in minds with equal information (and so on), can be conflicting, depending on the history of the development of the persons: their past identifications, their past rewards and punishments. The doctors, then, disagree. But how does the currently available experimental evidence look? Does it favor the view of either theory, on this particular point? To this our answer must be: There is no *certainly* correct reading of the evidence, but it *appears* to favor the relativist answer to our question, for there is some reason to think that fundamental orientations may be adopted from parents in early life, and that these may have a permanent influence on attitudes; that identifications, emotional relations with important figures in one's life, and feelings of security play a role in the development of one's values; that certain things or events may be highly valued in compensation for the inaccessibility of other satisfactions at an earlier period, or as a result of deprivations. Then, if these things are true, we can specify some occurrences in the life of an individual that would have the effect that his attitudes now, whatever the information (and so on) of his present state of mind, would be different from what they would have been had his earlier experiences been different. Individuals with relevantly different earlier experiences, then, may be expected to have different attitudes, despite identical qualifications with respect to knowledge, impartiality, and so forth.[8]

On the whole, then, the relativist is better able to claim the support of contemporary psychological theory and research than is his adversary. However, the issue is not closed.

The facts of anthropology are also relevant to our question, and in the following way. In the first place, we have already noticed (p. 109) that studies of cultural change in primitive societies suggest that facts like personal conflicts and maladjustments, the attitudes of one's close relatives (for example, whether favorably oriented toward White civilization), and personal success in achieving status in one's group or outside one's group (for example, with White men) play an important role in the development of the values of adults. This finding is some support for our reading of the observational evidence of psychology. In the second place, there is the fact that various groups have different values. The mere fact that different ethical standards exist in different societies, of course, by itself proves nothing relevant to our present problem. Nevertheless, something important is proved if the facts bear testimony that different standards can prevail even if different groups have the *same beliefs* about the relevant event or act, and if there is no reason to suppose that the group standards reflect group differences in respect of other "qualifications." (We must remember that attitudes common to a group cannot usually be discounted as being a result of personal interest or of an abnormal frame of mind.) The fact of variation of group standards, in these circumstances, would tend to show that attitudes are a function of such variables, that attitudes could differ even if our "ideal qualifications" were all met.

Is there such variation of group standards? We have seen that there is one area of ethical opinion where there is diversity in appraisal and at the same time possible identity of belief about the action—that about the treatment of animals. On the whole, primitive groups show little feeling that it is wrong to cause pain to animals, whereas the columns of *The New York*

---

[8] We should not, however, overlook the possibility that an individual might, if he knew that an attitude of his was a result of some type of early experience (for example, a high valuation of knowledge being a result of the unsatisfactoriness of his personal relations at an earlier period of development), to some extent lose this attitude. In other words, perhaps self-understanding in the sense of understanding the genesis of one's own values is a fact relevant to what one's present attitudes will be. It is possible that any two individuals, otherwise equally "qualified," would in fact always have the same attitudes toward everything at the conclusion of a careful psychological treatment in which each acquired complete self-understanding. Is there evidence, from psychoanalysts or other specialists in personality theory, that points in this direction? The writer does not know.

Times are testimony to the fact that many persons in the U.S.A. take a vigorous interest in what goes on in slaughterhouses. We have already mentioned some details about the attitudes of primitive groups (p. 103). Nevertheless, we cannot be sure that attitudes of the groups here in question really do fulfill our "qualifications" equally well. Primitive peoples rarely make pets of the animals they maltreat. There is at least some question whether they have a vivid imagination of what the suffering of an animal is like, comparable to that of the authors of letters to the *Times*. The writer has assured himself by personal investigation that there is no definite discrepancy between the Hopi *beliefs*, about the effects of maltreating animals, and those of what seems a representative sample of educated White Americans. Degrees of *vividness* of belief, however, do not lend themselves to objective investigation, and it is not clear how we may definitely answer questions about them, either way. Perhaps the sanest conclusion is just to say that, as far as can be decided objectively, groups do sometimes make divergent appraisals when they have identical beliefs about the objects, but that the difficulties of investigation justify a healthy degree of skepticism about the conclusiveness of the inquiry.

The fact that objective inquiry is difficult naturally works both ways. It prevents us from asserting confidently that, where there are differences of appraisal, there is still identity of factual belief. But equally it prevents us from denying confidently that there is identity of belief, where appraisals differ.

The anthropological evidence, taken by itself, then, does not give a *conclusive* answer to our question. At the present time, the anthropologist does not have two social groups of which he can say definitely: "These groups have exactly the same beliefs about action *A*, on all points that could be seriously viewed as ethically relevant. But their views—attitudes—about the morality of the acts are vastly different." Whether, everything considered, the relativist reading of the facts is not the more balanced judgment, is another question. The writer is inclined to think it is the better judgment.

If we agree that the ethical standards of groups are not a function solely of their beliefs (or the vividness of these), it is reasonable to suppose that "ideally qualified" attitudes may well conflict with respect to the very same act or event. To say this is to say that there is reason to suppose that nonmethodological relativism is correct.

4. ETHICAL UNIVERSALS

Thus far we have talked as if the truth of nonmethodological relativism were a black-and-white matter: either there are conflicts of justified ethical judgment in certain conditions or there are not. If there are, then relativism is correct; if there are not, then relativism is mistaken.

But to talk in this way is to conceive of the issue too indiscriminately, for it overlooks the fact that, whereas some conflicting ethical judgments may be equally valid in some areas of living and thinking, the same may not be the case in other areas. In other words, whereas it may be true that conflicting opinions are equally valid on the subject of cruelty to animals or sexual behavior, the same may not at all be the case when we come to topics like human rights.[9]

There are some more detailed questions, then, that we may well ask ourselves. For instance. we may ask: Is relativism true for *all* topics of moral assessment, for perhaps fifty per cent, or perhaps for only one per cent? Or again, is relativism true for all topics except perhaps for those about which we have no strong feelings anyway, or is it true also for some topics (for example, slavery) of strong concern to us? Or, and this is obviously the most important issue, on *exactly which topics* are conflicting ethical views supportable, and on which topics must we say that all valid views are in agreement?

The last of these questions will be matter for inquiry in the following chapters of this book, for in large part the job of answering it is the job of normative ethics. If, after examination of the facts, we conclude that there cannot be two valid opinions on some principles, we shall have shown by implication that there are many specific matters for which a relativistic view is indefensible. Of course, our examination may have the contrary effect. We may find out that some arguments, which have been thought to establish some ethical principles beyond question, really do not do so; and hence we must conclude that, as far as we can see, the field for valid disagreement is much wider than had been thought.

The less specific questions—about the proportion of topics on which there may be conflicting but equally valid opinions, and about the relative importance of the topics on which conflicting moral views appear to be defensible—are of secondary import. Nevertheless, it is of interest to know the opinion of social scientists on these issues.

On this matter there has been a marked change of opinion among social scientists in the past twenty years. There was a time when anthropologists like Ruth Benedict proclaimed the equal validity of the most diverse modes of living and ideals for humanity. The megalomania of the Kwakiutl, the repressed sobriety of the Pueblo, and the paranoia of the Dobuan culture were different value systems; but it would be ethnocentric, she thought, to make judgments about the relative merits of the systems. Since that time, however, anthropologists have turned attention to the similarities

[9] Even if one dismissed the concept of "validity" in ethics altogether, as is done by methodological relativism, one could still point out that in fact, in some areas, there are no disagreements. Whether the fact that there are is "theoretically" important is a question. But perhaps it is morally more supportable to impose legal restrictions on conduct that all persons agree should be prohibited, than on conduct about the morality of which there is genuine difference of opinion.

between societies, and to the functioning of social systems, to the analysis of institutions in terms of their capacity to minister to essential human wants and the maintenance of the social group as a continuing entity. These new interests have led to the following results.

First, it has come to be agreed that certain features of a culture system are essential for the maintenance of life, and that a system of values that permits and sanctions these forms is inevitable in society.[10] For instance, every society must provide for mating and for the rearing of offspring. Again, it must provide for the education of the offspring in the performance of those tasks that are necessary for survival. Moreover, in a complex society there must be differentiation of jobs, assignment of individuals to these jobs and the means for training them for adequate performance, and provision of motivation to do the jobs. Sufficient security must be provided to prevent serious disruption of activities, for example, security against violent attack. And so on.

It must be no surprise, therefore, to find that certain institutional forms are present in all societies: such as the family with its responsibilities for training children and caring for the aged, division of labor between the sexes (and occupational differences in more complex societies), games or art or dance, and so on.[11]

Second, anthropologists have come to find much more common ground in the value systems of different groups than they formerly did. As Professor Kluckhohn recently put it:

> Every culture has a concept of murder, distinguishing this from execution, killing in war, and other "justifiable homicides." The notions of incest and other regulations upon sexual behavior, of prohibitions upon untruth under defined circumstances, of restitution and reciprocity, of mutual obligations between parents and children—these and many other moral concepts are altogether universal.[12]

There are other universals we could mention: disapproval of rape, the ideal for marriage of a lifelong union between spouses, the demand for loyalty to one's own social group, recognition that the interests of the individual are in the end subordinate to those of the group. Ralph Linton wrote that "all societies attach high value to reciprocity and to fair dealing"—with some exceptions, such as *caveat emptor*. Again, parents are universally expected to train children; the child, for his part, is expected to be obedient and to render care in the old age of his parents. Knowledge is universally valued,

10 See D. F. Aberle, *et al.*, "The Functional Prerequisites for a Society," *Ethics*, LIX (1949), 100–11.

11 See G. P. Murdock, "The Common Denominator of Cultures," in R. Linton (ed.), *The Science of Man in the World Crisis* (New York: Columbia University Press, 1945); and C. Kluckhohn, "Universal Categories of Culture," in A. L. Kroeber (ed.), *Anthropology Today* (Chicago: University of Chicago Press, 1953).

12 C. Kluckhohn, "Ethical Relativity: Sic et Non," *Journal of Philosophy*, LII (1955), 663–77.

as is the escape from the pressures of reality provided by games, literature, art, dance, and music.[13]

At the same time, anthropologists agree that, to quote Kluckhohn, "variation rages rampant as to details of prescribed behavior, instrumentalities, and sanctions." Linton wrote, "If universal values exist, they must be sought for at the level of the deepest and most generalized conceptual values, those which stand in closest relation to the individual needs and social imperatives shared by the whole of mankind."[14]

Linton has also suggested that *basic* values tend to be more matters of universal agreement than do superficial values:

> In any study of values, it soon becomes evident that the values held by a particular society are arranged in a hierarchy of importance, strong emotional affect being associated with some, little emotional affect with others. Those with which strong affect is associated tend to be reflected in numerous concepts and behavior patterns. They are usually associated with the satisfaction of the basic needs of individuals, both physical and psychological, and the fulfillment of the conditions necessary for the continuation and effective functioning of societies. They may be termed *basic values*. At the other end of the scale lie values which find very limited expression and carry little emotional affect. Such would be the transitory value attaching to a particular style of clothing while it was in fashion. These may be termed *superficial values*. Between these two extremes lie a continuous series of values carrying varying degrees of emotional affect and expressed in culture patterns of varying number and functional importance.
>
> A comparative study of a large number of cultures indicates that the *basic values* of all societies include many of the same elements. Differences increase as one moves toward the superficial end of the scale.[15]

This is not to say there are no divergencies between groups on fundamental matters. Raymond Firth reports that human life has only a small sentimental value among the Chinese and the Tikopia; but even so, he remarks that "in all human societies there is a basic moral view that it is good as a general rule to attempt to preserve human life."[16]

What is proved by these observations of anthropologists? First, that there is much agreement about values, especially important values, which provides some basis for the resolution of disputes, even if we set aside completely considerations of validity, and assume there is no such thing as a "valid" value. Second, some values, or some institutions with their supporting values, are so inevitable, given human nature and the human situ-

[13] See Ralph Linton, "The Problem of Universal Values," in R. F. Spencer (ed.), *Method and Perspective in Anthropology* (Minneapolis: University of Minnesota Press, 1954).

[14] *Ibid.*, p. 152. It is not made quite clear what Linton means by a "conceptual" value. One example he gives is the value of "modesty," which can take numerous quite different forms. A conceptual value, he says, may not be consciously recognized by the group that has it. Presumably, it is a *general preference* that the anthropologist finds it fruitful to postulate, to account for classes of cultural phenomena.

[15] Mimeographed report, "Cultural Relativity," October, 1951.

[16] *Elements of Social Organization* (London: Watts & Co., 1951), p. 201.

ation in society as they are, that we can hardly anticipate serious questioning of them by anybody—much less any conflicting "qualified attitudes," that is, conflicting attitudes that are informed (and so on).

Thus, ethical relativism may be true, in the sense that there are *some* cases of conflicting ethical judgments that are equally valid; but it would be a mistake to take it as a truth with pervasive scope. Relativism as an emphasis is misleading, because it draws our attention away from the central identities, from widespread agreement on the items we care most about. Furthermore, the actual agreement on the central things suggests the possibility that, with better understanding of the facts, the scope of agreement would be much wider.

5. A SPECIAL BRAND OF ETHICS FOR RELATIVISTS?

So much, then, for the truth and scope of the relativist principle: "There are conflicting ethical opinions that are equally valid."

Acceptance of this principle, we have said, by our definition makes one an "ethical relativist." But we noted at the beginning of this chapter that relativists often espouse some further thesis—a particular ethical commitment, which they may regard as being implied by the foregoing principle of relativism. Protagoras, we saw, urged that people *should* follow the conventions of their group. An executive committee of the American Anthropological Association, in a published statement on human rights, included the remark that "*respect* for differences between cultures is *validated* by the scientific fact that no technique of qualitatively evaluating cultures has been discovered."[17] Also, Ruth Benedict closed her *Patterns of Culture* with these words:

> The recognition of cultural relativity carries with it its own values, which need not be those of the absolutist philosophies. It challenges customary opinions. . . . It rouses pessimism because it throws old formulae into confusion. . . . As soon as the new opinion is embraced as customary belief, it will be another trusted bulwark of the good life. We shall arrive then at a more realistic social faith, accepting as grounds of hope and as new bases for tolerance the coexisting and equally valid patterns of life which mankind has created for itself from the raw materials of existence.[18]

This same theme of tolerance was sounded by Professor Melville Herskovits, who wrote in an influential book: "The relativist point of view brings into relief the *validity* of every set of norms *for* the people whose lives are guided by them."[19]

[17] *American Anthropologist*, XLIX (1947), 539–43; italics mine.

[18] Ruth Benedict, *Patterns of Culture* (Boston: Houghton Mifflin Company, 1934), p. 278.

[19] *Man and His Works* (New York: Alfred A. Knopf, Inc., 1948), p. 76. Professor Asher Moore, in "Emotivism: Theory and Practice," *Journal of Philosophy*, LV (1958), 375–82, contends that the relativist thesis teaches the normative ideal of charity toward the ethical views of others.

Other inferences from the relativist view are different. As the writer has heard some students put it, "If all moral codes are equally valid, why should one not change to a code that is somewhat *less demanding* on the individual?"

Are there really any such *ethical consequences* of the relativist thesis we have been discussing? Or, irrespective of whether these views are implied by relativism, are they defensible on their own merits as part of an ethical creed for relativists? To try to answer these questions is to engage in a discussion of *normative* ethics as distinct from critical ethics. But let us do this. Let us look at *tolerance* as an ideal for ethical relativists.

The first question we must ask is whether the advocate of tolerance as a creed for relativists is saying that tolerance is only one among "equally valid" conflicting ethical opinions. Does he, that is, say that *intolerance* is equally as valid as tolerance, or not? He could be saying this: "We relativists, for our part, espouse the value of tolerance. But, as scientists, we recognize that intolerance is equally valid." Is relativism with its plea for tolerance only a "point of view," like another culture? Or is tolerance a value securely founded on the methods of science?

Perhaps we do best to answer these questions by considering what relativists can *consistently* say, not what they actually do say. (We must remember that anthropologists are not familiar with the terminology of philosophers, and we should not read too much into the use of words like "valid" and "validated." Furthermore, very possibly the writers we have quoted had not considered their words carefully.)

Suppose one is a methodological relativist, a skeptic. Suppose he holds the emotive theory about the meaning and function of ethical language, and believes that there is no unique rational method for criticizing ethical opinions. In this case, he will have no use for the phrase "is a valid view" in ethics (except as a mode of expressing his own ethical views, tantamount to "That is right"), although he may say that various conflicting views are "equally valid," as a way of stating his metaethical theory that there is no unique rational method in ethics. Now, according to this view, the value of intolerance is as justified (or unjustified) as that of tolerance. So why should he advocate it? Certainly there can be no reason in the sense that the correctness of such a position follows from the facts of science; indeed, according to this theory *no* ethical thesis has this status. One who is a relativist might easily as well say, "Since no system is more valid than any other, let each of us advance his own!" So, *intolerance* could be the outcome of relativism. Nevertheless, there may be something about the relativist doctrine that tends to *incline the attitudes* of its advocates toward tolerance, not only in the sense of not condemning any moral systems, but in the sense of active advocacy of a policy of encouraging, say, members of primitive groups to retain their distinctive and traditional moral patterns. It may be that Ruth Benedict meant no more than this when she wrote that "recognition" of relativity "carries with it its own values." If there is this causal influence of the doctrine of relativism on the values of its advocates, we must simply recognize it. There is no inconsistency between relativism and praising tolerance (and so forth)—as there is no inconsistency between relativism and praising anything you please. It is consistent, then, (1) to be a relativist, (2) to be influenced causally by one's convictions in the direction of tolerance, and (3) to give expression to one's favorable attitudes to tolerance by praising tolerance. It is *not* consistent for a methodological relativist to claim that tolerance has a status of "greater validity" (in the sense we gave this term) than intolerance, though he may condemn intolerance, in moral language, to his heart's content. Further, it is *not* consistent for a methodological relativist to say that the correctness of the ideal of tolerance "follows" from the facts of science, or from the theoretical position of methodological relativism, or from any other fact.

But suppose one is less radical a relativist—a relativist of the nonmethodological variety. What then? In this case, one does not necessarily say that *all* moral judgments are only as valid as conflicting ones. At least, one is committed by the definition of "relativism" only to saying that some are so. One is, of course, also not committed by the definition to saying that *only* some moral judgments have this status. A nonmethodological relativist may be, as we suggested, a one hundred per cent relativist or only a one per cent relativist. The point is that he does think there is a "unique rational method" that in principle might identify some moral judgments as unacceptable; this leaves much room for difference of opinion about whether a few, or many, ethical judgments are only as valid as some competing ones. Now, the consequence is that a relativist *can* consistently say that *tolerance is justified*—that this matter is one about which it is not true that conflicting opinions are equally valid. He *can* hold this—although he *cannot* reasonably say that the relativistic thesis *logically entails* such a view; obviously it entails no such thing.

One may ask such a relativist, however, how he can justify *wholesale* tolerance, including tolerance for social practices about which there are *not* two conflicting and equally justified moral opinions—assuming he thinks that there are some points about which only one moral opinion is justified. Can he, for instance, justify tolerance for intolerance?

Our question, however, needs to be clarified. Indeed, one source of confusion about the present issue has been a failure to distinguish two quite different issues, and two corresponding senses of "tolerance." In one sense of "tolerance," we may speak of tolerating a man and his opinions, in the sense of feeling and showing respect for him and his opinions. But one can have respect for a man and his convictions, and nevertheless believe his views happen to be mistaken; one can respect a man and yet be motivated to try to change his views, or even, if the matter is serious, take action to place legal restrictions on his ability to put his opinions into practice. We may respect the conscientious objector in wartime; but we may find it necessary to make it a crime to preach his doctrine.

Tolerance in the first sense is a firmly entrenched part of the Anglo-American moral system, among relativists and absolutists alike. It is traditional to have respect for the sincere moral opinions of others even when we differ with them. We do not blame sincere conscientious objectors, even if we think them mistaken and confused. There are limits to such respect, however. If a man commits a hideous crime, and defends himself on the ground that his conscience told him to do it, we do not excuse him, but think so much the worse of his conscience for having advised him as it did. We regard him as a bad man, no better for what he chooses to call the advice of conscience. In other words, we think there is a certain range within which decent people can have differences of opinion; when a person goes beyond this range, we accuse him of rationalizing or insensitivity. Things are somewhat different when a person with whom we disagree comes from another culture. In such cases, we stretch the range of tolerance; we feel there is, on account of cultural background, an excuse for moral opinions or actions we should not tolerate from a member of our cultural tradition. Even here, however, the stretch is possibly not indefinite. For instance, if a headhunter took the life of a child with no mercy or qualms, what should we think? It is hard to say. At any rate, the point is that we do not *blame* people for their actions insofar as they are consonant with their own moral convictions—within certain limits.

Now, is it tolerance only in this sense that some relativists wish to advocate? If so, no one need quarrel with them—unless they say that the morality of tolerance is entailed by the thesis of relativism, or that it is the special preserve of relativists, which it certainly is not. But sometimes they seem to go further. When they say that a given people's standards are *valid* for them, they seem to be saying that we should *advise* or at least *not discourage* people from conforming to their traditional moral doctrines; that groups like the United Nations should *take no steps to interfere* with local practices like slavery or racial discrimination, no matter how horrible they may be. In other words, some relativists seem to advocate, *wholesale, condoning* the accepted practices of other peoples.

How can the relativist justify this? Let us repeat that no such moral statement is logically entailed by the thesis of methodological relativism. We may concede, of course, that there is perhaps a tendency for a relativist to develop favorable attitudes toward the distinctive practices of individual groups, and to be inclined to urge conformity to these practices (no matter how devastating to the welfare of the natives). We also agree that there is no inconsistency in this. But nonmethodological relativism leaves open the possibility that there are *not* two conflicting but equally valid opinions about slavery, or putting people to death on the basis of witchcraft accusations, or denying a person civil and political rights because of his color. Then, if there are not two equally valid opinions on these matters, how can the relativist advocate that we condone such practices, wholesale? If the relativist view on these matters is to be justified, he has no alternative but to argue each issue on its merits, on the basis of evaluated moral principles, and unless conflicting opinions are equally valid on *every* issue, the relativist is not justified in advocating wholesale tolerance for everything, in this second sense of "tolerance," unless there is some general moral argument for condoning the accepted practices of other groups.

Some relativists do offer such a general moral argument for tolerance in this sense. Let us look at it. Briefly, it is that every working set of institutions is better for its practitioners than chaos, for every such set of institutions serves important functions, else the group would not have managed to survive. Now, it is argued, one should avoid interfering with such systems, because interference may destroy.

This reasoning, however, is unimpressive. It takes for granted a monolithic cohesion and inflexibility of institutional systems that is unproved. Why will a whole way of life collapse if we forbid headhunting, abolish slavery, forbid death penalties for conviction on witchcraft charges? Why must any interference be crippling to a way of life? It is far from obvious why there should not be interference to root out an institution that produces slavery.

Methodological relativism, then, may lead (psychologically, not logically) to advocating tolerance; but it is inconsistent for such a relativist to claim that tolerance has any objective superiority to intolerance. *Nonmethodological* relativism *permits* saying that tolerance is valid and intolerance not. But equally it leaves open the possibility of determining the one and only one justified opinion on many ethical issues. Therefore, it is not easy to see how a relativist is justified in a wholesale advocacy of tolerance in the sense of condoning unjustifiable behavior unless he produces some reasons that have as yet not been produced.

Let us consider the question, "If all moral codes are equally valid, why should one not change to a code that is somewhat *less demanding* on the individual?" In reply to this, two comments are pertinent. In the first place, we have already noticed (Chapter 4) that the ethical convictions of our social group are by no means necessarily correct. If we have doubts about a given standard, we can review it, apply the "rational" methods of ethical reflection to it; and if it does not stand up, then it would seem that normally the thing to do is to admit it and to start practicing the standard that can be justified (although whether we should raises a further moral issue). If a standard is repressive and makes no sense, it needs review; and we do not have to go afield and find a society with different standards, to have reason to question the prevailing convictions of our group. But there is a second point. Suppose we have reviewed some issue, and have applied the "standard" method, and have come to the conclusion that people *should* do a certain thing. However, as it happens, we *prefer* to do something else. Further, suppose we find another society with a valid standard that permits us to do what we want to do. Does relativism justify our doing what we wish to do? It is not obvious that it does, for, if we have reviewed the problem with the "standard" method and have come to a certain conclusion, there is certainly question whether the code of this other society *is* "equally valid." It is not impossible that there could be reason to think it so; and it is puzzling whether, if this situation did arise, there would be an obligation to follow one's own assessment of the situation. Perhaps there is a moral principle: "Each person is obligated to follow the judgment arrived at by his own application of the standard method." Whether there is, perhaps we can decide later.

As a result of all this discussion, what do we conclude theoretically, in our critical ethics? First, we reject methodological relativism, on the ground that in the preceding chapter we showed that there is a "standard" method for evaluating moral statements, and that there are good and sufficient reasons for using this method. But second, we decided that non-methodological relativism is not inconsistent with our having a "standard" method—although to decide this we had to discuss further what the standard method is. Moreover, we decided that, although the issue is a fine one, the evidence rather supports the view that different persons could apply the standard method properly and come out with conflicting answers to *some* ethical questions. To this extent, we agree with the view of the nonmethodological relativist. However, to say this, is not to say that there can be two conflicting but equally valid opinions on all, or many, or even important ethical issues. The serious question is: On what ethical issues can we show that one and only one opinion is correct? But this question is the question of normative ethics, and to this topic we now turn.

FURTHER READING

On relativism and its difficulties:

M. Herskovits, *Man and His Works* (New York: Alfred A. Knopf, Inc., 1948), chap. 5.

"Statement on Human Rights," *American Anthropologist*, XLIX (1947), 539–43.

E. Westermarck, *The Origin and Development of the Moral Ideas* (New York: The Macmillan Company, 1906), I, chaps. 1–5.

———, *Ethical Relativity* (New York: Harcourt, Brace & Company, 1932), chap. 5.

R. Firth, *Elements of Social Organization* (London: Watts & Co., 1951), chap. 6.

Ruth Benedict, *Patterns of Culture* (Boston: Houghton Mifflin Company, 1934).

———, "Anthropology and the Abnormal," *Journal of General Psychology*, X (1934), 59–82.

R. Brandt, *Hopi Ethics: A Theoretical Analysis* (Chicago: University of Chicago Press, 1954), pp. 87–90, chap. 16.

Plato, *Gorgias*, 482–84.

W. G. Sumner, *Folkways* (Boston: Ginn & Co., 1934).

P. Taylor, "Four Types of Ethical Relativism," *Philosophical Review*, LXIII (1954), 500–16.

———, "Social Science and Ethical Relativism," *Journal of Philosophy*, LV (1958), 32–43.

C. Kluckhohn, "Ethical Relativity," *Journal of Philosophy*, LII (1955), 663–77. An anthropologist's summary of the evidence.

A. Moore, "Emotivism: Theory and Practice," *Journal of Philosophy*, LV (1958), 375–82.

K. Duncker, "Ethical Relativity?" *Mind*, XLVIII (1939), 39–56. Doubts the evidence for relativism.

W. T. Stace, *The Concept of Morals* (New York: The Macmillan Company, 1937), chap. 1. An elementary statement of a relativist argument.

S. E. Asch, *Social Psychology* (Englewood Cliffs, N.J.: Prentice-Hall, Inc., 1952), chaps. 12 and 13. Criticism on the basis of Gestalt theory.

On ethical universals and the conditions for society:

R. Linton, "Universal Ethical Principles: an Anthropological View," in R. N. Anshen (ed.), *Moral Principles of Action* (New York: Harper & Brothers, 1952).

———, "The Problem of Universal Values," in R. F. Spencer (ed.), *Method and Perspective in Anthropology* (Minneapolis: University of Minnesota Press, 1954).

C. Kluckhohn, "Universal Categories of Culture," in A. L. Kroeber (ed.), *Anthropology Today* (Chicago: University of Chicago Press, 1953).

———, "Culture and Behavior," in G. Lindzey (ed.), *Handbook of Social Psychology* (Cambridge: Addison-Wesley Publishing Co., 1954), pp. 921–76.

D. F. Aberle, A. K. Cohen, A. K. Davis, M. J. Levy, and F. X. Sutton, "The Functional Prerequisites of a Society," *Ethics*, LIX (1950), 100–111.

B. Malinowski, *Scientific Theory of Culture* (Chapel Hill: The University of North Carolina Press, 1944), chaps. 8–11.

12

Things Worthwhile in Themselves: (A) Enjoyments

Thus far we have been discussing problems of *critical* ethics, problems about the meaning and function of ethical statements, about the sense in which, and the extent to which, they can be supported or confirmed or justified. It is time now to leave this area and examine the normative problems of ethics—questions like, "What kinds of things are desirable or worthwhile?" and "Which kinds of acts are morally wrong?" and "Do men possess any inalienable rights?" A major purpose for seeking to resolve the critical problems of ethics is to prepare ourselves for intelligent reflection on these normative, practical problems. (We shall, however, have to discuss critical problems further from time to time.)

Philosophers often speak as if the goal of normative discussion is to work out a "theory" of ethics. But what kind of "theory"? Ideally a normative "theory" consists of a set of *general* principles analogous to the axioms of a geometric system. That is, ideally it comprises a set of *correct* or valid *general* principles, as *brief and simple* as possible compatibly with *completeness* in the sense that these principles, when conjoined with true nonethical statements, would logically imply every ethical statement that is correct or valid. Such an ideal for a system must be our guide.

Can we describe further what this system will be like? One thing can be said. The system must contain *at least* as many distinct basic principles as there are different ethical concepts. For instance, suppose "it is desirable that" means something different from "it is wrong that" or "it is obligatory for," in the sense that the former cannot be defined in terms of either of the latter, and vice versa. Then, however many principles our system contains to the effect that a certain thing is wrong or obligatory, such principles will never imply anything about what is desirable or good; no formal deduction of the latter from the former will be possible, no matter how many nonethical statements are at our disposal, as additional premises. Nor will principles about what is desirable or good imply anything about what is wrong or obligatory. For every distinct predicate in ethics there must be at least one principle in the system, if it is to be complete.

Philosophers have displayed different degrees of optimism about the prospects of stating such a system. Some have not only supposed that such a system can be achieved; they have thought that they achieved it. Indeed, some philosophers have thought that the whole system can be written down in about two lines. Others have been less sanguine.

The following chapters make no pretense at the completeness some philosophers think has been attained. We shall sketch out what appear to be the basic principles as best we can; but in our opinion there are many others we do not mention, and what is worse, some of the principles we do state are at best approximations, shorn of the qualifications required for accuracy. Moreover, at some points the facts supporting relativism should make us tremble; perhaps we are stating what is only true for us.

One reason for incompleteness we can state now: It is that decisions require judgments comparing alternative courses of action, each with its own values and disvalues; and each of these comparisons presents a somewhat unique problem whose solution is only partly determined by any simple general principles we can state. It is as if someone gave us a thousand objects, differing in color and shape and size, and instructed us to arrange them in an order of similarity; all the principles we had about which colors resemble which, or which shapes most resemble which, and so on, would be of only limited value when set the job of judging the *total* similarity.

Since the ethical problems that face individuals are often quite unique, requiring a total appraisal of many factors, no philosophical book can be made to serve, like a telephone directory, as a source of clear-cut answers. What the philosopher can do is trace out a few helpful lines of thinking, set a few landmarks at points where the bulk of historical tradition suggests people are apt to be puzzled. He can provide a model of analytical thinking, about typical problems, that may prove acceptable to others and helpful in their thinking. He cannot do more.

In the present chapter, we shall commence our exploration of some principles about what things are desirable or worthwhile—or, more particularly, things that are "intrinsically" desirable, in a sense to be defined. We shall consider the simplest and historically most influential of such principles: that one and only one thing is intrinsically worthwhile, and that this is pleasure or enjoyment.

1. ARE NORMATIVE PRINCIPLES JUST "MATTERS OF OPINION"?

Before considering this question, however, we had better examine another that may be troubling the reader. "How," he may be asking, "can we proceed to evaluate ethical principles in any objective and fruitful way? In the first place, I have not been convinced by all of your reasoning, and I am not at all sure I agree with all of your conclusions. Second, you in any case admit that ethical principles must be evaluated, to some extent at least, by an appeal to *attitudes*. And, since attitudes may vary, doesn't this mean that you really can't *establish* anything at all? Perhaps you are getting ready to give expression to your own attitudes, in which I happen not to have much interest. Isn't it true that you are without the means of convincing anybody who really disagrees with you, on *any* point of normative ethics whatsoever?"

Let us consider whether things are really as hopeless as these questions suggest they are.

First, is it true that we cannot proceed, if the reader has not been convinced of all our conclusions? Not at all, for there are certain essential points of which he will have been convinced. He will, for instance, have been convinced that one cannot answer the questions of ethics simply by inquiring about the ethical opinions of other persons in one's social group. He will have been convinced that one cannot answer them simply by searching revelations. He will have been convinced that one cannot answer them by "hunches," by one's particular feelings of obligation (or guilt) on particular occasions, as if these experiences were final, irrespective of whether they comprise a consistent system. Furthermore, he will have been convinced that valid ethical principles must be *general* (applicable *for everybody at all times* in a relevantly similar situation), and devoid of proper names, statable in terms that refer only to abstract properties. Also, we think, it will be conceded that if ethical principles are "testable" by attitudes (preferences, feelings of obligation, and so on) at all, the attitudes must be *impartial* attitudes. There is a further negative point; we think we can tentatively assume—and we shall support this view further as we go along—that the substantive issues of normative ethics are not settled just by *definition*, as R. B. Perry and some other naturalists would have it. (We need not, however, quarrel seriously with Westermarck or the Ideal Observer theory, for reasons that may be apparent.) So much, at least, is solid ground.

One may think, however, that more agreement on metaethics is necessary, if discussion of normative problems is to be fruitful. But is this so? We do not think it is. Unconverted nonnaturalists, for instance, can talk with us quite successfully, if only they will read "intuition" where we write "attitude" ("preference," "feelings," and so on) and will make further minor obvious adjustments. Exponents of a "rule-utilitarian" methodology are, it is true, in somewhat more serious disagreement with us; but their view concerns only one problem, rules of right and wrong (or obligations). We shall discuss it in further detail at the relevant point, and we shall see that the difference in result would be small in practical consequence if we agreed with them. *Prima facie,* however, the emotive theory as usually formulated is a real obstacle. Can we talk normative ethics with a hardy emotive theorist?

Of course we can. Indeed, we can probably do this even if he does not concede that ethical statements are properly "tested" only by compatibility with impartial attitudes. Even if he insists that there is no such thing as a "valid" moral principle at all, it is highly probable that his *attitudes* will be such that he will refrain from urging an ethical statement if it is pointed out that it is not supported by his impartial attitudes. Moreover, even if the emotive theorist does not think an ethical statement is "valid" only if the attitude expressed by it is well informed, he will still *want* his attitudes to be informed; for he will not want to encourage today, by his ethical statements, what he will want (because of unexpected information) to discourage tomorrow. He will want to enlighten his attitudes by exposure to the facts. Again, we need not argue with him whether an ethical statement is warranted only if the corresponding attitude is one the speaker would have had in a "normal" frame of mind; the emotive theorist who reads this book will in fact *be* in a normal frame of mind, or at least not in any abnormal state likely to be relevant to the issues we are considering. Thus, we do not have to argue with him whether an ethical statement is tenable only if it is coherent with his normal attitudes; for the issue need not arise. Furthermore, the emotive theorist, like everyone who has reflected seriously, will want a *consistent* set of principles; he will not want to tear down with one hand what he builds up with the other.

Any line of reasoning about ethical principles, then, that tends to show that denial of a certain ethical statement will result in one's ethical principles failing to satisfy the Qualified Attitude Method—a convincing point for anyone who accepts the conclusions of Chapter 10—will probably prove convincing also both to unconverted nonnaturalists and the most radical advocates of the emotive theory. They will not, of course, acknowledge the same epistemological status for any conclusions to which such reasoning might lead them, as we should want to claim. No matter: The reasoning will be convincing, the kind that they too, on their theories, will want to take into account in coming to normative conclusions.

What can we say about the doubter's second point? Is it true that the only "reasoning" we can use, when we come to the normative problems of ethics, is the parading of our own attitudes, and the expression of hope —perhaps in an emotively charged way—that the attitudes of others will agree?

In this suggestion there is an element of truth, for we have argued that what one has to do, in order to evaluate a suggested ethical principle, is to inquire whether it can be a member of a consistent set of abstract general principles, not excessively complex, which are coherent with one's attitudes as they would be if one were completely informed, impartial, and in a normal frame of mind. We have also conceded that the attitudes of different people may be and probably are somewhat different, and might be so even when "corrected" by more knowledge, complete impartiality, and a calm state of mind. Thus, the principle that is valid for you may not, we have conceded, be also valid for me—and the reason being one of a fundamental difference between our attitudes.

We must, therefore, admit the importance of attitudes for ethical thinking, and that some differences of ethical opinion perhaps cannot be resolved except by inducing one person to change his attitudes.

But it by no means follows that all that happens in a normative discussion is that one person tells how he feels, and another replies by telling how he feels. Such an inference would be absurd. There is enormous scope for reasoning in normative ethics, and possibly some points are open to demonstration.

What sort of reasoning? Let us review some kinds of points that can be made.

1. One thing we can do is show that a set of principles is inconsistent. It is true that, since people seldom contradict themselves overtly, pointing out inconsistencies may not seem to take us far. But we must not forget that the chain of implication, leading from one principle (via factual or mathematical principles all of which are accepted by all parties) to another principle may be long and devious, and gross oversights may pass unnoticed.

2. Next, sometimes a principle may be shown to contain inherently unintelligible notions, when it is formulated precisely. For instance, take "One state of affairs is better than another if and only if it contains a greater amount of pleasure." It may be that, given the speaker's view of pleasure, it is *impossible* to determine when one thing "contains a greater amount of pleasure" than another, so that no *meaning* can be assigned to the expression "greater amount of pleasure." Would this principle not then stand refuted? If not, why not?

Sometimes something like the opposite of this can be done. Sometimes a person's only reason for believing a certain principle is that he thinks there is no clearly statable alternative. If we produce such an alternative, his reasoning is undermined. (His principle is not refuted, but it is placed in doubt.)

3. It may be possible to show that certain ethical principles by themselves or conjoined with true factual statements, imply an ethical statement that is incoherent with the impartial attitudes of everyone, and would be repudiated by everyone who understood the situation. We can draw this to a person's attention, and possibly, in occasional instances, we can do more. We may be able not only to point to common-sense reasons for assuming unanimity of "qualified" attitudes on a certain point, but also to show that psychological theory stands massed behind the conclusion that

this is so. We can direct anyone who doubts it to review the facts of psychology.

4. Sometimes a person may be convinced that a certain set of principles must be accepted, but be in doubt about a particular application of the principles. For instance, there has been controversy about exactly what follows, for the ideal distribution of economic goods, if a utilitarian basic principle is accepted. Part of the job of normative ethics is to clear up such matters.

5. Sometimes a *particular* ethical judgment can be shown to be mistaken by surveying the various general principles by which it might be supported (and we have agreed that it must be supported by *some* principles general in scope), and by showing that the implications of none of these are compatible with criticized attitudes.

6. Sometimes a controversy can be settled simply by showing that there was genuine misunderstanding, that one party was arguing for one proposition and the other was arguing against a different one. For instance, one person may think an action is wrong because of the motives of one party involved; someone else may think the action right. The whole issue may be cleared up when it is shown that there are several senses of "wrong," and that a party's motives are relevant to whether it is wrong in one sense, but not to whether it is wrong in a different sense. When the distinction is pointed out, the issue has been genuinely settled.

How far will such methods take us? It is conceivable that they will not take us far, that very early in any controversy we shall meet conflicting attitudes, and rational argument must come to a halt. But *will* this happen? We must wait and see what happens when we try. It may well be that, if we think through the issues patiently, we shall be able to reach agreement, to reach principles consistent with or required by the impartial (and so on) attitudes of all. Or, at least it may be that we can do so on the central issues, the strategic questions about which controversy has raged historically.

At any rate, it is a misunderstanding of the type of reasoning typical of normative ethics, to suppose that normative reasoning is just a matter of exhibiting how one feels.

2. THE DESIRABLE AND THE INTRINSICALLY DESIRABLE

Our first normative question is: "What things are worthwhile (or desirable) in themselves?" Or, to use a more technical term that we shall explain, "What things are *intrinsically* worthwhile (or desirable)?" In the present chapter we shall examine one answer to this question, the theory of *ethical hedonism:* "A thing is intrinsically desirable (undesirable) if and only if and to the degree that it is pleasant (unpleasant)." This theory has been enormously influential historically. Among its supporters have been Epicurus, John Locke, Thomas Hobbes, David Hume, Jeremy Bentham, Henry Sidgwick, and many contemporary writers. The theory has also had its critics: Plato, Aristotle, Kant, T. H. Green, G. E. Moore, and many (perhaps most) philosophers living at the present time.

We shall begin by explaining the theory as carefully as we can, commencing with a discussion of the phrase "intrinsically desirable" and following with an examination of what is or reasonably could be meant by "pleasant." We shall then consider a psychological argument often used to support the thesis: the argument from "psychological hedonism." Next, we shall survey other reasons for and against the theory. Finally, we shall examine a puzzle, often supposed to constitute a serious difficulty for the theory and of great interest—particularly to economists—on its own account: the problem of the measurement of "quantities" of pleasure.

Let us begin with the term "desirable." This word is a close synonym of "worthwhile" and "valuable" (not in the sense of "expensive" but in the sense of the phrase "a valuable experience"). It is also closely related to "good." To say that something "is a good thing" is nearly if not quite the same as to say it "is a desirable thing."[1]

"Desirable" has a close relation to "better." Indeed, the technically simplest thing would be to take "better than" as our basic term, and to define "desirable" in terms of it. For instance, we might say that "It is desirable for a cure for cancer to be discovered" is the same as "It would be better for a cancer-cure to be discovered than for none to be discovered." Then, since "*x* is better than *y*" seems to mean much the same as "*x* is preferable to *y*," we might also define "is desirable" in terms of "preferable." The thesis of ethical hedonism could be restated in terms of "preferable." For instance, we might say: "The existence of something is intrinsically preferable to its nonexistence, if and only if and to the degree that it is pleasant." (Analogously for "unpleasant.")

Obviously "is desirable" has a meaning different from "is A's duty" or "is A's obligation," for we can say, "It is highly desirable for a cure for cancer to be discovered," although we can hardly say it is anybody's obligation to discover it, although doubtless it is the obligation of people to *try* to discover it. Again, we can say of an *act* that its performance is desirable, even though we may not think it is anyone's duty to do so (in a

---

[1] Notice that the predicative use that we here have in mind, "is desirable" or "is a desirable thing," is not the same as the adjectival use, for example "is a desirable addition to the football team," which is somewhat similar to the adjectival use of "good," for example, "a good knife." (We count "is a desirable thing" as predicative, since "thing" does not refer to any specific kind of thing or class.) The adjectival use is narrower, and perhaps can be defined in terms of the predicative use. For instance, "John is a desirable man for the football team" might be explained as "It would be a desirable thing to add John to the football team."

Many philosophers today concentrate their analysis of value terms on the adjectival use of "good." There is no harm in this, provided this procedure does not blind one to the real and important traditional problems.

sense that would imply that the person is properly subject to moral criticism or punishment if he fails); for instance, it may be a desirable thing for me to learn to play the violin because it would be relaxing and would secure for me much enjoyment, but it is hardly my moral duty to learn to play. "Obligation" and "duty" also differ in having a necessary relation to people; being obligated is always a property of somebody. But we can say, "A toll-road all the way from New York to San Francisco would be a desirable thing."

Can we offer any more positive and specific account of what "is desirable" does mean? If our quasi-naturalist suggestion at the end of Chapter 10 is correct, then "*x* is desirable" means "desiring *x* satisfies all the conditions that would be set, as a general policy, for the endorsement of attitudes governing or appraising choices or actions, by anyone who was intelligent and factually informed and had thought through the problems of the possible different general policies for the endorsement of such attitudes." We might abbreviate all this by saying that "*x* is desirable" means that "desiring *x* is justified."

More important for our present purposes is the question of how we may decide whether anything is desirable (or something preferable to something else). If our proposals of Chapter 10 were correct, this is a question of whether a general abstract (no proper names) principle to that effect can be incorporated in a consistent and complete set of principles, which are coherent with our total choices, preferences, desires, likings, and approvals, when we are fully informed and impartial but otherwise in a normal state of mind.

What is meant by "*intrinsically* desirable"? To say that something is intrinsically desirable is to say that it is desirable, taken just for itself, viewed abstractly, and in particular, viewed without respect to any consequences its existence will or may produce. For instance, we should not say that having an appendectomy is intrinsically desirable. Doubtless having one is a good thing, if one has appendicitis. But it is desirable, not just for itself, but because of its consequences, in the preservation of the patient's life and avoidance of pain. Or, owning a hi-fi set is hardly intrinsically desirable. The point of owning such a set lies in its consequences: the production of sounds more similar to actual musical performances.

We can put this in another way. If anything is desirable, it is so because of the kind of thing it is, because of the properties it has or relations within which it stands. Now, some of the properties that make a thing desirable do not involve anything beyond the thing or event or state of affairs said to be desirable; they are what they are independently of the remainder of the world, in the sense that it would be logically possible for the rest of the world to be different, but for them to remain the same. (The property of causing some future event is not one of these.) Such properties we can call intrinsic, and we can say that something—an event, state of affairs, or thing—is intrinsically desirable if it is desirable in view of its intrinsic properties alone.

The term "instrumentally desirable" contrasts with "intrinsically desirable." To be instrumentally desirable is to be desirable on account of actual or expectable effects; so that an appendectomy is instrumentally desirable in view of what it will bring about. Presumably, something is instrumentally desirable only because the expected results, immediate or remote, are intrinsically desirable.

Something can be both intrinsically and instrumentally desirable at once. Consider a child who is swinging, in a rapturous state of enjoyment. We shall probably think that being in this state of mind (and perhaps body) is worthwhile for itself alone. To be in a state of rapturous enjoyment of the experience of swinging is for one's state of mind to have an intrinsic property, on account of which the child's experience is desirable. So we shall say that the child's experience is of intrinsic worth. But his experience is perhaps instrumentally desirable as well, for it may help to make him a more relaxed, better-adjusted person in the future.

The ethical hedonist does not for a moment deny that things other than pleasant ones are desirable; indeed, he concedes that unpleasant things may be desirable for other reasons and that pleasant ones may be undesirable. At least, he would be very foolish if he denied these things. Obviously getting knowledge, or having an appendectomy, or beginning with the violin may be desirable, even if they are not intrinsically desirable. All the hedonist is saying is that a thing is *intrinsically* desirable if and only if and to the degree that it is pleasant. The hedonist's thesis, then, is only about what is intrinsically desirable; but it is of no less importance for that fact.

3. WHAT IS PLEASURE?

A person is a *monist* about values if he thinks there is only one property the possession of which to some degree makes a thing intrinsically valuable. A person is a *pluralist* about values if he thinks there is more than one property whose presence in an object can make a difference to the object's intrinsic worth. Hedonism is a form of monism, at least if we count both pleasantness and unpleasantness as simply degrees of one kind of property (otherwise it is dualism). Usually, critics of hedonism are pluralists; but a nonhedonist could be a monist, thinking, perhaps, that knowledge or quality of character is the only property that makes something intrinsically worthwhile.

What kinds of thing might a nonhedonist think affect intrinsic worth? Such things as knowledge, strength of character or the possession of various virtues, human life, kindly deeds, suffering for one's community, keeping a promise it is hard to keep, grateful recognition of services done, beauty even if not enjoyed by anyone, a distribution of happiness among people in proportion to their merits. Some of these, we see, are properties of single conscious organisms (for example, knowledge and being alive); persons who confine "good-making" (those that affect intrinsic worth) qualities to this sort are *personalists* about values. Others of these are not properties of single conscious organisms (for example, the distribution of happiness according to merit); writers who believe there are "good-making" qualities of this kind, we shall call *impersonalists* about values (although the term may be misleading, since no impersonalist fails to allow that states of persons are of intrinsic worth). Correspondingly, we shall speak of *personal* and *impersonal* "good-making" qualities. Obviously, a hedonist is not only a monist but a personalist in his view about what makes for intrinsic worth. We might say that a personalist about values is one who counts only states of *welfare* as having intrinsic worth; but "welfare" is itself a rather vague term, although one widely used.

The controversy between hedonists and antihedonists may seem largely theoretical, since for the most part they agree on what is worthwhile, differing only as to the intrinsically worthwhile. But there are practical implications of importance, too. For instance, a nonhedonist may oppose euthanasia because he thinks life has intrinsic value even when it is unpleasant, or on the ground that suffering builds character (which he thinks has intrinsic worth). On the other hand, the hedonist, although he agrees that *normally* life and character are worthwhile, because they make for states of happiness, nevertheless thinks these things have no value when they can no longer add to happiness. He sees no possible value in life or character *per se*, and hence will be more favorably inclined to euthanasia. Hedonists and nonhedonists are apt to be found on opposite sides of other moral questions, for similar reasons.

If we are to assess the hedonist view fairly, we must first of all ask what pleasure is. Unfortunately the term "pleasure" has a slightly bad name; it makes people think only of wine, women, and song. The hedonists have certainly not intended this; and perhaps, at present, the word "enjoyment" is closer to their meaning than "pleasure." We do say, "I enjoyed working for the election of Mr. A." The hedonist means to include such enjoyments as kinds of pleasure. With this understood, let us ask what "pleasant" (or "enjoyable") means.

We certainly know how to apply these words, how to decide, at least in many cases, whether something is pleasant or not. Most people will say without hesitation that it is pleasant to eat ice cream, smell flowers, and get warm by the fire when one is cold. Most people will also say without hesitation that it is unpleasant to swallow castor oil, hear someone brag, or have unfavorable comments made about oneself. Often, of course, it is not easy to say whether one is enjoying oneself or not.

We know, then, how to classify many experiences as pleasant or unpleasant, but it is not easy to say exactly what we are saying about an experience when we so classify it. Nor is this difficulty purely a layman's problem; it has vexed psychologists just as much, and there have been various theories about it.

There is virtual unanimity today that pleasantness is not an element of experience like a color patch or a sound. Just try to examine pleasantness by itself, in the way you can inspect a red patch by itself. It cannot be done. Pleasantness always seems to be the pleasantness *of* something, of an activity, or some other elements of experience. But if it is not a distinct element of experience (like a red patch), then what is it? Of the several theories about this, two are worth developing.

The first starts by pointing to the dimensions of a sensory experience— a "dimension" being something like the pitch or loudness of a sound, or the shade, brightness, or saturation of a color. The dimensions of a sound, like pleasure, are not distinct elements of experience; but they are some- how discriminable aspects of elements of experience that enable us to order experiences in series (from high to low pitch). Pleasantness is not exactly like these dimensions, for if a dimension is reduced to zero the element of which it is a dimension disappears altogether (just as a stick disappears when we reduce it to zero-length); but an experience can per- fectly well exist without being either pleasant or unpleasant. Still, the analogy may be a good one: pleasantness is, like these dimensions, a "higher-order" quality that pervades, and enables us to order, complexes of experience (tastes, emotions), as more or less pleasant.

If we think of pleasantness in this way, we can understand why some writers, like John Stuart Mill, have spoken of "different kinds" of pleas- ure, for when some experience has the quality of pleasantness, it is natural to call the whole experience (for example, the pleasant taste) "a pleasure." Then we can say, as Mill does, that one pleasure is different from another when the pleasantness adheres to a different kind of complex: a pleasant taste will be one kind of pleasure, and the pleasant reading of a novel will be another kind of pleasure.

Psychologists who have defended this general view of pleasure have held differing opinions about which parts of experience can have this pervading quality of pleasantness–unpleasantness. Some have said that only feeling elements (joy, fear, anger, itches) qualify; others have said "bright" feelings in the chest, "dull" feelings in the lower back; others, complexes or patterns of sensation; still others, the *total* momentary ex- perience.

This theory makes some sense, but it is somewhat unsatisfactory, and there is a trend away from it at the present time. The prime objection to it is that the alleged dimension-like quality is so elusive, if not entirely elu- sive, when we try to inspect it. It seems to be unlike the other "dimensions" of experience in this respect. Many have come to suspect that it is quite imaginary to suppose there is any such dimension of experience. What, then, could we be meaning by the phrase "is pleasant"? Obviously we classify experiences as pleasant or unpleasant on *some* basis within experience. This leads us to a different theory.

According to this second view, "*x* is pleasant" simply means, "*x* is a part of my experience that I wish to continue on its own account," and "x *was* pleasant" means "*x* was a part of my experience that I wished at the time to continue on its own account." The *intensity* of the pleasure can then be identified with the intensity of this wishing to continue. But "wishing" in what sense? It is not, of course, necessarily in the sense of conscious thoughts; rather, it is in the sense of wanting (not necessarily longing), of being motivated. In other words, the person "enjoying" his experience is having an experience that he *would take steps to prolong* on its own account, if he could—the interruption of such an experience would annoy him and he would avoid it if he could. So far this seems true to life. We do want to linger with pleasant experiences (other things being equal). Even rats will drink more than usual if their water has a little sugar in it—just as we may drink more cold ginger ale on a hot afternoon than we would warm water. This theory too, like the former one, explains why people talk of "different kinds of pleasure," for there are different kinds of experience that we wish to prolong.

Another proposal, very similar to this, is that saying something "is pleasant" is to say that it elicits effortless heed or attention, absorption in what we are doing or experiencing. Thus, if we are absorbed in a book (not compelling ourselves to plough through it), we can say we are "enjoying" the book, and that reading it is "pleasant."

These last theories, as stated, however, seem to leave something out, for it seems that always when we like an experience for itself (or are absorbed with it), there is always some "subjective" experience present. If hearing some news is pleasant, there is always some emotion present, some swelling of pride, some joy, and so forth. Or, if some homely event like scratching a mosquito bite is pleasant, there is an itch or a tickle present. Or, if hearing some news is unpleasant, there is perhaps a thrill of grief or disappointment. And, of course, pain is unpleasant. In each case, the experience includes a "subjective" element, in the sense of elements in experience that are *not* ostensibly public events or parts of physical objects in the way some parts of our experience are ostensibly the surfaces of pictures, or in the way in which a thunder-clap is public. Such subjective elements not only belong to all segments of experience that we like for themselves, but seem to be correlated with "enjoyment" in the sense that there are never differences in degree of enjoyment without there being differences in the kind or intensity of these subjective elements.

We can include this point in the preceding proposal about pleasantness by saying that "is pleasant" is to have the same sense as "is a part of an experience, containing a subjective element, which one wishes at the time to prolong (or in which one is absorbed without effort) for itself."

This second theory seems less mysterious than the first, and we therefore adopt it. Let us restate the thesis of the hedonist accordingly. He is saying, then, that something is intrinsically desirable (undesirable) if and only if and to the degree that it is an experience with a subjective element that the person at the time wants to prolong (terminate or avoid) for itself. If course, "to the degree that" can refer only to the strength of the desire to prolong or terminate. In brief, the intrinsically good consists of *liked* experiences containing a subjective or feeling element.

The hedonist theory, formulated thus, sets no restriction on the kinds of enjoyment. A person may enjoy wine, women, and song; but equally he may enjoy working at his job, solving crossword puzzles, helping his neighbor repair a fence, and so on. What the hedonist is *denying* is that anything is intrinsically worthwhile if it is not somebody's experience at all, and if it is not enjoyable to the person who has it (for it is the fact that it is enjoyed that makes it intrinsically worthwhile).

We must not forget that identical physical transactions (ignoring subtler physical processes on the microscopic level) are not always identically pleasant. Drinking water is more pleasant when we are thirsty. The experience of drinking (and the underlying physiology) of course is different in the two cases. It is an interesting question whether the same *experience* might carry different degrees of pleasantness in different persons; some philosophers (for example, G. E. Moore) have thought it could. Indeed, it is *logically* possible for there to be human beings who like toothaches and pains, and dislike sex. On the *second* theory of pleasure, it is not logically possible for a person to dislike pleasure; on the first theory this is possible.

4. PSYCHOLOGICAL HEDONISM

The hedonist's thesis has plausibility. On the whole, we do think it a good thing for people to have enjoyable experiences, and for them not to have disagreeable ones. When we are planning our children's education, one thing that we have in mind is whether a certain kind of education will enhance the future enjoyments of the child, and we avoid a course of action likely to cause an unhappy future. Enjoyable experiences, we think, are at least highly important components of whatever it is that makes living worthwhile. If we tend to question the hedonist's thesis, it is because of its scope and its exclusiveness: the claim that *every* kind of enjoyment is intrinsically good; the claim that nothing *but* enjoyment makes a difference to the intrinsic desirability of a thing.

But is there reason to suppose that the hedonist's thesis true or valid? Historically, in many writers have thought there is good reason for this conclusion and that it lies in the psychology of motivation. Diogenes Laertius, for instance, wrote of Epicurus:

> And as proof that pleasure is the end he adduces the fact that living things, so soon as they are born, are well content with pleasure and are at enmity with pain, by the prompting of nature and apart from reason. Left to our own feelings, then, we shun pain. . . . And we choose the virtues too on account of pleasure and not for their own sake, as we take medicine for the sake of health.[2]

Much the same reasoning has been used by other hedonists, including Jeremy Bentham and John Stuart Mill. The type of psychological theory of motivation that Epicurus supported is generally classified under the title "psychological hedonism."

We must examine this psychological theory and its alleged implication of the truth of ethical hedonism.

Unfortunately, several different propositions have been called "psychological hedonism" by various writers. For this and other reasons, the term is a confusing one, and we shall drop it altogether, in favor of more descriptive phrases. But before doing so, it is helpful to note a definition of it proposed by Henry Sidgwick,[3] which we can expand in such a way as to show the relationsihp of the three distinct theories we shall discuss. Sidgwick said that psychological hedonism is the view "that volition is always determined by pleasures or pains actual or prospective." Let us change his phrasing to read that psychological hedonism is the view that "volition *or desire* is always determined by pleasures or pains *prospective, actual,* or *past.*" The theory is significantly different depending on whether the thesis is that volition and desire are determined by prospective, actual, or past pleasures and displeasures. Let us examine three types of psychological hedonism in this order.

The Pleasure Theory of Goals. The most important form of the theory asserts that a person wants (is motivated to produce) a state of affairs if and only if he believes that it will be enjoyable to him, or will produce enjoyment for himself or at least avoid a disagreeable state of affairs; and he will prefer one state of affairs to another if and only if he thinks it will be more enjoyable, or produce more enjoyment, all things considered, for himself. This theory has sometimes been called "psychological hedonism of the future."

The theory, of course, is not saying anything so absurd as that we are not motivated to do something unless we say to ourselves, "Now this is going to be fun." Rather, the term "believe" is to be taken broadly, so as to include a more-or-less unconscious "taking for granted." Further, the theory

---

[2] Diogenes Laertius, *Lives of Eminent Philosophers*, R. D. Hicks (trans.) (London: William Heinemann, Ltd., 1925), Bk. X, pp. 137–38.

[3] *The Methods of Ethics* (London: Macmillan & Co., Ltd., 1922), p. 40.

should be viewed as a proposal about purposive behavior only, not about reflex or purely habitual behavior. Finally, "wanting" or "preferring" or "being motivated to . . ." are not to be taken as referring to that mildly unpleasant internal episode that we sometimes call "longing" or "craving." Rather, it is readiness to expend energy in action. It is also readiness to respond to news that an object is lost (for example, someone else has married the beautiful queen) with some disappointment, at least unless one never expected to achieve it anyway. It is readiness to respond with some joy to the news that some goal is now sure, at least unless one has been certain of getting it all along.

The Pleasure Theory of Goals, then, is saying that personal pleasure is one's only ultimate goal, in the sense that belief that one can obtain pleasure by a certain course of action is a necessary and sufficient condition for being motivated to act, and that one will be more strongly motivated toward one of alternative courses of action if and only if one believes it will procure more net enjoyment. As Jeremy Bentham put it, everyone is "led to pursue that line of conduct which, according to his view of the case, taken by him at the moment, will be in the highest degree contributory to his own greatest happiness."[4]

There are two questions we must ask ourselves about the Pleasure Theory of Goals. First, would its truth establish ethical hedonism? Second, is there reason to think that it is true? Let us look at this.

We need not examine the various forms of reasoning that have been used to extract ethical hedonism from this theory of motivation. The description of Epicurus' thinking is an example. But we should notice that conceivably a theory of motivation *could* lead to an ethical doctrine, for we have argued that a principle to the effect that things of a certain kind are desirable would be established, roughly, if it is coherent with what we *want or favor* when we are fully informed, and in an impartial but otherwise normal frame of mind. So, if a psychological theory of motivation could somehow show, say, that everybody in every condition of mind whatsoever wants pleasant states of affairs and nothing else, the hedonist ethical thesis would be established. For no matter how fully informed or impartial or otherwise normal we might be, we should still be interested in states of enjoyment and nothing else.

Does the Pleasure Theory of Goals have this implication? Not quite; there is a difficulty about the inference, because of the fact that the theory implies that no one is ever *impartial*. Nevertheless, we need not become too puzzled over just what is implied by the Pleasure Theory of Goals, for there are solid grounds for questioning whether the theory is true. Let us examine the evidence on this matter.

[4] Jeremy Bentham, *Constitutional Code*, Introduction, in *The Works of Jeremy Bentham*, John Bowring (ed.), (Edinburgh: William Tait, 1843), vol. IX, p. 5.

If we *ask* people what they think is worthwhile in life, what are their goals, things will probably be mentioned rather similar to those suggested by the Hopi to the writer (p. 96): things like a good harvest, having money, being liked by other people, having good health, not dying before one's time, having skills and talents, and so on. Such things are not like "just anything insofar as it is pleasant or avoids the disagreeable." It *sounds* as if the thought of obtaining some goal other than pleasure might be motivating. But, it may be said, of course people who say these things know and take for granted that the getting of these things will be pleasant, or bring pleasure; and they would not continue to take an interest in them if they changed their view on this.

The Pleasure Theory of Goals can be supported by pointing to the fact that we all do take an interest in having fun. If you say to me, "Let's take the evening off and go out and have some fun," my interest will be aroused, without your specifying at all what you have in mind to do. Moreover, if my physician, in the course of giving me a physical examination, says, "I am afraid what we are going to do next will be rather unpleasant," then I at once rather prefer that he should not do whatever he has in mind to do, even though I don't know what in particular it's going to be. We do avoid many things just because we think they will be unpleasant: getting a shock, going without dinner, sitting for several hours during the night in a railroad station. Also, we seek and want many things because we think they will be pleasant.

But are there never cases of desiring something, of being motivated to attain a certain end, when we have *no* expectations about whether the event will be pleasant for us, or think definitely there will *not* be pleasure in it for us? Are there *never* cases of being motivated to attain a certain end, even despite the expectation that the event will be, on balance, *less* pleasant for us than some alternative?

There certainly appear to be such cases. For instance, ask yourself whether Churchill and Truman take a lively interest in the verdict of posterity about their conduct in high office. Do they take *no* interest in what happens after their decease, that is, beyond the point after which they will get no pleasure from whatever happens? The impression one gets is that their interest is not limited in this fashion. One might say that perhaps these men imagine themselves flitting about observing earthly events after their demise, reading death notices, and so forth; but this hypothesis is an unlikely one. Ask yourself: "Would I expend *no* energy to secure myself an important niche in human history—even if so doing would add nothing to lifetime pleasures?" It seems rather obvious that a person can be motivated by certain ends, irrespective of his belief that achieving the end will bring him pleasure.

Moreover, is it not blind to deny that people have made and carried out decisions that they regarded as likely to bring personal disaster? "The boy stood on the burning deck. . . ." Foolishly, to be sure, in his case. Still, people have taken a stand for what they thought was duty or principle; and it is hard to imagine they can have supposed it was a way of advancing their personal benefit. Events in wartime are the most obvious ones. Are men who volunteer for the dangerous mission of blowing up a bridge inside enemy lines merely looking for a thrill? On a humbler level, consider housewives who beat down tin cans in order to save metal, or persons who were denied a hotel room or a pair of stockings because they would not stoop to bribery. Here is discomfort deliberately accepted, for the sake of principle or a cause.

Ethical hedonism may be tenable, but the Pleasure Theory of Goals is just too simple. Perhaps people ought to take an interest only in pleasure or even their own personal pleasure. But they don't. They sometimes sacrifice their pleasure for some intangible goal like posthumous recognition; or they sacrifice it for a principle, or for the happiness of others.

In the face of obvious points like these, the advocate of the Pleasure Theory of Goals is apt to argue: "People who make sacrifices do so because they know they wouldn't be happy if they didn't." Thus, after all, it is said, these people are only doing what they think will make them happy or avoid unhappiness. Now, it is true that sometimes people stick to their principles (and so forth) because they think they'll be unhappy if they don't. But can one seriously urge that this is *always* the case? Surely some people stick to their principles when they have not given thought, one way or the other, to whether so doing will make them happier. Indeed, a person who argues in this way overlooks a major point. He overlooks the fact that in many cases disappointment at, say, failing to live up to one's principles or proud joy in having done so are not the driving forces of motivation but *symptoms* that living by one's principles is wanted for itself. It is *because* a person is concerned about standards and ideals that he is disconcerted when he fails and overjoyed when he succeeds. It is the very opposite of the truth to say that what he wanted was to avoid the disagreeable and have the pleasant.

The Pleasure Theory of Goals, however, has a peculiar fascination for some minds. Some people will argue stubbornly for the theory in the face of the most obvious counterevidence. We cannot mention all possible arguments they might advance. But we can do this. We can ask: Do you regard the Pleasure Theory of Goals as a thesis of empirical science, supported by evidence of observation—or just as true by definition? If you think it is true by definition, explain why it is. (No explanation will be forthcoming.) If not true by definition, please explain what *kind of evidence in principle* you would accept as *disproving* the theory. If there is *no* such *possible* evidence, how can your thesis be a thesis of empirical science at all? (Imagine a physicist proposing a theory and saying there *could* not be counterevidence!) We can confidently anticipate that the Pleasure Theorist will *not* be able to describe any kind of empirical evidence he would accept as refutation of his theory—or if he does, it will not be difficult to produce the very evidence he is inviting.

The Pleasure Theory of Goals, then, is insupportable. Nor, we may note, is it a theory that has captured the attention of psychologists. One looks in vain through the volumes of modern psychology in search of such a view. True, some psychologists *call* themselves psychological hedonists, but what they mean, as we shall see shortly, is quite different from the thesis we have been considering.

Perhaps some people have been attracted to the Pleasure Theory of Goals because they did not distinguish it carefully from other, more plausible, contentions. Jeremy Bentham, for instance, made this mistake. What are these related theories?

Motivation by Pleasant Thoughts. The next theory, sometimes called "psychological hedonism of the present," is this: A person is motivated to produce a certain state of affairs if and only if the thought of it is pleasant or attractive to him (or the opposite); and a person will prefer one course of action to another if and only if the thought of what it will bring about is more attractive or pleasant than the thought of what other possibles acts will bring about. We shall call this the "Motivation by Pleasant Thoughts" theory. It differs from the first theory in this way: the first theory roughly tied motivation to the expectation of future pleasure, whereas this theory ties it to pleasant thoughts. Since thoughts of future pleasant activities are likely to be pleasant thoughts, the two theories are easily confused.

This second theory, however, whether true or not, has no bearing on the topic of our interest. Its truth does not weigh either for or against the doctrine of ethical hedonism. It does not tend to show that people (or, specifically, informed, impartial people) take an interest in events only insofar as they are believed to be pleasant. Even if it is granted that we take an interest in producing an event only if the idea of it is pleasant, it need not be true that the idea of an event is pleasant only if the idea is an idea of a pleasant experience. The thoughts of attaining knowledge, or stature as a person, or of fame after one's decease, or of speed as a runner, or skill as a pianist, and so forth, may all be pleasant thoughts.[5]

Conditioning by Pleasant Experiences. Neither of the foregoing theories is of much interest to psychologists today. A third theory, however, does have support. Roughly, this theory states that the strength of one's present interest in a particular kind of occurrence is a function of past enjoyments. Sometimes this doctrine is called "psychological hedonism of the past."

---

[5] It is fairly obvious that the thought of *someone else* suffering can be highly unpleasant. If so, this theory, unlike the previous one, does not limit our interest to pleasant and unpleasant states of ourselves.

Let us, however, call it the "Conditioning by Pleasant Experiences" theory.[6] A simple example to illustrate the theory is the following. A person stops in at a restaurant or bar for some refreshment. What does he order? There are complications, of course, such as prices, what other people are ordering, a desire to experiment, and so forth. But forgetting such matters, it seems plausible to say that whether he orders a milkshake, ginger ale, a glass of beer, or a Tom Collins will depend on previous enjoyments of the drink in similar situations. For this example, the theory seems true to life.

It will simplify our task of examining this theory if we remind ourselves that our interest in it is quite specific. What we need to know for our assessment of ethical hedonism is whether a perfectly informed (discriminating) person would prefer one thing, *for itself*, to another thing, if and only if the pleasantness of the former were greater than that of the latter. The interest of the Conditioning by Pleasant Experiences Theory lies in the fact that it might imply that the laws of preference-learning are such that this is true.

Let us consider the theory with our specific interest in mind. Two main things should be said. First, theories and facts in psychology raise serious doubts about the theory. We have reviewed the major psychological theories about the learning of values (and preferences and motives) in Chapter 6, although we did not there mention the hedonistic theories of P. T. Young and L. T. Troland. We saw that there are today many conflicting theories about this process. In particular there are disagreements between Gestalt theories and Hull-type theories (which can be taken to regard learning as a function of enjoyments, namely, drive reductions). Practically all the experimental evidence in support of a Gestalt theory of values has weight against the Conditioning by Pleasant Experiences theory. Second, the theory itself, on careful inspection, seems to allow that people can learn to value things that are *not pleasant and are not supposed by them to be pleasant*. Why? The reason is that the "past enjoyments" which influence present preferences may include such things as praise by parents, the joy of being able to think of oneself as being like an admired person, the pleasure of being able to think of one's system of values as consistent, and so on. Past enjoyments can very well, according to the theory, cause a person to take an interest in such things as having character traits like chastity, self-discipline, and control of the temper. So, on the one hand the Conditioning

---

[6] See, for instance, P. T. Young, "The Role of Hedonic Processes in the Organization of Behavior," *Psychological Review*, LIX (1952), 249–62; "Food-seeking Drive, Affective Process and Learning," *Psychological Review*, LVI (1949), 98–121. Also L. T. Troland, *Fundamentals of Human Motivation* (D. Van Nostrand Company, Inc., 1932), chap. 16; E. C. Tolman, "There Is More than One Kind of Learning," *Psychological Review*, LVI (1949), 144–55. If drive reduction (*supra*, p. 135) is thought to be subjectively represented by pleasure, then Clark Hull's theory can be viewed as a theory of this type.

by Pleasant Experiences Theory is in conflict with some major theories of learning and with substantial pieces of experimental evidence; and on the other hand the theory implies that people can acquire interests in things that are not inherently enjoyable.

Contemporary psychological theory, then, does not establish ethical hedonism.

5. SOME DIFFICULTIES FOR HEDONISM

The attempt to establish ethical hedonism by appeal to a general theory of human motivation is a failure, at least at present.

There is a second line of reasoning that has been used to establish ethical hedonism in an even simpler way; this merits brief attention. This second line of reasoning simply is the claim that ethical hedonism is *true by definition*. In order to use this reasoning, one must, of course, be prepared to be a naturalist, at least about the term "desirable." The essence of the theory is simply that "intrinsically desirable" means the same as "pleasant"; and if so, then of course the thesis of hedonism is necessarily true. We remember that Spinoza said "By *good* I here mean every kind of pleasure, and all that conduces thereto. . . ." And John Locke wrote: "That we call 'good,' which is apt to cause or increase pleasure. . . ." Among contemporary writers, such a view appears to be defended by no less eminent a philosopher than C. I. Lewis.[7] A naturalistic definition of this sort is rather similar to the view held by R. B. Perry, which we have described.

It is perhaps obvious that "pleasant" does not *overtly* (p. 163) have the same meaning as "intrinsically desirable." If the proposal of these philosophers is correct, then, it must be that what is asserted is only that the two terms mean the same, although not overtly. We are familiar with the methods by which this claim is to be tested. How does their proposal survive such tests? The answer is that it does not survive, for, as we shall see shortly, it is possible, or even probable, that some things are intrinsically *more* desirable than others, when their pleasantness is no greater (or at least it is doubtful whether it is); and there is some possibility, at least, that some things that are pleasant are intrinsically *undesirable*. Possibly the reader

---

[7] See *An Analysis of Knowledge and Valuation* (LaSalle Ill.: Open Court Publishing Co., 1946), chap. 13; John Reid, *A Theory of Value* (New York: Charles Scribner's Sons, 1938), *passim*; G. F. Hourani, *Ethical Value* (Ann Arbor: University of Michigan Press, 1956), chap. 5. W. T. Stace has gone somewhat further in proposing a hedonistic definition of "right" and "wrong." He says: "The kind of actions which tend to increase human happiness are the kind of actions which are called right; while those which tend to increase human unhappiness are those which are called wrong. And I believe that this is what we *mean* by such terms as right and wrong; and that we mean nothing else, nothing in addition to this." *The Concept of Morals* (New York: The Macmillan Company, 1937), p. 112. These writers do not necessarily share our concept of pleasantness. Stace, moreover, distinguishes "happiness" from "pleasure."

will not be convinced by these reflections, but if he is, then he must grant that, if a naturalistic definition of "desirable" is tenable at all, it must be so complex that the main thesis of hedonism is not just true by definition.

How then may hedonism be defended? Well, we can state the thesis clearly. We can consider the major historical objections that have been raised against the hedonistic thesis, and consider whether they would have been raised but for misunderstandings. We can then ask ourselves whether persons who are disabused of misunderstandings would care for anything but enjoyment, for itself. If a fair answer to these questions must be negative, then we have established hedonism as well as we can establish any theory in this area. If a fair answer is affirmative, then we shall not wish to defend hedonism in any case, but perhaps we shall be able to defend a slightly more complex view that does justice to the claims of hedonism. Let us see what can be done.

We have defined "ethical hedonism" as the view that "a thing is intrinsically desirable (undesirable) if and only if and to the degree that it is pleasant (unpleasant)." This statement is somewhat compact, and it may be helpful to expand it. It is equivalent, clearly, to the following propositions. (*a*) Everything that is pleasant is intrinsically desirable. (*b*) Everything that is unpleasant is intrinsically undesirable. (*c*) Nothing that is neither pleasant nor unpleasant has intrinsic worth. (*d*) Anything that is more pleasant than something else (or more unpleasant) is more desirable (more undesirable) intrinsically than that other thing.

We shall shortly consider exceptions that have been taken to principles (*a*) and (*b*); in the following chapter we shall examine alleged counter-examples to principles (*c*) and (*d*).

It would be a misfortune to think that more is at stake in these coming considerations than actually is the case. Suppose we found that something is pleasant but *not* intrinsically desirable. What would follow? *Not*, as some have thought, that pleasantness is *never* of intrinsic worth, or that the addition of pleasantness to an experience *never* makes it better. To draw such inferences would be absurd: it would be like saying that because *some* promises (for example, ones made under duress) are ones we are not obligated to fulfill, therefore making a promise *never* creates an obligation. Not at all; what we conclude in the case of promises is that *some* types of promises must be fulfilled except where other features in a situation impose stronger conflicting obligations. The same is true for hedonism. To show that pleasure in some contexts is not good is to show simply that; it shows that the hedonistic thesis as stated requires some complication, and no more. Whether a thesis, thus complicated, is properly still called "hedonism" is another matter.

Why have philosophers questioned proposition (*a*)? They have done so because they think there are obvious cases of pleasant states of mind that a thoughtful person would prefer not to occur. Thus, they have supposed reflective people will not only be indifferent to certain kinds of pleasure; they positively will object to them. If so, and assuming these "thoughtful" people are fully informed, impartial, and in a calm frame of mind, the inference is correct that we must allow there are exceptions to thesis (*a*), and that this thesis must be reformulated to take account of them.

Among the alleged obvious counterexamples to thesis (*a*), the most plausible that has been presented is that of enjoyment of the suffering of others, and we shall confine our examination to it.

Let us take a case. Not too long ago, the writer has been informed, in some parts of Germany executions of criminals were performed publicly. The event was a social occasion of some interest, and women might attend —occupy "box seats"—in evening dress. (We might recall the knitting women of French Revolutionary days.) Execution was by the method of beheading. The prisoner was led in with hands tied behind his back. He was thrust down onto his knees, with head and neck across a block. His head was then severed with a blow of a sword. Evidently the ladies present got some sort of thrill out of the occasion; or at least the officer-husbands who escorted them must have done so, else it is not easy to see why there was a practice of attending. But we need not concern ourselves with whether in fact the occasion was enjoyed. The point of some philosophers is: *If* it was enjoyed, the enjoyment was an intrinsically undesirable one.

We may make this example more extreme. Suppose there were someone present who personally knew the prisoner and disliked him. And suppose this person noted every sign of terror, every flinching at the indignity, every sign of pain in the prisoner; and suppose he relished all, that each symptom gave him a thrill. "Very well," some philosophers will say, "obviously such pleasures are bad, and the more intense the pleasures are, the worse."

The critic's case unquestionably has some plausibility. Has the defender of thesis (*a*) an answer? He can say this. He can agree that it would be better if these pleasures did not occur. But *not* because they are intrinsically undesirable. It would be better if they did not occur, because the reason for their occurrence is the existence of an unhealthy mind, an insensitive and callous mind, which may confidently be expected in the long run to cause unhappiness among sentient beings. The pleasure in the execution is not bad; it is only a symptom of something, but the thing of which it is a symptom is undesirable—not intrinsically undesirable, but undesirable because of its probable effects on happiness. So, the hedonist will say, the critic has failed to make a crucial distinction. The critic is right that it would be better if there were no pleasures of this sort, but only because it is undesirable that there should be the minds that have them. The pleasure taken *just for itself*, however, is harmless and indeed desirable; *intrinsically* it is good.

Let us turn to thesis (*b*). The hedonist says that there are **no unpleasant** experiences that are intrinsically worthwhile. The critics of hedonism have suggested that *merited punishment* is unpleasant, but of intrinsic value.

To see the point of this controversy, let us take a homely case. Suppose some large boy plagues a shy little fellow, terrorizes him on the way home from school, beats him up, bloodies his nose, sends him home frightened and in tears. Now suppose that the elder brother of the victim rises to the occasion, sallies forth to meet the culprit, denounces him for his behavior, and proceeds to pay him back in kind, with good measure. The critic of hedonism will applaud. And he will say this: It is *intrinsically better* for the bully to have suffered this beating, *even if it does not lead him to mend his ways,* than for the offense to have gone unpunished.

Is the critic right? The hedonist will say "No." This is not to say the hedonist will not applaud the elder brother's action. He will. He will do so because he thinks there is good reason for expecting that the beating will lead the bully to stop and think, perhaps to mend his ways; and it will lead other would-be bullies to stop and think. And so on. But the hedonist will say, if you confine your attention to the beating alone, and ask yourself whether you could want just that to happen, quite irrespective of these consequences, you must say "No." If one takes this brief strand of the bully's existence (the beating), and look at it just for itself, or even just in connection with the past but ignoring future consequences, it is made worse by the pain, not better.

A decision between the hedonist and his critic on this point will not be attempted here. The controversy raises large issues, and we shall not be able to assess them adequately until much later (Chapter 19).

But how shattering is it to the hedonist, if both the critic's points must be accepted? Well, if they are, the hedonist must revise his thesis, perhaps as follows: (*a*) Everything that is pleasant, except for enjoyments of the suffering of others, is intrinsically desirable. (*b*) Everything that is unpleasant, except for merited punishment, is intrinsically undesirable. These are less simple than the originals, but we can make do with them; and life is not simple anyway. If hedonism is right but for these modifications, it is not far from true.

Unfortunately for the hedonist, more serious difficulties are still to come: evidence that various other properties besides pleasantness make a difference to intrinsic worth. Moreover, perhaps there are other exceptions, in addition to those mentioned, to the principle that pleasant things are of intrinsic worth. If all these objections are accepted, the hedonist's thesis is substantially reduced in scope. What could be defended might be something much like this: "If pleasure (displeasure) is present in a complex whole, then, except for the cases of . . . , the whole is of greater (less) intrinsic worth, and the more so the more intense the pleasure (displeasure)." Such a principle appears defensible, but it is not nearly as interesting a principle as the more radical initial proposal of the hedonist. Nor would a person who accepted it properly be called a "hedonist."

There is a more general criticism of the hedonist stand that has aroused a sympathetic echo in many thoughtful persons. This is the fact that pleasures are transitory. Suppose a person promises his family that he will take them out for a birthday dinner. He does so, and everyone enjoys himself. But the next morning he awakens $50 poorer, with nothing to show for his expense except not very interesting recollections. The enjoyments of the evening are fully gone, and the man may ask himself if there was a point in spending for them. More generally, a person may wonder whether there can be worth in a series of enjoyments, none of which can be captured, but each of which exists for its moment and then is gone forever. Is this the only worth in life? Why should a person take an interest in things like this?

The hedonist may reply, however, that this thinking is convincing only because we overlook certain facts. In the first place, the same argument would prove that pain is not a bad thing, because it is merely transitory; but no one will take this seriously. Second, there is a sense in which everything is transitory: knowledge, character, reputation, anything you wish to mention. Life has an end; and all of these, except one's influence, are dissipated. Third, the hedonist will point out that enjoyments can be prolonged and recurrent. He will insist that various things we can achieve in life are conditions of recurrent joys: knowledge, friends, an interesting job, absorbing commitments in the life of the community. If we achieve these things, then not only sporadic pleasures but recurrent joys and persistent happiness will accompany them. The hedonist concludes that a thoughtful person who takes all these things into account will not be deterred, by talk of transitoriness, from approving enjoyable experiences for themselves, and wishing for nothing else for itself.

6. THE CONCEPT OF A "SUM" OF PLEASURES

The hedonist, we have seen, asserts that one state of affairs is intrinsically better than, or preferable to, another state of affairs if and only if it is more pleasant. This seems simple enough, if all the hedonist intends to claim is that your state of mind *at the present moment* is intrinsically better than mine if and only it is a more pleasant state of mind. But actually hedonists have had something more complex (and useful) in mind when they talked of the relative intrinsic worth of different states of affairs. They have wanted to discuss whether the experience of a week at the shore is pleasanter and therefore intrinsically better than a week in New York spent at theaters and art galleries. They have wanted to discuss whether one system of economic distribution or government makes for a pleasanter, and hence intrinsically better kind of life for everybody concerned. They have (rightly) thought that it is questions like these with which practical decision is concerned.

When one raises questions as to which one of such complex states of affairs is pleasanter (and therefore, according to the hedonist, intrinsically better), problems arise. First, there is the practical problem that it is difficult to estimate how enjoyable certain future experiences (like a week at the shore) will be for other people or even for ourselves, if we base our inferences, as we must, upon past experiences. People are different from one another in likes and dislikes; their likes change from one period of life to another; they are apt to forget the unpleasant side of past experiences, and so on.[8] But there is a second and more interesting problem, a theoretical difficulty: that it may be *meaningless* to talk of the "total" pleasantness of such complex states of affairs (extended over stretches of time and involving many people), or of one collection of experiences being "more pleasant" than another. This second issue is an intriguing one, and obviously is crucial for the hedonist who wants to make interesting comparisons of the relative pleasantness of modes of life or systems of cultural organization. We must look into this.

What exactly is the difficulty?

Let us begin with our explanation of "is pleasant." We suggested that "x is pleasant" is to say the same as "x is an experience with a feeling element that the person wants to prolong at the time." (It would make no difference if we adopted the alternative, quality view of pleasure.) As a consequence, to say that "x is more intensely pleasant than y" presumably is the same as to say, "x and y are both experiences with feeling elements, and the wish of the subject of x to prolong x at the time is more intense than the wish of the subject of y to prolong y at the time." Now, there is a problem about how to decide that the wish of one person to prolong his experience is stronger than the wish of another person to prolong his experience. But for the present we shall avoid this by assuming that both experiences belong to the same person, and that he can remember how he felt about prolongation of his past experiences and can tell us which one he wished more strongly to prolong.

We know, then, what it means to say that one person's experience at one moment is more intensely pleasant than some person's experience at the same or another time. However, this does not tell us what it might mean to say, "x's *hour* at the theater was pleasanter than y's *hour* at the shore." (Assume, for the moment, that x and y are the same person.) Is there any meaning in such comparative judgments about the total pleasantness of *stretches* of experience?

This is the main theoretical issue, and we must see to what extent we can answer this question.

---

[8] These difficulties are discussed with great care and fairness by the hedonist, Henry Sidgwick, *op. cit.*, Bk. II, chap. 3.

We can give a meaning to "was pleasanter than" for this type of context in two types of case.

First, we are ready to say that x's hour as a whole was more pleasant than y's hour as a whole *if at no instant during the hour x's enjoyment was less intense than y's, and if at some instants during the hour x's enjoyment was more intense than y's.* This relationship of pleasure levels during the hour is a sufficient condition for saying that x's hour as a whole was more pleasant; and this fact gives us a partial explanation of the *meaning* of the phrase in which we are interested. Figure 1 is a graphical example of pleasure-levels during hours for which x's pleasure was greater than y's.

Second, we are ready to say that x's hour at the theater was more pleasant than y's hour at the shore, even in case at some instants during the hour y's pleasure-level was higher than x's, *provided that,* by *rearranging the segments* of the hour, we can have the situation of the foregoing first type of case. Figures 2 and 3 illustrate an example of such a rearrangement. It is doubtless intuitively less clear that we should be willing to say that x's theater-hour was pleasanter than y's shore-hour under these conditions; but on reflection we shall see that we are indeed willing to do this. This provides a further partial explanation of the meaning of the phrase of interest to us.[9]

However, can *all* comparison problems be handled in this way, so that we get an example of our first situation by rearrangement of segments of the curves? Unfortunately, they cannot. Figure 4 illustrates a simple case in which rearrangement will not give this result. Is there any way in which we can show that one of these hours is more pleasant than the other? We could, if we had some objective way of proving that the amount by which the theater-hour enjoyment exceeds that of the shore-hour (Area A) is greater than the amount by which the shore-hour exceeds the theater-hour (area B)—or rather, if we could provide a *meaning* for statements of this sort. But this cannot be done by the ordinary methods used for calculating the areas under curves, for, although our graph necessarily locates these curves in specific places, that is, with specific heights, our evidence justifies us only in placing one point of a curve higher or lower than some other point (through comparative judgments about the relative strength of a desire to prolong the experience), but not in placing it higher or lower than

---

[9] Of course, if we actually rearranged the temporal position of the experiences, we should probably modify the pleasure-levels. For instance, if you work hard for something first and then enjoy it, the pleasure levels of the different experiences may be quite different from the case where you enjoy something first, and then must work hard to pay for it. In the second case, the pleasures of anticipation may not have the same importance.

But the rearrangement we are suggesting is not of this sort. The rearranging is only a convenience of exposition. What is being suggested is that we are prepared to say that one pleasure as a whole is greater than the others *if* we can *match* segments from each in such a way that no segment of the first is lower than its matching segment from the second, and that some segments of the first are higher than the matching segment of the second.

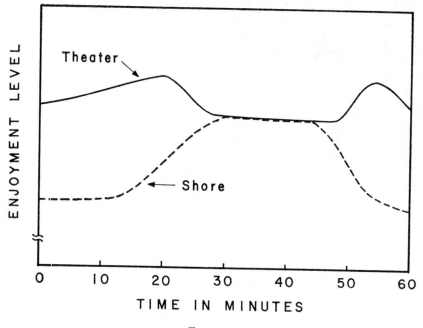

FIGURE 1

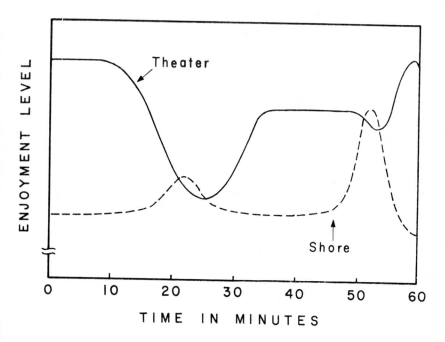

FIGURE 2

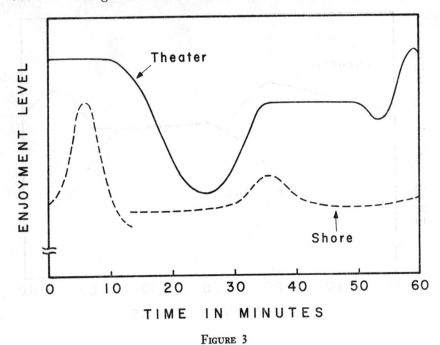

FIGURE 3

FIGURE 4

the other curve to *any specific extent* except as a rough representation of our intuitive feelings that the one desire was only slightly, considerably, or very much greater than the other.[10]

To see the difficulty, let us look at a simple analogue. Suppose we have six red stones, and six black stones (each corresponding to a ten-minute period of pleasant experience). And suppose we know that the black stones are all of equal weight. Moreover, two of the red stones are much heavier than the black stones, but the four other red stones are a bit lighter than the black stones. And suppose this is *all* we know. Could we then answer the question whether the red stones as a group weigh more than the black stones as a group? Obviously not. But of course we can answer the question without difficulty, for we can simply load the red stones onto one pan of a balance, and the black stones onto the other, and the issue is settled by observing which pan sinks.[11]

[10] The shape of the curve must also preserve the relative hedonic level of all the moments represented by the curve, so that each point represents an intensity of enjoyment equal in level to that of other points represented as at the same level on the graph, higher than those the graph shows as below it, lower than those the graph shows above it. But this condition would still be met if we flattened the curve outlining the upper part of area A, above, in such a way as to make the graphical area smaller than that of B. It has been supposed that we can circumvent the foregoing difficulty in the following way. First, we represent the hedonic (enjoyment) level of any experience that is neither pleasant nor unpleasant by assigning it a y-coordinate of 0. Then we change the experience until its pleasantness is just noticeable, and we assign to the hedonic level that is the least that is noticeably different from the 0-level, the value 1, on the y-coordinate. The pleasure level that is just noticeably more agreeable than level 1, we assign to level 2. And so on. It is then assumed that the smallest discernible differences between levels are equal in magnitude throughout, so that the correlation of levels with the integers is justified. After the position of any enjoyment level has thus been fixed, we can graph a particular experience by matching it with the standard—just as we can give a name to a given color by matching it with the named colors on a color card. (For simplicity we ignore the obvious difficulties, for example, that we cannot depict the various enjoyment levels on a standard card.) Then the areas (like A and B in our graph) will have the same relative size on any graph, and it will be possible to say which one is larger.

The crucial difficulty is the assumption that the least discriminable differences are "equal in magnitude." To make this clear, let us suppose someone says that ten minutes of pleasure at level 1 are equal to five minutes pleasure at level 2. We can then choose to doubt this, and ask him to show why we should not do so. How would he show we are mistaken? If anyone doubts whether ten 1-pound weights are equal to five 2-pound weights, he can be answered by placing them on a balance. The balance (which by definition shows us "equal weights") proves that the assignment of numerical values to weights and the application of arithmetic in calculations about them is consistent and confirmed by its predictive success. How can an equivalent confirmation be provided for the assumption in our case? There is no device here, comparable to a balance, that can show that the two segments are equal (by definition of "equally pleasant"). In principle, then, the assumption eludes empirical assessment, and must be adjudged arbitrary and indefensible.

[11] Of course, we can also weigh each stone individually, and then add up. But in principle the calibration of a scales requires that we can assign numbers to standard objects by the device of balancing *groups* of objects on a balance scales. What is done is in principle the same as what is suggested in the text, and we shall ignore this alternative.

There is no comparable procedure for comparing the relative size of the areas of pleasure of interest to us; and correspondingly there is no definite meaning that we can assign, in this situation, to the statement that the hour at the theater was pleasanter than the hour at the shore. Thus, the critics of the hedonist are correct in their contention that it may be meaningless to say that last Saturday evening's theater party was more or less pleasant than the previous Saturday evening's stay at the shore. As a result, the hedonist is prevented from predicting that money spent for an evening at the theater would purchase more or less enjoyment than money spent for a few hours at the shore, if the prediction is to be based on previous experiences.

Need the hedonist feel particularly embarrassed by this? In other words, is our result an *objection* to the thesis of hedonism? Not obviously. It is true that the result at which we have arrived implies that the hedonist is in principle debarred, in some cases, from asserting that one experience is preferable to another (for he says one is preferable if and only if it is more pleasant). But this may not be shocking. Perhaps it is unduly presumptuous to suppose that we can always know that one event is preferable to another. It *would* be embarrassing for the hedonist, however—indeed would definitively refute him—if we happen to *know* that some things are preferable to some other things, although it is in principle impossible to say that one is more pleasant than the other. But do we really have such information?[12]

The problem we have been discussing has been a somewhat simplified one. It has assumed that the pleasureable experiences of one and the same person are being compared, and that this person's judgments based on recollections are a reasonably reliable source about relative intensity of enjoyment. In practice, however, we must try to solve interpersonal problems. We must decide whether we are spending our scarce money better by sending one son to a baseball game or the other to an art exhibit. For this problem, the judgment of one person about his past experiences does not give sufficient guidance. We must estimate the future enjoyments of each by appeal to past enjoyments of the two; we must be able to judge whether one son has enjoyed baseball games in the past more or less than the other has enjoyed art galleries. Economists are faced by greatly magnified problems

---

[12] It has recently been suggested that we might analyze "x is more pleasant than y" (where x and y are both experiences of the same person) as meaning "the subject of both experiences prefers x to y." There are difficulties about the meaning of "prefer." Does it mean "would prefer to *repeat* an experience like"? or "remembers with more relish"? Again, it is quite conceivable that a person will recall past experiences with different degrees of relish, depending on the level of his appetite at the time. If, however, we grant enough assumptions (including the assumption that one's preference order is always the same, and that we can make consistent preference judgments relating every moment of experience to every other one and to every combination of them), the described difficulty for the hedonist can be altogether removed. See Robert McNaughton, "A Metrical Concept of Happiness," *Philosophy and Phenomenological Research*, XIV (1953), 172–83; and Davidson, McKinsey, and Suppes, "Outlines of a Formal Theory of Value, I," *Philosophy of Science*, XXII (1955), 140–60. See also the bibliography at the end of the latter paper.

of a similar sort, for example, when they are asked to judge whether an inflationary monetary policy should be adopted, in view of possible hardships on some people.

If there is an objective method for making interpersonal comparisons of intensity of enjoyment, then we can extend our foregoing conclusions from the case of one person to the case of two or many persons. But is there such a method? We must postpone an answer to this question to the final pages of the following chapter.

7. SCIENCE AND THE LIFE OF PLEASURE

So far hedonism has come out of our discussion fairly well. It will not do as well in the following chapter, however, where we expect to convince the reader that some things in addition to being enjoyable affect the intrinsic worth of things. Even so we shall want to say that enjoyment is one thing that affects the intrinsic worth of something. Perhaps, in the end, we can even say that it will be rare if ever that an unhappy or wretched life can count as being of intrinsic worth, and that moments of enjoyment are a major determinant of whether an experience is worthwhile in itself.

There is enough truth in hedonism, then, to make it worth our while to give some thought to the question of how to achieve the most enjoyable kind of life. We can well ask ourselves: "Am I living in a way that will give me (and others) as much enjoyment as is possible? If not, what wants alteration?" Also, we can well ask of our society: "Are our institutions and customs ones best suited for maximizing enjoyment, combating wretchedness? If not, which should be modified and how?" Despite problems of interpersonal measurements, such questions can sometimes be given definite answers.[13]

The proper strategy for realizing the most desirable state of affairs, if hedonism is true, will be to adopt those modes of living that, given the results of science about the conditions of enjoyment and unhappiness, are on the whole most likely to maximize enjoyments in the long run. Of course, we cannot have certainty here. Sometimes the course of action most likely to maximize happiness, given the evidence, will in fact fail to do so as well as some other course of action would have done. But, if our aim is to maximize happiness, there is no consistent alternative to doing what is most likely to achieve this end, given the evidence available—no consistent alternative to drawing inferences about what is best from our ethical (hedonistic) premises conjoined with those factual premises we have best reason for believing.

Obviously, in some areas our information is too meager to enable us to

[13] Last century in England the posing of such questions and insistence on using the answers to them as a guide for legislation led to much social reform. For instance, it was (rightly) claimed that the factory system as it worked in 1850, was not the most efficient conceivable means for realizing happiness.

have much confidence about which one among possible plans is most likely to succeed. Sometimes we do: There is no question about the wisdom of administering anaesthetics. But sometimes we don't. We do not, for instance, know much about how to train ourselves or modify our institutions so as to reduce anxiety or fear. We do not know much about how to train ourselves to think through personal problems clearly, or to summon the resolution to take the steps required for rational solutions. Where information is unavailable, however, what is needed is more effort to obtain it; and however little we may have in some areas, a consistent hedonist will apply the knowledge he does have.

Every hedonist program for living will contain one feature that is worth our special notice—one emphasized by J. S. Mill. The hedonist will advocate permitting everyone freedom of speech and thought, and freedom to live generally after one's own preferred style, insofar as these are not incompatible with more pressing requirements of communal life. The reason for this is perhaps obvious. A major cause of why our patterns of life are not more productive of pleasure is doubtless that we have not thought of, much less tried out, other possibilities than those that are habitual. Thinking is work; and everyone has a tendency to become attached to his own manner of living and working. In this light, new ideas and the willingness to experiment are precious. It is from these that we may learn. Even if it seems obvious that some proposal is inadequate and misguided, or some experiment in living destined to produce less happiness than the accepted mode, Mill thought these must be permitted. If we do not allow ideas and experiences to prove themselves, we shall find ourselves quenching the truth with the untruth, the promising with the sterile; and we shall be condemned to a static conformity.

It is an interesting question whether we should say that, in the Western world and the United States particularly, information about the sources and conditions of happiness *is* being put to work, whether there is an energetic effort to acquire more such knowledge, whether we do permit the freedom of thought, speech, and experimentation in living that are important for progress. We might expect so, in the United States, in view of the fact that American culture is often characterized as materialistic and pleasure-seeking. One might expect, from such comments, a nation of devoted pleasure-seekers. Unfortunately, from the point of view of the hedonist, this is very far from true. It is, of course, a fact that in the United States there is a great deal of emphasis on amusement and recreation (mostly spectator recreation rather than sport). But if we look around us at our institutions and customs, some of them ones most intimately related to our happiness, we find much less intelligent application of actual knowledge, or search for relevant knowledge, than we might have expected. How far, for example, is the curriculum of our educational institutions planned on the basis of experimental evidence about the kind of training that conduces to happiness? Well, there is improvement; and if we look at the curriculum standard in some places, the hedonist may think that in the United States things are progressing very well. But the heavy hand of tradition is very much with us. Students are often required to do many things, ostensibly to develop more disciplined or rational habits of thinking, despite the complete absence of experimental or theoretical ground for supposing that performing these required tasks will have any such effect. There are many other questions we could raise. We know that a person's marriage and the choice of his occupation are actions that will affect his later happiness more than perhaps any others. How much are these matters left to chance, and to what extent are individuals given—and trained to use—systematic information that will enable them to make the wisest decision in these matters? Again, is it the custom for physicians to practice with the hedonistic ideal in mind, or, for example, do medicine and law conspire together to preserve the doctrine that every individual must be kept alive as long as possible, irrespective of his agonies and the suffering that the prolonging of his life will bring to others? As another example, there are many different laws about divorce in different states. It is doubtful, to say the least, whether all are equally ideal. How strong is the disposition, in our legislatures, to model them so as to contribute best to the attainment of human happiness? How much information, even, has been gathered about the influence of divorce on the personalities of children, as compared with the continuation of an unhappy household? Or, what is the rationale behind the custom assigning to men the sole right to take the initiative in forming acquaintances with the opposite sex? or in inviting to dance? How much happiness has been sacrificed on this particular altar, and for what reason? The hedonist who considers these and many others questions will, one fears, come to the conclusion that a vast amount of "pleasure-seeking" energy in the United States has been channeled into recreational activities, with a comparative lack of interest in those institutions that touch most deeply on human happiness. We must say "comparative," of course, for legislation in the past few years has markedly contributed at least to relieving the insecurities and anxieties deriving from the threat of no work and no income, costly sickness, and penniless old age—although the visitor at a nursing home may wonder about this last. But even in the area of recreation, one might ask whether there is much thoughtful planning in view of evidence. In the Eastern world, apparently, much pleasure is derived from looking at flowers and gardens, and from relaxed contemplation of life and the world. Perhaps some review of the pleasantest way to spend Saturday and Sunday is in order.

Philosophers have written widely—albeit the matter is not more within their competence than within that of other persons, and often not as much —on the form of life that is most likely to produce most happiness for everyone, in the long run. We cannot survey this literature here. However, some of the reflections of the early Greeks on the proper strategy for personal living for the hedonist are worth more than a moment's consideration by everyone, and we must say something of them.

One of the earliest hedonists, Aristippus (c. 435–356 B.C.), advocated primary attention to the pleasures of the body, on the ground that they are more intense (which seems correct). He also thought one should seize the pleasures of the moment, since life is uncertain and one may miss the pleasures put off till the morrow. (His view bears consideration by those who always save and feel guilty if they permit themselves a luxury.) Epicurus (342–270 B.C.), in contrast, wrote: "It is not continuous drinkings and revellings, nor the satisfaction of lusts, nor the enjoyment of fish and other luxuries of the wealthy table, which produce a happy life, but sober reasoning, searching out the motives for all choice and avoidance, and banishing mere opinions, to which are due the greatest disturbance of the spirit."[14] Evidently, Epicurus thought that the satisfaction of bodily appetites is less important for a happy life than the acquisition of some kinds of knowledge and intellectual habits. Why? The reason lay in his concept of enjoyment and its conditions. Epicurus supposed that the highest degree of pleasure is simply complete relief or release from unpleasant want or anxiety; it is the stilling of desires and anxieties or fear. The most effective way to be happy, then, is to take steps to avoid unfulfilled longing and anxiety or fear. How will one do this? On the one hand, Epicurus thought that scientific reflection about man and his destiny is called for, since this will banish the worst of all anxieties, that of fear of death. But there must also be rational discipline of one's desires. Some human needs, he recognized, like those for food or drink or companionship, are insistent and must be satisfied on pain of unavoidable distress. But other wants, he thought, are subject to control. Of these, he thought it important to stamp out those whose satisfaction is so uncertain or so unlikely that their existence will almost certainly in the long run be a source of pain. Epicurus was probably on the timorous side in his conclusions about which interests are liable to be a source of pain, for we find him saying that "the most unalloyed source of protection from men . . . is the immunity which results from a quiet life and retirement from the world." And, he goes on, "He who has learned the limits of life knows that that which removes the pain due to want and makes the whole of life complete is easy to obtain; so that there is no need of actions which involve competition." It looks, then, as if Epicurus underrated the joys of action and achievement, and doubtless others. He further overlooked the fact that the bodily pleasures like eating and sex are not merely cessation of longing but positive pleasure (irrespective of whether this pleasure is, as some psychologists think, the subjective feeling of physiological "tension reduction"); and he overlooked the fact that some enjoy-

14 "Letter to Menoeceus," C. Bailey (trans.), in W. J. Oates, *The Stoic and Epicurean Philosophers* (New York: Random House, 1940, p. 32.

ments like aesthetic pleasure cannot well be simply release from unpleasant longing since they are not preceded by any identifiable state of longing. Nevertheless, of course, Epicurus was right that part of the strategy for obtaining happiness is to stamp out or redirect certain desires that are unrealistic or likely to bring unhappiness in the long run. Incidentally, "Epicureanism" does not deserve the reputation it sometimes has for selfish indifference to other people. Epicurus wrote: "It is not possible to live pleasantly without living prudently and honourably and justly, nor again to live a life of prudence, honour, and justice without living pleasantly."[15]

The reflections of men like Epicurus, on the strategy for maximizing happiness, are worth reflection. Even truisms are easily overlooked. But in a complex modern world, and after the rise of psychology and the social sciences, we can and should look for something more sophisticated and better founded in observation. The sciences of psychology and psychiatry certainly bear on this, as do economics (especially the theory about the economic organization that will maximize welfare), political science (especially the theory about governmental forms that tend to maximize welfare in certain circumstances), sociology, jurisprudence, and anthropology. So, in the modern world, after we have read Epicurus (and, if our taste is good, also Thomas Hobbes and John Stuart Mill and Henry Sidgwick), we might—if we do so with a very critical eye—pick up Margaret Mead, or Clyde Kluckhohn, Erich Fromm, Gordon Allport, Karen Horney, or any one of a multitude of others, as a source of concrete facts (liberally sprinkled with fiction, in some cases) and at least proposals about how these facts bear upon intelligent planning of life. The literature of academic psychology is not as rich as one might expect, in discussion of the implications of theory for how to maximize enjoyment. Perhaps the most outstanding exception to this is the work of Gordon Allport, who argues for the importance to the individual of acquisition of unselfish interests, of an objective appraisal of oneself and one's capacities, and of the working out of a personal philosophy of the world and life.[16]

It would be helpful if there were a serious manual showing what experimental and theoretical science really imply we should support if we are interested in human happiness. However, no such manual exists, despite the proliferation of advice from persons unqualified to speak about what has been demonstrated and what has not been. There is no alternative, for anyone young enough to wish to improve chances for happiness for himself and society, to having one's own look at theoretical treatises in psychology and the social sciences, at least. One thing a liberal education is for is precisely to provide such a look.

[15] According to him, just law or custom is a set of regulations of interpersonal relations, which has the aim (and, if really warranted, normally the result) of promoting human happiness so far as it is affected by interpersonal relations.

[16] *Personality* (New York: Henry Holt & Company, Inc., 1937), chap. 8.

FURTHER READING

On the nature of pleasure and psychological hedonism:

K. Duncker, "Pleasure, Emotion, and Striving," *Philosophy and Phenomenological Research*, I (1940), 391–430. A brilliant analysis by a psychologist.

C. D. Broad, *Five Types of Ethical Theory* (New York: Harcourt, Brace & Company, 1934), pp. 180–91.

———, "Egoism as a Theory of Human Motives," in *Ethics and the History of Philosophy* (London: Routledge & Kegan Paul Ltd., 1952).

P. Nowell-Smith, *Ethics* (Baltimore: Penguin Books, Inc., 1954), chaps. 8–10.

G. Ryle, *Dilemmas* (Cambridge, Eng.: Cambridge University Press, 1954), chap. 4.

G. Ryle and W. B. Gallie, "Pleasure" (symposium), The Aristotelian Society, Supplementary volume XXVIII (1954), 135–64.

T. Penelhum, "The Logic of Pleasure," *Philosophy and Phenomenological Research*, XVII (1957), 488–503.

P. T. Young, "The Role of Hedonic Processes in the Organization of Behavior," *Psychological Review*, LIX (1952).

L. T. Troland, *Fundamentals of Human Motivation* (New York: D. Van Nostrand Company, Inc., 1928), chap. 16.

J. G. Beebe-Center, *The Psychology of Pleasantness and Unpleasantness* (New York: D. Van Nostrand Company, Inc., 1932), pp. 394–417.

On ethical hedonism:

Epicurus, in Diogenes Laertius, *Lives of Eminent Philosophers* (London: William Heinemann, Ltd., 1925), X, pp. 117 ff.

Aristippus, in *ibid.*, II, 65–104.

J. Bentham, *Principles of Morals and Legislation*, chaps. 1–4.

J. S. Mill, *Utilitarianism*, chaps. 2, 4.

R. Blake, "Why not Hedonism?" *Ethics*, XXXVII (1926), 1–18.

F. C. Sharp, *Ethics* (New York: Appleton-Century-Crofts, Inc., 1928), chap. 19.

H. Sidgwick, *Methods of Ethics* (London: Macmillan & Co., Ltd., 1922), Bk. III, chap. 14.

L. Garvin, *A Modern Introduction to Ethics* (New York: Houghton Mifflin Company, 1953), chap. 11.

Philip Rice, *On the Knowledge of Good and Evil* (New York: Random House, 1955), chap. 11 and pp. 266–78.

C. D. Broad, *Five Types of Ethical Theory*, *op. cit.*, pp. 227–39. A criticism.

E. F. Carritt, *Ethical and Political Thinking* (Oxford: Clarendon Press, 1947), pp. 58–65, chap. 8. A criticism.

G. E. Moore, *Principia Ethica* (Cambridge, Eng.: Cambridge University Press, 1929), sections 36–57.

———, *Ethics* (Oxford: Oxford University Press, 1949), chaps. 1–2.

A. C. Ewing, *Ethics* (London: English Universities Press, 1953), chap. 3. A criticism.

On comparisons and measurement of pleasures:

H. Sidgwick, *The Methods of Ethics*, *op. cit.*, Bk. II, chap. 3.

J. Bentham, *The Principles of Morals and Legislation*, *op. cit.*, chap. 4.

R. B. Perry, *General Theory of Value* (New York: Longmans, Green & Co., Inc., 1926), chaps. 21–22.

F. C. Sharp, *Ethics, op. cit.*, chap. 20.

M. Cohen and E. Nagel, *Introduction to Logic and Scientific Method* (New York: Harcourt, Brace & Company, 1936), pp. 293–98.

R. McNaughton, "A Metrical Conception of Happiness," *Philosophy and Phenomenological Research*, XIV (1954), 172–83.

D. Davidson, J. M. McKinsey, and P. Suppes, "Outlines of a Formal Theory of Value, I," *Philosophy of Science*, XXII (1955), 140–60.

13

Things Worthwhile in Themselves:
(By Pluralist Theories)

Hedonism is a sweeping and exclusive theory. It does not merely assert that most enjoyable experiences are intrinsically desirable, and that most disagreeable experiences are intrinsically undesirable. Such a claim would hardly be contested. No, it says not simply "most" but absolutely "all." This larger claim, we have seen, has aroused objections. But hedonism goes much further still. It alleges that absolutely nothing has intrinsic worth except as it is either pleasant or unpleasant; and that something is more (or less) desirable intrinsically than something else, if and only if the former is more (or less) pleasant than the latter. In general, the hedonist says, nothing but pleasure and displeasure makes a difference as to whether something is intrinsically good or bad.

Hedonism in this sense has been criticized as too narrow by a long line of distinguished philosophers, beginning at least with Plato and Aristotle. For the most part, these philosophers have not been monists (p. 303), but pluralists: they have said there are various types of thing that make a difference to intrinsic worth. (A critic of hedonism of course *can* be a monist, saying, for example, that character is the only thing intrinsically good.) In the present chapter, we shall consider the claims of some of the other things they have said are of intrinsic worth. We shall confine ourselves to "personal" values (p. 304), leaving for a later point the question whether anything is intrinsically desirable that is not a state of a minded-organism.

We shall begin with the question whether *knowledge* is intrinsically worthwhile. We shall discuss this relatively at length, partly because the intrinsic worth of knowledge has been very widely acclaimed, and partly because we need a model showing how an analysis of such questions should proceed. With this discussion before us, we shall examine whether various other kinds of experiences, or states of persons, are intrinsically worthwhile;

332

we shall pay particular attention to the claims of character and the performance of good deeds. Finally, we shall consider how far it is possible to decide rationally which is best, if we must compare several complexes each containing several different kinds of thing (for example, knowledge, character, pleasure) all intrinsically worthwhile.

For the purpose of determining which one among several complex states of affairs would be best, we need to know far more than just general principles to the effect that certain kinds of thing are intrinsically worthwhile to some degree. We need to know *how* worthwhile they are. Conclusions about the kinds of thing that are intrinsically desirable to some degree, then, are the merest beginning of a solution to practical problems; but they are of some help in reaching reasonable decisions about concrete—and more complex—problems.

1. IS KNOWLEDGE INTRINSICALLY DESIRABLE?

The hedonist says that something is intrinsically desirable if and only if and to the degree that it is pleasant. Such an extreme claim has rarely if ever[1] been made for knowledge; few if any have said that something is intrinsically desirable if and only if and to the degree that it is a state of knowledge. Only a more modest claim has been made: that a state of knowledge is one thing of intrinsic value, or at least that a state of knowledge is one thing that enhances the intrinsic worth of wholes of which it is a part. Our present question is whether this modest claim is well founded.

How shall we answer this question? As usual, by considering whether we can frame a general statement asserting the intrinsic worth of knowledge, as a consistent part of a not excessively complex system of general ethical statements, which is coherent with our relevant attitudes (in this case, our desires or preferences) when these are fully informed, and products of a calm and normal frame of mind.

Exactly what principle shall we evaluate? In order to get such a principle before us, we need first to get clear what we mean by "knowledge." To have knowledge, obviously, is to have *beliefs*. But not *false* beliefs. So, to have knowledge is to have some true beliefs. What more, or does "knowledge" mean just "true belief"? Surely something more: We would not say that a person had knowledge that a certain future event would occur, even if he correctly believed it would, if he had no reasons for his belief, or if his reasons were very bad ones. A suggestible person might have believed correctly that Lincoln would be assassinated on a certain day, for no better reason than that he dreamed he would; but we would not say he *knew* this would happen—not in the way F. D. Roosevelt knew that the invasion of France from Britain would occur in a certain month, after having partici-

[1] Plato represents Socrates as coming very close, in *Meno* 88, and possibly Spinoza should be taken to advocate this view.

pated in drawing up the plans. "Knowing" that something is the case is be-lieving correctly that it is, for the reason that one is familiar with the evi-dence and understands the relation of the evidence to the proposition be-lieved. Science, of course, is the paradigm case of "knowledge" in this sense.

There are other kinds of "knowing." For instance, there is knowing how to swim or to ride a bicycle; there is knowing a certain poem in the sense of being able to recite it; there is knowing a language, in the sense of being able to speak and understand it accurately. More generally, there is know-ing *how* to do all sorts of things, as contrasted with knowing *that* certain statements are true (knowledge in the sense of the previous paragraph). *We are presently concerned only with knowledge in the sense of "knowing that. . . ."*

Do we mean by "knowledge," in this sense, a *conscious* experience, or not? Not exactly, for we want to say that a mathematician has his mathe-matical knowledge when he is asleep or playing golf; he has it in the way in which he has his knowledge of how to ride a bicycle when he is walking. To have knowledge is to have cash in the bank, on which one *can* draw, even if one is not spending now. But to say this is to show only one side of the pic-ture. Just as money in the bank is not of much interest if you can never draw it out, so knowledge in the sense of capacity to think certain thoughts, make certain points, would not be of much interest if we were not allowed to draw on it. Suppose a person suffered a blow on the head and lost his capacity to draw on what he knew; the fact that *unconsciously* it was there, and perhaps could be tapped under hypnosis, might be of little interest. What we mean by "knowledge," then, is having a reserve of true beliefs (and so on) on which one may and does continuously make drafts; it is *both* the fact that conscious thinking and experience are in-formed, *and* the fact that the reserve hovers in the background, waiting to be called upon when need arises.

Knowing in this sense is to be distinguished from discovering, just as a hunter's having a deer over his shoulder is different from hunting. Discov-ering is perhaps a good thing in itself; at least, there are pleasures in pursuing ideas comparable to those of pursuing game. But, for clarity, let us dis-tinguish the state of knowing from the pursuit of knowledge. Our present concern is with the former.

It may be suggested that knowing something is a species of enjoyment, or at least that knowledge contains enjoyment as an essential part; and it has been said or implied that knowledge is a "part of" happiness. This sug-gestion is erroneous. Clearly, knowledge *as a reserve* is not a conscious experience at all, much less one with a feeling element, which one wishes at the time to prolong on its own account. But even conscious thinking in-formed by true beliefs and awareness of their evidential basis must be dis-tinguished from enjoyment and does not, as such or necessarily, contain enjoyment as a part. An informed state of thinking need not be a state of mind that contains feeling elements at all. Further, although knowledgeable thinking is often or normally pleasurable partly because it is knowledgeable, it is sometimes quite unpleasant—as when we recall some disagreeable fact about ourselves.

What principle about knowledge, then, shall we assess? Let us consider this one: "There are *some* kinds of knowledge which as such (without regard to any pleasure that may be felt in knowing) are of intrinsic worth, or at least which enhance the intrinsic value of wholes of which they are a part." This proposition is a weak one: It does not specify *which* kinds of knowledge are worthwhile, and we have to know this in order to make practical application of a principle; much less does it say that *all* knowledge is of intrinsic worth. What our principle does is just *deny* that there are *no* kinds of knowledge that are of intrinsic worth.

We must now consider whether this principle comports with the criticized preferences or attitudes of men.

There is *prima facie* support in our attitudes for the intrinsic worth of knowledge; we do seem to want at least some knowledge on its own account. For instance, we hear the song of a bird we cannot see; we then wish we were enough of an ornithologist to be able to recognize its kind. We are curious about the kinds of animate life in the depths of the sea, and what mode of existence they may have; we purchase and read a book. We hate to think that our child might live and die without ever knowing what reasons human beings have put forth for accepting the principles of empirical science, or for accepting geometry, or for believing theological propositions; and we urge him to read Plato, hoping his interest will be aroused. These cases *look* like an interest in certain pieces of knowledge for their own sake. What else? It looks, then, as if the denial that *any* knowledge has intrinsic worth would be incoherent with our attitudes. And this, we think, is true.

One may object, however, to drawing inferences from such interest on several grounds. (1) It may be objected that these interests are not interests in any piece of knowledge *for its own sake*. This objection may be specified more fully in the form of three separate objections. (1*a*) It may be said that interest in knowledge is always interest in knowledge as a *means to other ends*. (1*b*) It may be said the interest is not really an interest in *knowledge*, but rather in the *enjoyment* of getting or having knowledge, or in *ridding ourselves of the discomfort* of unsatisfied curiosity. (1*c*) It may be claimed that the interest is not in knowledge as such at all, but only in *oneself having* certain pieces of information. (2) An entirely different objection may be raised. It may be said that any interest in knowledge for itself, just as such, would evaporate in a person who was well informed and made important distinctions. Let us consider these points in order.

1*a*. Are we interested in pieces of knowledge only as a means to other ends? It is true that almost every piece of knowledge is a potential means to other goods. One cannot enlarge one's salary by possessing odd bits of information about the bottom of the sea, but one may, as a result of having them, scintillate at a cocktail party. Furthermore, if we ask ourselves if we would want a piece of knowledge if we would be forever debarred from conversing about the matter with another person, we must concede that we have some inclination to answer in the negative. Knowledge is thickly interwoven with other goals. Yet, when we abstract the having of certain pieces of knowledge from these other goals, does our interest in it drop to zero? It doesn't seem to. Are there not pieces of our knowledge we would not willingly give up, for no return, even aside from their contribution to other goods? Would we, for instance, willingly part with our knowledge of the foundations of science, of the status of the principles of theology, of the evidence for different estimates of the nature and destiny of man? The right answer to this question seems to be in the negative.

1*b*. But are we making the different mistake of confusing an interest in knowledge for itself with an interest in the enjoyment of getting or having knowledge (or reflecting knowledgeably), or an interest in ridding ourselves of the discomfort of unsatisfied curiosity? Of course, we must concede that it *is* often or normally enjoyable to learn things (especially if we discover them for ourselves) and to think or discourse with knowledge; and we *are* restless when we are puzzled by some problem and cannot find the solution, or if we think some of our opinions are based on ignorance.

The issue is a subtle one, and we must remind ourselves what it is to *desire something for itself* (pp. 309 and 302). To desire something for itself, then, is for the thought of *it*—excluding or disregarding its consequences and any other extrinsic properties of the thing—to motivate to action, for the thought of loss of it to disturb us, for the thought that *it* is coming to please us (if we have not anticipated it all along). We must ask ourselves, then, whether the thought of having some piece of knowledge is motivating irrespective of belief about the enjoyment of getting or having it; and similarly for the thought of losing some knowledge we have, or for the judgment that we shall now have the opportunity to get a certain piece (or field) of knowledge. Sometimes, obviously, it is. A new book comes out, with a chapter on some topic about which we have long puzzled; we pick it up greedily—and it is no precondition of our interest that we rehearse to ourselves that reading this chapter is going to be fun, or even that we ever have considered whether it would or not. Indeed, one may read an original chapter by a respected author with such zest, even if one knows full well that it may contain a painful demonstration that some view of the reader, perhaps one already in print, is mistaken and too simple-minded! But perhaps we are confusing the interest in some piece of knowledge with an interest in getting rid of the discomfort of unsatisfied curiosity? Well, certainly we do not have to *think* of ridding ourselves of unpleasant sensations in order to be motivated to solve a crossword puzzle. Indeed, do we ever think seriously about how to rid ourselves of these sensations in the way in which we do wonder how to rid ourselves of a stomach-ache or an itch? Indeed, there is question whether the "itch" of curiosity is really unpleasant. Do we really want to rid ourselves of this kind of experience? (If we don't, then by definition it is not unpleasant!) It seems rather that our interest in knowledge is sometimes high enough that we are glad to be tormented by any curiosity we may have, in order not to lose our motivation to get knowledge.

1c. But is our interest in knowledge as such, or in *our* having certain pieces of knowledge?[2] One may wonder about this particularly because people do not yearn much for knowledge completely beyond their ken unless they think they ought to have it; the possibility of proving a theorem in economics does not tickle the imagination of persons to whom economics is totally unfamiliar. What seems rather to be the case is that people are curious about whatever is just over the horizon of their intellectual world, whatever the horizons of this world may be. This suggests a Gestalt-type possibility: that the existence of "gaps" in our stock of ideas generates an interest in the filling of these gaps *for us*, but hardly anything so transcendent as an interest in everyone possessing such knowledge.

Do we, then, take an interest in everybody having some bits of knowledge? Not to the extent, certainly, to which we take an interest in it for ourselves. Also, we do not necessarily want others to have all the particular pieces we wish for ourselves: we don't seriously wish everyone to know how a certain mystery story comes out, although at the time we take a strong interest in this for ourselves. Yet it does seem that there are certain kinds of knowledge we do wish everyone to have—not isolated bits, as if there were value in memorizing paragraphs from Keynes on economic theory, without understanding what they mean, but systems of knowledge: the understanding of the physical and social world, of man's nature, of science and the evidence for scientific theory, and so on. These we wish all to have. That we do so is doubtless part of the basis for advocating a "liberal" education and requiring acquaintance with certain fields of

---

[2] One might argue that we need not establish that the interest is not just in *our* having knowledge, for, it may be said, even if our interest is only in getting knowledge for ourselves, we still have a case of something intrinsically worthwhile that is different from enjoyment. But is this so? What then is the principle—that *my* having some kinds of knowledge is intrinsically worthwhile? But then the principle contains a proper name, and we agreed (Chapter 2) that valid ethical principles must be statable without the use of proper names.

A critic might, however, then go on to question whether the "requirement of generality" was properly extended not only to specifically moral judgments (judgments of obligation, of rights, of reprehensibility or moral admirableness) but also to judgments of intrinsic worth or desirability. And one must admit that the arguments used to support this principle do not all apply to judgments of intrinsic worth.

If we agree with the critic, the effect would be a reduction in the requirement for accepting something as intrinsically desirable, and consequently a probable enlargement of the list of intrinsic goods.

knowledge. Nor is the reason for this simply that we wish everybody to have some common areas about which he can *converse* with other people.

One might question all of this reasoning, and say that what we want for others is simply *whatever* they may wish to have (so long as getting it does not conflict with the realization of the desires of others), or whatever they would not wish to be without if they experienced having it. But this alternative principle we have questioned long ago (p. 172).

2. We come now to the question of whether, granted we have an interest in knowledge for its own sake, this interest would evaporate if we had relevant information and made appropriate distinctions. But what distinctions, and what information might have this effect?

Perhaps what is meant is information that our interest in knowledge is solely a result of having been spanked for not mastering our first-grade work, or of having been praised for academic achievement before the age of ten. But such "information" would in fact be misinformation, for it is not for nothing that many psychologists have postulated an exploratory or curiosity drive in some animals, including men. Even the lowly rat, when placed in a new environment, takes an interest in getting oriented, in wandering about, in manipulating unfamiliar objects, apparently without reference to the level of his sex or hunger drives. A hungry monkey will leave his meal in order to look out a window at interesting visual stimuli.[3] There is no reason to think human beings are different in this respect. Interest in knowledge has a firmer basis in human nature than the goadings of our teachers.

Interest in knowledge, like everything human, has its causes. It is possible that familiarity with these, whatever they are, would cause the interest to decline. However, there is no positive reason for supposing this is so. Would it be contended that information about the causes of why men seek enjoyments and avoid pain would end the interest in these experiences? Not at all. Why then should it be different with the case of knowledge? Is our wish to know what kind of bird is emitting those notes diminished by the reflection that, if our constitutional makeup were different, we probably would not care? Suppose a person takes up coin-collecting as a hobby because he is deprived in other ways—because he is not valued by other persons, for example, and is lonely. And suppose, in time, he becomes fascinated with his hobby. Is it likely that reflection on the origins of his interest will decrease his eagerness for information about a certain type of coin he has just acquired? Possibly, but surely we should need to see the evidence. So, we ask again, what information might we get that would probably reduce our interest in knowledge?

Interest in some knowledge, then, stands up to criticism. It seems we are

---

[3] See H. F. Harlow, in *University of Nebraska Symposium on Motivation* (Lincoln, Nebr.: University of Nebraska Press, 1953), pp. 24–49.

justified in saying, at the least, that some knowledge adds to the intrinsic desirability of wholes of which it is a part.

However, having said this, we need not inflate the importance of knowledge beyond all reason. Let us consider how important, relatively, our criticized interest in knowledge is. Let us take a homely example. Suppose you have read a biography of Lincoln. What pleasure would induce you to accept permanent forgetfulness of everything that happened in the twenty-second year of his life? A milkshake? Certainly not. An evening at the symphony? Perhaps. A month's vacation in January, doing nothing but relaxing and playing tennis in an agreeable spot in Florida? Definitely; although the example is not a fair one, since a month's relaxation would give time to read many other books.

Philosophers have thought that different kinds of knowledge may have different values. This seems to be true. Indeed, some knowledge seems to be completely without intrinsic value. For instance, there are some things about a person that should perhaps remain his private property, and perhaps are better *unknown* to others. Take the gruesome details of death. Doubtless we should know what these details sometimes are or may be, but we shall scarcely urge them for the columns of the newspapers. Furthermore, some knowledge that does have intrinsic value seems more important than other knowledge also with intrinsic worth. In general, it seems that we have a keener interest in those pieces of knowledge that are more significant, more capable of integrating our thinking and experience, more capable of illumination. Some philosophers have thought it better to have general, theoretical, abstract knowledge than particular, practical, rather vague knowledge. But it seems doubtful that they are correct. It is true that if we wish to point to paradigms of knowledge, we shall turn to the theorems of mathematics or the principles of physics. But why should the principles of arithmetic or physics be more worth knowing than the vaguer principles of psychology or anthropology? Further, why should a general principle be more worth knowing than some particular fact, such as the influence of the thought of Karl Marx or J. M. Keynes? It is true that, according to our conclusions, the value of a piece of knowledge is not decided by our preferences just as they stand, but by these as they would be if we were cognitively equipped to appreciate the knowledge in question. It is possible that if we were better mathematicians we would rate the principles of mathematics and physics as highly as some philosophers have done. But this is doubtful.

We must beware of inferring, from conclusions about what kind of knowledge has the greatest intrinsic worth, that we should turn our attention to mastering the pieces of knowledge most worthwhile intrinsically. This is not so. For one thing, each of us has a job to do, and requirements of doing this job well (and we must do so if we are to have the means for doing worthwhile things) may preclude such expenditure of time. Furthermore, we must remember that a piece of knowledge that is valuable in the context of a broad intellectual background may have no more worth taken by itself than a tennis racket without balls or net. Moreover, the agonies of mastering material not congenial to our intellectual bent is the very opposite of a value; hence, it may be better if we read Margaret Mead with enjoyment than if we wrestle with Gödel's proofs.

2. MISCELLANEOUS INTRINSIC GOODS

A somewhat bewildering prospect emerges once we have satisfied ourselves that some kinds of knowledge are, along with some kinds of enjoyment, intrinsically worthwhile. Once we think of it, we see that there are many candidates with some credentials for the status of intrinsic worth: life itself, aesthetic contemplation, friendship, traits of character, and many more. Moreover, how shall we know when we have exhausted the list of candidates with credentials that should be examined? And must we really consider each candidate?

We have to agree, unfortunately, that the job is a large one, and that there is no easy way of reducing its proportions. Indeed, the job in practical life is bigger: we have to make judgments of the comparative intrinsic worth of complex sets of events—something we do not settle by deciding which kinds of things have some intrinsic worth.

We can here, of course, examine the claims of only a limited number of types of thing; and this we must do briefly.

Our examination of whether knowledge has intrinsic worth provides a model for our investigation of other possible intrinsic goods, such as "being loved by other persons." We shall want to ask of them whether there is some principle about their intrinsic worth—perhaps only the vague one that *some* species of a kind are intrinsically worthwhile—that comports with our "qualified" interests or desires. Further, in deciding this, we want more particularly to know (1a) whether we take an interest in these things for themselves or just as means to other things; (1b) whether we want *these* things or rather just the enjoyment of them, or the riddance of the unpleasant uneasiness of not having them; (1c) whether we want them not just for ourselves but for others too; and (2) whether our interests would continue even if we had all relevant information and were in a calm and impartial state of mind.

What candidates for the status of intrinsic value should we examine? Perhaps the most helpful source of suggestions is the work of personality psychologists, who have had much to say about the interests we must ascribe to people if we are to understand their behavior.[4] Anthropologists, too, have recently had something to say about interests that are common to mankind. If we survey these sources, we shall emerge with a list of can-

---

[4] For a rich list of suggestions, see H. A. Murray *et al.*, *Explorations in Personality* (New York: Oxford University Press, 1938).

didates including the following: oxygen, food of various kinds, water, elimination, sex, preservation of life, clothing, health, money, security, novel experiences, human company, being accepted and respected by others, being loved by others, play and recreation, achievement, aesthetic creation and contemplation, being remembered after death, and being able to respect oneself for one's talents or skills. This list is quite long enough for our present purposes.

Which ones of these must be eliminated from consideration as intrinsic values?

1*a*. Some of these objects are wanted only as means to other things. Money, for instance, is usually wanted only because of what we can purchase with it, because it gives security. Fancy how gratified we would be if we found a buried treasure on an island where money was not used and which had no contact with the outside world. The same is true for health—depending, of course, on how we define the term. Our interest in health seems to be an interest in having the conditions for zestful activity, for self-enjoyment. If our physician tells us our liver is out of order, or that our blood pressure is too high, but we have unbounded energy and have never enjoyed ourselves more, and we are assured that our eventual demise is in no way hastened by these "disorders," we shall say that, although in theory our physician may be right in thinking our health is not perfect, the kind of ill-health he has in mind is of no concern to us. Again, the same is true for clothing. Imagine being shipwrecked on a desert island, where clothing made us uncomfortably warm and sticky, where the available garments had no aesthetic or ostentation appeal (or perhaps where we had no interest in the possible admirers of our attire). How much would we wear?

1*b*. Some of these supposed objects of interest, again, are not really wanted; what is really wanted is either riddance of the discomfort that getting them will make possible, or just the enjoyment we know activities of consumption will give us. Take, for example, food. At least sometimes we would much rather do something else than eat, and indeed the idea of eating is not attractive to us; but we want to get rid of the increasing bodily discomfort, in order to get on with some job more effectively. We want to be rid of the unpleasant hunger, but we do not particularly want to eat.[5] Sometimes, again, food is desired only as a means to the enjoyment of consuming. For instance, I may not have any hunger at three o'clock this afternoon, but at that time I may be motivated to arrange a dinner at an exotic restaurant, for Friday evening, in the belief the enjoyment will be worth it. The experience of eating in such circumstances has been enjoyable in the past; we arrange a similar occasion for the future in the belief

[5] This is very different from the case of wanting somebody's company, and being miserable because one cannot have it. Here one *both* wants the other person's company, *and* also wishes one were not so miserable on account of not being able to have it.

that the future will be as pleasant as the past. In such cases, we don't desire the eating for itself; what motivates us is the prospective enjoyment of the event. Do we ever desire food or eating for itself at all? Perhaps when we are really deprived, and start having dreams of steaks?

1c. Other objects of interest are wanted for themselves and not just as ways of ridding ourselves of unpleasant organic sensations or as ways of having the pleasure of consuming something; but we can hardly count them as things of intrinsic worth, because we don't want them for everybody, and a corresponding principle would be infected with proper names. Take, for example, one's ambition to beat a certain person at tennis. It isn't that one wants everybody else to beat him too; far from it. Thus, the goal of my beating Mr. A at tennis is not qualified as an intrinsic value. But note that this event is not wished as a means to some other end; it will not bring a raise in salary, nor will Mr. A necessarily like one any better for having beaten him. Further, we are not troubled by unpleasant organic sensations of which we wish to rid ourselves by beating Mr. A; nor do we want this event just for the pleasure it will give us.

2. But there are various things we want that are not eliminated from the class of intrinsic values by such considerations as these. Take, for instance, the desire to be remembered after death. Surely we want this for itself, not as a means to some further end; obviously there is no consumption pleasure this event can bring us; nor is the event a way of ridding ourselves of unpleasant organic sensations; and perhaps we wish as much for everybody— since it at least slightly appalls us to think of a living, conscious being vanishing without a trace. However, can we really count this event as being of intrinsic worth? Does the desire stand up in calm moments, in the face of all the information? Perhaps the wish is a remnant of childish thinking. Perhaps it vanishes, when we think clearly how death is a necessary fate of all living things, a destiny of everyone alike.

Suppose, then, we consider, for each one of the many interests we have listed, whether it passes all these tests. How many remain? Does preservation of life? This is doubtful—if we are careful to abstract sheer life from the presence of an active mind endowed with memory, not overcome with pain. Take novel experiences. Do we want these for themselves, or only because they give enjoyment—enjoyment that can be revived by recollections? We need not settle on any final list as a partial list of successful candidates, and certainly ought not, without more discussion of each one individually. Still, some seem to have a better claim than others, and perhaps they merit the reader's reflection: the preservation not just of life but of mind with memory; the company of friends; achievements over obstacles; the contemplation of beautiful things. Perhaps many additions are in order; and perhaps some deletions. Nor should we forget the possibility that one person may properly include some event that another person properly omits; to some extent perhaps relativism holds sway.

3. CHARACTER TRAITS AS INTRINSICALLY DESIRABLE

Our reflections on what is of intrinsic worth have ignored one issue that historically has received much attention: whether certain traits of character (for example, conscientiousness) are intrinsically worthwhile, and others (for example, cruelty) intrinsically undesirable; and whether the exercise of such traits (kindly deeds, cruel actions) is of intrinsic value. Ever since at least the time of the Stoics, important philosophers from time to time have advocated that such things are intrinsically valuable, and indeed values of the very first importance. This issue merits separate consideration.

We need not concern ourselves until later with the question of how exactly "trait of character" is to be defined, as distinct from the more comprehensive term "trait of personality." There is a difference, and nobody would classify intelligence, energy, or sense of humor as traits of "character." Our present question, however, can without prejudice be stated broadly as simply the question of whether *some* traits of mind (other than knowledge), or the exercise of them, can be counted as of intrinsic worth.

In order to answer this question, let us select as favorable an example as we can, and stake the whole issue on it. It will be most convincing if we consider the *exercise* of a trait of character.[6]

Let us consider an event that might have happened at the sinking of the *Titanic.* Let us suppose that when the last lifeboat was filled and about to be lowered, a person appeared who clearly ought to be among the occupants of the boat. Let us suppose further that there was one person in the boat who had less claim than any others to be in it. And let us suppose that at this point that person, taking in the situation, quietly arose and removed himself, offering his place to the newcomer. We need not inquire *what* trait of character he exercised. Let us ask only: Does such an action have intrinsic worth?

We must ask about this example what we have been asking about the candidates for the status of intrinsic value generally: Is there a corresponding general principle that comports with our qualified attitudes of preference or approval? Of the four more specific questions into which we broke this one down, the answers to two (1*b* and 1*c*) are obviously in the affirmative. So, the specific questions that are serious and relevant for our example are: (1*a*) Do we prefer this sort of thing to happen—say, as compared with the person being compelled to leave the boat at gun-point—for itself, or only as a means to other ends? and (2), would our interest continue even

---

[6] Some philosophers definitely hold that traits of character are intrinsically worthwhile even if and when they are not exercised. See W. D. Ross, *Foundations of Ethics* (Oxford: Clarendon Press, 1939), p. 292. For a contrary view, and an interesting examination of the whole question, see G. E. Moore, *Principia Ethica* (Cambridge, Eng.: Cambridge University Press, 1929), pp. 171 ff.

if we had all relevant information, and were in a calm and impartial state of mind?

1*a*. Do we want or prefer this kind of action *for itself?* Of course, we recognize that it is advantageous, from the point of view of society, that people do voluntarily what must be done in any case. In our example, it would be embarrassing and distasteful to all present, if the morally necessary move were taken only in the face of force. But in this instance, our preference for what occurred seems to be independent of thoughts about convenience to society and the embarrassment of onlookers. As A. C. Ewing has remarked, we would feel the same if we did not think of anyone as present, as in the case of a person who relinquished a plank for the benefit of someone he regarded as more deserving—and irrespective of whether both eventually were drowned. Hence, it does seem that we prefer the action for itself.

2. Would we feel differently if we had all relevant information, and thought of the matter with all possible detachment? Suppose it could be shown, as David Hume thought it could, that all our moral preferences are guided by the convenience of society; that, through tradition and parental training, the wants of society are served by the development in us of preferences like this. Or, suppose it could be shown that our tendency to feel thus is a generalization of a tendency to protect our younger sister? We do not know these things. But if we did, would we feel differently? It is hard to say. Perhaps individuals will differ among themselves. Most people, one suspects, will not be moved by such information.

Yet perhaps this is not the end of the matter. Henry Sidgwick, the ablest historical exponent of hedonism, wrote that when he sat down in a cool hour, he could "only justify" to himself the importance attached to traits of character or fine deeds by their "conduciveness, in one way or another, to the happiness of sentient beings."[7] He then went on to argue, in support of the hedonist estimate of character traits as being only instrumentally desirable, that most people value character traits "in proportion" to the extent of their expected long-range contribution to happiness. But what is proved, if his point is roughly true? Doubtless that there must be some *historical* connection between our prizing qualities of mind and their effects, or supposed effects, in enhancing human happiness. But suppose there is. It need not result, from the fact that there is or that we know there is, that we shall prize the traits any less on their own account—and this is the crucial issue. But his point, if accepted as true, may suggest something more directly pertinent. Suppose our prizing of traits of character corresponds roughly with the estimates of instrumental value a rational hedonist would

---

[7] *Op. cit.*, p. 401. Sidgwick admitted that he did cherish good deeds for themselves; but he regarded this as irrational, apart from further justification. He seems to have overlooked the fact that in the end *no* judgments of intrinsic good are rational in the sense of being able to be justified by showing that the object is a means to other ends.

make for them. Might not such a correspondence raise a question whether we do really prize these things for themselves? Perhaps we only *think* we do; perhaps we prize these traits of character, but are mistaken in thinking that we do so when we totally disregard the consequences, the extrinsic properties of these traits. Perhaps, if we really did not assume that these traits normally have certain favorable effects on interpersonal relations, the traits would no longer be prized. Could those who think they value traits of character just for themselves be making a mistake of introspection?

What would Sidgwick say of our *Titanic* case? He might say this: that the only value of the act is its instrumental value—the fact that it avoided embarrassment, and so forth. He might also say that our foregoing analysis of our attitudes was mistaken on account of a confusion—our failure to distinguish clearly between the event by itself and the fact that the person's action was a symptom of a trait of mind that has great instrumental value, so that if the act had not occurred, an instrumentally very important trait was absent. He might say that if we really disregarded the fact that an act occurred that was a symptom of a trait of mind highly important because of its normal consequences, we would not really have prized the action except for its actual consequences. Sidgwick, in effect, might ask us to review the matter again, after having drawn carefully the relevant distinctions, and consider whether we still continue to want this sort of behavior, as compared with alternatives, just for itself.

Very well, then; the distinction has been pointed out. Let us review again what our preferences are. Doubtless the introspection called for is a difficult one, and it is fortunate that our further argument does not turn on how we decide. The writer is inclined to think Sidgwick was wrong, but there is no further argument to prove he was.

Happily, the disagreements about whether traits of character and the manifestation of them in action are *intrinsically* worthwhile do not much affect the questions of what traits are just worthwhile, and what can be done for their encouragement. On this there is almost universal agreement. Roughly, the traits of mind that are desirable are those the exercise of which in living enhances the realization of other goods in life: including courage, self-discipline, wisdom, respect for and thoughtfulness about the welfare of other conscious beings, fairness and impartiality, conscientiousness (concern to fulfill one's obligations), veracity, kindliness, prudence, honesty, reliability, persistence, and tolerance. The importance of these has long been recognized.

The question of how desirable traits of mind, such as these, can effectively be developed, is a matter for psychology. But we can say this much: We shall have done at least almost all of what psychology today recommends that we do, if we get children to act as if they had these qualities (that is, practice them), if we can get them to see the point of behavior in these ways, and if we reward them for manifesting these qualities in their conduct.

4. COMPARATIVE JUDGMENTS OF VALUE

If we have a list of all the things that are intrinsically worthwhile, we still do not have all the information needed for rational decisions. It is not enough to know that enjoyableness, being an item of knowledge, and others, all contribute to the value of a situation. What we need to know is which one, of various complex situations containing different amounts of these various worthwhile items, is the best. We cannot deduce this from general principles to the effect that certain kinds of thing are intrinsically worthwhile. Suppose one is a professor deciding whether to spend a sabbatical year in Los Angeles or in Oxford. There are many things to be considered: whether one's family will survive the chill of Oxford houses; whether books will be equally as accessible in the Oxford library; whether one will have more good ideas in Oxford, given the stimulation of many active minds and the frosty atmosphere of one's study; whether a year in England will promote the development of one's children, as persons; whether the joys of exploring the English countryside will compensate for the loss of sunny hours on California beaches; and so on. It will be cold comfort to a man faced with such a choice, to assure him that enjoyment, knowledge, the development of character (and so forth) are all good or indeed intrinsically good. This, perhaps, he did not doubt. But his problem is one of weighing. Suppose a man has to decide which of two piles of stones, each composed of some sandstone and some granite, is of greater weight. We do not help him much by assuring him that both granite and sandstone do make some difference on a scales.

Is such weighing possible, and if so how?

Some philosophers have despaired of answering this question. It is not merely that they have felt it beyond our powers to give a rational answer to specific questions; they have sometimes thought it impossible to explain the *meaning* of "*x* is better than *y*" or at least to develop a reliable method for deciding whether one complex state of affairs is better than another, if there are intrinsically good things of entirely different kinds. If only one kind of thing is intrinsically good, they thought, then we can determine which complex situation is best by finding which contains *more* of that kind of thing; but if there are different kinds of thing intrinsically good, then the question of deciding which situation is better is a baffling one.[8]

We must certainly try to solve this problem, whether in principle there is a *meaning* in comparative judgments of worth or a rational *method* for confirming such judgments, if there are many different kinds of thing, all of intrinsic worth.

---

[8] Even if there is only one kind of thing that is intrinsically worthwhile, some comparative judgments may be in principle unconfirmable. We saw in the previous chapter that we can in principle decide whether one thing is more pleasant than another, only in certain types of situation.

If our metaethical conclusions have been correct, the first question—that of the *meaning* of comparative judgments—is already disposed of, for "the total situation *x* is the *best* we can produce" means the same as "the total situation *x* is *better* than (preferable to) any other one we can produce." We have already explained (p. 301) the meaning of such expressions. Moreover, in principle we know the method for answering such questions. It is a matter of forming a preference for one total situation in comparison with others that could be produced. (What situations can be produced is a question for science or common sense; it raises no special questions for ethical theory.) Further, it is a matter of rectifying this preference to make it agree with what it would be if we were fully informed, impartial, and in a normal state of mind; and to make it agree with the abstract general principles that cohere with our other rectified preferences. In other words, if there is a rectified or "qualified" preference for *A* over *B*, then *A* is better than *B*—and this wholly irrespective of the internal complexity of either total situation.

Why, then, is there a difficulty? The answer is: there is *not* a difficulty in principle—*unless one mistakenly assumes* that judgments, comparing the worth of complex wholes, must somehow be *deducible* from a set of premises including, as ethical premises, *only general statements that various abstract kinds of thing are intrinsically worthwhile to some extent.* If this last is set as the job, the job cannot be done. But there is no reason why one must set oneself this job.

Still, there is a serious practical problem. When the issues are complex—as in the case of the professor deciding where to spend his sabbatical year, and more so in the case of a legislator trying to decide whether he ought to support an inflationary monetary policy—it is difficult if not impossible to get all the relevant factors before the mind at once, and to form a preferential attitude to some total alternative. We know our attitudes are sometimes not "qualified," for the one we form today may be the opposite of the one we have tomorrow, when deliberating about a single choice. Sometimes, too, our attitudes or decisions are inconsistent with each other in other ways. Thus, there is reason to look about for some more "objective" procedure for weighing such sets of values. Is there anything we can do? One thing we shall find is that *in many cases* we *can* answer our question on the basis of a few general principles about what is intrinsically worthwhile, after all. Let us consider what can be done.

What do we actually do, in such problem situations? Take our professor. If he is not of the impulsive type, he will get out paper and pencil and list the pros and cons of each alternative. He can ask himself: How does the *enjoyment* of one way of doing this compare with the other? How do the alternatives compare when only their promise of knowledge is considered: addition to historical learning, and original ideas? How will the alternatives affect the values, the character structures, of the children? (Each of these questions can be broken down again into several subquestions.) These questions are more manageable, since each asks about only the amount of one type of thing known to be worthwhile; and presumably they usually can be answered. (If none of them can be, then the hedonist and other monistic theories are no better off, as far as comparisons of complex objects are concerned, than are pluralistic theories.) Then, if all of these more specific questions are answered favorably to the same one of the alternatives, the over-all question takes care of itself. It is then obvious what over-all preference a person would have if he had all these issues clearly before his mind at once.

There are some more specific things that can be said in general terms, along the lines of the foregoing example, about how total situations can be broken down and reliable over-all comparisons of worth based on comparisons of the worth of specific pairs of elements. (1) Let us assume we wish to compare two situations, A and B. Suppose A contains exactly the same things or events that B contains, as far as things of worth are concerned (as two journeys might have, if they differ only in taking somewhat different routes), except that A has at least one additional element of value (or B at least one additional, undesirable element). A is then better than B. (2) Suppose that A and B do not contain the same events, but we can make accurate comparisons of the amounts of things of intrinsic worth of the same type in each. For instance, suppose the events are dissimilar, but we can say that each will give approximately the same amount of pleasure; or we can say that the amount of knowledge to be derived from each is about the same, although the books to be read are different.[9] Suppose then we can say that the amount or sum of each class of valuable things (pleasure, knowledge, and so forth) in A is not less than the corresponding class in B, and that the sum of at least one such class in A is greater than that in B. Then again A is better than B.

We shall naturally feel we are on soundest ground if we can decide an issue by appeal to the first method. Application of the second is more precarious, but at least comparisons only of things of the same type are involved. Moreover, it will not be questioned that, at least in many cases, we can decide that there is more pleasure to be got from one course of action than from another, and hence that the pleasure value is greater. Nor, in fact, is there more difficulty with some other sorts of thing. Take knowledge, for example. It would be absurd to say that we do not know that reading the works of Aristotle gives more knowledge than reading the works of Cicero. There is just far more content in Aristotle. These methods can be used, of course, if our only ethical premises are of the form we have been assessing: "Pleasure (with certain exceptions) is intrinsically worth-

---

[9] There are complications if some of the types of knowledge are of greater worth than others.

while"; "Knowledge (with certain exceptions) is intrinsically worthwhile"; and so on.

There is another method. (3) Suppose we cannot proceed as in (2), because, say, A and B contain no similar elements. Suppose, however, that every element of worth in B can be matched, from the standpoint of worth, with some element of worth in A in such a way that no element of B exceeds the matched element of A in worth. And suppose that some of the elements in A are superior in value to the matched elements from B; or that there are positively (and no negatively) valuable elements in A that are not matched with any corresponding element of worth in B. Then again, A is better. This third method requires judgments of the *comparative worth* of things of different kinds, but use of it makes the comparisons simpler than the comparisons of two complex objects or trains of events as wholes. It would be extraordinary to say that no such simple judgments of comparison are tenable at all. We have already suggested that *some* such judgments can be made: that knowledge of what happened to Lincoln during his twenty-second year is intrinsically more worthwhile than the enjoyment of a milkshake, but less so than the enjoyment of a month's holiday in a pleasant clime in January. Unfortunately, comparisons we must sometimes make are not so easy.

We may infer that, even if "pluralism" is right in saying that different kinds of thing are intrinsically worthwhile, there are still some situations in which a reliable comparative judgment of value can definitely be made (by method no. 1). There are other situations in which it is possible (by method no. 2) to make such judgments validly if we can make judgments of *amount* comparing objects of similar kind (as the hedonist thinks we can for pleasure). Still other over-all comparisons are reliably made (by method no. 3) if we can make correct comparative judgments of worth for individual parts of one situation, in relation to matching parts of another situation.

There are various other principles, obviously acceptable, that to some extent will supplement those we have listed. (a) It makes no difference whether the events of worth occur in the experience of one person or in different persons. (But we must be careful: one piece of information in one mind and another in another mind may be together not nearly so valuable as both in one mind, and related.) (b) If one event is more worthwhile than another, the former is better than a part of the latter. For example, if a piece of biographical knowledge is more worthwhile than the enjoyment of a milkshake, it is *a fortiori* better than the smaller enjoyment of half a milkshake. (c) If one event is more valuable than another, then the former is better than a fifty-fifty chance of the second, provided the first object has positive value, namely, is better than nothing at all. (d) If A is better than B, and B is better than C, then A is better than C. (e) If A is better than B, then anything exactly like A in abstract properties is better than anything exactly like B in abstract properties. (The first of these principles might be taken as a corollary of this one.)

When we have made fullest use of all these principles, however, there will still be situations about which we cannot say that one is either better, or worse, or equal in value to, the other. Suppose, for instance, we match all the elements of A and B except for two of A and one of B, and the matched elements strike us as roughly equal. But the unmatched value of B is substantial; the unmatched values of A are smaller. Is the "sum" of the latter greater than that of the former? Our methods and principles provide us no way of deciding.

Moreover, no matter how careful we are in an *over-all* comparison, it seems that there are comparisons that we cannot seriously claim to be reliable. Take, for instance, our earlier statement that the enjoyments of a month's vacation in Florida in midwinter are intrinsically more worthwhile than the knowledge to be got by reading a biography of Lincoln's twenty-second year. But suppose we tried to fix the precise number of vacation hours which is equal in value to this knowledge. Clearly we cannot. Or suppose we wished to compare the value of this knowledge with that of a *chance* of a vacation: a 50–50 or a 25–75 chance. Could we pick a precise chance of having the month's vacation that is exactly equal to the knowledge of Lincoln? Obviously not.[10] (We are here not comparing intrinsic values, but a value with a *chance* of an intrinsic value; life, however, does pose such problems, and it seems sensible to say that there could be a "qualified" preference one way or the other.)

Our conclusion, in summary, is that, if "pluralism" is right, in some situations reliable comparative judgments of value can be made; but in other situations such judgments cannot be made. This is probably what we should have expected!

There is a final difficulty we postponed from the previous chapter. Comparative judgments of worth presuppose the possibility of knowing the character or nature of the situations being compared. But sometimes, when the things being compared are the experiences of different persons, this supposition may not correspond with fact. For instance, suppose we have the price of only one movie, and have the choice of financing either our son or our daughter, but not both. How shall we decide this? We must know the net difference that attendance at the movie will make for each. Clearly, inferences on this point must be based on past experience. Such inferences, on some points, can without doubt be drawn. For instance, if our son is five years older than our daughter, we can properly anticipate that

---

[10] If we always could—and if some other simpler and more plausible propositions were granted—then we would talk of "quantities" of value, at least in the sense of an "interval scale." See Davidson, McKinsey, and Suppes, "Outlines of a Formal Theory of Value, I," *Philosophy of Science*, XXII (1955), 140–60; and R. McNaughton, "A Metrical Concept of Happiness," *Philosophy and Phenomenological Research*, XIV (1953), 172–83.

he will understand, say, certain historical features of the film, whereas our daughter will not. From certain types of film, then, our older son will definitely learn more. But how shall we make estimates about the level of sheer enjoyment of the film, extrapolating from experiences in the past? This is difficult. We might draw inferences from the fact that our daughter has been willing to spend her own money for movies in the past, whereas our son has not; but perhaps this fact reflects, not different levels of enjoyment, but different valuations of money. Or, perhaps in the past our son has been willing to forego five milkshakes for a movie, whereas our daughter has not been; but this evidence may show merely that our daughter likes milkshakes more than does our son. Is there, then, *any* way in which we may compare intensities of satisfaction in two persons? The question is an exceedingly important one, assuming that enjoyment is a major determinant of whether a situation is worthwhile.

Obviously, precision is here out of the question. It would be foolish to say, however, that we know nothing. For instance, it would be foolish to say that it is doubtful whether it is more uncomfortable for our daughter to swallow a stomach tube than it is for our son to eat ice cream of a flavor he does not like.

How can we properly draw such inferences? It is a proper assumption that hedonic levels are connected by natural law both with complex neural or physiological structures and with other kinds of observable event, so that the possibility of deviations from the normal can be cross-checked in various ways. Thus, if a Hindu mystic reports mild enjoyment from having the soles of his feet seared by fire, we believe him if we find great calluses on the bottom of his feet; but if we find no such calluses, and if delicate instruments show marked alterations in his blood pressure, pulse rate, and perspiration, we conclude he is lying to us. In general, we are thus justified in inferring that another person's hedonic level will approximate to what ours would be in a similar situation, unless there is special evidence to the contrary. It is possible, of course, that a man who has had no food for twenty-four hours is perfectly happy; but we want special evidence—information about training, peculiar constitutional features, expressive behavior—in order to find this plausible. It is possible, also, that a Negro child does not suffer appreciably if he goes to school and is snubbed and ridiculed by other children, treated harshly by the teachers, made to sit by himself at lunch, and spat upon in the hallways; but, barring nonexistent evidence correlating emotion with skin color, belief that he does not suffer is absurd. Then, can we or can't we say anything about whether our son or our daughter will enjoy the movie more? The answer is that sometimes we can and sometimes we can't: a mystery thriller will only frighten our daughter and she would much prefer not to go; and a nature film may bore her. On the other hand, a Disney film about the adventures of a baby elephant might send her into raptures, whereas our son would feel the whole thing a bit unsophisticated for his age. On the other hand, a simple Bob Hope comedy might be enjoyable for both, and if we have to choose, we had better toss a coin.

The exact logic of such inferences is a complex and controversial matter. But we must be careful not to accept a line of reasoning such that, if we followed it consistently, we would be committed to holding there is no reason to think other persons have conscious experiences at all. The conclusion must be that we can make many reliable judgments about the experiences of other persons, even about comparative pleasure level; but in other cases our judgments are little more than guesses.

FURTHER READING

Plato, *Philebus*

Aristotle, *Nicomachaean Ethics*, Bks. I, X.

G. E. Moore, *Principia Ethica* (Cambridge, Eng.: Cambridge University Press, 1929), chap. 6.

———, *Ethics* (Oxford: Oxford University Press, 1949), chaps. 1, 2.

E. F. Carritt, *Ethical and Political Thinking* (Oxford: Clarendon Press, 1947), chap. 7.

W. D. Ross, *The Right and the Good* (Oxford: Clarendon Press, 1930), chap. 5.

———, *Foundations of Ethics* (Oxford: Clarendon Press, 1939), pp. 275–308.

H. Rashdall, *Theory of Good and Evil* (Oxford: Oxford University Press, 1924), I, chap. 7.

W. G. Everett, *Moral Values* (New York: Henry Holt & Company, Inc., 1928), chap. 7.

P. Nowell-Smith, *Ethics* (Baltimore: Penguin Books, Inc., 1954), chap. 17.

14

Moral Obligation and Personal Interest

The question of what things are intrinsically desirable strikes some people as hardly an "ethical" question at all, although historically it has been a major preoccupation of writers on ethics. In contrast, questions about what is right or wrong, what is our duty, what is our obligation, what we ought to do, what is immoral conduct, are universally viewed as central questions of ethics. We must now consider these questions.

The number of different ethical words used in these peculiarly ethical questions—"wrong," "duty," "obligation," and so on—suggests that correspondingly many distinct problems of theory must be faced by normative ethics. Fortunately, however, there are only two distinct central ideas or concepts to be considered, one of which will be discussed in the present chapter and the following chapter, and the other in Chapter 18. (Others will be discussed, but in the end, as we shall see, they are reducible to these two.) The first of these is the idea of *moral obligation*. Most of the questions mentioned in the preceding paragraph can be correctly viewed as, at least approximately, questions about moral obligation.

In order to see that most of the questions listed can be viewed as questions about moral obligation, we have only to notice how a sentence about moral obligation is approximately translatable into a sentence substituting one of the other words for "moral obligation," and vice versa. For instance, take "Everything considered, I think your moral obligation is to do what you promised to do." This is approximately the same as, "Everything considered, I think it would be *wrong* for you *not* to do what you promised." Or, "Everything considered, I think it would *not* be *right* for you *not* to do what you promised." Or, "Everything considered, I think you *ought* to do what you promised." (But this is not the same unless the context makes clear that the "ought" is a moral "ought." Sometimes "you ought"

353

just means "it would be best if you. . . .") Or finally, "Everything considered, I think it is your *duty* to do what you promised."[1]

In previous chapters, we have examined several theories about what is intrinsically desirable—that is, several proposals, of a general nature, about what kinds of things are intrinsically desirable. There are comparable theories about what is morally obligatory. Of course, in view of the relations of meaning among "moral obligation," "wrong," and so on, these theories are equally theories about what is right or wrong, and so on. These proposals must now be stated and considered.

It may be helpful to explain briefly what are the major types of normative theory about moral obligation (the analogues of hedonist and pluralist theories about what is intrinsically desirable), in order to see where we shall be going in the present and in the following chapter. There are two major *types* of theory: what we shall call "result" theories, and what we shall call "formalist" theories. (Result theories are often called "teleological," and formalist theories "deontological," but we shall not use these terms.) What is common to result theories is the view that one's over-all moral obligation depends *entirely* on the intrinsic worth of the actual or expectable results of the various acts one might perform at a given time; for instance, one form of theory says one is always morally obligated to act so as to produce results of maximum intrinsic worth.[2] Formalist theories assert that the thesis of result theories is too simple, and they have in common the view that one's moral obligations are dependent on some other things about one's situation in addition to (or perhaps, instead of) the intrinsic value of the actual or expectable results of one's act; for instance, a formalist theory may say that one is morally obligated to keep one's promises irrespective of the consequences of keeping or breaking them. The *nature* of an act (that is, whether it is a lie or a breach of promise—something

---

[1] We should emphasize that these translations are approximate only, and that following the pattern above would sometimes violate the subleties of English idiom. For instance, we might say, "It would be wrong to assault your mother-in-law," but hardly, "It is your duty not to assault your mother-in-law." "Duty" is most naturally used where there are some positive performances recognized as pertaining to an office or social role, for example, "It is your duty as the boy's father to speak to him about his conduct." Thus, "duty" in moral contexts is ordinarily closely related to and continuous with talk of the "duties of the governor," meaning here the performances recognized as involved in a satisfactory fulfillment of one's job, the set of activities one has committed oneself to perform in accepting a status or position. Moreover, we use "duty" where we can speak of someone *to whom* we have the duty, for example, one's duty to one's employer or to one's country. On the other hand, it is difficult to generalize, and "duty" can be used correctly when these conditions do not obtain. Somewhat similar things may be said of "moral obligation."

We shall, however, in the following discussion ignore these subtleties and assume that the foregoing suggested approximate equivalences are correct.

[2] We can count the act itself (with its intrinsic worth) as part of the "consequence," if we wish, even though we ordinarily think of the results of an act as coming subsequent to the act. Whether or not it is important to speak in this way depends on how we use the word "act"—whether to refer to a whole event, such as the execution of a kidnaping, or simply to an initiating decision or resolution.

about it different from the intrinsic worth of actual or expected consequences) is held by formalists to be sometimes an important fact bearing on
whether there is a moral obligation to perform or avoid it.

Result theories fall into two species. *Egoist* theories hold that one is
morally obligated to perform a certain act if and only if so doing will
(actually or expectably) produce a state of *oneself* that is of maximum
intrinsic worth, for example, by maximizing one's enjoyment, satisfying
one's desires fully, and so on. *Universal* theories roughly hold that it is
morally obligatory to perform a given act if and only if performing it
will (actually or expectably) produce more intrinsic good *in general* than
any other act the agent could perform instead.

Result theories may be subdivided further, according as they adopt
hedonist, personal pluralist, or impersonal pluralist views about what is
intrinsically good. Thus, we end up with five subspecies of result-theory:
(1) egoistic hedonism; (2) egoistic personal pluralism; (3) universal hedonism (usually called "hedonistic utilitarianism" or even just "utilitarianism");
(4) universal personal pluralism (often called "ideal utilitarianism"); and
(5) universal impersonal pluralism.[3] Some of the names we are giving these
theories are long and barbarous; fortunately, we shall not have much
occasion to use them. One should particularly notice that only the first
two types of universal theory are called "utilitarian"; this conforms to
practice and, as we shall see, to an important point about the spirit of the
several theories. What the two forms of utilitarianism have in common,
as contrasted with the other universalist theory, is the view that an act
is right if and only if it will (actually or expectably) maximize the *welfare*
(in the sense of intrinsically desirable states) of sentient beings.

There is also, however, a group of compromise theories, which form a
bridge between the universal result theories and formalism. We have already described ("p. 253) a form of such theories under the title of "rule-
utilitarianism."[4] Roughly, these theories agree with formalism that what is
obligatory does not depend entirely on the intrinsic value of the results (actual or expectable) of the various things an agent might do at a particular
time; one's obligation is rather to conform one's behavior to certain rules
(for example, about telling the truth), but the rules to which one must conform are ones such that there would be best results (actually or expectably)
if *everyone* conformed to them. So, in a sense the value of results is the ultimate reason why acts are right or wrong (just as result theories say), but
yet not in a direct way (and as a result, the theories are close to formalism).
There can be hedonist and personal pluralist forms of this type of theory.

[3] Since we have already weighed the merits of hedonism and personal pluralism,
we shall not discuss this issue further. Thus we shall mostly ignore the differences
between theories (1) and (2), and (3) and (4).

[4] In the previous context we treated it as a theory about the basic method for
answering ethical questions. But we must also view it as a general theory of obligation;
and as such it is a most impressive theory.

There can even be an impersonal pluralist form; only, in order to conform with our use of "utilitarian" in the case of result theories, we shall not call this a form of "rule-utilitarianism," but rather use the term "extended rule-utilitarianism."

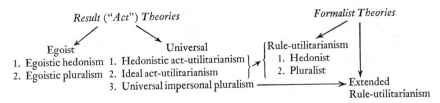

THEORIES OF MORAL OBLIGATION

Result ("Act") Theories   *Formalist Theories*

Egoist   Universal   Rule-utilitarianism
1. Egoistic hedonism   1. Hedonistic act-utilitarianism   1. Hedonist
2. Egoistic pluralism   2. Ideal act-utilitarianism   2. Pluralist
           3. Universal impersonal pluralism   Extended
                                               Rule-utilitarianism

FIGURE 5.

Figure 5 may help keep in mind the relations of the various theories.

Before we can profitably examine these theories, however, we must examine the concept of moral obligation itself—just as, in preface to our discussion of theories about what is intrinsically desirable, we had to discuss the concept of the intrinsically desirable. Unfortunately, the concept of moral obligation and its relation to that of the intrinsically desirable is puzzling.

1. THE CONCEPT OF MORAL OBLIGATION

Most writers on ethics have recognized a distinction between terms like "morally obligatory," "duty," and "wrong" on the one hand, and "is a desirable thing," "is a good thing," and "is worthwhile" on the other. One of the jobs of metaethical theory (and we are back in metaethics again when we discuss this topic) is to clarify the difference.

It is obvious that there is no simple identity of meaning between any term from the first group and any from the second group. Take, for instance, "morally obligatory" and "is a desirable thing." One difference between them is that "is morally obligatory" applies only to persons: We must always say "Mr. X is morally obligated to do. . . ." Again, if it is morally obligatory for someone to do something, it must in some sense be possible for him to do it; but we can perfectly well say it is (or at least, that it would be) desirable for somebody to do something, even if it is quite clear that he cannot. Again, it may be desirable for me to do a certain thing (for example, learn to play the violin), and it may also be possible for me to do it; but there may still be no obligation.

It has sometimes been thought that, although there is no simple identity of meaning between words of the first set and those of the second, still words of the first set can be defined in terms of words of the second *along with nonethical concepts.* For instance, the nonnaturalist G. E. Moore once urged:

> What I wish first to point out is that "right" does and can mean nothing but "cause of a good result," and is thus identical with "useful"; whence it follows that the end always will justify the means, and that no action which is not justified by its results can be right. . . . That the assertion "I am morally bound to perform this action" is identical with the assertion "This action will produce the greatest possible amount of good in the Universe" has already been briefly shewn . . . ; but it is important to insist that this fundamental point is demonstrably certain. . . . Our "duty," therefore, can only be defined as that action, which will cause more good to exist in the Universe than any possible alternative. And what is "right" or "morally permissible" only differs from this, as what will *not* cause *less* good than any possible alternative.[5]

A rather similar proposal has been made by R. B. Perry (*supra*, p. 170). Such definitions have the extremely important consequence that they make a universal form of result theory true by definition.

The critic of naturalism in ethics need not object to such definitions, since they are not naturalistic definitions; they propose only that an ethical word can be defined by a phrase that also contains an ethical word. Nevertheless, it can be shown that such definitions are incorrect. Moore's definition, for instance, clearly does not fit the most usual senses of "duty." For instance, suppose someone's will contains a provision bequeathing the sum of $100,000 to a college for the provision of scholarships for students who are not Negroes or Jews. It might be quite clear that the administrative officers of the college could produce the most good by accepting the money on behalf of the college. But it is obviously a debatable question whether they are not obligated to refuse to accept money offered on such terms. Consider another example. Suppose a college has accepted a bequest of $100,000, the income of which is to be used for postgraduate fellowships for students planning to enter the ministry, or for members of the Presbyterian Church. Furthermore, suppose the terms of the bequest do not legally bind the college to use the money in this particular way; but the terms request this, and the will had been written on the understanding (given in an oral promise by the president of the institution) that the money would be so used. Finally, suppose that, as time goes on, there are relatively few well-qualified students who meet the conditions of the will, and it becomes clear that more good would be produced if the college abandoned the attempt to confine use of the money to fellowships for students who are Presbyterians or candidates for the ministry. Is it then equally obvious that the college is morally free to act accordingly—or that it is the duty of the college to do so? Obviously not. Indeed, the reader

[5] *Principia Ethica* (Cambridge, Eng.: Cambridge University Press, 1929), pp. 147–48. For a statement of Moore's more recent view, see P. A. Schilpp (ed.), *The Philosophy of G. E. Moore* (Evanston, Ill.: Northwestern University Press, 1942), pp. 596 ff.

will be convinced, as we go on, that there is *no* ordinary sense of "duty" in which he is prepared to say that some things that Moore's definition implies are our duty are actually our duty.

What then do we mean by "is morally obligated to"? One thing we seem to mean by "morally obligated" is "morally bound," so that it is not open to one to decline to do what one is obligated to do—and this irrespective of any other consideration.

But "bound" in what sense? Not in the sense of "causally necessitated": a person may be morally bound to do something and yet fail to do it. Thus, being morally bound does not imply that it is impossible to do otherwise. Furthermore, not in the sense of "legally bound." Doubtless usually it is one's moral obligation to obey the law. However, there can be a moral obligation to break the law, and there are many occasions when we have a moral obligation to do something that legally we are not required to do. Again, not in the sense of being "obligated by someone." Some people have thought there can be no obligation unless some being, usually God, obliges us to do something, in the sense of "requires us to do it on pain of punishment." At present, however, at least most people use "moral obligation" in such a way that it is proper to say one is morally obligated even if no one requires.

One proposal for a definition of "duty" and "obligation" that has the virtue of making clear a sense in which we are bound is rather like Moore's definition above, in being a proposal that all the moral-obligation words are explainable by means of ethical words of another type (but not now from the "good"–"desirable" class): "morally culpable," "morally blameworthy," "reprehensible," and so on.[6] Roughly, the suggestion of some philosophers is that "It is your duty to do *A*" means "If you don't do *A*, you will be morally culpable." Or, to take the most subtle of such suggestions, "It is your duty to do *A*" is said to mean "*A* is the one act you can perform with the result that you will escape all moral blame (culpability) except possibly on grounds of your motivation."[7] If this definition is

[6] These terms will be discussed in Chapter 18. Roughly, to be morally culpable on account of something is for one to be justifiably an object of censure, disapproval, or criticism on account of it. Whatever is morally culpable must also show a defect of character.

[7] The reason for the exception is this. Suppose a person does his duty, for example, takes his son to the circus when he has promised to do so. But suppose that the only reason he does so is that he expects to meet a certain person at the circus, and that he would not have kept his promise (which we may suppose, for the sake of the argument, it is his duty to keep) but for this expectation. In this case, his act is open to moral criticism on account of his motivation, even though the person does what it is his duty to do.

This definition was suggested to the writer by Professor Wilfrid Sellars. Professor Sellars, however, has rather complex views about the meaning of "moral culpability," so that what he means by the definition perhaps differs somewhat from what the reader will understand by the definition. It is not suggested that the critical remarks below are validly applicable to the definition as Professor Sellars understands it.

correct, the sense in which we are "bound," when we are obligated, is clear, for moral people are eager to avoid being morally culpable, and whatever must be done to avoid this, they will feel they *must* do.

Is this sort of definition acceptable? We must certainly concede that it is a helpful proposal. Even if it is not correct as a definition, the suggestion calls our attention to the fact that it is at least very often true that we are morally culpable if we fail to do our duty. As a result, any statement that something is our duty at least *implies* (in a familiar sense) that we shall be culpable if we fail to do it. This fact, then, would be a partial explanation of why we properly think we are "bound" to do something if we think it is our duty to do it. This much of the suggestion, at least, we must hold to firmly as being true and helpful.

Whether the definition is correct is a matter not easy to assess, and what we shall be saying later need be altered only at a few points by anyone who thinks it is. Some examples, however, raise serious question. (1) Suppose we think it a certain executive's duty to discharge a person who is a long-time employee and friend. But the executive, being a kindly person, is never quite able to bring himself to do it. In this case, the very virtues of his character are a defect for the job at hand. He does not, then, do his duty. But should we think him morally culpable? (2) Suppose a man is convinced that it is wrong for a person to marry his deceased wife's sister. Therefore, he refuses to give his daughter permission to marry her widowed brother-in-law, a man whom she loves, and who wishes to marry her. We would say that, in the circumstances, it was (at least probably) his duty to give his permission, and that he was just mistaken in his views. But, if his conviction was an honest one, should we say he was morally culpable for governing his conduct accordingly? It seems we can say it *was* his duty to give permission, but that he is not necessarily culpable for failing to give it. If either of these examples is well taken, the definition is incorrect.

It seems, then, that it is impossible to define words of the "duty" type in terms of words either of the "desirable" type or of the "morally culpable" type. Fortunately, there is another way of looking at their meanings. Let us ask ourselves, along the lines discussed in Chapter 10, how we *correct* our judgments about duty or obligation—and in particular with what "qualified attitudes" we expect our judgments or principles about duty and obligation to be coherent or compatible. Then perhaps we can find a "quasi-naturalist" definition of these terms with which we can be satisfied (or a comparable view of one of the other types suggested at the end of Chapter 10).

Against what attitudes do we test our judgments of duty or obligation? Not, it seems, against just our "qualified" desires or preferences, as we test judgments of what is worthwhile. It seems we test them against our attitudes of two kinds. First, we test them against our own "feelings of obligation" in the sense described in our discussion of psychology (pp. 117 ff.)—

impulses to act that are independent of our "subjective wants," and that tend to be succeeded by feelings of guilt or remorse if we fail to obey them. It seems that if we have such an impulse in response to our view of a total situation, and think it "qualified" (in the sense of Chapter 10), then we say we have an obligation to do what it impels us to do. On the other hand, we also test our judgments of obligation against *impulses to demand* that someone else do something—an "impulse to demand" in the sense of one that is, again, independent of our "subjective wants," and is a readiness to *compel* the action in question by some sort of sanction if that is feasible and to be indignant at the person if he fails to perform the act in question. We say, again, that someone else has an obligation to do something (and that we are obligated to do the same in the same circumstances), if we feel such a "demand" on him to perform this act, and think the attitude is "qualified" (in the sense of Chapter 10).[8]

If these are the relevant attitudes against which we test our judgments of obligation, then, if we want to have a definition and if we are prepared to follow the suggestions of Chapter 10, we can venture the proposal that "X is morally obligated over all to do A" means "it is objectively justified for X to feel obligated to do A, and for other persons to demand that he do A," where "objectively justified" is a substitute for the long phrase on p. 265, including "satisfies all the conditions . . . endorsement of such attitudes."

This explanation of "moral obligation" permits us to speak of different stringencies of duty or obligation. Furthermore, we do speak in this way: Sometimes we say our duty is very compelling, whereas at other times we regard it as fairly slight. Our explanation permits this, because feelings of obligation and demand can vary in strength, and the sanction we are prepared to use may be strong or weak.

According to this view, we are "bound" when we are obligated, in the sense that a feeling of obligation (including a tendency to feel guilt if we fail) is objectively justified, and in the sense that a demanding attitude by others is also objectively justified (including a tendency to be indignant if we fail). Is this not enough?

So far, so good. But now we run into a puzzle.

Moral obligation and the agent's beliefs. The definition of "moral obligation" we have outlined makes it possible for a person to make mistakes about his obligation. He may *think* his feeling of obligation is "objectively justified" when in fact it is not. This seems acceptable; we do think that people are sometimes mistaken about their duty or obligations. Furthermore, our

---

[8] There is one exception to this. In order to test whether another person really is obligated to perform a certain act, we must ignore one set of facts—the agent's own beliefs about what he ought to do, and also any errors or incompleteness in his own view of the facts of his situation. These facts about the agent are, as we shall see, relevant for deciding whether his act, after he performs it, was blameworthy or reprehensible. But they are not relevant for deciding what he really ought to do.

theory of the justification of judgments about obligation is, roughly, that a judgment that one is morally obligated to do something is correct if and only if it is consistent with a complete set of general principles of obligation which are coherent with what our corresponding attitudes would be if we were impartial, fully-informed, and in a normal frame of mind. All of this seems plausible. Yet there is something wrong, as two examples will make clear.

First, suppose a physician examined a patient suffering from allergies in 1920, when nothing was known of allergies. The physician advised and performed a series of operations (on the patient's nose and sinuses, for example) at considerable cost to the patient in suffering and money. Was the physician's behavior consistent with his moral obligations? We certainly incline to say it was. According to our total theory, as described above, however, it seems he did *not* do his duty, since, if he had been fully informed (including information about allergies), he would have felt obligated to treat for allergies.

Second, suppose a driver is approaching a crossroad, where trees and buildings block his vision of traffic on the other road. Ought he to stop, or may he drive across at sixty miles an hour if he is in a hurry? We think his moral obligation is to stop, irrespective of whether there *is* traffic on the other road, because he does not *know* whether there is or not. Not, however, according to our total theory, for a person who was fully informed (including information about the presence of traffic on the other road) would presumably *not* feel an obligation to stop if there were no traffic. So, according to our theory he need not stop if there is in fact no traffic on the other road. Something seems wrong in both these cases.

In order to unravel this tangle, we must pay attention to two things: first, the contexts in which we make statements about a person's duty or obligation (our own or others'); and second, the different causes, some culpable and some not, on account of which a person's conduct may diverge from the course of duty.

There are two main types of context in which we make statements of obligation. First, we may make them before an action has taken place, when we are raising questions about, or reporting our beliefs about what we or others ought to do, or giving advice to others about what they should do. We are looking to the future, to what is *to be* done. Let us call these contexts of "advice" (to ourselves or others).[9] For instance, suppose we are puzzling about what our duty is. Suppose the physician of our previous example asks himself, "How ought I to treat this patient?" Or, suppose an aunt of ours is penniless, and falls ill. Either her relatives support her, or she must go to a

---

[9] My attention was first called to the importance of the contexts in which obligation-statements are made, for an understanding of the present puzzle, by Dr. Jerome Schneewind.

charitable institution. We are one of the nearest relatives. We ask ourselves, "Is it our *duty* to offer a substantial contribution?"

For contexts of this sort, the total theory of statements about duty, as
described above, fits very well. It is plausible to say that we are asking
whether feeling obligated is "objectively justified" in the sense of "meeting all the conditions . . . ," and to say that the conditions it has to meet
include that of being the feeling one would have if one were fully informed
and knew all the relevant facts.[10] The same thing can be said about statements in which we express our decision after we have finally reached it:
"After reflection, I have decided that my duty probably is to do this certain
thing." The physician, for instance, when he has decided he ought to operate, is saying something which our total above theory fits very well, when
he says, "This is what I probably ought to recommend"—however mistaken
he may be in what he thinks. It is reasonable to construe him to be asserting
that his attitude is objectively justified, and to say that it *is* justified if it
meets the conditions of the Qualified Attitude Method.

For convenience, we shall say that a person is using "duty" or "obligation" in the *objective sense*, if he is using it in this way.

There is a second and quite different type of context in which statements
of obligation are made. Those of this type we may call "post mortem" contexts. They are contexts in which we are criticizing, condemning, or defending agents, ourselves or others. In order to understand these contexts,
we should note that there are different causes why a person may fail to do
his duty in the above objective sense. These causes are different in an important way, from a moral point of view, since failure to do one's objective
duty for some reasons reflects on one's character and is culpable, whereas
failure to do one's objective duty for other reasons does not. (The theory of
what is morally culpable will be discussed in Chapter 18; but we shall anticipate our results there, on some obvious points.)

There are two major reasons why people fail to do their objective duty.
One is that they do not know what it is. Ignorance of objective duty
may itself be a reflection on character: for example, if the reason for one's
ignorance is lack of interest in doing one's duty, or rationalizing reflection
influenced by extreme self-centeredness. Ignorance of objective duty may
not, however, be a reflection on character: for instance, if the reason is misinformation about the facts when the facts are inaccessible or so difficult to determine that it is not obligatory to ascertain them for the sake of
deciding the question at hand.

The second reason why people fail to do their objective duty is moti-

10 Also we are asking whether the "objectively justified" attitudes of others toward
us would be attitudes of demanding that we do a certain thing. If so, it is plausible to
suppose that we want to know whether such attitudes would be demanding attitudes
if they "met all the conditions," including the one of being the attitude of a mind
aware of all the relevant facts—except for ignoring what we think we ought to do,
and the errors of our beliefs about the facts of the situation.

vational: They know what their duty is, but lack a desire to do it, or else are strongly motivated to do something conflicting with it. Usually a person who fails to do his duty for this reason is morally culpable; he has failed on account of some defect of character—perhaps lack of conscientiousness, or self-centeredness. But he need not always be culpable; clearly we judge quite leniently—if we condemn at all—a person who fails to do his duty because of affection for other persons.

A sincere conscientious objector, we may notice, fails to do his duty (assuming his reasoning leads to false ethical conclusions) for the first reason, and nonculpably; a man who poses as a conscientious objector merely because he hates the thought of service in the army fails to do his objective duty for the second reason, and culpably.

It is clear that a man of good character will always do two things. First, being a conscientious person, he will try to find out his objective obligation, what he must do to satisfy the just claims of other people, what it is objectively right for him to do. Second, after coming to a careful decision about what his duty is (the degree of care depending on the importance of the issue), he will do what he believes to be his duty. (We have noted minor possible exceptions to this last.) He will then necessarily escape censure: no mistake he has made can be attributed to a defect of character.

Let us now return to our examination of the contexts in which statements about duty or obligation are made. Some of these contexts, we said, are post-mortem contexts; in them we are criticizing or defending, condemning or excusing. For instance, we may defend the physician who operated because of nonculpable ignorance, saying, "He really did all that duty required. How could he have done more?" What in effect we are saying is that failure to do objective duty is no reflection on his character; perhaps we are implying that he would have been culpable if he failed to operate. We are not *advising anyone what to do,* but excusing an action in the past. Or, again, we may criticize the driver who traversed a crossing at sixty miles an hour when he could not see oncoming traffic, even though no accident occurred. We say: "He didn't do what his duty required." Why? We must concede that he did his objective duty. He did not, however, do what a morally perfect man would have done, since either he failed to reflect at all on what his duty was, or else he failed to do what he thought was his duty. Again, we are not advising anyone what to do; we are condemning for past behavior.

There are hybrid situations which are neither advising nor post-mortem situations. Suppose a man has been agonizing about whether it is right to join the armed forces, and has concluded that the most tenable position is that of the conscientious objector. But now he must act; today he must appear before his draft board and register, as a conscientious objector or not. Suppose, further, he is still enough perplexed that he asks our advice about what he should do. Suppose, finally, that we think his conclusion is mistaken; we think his duty is to join the armed forces. What should we say to him? We may not wish to reopen all the issues; we have been over that ground many times before. We also don't want to encourage him to go against his conscience. So, perhaps we shall say: "Since you are honestly convinced that this is your obligation, it is your *duty* to act accordingly." In this case, we are advising him, but we are not stating what we think is his objective duty. We are advising him by way of telling him that, in his peculiar circumstances, he will be free of moral blame if he refuses to join, and that, perhaps, he will be subject to moral blame if he does join —since joining presumably will, in his situation, show a defect of character.

In a way, there is no difficulty about all this. Contexts of advice normally pose one problem: whether a feeling of obligation or a demand that someone else do something is objectively justified. Post-mortem contexts normally pose a different problem: whether an attitude of remorse or a condemning attitude toward someone else is objectively justified. Further-more, we know how to answer these questions—by the Qualified Attitude Method. The only difficulty is a kind of lexicographical difficulty: what we are to say about the *meaning* of "duty" and "obligation" as they are used in these various contexts. If we used them only in contexts of advice, there would be no puzzle, since our definition of them (in the objective sense) fits nicely. But the fact is that we also use them in post-mortem and hybrid contexts—not a surprising fact, when we consider the close connec-tions between contexts of advice and post-mortem contexts. So, there is the question whether our above account of their meaning and justification is adequate for all these contexts. If it is not, then what must we add?

A great deal has been written about this problem in the past fifty years. The most usual solution at present is to hold that "duty" and "obliga-tion" have *several senses*. If so, of course, ideally we should supply a defini-tion for each of these several senses. It is simplest to follow the tradition on this matter, although it is misleading to say that these senses are quite dis-tinct in the way in which "grip" has several senses. Yet there is a kind of shift of sense from one context to another, and to speak of this as a shift of "sense" is simpler and less misleading than any other mode of descrip-tion. What are these senses?[11]

1. *The objective sense.* We have described this sense above. This sense is for our purposes the most important one, for it is best to construe theories

[11] A noncognitivist would rightly emphasize the fact that these words express different attitudes, directed toward different problems or situations, in the different contexts. In one context I may be expressing a feeling of obligation of my own or making a demand on someone else; in another context I may be expressing remorse or indignation. In each case, if our conclusions in Chapter 10 were correct, we are claiming that our attitude is justified in the sense that it can meet certain conditions; and our discussion of the Qualified Attitude Method is a proposal about what in fact these conditions are.

like egoism, utilitarianism, and formalism, as theories about what is our duty or obligation in this sense.

2. *The subjective sense.* We have agreed that when we say the physician did "his duty," we cannot be using "duty" in the objective sense (unless we know nothing about allergies either, and are defending his action as objectively correct).[12]

In what sense, then, are we using it? One suggestion about this we propose to call the "subjective" sense. According to this proposal, "did his duty" in this sense means "did what would have been his duty in the objective sense, if the facts of the particular situation had been as he thought they were, except for corrections he would have made if he had explored the situation as thoroughly as a man of good character would have done in the circumstances." In this sense the physician did his duty, and the driver did not, and our original problem is resolved.

It is interesting to notice that in this sense there may be a subjective obligation to do (or at least to try to do) what is in fact impossible. (If succeeding is impossible, there is no *objective* duty even to try.) Thus, if a man finds a log across a railway track that will cause a serious accident, and if he thinks he can remove it, he is subjectively obligated to do so (or at least to try). After he has tried and learned that he cannot move it, he no longer has a subjective obligation to do or try.

On occasion, in later chapters, it will be convenient to say that something is someone's "subjective obligation" or "subjective duty"; when we do we shall mean that the something *would* be the person's objective duty if the facts . . . and so on, as above. In other words, we shall find it convenient to make use of the concept of subjective duty. Nevertheless, it is not necessary to subscribe to the view that actual statements of ordinary people, in which "duty" or "obligation" occurs, must be construed in this suggested sense. It may be that it is simpler, in view of the total context, to construe "did his duty," in the case of the physician, to mean simply, "was not reprehensible for doing what he did, and in the total circumstances would have been reprehensible had he failed to do what he did."

3. *The putative sense.* Many philosophers have supposed there is still a third sense of "duty" and "obligation." Suppose a man sincerely thinks it is his (objective) duty to do *A*. But, we think, he is mistaken in this, and not just because he is mistaken about the facts of the situation but because

---

[12] It is a mistake to suppose we never use "duty" in the objective sense in post-mortem contexts. We can defend a person against attack by saying that he did what was really the right thing. Suppose someone is criticized for telling a lie. We may defend his character by saying that he was only thoughtless, or something of the sort. But we may defend him by saying that what he did was exactly the right thing to do in the circumstances. If we do, we are using "right" in the objective sense. We shall be using it in some other sense only if we do not think that what he did was objectively right. There is no simple correlation between the type of context and the sense of these terms; but if there were not these different types of contexts presumably the terms would not be used in the different ways in which they are used.

he holds the wrong moral principles. (Unlike the case of subjective duty, his mistake is not just a mistake, say, about the facts, but a mistake in moral principle or reasoning.) Consider, for example, the man who (p. 359), because he thinks it wrong for a person to marry his deceased wife's sister, concludes it would be wrong for him to give permission for his daughter to marry her widowed brother-in-law. Now, these philosophers say that in this situation, if we think the man is doing what he honestly believes is his (objective) duty, we say, "He is really doing his *duty*"—evidently in still a third sense of "duty." In fact, it is often said that, *whenever* a man honestly thinks it is his objective duty to do *A*, then it *is* his duty in this third sense to do *A*. This sense is called the "putative" sense of "duty."

What shall we say to this? First let us notice that it is not true that we think it is always a person's duty, in some sense, to do what he thinks is his duty. Suppose a prisoner of war thinks it his duty not to give any information to the enemy, however valueless, even under the most extreme torture. Do we think that his thinking so makes it so in *any* sense? Or, suppose an obviously confused person tells us he has concluded he ought to commit suicide. Do we necessarily think it is his duty in *any* sense? Not at all.

Yet it is true that we sometimes use "duty" in a way—as in the "hybrid" situation described above—that is different from both the objective sense and the subjective sense. We shall not try to formulate a theory of its meaning, however, for an obvious reason. This sense of "duty" is not relevant for getting clear what our duty is—for nothing is our duty in this sense, apparently, except when we already have made up our minds about our duty. This sense of "duty" is relevant only at the end of our inquiry into what our duty is in some other sense; and it is not going to help us in this inquiry. What we want now is to find out what is our duty in some sense other than that of the statement "I did my *duty* because I thought I was doing it." For the present, then, we ignore the question of this supposed third sense of "duty." Later we shall discuss the concept of moral culpability, and under what conditions we are morally culpable—presumably, much the same topic.

In fact, we need not concern ourselves about what is our "subjective duty" either. There are only two concepts we need for ethics: that of objective duty or obligation, and that of moral culpability or reprehensibility or blameworthiness (discussed in Chapter 18). All the points people ever make by using "duty" in some other way can be made quite well by some locution containing "duty" in the objective sense, or "morally reprehensible."

A person might say that the subjective or the putative sense of "duty" is more important, for don't we think that what a person really ought to do is his duty in the subjective or putative, not in the objective sense? For instance, don't we think the driver ought to stop at the crossroad, irrespective of what a better-informed person might advise? And oughtn't the conscientious objector to follow his conscience?

But such argument is confused. In the first place, it overlooks the fact that, *for the agent*, the question whether he should do his duty in the objective or some other sense *cannot arise*. It arises only for hindsight, or for other persons better placed to know the facts, for obviously the agent is never in a position to distinguish between what the facts really are (or what his duty really is) and what he thinks they are (or what he thinks his duty is). He can never say: "My objective duty is to do a certain thing, but my subjective (or putative) duty is to do something else." When he is deciding, he can only ask what is his duty in the objective sense; and he will try to do this if he is a moral man. In the second place, for purposes of deciding whether a man is *morally culpable*, it is more important to know whether he did his subjective or putative duty than whether he did his objective duty. But if we want to know whether a man did his objective duty, then whether he did these other things is obviously not more important. In the third place, if we know the general principles of objective duty, we can easily draw inferences about a person's subjective duty. The reason for this is that it is a person's subjective duty to do A if and only if doing A would have been his objective duty if the particular facts of the situation had been what he believed them to be, or would have believed them to be if he had explored the situation as a man of character would do. So, if we know what a person responsibly thinks about the facts of his particular situation, and if we know the correct principles of objective duty, we can infer his subjective duty. So, since the true principles of objective duty are decisive for what is a person's subjective duty, we may explore the principles of the former in order to determine the true principles of the latter.

From now on, then, we shall confine our discussion to general principles about duty in the objective sense. Utilitarianism, for instance, as ordinarily stated is such a principle.

Prima facie obligation (or duty) and over-all obligation (or duty). There is one further concept we need to clarify before examining the major normative theories.

So far, we have been talking as if whenever we use "obligation" or "duty" in a sentence, we are using it in the sense of "over-all duty"—as in the sentence, "Everything considered, I think your obligation is to keep your promise." But this is not correct, for we can say, "I agree that I have *an obligation* to do what I promised (for example, go on a fishing trip with someone), but my wife has been taken seriously ill and there is no one but me to take care of her. So I have *a stronger obligation* to stay at home." Some philosophers have spoken of obligations in this sense as "prima facie obligations" or "prima facie duties."

What is a "prima facie obligation"? Fortunately, we can explain this in terms of "over-all obligation," the kind of obligation we have been discussing. Suppose I notice, in some situation where I am obligated to do A, that I would not have been obligated but for the factor F. For instance, I notice that I would not have been obligated to attend a certain dinner, if I had not promised I would do so. Let us then think of these two things as forming a pair: the factor F (the promise) and the obligation A (to do what I promised). Now suppose we find, on reflection, that almost always when the first member is present in a situation, the second member also is (that is, there is an *over-all* obligation to do a certain thing). Thus, for instance, almost always when I have promised to do A, I am obligated over-all to do A. Now this may not always be so. But suppose that, whenever it is not so, there is always some other similar pair present in the situation. For instance, when I have made a promise to do A, but do not have an over-all obligation to do A, we can identify some other factor present that generally creates obligations just as promises do—for instance, my wife being ill and there being no one but me to take care of her. Now, when there is such a pair— a factor in situations and a universally corresponding obligation except when some other factor is present that normally creates over-all obligations of a kind to conflict with the first one—we shall speak of the factor in the situation as "obligation-creating," and we shall say there is a *prima facie obligation* to do A on account of F, even in situations where there is in fact an over-all obligation to do something that conflicts with doing A.[13]

Very often, if not always, when we have a *prima facie* obligation to do something in a situation but our over-all obligation is to do something conflicting, further future obligations are created. For instance, if I must break a promise, then at least I have a new prima facie obligation to apologize, make amends, and so on.

It is in this sense of "prima facie obligation" that it is correct to say, as we suggested above people do, that there is "an obligation" to do what I promised, or that there is a "stronger obligation" to stay at home.

Prima facie obligations differ from over-all duty in an interesting way, in that there is no over-all duty to do the impossible but there can be a prima facie obligation to do not what is inherently impossible but what cannot be done consistently with meeting all other prima facie obligations. This is a result of what we mean by a "prima facie" obligation—that it is what would be an over-all obligation if there were no conflicting stronger obligations.

---

[13] See W. D. Ross, *The Right and the Good* (Oxford: Clarendon Press, 1930), pp. 19 ff.

Notice that if we are ever in a position to say that we have a prima facie obligation to do A on account of F, we are in a position to say that *always* there is a prima facie obligation to do A on account of F, for any evidence we have against the universal statement counts against our right to speak of a prima facie obligation being present at all.

2. EGOISM: WE ARE OBLIGATED ONLY TO BENEFIT OURSELVES

After our long excursus into the meaning of "moral obligation" and the relevance of the agent's beliefs for his obligations, we turn now to the major theories about our obligations: the egoisms, the utilitarianisms, and formalism. We begin with egoism.

What exactly is the egoist theory in ethics? Egoism, we have seen, is a theory about moral obligations, and it is a form of result theory. But what form? It might be suggested that an egoist is a person who asserts the following general principle: "A person is morally obligated over all to perform an act *A* if and only if performing *A* will produce states of *me* [the egoist speaker] that are of maximum intrinsic worth." (Or, if one likes, "of maximum pleasure.") But this principle is not an ethical principle at all, because it contains a proper name, "me." So, if the reader is convinced that a statement is acceptable as an ethical principle only if it can be formulated without proper names, he need not expend time considering this principle. In any case, one can ask why we should all serve the welfare of some particular person. (Perhaps God could reasonably assert such a principle.) Why not somebody else? Certainly it is not easy to see how a person who defends this principle will go about convincing someone else!

The egoist principle we can take seriously is rather this one: "A person is obligated over all to perform an action *A* if and only if *A* is, among all the actions he can perform, the one that will produce states of himself of maximum intrinsic worth." In this form, the principle contains no proper names. It does not ask everybody to serve some particular person; it proposes, rather, that each of us look out simply for himself. (This will, of course, include one's loved ones; one will seek their welfare as a way of enhancing the happiness of oneself.) The practical implications of the principle naturally differ widely, depending on one's views about what is of intrinsic worth: whether just pleasure, or knowledge, or character, and so forth.[14]

In this form the principle has been rather widely held. Plato, in the *Republic*, seems to assume that one can justify a person's performing an act only if one can show how it is to his advantage to perform it. John Gay, a theological writer of the early eighteenth century, went so far as to urge roughly that it is true by definition, saying that "obligation" simply "is the

---

[14] One must be careful not to adopt a *circular* theory. Suppose one thinks—as some have—that *character* is the only intrinsic good. Then, according to egoist theory, one is to act so as to acquire a character of maximum value. But now, what kind of personality structure is a "character of maximum value"? Suppose one says it is a character *disposed to do one's moral duty*. But what kind of character is this? One's duty is to develop ideal character; but ideal character consists in readiness to do one's duty. Obviously something is wrong with this kind of reasoning. Each of the two basic concepts is defined in terms of the other, and consequently we are given no instruction whatever about what we ought to do.

This kind of circular thinking is to be found at crucial points in the writing of the important nineteenth-century self-realizationist, T. H. Green.

necessity of doing or omitting any action in order to be happy: i.e., when there is such a relation between an Agent and an action that the Agent cannot be happy without doing or omitting that action, then the agent is said to be obliged to do or omit that action."[15] More important, Thomas Hobbes wrote in a famous passage:

> Every man is desirous of what is good for him, and shuns what is evil, but chiefly the chiefest of natural evils, which is death; and this he doth by a certain impulsion of nature, no less than that whereby a stone moves downward. It is therefore neither absurd nor reprehensible, neither against the dictates of true reason, for a man to use all his endeavors to preserve and defend his body and the members thereof from death and sorrows. But that which is not contrary to right reason, that all men account to be done justly, and with right.[16]

If the thesis of egoism is correct, many people have apparently made serious mistakes about their duty. The Roman Regulus, for instance, was a captive of Carthage and was permitted to visit Rome, on his word of honor that he would return. Regulus considered that he must go back to Carthage as he had promised; he did so, and was cruelly put to death. If egoism is correct, it was wrong for Regulus to sacrifice himself. To take a less extreme example, many soldiers in wartime have felt it their duty to volunteer for a mission with an almost certainly fatal outcome. Assuming that they could enjoy years of happiness if they lived, it is not easy to see how an egoist could justify such generous offers. What possible intrinsic value of a personal sort would be realized by this act of sacrifice, which could compare in value with years of happy family life? If a person were already suffering from cancer, then of course matters might be different.

But is egoism true or false? Let us consider the pros and cons.

The egoist thesis may be supported by reasoning quite similar to that of the ethical hedonist: (*a*) by a logical and (*b*) by a psychological argument.

The logical argument is simply the proposal that the thesis is true by definition—as it would be, if John Gay's definition of "moral obligation" were correct. But if the proposal about "moral obligation" urged in the preceding pages is accepted, then egoism is *not* true by definition. The egoist who makes the claim that it is, then, must have a rival definition of his own. What will this be, and will it survive the tests for identity of meaning discussed in Chapter 7? We need not survey possible definitions, if we can convince the reader that he is sometimes definitely ready to *say* either that some act is morally obligatory when he knows it would not serve his welfare, or that at least it is doubtful whether it is obligatory. In either case, the meaning of "morally obligatory," as used by the reader, is not such that to

[15] *Concerning the Fundamental Principle of Virtue or Morality*, first published in 1731, reprinted in part in L. A. Selby-Bigge, *British Moralists*, II (Oxford: Clarendon Press, 1897), p. 273.

[16] Thomas Hobbes, *Philosophical Rudiments Concerning Government*, in F. J. E. Woodbridge (ed.), *Selections* (New York: Charles Scribner's Sons, 1930), pp. 263–64.

say that an act is morally obligatory implies that it will serve his welfare. Whether the discussion of the following pages does convince the reader of this, he himself must decide.

The psychological argument for egoism is somewhat similar to the psychological argument for hedonism. It is convenient to consider two forms it may take. (1) The first argument begins by assuming a psychological thesis very similar to the Pleasure Theory of Goals (pp. 308 ff.). The thesis asserts (like Hobbes, as quoted above) that a person is motivated to produce a certain situation if and only if he believes it will be, or produce, a desirable state of himself; and he will be motivated to produce one situation in preference to another if and only if he believes it will be, or produce, on balance, a more desirable state of himself. Starting from this thesis as a premise, then, it may be argued (assuming a view of "morally obligated" similar to that urged by us), that, since a person is motivated only to produce desirable states of himself, he will hardly "feel obligated" to act, or "demand" that others act, in a way that will conflict with what he thinks is his own welfare. Hence, by our definition he will be obligated only to serve his own welfare.

This reasoning is subject to serious objections. In the first place, what it supports is the illicit "proper name" form of egoism, not egoism proper. We would have a support for egoism proper, only if the psychological theory implied both that one will feel obligated to seek only one's own welfare and that one *will demand of others that they seek their own welfare*. But the psychological theory, as stated, implies that a person will demand of others that they seek *his* own welfare. Another way of putting the matter is to say that the psychological theory implies that no one is ever impartial; so that it becomes speculative to inquire what a person would demand of others, or feel obligated to do himself, if he were impartial. In the second place, the psychological theory is bad psychology, and for reasons approximately identical with those mentioned above (pp. 310 ff.) as objections to the Pleasure Theory of Goals. Of course, the theory is less narrow than the Pleasure Theory of Goals; the goal of conduct is said to be only *some desirable* state of the self, not necessarily a pleasant state. Hence, it is not so obviously discrepant with the facts. But still there are many examples of actual motivation in conflict with the theory: the boy who stood on the burning deck, the secure person who gives handsomely in support of a cause, perhaps even the desire for posthumous fame. (Is posthumous fame a desirable state of oneself?) Ordinarily we distinguish between acts aimed at the agent's welfare and those we think are (perhaps foolishly) intended to enhance the welfare of others. Why should we abolish this distinction?[17] But perhaps the most fatal thrust against the theory is simply to ask what

[17] For a careful examination of the confusions of the theory, see C. D. Broad, "Egoism as a Theory of Human Motives," *Hibbert Journal*, XLVIII (1949–50), 105–14.

kind of observational evidence would, in principle, be accepted as evidence against the theory. Confronted with this demand, the advocate of the egoist thesis in psychology must either admit his view is not an empirical theory in psychology at all, or else he will cite possible kinds of counterevidence —in which case his requested kind of evidence can be cited in abundance.

2. A second psychological argument runs as follows. The first premise is the theory of motivation we have just criticized. It is next pointed out that it follows, from this theory of motivation, that a person *can* (in view of psychological causal laws) act only in such a way as he thinks will promote his own welfare. Now, it is pointed out, nonegoist ethical principles imply that it is sometimes a man's duty to sacrifice his own welfare. Hence, if nonegoist theories are right, it is a man's duty sometimes to do what it has just been shown he *cannot* do. But obviously it is never one's duty to do the *impossible*. Hence, the nonegoist assumption that a man can have a duty to sacrifice his welfare must be mistaken.

This argument is unsound, for other reasons beyond the fact that its psychological premise is unacceptable. First, is it really true that it is never a man's duty to do something if doing it is *impossible only because he does not desire to do it?* This is certainly not obvious. What is obvious is that it is never a man's duty to do something he cannot do no matter how hard he tries. Second, *if* this argument were valid at all, it would prove far more than it claims to do: It would prove that it is not a person's duty to do *anything* he does not do. Whatever a person does, presumably (we shall discuss this in Chapter 20) his action is an instance of some causal law; and we can say that, in the total circumstances, it was causally impossible that he act in a way other than he did. Thus, if it is never a man's duty to do anything he causally cannot do, it cannot be his duty to do anything he in fact does not do. But this is absurd. We happen to know there are many cases of people failing to do their duty.

The logical and psychological supports of egoism, then, break down, just as such arguments for hedonism broke down. However, egoism may nevertheless be true; or at least perhaps its falsity—if it is false—cannot be shown. Do the criticisms of egoism emerge any better than the reasoning in its favor? There are three main reasons worth consideration.[18]

1. It has been argued that egoism is paradoxical. On the one hand, the egoist purports to believe the thesis of egoism. But if he does, then it must be that he is given to preaching it, to promulgating it, for, it is said, "Is not to believe that someone should act in a certain way to try to persuade him to do so? . . . In so far as we believe that Tom should do so-and-so, we

---

[18] G. E. Moore once argued (*Principia Ethica*, pp. 96 ff.) that egoism is self-contradictory, but his reasoning seems plausible only because he implicitly assumed the truth of universalism, as has been shown by C. D. Broad, in P. A. Schilpp (ed.), *The Philosophy of G. E. Moore* (Evanston, Ill.: Northwestern University Press, 1942), pp. 43–57.

have a tendency to induce him to do so-and-so."[19] But, the critic goes on, by his own doctrine the egoist is enjoined not to do anything that will tend to diminish his own welfare. And preaching egoism will diminish the egoist's own welfare, for it will incline others to look after themselves and not after him. Acceptance of egoism, then, both implies that one will preach it, and at the same time that it is one's moral duty not to do so.

The egoist can avoid this pitfall, however, by declining to adopt that thesis of the emotive theory of ethics, to the effect that we cannot believe that someone is obligated to do something unless we stand ready to try to persuade him to act in this way (p. 207). To believe is one thing; to state to try to persuade, is a different thing. The egoist can believe the thesis of egoism, but refuse to state his views publicly on moral grounds, because so doing would diminish his own welfare, just as the argument said it would. (He can, however, state it among friends, among those persons whose welfare is thickly interwoven with his own.) Where is the paradox?

2. It may be argued that egoism gives inconsistent directives, like telling a person both to open and to close the door, at the same time. Suppose two knights are competing for the hand of a beautiful maiden, who likes both equally. Then does not egoism direct the one, implicitly: "Kill your rival and have the maiden for yourself"? And does it not direct the other, implicitly: "Kill your rival and have the maiden for yourself"? But both directives cannot be followed. Therefore egoism is an inconsistent theory.

This objection, however, is mistaken. What egoism says is, "It is one's duty always to do what will in the circumstances maximize one's own welfare." Will the two knights, then, have conflicting duties? Obviously not. If they engage in mortal combat, one of them is logically bound to die, and possibly both will die. The weaker one, the one who will be killed, can then hardly be obligated (by the directive above) to engage in combat. What is his duty? To get the best deal possible in the circumstances. The duty of the stronger one, similarly, will be to get the most satisfactory situation for himself. Possibly, but not likely, his interest will require that he kill his rival. Probably a cooperative compact will best serve the interest of each. Clearly there will be no conflict in directives.[20]

3. The first two objections to egoism miss the mark. The third, however, is fatal, and we must examine it closely.

[19] Brian Medlin, "Ultimate Principles and Ethical Egoism," *Australasian Journal of Philosophy*, XXXV (1957), 111–18.

[20] The subjective obligations of the two knights could be conflicting, for example, if each thought he could defeat the other in battle. But *any* normative principles can yield conflicting directives, if applied on the basis of contradictory factual assumptions.

One might construe egoism in a slightly different way, as holding, "It is a person's objective duty always to do what in the circumstances, and on the evidence available to him, will *probably* maximize his welfare." In this case, egoism might imply conflicting duties for different people. But again, if other theories were so construed, the result would be the same for them.

Part of the "standard test" for ethical principles—part of the "Qualified Attitude Method" for assessing ethical statements—is examining whether they cohere with, are compatible with, our criticized, "qualified" attitudes. In this instance, that of a principle about moral obligation, we have to test the principle against our "qualified" feelings of obligation, our "qualified" demands that other people act in a certain way.

Let us then ask ourselves: What could our *motivation possibly* be like, in order for our "qualified" attitudes to be coherent with the principle of *egoism?* It could not be just selfish: although a selfish man might feel obligated to promote his own interests (or at least not feel obligated not to),[21] he would not be inclined to demand that other people concern themselves only with their own welfare. Nor could it be *purely* benevolent: a purely benevolent person would neither feel obligated simply to promote his own interests, nor demand of others that they be concerned only with their own interests; on the contrary, he would feel obligated to sacrifice his own interests to those of others, and he would demand that others stand ready to sacrifice their interests, when they conflict with more important interests of other people. What kind of motivation, then, must it be? Very peculiar.[22] We must be *partial to agents,* but only with respect to their *own acts.* We must demand that an agent take that course which maximizes his own welfare. Agent A, let us say, is to serve himself when he acts. But we must have no interest in an agent, in relation to the acts of other agents. Agent A is forgotten when Agent B is deliberating. We must approve of Agent A concerning himself only with his own interest; but we must also approve of Agent B ignoring the interests of Agent A altogether. So long as Agent A is agent, *his* interests are the only ones that count; but when Agent A is patient, affected by the acts of others, his interests do not count at all. When Agent A is acting, he can cost another man his life in order to save himself a scratch; but when Agent B is acting, he can cost Agent A his life in order to save himself a scratch. And, of course, our "qualified" attitudes must be the same, if we ourselves happen to be either Agent A or Agent B.

Now, is there really anybody whose attitudes run in this peculiar mold? It is difficult to believe there is. One must ask oneself whether one's attitudes really are what they must be if the egoist principle is to pass inspection. Obviously they are not. Certainly we are concerned about the effects of the acts of others on *us,* and are more than ready to demand that others refrain from acting in ways that will hurt us (especially for only minor advantages to themselves). In general, we are ready to demand that people refrain from doing what will hurt others; and it is only in special circumstances that our

---

[21] Or more likely, as we have explained a "feeling of obligation," a perfectly selfish person would have no such experience at all. See p. 118.

[22] It might be that of a benevolent man who thinks the interests of all are best served, in the long run, if each concerns himself solely with his own interests. In this case, the basic moral principle is utilitarian.

feelings are changed even by the reflection that hurting someone else was necessary in order for the agent to avoid a greater injury to himself. Further, we do feel obligated to avoid injury to other persons, even for the sake of a considerable advantage to ourselves.

One might reply, of course, that if only our attitudes were "qualified," they would conform to the pattern of egoism. However, it is difficult to imagine what reasoning might support such a view.

The egoist theory about moral obligation, then, is mistaken.

3. IS IT REASONABLE TO SACRIFICE PERSONAL INTEREST FOR THE SAKE OF DUTY?

Since egoism is mistaken, it will presumably at least sometimes be our over-all obligation to do something that conflicts with our personal interests. There is a question that one may raise about such instances, a question that almost everyone must have asked himself seriously at one time or another. This question is: "Granted that is my duty, is it *reasonable* for me to do it?" Or, in general, we may ask: "Is it *reasonable* for me to do my duty if it conflicts seriously with my personal welfare?" Perhaps the question is a confused one, but it is a natural one that we cannot ignore.

If the question of whether it is reasonable to sacrifice personal interest for the sake of duty is to be answered, we must decide what the question is. It is not necessary that everybody raise the same question with these words, but unless a given individual fixes on some definite question, he cannot expect an answer. Perhaps such questions are not intellectual questions at all, but expressions of nameless anxieties or hesitations, fundamentally emotional. In this case, there is nothing to be answered, but perhaps something it is well to bring to light.

What might a person mean by, "Is it *reasonable* to choose x in preference to y"? He might mean any of the following: (1) "Would it be logically inconsistent to choose y in preference to x?" (2) "Is preferring x required in order to satisfy my present wishes?" (3) "In the long run, will doing x make me happier than doing y?" (4) "Would the choice of x in preference to y satisfy my reflective preferences better than the reverse?" (5) "Would the choice of x in preference to y satisfy better my preferences as they would be if I were a person who measured up completely to my moral ideals?" Doubtless there are many somewhat similar questions he might be raising.

We cannot consider what is the proper answer to all these questions. But perhaps formulation (4) will strike the reader as being of interest. Let us consider it. Our question, then, is: "Given that doing x is my duty, and that doing some conflicting act y will maximize my personal welfare, will the performance of x instead of y satisfy my reflective preferences better?" There are several things to say.

In the first place, it is clear enough why *society* may demand that we do our duty: Society may be expected to insist on observance of rules, obedience to which will serve the general welfare best. So, irrespective of what is "reasonable" for me, it is reasonable for society to insist that I do my duty. This consideration does not answer our question; but we must bear it in mind.

In the second place, we must also observe that, although avoiding a particular duty might serve personal interest, in the long run the practice of doing what is our duty does not conflict with personal interest but rather serves it. For the most part, doing our duty consists in not taking unfair advantage of other persons, and in giving assistance to those in need, especially to those for whose condition of need we are responsible. A willingness to do these things is the precondition of a happy social relationship; tolerable family life and friendship are not possible without it. We cannot generalize for all persons and all possible situations, but generally a practice of complete fulfillment of one's obligations to family and acquaintances is in the long run more than repaid in satisfaction. It is true that failure to contribute to charities, cutting corners on one's income tax, padding expense accounts, ignoring debts that the creditor cannot well enforce, and so on, may not be costly, at least directly. But such behavior is likely to be duplicated by one's children, in whom one prefers not to see it. Also, the cultivation of wide interests in human beings and in causes that serve human welfare is one of the most reliable sources of satisfaction. On the whole, then, a long-range view of the matter suggests that performance of duty usually does not conflict with personal interest. Thus, our troubling question arises less often than we might at first suppose.

But suppose it does arise; suppose duty requires that I volunteer to undertake a hazardous mission in wartime. Here, there clearly is a conflict with personal interest. Is it reasonable (in our sense above) to volunteer?

It is in a different sense. It is reasonable in the sense that it would have been a prudent choice, at the start of life, to agree to follow all the rules of obligation, provided others would do the same. This would have been a prudent choice, for a system in which everybody followed the rules of duty would (we assume) maximize the general welfare, and hence maximize an individual's *prospects* of welfare. It is true that committing oneself to such a system *might* work out badly for one in the long run; it might turn out that the requirements of the system for a given person (for example, one who is killed on a hazardous mission at an early age) will be so costly that the benefits of participation are not a recompense. But the *chances* are that it will not be so costly; and a prudent man would bind himself to do his duty, whatever it might turn out to be, if others would do likewise. So, doing one's duty is reasonable in the sense that one's prospects for welfare (in view of the fact that many "utility-curves" will be higher in the conformity-to-duty system than in any alternative) are maximized by participating in a system in which one is committed, from the outset of life, to doing one's duty if others do the same.[23]

Still, although it is reasonable in this sense to do one's duty, we must remember that we are not—when faced with a particular decision—trying to decide whether to commit ourselves to a system of living in conformity with rules, when we don't as yet know what the rules will require of us. When we decide to undertake a hazardous mission, we are not making a choice that will probably work out well for our personal interests; we are making one that will in all probability end our lives. Can we say, then, that it will satisfy our "reflective preferences" to choose now, in these circumstances, a course of action that risks almost certain death, that minimizes our prospects of personal welfare? It is not obvious that the answer is affirmative; and if it is negative, then in some cases it *may be* unreasonable, in our selected sense above, to do our duty.

But we must be very careful not to take a misleadingly narrow view of the nature of our "reflective preferences." Reflective preference need not favor our personal interests. Most people, if they had a clear choice to make between their own lives and those of their children, would without hesitation prefer the latter. Such a choice would not serve personal interest in the sense of being a selection of that one, among possible lives for themselves, of maximum intrinsic value. It might be a selection of a life, for themselves, of minimum intrinsic value. But of the *total* possibilities among which choice must be made, it might still be the choice of reflective preferences.

Some people value the welfare of sentient creatures generally, value justice and a social system in which the rights of all are recognized, and so on, much as most parents value the lives and well-being of their children. Consequently, if they had to choose between these things and their own welfare, they would prefer the former. They prefer a combination of low welfare for themselves plus a just social system to a combination of high welfare for themselves plus an unjust social system. Not, of course, that they prefer low welfare for themselves to a high degree of welfare for themselves, just for its own sake; but if the combinations between which choice must be made are as stated, then they prefer the combination containing the low level value for themselves. Where this is true, then, it is "reasonable" for them, in our selected sense of "reasonable," to put duty ahead of personal welfare.

If this analysis of the problem is correct, it is not possible, on the evidence available, to give one answer, suitable for everybody, to the question whether it is "reasonable" to do one's duty when it conflicts with personal interest. The correct answer may vary from one person to another. It depends on what kind of person one is, what one cares about. For a com-

---

[23] I am indebted to Dr. Michael Scriven for this way of thinking about the matter. Essentially the same concept occurred in an earlier context, as part of the reason for testing ethical judgments by the Qualified Attitude Method, p. 263.

pletely selfish man, dutiful choices that conflict with personal interest will not be reasonable; for a generous and sympathetic man, they very often will be.

It is, of course, no defense of one's failure to do one's duty, before others or society, to say that doing so is not "reasonable" for one in this sense. The act would not be one's *duty*, if feeling obligated to do it—and others demanding that one do it—were not *justified*. Thus, although it may not be "reasonable" for the agent to do his duty in this sense, it *is* "reasonable" for society to compel him to do it, or to punish or condemn him if he fails.

FURTHER READING

On the meaning of "moral obligation":

W. D. Ross, *The Right and the Good* (Oxford: Clarendon Press, 1930), chap. 1.
A. C. Ewing, *The Definition of Good* (New York: The Macmillan Company, 1947), chaps. 4–5.
G. E. Moore, in P. Schilpp (ed.) *The Philosophy of G. E. Moore* (Evanston, Ill.: Northwestern University Press, 1942), pp. 597–601.
———, *Principia Ethica* (Cambridge, Eng.: Cambridge University Press, 1929), pp. 23–27, 146–48, 152–54, 167–70.
H. Sidgwick, *The Methods of Ethics* (London: Macmillan & Co., Ltd., 1922), Bk. I, chaps. 3, 9.
P. Nowell-Smith, *Ethics* (Baltimore: Penguin Books, Inc., 1954), chaps. 13–16, pp. 306–14.
R. M. Hare, *The Language of Morals* (Oxford: Clarendon Press, 1952), chaps. 10, 12.
C. L. Stevenson, *Ethics and Language* (New Haven: Yale University Press, 1944), pp. 97 ff.
H. A. Prichard, *Moral Obligation* (Oxford: Clarendon Press, 1949, chap. 5, sects. 1, 2, 6, 7.
W. D. Falk, " 'Ought' and Motivation," in W. Sellars and J. Hospers, *Readings in Ethical Theory* (New York: Appleton-Century-Crofts, Inc., 1952).
W. K. Frankena, "Obligation and Motivation in Recent Moral Philosophy," in A. I. Melden (ed.), *Essays in Moral Philosophy* (Seattle: University of Washington Press, 1958).
H. L. A. Hart, "Legal and Moral Obligation," in A. I. Melden (ed.), *Essays in Moral Philosophy*.
Sesonske, Alexander, *Value and Obligation*, University of California Publications in Philosophy (Berkeley: University of California Press, 1957), XXXI, No. 1, pp. 1–124.

On the sense of "duty" and "obligation":

H. A. Prichard, *Moral Obligation*, chap. 2.
A. C. Ewing, *The Definition of Good*, pp. 118–44.
E. F. Carritt, *Ethical and Political Thinking* (Oxford: Clarendon Press, 1947), pp. 14–27.
W. D. Ross, *Foundations of Ethics* (Oxford: Clarendon Press, 1939), chap. 7.
G. E. Moore, *Ethics* (Oxford: Oxford University Press, 1949), chap. 5.
W. J. Rees, "The General Nature of a Moral Duty," *Philosophy*, XXVIII (1953), 41–57.

K. Baier, "Doing my Duty," *Philosophy*, XXVII (1952), 253–60.
H. Nystedt, "The Problem of Duty and Knowledge," *Philosophy*, XXVI (1951), 333–46.
H. D. Lewis, "Obedience to Conscience," *Mind*, LIV (1945), 227–53.
W. K. Frankena, "Obligation and Ability," in M. Black (ed.), *Philosophical Analysis* (Ithaca: Cornell University Press, 1950).

On egoism:

C. D. Broad, *Five Types of Ethical Theory*, pp. 161–77.
———, P. Schilpp (ed.), *The Philosophy of G. E. Moore* (Evanston, Ill.: Northwestern University Press, 1942), pp. 43–57.
G. E. Moore, *Principia Ethica*, sect. 58–65.
F. C. Sharp, *Ethics* (New York: Appleton-Century-Crofts, Inc., 1928), chaps. 22, 23.
H. Rashdall, *Theory of Good and Evil* (Oxford: Oxford University Press, 1924), vol. I, pp. 44–63.
A. C. Ewing, *Ethics* (London: English Universities Press, 1953), chap. 2.
J. A. Brunton, "Egoism and Morality," *Philosophical Quarterly*, VI (1956), 289–303.
B. Medlin, "Ultimate Principles and Ethical Egoism," *Australasian Journal of Philosophy*, XXXV (1957), 111–18.

15

Moral Obligation and General Welfare

The most important problem of normative ethics now faces us: a choice among the major theories about when we are morally obligated to do something—among the result theories (excluding the egoisms) and the formalist theories. The central problem (but not the only one) to be solved is that of the exact relevance of general welfare for moral obligation.

If we look at the concrete teaching about moral obligation common in our society, we get the impression that the general welfare is at best only of secondary relevance for obligation. The Ten Commandments do not mention it explicitly (nor does the Golden Rule, although it is closer). Rather, they tell us not to worship (or build) "graven images," to keep the Sabbath day holy, to honor our fathers and mothers, not to kill or steal or commit adultery or bear false witness or covet anything belonging to our neighbors. Similarly, the advice we give our children is at least partly in the form of rather specific directives or prohibitions, which do not mention general welfare—for example, "Don't ask people personal questions"; "Don't take another person's property"; "Always tell the truth except. . . ."

Are specific principles like these the ultimate principles of obligation or duty? Or, is it true, as some hold, that there is only one true principle about duty—such as that we ought to act so as to maximize welfare?

1. ACT-UTILITARIANISM: ITS FORCE AND PROBLEMS

The simplest answer to these questions is that of two kinds of utilitarian theory: hedonistic utilitarianism and ideal utilitarianism. These two forms of universal result theory (see the table on p. 356) we shall group together under the title of "act-utilitarianism." What they have in common is roughly the view that it is an agent's duty (in the objective sense) to perform a specific act on a specific occasion if and only if so doing will (actually or probably) produce a state of conscious beings that is of maximum intrinsic worth, as compared with what would have been produced by other acts the agent could have performed instead. The two types differ between themselves about what states of conscious beings are intrinsically desirable: the hedonist holds that only states of pleasure are so, whereas the ideal utilitarian holds that other states of conscious beings are also intrinsically worthwhile, as we have seen in earlier chapters. We shall ignore this difference in the present chapter.[1]

We begin with an examination of act-utilitarianism. The first thing we must do is state the theory precisely. To do this may seem simple, but unfortunately there is a problem we must face. Roughly, the problem is as follows: Shall we construe the act-utilitarian theory as saying (*a*) that a person's (objective) duty is to perform that act whose performance will *actually* produce a state of conscious beings of maximum intrinsic worth, as compared with what would in fact be produced by other actions he could perform instead? Or, (*b*) is he saying that a person's (objective) duty is to perform that act whose performance will, roughly, *on the available evidence probably* produce a state of conscious beings of maximum intrinsic worth (and so on as before)? Consider an example. Suppose a surgeon is weighing whether to perform a certain operation on a patient's heart. The basic known facts are that a successful operation will work a complete cure, whereas without the operation the patient must be permanently confined to bed; but the operation is a dangerous one, the mortality rate being 60 per cent. Now, is the act-utilitarian saying that the surgeon's (objective) duty is to perform the operation if and only if *in fact* so doing will produce the best results (namely, if and only if the patient will in fact survive)? Or, is he saying that the surgeon's (objective) duty is to perform the operation if and only if so doing is the "best bet," has the "best promise," has the highest "product" of probability $\times$ value? Or, to use a phrase we shall employ, if and only if operating has *maximal net expectable utility?*

There would be a gain in consistency and neatness if we interpreted it in the former way.[2] But there is a considerable advantage in construing the

---

[1] One might urge that it would be more consistent to count "universalist impersonal pluralism" as a form of utilitarianism. It is more illuminating, however, to treat it separately, in connection with formalism. Its spirit is closer to formalism than to the other universalist theories.

Some writers use "utilitarian" to mean more specifically "hedonistic utilitarian." The reader should be alert to such specialized uses. Many "refutations" of utilitarianisms are aimed at the hedonistic features, and do not touch the utilitarianism at all.

[2] Given the way in which we have explained "objective duty," it is more consistent, since we are construing utilitarianism as a theory about what our objective duty is, to interpret it in the *former* way. The reason why is complex, and we shall omit statement of it here. We interpret it in the second way mainly because so doing provides a better model of a reasonable way to decide what is one's duty (or probably one's duty), for readers who may be attracted by utilitarianism.

This decision makes no difference, however, to our appraisal of the theory. The arguments adduced in criticism of the theory are effective in whichever way we interpret it, although sometimes minor adjustments need to be made (usually simply theory in the second way. Partly the gain is pragmatic: in that our discussion will better illumine the reasoning we all have to perform in life. Partly the gain is in historical truth, for we shall be assessing a theory closer to what the great utilitarians, such as Bentham, actually held. We shall, therefore, construe the theory in the *second* way.

Let us then state the thesis of act-utilitarianism as follows: "If doing A has, among all the things X can do, the maximum net expectable utility, then it is X's objective duty to do A."

But what exactly is "maximum net expectable utility"? How shall we, in principle, decide that doing a particular A has maximum net expectable utility? To give the proposed formulation of the utilitarian thesis definite content, we must explain this.

We can limit our explanation to a definition of what it means to say that doing A has "greater net expectable utility" than has doing B, since "maximum" merely means "greater than that of any other course of action."

In order to determine which has "greater net expectable utility" (and the procedure for determining this may be taken as defining the meaning of the phrase), the first thing to do is consider the things that, on the basis of available evidence, have more than a negligible probability of happening if A is done, and which are different from what probably will happen if B is done. All the things that will in all probability be the same, whatever we do, may be ignored; so, although what we do now may have important repercussions a thousand years from now—like the statements of Jesus, or the writings of Plato and Aristotle—the probability now that such things will occur is negligible. So we consider, then, two sets of things: events likely to happen (with the estimated probabilities attached) if A but not B is done, and events likely to happen if B but not A is done. This gives us a view of what difference it makes which course of action is taken.

Let us call one set "the expectable consequences of A" and the other set the "expectable consequences of B." How, then, do we decide which has the greater net expectable utility? Fortunately, this question has already been answered in Chapter 13. That set of consequences (with probabilities attached) has greater net expectable utility which is *better*, that is, which would be the object of a justified preference. (See pp. 346–50). There can be a justified preference, we have already noted, not only for one situation over another, but for one situation with a probability attached, over another situation with another probability attached. Whichever set of ex-

---

striking the word "expectable" from the phrase "net expectable utility") in order for the reasoning to be equally effective against the theory, as construed in the first sense.

When we come to "rule-utilitarianism" later in the chapter, we shall construe it in a parallel way. There too, we have a choice. One could decide differently, and the arguments used in appraisal of the theory would be equally effective.

Incidentally, we could have defined "egoism" in this second way, but our objection to it would still have been fatal.

pectable consequences has the capacity of eliciting such justified preference, we shall say has "greater net expectable utility." Whether one set of consequences has a greater net expectable utility than another, then, is a matter of fact about which a person can have a correct or incorrect opinion.[3]

The utilitarian must concede that it may be no easy matter to decide which act has maximum net expectable utility, that is, which one from the sets of states of conscious organisms that would result from different possible actions (and ignoring questions of distribution, that is, which conscious organisms were affected) is best, that is, would be justifiably preferred.[4] In order to be as accurate as possible in one's estimate of which act has maximum net expectable utility, one will naturally use all the devices of matching, and the other principles formulated at the end of Chapter 13. The hedonist, of course, because he holds that only states of pleasure are of intrinsic worth, can say that for him the problem is somewhat simplified, since a preference for one state can be justified on the basis of an examination of the intensities and durations of pleasure-effects alone. But the hedonist—and this point is an important one—cannot regard the problem of determining maximum net expectable utility as simply one of deciding which course of action will produce *most pleasure* and viewing this course as one's obligation. He must concede that the problem is one of balancing one set of pleasures with certain probabilities attached against another set of pleasures with different probabilities, so that, except in

---

[3] There is a necessary reservation about the use of the phrase "have a correct opinion." If we are relativists, the possibility is open that a course of action will be correctly said to have greater net expectable utility by one person, and less (than some alternative) by another person.

It may be suggested that the existence of a "correct" opinion is further compromised by the fact that probability is always relative to the available evidence. But at the time when a decision must be made, the "evidence available" will be approximately the same for any person involved; and we shall assume that there is, therefore, a fixed base of "evidence" for probability determinations, and hence that the probabilities correctly assigned any event in a given set will be determinate, for a given problem. If it is questioned whether probabilities can be assigned in an objective manner, then matters are not greatly altered; for now the choice is simply between sets of consequences, not now with a definite probability assigned each member of the set, but with a certain specifiable piece of evidence as the ground for expectation of each member of the set. In principle, there is still no question except that of what preferences are justified; indeed, this manner of stating the problem probably is closer to life—since no one ordinarily does us the favor of working out the probabilities of the members of the sets between which we choose, and we make the choices on the basis of rough familiarity with the favorable and unfavorable evidence.

The critical reader may wonder whether these qualifications do not go a long way toward erasing the difference between what is a person's "objective" duty and what is his "subjective" duty. And, of course, this is correct. But there is still a difference between the act which *has* maximum expectable net utility and the one the agent *thinks* has maximum net expectable utility.

[4] It is assumed that the choice is made between sets of experiences, ignoring who has the experiences, and thus ignoring questions of one distribution of enjoyments being better than another. If this assumption is not made, the distinction between the utilitarian theories and universal impersonal pluralism is erased.

special cases, ability to compare situations for "greater pleasure" will not solve the relevant problem, and he must, like nonhedonists, appeal to preferences for a decision as to which action has maximum net expectable utility.

The foregoing complications in the utilitarian thesis are unfortunate but necessary. It is important to see that they *are* necessary. Many people have been attracted by the utilitarian thesis because they supposed that, once general decisions about what general kinds of thing are intrinsically worthwhile have been made, the utilitarian can leave the job of deciding what is one's duty to empirical science. But this is mistaken, at least for all those cases in which the intrinsic values of sets of consequences have to be balanced against probabilities of getting them. In the cases where such comparisons are required, it is not easy to see how the utilitarian's procedure for determining one's duty is in any respect simpler than that of nonutilitarians.

So much, then, by way of explanation of the utilitarian thesis that it is always a person's duty to do *A*, if and only if doing *A* has, among all the things he can do, the maximum net expectable utility.

The utilitarian naturally thinks we must take into account the less obvious as well as the more obvious consequences. Suppose, for instance, Mr. X asks me whether I know the size of Mr. Y's salary, which I do. It would be an unfair caricature of utilitarianism to suppose it is committed to holding that it is my duty to lie, in view of the embarrassment that will arise if I admit I do know, but then have to explain that I prefer not to publicize my information. One of the utilities to be considered is that of mutual forthrightness among human beings. Another is the effect of a lie on my habits, the building up of a habit of taking the easy way. In general it is probably not often that the utilitarian formula implies that a lie is one's duty.

Does the utilitarian formula leave any place for moral maxims like "Keep your promises" and "Always tell the truth"? Yes, these maxims can be regarded as directives that for the most part point out what is a person's duty. They are rules of thumb. They are properly taught to children and used by everybody as a rough timesaving guide for ordinary decisions. Moreover, since we are all prone to rationalizing in our own favor, they are apt to be a better guide to our duty in complex cases than is our on-the-spot reflection. However, we are not to be enslaved to them. When there is good ground for thinking the maximum net expectable utility will be produced by an act that violates them, then we should depart from them. Such a rule is to be disregarded without hesitation, when it clearly conflicts with the general welfare.

It is far from the truth, however, that the utilitarian need regard *all* generally accepted moral maxims as having this status. He may regard some of them as simply mistaken. Utilitarians can, of course, disagree among themselves about which ones are mistaken, but traditional rules about marriage and divorce, sexual relations, and birth control and euthanasia, are among those apt to arouse suspicion in the utilitarian. Hedonistic utilitarians generally are more prone to question these rules than are the ideal utilitarians. Some ideal utilitarians (for example, Hastings Rashdall) think that qualities of character like veracity, sexual purity, and temperance have great intrinsic value on their own account. Naturally, they urge the corresponding moral rules with more conviction than a hedonist is apt to feel.

Incidentally, as the utilitarian Henry Sidgwick argued in detail, the utilitarian formula implies that people should sometimes publicly urge universal obedience to moral rules other than the utilitarian formula. Why? The basic point is that most people are not only prone to rationalize but are rather clumsy at abstract thought. Thus, a given individual's greatest contribution to realizing maximum net expectable utility may be to get others to follow simple rules in their moral thinking. Indeed, since it is a moral question whether one is to calculate one's duty by thinking a problem through in accordance with the utilitarian formula, or merely following some simple moral rule, the utilitarian formula presumably tells us that the answer to the question, "Is it my duty in this case to calculate or to follow a moral rule?" is sometimes that it is one's duty *not* to calculate.[5]

Now that we have explained what the act-utilitarian thesis is, we must assess it.

How shall we decide whether the act-utilitarian thesis is true? Since the thesis is a universal normative statement, we must see whether there are exceptions, or probable exceptions to it. If there are, then it is false—although it might be more nearly true than any one of the other major theories. Or contrariwise, we may find reasons for supposing that there are no exceptions to it. Finding exceptions to it, of course, presupposes that we have some method for determining what our duty is, aside from relying on the utilitarian formula. And we do. As we have seen, every statement of obligation must be tested against our "qualified" feelings of obligation or inclinations to demand certain behavior of all persons. It must be tested by whether it fits in with a system of consistent principles of duty, of universal form, which are coherent with our feelings of obligation and inclinations to make demands on others, as they are when we are fully informed, impartial, and in a normal frame of mind. So our question, roughly, is this: Are the acts that we must view as our obligation or duty, as a result of a process of thinking of this sort, identical with the ones that the thesis of utilitarianism asserts are our duty? Let us look at some pros and cons. We begin with points favorable to utilitarianism.

1. The most impressive line of reasoning is this. Many people have asked themselves: "How can it possibly be my duty to do something less than the most good I can do? How can it be wrong to do the greatest amount

[5] But see A. Duncan-Jones, "Utilitarianism and Rules," *Philosophical Quarterly*, VII (1957), 364–67.

of good?" They have gone on in similar vein: "A person *explains* why he has a duty to do something if he shows that it is necessary in order to maximize the welfare of sentient beings. The utilitarian's thesis about duty, then, is an intelligible one. The nonutilitarian, however, has a bundle of rules about duty for which he can give no such explanation. And isn't one being just a slave to traditional rules if one doesn't demand that the rules be supported by showing their connection with welfare? Nonutilitarians are surely thoughtless worshipers of traditional rules."

This reasoning has force. It is doubtful whether we think any action is wrong if *nobody's* welfare is in any way adversely affected by it. Moreover, "qualified" feelings of obligation or of demand on others might surely be expected to be influenced by whether or not an action will cause harm— and perhaps by nothing else?

The point is sufficiently serious that we shall not try to assess it at the present stage. Rule-Utilitarianism has been in good part inspired by desire to formulate a near-formalist system that is not open, at least not as much, to this objection.

2. The second line of support for the utilitarian thesis is simply the question, "What is your alternative?" Obviously the alternative, if we ignore the possibility of rule-utilitarianism for the present, must be a *set* of rules, probably including a rule about doing good where one can. But what will these rules be like? Moreover, if there are several rules, the set must provide directions as to what we are to do when two rules conflict, for example, if "Your duty is always to tell the truth" conflicts with "Your duty is always to keep your promises." Evidently, the set must contain higher-order rules, telling us what to do if the lower-order rules conflict; and perhaps third-order rules telling what to do if the second-order rules conflict; and so on up. One would like to see some plausible concrete proposals for such a set of rules.

Leaving aside the complications of higher-order rules, do we really know any nonutilitarian first-order rules that we can take seriously? No matter how such rules are framed, they seem objectionable. Take, for instance, "It is your prima facie duty (namely, duty when no stronger moral consideration overrides) to tell the truth." But do we really believe this rule? Suppose I am talking with a shrewd real-estate dealer about the purchase of a piece of property. He asks me to name a figure that is the highest I am prepared to offer, but expecting all the time that I shall only be making a *bargaining* offer, being willing to make some further concession if the seller makes one. Am I then bound prima facie to speak the truth? Or, if someone asks me a personal question, and I think of a way of giving a literally true answer, which, however, will lead him to infer something that is false, is there a prima facie obligation to avoid leading him into such inferences?

Much the same questions could be raised about the rule, "It is your prima facie obligation to keep your promises." Is this rule as stated to be applied to promises made under duress? Or promises made in a joking vein? Or promises made to a person who, since you made promises to him, has ignored his promises made to you? Or promises made on a mistaken assumption—for instance, if I promise to give $10,000 to a college for a certain purpose but, before the money is paid, a gift from another donor is announced, for the same purpose, and in the sum of $10,000,000, a sum sufficient to realize completely the goal I had in mind?

Suppose we have to agree that few, if any, nonutilitarian principles have been stated—much less a complete set of them, with higher-order rules giving directions for conflicts between the other rules—with all the qualifications and exceptions we think are necessary. Does this fact not destroy the case of the nonutilitarians, by showing that their own positive view does not even admit of being stated? This argument, again, has weight, and we postpone attempting to assess it.

Let us now look at the other side of the situation, at the problems of act-utilitarianism. The main, but not the only, difficulty is that act-utilitarianism has erroneous implications about what is obligatory. Let us consider some examples.

1. Let us suppose that Mr. X is considering whether it is his duty to hasten his father's death. Let us suppose further that Mr. X's father is well-to-do, whereas the son is poor. The father gives the son no money, and the son and his family are continually missing the joys of life because they do not have the means to pay for them. Furthermore, the father is ill and requires nursing care. The cost of nursing care is rapidly eating into the father's capital. Moreover, the father himself gets no joy from life. He must take drugs to make life tolerable, and his physician says that his condition will gradually become worse, although death is still several years away.

On the utilitarian theory, it can well be (and on the hedonistic form, certainly will be) the son's duty to bring about the demise of his father, provided he can do this so that his deed will be undetected (thereby avoiding legal calamities for himself and his family, and not weakening the general confidence of fathers in their sons). But would this in fact be his duty? It does not seem so. We may perhaps hesitate to say that the father would be wrong in ending his own life, and conceivably some will say it is his duty to do so; but it is doubtful if anybody will say that the son's duty is to take the matter into his own hands as soon as it becomes clear that the public (primarily his own) welfare will be served by so doing.[6]

2. Suppose a widow with a ten-year-old daughter has been supporting herself and her child by her earnings as a teacher. However, her earnings are so low that she is not able to purchase adequate life insurance or save against the future. Let us suppose further that she has no near relatives, has

---

[6] The act-utilitarian can consistently say we should *condemn* such an act, if it is detected, as a means of promoting the security of fathers.

recently moved into a large community, and that you and your family, her neighbors, are her only friends. Now suppose she is suddenly taken ill, and it is immediately clear that her illness will be fatal. She asks you if you will see to the care of her daughter, so that she will not have to go to an institution. Wisely or unwisely, you promise you will do so. The question then is: Does the making of such a promise affect your obligation to act more than utilitarian theory permits? Does the making of such a promise create a prima facie (p. 367) obligation toward the child, whereas the act-utilitarian theory implies that it does not?

Most people, if not all persons, will agree that the making of the promise does create a prima facie obligation. Further, they will feel that it imposes a stronger obligation to provide for the girl than there is to care for other persons similarly circumstanced whom one has not promised to care for.

In contrast, the act-utilitarian formula holds that the promise is of weight only if and insofar as the fact of having made it affects the relative expectable utilities of various courses of action. If it so happens that the fact of having made the promise does not affect the relative expectable utilities (for example, if no one knows about the promise, and hence will not be disappointed by failure to keep it), then the promise is of no moral effect whatever. Consequently, because sometimes it will not be of *any* weight for this reason, the act-utilitarian cannot say that there is a prima facie obligation to keep promises (that is, can't say it is *always* one's duty to keep them, when there is no conflicting prima facie obligation).

There are many parallel difficulties for the act-utilitarian. We think we have strong prima facie obligations to our children, our parents, and our wives, that we do not have to others, and that derive from the special relation in which we stand to them. We think that, if we have accidently caused the injury of another person, we have a prima facie obligation to be solicitous, to send flowers, and so on, which we would not have if we merely read about the injury in the newspaper. Or, if a friend has done us the favor of reading and criticizing the manuscript of our book, we think we have a prima facie obligation to read and criticize the manuscript of his book, which we do not have toward others, even if we think the manuscripts of others would interest or profit us more. Furthermore, in all these cases, it is plausible to conclude not merely that we think we have these prima facie obligations, but that we really do have them—and that our duty is, therefore, affected by more things than net expectable utility.

What is the utilitarian answer to these considerations? One thing act-utilitarians do is to argue that there is no discrepancy between actual obligation and the implications of their theory when remoter consequences are taken into account. But just what *will* be the disastrous consequences of ignoring your promise to the widow? The act-utilitarian is apt to say to this: "Don't forget the effect on your own character, the increased tendency to take promises less seriously." But he does not want us, surely, to develop a habit of undiscriminating concern to keep our promises. On his theory, such a habit will lead us to neglect our duty. What we must learn is a habit of keeping those promises that on the act-utilitarian principle we ought to keep. (He can say, of course, that stupid people had better be urged to keep *all* promises, for otherwise they may neglect ones they ought to keep on utilitarian grounds.) The ideal utilitarian sometimes argues that we should keep our promises because this builds our own characters, thereby realizing the intrinsically valuable quality of fidelity. But *is* undiscriminating fidelity of intrinsic worth? Would it not be much better to develop the trait of keeping faithfully those promises it is right to keep, and not those it is wrong to keep?

In general, then, it seems that W. D. Ross, a leading critic of utilitarianism, is well justified in the following comment.

> The essential defect of the "ideal utilitarian" theory is that it ignores, or at least does not do full justice to, the highly personal character of duty. If the only duty is to produce the maximum of good, the question who is to have the good—whether it is myself, or my benefactor, or a person to whom I have made a promise to confer that good on him, or a mere fellow man to whom I stand in no such special relation—should make no difference to my having a duty to produce that good. But we are all in fact sure that it makes a vast difference.[7]

3. The act-utilitarian thesis is in conflict with the fact that we have certain obligations connected with social and economic justice. The matter is a complex one, and we cannot examine the problems carefully until Chapter 16. But it may be convincing to observe now that many people have thought that, if a divine being had the power to guide the distribution of joy in the world, he should distribute it equally (or perhaps compensate for the past, to virtuous people who have sacrificed themselves for the public good), and not arbitrarily favor individuals whom he happened to fancy—and this even if his playing favorites did not diminish the total amount of welfare in the world. On this question, however, the act-utilitarian must say that any distribution is equally satisfactory, as long as the total amount of joy is undiminished. Again, many people have thought that if a man had a family of four, but could increase the total amount of welfare by increasing it to eight, albeit at severe cost to the average welfare of the initial four, it would obviously be immoral for him to have a larger family. However, the act-utilitarian must say that any act that maximized the total welfare is one's duty.

4. Suppose that, in wartime England, people are requested, as a measure essential for the war effort, to conserve electricity and gas by having a maximum temperature of 50 degrees F. in their homes. A utilitarian Frenchman living in England at the time, however, argues as follows: "All the good moral British obviously will pay scrupulous attention to conforming

[7] *The Right and the Good* (Oxford: Clarendon Press, 1930), p. 22.

with this request. The war effort is sure not to suffer from a shortage of electricity and gas. Now, it will make no difference to the war effort whether I personally use a bit more gas, but it will make a great deal of difference to my comfort. So, since the public welfare will be maximized by my using gas to keep the temperature up to 70 degrees F. in my home, it is my duty to use the gas."

According to the act-utilitarian theory, this argument is perfectly valid. But we should not take it seriously in fact. Why not? At least part of the reason is that we think that, if a sacrifice has to be made for the public good, all should share in it equally. Imagine the outcry in Britain, if it became known that members of the Cabinet, who knew that electricity and gas were in good supply because of the country's willingness to sacrifice, used this argument to justify using whatever power was necessary to keep their homes comfortable.

5. The foregoing example discloses a further difficulty. *Every* Englishman can also argue that what he personally does will in all probability have a negligible effect on the war effort; and therefore, by the utilitarian principle, any substantial benefit from self-indulgent behavior will justify it. It is true that losing the war must be judged an enormous calamity that cannot be risked; if the chance were one in ten million that the war would be lost by one's self-indulgence, one should not take the risk. But this is not the case; if other people decide on self-indulgence, too, and the war is lost on that account, one will still conclude that it would have made no difference if one had abstained oneself. But, if *everybody* follows this act-utilitarian reasoning, the war will be lost, with disastrous effects for everybody. Thus, universal obedience of the act-utilitarian directive to seek the public good may well cause great public harm. The point may be put in a general way. Suppose there is some kind of behavior (for example, truthfulness) the practice of which by the vast majority of people is highly valuable although deviation by occasional individuals may have good effects, on balance. The act-utilitarian thesis justifies any individual in deviating from this practice whenever the net expectable utility of *his* deviation exceeds that of *his* conformity.

Suppose everyone followed the act-utilitarian principle in behavior. This would mean that every time one answered a question, even under oath, one must think it one's duty to answer falsely if one thinks so doing will serve the public (including one's own) good. It would mean that when one has contracted to do something and the time has arrived for performance, one must raise the question of whether performance will really have maximum net expectable utility, everything considered. It would mean that when one's parents fall ill and are in need of assistance, one must think one ought not to help them if the net expectable utility of so doing is less than the net expectable utility of spending one's money and time in some other way.

But if people really thought and acted in this way, no one could have assurance about what might happen on important occasions in the future. Institutions would be undermined. (Take marriage: A man would feel it his duty to commit adultery, if the net expectable utility—assuming it could be kept secret—would exceed that of refraining!) A great number of people, if not everyone, would feel insecure.

If the act-utilitarian, then, criticizes the formalist on the ground that the formalist cannot explain *why* we should do certain things like keep promises, and so on, when doing so does more harm than good, one reply the formalist might make is that at least the practice of following his principles will secure the long-range public good, whereas the practice of everybody following the act-utilitarian principle will lead to harm and injustice. Our "qualified" attitudes will hardly be comfortable with these implications of the thesis of act-utilitarianism.[8]

2. THE FORMALIST THEORY STATED

Formalist theories have in common (this is true by definition of "formalism") opposition to act-utilitarianism; they all make some assertion about duty or obligation in conflict with the thesis of act-utilitarianism. Whether an act is right or wrong, they say, is not determined solely by its relative net expectable utility, although this may be acknowledged to be one thing about it that is relevant to its rightness. Positively, formalist theories assert some general principles, different from the act-utilitarian principle, about what acts are right or wrong. As a result, formalist theories assert that there

[8] The act-utilitarian is apt to reply to the foregoing by an invalid argument. He will say that the person who uses the reasoning above to justify using gas and electricity is reasoning very badly. He is ignoring the risk that others may do likewise. There is a chance, say, one in a million, that many others will decide as he does, and if so the war will be lost, and he will, along with the million others, have the responsibility for that. He will be responsible for about a millionth of the calamity of losing the war. Considering this risk and the size of the calamity, the net expectable disutility of using the gas will be very large; and hence he will not use it. (And, it is concluded, the act-utilitarian principle is not responsible for unintelligent application of it; if the principle is used intelligently, it will *not* lead to bad consequences.)

The trouble with this argument is that, if the million others decide to use the gas, it makes no difference what I do. The war will be lost anyway.

Act-utilitarians are apt to forget that their principle is not, "It is your duty to do that act, the decision to do which by *everyone* in your situation would maximize the total net expectable utility, as compared with a different decision by *everybody*," but "It is your duty to do that act whose performance by *you* will maximize net expectable utility." (This second principle does not violate the proscription of proper names, since we can replace "your" and "you" by "anyone's" and "his.") There are very different.

For a detailed discussion of the difficulty, see R. F. Harrod, "Utilitarianism Revised," *Mind*, XLV (1936), 137–56; Jonathan Harrison, "Utilitarianism, Universalisation and Our Duty to be Just," *Proceedings*, The Aristotelian Society, 1952–53, pp. 105–34; A. C. Ewing, "Suppose Everybody Acted Like Me," *Philosophy*, XXVIII (1953), 16–29; J. J. C. Smart, "Extreme and Restricted Utilitarianism," *Philosophical Quarterly*, VI (1956), 344–54.

are several basic principles about obligation, whereas act-utilitarianism thinks there is only one.

An early but sophisticated formalist theory was proposed by Bishop Joseph Butler (1692–1752), who wrote as follows:

> Benevolence, and the want of it, singly considered, are in no sort the whole of virtue and vice. For if this were the case, . . . our moral sense would be indifferent to everything, neither approve of benevolence to some persons rather than to others, nor disapprove injustice and falsehood upon any other account, than merely as an overbalance of happiness was foreseen likely to be produced by the first, and of misery by the second. But now, on the contrary . . . suppose one man should, by fraud or violence, take from another the fruit of his labour, with intent to give it to a third, who he thought would have as much pleasure from it as would balance the pleasure which the first possessor would have had in the enjoyment, and his vexation in the loss of it; suppose, also, that no bad consequences would follow; yet such an action would surely be vicious. . . . The fact then appears to be, that we are constituted so as to condemn falsehood, unprovoked violence, injustice, and to approve of benevolence to some preferably to others, abstracted from all consideration, which conduct is likeliest to produce an overbalance of happiness or misery.[9]

Formalists prior to the present century did not provide a precise or comprehensive statement of the substantive principles about obligation. Nor did they put forward a precise theory about what is one's over-all obligation in case the basic principles give conflicting advice for a given situation. We shall do well, then, if we wish to examine a well-developed and plausible alternative to a result theory, to concentrate attention on contemporary formalism and in particular on the most convincing of twentieth century formalist theories, that of W. D. Ross, for many years the Provost of Oriel College, Oxford.

A major part of Ross's theory is the assertion of a list of *prima facie obligations* (in the sense defined above, p. 367). These are as follows: (1) There is an obligation of fidelity, that is, of keeping our promises or engagements. (Ross thinks the obligation to tell the truth is a case of this, since when one enters into a conversation there is an implicit promise to speak the truth.) (2) There is an obligation to make reparation to people for any injury we may wrongfully have caused them. (3) There is an obligation to render services to others in return for services rendered us by them. (4) There is an obligation to assist and not prevent a distribution of happiness in accordance with merit. (5) There is an obligation to do whatever good we can for others, to make the condition of other persons better in respect of virtue, intelligence, and pleasure. (6) There is also an obligation to improve ourselves, to "improve our own condition in respect

---

9 *Dissertation upon Virtue*, 1736, reprinted in A. Selby-Bigge (ed.), *British Moralists* (Oxford: Clarendon Press, 1897), I, pp. 251–52.

of virtue or of intelligence." (7) Finally, there is an obligation not to injure other people.[10]

What is the relation of these prima facie obligations to one's over-all duty in a particular case? Ross' view is that if, in a given situation, prima facie obligations do not prescribe incompatible actions, then one's over-all duty is to fulfill these obligations, whatever they may be. (This is true by definition of "prima facie obligation.") But suppose prima facie obligations conflict? Ross' theory proposes one general second-order principle to deal with such situations. This is: "That act is one's duty which has the greatest balance of prima facie rightness over prima facie wrongness"; or, in the case where only two prima facie obligations conflict: "That act is one's duty which is in accord with the more stringent prima facie obligation." But which is the "more stringent" obligation? Ross' list of prima facie obligations tells us nothing of relative stringencies; and indeed Ross thinks that we cannot frame any simple generalizations on this point, for the stringency of a prima facie obligation varies with the circumstances. However, he thinks that very often we do know which the more stringent is; and there are some rough generalizations we can make, for example, that the obligation not to injure others is usually more stringent than the obligation to do good.[11]

In essence, this is Ross' theory.

Ross' system is incomplete in the sense that it is not possible to infer, from the principles he explicitly states, what is our duty in a particular situation (except for the special case where there is not conflict of prima facie obligations), even when full factual information is available, and when it is known which act would maximize the welfare of sentient beings. We cannot infer what our duty is, in all cases, from his stated principles, even with full factual information at our disposal, because he does not give

---

[10] *The Right and the Good* (Oxford: Clarendon Press, 1930), chap. 2; and *Foundations of Ethics* (Oxford: Clarendon Press, 1939), chaps. 4, 5. See also E. F. Carritt, *Ethical and Political thinking* (Oxford: Clarendon Press, 1947), especially chaps. 9, 10.

[11] A serious question is what *meaning* can be ascribed to the term "more stringent obligation." The answer seems to be this. We have already explained (p. 360) that we can speak meaningfully of different stringencies or strengths of over-all duty or obligation. Now, suppose in a given situation we find we have both a prima facie obligation to do *A*, and also to do *B*, which is incompatible with *A*. How do we find which is "more stringent"? Well, we can ask ourselves how strong would have been our duty to do *A* if the other prima facie obligation had not been present, and similarly about our duty to do *B*. We can then make a direct comparative judgment about which duty would have been stronger. The one that would have been stronger is also stronger as prima facie obligation—and it is what this stronger obligation requires that is our duty in the situation.

But when Ross talks of a "balance" of prima facie rightness as compared with prima facie wrongness, and an act being the over-all right one that has the greatest such balance, Ross seems to be making use of quantitative conceptions that he certainly has not explained, and are of doubtful value here. But his view has a right to be as good as that of the pluralist about values. See the explanation on p. 350, especially the footnote.

us the second-order (much less third-order) principles necessary for determining our obligation over all, when prima facie obligations conflict.

There are other respects in which Ross' theory is probably incomplete. For one thing, it is doubtful whether his statement of the basic prima facie obligations includes all the qualifications and exceptions that ought to be included. In the second place, it is doubtful whether there are not more prima facie obligations in addition to those he has described. For instance, it may be thought that parents have obligations to their children on account of being responsible for the children's existence. Again, it has been thought that incestuous sexual relations are wrong, along with "unnatural" sexual relations, especially with animals. Incompleteness of these sorts is not inherent in a formalist system, however; with some effort it should be possible to produce a list of distinct obligations, and to add qualifications and exceptions to them, so as to reach at least a quite high level of accuracy in the description of the basic prima facie obligations.

The task of adding a list of second-order principles suited to adjudicate conflicts of the prima facie obligations is much more difficult. It seems unlikely that a formalist system will be stated, at least in the near future, which makes any substantial progress in the completion of this indefinitely large task of listing such principles, one by one.

At an earlier stage we suggested that one objection to the formalist view is that a formalist view simply eludes complete and accurate statement, that in principle a complete formalist system cannot be put on paper. This critical point is well-taken: it does seem that no complete set of formalist principles will be, or even can be, set down in black and white.

Is this objection, however, a sufficient reason for rejecting Ross' view or the formalist type of ethical theory? No, it is not. There are several reasons for this conclusion. (1) The adoption of a formalist theory, with its necessary incompleteness, does not have the result that we cannot know the answer to particular moral questions. We can learn this by the method we have described repeatedly, that of ascertaining what we would probably feel obligated to do if we were a person of "qualified" attitudes. Incidentally, the various helps for deciding such questions, which we described at the end of Chapter 13, can be utilized, with suitable modifications, for solutions of problems about our duty. (2) The formalist need not state a complete system of true moral principles in order to make his main point —that the act-utilitarian principle is unacceptable, and that there are other principles which must be adopted in its stead. It is enough if he provides convincing samples of nonutilitarian principles; he is not logically required to state them all. Indeed, there is some question whether a moral philosopher ought, in order to do his professional job well, to produce a telephone-book-like directory listing all these moral principles. It would seem that his main job is done if he argues for and states some broad strategic principles, and sets forth carefully some models for ethical reasoning. His job is not to provide a manual for moral decisions; it would be presumptuous of him to try to do so. (3) In any case it should be noticed that the utilitarian, most obviously the ideal utilitarian, must concede that his theory suffers from an incompleteness essentially the same as that from which the formalist theory suffers. Why? The ideal utilitarian only tells us that, in general, certain things are intrinsically worth while, for example, knowledge; but it is impossible to infer from such general principles whether, for instance, a specific piece of knowledge is worth the effort it would take to acquire it. Comparative judgments of intrinsic worth do not *follow* from the rather general statements of the ideal utilitarian; his theory as stated does not allow us to infer deductively the relative merits of two complex states of affairs. (We have seen that there is a comparable difficulty even for the hedonist, if he has to compare for worth two sets of consequences which are less than certain.) Ross' theory simply has this incompleteness at two points. He has it first because he is a pluralist about values and, hence, has the ideal utilitarian's difficulty in deciding which act will produce more good. Then, in addition, his theory has a similar incompleteness in that the abstract statements of the major prima facie obligations do not by themselves enable one to infer which course of action, where prima facie obligations conflict, satisfies all our prima facie obligations best.

The formalist theory as stated by Ross, then, is incomplete in some ways, and a theory of this type can never be completely perfected. But this kind of incompleteness is no serious defect, or at least is no conclusive reason for rejecting the theory.

Let us now take leave of the formalist theory, and look briefly at the theory we have called "universalist impersonal pluralism." This theory accepts the main thesis of act-utilitarianism, that it is one's duty to do whatever act is the one, among all the possible ones, that will produce maximum net expectable utility. As such, the theory should perhaps be classified as a form of utilitarianism. However, the forms the theory has taken historically affiliate it closely with formalism. The reason its spirit is close to formalism is the following. Advocates of the theory have been attracted to it primarily because it permits one, through an extension of the list of intrinsic values to various "impersonal" things, to be an act-utilitarian and yet to share all the views about over-all obligations which formalists put forward. Adherents of the theory, for instance, suggest that among the things of intrinsic worth are keeping promises, making return for benefits rendered, distribution of happiness to people in accordance with their merit, and so on. In other words, it is sometimes held that the very situations Ross says we are prima facie obligated to bring about are of *intrinsic* value! If they are, then the act-utilitarian formula to "act so as to produce the most good possible" will direct us to do exactly what the formalist says we ought to

do. Act-utilitarianism and formalism, then, are reconciled.[12] This theory
agrees with act-utilitarianism that there is only one principle of duty,
the act-utilitarian principle; it differs with hedonism and personal pluralism
in extending the list of intrinsic values. It agrees with Ross about what our
duties are, as contrasted with the simpler views of traditional utilitarians.

Should we not welcome this theory as a happy solution of our problems?
In fact, we *do* welcome part of it. At a later point we shall agree that there
is one impersonal intrinsic good—equality of welfare. Unfortunately, however, it is difficult to convince oneself that all those things are intrinsically
worthwhile which the theory must say are so, if it is to have the capacity
to reconcile utilitarianism and formalism which has attracted philosophers
to it. Can one say that the fulfillment of a promise is intrinsically worth
while? The answer to this question is not quite obviously negative; but
certainly one can doubt that it is affirmative.[13] At least many people have
thought it foolish to claim that keeping a promise is intrinsically worth
while in the way in which enjoyment and perhaps knowledge are so.

We shall not discuss this possible theory further, however, partly because it is so similar to formalism, and partly because we shall shortly
describe a theory very similar to it, but somewhat simpler—a theory we
shall call "extended rule-utilitarianism."

3. THE COMPROMISE: RULE-UTILITARIANISM

Many philosophers today are convinced both by objections to formalism
and by objections to act-utilitarianism. They are therefore attracted by a
compromise theory, which we shall call "rule-utilitarianism."[14]

This theory, a product of the last decade, is not a novel one. We find
statements of it in J. S. Mill and John Austin in the nineteenth century; and
indeed we find at least traces of it much earlier, in discussions of the nature
and function of law by the early Greeks. But in the earlier statements of it
we do not find it sharply defined, as an alternative to act-utilitarianism.
Clear formulations of it have been the work of the past few years.

Let us begin with as exact a statement of the theory as is possible. Unfortunately, no exact statement will represent accurately the views of all
who advocate this general type of theory, for the precise suggestions they
have put forward have varied considerably. But there is an exact formulation that is at least as convincing as any others that have been suggested.

The thesis of rule-utilitarianism may be formulated thus: "It is obligatory over all for an agent to perform an act *A* if and only if the prescription that it be performed ['Do *A!*'] follows logically from a complete de-

---

12 A. C. Ewing thinks such a reconciliation is required by close attention to the
meanings of "good" and "ought." See *The Definition of Good*, chap. 6.

13 See, for instance, W. D. Ross, *Foundations of Ethics*, pp. 74, 289.

14 On p. 253, it was formulated, not as a general statement about what acts are
obligatory, but as a *method* for determining which acts are obligatory.

scription of the agent's situation plus ideal prescriptions for his community; and ideal prescriptions for his community are that set of universal imperatives [of the form 'Do A in circumstances C'] containing no proper names, which is (a) complete[15] and as economical in distinct imperatives and in concepts as is compatible with completeness, and such that (b) a conscientious effort to obey it, by everyone in the agent's community, would have greater net expectable utility than similar effort to obey any other set of imperatives."[16]

A rough example of the application of this thesis is as follows. Suppose I have made a promise to do A, and I wonder whether I should really do A. Now, presumably the set of imperatives, universal conscientious effort to conform with which will have maximum net expectable utility in my community, will contain a directive rather like (but with some qualifications), "If a person has made a promise to do x, then let him do x!" This set of ideal prescriptions, then, plus the description of my situation (as having made a promise to do A), thus entails the prescription, "Do A!" And, by the thesis, I am therefore obligated over all to do A.

It may be helpful to draw an analogy between this theory and the application of laws to particular cases. Laws are general, and they are made by legislators, undoubtedly with utilitarian considerations in mind. But when judges apply the law, they do not construe their job as one of deciding particular cases by appeal to utilities (as if act-utilitarianism were the principle judges should follow); they regard their job as one of following the direction of the general law for the particular case. Now, morality is an informal analogue of law, and the rule-utilitarian is saying that we should decide particular cases by following general prescriptions but that whether a given general prescription should be adopted depends roughly on the utility of its being generally obeyed.

Such a view to some extent avoids the main objection to formalism, for it links moral principles to welfare; general prescriptions are not to be adopted unless observance of them will probably do good. But it also escapes at least most of the objections to act-utilitarianism; its implications are closer to reflective conclusions about obligations. Take our second objection above, to the implications of act-utilitarian theory about the bindingness of promises. On the rule-utilitarian theory, if we make a promise to a widow to care for her daughter, we are bound not just to the extent

---

[15] A "complete" set is one that does not fail to supply direction for any decision one may have to make.

[16] The expectable utilities of everyone obeying a given rule will include not only direct benefits, but the indirect benefits of being able to plan on other people doing a certain thing in certain circumstances. An alternate formulation very similar to the foregoing is this: "If the doing of A by everyone in your community who might find himself in circumstances like yours would have greater net expectable utility than any other act that might be performed in such circumstances, then it is your obligation to do A."

that we must do whatever will produce best consequences (so that we are bound, perhaps, to do just what we would otherwise have been bound to do if we had not made the promise); we are bound to do whatever it would have the best consequences for *everyone* to do in similar situations. This—especially in view of the value of people being able to rely on promises—may be to honor the promise in many situations for which act-utilitarians would not prescribe honoring the promise.

Several points about the foregoing theory require explanation.

1. It is perhaps obvious why the theory is called "rule-utilitarianism." The theory holds that there are many general ideal prescriptions that determine whether a given act is obligatory over all, and none of them is identical with the thesis of act-utilitarianism. On the other hand, the theory is properly called "utilitarian" in view of the fact that it states that those prescriptions should be followed, universal effort to conform with which would maximize expectable utility.

2. The theory leaves open the possibility that the system of prescriptions that defines whether an agent's act is right or wrong will differ from one agent to another, depending on the community to which he belongs. It leaves open the possibility that for one community with its material environment, institutions, and pervasive beliefs, conformity with one set of ideal prescriptions would be best; whereas for another community with different material environment (and so on), conformity with a different set of prescriptions would be best. The theory does not require that this be so, however. It also leaves open the possibility that the same set of prescriptions will do for all.

3. The prescriptions included in these systems will presumably not be simple, like "Always tell the truth!" or, "If you have made a promise to do *x*, and the promise was not made under duress and was not based on deliberate misrepresentations by the promisee, then do *x*." There is no restriction on the complexity of the principles, or on their number, which may be quite large. Nor is there any restriction on the kind of property to which a prescription may refer.

4. How will this theory dispose of cases of conflict of obligations? Suppose, for instance, one prescription tells us, roughly, to keep our promises, and another tells us, roughly, to do whatever good we can; and suppose a case arises in which keeping a promise will prevent the doing of a great deal of good. What is one then required to do, according to the theory?

The simplest answer is that a set of prescriptions is not complete if it does not contain a prescription for every specific kind of problem. A complete set of prescriptions, then, must contain prescriptions giving directions for cases of possible conflict between the simpler prescriptions. And, of course, these conflict-resolving prescriptions will, like all the prescriptions in the set, be ones conscientious adherence to which in the circumstances envisaged will maximize the net expectable welfare of the group. Conceivably these conflict-resolving prescriptions might themselves conflict with each other; and if they may, then obviously there must be even more complex and specific prescriptions added to the list, if it is to be complete.[17]

5. A critic of the theory might object that the theory is not of much use, if it is intended as a scheme for helping agents find out their duty, for nobody knows what are the ideal prescriptions that determine anyone's overall obligations—and indeed a complete set of them might have to be infinitely complex. But to this, the advocate of the theory can reply that the critic is taking an overly pessimistic view. It is true that probably no one is familiar with the complete detail of any such system. However, presumably almost everyone knows a first approximation at least to part of it. Moreover, for purposes of practice, all a person needs to know is one part of it, the part of it relevant to any concrete decisions he has to make. For instance, it is not such an impossible job to know, with at least a substantial degree of probability, whether the net expectable utility would be greater if a certain type of contract were universally honored, as compared with not honoring it.

There are two more specific questions likely to be raised about such a theory, whose answer will help us understand it. These are the following. First, suppose a man thought that the best possible system of rules for his community would include the prescription that no individuals support their parents in their old age, but that all the elderly be supported by the state, out of taxes. (Perhaps he would be right in this.) The question is then this: If this is correct, is one then relieved of one's obligation to support one's parents, as the social system now stands? The correct answer is negative, for we must distinguish two questions. (1) Given a community in which it is established practice for children to support their parents and where there are no other institutional arrangements, would it have maximum net utility for everybody to stop supporting parents? The answer is obviously, "No." (2) But, given this same kind of community, would it have maximum net utility for everyone to start advocating and doing all in his power to introduce a legal system of institutional tax-supported care for the elderly? The answer to this may well be, "Yes." If we

---

[17] One might ask how it is possible to construct the system, so that the conflict-resolving prescriptions don't contradict the others. For instance, one prescription might be "Keep your promises." Suppose then we introduce a conflict-resolving prescription, perhaps roughly, "In cases such that breaking promises would, on the average, do more good than keeping them, everything considered, break the promise!" These two prescriptions conflict. This can be avoided by adding to every prescription (except to the most specific ones of the set) "except where otherwise specified by a more specific rule of this set." Another possible type of system might attach different numerical *weights* to different principles, and specify in the general formulation that the act a given agent is required to do is the one called for by the greatest weight of prescriptions. The weights, then, could be assigned on the basis of utility. A formulation of this sort could be rather similar to Ross' remarks about the relation of prima facie to over-all duty.

distinguish the two issues carefully, the theory does not lead to obviously wrong conclusions.

There is a second question, about the implications of the theory for cases such that the agent happens to know whether or not other people will in fact obey an ideal rule. Suppose, to take a simple case, an agent knows that it would be better for everyone (except persons with some urgent business) to refrain from cutting across the grass of a park. But he also happens to know that no one (except possibly himself) will in fact hesitate to cut across the grass when it suits his convenience—and knows that in fact the grass in the park is going to be, or is already, in an unpleasing condition. Should there be a rule prescribing that he (anyone who knows this) now may walk on the grass also, since this will have most net utility in a society where the grass will be spoiled anyway? Or, take the opposite case. Suppose he knows that practically everybody else will scrupulously avoid crossing the grass, and therefore nothing will be gained by his refraining from walking on it since the grass will be in fine shape anyway. Should there again be a special rule prescribing that he (anyone who knows this) walk on the grass if it suits his advantage, this time because so doing by everybody in a situation like his will produce a net gain in utility in a society where the grass is carefully provided for? The most thoughtful defenders of the theory who have considered the matter have answered both these questions in the affirmative.

4. FORMALISM OR RULE-UTILITARIANISM?

Assuming that the objections to act-utilitarianism are conclusive, the choice of a general theory of obligation seems to lie between some kind of formalism and at least something like rule-utilitarianism. Let us consider the pros and cons of such a choice.

The first thing we must do is get clear the exact connection between the two theories. And here we may be surprised to notice that, if we define formalism (as up to now we have been doing) simply as a counter to act-utilitarianism, as the thesis that the rightness or wrongness of an act is *not* a function solely of the intrinsic value of the consequences of *that act*, then rule-utilitarianism turns out to be a species of formalism. Since it is convenient to distinguish the two theories, however, from now on we shall understand by "formalism" the view that the rightness or wrongness of an act is *not determined solely* by the intrinsic worth of the consequences of that act or of any other act or *class of acts*. Formalism and rule-utilitarianism, then, are different theories, although in many ways closely related.

Act-utilitarians, however, regard rule-utilitarianism and formalism as two of a kind, for both theories imply that in some cases an agent may be obligated to do something when he knows that he could realize more welfare in the circumstances by doing something else. The rule-utilitarian, for instance, will sometimes say a promise is morally binding because in the long run it would have better consequences if everybody kept promises in circumstances like the case at hand, although actually more good in the particular instance would be done by breaking the promise. Both theories, then, are accused of "rule-worship" by act-utilitarians.

But exactly what are the differences between rule-utilitarianism and formalism as a *type* of theory (not necessarily exactly like Ross' theory), if we define "formalism" as we have just suggested?

1. The rule-utilitarian holds (like the act-utilitarian) that we need only *one* moral principle, which says that an act is obligatory if and only if the act has a certain property that can be defined without any reference to principles of obligation or duty. Formalism says we need more than one. Formalisms are essentially many-principle theories; therefore, they essentially require more than one *order* of principle, since there must be higher-order principles stating what is one's over-all duty when there is a conflict of other principles, or if none of the first-order principles applies.[18]

2. There is a sense in which rule-utilitarianism is a more complete normative system than is any formalist system. Because ideally complete formalist systems must have rather complex first-order rules, and probably many of them, and also, if everything is written out, many super-rules specifying priorities when the first-order rules conflict, actual formalist theories, like Ross', give only sketches, or parts of a system. Now, rule-utilitarianism in a sense does no more: It does not write out the details of any set of "ideal rules" for a society. Such a set would be as complex as an ideal formalist system. Moreover, the application of the formula requires knowledge about which classes of acts would have best results, with all the problems for such judgments that we discussed at the end of Chapter 13. But the theory is more complete in one sense: It gives a specific formula telling us exactly what property any "ideal rule" must have. Thus, if we want to know whether certain types of promises should be honored, there is a substantive rule telling us the answer.

3. A rule-utilitarian may consistently claim that his general formula is true for all persons everywhere, but think that any more specific moral principles vary from one community to another. The reason for this is that the "ideal rules" for a given community are fixed by whether conscientious following of certain prescriptions *in that community* would have maximum net expectable utility, and the prescriptions that have this property in one

---

[18] Kant is a formalist, and at the same time it may be said that he has only one principle, the one described in Chapter 2 (that an act is morally permissible if and only if its maxim is universalizable). If so, Kant is a formalist with only one principle, very like the rule-utilitarian principle. But is seems more illuminating to regard his principle as a *test* for moral principles (rather like the Qualified Attitude Method) than as itself a substantive moral principle. In this case his moral principles would be statements like "It is wrong to commit suicide in order to escape unhappiness or pain" and "It is wrong to borrow money if one knows one will not be able to repay it."

community need not have it in another. "Always tell the truth" may qualify as an ideal prescription in one society and not in another. Correspondingly, "It is always wrong to lie" may be a true moral principle in one society but not in another.

The rule-utilitarian can say that moral principles that are more specific than his supreme principle are in a sense relative to the society; but this does not make him a relativist in our sense (Chapter 11).

Is anything like this possible for a formalist? Ross, of course, thinks that principles such as "If one has made a promise, it is prima facie obligatory to keep it" are valid for all peoples. Subsidiary secondary principles, however, can consistently be said to vary from one society to another.[19] A formalist can say that the basic, primary principles are also different in different societies, but if so he must be a relativist, because he has no supreme universally valid principle corresponding to the rule-utilitarian's principle.

In view of these differences, which theory has the advantage?

1. The fact that rule-utilitarianism is a more complete theory gives it a pragmatic edge over the formalisms.

2. Many philosophers are convinced that no set of principles as specific as those Ross lists is true for all peoples. Consider for example: "Parents are prima facie obligated to care for their children." This principle is not apt to cohere with the "qualified" attitudes of members of a matriarchal society, in which the male blood-relatives of the mother of a child are charged with the responsibility of a child's education; or, of a Platonic society, in which the state takes over the education of all children. As a consequence, some philosophers emphasize that a formalist like Ross cannot claim that ethical principles like those he regards as the basic principles of obligation are self-evident, although the rule-utilitarian formula can plausibly be said to be self-evident. Furthermore, they say that a formalist like Ross must, in view of these facts, be a relativist. Ross himself would presumably regard these as serious difficulties, since he both criticizes relativism and holds the rational self-evidence theory of moral knowledge.

What reply might a formalist make? First, he might question the factual basis of the criticism. He might say that, however it may be with some ethical principles like the above example (the obligation of parents to care for their children), in fact the *fundamental* principles can be said to be valid for everyone, in the sense that they cohere with the "qualified" attitudes of people everywhere. We shall not attempt to decide whether this reply is well-taken. Second, a formalist may admit the charges, but deny their force. He may say that he does not propose to defend a rational self-evidence theory—and for this, of course, we shall applaud him. Furthermore,

[19] For instance, suppose he held that a basic principle is: "There is an obligation to keep all promises." Suppose further that in society *A* there is a universal implicit promise always to tell the truth when one speaks, but in society *B* there is no such understanding. Then he could say, "There is an obligation to tell the truth in society *A* but not in society *B*."

he may concede the truth of relativism—while emphasizing, doubtless, that the differences between the principles valid in different societies is rather small.

If the rule-utilitarian charge is correct, that there is *no* set of abstract principles of a level of concreteness comparable to Ross' which is consistent with the "qualified" attitudes of all people everywhere, and *if* the claim for the rule-utilitarian formula is correct, that it is consistent with and implies (when combined with true factual propositions) the ethical judgments valid among all peoples, then rule-utilitarianism gains considerably in stature. We cannot, of course, say that formalism is erroneous, in the sense that the principles asserted are not valid. But if the rule-utilitarian theory has the advantage on the points just mentioned, the rule-utilitarian theory is a much *simpler* theory. We should emphasize: It is a *much* simpler theory. Furthermore, simplicity is a good reason for preferring one of a pair of theories, if the two are equal in other respects.

3. Act-utilitarians object to both theories as cases of "rule-worship." The rule-utilitarian, however, ties moral obligation to welfare in a way in which formalism does not, since an act is obligatory only if uniform acceptance of a corresponding rule would maximize expectable utility. Is this not an important advantage for rule-utilitarianism? The formalist must admit that he does not link obligation with welfare as closely as does the rule-utilitarian, although he may properly object to the connotations of the pejorative phrase "rule-worshiper." He will go on, however, to argue that the rule-utilitarian just happens to be mistaken in thinking that moral obligation is as closely connected with the general welfare as he does.

4. Let us now consider what the formalist can say in defense of this view. Sometimes, the formalist may say, we are in fact obligated to do things the rule-utilitarian's formula says we are not obligated to do. In other words, the general formula happens to be false.

Is this charge correct? Are the implications of the rule-utilitarian formula anywhere discrepant with our actual obligations?[20]

The point of primary difficulty for the rule-utilitarian appears to be the implications of his theory for the *distribution* of welfare. The rule-utilitarian, we recall, approves of *any* rule for distributing welfare so long as it does not bring about *less* welfare than some alternative rule. But *is* every rule that satisfies this condition consistent with what we know about our obligations? It is doubtful whether this is true. We shall examine the dif-

---

[20] We must remember that any specific formalist theory may also show such discrepancies. However, a formalist is not committed, by his formalism, to any specific list of obligations—only to the view that obligations are not determined solely by any utilitarian formula. So, rule-utilitarianism is open to criticism in a way that formalism is not.

A formalist might agree with the statements about obligation implied by the rule-utilitarian formula, except on a very small number of points—indeed, on just one point.

ficulty more precisely in the following chapter where we shall consider the question of how economic goods must be distributed in order that the distribution be just. For the present, however, it must suffice to point to two examples for which the rule-utilitarian formula appears to be discrepant with our actual obligations having to do with distributions. First, the examples described as difficulties for act-utilitarianism on this score, earlier in this chapter (p. 389), seem equally to be difficulties for rule-utilitarianism. The second example is rather similar. At the end of our discussion of rule-utilitarianism (p. 390) we saw that, according to this theory, if a person happened to know that nearly everybody else was in fact going to make a sacrifice that no one wants to make, and if he knew that, as a result, a similar sacrifice by him was not really essential for the public welfare, then he need not make it. The Frenchman who is deliberating about whether to use electricity and gas if all the good English are certain to refrain is a case in point. According to the theory, since it really does no good for him to make the sacrifice (and such sacrifices do no good when they are made by *everybody* in his position), he need not make the sacrifice; indeed, it is his obligation not to. But such a conclusion seems dubious. It looks as if, perhaps, a "qualified" person would approve of *everybody* making a sacrifice equally, if almost all have to make it, except some with a special reason—and a "qualified" person would not count it a special reason that one happens to know that all others are obeying cheerfully. Thus the fourth objection to act-utilitarianism (p. 389) also has force against rule-utilitarianism.

These discrepancies with what appear to be our real obligations occur not only in the case of the hedonistic rule-utilitarian; they are difficulties for the personal pluralist as well. They could be avoided if the rule-utilitarian could only borrow just a little from the impersonal pluralist theory. If only, without going to the length of asserting that it is intrinsically good to keep promises, repay favors, and so on, he could count just one or two impersonal states of affairs as having intrinsic worth—say, for one thing, an *equal* distribution of welfare—then his problems would be solved. However, he cannot do this. At least, he cannot do it consistently with being a "rule-utilitarian" in our sense, for we have defined a "rule-utilitarian" as a person who is either a hedonist or a personal pluralist in his view about what is intrinsically worthwhile. In order to adopt the theory that we suggest is plausible, we have to resort to the position we call "extended rule-utilitarianism."

If these objections to the implications of rule-utilitarianism are well-taken, there is good reason for abandoning rule-utilitarianism in favor of extended rule-utilitarianism—or else formalism.

Some of the first three reasons carry a certain amount of force in favor of either extended rule-utilitarianism or straight rule-utilitarianism (which is still in the running if the reader is unsympathetic with the objections of the fourth point). In view of them it seems reasonable to adopt one or the other of the rule-utilitarian theories, unless further difficulties are discovered. This is our conclusion.

Some philosophers will probably think that we must "extend" extended rule-utilitarianism much more if it is to be plausible. They will say that otherwise we would be committed to many more exceptions to the rule of keeping promises, and so forth, than are in fact justified—and this is possible. We need to have such matters argued in detail. But until it has been shown that we need further "extensions," there seems to be justification for tentatively adopting extended rule-utilitarianism as substantially correct.

FURTHER READINGS

On act-utilitarianism:

G. E. Moore, *Principia Ethica* (Cambridge, Eng.: Cambridge University Press, 1929), pp. 146–71.

H. Rashdall, *Theory of Good and Evil* (Oxford: Clarendon Press, 1924), vol. I, chaps. 4, 7.

J. Bentham, *Principles of Morals and Legislation,* chaps. 1–4.

J. S. Mill, *Utilitarianism,* chaps. 1–2 (but see J. O. Urmson, below).

H. Sidgwick, *The Methods of Ethics* (London: Macmillan & Co., Ltd., 1922), Bk. I, chap. 9; Bk. II, chap. 1; Bk. III, chaps. 11, 13; Bk. IV, chaps. 2–5. This is the most substantial discussion of the point of view.

C. D. Broad, *Five Types of Ethical Theory* (New York: Harcourt, Brace & Company, 1934), chap. 6. A helpful analysis of Sidgwick's theory.

S. M. Brown, Jr., "Utilitarianism and Moral Obligation," *Philosophical Review,* LXI (1952), 299–311. Comments by C. A. Baylis and John Ladd, *ibid.,* pp. 320–30. Brown is critical of act-utilitarianism.

A. I. Melden, "Two Comments about Utilitarianism," *Philosophical Review,* LX (1952), 508–24.

A. Duncan-Jones, "Utilitarianism and Rules," *Philosophical Quarterly,* VII (1957), 364–67. A criticism.

A. C. Ewing, *Ethics* (London: English Universities Press, 1953), chap. 5.

On formalism:

W. D. Ross, *The Right and the Good* (Oxford: Clarendon Press, 1930), pp. 16–41.

———, *Foundations of Ethics* (Oxford: Clarendon Press, 1939), chaps. 4–6. Statements by the leading modern formalist.

J. Butler, *Dissertation upon Virtue,* 1736, reprinted in L. A. Selby-Bigge (ed.), *British Moralists* (Oxford: Clarendon Press, 1897), vol. I. An influential formalist.

W. Pickard-Cambridge, "Two Problems about Duty," *Mind,* XLI (1932), 145–72, 311–340. A criticism of Ross.

A. C. Ewing, "Utilitarianism," *Ethics,* LVIII (1947), 100–111.

———, *The Definition of Good* (New York: The Macmillan Company, 1947), chap. 6.

———, *Ethics* (London: English Universities Press, 1953), chap. 5. A position claiming to reconcile utilitarianism and formalism.

On rule-utilitarianism:

J. O. Urmson, "The Interpretation of the Philosophy of J. S. Mill," *Philosophical Quarterly*, III (1953), 33–40.

J. D. Mabbott, "Moral Rules," *Proceedings of the British Academy*, XXXIX (1953), 97–117.

———, "Interpretations of Mill's Utilitarianism," *Philosophical Quarterly*, VI (1956), 115–20.

S. E. Toulmin, *An Examination of the Place of Reason in Ethics* (Cambridge, Eng.: Cambridge University Press, 1950), chap. 11.

R. F. Harrod, "Utilitarianism Revised," *Mind*, XLV (1936), 137–56.

J. Rawls, "Two Concepts of Rules," *Philosophical Review*, LXIV (1955), 3–32.

C. A. Campbell, "Moral Intuition and the Principle of Self-Realization," *Proceedings of the British Academy*, XXXIV (1948).

J. Harrison, "Utilitarianism, Universalization, and Our Duty to Be Just," *Proceedings*, The Aristotelian Society, 1952–53.

M. G. Singer, "Moral Rules and Principles," in A. I. Melden (ed.), *Essays in Moral Philosophy* (Seattle: University of Washington Press, 1958).

A. K. Stout, "Suppose Everybody Did the Same," *Australasian Journal of Philosophy*, XXXII (1954), 1–29.

P. Nowell-Smith, *Ethics* (Baltimore: Penguin Books, Inc., 1954), chaps. 15, 16.

A. C. Ewing, "Suppose Everybody Acted Like Me," *Philosophy*, XXVIII (1953), 16–29.

J. J. C. Smart, "Extreme and Restricted Utilitarianism," *Philosophical Quarterly*, VI (1956), 344–54. A vigorous criticism of the view.

H. J. McCloskey, "An Examination of Restricted Utilitarianism," *Philosophical Review*, LXVI (1957), 466–85. Another criticism.

A. MacBeath, *Experiments in Living* (London: Macmillan & Co., Ltd., 1952), chap. 2.

16

Distributive Justice

Suppose we have a set of rather abstract ethical principles before us, and we are wondering whether it can be at least the framework of the true set of basic ethical axioms. How shall we appraise such a set of principles? Certainly one relevant thing to do is work out its implications for some areas of living about which we have concrete and well-structured opinions about what conduct is right or wrong. If we bring our abstract principles into contact with such concrete convictions about right and wrong conduct, we may find that our abstract theory is seriously in disagreement with our views about more concrete problems—views firmly supported (as it seems) by our "qualified" attitudes. If so, our axiom system may need modification. But conversely, there may be an opposite result: We may see that no possible general principles are compatible with our views about more concrete problems—or at least no general principles that we are prepared to advocate in view of their implications for other areas. In this case, it is our ideas about concrete problems that need change. Either way, the comparison of our opinions about concrete social problems with tentatively adopted basic principles of ethics is likely to be fruitful.

In view of this fact, we shall now bring abstract basic principles into contact with well-structured opinions about what is right or wrong in two areas: the system of criminal justice, and the system of economic distribution. We begin with the system of economic distribution.

The present chapter, despite the fact that it will deal primarily with the problem of a morally justifiable system of distribution of income, has been given the title "distributive justice." It could have been entitled "economic justice" or "justice in the allocation of income." But a broader title has been chosen deliberately, to emphasize that there are more things than money that people want, and that are distributed, equally or unequally. Moreover, there is as much a problem of the morally justifiable distribution of these things, as there is of money. What are some of these things? Some jobs are more interesting than others, are more challenging, permit longer vacations, assure the incumbent more power and prestige than others. People want interesting friends. They want to live in an aesthetically pleasing environment. They want access to books, and to the education that enables them to enjoy books. They want to be married to an interesting and congenial partner. They want love and affection. And so on. Some of these things can be purchased, so that how they are distributed is closely connected with how money is distributed. Others, however, cannot. The fact that some people have much of these things and some little is also, in some cases, a fact that is not subject to control; for instance, some people have far more than an equal share of good things because they have been born with a charming personality, and personality and its effects are beyond control. The distribution of others of these things, however, can be controlled: whether certain jobs are open to both sexes and to members of all races; whether women have opportunities to form friendships, or to find a congenial marriage partner, equal to those of men; how the dirty and dangerous jobs are distributed in a captain's company in the army; how a teacher allocates his time and interest among his students; and how a parent divides time and affection among the children. Where anything can be controlled, it can be directed by principle. Further, in any case where some distribution can be directed by principle, there is the question of what principle or principles are defensible. There are questions of "justice" in all these areas, and the answer to such questions —the principles of just distribution—are much the same as they are for the specific area on which we shall concentrate, that of distribution of income.

We must bear in mind, then, that many of the principles of economic justice have a wider application for the distribution of other goods, some perhaps more important than economic goods. We may hope to get from any examination of the theory of economic justice some broad principles that we can view as principles for distributions of good things generally, where such distributions can be controlled.

1. THE MEANING OF "JUST"

The reader may say: "The term 'justice' has appeared several times in the preceding pages. This I do not understand. Notions like 'principles about obligation' have been explained. Also, everyone understands what is meant by 'economic institutions,' and by talk about laws and procedures concerning the treatment of criminals. But what is this about 'justice'?"

This question is well taken; "justice" has not been explained. We also could get on without mentioning it, for if we have justified beliefs about what is right and wrong, what we ought to do or are obligated to do, we can hardly need more, as far as practice is concerned. If we already know what we ought to do, we know how to act, irrespective of further talk about justice. Still, the terms "just" and "justice" and their negatives play an important role in discourse, and we cannot well ignore them altogether. Let us concern ourselves primarily with "just" and "justly," and their negatives.

Unfortunately, the ease of defining a word often varies inversely with its importance in a language, and these words are an example. We know how to use them well enough in various contexts, but we cannot identify a precise property of all these situations, to which the terms can be taken to refer. Rather, there is a family of related meanings, and if we select one of these as "the" meaning, we find that it is rather forced to view this as what was meant in certain contexts. If we define the word at all, the best we can do is choose a central core that is not an entirely accurate account of some usages, but is accurate for many important uses and closely related to all.

But let us look at some details. The first thing to notice is that to act "unjustly" is not to act in a specific manner, such as to "lie." We might define the verb "lie" as meaning "deliberately to state falsely," a very definite kind of action. To "act unjustly" is vaguer or more abstract: There are many things we can do that are unjust.

Is "unjust" then an ethical term like "wrong"? Should we regard it really as an "obligation word"? This seems plausible at first, but it is clear that we can act wrongly without acting unjustly: incest, for instance, may be wrong but it is not unjust. The terms "just" and "unjust" simply do not apply. "Is wrong," then, does not imply "is unjust." Hence, "unjust" is not just a synonym of "wrong." But can we perhaps say something much weaker: that "is unjust" in some sense implies "is wrong"? Can we at least say that in every case where we are seriously willing to say an action is unjust, we are also willing to criticize it as being wrong?

The correct answer to these questions is affirmative, although we might be led to doubt it by the fact that sometimes it is not wrong to produce a situation that is to some extent unjust. For instance, we sometimes say that it is right to pass a law that works a "certain injustice" (although we do not think of the law as being an unjust law). Consider this case. Suppose a farmer, fearing a shortage of labor at harvest time, engages with three men in April to work for him in August at $20 per day, but then, in August when the labor market is unexpectedly flooded, hires ten more men at $10 per day. And suppose one of the ten complains that this arrangement is unjust, and demands that all be paid $20 a day. We would agree that there is a "certain injustice" in the situation. However, we also think that the farmer on the one hand is obligated to keep his promise, and on the other hand is not obligated to pay more than the going rates. So, although his arrangements produce a somewhat unjust situation, he did not act wrongly; and similarly we do not say he acted unjustly. It is not clear that we ever use "acted unjustly" correctly, when we cannot also correctly say "acted wrongly."[1]

What, then, roughly does it mean to "act unjustly"? Roughly, it seems that "act unjustly" means the same as "treat persons unequally, in some matter that involves the distribution of things that are good or bad, except as the inequality is required by moral considerations [principles] with substantial weight in the circumstances."

This definition implies that "just" is limited to cases of allocation of some sort, as distinct from other types of wrong action. It also implies that injustice is essentially unequal treatment, thereby conforming with a tradition that holds that equity is essentially a matter of equality. Moreover, the phrase "treat unequally in matters involving allocations of good and bad things" is so general as to permit application in widely different sorts of context; it permits us to accept an ancient adage that "justice is giving every man his due," a statement also susceptible of quite broad interpretation. All these implications, so far, seem quite plausible. Moreover, the definition enables us to understand the close connection between "is unjust" and "is wrong," given the assumption that we think for some reason that it is wrong to treat people unequally without some reason of moral principle—as we apparently do think. (Whether this assumption is a basic principle or an implication of other basic principles, we shall be deciding later in this chapter.)

Some uses of "unjust" appear to be somewhat more specialized, but we can view these as extensions of the foregoing core meaning, with specific connotations understandable in the context. For instance, "He stated the case unjustly." Here "state unjustly" seems to mean "state inaccurately, in a biased way, so as to give a misleading impression." But this is only a specialized extension of the core meaning, for "stated unjustly" is used only when different parties have an interest in how a situation is understood (we don't say that an inaccurate statement in a physics textbook is "unjust"); and to state the facts unjustly is to state them in such a way as to place one party at a disadvantage, without any moral justification. Again, we speak of an "unjust trial," meaning perhaps "a trial in which the rules of evidence, and so on, have not been scrupulously adhered to." But again, the core sense is present: Assuming that these rules are adhered to in most cases and work to the disadvantage of someone when they are not, departure from them is unjust in the core sense. Or again, we speak of an "unjust verdict," meaning a "verdict palpably out of line with the evidence." But we assume that when a verdict is thus out of line with the evidence there

---

[1] Possibly we should recognize "subjective" and "objective" senses of "acted unjustly" as we did of "wrong" and "obligation."

has been unequal treatment in some way; thus, the verdict is still unjust in our core sense.[2]

It seems, in like manner, that when we speak of "unjust" differences in income (or in taxes) we are using "unjust" in our core sense.

2. QUESTIONS OF ECONOMIC JUSTICE REQUIRE ASSESSMENT OF THE SOCIAL ORDER

We must now face the question of the ethical principles relevant to the distribution of economic goods. We want a complete set of the true principles relevant to such distribution.

Any discussion of the basic ethical principles of economic distributions is likely to seem abstract and utopian, however, unless we see that our usual abbreviated procedure for deciding questions of economic justice really does not go to the heart of the matter. Ordinarily we try to answer questions about economic justice while taking for granted a complex institutional framework, and without questioning or assessing the framework itself. If we do this, we overlook the main relevant principles. Let us see how this is true.

What sorts of questions about economic justice are we accustomed to debate? Simple ones like these: Was the plumber justified in charging us $10 to replace the washer? Was the barber justified in raising the price of haircuts to $1.50? Was the physician justified in raising the price of office visits from $3 to $5?

Normally, how do we answer these questions? We say the plumber was unjustified if he charged our neighbor only $2 for the same service; or if most plumbers ask the same amount, we may still regard the charge as unjustified ("they are a gang of racketeers"), if the going rate in the area, for services demanding the skill and training of a plumber, is substantially less for jobs requiring similar equipment and time. Even wage arbitrators normally fix wages by reference to the wages paid by "leaders" in the industry, as rectified by the general wage pattern for the particular area. Or, take the increase in charges by the physician and the barber. We are apt to argue thus: The general level of costs has gone up 60 per cent; so a comparable increase in their charges is not out of line.

But do these simple considerations really settle the matter? Not at all. Take the case of the plumber. When we have shown that he is being paid approximately what others in the area get for comparable services, some questions are still unanswered. In a highly unionized area, for example, where comparable trades all enforce standard prices, the customary

---

[2] When we use the phrase "unjust to," we specify the party that received the disadvantage of the unjust treatment. We also speak of the act as being unjust, if someone receives preference arbitrarily; but of course we don't say this was "unjust to" him.

charges for *all* comparable services may be too high, as compared with the average incomes of nonunionized occupations like farming, teaching, medicine, store-clerking, and so on. What we do in our ordinary thinking about the plumber—and the same for the barber and the physician—is settle particular issues by noticing whether in a particular case there is deviation from some standard that seems relevant; the standard itself remains unquestioned. But, as in the case of the plumber, the standard may need to be questioned; or at least there is no reason why we should not question it. If we do question it, we then find ourselves facing more fundamental problems.

It may seem merely unreasonable to push matters back so far. In many cases, however, there are larger issues of serious practical moment that require our tackling the fundamental questions. For instance, in recent years there has been a good deal of writing to the effect that educators and scientists as a group are paid less than they ought to be. Now, do we settle this issue simply by showing whether their salaries have increased comparably with the cost of living, or with the increase of wages in other occupations? Not at all. It is possible, for one thing, that the scientist's share in the national income has *always* been less (or more) than it ought to have been. If so, we do not set it right just by increasing it so that the share of the national income remains roughly what it was twenty years ago. The same sort of fundamental issue is raised if a union, say the United Auto Workers, should claim that the stockholders have been receiving too high a proportion of the corporate profits, and that dividends should be reduced in order to permit higher wages—or perhaps to permit lower prices for automobiles.

There is no way to answer these more fundamental questions without going back to the basic principles that justify economic distributions. We must view the economy as a whole, with the place of a given group of workers in it, and then employ basic ethical principles to determine the rightful share of a worker. Such a job, of course, is a difficult one, and it is understandable that wage arbitrators decide wage cases by appeal to precedents whenever they can find one.

Philosophers' discussions of economic justice have been concerned with these fundamental issues. They are apt to seem out of touch with facts because, in getting down to the basic principles and issues, they do not take for granted that any customary distribution of income among various occupational groups is a standard to be accepted without question—and do not even take for granted the sanctity of an open market, unregulated by government, as a means for deciding questions about the appropriate wage for a worker or class of workers. Such discussions, however, are not irrelevant to the real issues; they deal precisely with the problems that must be faced if we are to have a firmly established and systematic theory.

3. THE UTILITARIAN THEORY OF DISTRIBUTION

Utilitarian thinking about economic justice has had a large place in modern thinking on our topic, and with good reason, as we shall see. It will be expeditious, therefore, for us to begin with the implications of utilitarianism for the distribution of economic goods. We shall then consider whether at some points it is in conflict with justified convictions about distribution, and we shall examine the merits of some other principles that can be used to supplement it, or that might be substituted for the utilitarian principle.

Shall we consider act-utilitarianism or rule-utilitarianism? Since our conclusion has been that rule-utilitarianism is a more defensible theory, it seems best to confine our attention, in large measure, to it.[3]

We recall, then, that the thesis of rule-utilitarianism is, roughly, that an act is a person's duty if and only it it is required by the ideal rules for his community—those the conscientious following of which would have maximum net expectable utility. But this thesis says nothing about institutions or customs or laws; it is an assertion about the *acts* that are a person's duty. So we must ask ourselves how such a principle about which acts are obligatory or right or wrong has implications for the system of economic distribution.

It obviously does, and in several ways. First, an "economic system" is partly a matter of law: about taxation of various kinds, about contracts that are in the public interest, about relations between employers and employees and the union, about the ownership of property, and so on. Laws are enacted by human beings. As a result, the utilitarian formula bears on them, because it is a formula stating the duty of any person in a position to enact laws: as a principle about right acts, it is necessarily a principle about right enactments. Second, much the same can be said about persons who are in a position to influence the economic system insofar as it is a matter of custom or of agreements that are not legal enactments (for example, agreements between unions and employers). The utilitarian formula has implications about how persons in a position to do so should try to modify (or maintain) the system of distribution. Third, there are officials whose job is to effectuate law, agreement, or custom in particular cases, and who have a certain amount of discretion. The utilitarian formula, as a formula about how we ought to act, is a formula that has implications about the discretionary decisions of these men. (In case of gross conflict between moral principle and law or agreement, it could be an official's duty to subvert the very laws or agreements he is supposed to effectuate.) Finally, all of us as private citizens must repeatedly make allocations of economic goods:

---

[3] Our reflections on principles supplementary to the utilitarian principle, and on possible substitutes for it, will bring us back to the question of how far rule-utilitarianism must be "extended" in order to be an acceptable theory.

in our dealings with our children, when we employ the neighbor's son to mow our lawn, and so on. The utilitarian formula obviously applies to our acts in this capacity. So, while the utilitarian formula is a formula about right acts, it is implicitly a formula about economic institutions.

Exactly what does the utilitarian formula imply about the proper principles for the distribution of income? In general, of course, the direction is: "Distribute according to those rules, a universal conscientious effort to follow which will maximize net expectable utility."[4]

But "distribute" what? Not *welfare;* only God, perhaps, can distribute that. It must, then, be something material. One proposal could be: Distribute the year's produce—all the beans and beets and automobiles, and so on. However, the utilitarian can show that the best thing to distribute is *money*, for if we give individuals power to purchase a portion of the material products that have been produced, we shall tend to maximize utility. Presumably, the individual, within certain limits, can be counted upon to allocate his expenditures so as to maximize the welfare he will get from his share of the purchasing power. (There are limitations: We require all children to enjoy the benefits of education. We purchase police and fire protection for all. We require everyone to connect to the community sewerage system. And so on.) Let us agree, then, roughly—and this is not debated—that what is to be distributed is money.

We should notice that in one respect the utilitarian formula for distri-

---

[4] There is a complication here. In a complex society, the rules for economic distribution cannot be wholly *moral* rules. They can for some contexts, for example, intrafamily relations. But elsewhere they are of such importance that they must take the form of law, or of agreements having legal force. And when they are, they have some moral force simply by having such a status. So, in a society where one form of distribution has the sanction of law, we cannot simply say that, where this form differs from ideal law—what the law would be if it were the correct and defensible one from a moral point of view—an individual's obligation is to ignore the law and conform to the ideal system of distribution. It would be chaotic if everyone did this. There is an obligation, then, to conform to law except in extreme cases; the force of the "ideal" is in our obligation to change the law.

It is convenient and illuminating, however, to ignore this complication for the most part, and simply ask ourselves what are rules or prescriptions for distribution such that, if everyone conscientiously followed them, welfare would be maximized, and assume that behavior deviating from such rules is wrong. Thus, the application of rule-utilitarianism to distributions is brought into line with thinking about keeping promises, and so on.

Actually, we have already been making comparable simplifications in the previous chapter, for keeping of contracts, making restitution for injury, and so forth, are matters of law as well as of morals.

Incidentally, the *act*-utilitarian is in a disagreeably paradoxical position on the point of disposal of his own income. His theory has the implications of rule-utilitarianism on the issue of what *laws* he should support. But when it comes to his own income, his formula directs him to spend it for the general good. If it will do more good to give half of his $100-per-week income to charity, in place of giving his family a pleasant place to live, then he ought to do so. Nor can he argue on the ground that the incentive system would break down, that it would be bad if everyone did this. What would happen if everybody else did something is irrelevant, on his theory, to whether he should do it.

bution is a ruggedly egalitarian one. It counts the utility or welfare of everyone as equal. No consideration is paid to *who is* to have the welfare. No distinction is made between the king and the pauper. Welfare is counted simply as welfare, mine as much as yours. (Nothing is changed in all this if we are hedonists and write "pleasure" instead of "welfare.") The theory is as democratic as arithmetic. As Bentham said, "Everyone is to count for one, and no one for more than one." *Quantity* of welfare, irrespective of persons, is the fundamental aim of action.

In another respect, however, the utilitarian formula is not egalitarian. It does not recognize *equality of welfare* as intrinsically worthwhile. According to the formula, *if quantity* of welfare can be raised by a grossly unequal distribution—for instance, as in an efficient system of slavery—then we have to favor inequality. Equality, on the utilitarian scheme, is the servant of quantity of welfare, and is to be sacrificed to the slightest gain in quantity of welfare. In practice, however, as we shall see, most utilitarians think that inequalities of distribution tend to *reduce* the total welfare; so that in practice most utilitarians favor equal money distributions except as there are special reasons to the contrary.

But let us now look at the implications of the utilitarian formula. It directs us to follow those rules of distribution, a conscientious effort to follow which will maximize net expectable utility. But what are such rules? Are there any facts that may properly lead us to think that following some rules maximizes expectable utility, as compared with others?

Six lines of reasoning on this point are worth our attention.

1. One important line of reasoning purports to show that an *equal* distribution of income tends to maximize net expectable utility. Utilitarians who accept this reasoning hold, therefore, that equality of distribution has a strong initial claim on public policy. Deviations from it may be proper in special cases; they are proper insofar as inequalities are necessary in order to maintain a large quantity of goods available for distribution. But equal distribution is the basic rule, and deviations from it must be justified.

Since the argument is highly important if true, and seems to be a common-sense way of thinking, we shall examine it in some detail.

The first premise of the argument is that, after a certain amount of, say, weekly income, the utility of an extra dollar declines. Why? Consider a boy's weekly income. Suppose he receives two dollars a week. What will he spend this on? The things he wants most—the things he thinks (probably correctly) will give him most welfare. Perhaps these two dollars will go for a date with his favorite girl, or for milkshakes at the drugstore. (If he is dating, we may have to go beyond the first two dollars before we find a decline in utility.) Suppose then we raise his allowance to four dollars a week. What will he purchase with his third and fourth dollars? Things that he thinks (probably correctly) will give him less welfare than those he paid for with the first two dollars, but which he wants more than anything else he doesn't have. We must believe, then, that the total welfare purchased by the third and fourth dollar is not as great as that purchased by the first two dollars. If, therefore, we made a graph of the welfare he purchases with his money (see Figure 6), in which the areas of the columns represent the welfare purchased by each dollar, we would find that the curve bounding the tops of these areas slopes downwards to the right, after the first couple of dollars.[5] On the basis of such reasoning, it is justifiable to conclude generally (so the first premise assumes) that the utility of income tends to decline after the first few dollars. Or, to use technical terms, after a certain point (perhaps, in the case of an adult, the point of a "living wage") the marginal utility of money declines.

X – DOLLAR INCOME

Figure 6

Such is the first premise. Is the premise really sound? There are complications. For instance, suppose the boy wants very badly to play tennis. In order to play, he needs $2 for balls, and $15 for a racket. He cannot play until he has both. If we figured out the utility of having $2, $4, $6, we might find our curve sloping downwards rapidly. But if we drew a curve for $17, things would look very different. Or, if we compared the utility of $16 with that of $17, we would find a great disparity, so that the additional welfare purchased by the seventeenth dollar would be very high indeed. The serious question is whether there is a comparable phenomenon, every week, for the man with an annual income of $20,000 or $50,000. Can we say that his ambition to purchase a large and ostentatious home, or to have a $50,000 yacht, or to own several Cadillacs, or to have a fine collection of paintings, or to have a stamp or record collection, and so on, is such that we can say that the marginal utility of his income either does not decline at all, or declines very, very late? Or, perhaps some people simply get a tremendous thrill out of having a big income, and out of having large investments, and playing with them in the

[5] Figure 6 does not assign numbers to the y-axis, since it is not proposed (in view of the arguments at the ends of Chapters 12 and 13) that utility can be measured in numerical units. In order to emphasize the point, the columns are broken at the bottom.

stock market. Again, perhaps the marginal utility of income does not decline for such persons. (Marginal utility of income is very different from the marginal utility of goods: Beyond a certain number of potatoes, for example, the marginal utility of potatoes, for purposes of consumption, declines very rapidly.)

Nevertheless, it is plausible to suppose that the normal thing is for marginal utility of income to decline, and fairly early after the income is reached that the Department of Labor says gives "a modest but adequate standard of living."

The second premise is that we cannot compare the utility curves of different individuals in respect of relative height—or at least that it is not normally feasible to try to determine the optimum distribution of income on the basis of such comparisons. This premise, again, is plausible. Imagine my trying to convince an official that I should get more out of an additional $10 of weekly income, than you would! There are doubtless exceptional cases where such claim can be made out, for example, if I have cancer and need the money for the purchase of drugs.

Now, how does the argument move from these premises to the conclusion that—ignoring effects on production—one is *likely* to get more welfare by an equal distribution of income? The reasoning is best explained by a graph. Consider Figure 7, which represents *possible* utility curves of A

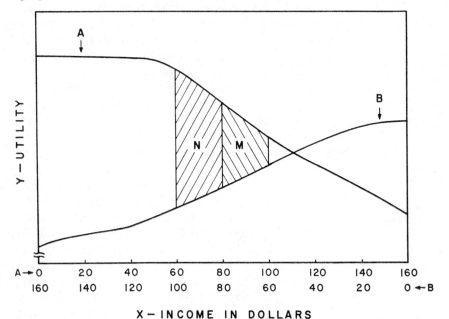

FIGURE 7*

* Adapted from A. P. Lerner, *The Economics of Control* (New York: The Macmillan Company, 1947), chap. 3, fig. 1. Used by permission.

and B, for weekly incomes ranging from $0 to $160. (We do not assume we can normally know any such facts as are represented by the graph; but we can understand what the graph *means*.) The area under either curve, from 0 to any point, represents the total utility of income up to that point. Thus, the total utility of the first $40 of A's income is represented by the area under A's curve up to the point above the $40 mark. (B's income is represented as starting from the opposite side.) For reasons stated in Chapters 12 and 13, we cannot think of either curve as having any numerically reprehensible distance above the *x*-axis; hence, whether the slope is represented as steep or gradual is arbitrary.

According to the first premise, A's curve must slope downwards to the right (after an initial horizontal line), and B's curve must slope downwards to the left (after an initial horizontal line). For simplicity, we eliminate possible humps in the curves, and we assume the two curves cross. The argument is unaffected by these simplifications.

Suppose, now, these curves represent accurately the utility curves of A and B. Then what distribution of income between them will maximize their joint utility? Obviously, distribution at the point where the two curves cross, for if income is distributed in this way, there will be a maximum area under the curves (since A's curve is higher to the left of the intersection, and B's is higher to the right.) If we divided equally, we would lose—all the area between the two curves between the line above the $80 mark and the point of intersection. Unfortunately, however, we *do not know* (by the second premise) where the curves intersect. And since we don't, presumably if we try to distribute unequally, we shall make mistakes about half the time—half the time we shall rightly give extra to the person with the higher utility curve and hence gain, and half the time give extra to the person with the lower utility curve, and thus lose. *As a result, on the average we shall lose utility if we depart from equal distributions.* Why? Suppose we give an extra $20 to A, and $20 less to B. This is a gain in total utility, equal to the shaded area M. But suppose— and this is equally probable—we make the mistake of giving an extra $20 to B, and $20 less to A. Then we lose in total utility, by the amount of the hatched portion N. Now the thing we notice is that the area of N is larger than the area of M; therefore, if we make the one arrangement one week and the opposite arrangement the following week, the total utility is *lower than* we would have got by an equal distribution both weeks, by the difference between the areas N and M. Since we do not, in general, know the relative positions of the curves of the two individuals, on the average any deviation from an equal distribution will work out at a loss, although we cannot say how large the loss will be. So, we shall get maximum net expectable utility, given the knowledge we have, by dividing income equally between A and B.

The argument can be generalized for any number of individuals. An equal distribution has maximum net expectable utility—for the present setting aside possible effects of inequality on production, and so on. Therefore, rule-utilitarianism must recognize an initial foundation for the view that equality should be the rule guiding income distributions.[6]

Is this complex argument sound? Economists are divided. Most appear to agree with the conclusion of the argument, that equality of income should be an aim of national policy, so far as this will not produce loss of utility because of unfavorable effects on production. Indeed, some economists are inclined to reject utilitarianism just because they think it cannot justify the degree of equality they think is right. But on the whole, economists appear to be dubious of the details of the foregoing argument, and many of them justify the progressive income tax and a steep inheritance tax by different lines of reasoning—for example, by saying simply that there is no other practicable way of getting the money, or that heavy taxation of the wealthy is necessary if their *real sacrifice* in support of government is to be comparable with that of the less well-to-do. (The theory that the rich must pay more in order to make an equal sacrifice, however, relies on reasoning practically the same as that above. But this theory is not committed in principle to the desirability of equalizing incomes where practicable.)[7] Economists who criticize the foregoing form of reasoning, however, do not present cogent objections to its logic, and it appears that it ought to be accepted.

The foregoing argument does not show precisely *how much* utility is probably lost by any given amount of inequality. The conclusion to which it commits us is, therefore, only that equality of income is one thing with good consequences, other things being equal. But we must be careful not to underestimate the amount of welfare that is lost by inequalities of income. It is hardly sensible to deny that there is a great difference between what an extra $100 will buy in welfare for a wealthy man who already has two Cadillacs and a yacht, and what it will buy for a poor man whose family is hungry or improperly clothed or whose children must stop their education and begin work at the age of sixteen.

2. There are other disutilities in a system of income allocation that permits large inequalities: the resentments of those who are paid less well despite no lack of industry on their part; the snobbishness and competition

[6] The foregoing formulation is due to A. P. Lerner, *The Economics of Control* (New York: The Macmillan Company, 1947), chap. 3. For a criticism and more rigorous restatement, see Milton Friedman, "Lerner on the Economics of Control," *Journal of Political Economy*, LV (1947), 405–16. See also G. J. Stigler, *Five Lectures on Economic Problems* (New York: The Macmillan Company, 1950).

[7] There is a substantial literature on how a progressive income tax may be justified. The most helpful discussions of this subject are: W. J. Blum and H. Kalven, *The Uneasy Case for Progressive Taxation* (Chicago: University of Chicago Press, 1953); R. J. Lampman, "Recent Thought on Egalitarianism," *Quarterly Journal of Economics*, LXXI (1957), 234–66; E. D. Fagan, "Recent and Contemporary Theories of Progressive Taxation," *Journal of Political Economy*, XLVI (1938), 457–98.

in ostentation of those who have the largest incomes; the tendency of the wealthy to lose contact with the values of hard work and achievement in favor of the passive joys of recreation (golf, yachts, travel, and so forth); the decline of social concern among the wealthy.

The consistent utilitarian, everything considered, will conclude that approximate equality of income should be a substantial aim of policy, to be deviated from only where the benefits of inequality are shown to be considerable.

3. We now come to the other side of the ledger: considerations that will incline the utilitarian toward a system that will foster or at least permit some inequalities of income. The first consideration is one implicit in the foregoing argument for equality on the ground of declining marginal utility of income. It will be recalled that we admitted, in connection with the second premise of that argument, that in some types of case it is possible to show, without the necessity of highly subjective reasoning, that utility is probably increased by inequalities of income. For instance, a person in pain will get more utility from the purchase of drugs than can the average person from the same amount of money. So, in principle, we may admit that unequal incomes can sometimes be justified on the basis of partially-known utility curves. Sometimes such reasoning has been carried to great lengths; sometimes it has been argued that people with sensitive taste ought to be subsidized in order to purchase the exquisite aesthetic enjoyments of which they alone are capable. Such proposals, however, must be dismissed on the ground that, at best, the required adjudications would be too subjective to be entrusted to public agencies. A sensible man will be very careful about making claims on the basis of peculiarities of his utility curve.

4. We come now to a more important matter. It can be claimed with much plausibility that net expectable utility will be increased if we permit inequality of income—whatever inequality is needed to serve as an incentive for industry and vigorous use of intelligence in one's occupation. It is a question of fact, of course, and one that in principle can be answered by the methods of science, *how great* inequalities of income must be permitted in order to provide satisfactory incentive. But there is much simple evidence of the incentive value of pecuniary inducements—for instance, the difference in one's son's motivation to mow the lawn when $2 is offered as compensation. On the other side, of course, is to be weighed the fact that many other motives for industry are observable, such as pride in personal achievement. The subject is one that needs further investigation, but in general there is reason to think that net expectable utility will be increased if some inequalities of income are permitted, on account of enhanced motivation to achieve.

5. A further and perhaps still more important argument for a system permitting inequalities is based on the efficiency of a system in which both human and material resources are allocated to producing objects or serv-

ices that people want. How is such efficient allocation of resources to be achieved? Theoretically, the open-market system of bidding for them solves the problem perfectly, and many economists doubt that any other system can solve it satisfactorily, at least without oppressive controls.

Let us see how the open-market system solves the problem. Suppose that (as is the case in India) there are far too many lawyers and far too few engineers. In a free-market economy, where labor sells for what it will bring, this situation tends to be rectified. The lawyers will compete for the work there is, so that fees are forced down; and in any case, the total amount of business to be divided among them is relatively fixed and small. Thus, the average income of the lawyer will be small. Among engineers the opposite situation will prevail. As a result college students, say, moved by the difference in prospective income, will tend to choose engineering as an occupation, until both occupations are relatively satisfactorily filled.

The open-market system is, however, only an approximate solution—as is shown by the fact that there are too many lawyers in India, and too many farmers in the U.S.A. There are various reasons for this: It is not easy to change occupations after one has already been trained; there are prestige factors that influence choice of occupation even in an open-market economy; and very often it is difficult to predict future prospects in a given occupation. Nevertheless, advocates of a free enterprise system argue that an open-market economy—with the price of wages determined solely by the forces of supply and demand—is the most satisfactory way of allocating labor (and raw materials) efficiently.

6. The final point is political. There are reasons, in the light of history, for wishing to avoid extreme power in government. It is desirable, therefore, to obtain decisions about the allocation of labor and natural resources —not to mention decisions about the size of income necessary for adequate incentive—by some other device than the deliberations of governmental agencies.

We must be careful, of course, not to go to absurd lengths in this reasoning. The present policy of the U.S. government, not to support farm prices beyond a certain percentage of parity, is in effect a method for reducing the number of farmers; whereas the device of supporting farm-prices beyond their market price is a means of keeping the occupation of farming overfilled. Further, in wartime there was rigid rationing of raw materials, and workers were not free to leave an important occupation. Yet, of course, tyranny has not resulted. There is risk in the centralization of governmental controls, and big government is likely to be inefficient, but some further measure of governmental control *could* be a good thing over-all, if the other gains were considerable.

Other reasons have been suggested why one form of income allocation or another may be expected to affect the general welfare favorably or adversely, but the foregoing ones are the most important. Let us sum them up. There are six facts that should affect estimates of the net expectable utility of a given system of distribution of income: (1) The fact that marginal utility of income tends to decline and, hence, that unequal distribution tends to decrease the utility that can be purchased; (2) the fact that inequalities produce snobbishness and discontent; (3) the fact that in special cases one man can purchase more utility with a given sum of money than can another person; (4) the fact that people tend to work harder if they believe their efforts will be rewarded by an extra share of income; (5) the fact that some method is needed for allocating labor and material resources efficiently; and (6) the fact that concentration of decisions in the hands of government is somewhat dangerous and likely to be inefficient.

If the foregoing facts are the major factors which determine whether one system of income allocation will affect general welfare more favorably than some other, then, if the utilitarian theory about obligations is correct, they are also the major facts relevant to the moral justification of a system of economic distribution. If utilitarianism is true, we ought to support that system of distribution which combines equality with inequality in such a way as will probably—in view of these various facts—maximize the net expectable utility of society.

4. SOME NONUTILITARIAN PRINCIPLES

The utilitarian theory of distribution is impressive. Practically everyone will admit that the considerations that utilitarian theory implies are strongly relevant for the justification of a system of income allocation, really are in fact strongly relevant. Nevertheless, it is at least doubtful whether the theory is not too simple. There are further principles with some claim to the status of at least necessary supplements to utilitarian reasoning. We must consider some of these principles in detail.

1. *The compensation of disutilities.* It is a recognized principle of just compensation that disagreeable, onerous, or hazardous work has a prima facie claim[8] to be compensated more highly than pleasant, easy, risk-free work. Labor arbitrators, for instance, have recognized the justice of a claim by tractor-drivers to receive extra compensation on account of the physical strain of their work; and they have compensated the workers in a

---

[8] In the case of these nonutilitarian principles, we shall generally speak of a "prima facie" claim for recompense on a certain basis, or a "prima facie" obligation on us to support a system that allocates rewards on a certain basis. The reason for this is that there might be, in every case, some other stronger conflicting consideration, so that, everything considered, the first prima facie claim to compensation must be ignored, or only partly met. For instance, if in the end we must support some kind of open-market economy, it may be that it will not be possible to recompense workers for the disutilities (or utilities) of their occupations, at least in any reasonably precise way.

fish-reduction plant for the fact that their work must be done in the presence of offensive odors.[9]

Does the utilitarian formula imply that such compensation should be made? Not obviously. The formula says that distribution should be made according to rules that, if followed, will maximize utility. But it does not necessarily maximize utility to give extra compensation to those whose work is hazardous, and so on.

However, it may be supposed that indirectly the formula requires such compensation, for, it may be said, the utilitarian is committed to some form of free-market determination of wages. However, in a free market, more must be paid for performance of work that is unpleasant, onerous, or hazardous. Why? Because each man will decide to sell his services for the job whose wages compare best with the services he is expected to perform. Workers will, therefore, not look favorably upon jobs that are hard or risky, unless extra compensation is involved, and such jobs will be difficult to fill. So, assuming there is demand that these jobs be done, compensation for them will be higher than for comparable jobs, in an open-market economy. Utilitarianism espouses an open-market economy, and therefore it implies what goes with such an economy—extra compensation for more hazardous, onerous, and disagreeable jobs. So the argument may run.

This reply is not successful, however, for the reason that the utilitarian formula, when taken in conjunction with *true* factual premises, by no means necessarily implies that we should try to realize an open-market economy precisely of a kind that will recompense a person for the disutilities of his occupation. Why? In the first place, of course, there is doubt whether it implies we should try to realize an open-market economy at all; whether it does is a question of subtle balancing of the disutility of inequality against the feasibility and dangers of a centrally-planned economic system. But let us assume it does. Why will the economy to be supported be one that will automatically recompense the disutilities of one's occupation? It will, admittedly, if what we should advocate is a market that is "perfect," "ideally free." But why must we suppose that the utilitarian formula implies that we should aim at an ideally-free market or even that such a market is *possible?* The kind of open market to which the Western world has been accustomed is far from perfect in this sense. Moreover, historically, the open market of the kind that has existed in the West has given the *lowest* remuneration to jobs that are hard, disagreeable, and irregular. In fact, the tradition has been such that the recompense for various types of jobs has only a faint resemblance to the recompense that theoretically would occur in a "perfect" market. It is only recently that the supply of unskilled labor has become sufficiently

---

[9] Irving Bernstein, *Arbitration of Wages* (Berkeley: University of California Press, 1954), pp. 90 ff. For thinking of a primitive group on the same problem, see R. B. Brandt, *Hopi Ethics*, pp. 230–34.

scarce that it has been necessary to increase compensation for disagreeable jobs in order to attract workers to take them.[10] Even today, company job analysts give serious weight only to skill, in assessing the relative wage proper for a given job.[11]

In view of past experiences with the open-market system, it is hard to believe that the utilitarian formula implies, given true factual propositions about the conditions a working economic system must satisfy, that we must aim to realize precisely that form of open-market economy that will recompense for the disutility of jobs. Therefore, unless we are prepared to say that "qualified" attitudes would not demand attention to such matters in fixing compensation, the utilitarian principle is unacceptable as it stands, and must at least be supplemented.

2. *A living wage.* There is a widespread feeling—surely with some claim to coherence with "qualified" attitudes—that every person, if he makes what contribution he can to the common welfare, has a prima facie claim to a "living wage" share of the national income. Exactly what a "living wage" amounts to is not a matter of agreement, but it is felt that there is a certain floor below which wages should not go, in terms of the cost of living; and that persons who enjoy high wages should be prepared to make a sacrifice in order to secure this minimum for all. What is objected to is not inequality as such, but inequality that requires some persons to live a miserable life.

This conviction is compatible with utilitarianism if the argument from the declining marginal utility of income is accepted: the conviction may be construed as the belief that the utility of income is very high, up to the point of a "living wage," and thereafter drops off steeply, and that therefore there are utilitarian reasons for securing a living wage for all.[12] If one does not accept the argument from the declining marginal utility of income, however, one seems to be faced with a clear choice between surrendering this conviction about the necessity for a living wage and surrendering a pure utilitarian theory of just wages.

The conviction carries some force, even when it takes a simpler form: the belief that we have a prima facie obligation to realize equal welfare on its own account. In order to appreciate this, let us note how we would feel about the following case. Suppose there were a group of a dozen

---

[10] See Barbara Wooton, *The Social Foundations of Wage Policy* (London: George Allen & Unwin, Ltd., 1955), chap 2.

[11] According to Professor John Turnbull of the University of Minnesota.

[12] A. C. Pigou recently expressed the view that after income attains a modest level, further increases are not very significant in producing welfare. "Some Aspects of Welfare Economics," *American Economic Review*, XLI (1951), 287–302.

Much has been written about the joys of the cottage as compared with the palace, but it is hard to believe that life is as joyful as it might be when one does not have a "living wage."

orphans in a home, and we decided to contribute $200 for a holiday. Would we think it proper if the administrators invested it all in one glorious long holiday for one boy—providing there was no special reason, such as illness, that clearly indicated such a step? Not at all. We would think the boys should all receive an equal if much shorter holiday—and this even if we thought that resentments could be prevented by keeping the whole thing secret.

3. *Equality of opportunity.* Some writers who apparently are not moved by the preceding argument think, however, that there is strong prima facie obligation to give all children an *equal opportunity* to get an advantageous position in the wage system. The reasoning is as follows.[13]

Suppose we have, as in fact we have, a social system in which there are unequal economic rewards—inequalities justified as necessary in order to provide incentive and an efficient allocation of talent. Presumably, then, some occupations that require a high degree of skill and ability, for example, those of surgeon or business executive, will receive relatively handsome rewards. Now, most people will want to occupy one of these prize posts, because these jobs, in addition to being economically well-rewarded, also tend to be inherently attractive; they are normally challenging, interesting, satisfactory to a person's desire for power and influence, and so on. (In fact, in view of the inherent utilities of such jobs, one might argue that their incumbents ought to receive a *lower* economic return!) Many, then, will want these posts, but few can get them. Now, some writers feel that we have a prima facie obligation to give each person *equal opportunity* to get one of these posts. They feel that, if only everyone has an equal start in life, so that where a person gets will depend at least mostly on how hard he runs, then we need not feel disturbed by the inequalities of reward. We can say that everyone had an equal chance at the prizes; if anyone did not get them, it is because he did not put forth the effort, so that he has only himself to blame.

We should notice, however, that the utilitarian, too, will advocate substantial equality of opportunity, in two respects. First, he will emphasize the utility of allocating human resources to places where they are most needed; therefore, he will insist that posts of importance be *open* to the persons best fitted to occupy them. (In general. But a utilitarian is not committed to advocating the abolition of monarchy, or filling the king's post by civil service examination. There are utilities besides efficiency to be considered.) Second, the utilitarian will defend the institution of free education for all, partly as a means to fuller enjoyment of life, and partly because it is important for society that good brains be trained irrespective of the economic position of one's parents. For the latter reason, at least,

---

[13] See, for instance, Blum and Kalven, *op. cit.,* pp. 85–90.

he will also defend free higher education for gifted persons. The utilitarian, then, will advocate substantial equality of opportunity.

The conclusion of the advocates of "equality of opportunity," then, is acceptable to the utilitarian. Their argument, their underlying ethical premise, however, appears to be nonutilitarian. This premise seems to be that we have an obligation to bring about *equality of welfare* except insofar as inequalities can be blamed on an individual's own lack of effort or motivation. (One might question whether this is their implicit premise. But what is the point of insisting on an *equal start* in life for everybody on grounds of justice, unless it is thought that unequal rewards are unjustified except when they are a result of the individual's own effort or lack of it?) As such, the basic principle has some similarity to the preceding "living wage" principle; what is distinctive about it is the implication that inequalities are justified when they can be attributed to the industry or sloth of the individual.

We shall not attempt to assess the force of the distinctive point of this basic principle. Undoubtedly it raises a responsive echo in most minds. However, since it is impossible to distinguish between that part of a person's achievement which is a result of industry and that which is a result of natural endowments, advantages in education and experience, and so on, the principle is not one that can be applied in the assessment of what a person's income ought to be.

4. *The claims of the physically or mentally subnormal.* It has been thought that we have a prima facie obligation to bring the aged, the sick, and even the imbecilic up to a modest standard of comfort, even if this requires not merely an equal share of income but a substantially larger than equal share. This conviction differs from the "living wage" view in that it advocates not merely a "cost of living" wage for everyone who works, but *a decent level of welfare for everyone*, with whatever sacrifice of luxuries this may require from others. However, we might well amalgamate the two convictions and say that there is just one conviction—that we have a prima facie obligation to achieve a certain *floor of welfare*, and that the incomes of better-situated persons must be reduced to whatever degree is necessary to support this minimum standard.[14]

The utilitarian need not disagree with the justice of a special claim of the sick or handicapped to be brought up to an equal level, *if* he is prepared to hold that in these cases money spent for them purchases more welfare than money spent in adding to the luxuries of the normal. Indeed, if he accepts the argument for equality on the basis of declining marginal utility of income, he will be disposed to accept the general idea of a floor for welfare, at least as an ideal with strong claims. The principle here in

[14] See the interesting essay by D. D. Raphael, "Equality and Equity," *Philosophy*, XXI (1946), 118–32.

question, then, need be classified as "nonutilitarian" only if we have in mind certain sorts of utilitarian.[15]

5. *The merits of valuable services.* Finally, it has been thought that individuals should be paid for their services in proportion to the "value" of the services rendered, just as we would stand ready to pay for a material article a price corresponding to its "worth."

This principle, at least when stated vaguely, has much appeal. Corporation reports to stockholders use it in justification of the size of the salaries of corporation officers. It is used to justify higher rewards for skilled than for unskilled workers. Also, should not the largest salaries go to those members of a university staff who by their teaching, research activities, committee work, fund-raising activities, and so forth, make the largest contribution to the life of the institution? Such thinking has been familiar in the pages of economic theory. Nor is it an idiosyncrasy of the Western industrialized world. For instance, the writer found that the Hopi think it is reasonable to make larger payments to a successful physician than to a successful carpenter or garageman, on the ground that the service performed is more important. "The one who works on human beings gets more," said one informant, "because life is more important than property."[16]

But what exactly *is* the principle? Suppose we take it to mean that a person should be paid all that his services are worth to the recipient, that is, all the recipient would be willing to pay rather than go without them. But this is absurd. If it were true, an aggressive company president who is responsible for an increase of profits to the extent of $5,000,000 a year, ought to be paid $5,000,000. But if so, then there would be no point in hiring him, since profits would remain the same. Moreover, we think that just return for a service should bear some relation to the cost of the service to the one who supplies it; thus, a man who saves a millionaire from drowning by throwing him a rope is hardly entitled to whatever the millionaire would pay rather than lose his life. It is evident, also, that the cost to the company president of his services to the company does not strike him as being in the $5,000,000 class, else it would not be true that he, and others equally competent, are willing to perform this service for much less than $5,000,000. Moreover, the plausibility of the principle is further reduced if we look at the matter in a different way. Why not say that salary is not a payment by one person for services rendered him by another person, but that salary is an allocation of national income? Then, in this case, it seems more proper, if we are going to pay on the basis of value of services, to appraise a service in terms of its worth to society as a whole.

---

[15] Utilitarians are perhaps more committed than others, at least unless they think life itself is an intrinsic value, to advocating euthanasia for cases where the degree of welfare cannot be made high except with very substantial expenditure; but that is another problem, different from the question of how income should be distributed among the living.

[16] *Hopi Ethics* (Chicago: University of Chicago Press, 1954), p. 232.

But if the principle is implausible when interpreted as the view that a person should be paid whatever the beneficiary is willing to pay rather than go without it, then how are we to interpret it?

Economists who have supported the principle have a subtle answer to this. A person should be paid in proportion to the *value* of services rendered, where "value" is defined as the price the service can actually command in an open market where one is free to contract one's service. The mechanism of the market will see to it that both benefit to the recipient and cost to the donor are represented in the price. Some years ago, one economist described the workings of an open market in the following way:

> Each receives a share which is supposed to represent the effective social importance of the function he performs directly or through some factor which society authorizes him to own. . . . Every economic income tends to approximate that quantity of goods which constitutes an expression of the marginal significance to people at large of the actual output—when competition is free, the natural output—of the type of service rendered by the receiver of said income, and which also, in the case of free competition, constitutes an expression of the net marginal disutility involved in furnishing said type of service.[17]

In other words, owing to the (supposed) fact that people will purchase a service at a given price only when it is preferred by them to other services available at that price, and owing to the (supposed) fact that people will sell their services at a price only when they cannot sell them elsewhere at a better price, the operation of the open market will make the price of a service correspond both with its marginal utility to buyers, and with its marginal disutility to sellers. Thus, it is supposed, the open market measures the value of services and sees to their just reward.

When the principle is interpreted in this way, however, it is far from convincing—far from conforming with our "qualified" attitudes. The principle that tells us that a man who is a patient and gifted teacher should be better remunerated strikes a sympathetic chord; but the principle that tells us that a bumbling economist is "worth" more than a good philosopher because economists are in short supply is much less successful. The principle as precisely interpreted tells us that the "worth" of a psychologist's service declines if too many people become psychologists and the market is glutted. It tells us that the way for a person to enhance the "worth" of his services is to do his best to keep others from entering the same occupation! This is not convincing.

Moreover, the principle is obviously not true (nobody claims it is) for a monopoly market, where prices can be controlled by a few buyers or sellers; hence, it does not apply to the services of prize-fighters, movie-stars, and perhaps top surgeons. It does not apply, for the same reason, to

---

[17] F. M. Taylor, *Principles of Economics* (Ann Arbor: University of Michigan Press 1925), pp. 440, 443.

the value of services of members of labor unions. Moreover, the principle is obviously not true where individuals cannot freely change their occupations or places of residence, in order to take advantage of higher wages. So, at best, one can claim that this principle can determine a just wage only for a limited range of jobs.

It seems, then, that the principle of reward in proportion to the "value" of services is not acceptable—certainly not as the single principle relevant to fixing wages—when interpreted in either of these two ways.

Yet there is some value in the principle, not as a nonutilitarian principle, a basic distinct ethical principle about distributions, but as an implication of utilitarianism. Given the fact that people are motivated by financial incentives, then an employer is justified on utilitarian grounds in rewarding fine services with extra recompense. Again, if we conclude on utilitarian grounds that some form of open-market system for labor must be used, as a means of allocating brains to positions where they are needed without elaborate governmental controls, then we shall have to say that the wage a person can command in such a "best" system is a "just" recompense. To say this would be very near to saying that a person's just recompense for services is whatever they can command in the open market.

5. CONCLUSIONS

With the main facts and arguments now behind us, there are three questions to be answered.

First: Everything considered, is rule-utilitarianism a satisfactory theory about the correct allocation of income? The answer seems to be "No." The reason for this answer is not the nonutilitarian argument for equality of opportunity, or the argument that services should be rewarded in accordance with their value; these principles do not seem required by our "qualified" attitudes. There does, however, seem to be a prima facie obligation to recompense people for the disutilities of their jobs; and—we *may* not need to add this if we accept the declining marginal utility reasoning—there is a prima facie obligation roughly to effectuate equality of welfare or at least to remove inequalities incompatible with a decent standard of living for all (certainly for the families of workers).

It seems, then, that we must choose between two theories: (1) a formalist theory according to which there is a prima facie obligation to do what will maximize welfare, and also a prima facie obligation to promote *equality of welfare*[18] in one way or another; and (2) an "extended" rule-utilitarian

[18] For simplicity, we are here including under "equality of welfare" both compensation for the disutilities of one's job, and the setting of a floor for welfare (the "living wage" argument, as well as the claim that the sick and others must be given special compensation in order to bring them up to a reasonable level of comfort)—and, if we wish, also the simple principal (p. 424) that we should aim at equality of welfare as such. This terminology enables us to say that the two main principles of economic justice are utility and equality of welfare.

theory that asserts that equality of welfare is intrinsically worthwhile. This is the result we reached at the conclusion of the preceding chapter.

The second question is quite different. Everything considered, what kind of economic system ought we to support? Here again there appears to be a choice between two major types: (1) a planned economy, with central decisions about the allocation of labor, compensation for a particular type of job, and so on, being made by a bureaucracy; and (2) an open-market free enterprise system. There are various possible subtypes of each, including compromises between the two.

Which choice one makes between these two is independent of one's choice between formalism and "extended" rule-utilitarianism. Nor would matters be much different if one were a straight rule-utilitarian or even an act-utilitarian.

What choice is to be made? Presumably we shall have to compromise, for the system that provides most incentive for production will clearly not be the one that gives most equal distribution of income. Further, the system that most efficiently allocates human resources to the points where they are most needed may not be the one that compensates exactly for the disutilities of one's job.

We need not here attempt to defend any particular system. Of course, thinking in the West in recent years has favored a free-market system for setting wages, subject to rather minor regulation, as a way of providing incentive and an efficient allocation of labor resources. It has favored an increasingly large assumption by government of certain responsibilities: care for the aged, the ill, and the unemployed (in Great Britain much more than in the United States). It has favored a progressive income tax as a device for paying the cost of (among other things) the newly-assumed responsibilities of government; and many thinkers favor this tax also because it reduces inequalities, although in the United States egalitarian sentiment seems less strong than elsewhere. It may be, however, that the system will have to be re-evaluated and changed in order to meet currently puzzling difficulties, such as inflationary spirals, alternating booms and recessions in business, and long-term inequities in the compensation of certain classes of workers, including government employees, teachers, small businessmen, and perhaps farmers.

Will the system that provides maximum net expectable utility (including in utility the value of equal welfare) be a "just" system? Well, we said that to act "unjustly" is to treat individuals unequally, except as the inequality is required by moral considerations of weight. In the present context, we may interpret this as meaning that an unjust allocation of money income would be an unequal money income except as inequality is required by moral considerations—in this case, the "moral considerations" are *equality of welfare* and *utility*. An allocation of income that is in accordance with the system required by equality and utility, then, will be a *just* allocation.[19]

We come now to our third question: What are the obligations of an individual in the present system—one that may not be exactly what it ought to be? For instance, suppose that one concludes that an ideal system of allocation is much more egalitarian than the present system. Does this mean it is one's duty to refuse to pay the doctor's bill, if one knows the doctor's income is larger than ideally it ought to be? Is a social security administrator to write out checks, irrespective of the law (until he is fired!), so as to bring the income of recipients of these checks up to a minimum decent standard? The "extended" rule-utilitarian will say: only under most exceptional circumstances. Things would be chaotic if everybody in such circumstances made free to take into his own hands the equalization of incomes. One may advocate the passage of laws regulating the profits of the doctor. Indeed, if the time is suitable, it might even be one's duty to join in a revolution, if the road to reform were wholly closed to less violent methods. In general, however, one must act within the framework of law and custom.

There is an opposite situation: that of the person who has more than his just share of the national income. Is he obligated to dispose of it? The question is not an easy one. The rule-utilitarian's answer to it would be: Do whatever it would do most good for everyone in your position to do! Presumably, it will not do most good for everyone in this position simply to give the excess over their just share to any and every charity.

There is one important point that we have altogether ignored so far. Let us conclude this chapter by dwelling on it. We have been talking so far as if the moral problem were simply the assessment of various systems for allocating the *national* income. This must now be modified. When we are asking which system of income allocation is just and best, we must take a world-wide point of view. We must say—if our final result was correct —that the just set of rules is the one that will serve both equality and utility for the whole of mankind. Thus, if a have-not nation raises a cry that it has been excluded from the benefits of world resources, its complaint is well taken, however ineffectual it may be, given contemporary nationalistic thinking.

Why? We have simply to ask ourselves whether our "qualified" attitudes—our informed, impartial (and so on) ones—would feel more obligated to take steps to provide for the welfare of an American than for the welfare of a Chinese. Or, if one agrees that "justice" means treating peo-

---

[19] This is true, whatever the actual inequalities—for these inequalities will be equitable. If the system is just, and I inherit a million dollars under the terms of the system, then I have my money justly! It would be unreasonable first to select a system of allocation as a just one, and then to question whether the application of the system works out justly.

ple equally except as there are morally cogent grounds for unequal treatment, one must ask whether then it can be just to prefer the welfare of Americans to that of Chinese. Anyone who thinks he can justify such preferences ought to step forward and give his reasons.

FURTHER READING

On distributive justice—philosophers:

D. D. Raphael, *Moral Judgment* (London: George Allen & Unwin, Ltd., 1955), pp. 62–67, 77–94.

——, "Equality and Equity," *Philosophy*, XXI (1946), 118–32.

H. Sidgwick, *The Methods of Ethics* (London: Macmillan & Co., Ltd., 1922), Bk. III, chaps. 5, 13; pp. 439–48.

——, *Elements of Politics* (4th ed.; London: Macmillan & Co., Ltd., 1929), chap. 10.

C. D. Broad, *Five Types of Ethical Theory* (New York: Harcourt, Brace & Company, 1934), pp. 246–53.

Hastings Rashdall, *Theory of Good and Evil* (Oxford: Clarendon Press, 1924), vol. I, chap. 8. A careful discussion.

Aristotle, *Nicomachaean Ethics*, Bk. V, chaps. 1–8.

David Hume, *Treatise of Human Nature*, Bk. III, Pt. 2.

——, *An Inquiry Concerning the Principles of Morals*, chap. 3, appendix 3.

L. Garvin, *A Modern Introduction to Ethics* (New York: Houghton Mifflin Company, 1953), pp. 447–50, 456–72.

J. S. Mill, *Utilitarianism*, chap. 5.

J. Rawls and E. Hall, *Journal of Philosophy* (symposium), LIV (1957), 653–70. An interesting statement of a very general view about justice.

J. Rawls, "Justice as Fairness," *Philosophical Review*, LXVII (1958), 164–94.

W. D. Lamont, *The Principles of Moral Judgment* (Oxford: Clarendon Press, 1946), chap. 5.

On distributive justice—economists:

A. C. Pigou, *Economics of Welfare* (London: Macmillan & Co., Ltd., 1932), Pt. I, chap. 8.

R. J. Lampman, "Recent Thought on Egalitarianism," *Quarterly Journal of Economics*, LXXI (1957), 234–66.

W. J. Blum and H. Kalven, *The Uneasy Case for Progressive Taxation* (Chicago: University of Chicago Press, 1953).

A. P. Lerner, *The Economics of Control* (New York: The Macmillan Company, 1947), chaps. 2, 3.

B. Wooton, *The Social Foundations of Wage Policy* (London: George Allen & Unwin, Ltd., 1955), chap. 6.

17

Human Rights

According to the Virginia Bill of Rights, "All men are by nature equally free and independent, and have certain inherent rights, . . . namely, the enjoyment of life and liberty, with the means of acquiring and possessing property, and pursuing and obtaining happiness and safety." This declaration that all men have certain rights is typical of many major political documents of the past two hundred years.

The concept of human rights has had an important place in thinking about the relation of man to government for a long time. But it also has a conspicuous place in the moral reflection and discourse of the average man. The stenographer may say of her employer, "He has no right to expect me to stay overtime every night." And a man may answer his wife's criticism of his provocative remarks at a cocktail party, "A man has a right to state his opinions."

The student of ethics could perhaps ignore the topic of human rights if he has a satisfactory theory of obligation. If we have a satisfactory theory about what we *ought to do*, we cannot have omitted anything of practical importance, that is, anything we have to know in order to know what we ought to do. Nevertheless, it would be a great mistake for us to pass by the subject of rights, both on account of the historical importance of the concept and because connecting this concept with other moral concepts can serve to clarify our conclusions and reasoning about what rights people have.

As in the case of the other moral terms, it is necessary to distinguish two types of question about rights. First, there are the metaethical questions: What does the word "rights" mean? How shall we confirm statements about rights? Secondly, there are the normative questions: What general statements can we make about rights? Are there any rights that every human being has, just as a human being, independent of membership in any

433

political society, independent of status, race, religion, and so on? These are the questions we shall try to answer.

1. THE CONCEPT OF RIGHTS

In an earlier chapter we debated some proposals to the effect that the expression "morally obligatory" could be defined in terms of "desirable" and "morally culpable." We decided against these. Although "morally obligatory" is a near-synonym of other ethical terms, for example, "moral duty" and "morally ought," it is not possible to define it by means of more distantly related moral terms, in such a way as to show a clarifying inter-relation of ethical concepts.

The position of "rights," however, is different. "Rights" is properly classified as an ethical term and, in general, is like the other ethical words in point of definability by a naturalistic definition. But it can be defined in terms of "moral obligation" plus certain nonethical concepts. The point is an important one, for its effect is that all the theories about what is morally obligatory—utilitarianism, formalism, rule-utilitarianism, and the others—are by implication also theories about human rights. Thus, we already have, by implication, a set of true general propositions about human rights, although doubtless it will take some thinking to see exactly what they are.

One might raise an initial objection to the very idea that "rights" is definable in terms of "obligation," on the ground that if it were, it would be inexplainable why language has both these terms, and also why their close relation is not more obvious than it is. If "rights" is definable in this way, why do many people say that there was no concept of rights at all until after the Middle Ages? Such questions are well taken. Let us answer them in order. In the first place, there are two words in the language for the same reason there is both an active and a passive voice: convenience. "Wilkes Booth shot Lincoln" uses the active voice; before it was known who shot Lincoln it was still possible to say, with the passive voice, "Lincoln has been shot." Of course, one could also say, "Somebody shot Lincoln"; but when the general character of the agency of some event is more obscure we need the passive. Similarly for rights and duties. "I have a right to be paid $10 by him" can naturally be replaced by "He has a moral obligation to pay me $10." But "I have a right to be heard" can only with awkwardness be replaced by something like "The people doing that shouting have an obligation to be quiet and let me speak." When we come to "Everyone has a right to an education," it is by no means easy to formulate a corresponding statement in terms of "obligation."

In reply to the second question we can explain why "rights" and "moral obligation" are not more obviously connected in meaning than they are. We can do so in this way. Take the phrase, "I have a *right to* speak";

this expression *does* seem equivalent to some statement about an obligation to let me speak. But, grammatically, the substantive "right" admits of a plural, so that we pass naturally to saying, "I have many rights, to . . . and. . . ." We then pass naturally to speaking of the collection of things to which we have a right as a group of "rights." Widespread ideas about the *kinds* of thing that belong to this collection (privileges, freedoms) then come to comprise part of the connotation of the word. As a result, if a person is asked the meaning of "certain inherent *rights*," he is apt to say that "rights" means "liberties" or "privileges," and to overlook the crucial point that a privilege, when it is a right, is a privilege that someone is *obligated* to respect. In consequence, "a right" seems close to "a liberty" instead of the converse of "moral obligation"; language has broken asunder the two concepts that logically belong together.[1]

We shall take the phrase "have a right to" as basic. What does the expression mean?

It will be helpful first to notice a parallel, between "have a *moral* right to" and "have a *legal* right to." What does the second phrase mean? Take "*Legally* I have a right to cut off those branches of my neighbor's tree that overhang my driveway." How might we explain this statement to a foreigner, if we were asked? First, we can say that the law will not stop me from cutting off the branches: There is no law forbidding me; my neighbor cannot win a suit for damages against me if I do; he cannot obtain an injunction ordering me to desist, or induce the police to force me to abstain. Second, the law *does* require others to abstain from interfering; it imposes on them a *legal duty* not to interfere. If my neighbor comes over onto my property with the intent of preventing me, physically, from sawing off the limbs, I shall be able to obtain the assistance of the police, or a court order commanding him to abstain. Of course, to say I have a legal right to do something is not to say I *must* do it. I am merely given the liberty to do so, if I wish. I am provided with what may be called a "sphere of autonomy"—an area in which I may freely do as I please.

This legal right is not altogether typical; for instance, there corresponds to it the legal duty of someone else simply to abstain from acting, not to perform in some positive way. Other rights are different, for example, my right to collect a debt, to which corresponds the fact that a specific individual has the legal duty to perform a definite action, namely, give me what I am owed. Still, our case is typical enough to give us a suggestion for a general definition of "have a legal right to." Roughly, what it is for me to have a legal right is for the legal system to impose a *legal duty on someone else*, in the sense that the system stands ready to compel or oblige this

---

[1] Somewhat the same thing has happened in the case of "duty" and "obligation." Take "His obligation is to" and "his family obligations." These parallels are worth further study.

someone else, on my "motion" or application, to act or refrain from acting in some way in respect of the thing to which I am said to have the right.

The phrase "have a moral right to" can be explained in parallel fashion. We can say, roughly, that to have a moral right to something is for *someone else to be morally obligated* (in the objective sense) to act or refrain from acting in some way in respect to the thing to which I am said to have the right, if I want him to. This definition, we shall see in a moment, is not *quite* right: It needs to be complicated in some ways. But it is roughly correct, not necessarily as a formulation *overtly* the same in meaning as "have a moral right to" (although it would not be absurd to claim that this is true), but at any rate as a formulation the same in meaning in the sense explained in Chapter 7.

We of course cannot *prove* that for one person to "have a moral right to" is roughly equivalent to such a claim about the moral obligations of someone else. We can never *prove* that *any* two expressions mean the same. However, there are two facts that give initial support to the proposal. First, on reflection we can notice that we always believe that, when one person has a moral right, some other person or persons have corresponding obligations. Indeed, this "correlativity" of rights and obligations has usually been admitted. But second, we should ask ourselves what *attitude* we might plausibly say "I have a right to" expresses, if we held an emotive theory of ethical terms. It is plausible to say it expresses an impartial *demanding* attitude, a readiness to compel corresponding behavior in others where this is feasible and to be indignant at them if they fail to do what is demanded. Similarly, we should ask ourselves what attitude we might plausibly say "You do have a right for me to . . ." expresses, if we held an emotive theory. A plausible answer to this would be: an impartial *feeling of obligation* (in the sense of Chapter 6) to do a certain thing for you. Now, if our proposals about "obligation" statements have been correct, these attitudes are also the very ones we should have to say are expressed by the corresponding "obligation" statements, if we espoused the emotive theory.

Let us now digress a moment from our concern with the definition of "have a moral right to," in order to insist on a point that is very likely obvious, but about which it is important that no mistake be made. To have a moral right is *utterly different* from having a legal right. I may have a legal right to something when I have no moral right (for example, to disfigure my neighbor's tree by removing the branches that overhang my property); and I may have a moral right to something to which I have no legal right (to be considered for a job without discrimination on grounds of race or religion). Indeed, one of the most important uses of statements of moral rights is in advocating that people be given legal rights they do not have. The Universal Declaration of Human Rights adopted by the General Assembly of the United Nations, in 1948, is a statement of moral rights many of which are in fact not legal rights in many countries. Moreover, what legal rights I have is a matter of which legal system has authority over my case, and what are the recognized laws and procedures of that system; if I am under the jurisdiction of *no* legal system, then I have *no* legal rights. This is not true in respect to moral rights: if I meet an utter stranger, anywhere on earth or off the earth, and he is in dire need or suffering, he has a moral right to my assistance, absolutely irrespective of any laws having jurisdiction over the territory in which we meet.

Let us now return to our job of explaining the meaning of "have a moral right to." We have said that the rough definition already suggested must be complicated somewhat. We must do this for two reasons.

First, in order to admit saying things like "I have a right to an education": To say I have a right to an education is not to imply simply that some person or persons are to *abstain* from doing something (such as refraining from interfering with my speaking), or yet to say that some person or persons are to perform some *specific* act (like paying me ten dollars). My having such a right implies roughly that each individual in my community has an obligation to do what he can, in view of his opportunities and capacities and other obligations, to secure and maintain a system in which I and persons in my position are provided an opportunity for education. We have to frame our definition so as to allow for this. (Things were simpler, as we shall see, in John Locke's days two hundred years ago; the concept of rights was simpler and this complication in the definition was not needed.)

Second, we need to distinguish *two senses* of "have a right to" parallel to the distinction already drawn between "over-all obligation" and "prima facie obligation." This distinction is necessary because there is a great deal of difference between a statement like "I have a right to be paid that $10 now" and a statement, as in the United Nations Declaration of Human Rights, that people have a right to exchange ideas freely—something we say correctly, even though we agree that there are occasions when it is not proper, everything considered, for people to exchange ideas freely (for instance, if to do so would cause a panic or a riot). The former statement, if true, implies that someone has an *over-all* obligation (to pay me $10). But the second does not; at least it does not imply that others in a position to control whether people may speak have an over-all obligation to permit them to "exchange ideas freely" on every occasion, no matter what the circumstances. The latter statement rather seems to mean something like this: "People have a right (in the *stronger* sense) to exchange ideas freely if and whenever no conflicting more urgent moral considerations stand in the way."

This second point is more important than may at first appear. It has sometimes been argued that human beings cannot be said to have "natural" rights such as the rights to life and freedom of action (which important political documents have claimed they have), on the ground that obviously these alleged rights must sometimes stand aside—lives and freedom of action must sometimes be sacrificed, in the total context. If we used "have a right to" only in the stronger sense, this argument would be cogent; it proves that there are few if any rights at all that are universal rights of man at all times and places. However, if we make the distinction—which we shall call the distinction between *prima facie* rights and *absolute* rights —this argument is undermined, and it becomes clear that the most it proves is that men do not always and everywhere have an *absolute* right, say, to life and liberty of action.

Let us now proceed with our definition: We begin with the *absolute* sense of "have a right to." We propose that "X has an absolute right to enjoy, have, or be secured in *y*" means the same as "It is someone's objective over-all obligation to secure X in, or in the possession of, or in the enjoyment of, *y*, if X wishes it."[2] In this definition, "someone" is to be taken broadly to include in its range not merely a particular human person or persons, but also corporate bodies and communities or nations. In these latter cases, however, we must construe the definition in a special way (partly in order to avoid saying that corporate bodies or collectives have moral obligations). In these cases, "someone is objectively obligated over all to" is to be construed to mean that the responsible members of the collective "person" are severally objectively duty-bound over all not to interfere with X's getting (and so forth) and furthermore, more positively, to cooperate substantially, to a degree depending upon position and opportunity, in establishing the means necessary to secure (and so forth) X, and others in his situation, in *y*.

What is it, then, to "have a prima facie right"? This term could be explained in terms of "have an absolute right," but it is simpler to define it directly in terms of "obligation." We want to define it in such a way that to say that we have a prima facie right to something (say, free speech) is consistent with saying that sometimes we ought not to be provided the thing or opportunity; further, we want to define it in such a way that, if

---

[2] Perhaps we should add "or *would* wish it if X considered his interests carefully." The final clause maintains that a right is an area of autonomy. Others are not obligated to perform for a person services that he does not want.

It also has an implication that we should note. Suppose I pay my brother $10,000 to care for our aunt until her death. He then is obligated to keep her in comfort. Does anyone have a corresponding right? Well, according to the foregoing, *she* does not, for, in the circumstances, he has an obligation to keep her in comfort not if *she* wishes it, but if I do; it is I who may release him from his obligation to care for her. Thus, the duty is *to* me, and I have the right. This consequence corresponds with what we think.

Incidentally, this final clause does not imply that I can alienate—transfer—all my rights. Some rights I can alienate; for instance, I can transfer my right to collect $5 from you, or I can forgive you the debt. But some rights, for example, the right to freedom, I may not be able to alienate. It is true that I need not exercise my right if I don't wish to. But it may be that I cannot, even if I wish, transfer my right or give up my right, now, to do something later if I wish.

and whenever there is *no* conflicting right or moral duty, it will follow that we have an absolute right. We propose, then, that "X has a prima facie right to enjoy, have, or be secured in y" means the same as "it is someone's objective prima facie obligation to secure X in, or in the possession of, or in the enjoyment of, y, if X wishes it." As before, we must construe the definition in a special way if the "someone" refers to a collective, such as the community or nation. We must construe it to mean that the responsible members of the collective "person" are severally objectively *prima facie* obligated not to interfere with X's getting (and so forth) y, and furthermore, more positively, are obligated over all to cooperate substantially, to a degree depending upon position and opportunity and other obligations, in establishing the means necessary to secure X (and others in his position) in y whenever X wishes, except on occasions when X's getting y conflicts with securing something for some other person or persons, the securing of which is more strongly obligatory.

When we have at least a prima facie *right to* something, we may speak of this thing as being *a right*. Hence, we may speak of all those liberties, immunities, and enablements to which we have a right, as being "our rights." Also, when anyone interferes with one of these rights, we may speak of "our rights being infringed."

Are there any reasons why we should suppose that the foregoing proposals are *not* correct explanations of the meaning of "have a right to"? It has sometimes been suggested that there are counterexamples that show that our explanation cannot be correct. Let us conclude by examining some of these.

1. It has been suggested that we sometimes have charitable duties, when the objects of our charity have no right to our benefactions. But, it is suggested, if the foregoing definitions were correct, then whenever we are obligated to give something to somebody, he could properly say he has a right to our gift. Hence, the definition must be mistaken. Is this correct? Suppose a beggar comes to the door. Suppose further, as the critics suggest, that he has *no moral right* to a gift. Does our definition then imply that we have no moral obligation to charity? No, what it implies is that we have no moral obligation to give to *him*. And this is true—assuming he has no right. We may very well have an obligation to give to charity as far as we are able, but not necessarily to him. Of course, *if* he is in dire need, and we are the only one in a position to help, then there is an obligation; but in this case it must surely be admitted that he has a *right* to our help, just as our definition implies. People in dire distress do have a right to assistance from those who can give it, corresponding to the moral obligation to give it to them.

2. It is sometimes said that we have obligations to animals, but that animals have no corresponding rights, although our definition implies they do if we have obligations to them. But why have animals no rights? Of

course, they cannot *claim* rights; but inability to claim does not destroy the right. It seems not unnatural to say that animals have rights, for example, the right not to be hurt without some good reason.[3]

3. It might be objected that people are objectively *obligated* to do only things it is possible to do, and that our definitions therefore imply that people have rights only to what it is possible to give them, whereas we often say that people have rights to what it is not possible to give them. For instance, the United Nations Declaration states that "everyone has the right to rest and leisure, including reasonable limitation of working hours and periodic holidays with pay." But, it may be said, it is obvious that it may not be possible at present, in all countries, to provide so much. According to the proposed definition, then, the critic may say, the statement of the Declaration must be just false, whereas we are not prepared to agree that this is true. Thus, the definition must be mistaken. But is there really an objection to the definition here? Not at all. On the contrary, the definition is helpful and clarifying, for on reflection we *are* inclined to say that if it *really is* impossible to provide so much in some countries, it is wishful thinking on the part of the Declaration to say that everyone has such a right *now*—at least, such an *absolute* right. But perhaps it would be possible to provide so much, but only at the sacrifice of other things, such as medical care, adequate food, and so on. In this case, the Declaration may be asserting correctly that everyone really has a prima facie right to what it mentions. Or again, it may be that the corresponding obligation belongs to the world-community of nations, which really could cooperate to supply so much for everybody now. In this case, again, the Declaration's statement can be accepted as being true. In no case is there ground for objecting to our definitions.

These objections to the foregoing definitions, then, appear not to be successful.

Of course, the claim that "has a right to" can be defined in terms of "morally obligated" does not imply that the definiens and the definiendum are identical in respect of overtones and connotations. They are not. One such difference is this. Almost everyone thinks of certain things as paradigm examples of human rights: freedom of speech, security against violence, security against ex post facto laws. When we claim anything as a right, therefore, we suggest a similarity to, proper classification with, these rights; one's claim is associated with rights like these. Again, the notion of a "right" has the overtone of something properly belonging to one, so that to ask for one's rights is not to ask for a favor or a gift any more than one asks a favor in expecting to possess or use one's house or land. What-

---

[3] Sometimes it is supposed that rights and duties are correlative in the sense that, whenever a being has rights, it also has obligations. And in this sense there is no correlativeness of rights and obligations in the case of animals, for, although animals have rights, they do not have moral obligations. But, of course, our definition does not imply that rights and duties are correlative in this sense.

ever is one's right is something one can demand without embarrassment. The sphere of one's rights is the sphere of one's rightful possessions. Despite the fact that "rights" has such overtones, however, a society with a language that had no term corresponding to "a right" might still be said to have the *concept* of a right, if it were recognized that people have the obligations toward others which are the ones that correspond with rights.

2. A THEORY ABOUT RIGHTS: JOHN LOCKE

Since statements about rights are so closely related to statements about obligations, we naturally find theories about rights representing all the major positions in ethics we have been discussing in this book. Among metaethical theories about "rights" are naturalisms, supernaturalism, nonnaturalism, and noncognitivisms. There are also the major types of normative theory about rights: egoistic theories, hedonistic and ideal utilitarian, formalist theories, and so on.

One might ask: What do the previous conclusions of this book commit us to, for the theory of rights? The answer is twofold. First, since we have urged that to make a statement about one person's right is in effect to make a statement about another person's obligation, we are committed to the view that a quasi-naturalist definition of the kind we suggested for "obligation" (in Chapters 10 and 14) can be provided for "has a right to." Of course, we must also say that the Qualified Attitude Method is the "standard" method for testing statements about rights and one that can be defended by persuasive reasons. Secondly, since we have suggested that extended rule-utilitarianism is the normative theory about obligations most worth developing and testing, we are also committed to suggesting that an extended rule-utilitarian theory about rights is most worth attention now. There are two essential points or theses of an extended rule-utilitarian theory about rights. First, a person will have an *absolute* right to something, roughly, if and only if a rule prescribing that a person in his circumstances be given, secured in (and so forth) a certain thing *no matter what* is among the ideal prescriptions of a community, the conscientious following of which by everyone in his community will maximize net expectable utility (but now counting as part of "utility" not only the welfare of persons but also the value of equality of welfare). Second, a person will have a *prima facie* right to something if and only if there is comparable status for a rule prescribing that a person in his circumstances be given, secured in (and so forth) something unless so doing conflicts with other rules to which the total system of ideal rules ascribes superior weight. At a later point we shall indicate in more detail some prescriptions that such a set of ideal rules would contain.

It will be useful, for the sake of perspective, to look briefly at a systematic theory about rights that has historically enjoyed considerable influence: that of John Locke (1632–1704).

In order to get a systematic view, let us begin with Locke's theory of the meaning of "has a right to." He does not define the term explicitly, and sometimes he seems to think it means simply "It is not inconsistent with moral law to. . . ." But it is clear that he thinks that if one man has a right to do or enjoy something, then no other man may rightfully interfere. His view in the end seems to be that "X has a right to have or enjoy *y*" means approximately, "It is morally right for X to have or enjoy *y*, and it is morally wrong for anyone to interfere with X's having or enjoying *y*." This view is very similar to the definition we have suggested above; but it is simpler—and can be because he recognized fewer rights than those we recognize at present, not rights like those to an education or a decent wage. There has been a very real change in the concept of "moral right" since Locke's day, corresponding with a changed view about the denotation of the term. Locke's definition was also simpler in another way: he did not distinguish between absolute and prima facie rights. The only rights he recognized at all were absolute rights, ones that could not be overridden (he thought) in any circumstances.

Locke's view of the relation of "has a right to" to "morally wrong" gives us, of course, only part of his metaethics; to understand it fully, we need to know his view about "wrong." Was he a naturalist, a supernaturalist, or what? Unfortunately, Locke's discussion of such points becomes rather vague. It is clear that he thought that there are true ethical principles, and that in some sense they can be known by reason. For instance, he says:

> The law of Nature stands as an eternal rule to all men, legislators as well as others. . . . It is certain that there is such a law, and that too as intelligible and plain to a rational creature and a studier of that law as the positive laws of commonwealths, nay, possibly plainer.[4]

But Locke does not explain clearly his view about the *meaning* of "morally wrong"—whether to say that something is wrong is to say that it is proscribed by God and will be punished by him, or to say that it is condemned by one's community, or what.[5] And we have to leave it at that.

In his normative ethics, Locke addresses himself to two questions: what duties and rights men have in a "state of nature," that is, prior to or outside of a politically organized society, and what duties and rights men have inside a politically organized society. Locke's theory about these questions is rather similar to that of W. D. Ross (about obligations), except that Locke does not have the concept of *prima facie* obligations (or rights). He thinks that outside of a politically organized society one is obligated to do or avoid doing various things. "No one ought to harm another in his life,

---

[4] *Two Treatises of Civil Government*, Bk. II, chaps. 10 and 2.
[5] See *An Essay Concerning Human Understanding*, Bk. II, chap. 28.

health, liberty or possessions" except as the other has committed some offense against the rights of others. One ought to do what one can to "preserve the rest of mankind, and not, unless it be to do justice on an offender, take away or impair the life, or what tends to the preservation of the life, the liberty, or goods of another." A man also "has no liberty to destroy himself, or so much as any creatures in his possession, but where some nobler use than its bare preservation calls for it."[6] Man is also forbidden to subject himself to any arbitrary power, because to do so is tantamount to taking his own life. Otherwise, a man may order his actions, possessions, and person as he sees fit.

A man's moral rights in the "state of nature" are the reverse side of this coin. He has a right to enjoy or do those things which others are obligated not to disturb him in, and which he is not enjoined not to do by moral law. Thus, he has a moral right to life (but not to take his own life), health, property (except that the life of one's animals may not be taken except for some "nobler" use), and otherwise liberty to do as he pleases where this does not infringe the rights of others—except, in each case, if he is himself a criminal, who has infringed the rights of others. Furthermore, a man has a right to see to the punishment of offenders against moral law. To these rights Locke thought there could be absolutely no exception in the state of nature; they are absolute rights and cannot be overridden.

Inside a politically organized society, things are somewhat different. Man *can* transfer some of his rights, and in fact he *has* done so, in return for security and convenience. The authority of government has its moral basis in this transfer. Which rights has man delegated to others? The right to defend his own life and that of others, except to such an extent as may be permitted by law; the right to punish criminals; and some right of ownership—whatever is necessary in order to pay one's share of the cost of government, provided there is specific authorization by properly elected representatives. These transferred rights are the rights—the sole rights—of government against its subjects.

The rights of the government are limited, since some rights were not transferred, and the untransferred rights can no more be transgressed justifiably by government than by an individual person.[7] The remaining individual rights are the rights to life, health, property (except as specified), and liberty except as limited by conflict with the like rights of others and the rights transferred to the state. Locke offers two reasons for his view that these rights have never been transferred to the government. First, he holds that men cannot reasonably be supposed to have transferred

---

[6] *Two Treatises,* Bk. II, chap. 2.

[7] He thinks that an unlimited monarchy has no moral rights at all; only a state controlled by the consent of the governed has a moral right to govern. Why? Because to consent to such a power is in effect to give away one's life, which one has no moral right to do.

rights if such a transfer would obviously make them worse off than they would have been without a political organization. Second, certain rights cannot have been transferred, because men never themselves had these rights, and they could not transfer what they never had. For instance, a man has no moral right to take his own life; hence, he cannot morally give another a right to take his life. "For nobody has an absolute arbitrary power over himself, or over any other, to destroy his own life, or take away the life or property of another." Thus, governments have a "power that hath no other end but preservation, and therefore can never have a right to destroy, enslave, or designedly to impoverish the subjects."[8]

Inside politically organized society, then, men still have their rights to life, property, health, and liberty of action (except as would infringe on the rights of others and the specific rights transferred to government). These must be respected on every occasion; they are absolute. These are also one's only rights within a commonwealth; one has rights *not to be interfered with* by man or government, but no right to education, a job, economic justice, or medical care.

Locke's *Two Treatises on Government* was published in 1690, and its affiliations with the political philosophy of the Declaration of Independence and the preamble of the U.S. Constitution, as well as with many other political documents of the eighteenth century, are many and obvious.

3. ARE THERE SPECIFIC NATURAL RIGHTS THAT ARE UNIVERSAL AND ABSOLUTE?

Many eighteenth century writers, including Locke and the authors of the Declaration of Independence, supposed that there are several specific "natural" rights that are universal and absolute—such as the rights to life, liberty, and property. How far can we give serious credence to this view today?

The answer to our question turns partly on what we mean by "natural" rights. Historically, this term has been used to refer to rights that are independent of enacted law—to rights which one has by virtue of "natural law." We have seen, however, that all *moral* rights are independent of enacted law; and so far, "natural right" is synonymous with "moral right." Ordinarily, however, the term "natural right" is used in a somewhat more special way. Locke, for instance, thought of natural rights as knowable by reason, in some sense; he also thought of them as somehow derivative from God's law for human conduct. In view of the discussions of earlier chapters, however, it is inadvisable to include these features in the concept of a "natural right"; we have concluded that ethical principle cannot be known by "reason"; and it is not obvious that we can properly view ethical principles as dependent on God's commands or law. Writers have also used

---

[8] *Ibid.,* chap. 11.

the term "natural rights" to mean "rights which belong universally to men just as men, and absolute" (in the above-mentioned sense). If this is what we mean, we are being redundant in asking whether there are "natural rights that are universal and absolute." In view of the reasons for distinguishing between "prima facie" and "absolute" rights, however, it is inconvenient for us to use "natural right" so as to connote absoluteness. It seems best, then, to use "natural right" to mean simply "moral right which belongs universally to men." If we conclude, then, that there are natural rights, we shall be asserting less than some historical writers who made this claim; but our usage has the virtue of keeping the term alive for asserting something which perhaps can be seriously claimed to be true.

Our original question can now be restated as the question whether there are *specific* natural (*universal* moral) rights which are *absolute*. Locke, for instance, thought there are.

People obviously *sometimes* have absolute rights, in the sense that in the total circumstances there is a corresponding over-all obligation. If it is an over-all obligation of Mr. X to pay me $10 now, if I want him to, then I have an absolute right, now, to be paid the $10 by him. This is an absolute right, and it is specific. But it is a right of a specific individual at a specific time; it is by no means a universal or natural right.[9] Locke and others have thought that there are specific things that *every* man has a right, and an absolute right, to do—so that there are *never* overriding moral reasons for not doing them or for being prevented from doing them. Locke believed that the rights to life, liberty, and property are absolute natural rights in this sense. Possibly F. D. Roosevelt believed that the Four Freedoms—from want, from fear, of speech, and of religion—were absolute natural rights. Is such a claim defensible?

In order to answer this question, we should look to the theories about obligation we have been discussing, and ask ourselves what absolute obligations people can be said to have; if we can identify these we can, presumably, fix the corresponding rights. A formalist like Ross, however, does not assert that there are *any* universal absolute obligations as distinct from prima facie obligations. The act-utilitarian, of course, does say that everyone has an absolute duty to do whatever he can to maximize the welfare of society; correspondingly, he will say that everyone has an absolute right, at every moment, to enjoy or be secured in everything that it is best for his society for him to enjoy or be secured in. So, there is one absolute natural right, if act-utilitarianism is an acceptable theory. But there are two facts which make this consequence less important: first, the fact that there are good reasons to doubt the validity of act-utilitarianism; and

[9] One could claim that there is a natural (universal) right to be paid whatever sum of money has been promised to one. But this is not an absolute right: The person who owes money may very well have other obligations which override the obligation to pay the one to whom it is owed. Moreover, it may be impossible to pay—and if it is, we can hardly say there is an absolute right to payment.

second, the fact that in any case this absolute right is not a right to any specific thing like life, liberty, or happiness. The rule-utilitarian, again, can say that everyone has absolute rights: rights to whatever the ideal prescriptions for his society command that he be given, no matter what. (And approximately the same for extended rule-utilitarianism.) It is not easy to say what these rights will be, however; and it is quite possible that they will not be the same in every society. In order to know what they are, we should have to work out at least part of the details of sets of ideal prescriptions for different societies. Until we have done this, we cannot say which, if any, specific rights are both universal and absolute.

The reason that stands in the way of asserting that any specific right is both universal and absolute is the same one that stands in the way of saying that any prima facie obligation must always be satisfied. This reason is the fact that, whatever specific right may be mentioned, there are conceivable circumstances in which other moral considerations will have a stronger justifiable claim on conduct. For instance, in time of war a man's right to life may have to stand aside. Again, a man's property may have to be destroyed if for some reason, in time of a flood, for instance, it is a menace to human life. What Justice Holmes has to say about the legal right to free speech in the United States also pertains to the moral right:

> The most stringent protection of free speech would not protect a man in falsely shouting fire in a theater, and causing a panic. It does not even protect a man from injunction against uttering words that may have all the effect of force. The question in every case is whether the words used are used in such circumstances and are of such a nature as to create a clear and present danger that they will bring about the substantive evils that Congress has a right to prevent. It is a question of proximity and degree.[10]

Substantially the same thing can be said about any other specific right one can mention: We can conceive of times when such rights must give way, and, therefore, they are only prima facie and not absolute rights.

It may be said that we can still defend, as absolute, specific rights such as freedom of speech as absolute natural rights, if only we *define* very carefully just what the right is, just what is sacrosanct. But will this suggestion work? Such a task would require that we state all the exceptions, all the circumstances, in which the right is not absolute. It seems very likely that this cannot be done. Of course, one can do it by adding on to the statement of what the right is, the rider: "unless there are stronger moral reasons for not securing a person in. . . ." But to say this is precisely to reduce the claim, from the claim that something is an absolute right, to the claim that it is a prima facie right. It is conceivable that we shall one day be able to offer a complete list of the types of exception, and if so then we could state some more specific rights. At present, however, it seems to go beyond

---

[10] *Schenck v. United States*, 249 U.S. 52.

our knowledge to say that there is an absolute natural right to any specific immunities, privileges, or enablements.

Recently it has been asserted that there is an absolute natural right to a specific, if complicated, liberty or privilege.[11] It has been asserted that everyone has a right to free activity without interference, except where there is a special moral justification for interference that is not based on the general nature of the activity being interfered with or the general character of the parties (such as nationality or race), but rather on some special relationship such as a previous free consent or promise, or else on the fact that one's activity interferes with the equal freedom of others. This proposal of an absolute specific right close to the traditional concept of a right to liberty of action is certainly interesting. But does it really escape vagueness or abstractness, any more than the rule-utilitarian principle? The author himself appears to admit that there may be other, at present unspecifiable, "special relationships" (such as being someone's child or wife) that can justify interference; but it is doubtful whether these special relationships can be completely listed. Moreover, if we agree with the modern tendency to move more and more toward a "welfare state," we shall simply be doubtful of the principle asserted, on the ground that it is by no means obvious what kinds of regulation and constraint may be in the service of the public interest.

It seems, then, that the only natural rights plausibly claimed to be absolute are ones that are not specifically described. It may be there are specific natural rights like the rights to life, liberty, and property traditionally claimed; but if so, they are prima facie, not absolute. At least this is what one must say at present. To say this, however, is not to deny that, as prima facie rights, the traditional rights may have great weight and may be overridden only in special situations. It may be that the eighteenth century writers erred only in claiming a bit too much.

4. TYPES OF SPECIFIC PRIMA FACIE NATURAL RIGHTS

It is more plausible to suppose that there are specific *prima facie* (not absolute) natural rights, and that the traditional rights to life, liberty and property are among these. But we must be careful. To say that there is a prima facie natural right is no small claim. To say that there is, is to say that, where there are no conflicting moral considerations, there is an absolute right; and this may not be defensible. When we were discussing the pro-

[11] By H. L. A. Hart, "Are There Any Natural Rights?" *Philosophical Review*, LXIV (1955), 175–91. In the same symposium, S. M. Brown, Jr., urged that there is an "unconditional and inalienable right to institutions which provide general protection to all high-order goods and permit each individual member of the community to place the burden of proof upon those who would deny him his good or interfere with his pursuit of it." In "Inalienable Rights," *Philosophical Review*, LXIV (1955), 192–211. This claim, however, is hardly a claim that there are specific rights, and is very similar to the thesis of the rule-utilitarian, as stated above.

posal that there is a prima facie obligation to keep one's promises, we saw that only a carefully qualified claim can be made, for example, that promises not made under duress, not made on the basis of deliberate misrepresentations, and so on, should be kept. Also, we doubted whether anybody has actually yet succeeded in stating exactly what our prima facie obligations are, with all the necessary qualifications and exceptions. Perhaps there are comparable problems about stating any specific prima facie rights. Exactly what is it that we want to say is an absolute right, providing there are not contrary special moral grounds?

We shall shortly describe three things that can possibly be claimed with warrant to be universal prima facie rights. First, however, it may be helpful to review the types of things that have been claimed, in recent years, to be prima facie rights of all human beings.

There are four major classes of (alleged) prima facie rights: (1) It has been claimed that there is a universal right to protection against violation of life, against personal physical assault, against torture or inhuman punishment by government or its agents, against arbitrary arrest, against presumption of guilt of any offense until after proof at a public trial with all the guarantees necessary for fairness, against servitude, against libelous or slanderous attack on reputation. (2) It has been claimed that there is a universal prima facie right to *equal capacity to plead one's case before courts of law:* to possession of effective legal means for preventing the violation of one's rights, to a standing before courts of law equal to that of any other persons in one's community. (3) It has been said that there is a universal prima facie right to *make one's desires felt in the government and law of the land:* to vote on laws either directly or through chosen representatives, to speak and publish one's thoughts freely, to hold peaceable assembly and association. Finally (4), it has been thought that there is a universal prima facie right to *the basic conditions of good living:* to freedom of movement; to marry a person of one's choice; to own property; to minimum conditions of subsistence, including food, clothing, housing, and medical care; to work in an occupation of one's choice, with fair remuneration and in the absence of discrimination; to an education.

Are these alleged rights really prima facie rights? Is it true that some person—or rather community, in these cases—is obligated not to interfere with anyone having these things, and rather is obligated to secure them, insofar as securing them does not conflict with stronger obligations?

There is certainly an initial plausibility in every case. All the things mentioned are either important kinds of welfare without which life is miserable, or else important conditions of welfare, at least in most circumstances. To secure these things is, therefore, at least in the normal case, to secure the basic conditions of a tolerable existence. Hence, the rule-utilitarian will wish to consider seriously including among his "ideal prescriptions" imperatives directing that these things be secured where they do not conflict with more important goods. Further, there is some reason to expect that a person with "qualified" attitudes will feel obligated not to prevent anyone from having these things, and to cooperate substantially in the securing of them for everyone.

Yet we must be careful. Do we really want to urge democratic elections as an obligation, unless there is some contrary moral consideration, in *absolutely* all conditions, for example, where the people of a nation are generally uneducated and their country is being rapidly developed by an enlightened monarch? Moreover, we would like to hear more. *How much* education is said to be a prima facie right? *What kind* of property may we claim a prima facie right to own? Certainly in the case of some of these rights we wish to have the claim clarified further before giving our full assent.

5. THREE PRIMA FACIE RIGHTS: LIFE, LIBERTY, AND PROPERTY

We need to know, then, in order to decide intelligently whether certain things can properly be claimed as universal or natural prima facie rights, just exactly what it is that is claimed as a right. Moreover, we shall have a clear picture of what we are accepting only if, further, we have some idea of the force of the prima facie right, or when a given right takes priority over other rights and vice versa.

Such questions are difficult, and deserve much thought and discussion. We can here hope only to offer some, doubtless quite incomplete, pertinent remarks about three prima facie rights.

The right to life. It is widely believed today that normal[12] human beings have a prima facie right not to be exposed to death through human agency, except in certain special situations, and that they have a prima facie right to whatever positive assistance is required for maintenance of life. Let us examine the two aspects of this right separately.

It will hardly be questioned that there is a prima facie right not to be deliberately (or by negligence) caused to die, although this right may have to stand aside where necessary for protection of the lives and important welfare of all, for example, in wartime. But are there *any* exceptional cases of the total absence or lapse of such a right? Many writers have supposed that there is such a lapse of right in the case of a person—a murderer—who has violated another's right to life. We shall discuss their theory in the following chapter. Are there other possible exceptions? May a man be killed at his own request?[13] Perhaps he may; but if so this will hardly be an

---

[12] The term "normal" is used in order to avoid questions about the status of special cases, such as those of Mongolian idiots or elderly people in the last stages of senile degeneration.

[13] Some years ago, in a railroad wreck, a man was inextricably entangled in the wreckage, which was burning. In great pain, he begged a policeman to shoot him. This the policeman refused to do, since it was against the law. As a result, the man suffered death by burning.

exception. If, as we have suggested, a right is always a sphere of autonomy, we cannot say that a man's right to life is infringed if he dies by his own hand, or at the hands of others at his request, for to have a right is for others to be obligated to do something for one *if one wishes;* and in this case one does not wish. Suicide and euthanasia, then, may be wrong; but they do not infringe human rights. Indeed, it seems to be the other way around: It seems more likely that the law infringes human rights when it prevents release from agony.

Let us turn now to the more positive side. Is there a prima facie right to protection from accident and disease, from premature loss of life owing to malnutrition? At present, it is recognized that if a person neglects to give vital assistance to another, which he might provide at no personal risk and with little cost to himself, he is seriously culpable. Nevertheless, there has traditionally been less agreement that the community must provide adequate protection of this sort, than that it should provide adequate police protection. Medical service has been viewed as a commodity that an individual may purchase as he can. Not that it is at present supposed that a person has no right to, say, necessary surgery irrespective of his ability to pay. A charity patient can command the services of a top surgeon (not of his choice, however, and sometimes not one who is adequate for the job); all that is denied him is certain comforts, and this is a matter of comfort, not of life. But it is still thought not unnatural that a person dissipate his life's savings to pay for a catastrophic illness, whereas it is not thought that an individual need dissipate his life's earnings in payment for protection if someone threatens him. In the one case, it is thought obligatory to provide protection irrespective of a person's capacity to pay; in the other case, it is not. It is worth reflecting whether both types of protection of life are not equally rights.[14]

The exact scope of the prima facie right to life seems still to be debatable.

The right to freedom of expression. The right to express one's ideas free of coercion or intimidation by persons or government can be viewed as one aspect of a general right to liberty of action.

Freedom of speech has nothing to do with freedom of thinking or conscience. Indeed, there cannot be interference with thinking or conscience, since one's inner thoughts are not observable by anyone but oneself. There can be influence on these, by propaganda, by control of the channels of information; but that is a different matter. Freedom of speech means freedom to *communicate,* either orally or in writing. Freedom of speech is not understood to mean that anyone is guaranteed an attentive audience,

[14] It may properly be said that basically the question is one about the distribution of income. One group believes that society is obligated to provide means for saving one's life only after one's own financial resources are completely exhausted; the other does not. But we can as well put the matter as a problem about the right to life: "Is it a human right that services necessary for protection of life be available to all *without charge?*"

or even that he is to be supplied with the financial means to advertise his views in a newspaper. "Freedom of speech" has been generally taken to mean the power to express or communicate one's thoughts as one wishes, unaffected by the coercion or intimidation of any other persons, whether by police, legal action, economic retaliation or the threat of it, or personal interference (for example, when an agitator appears at a meeting and tries to prevent one's being heard). Influence by bribes or promises is not a form of threat or coercion, and does not count as a limitation of freedom of speech.

But does expression of *any and every idea* have a strong claim to protection? To answer this, we must look at the reasons why there is a right to free speech at all.

One reason for the protection of expression of one's ideas is just the fact that people do want to communicate their thoughts and are frustrated if they cannot. A more important reason is that many of a person's wants can be satisfied only if he can obtain the cooperation of other persons; as a result, impediments to communication are frustrations of other desires as well. Moreover, preventing one person from expressing what he thinks may frustrate the wants of others, who may need the information he can give them. Third, society and institutions tend to stagnate if facts and ideas are not exchanged freely. Where there is not communication, people may not think of the possibilities for social change or the need for them; and facts relevant to their feasibility may not be accessible. Society will not know whether or in what way an institution may be harmful, unless those who are harmed can speak out.

These values are important, but do they justify unlimited freedom? Certainly not *absolute* freedom. We have already observed that freedom of speech must stand aside when this is necessary to protect against more urgent dangers, for example, a panic or a riot, at least if there is a "clear and present danger" of these. But does the expression of all ideas, the statement of anything (even deliberate falsification) have a prima facie right to protection? Is there a prima facie right to protection of obscene language, deliberate falsification, or the advocacy of political programs that would result in the abolition of institutions of government supporting liberty and free speech?

The rule-utilitarian will probably say that, if some of these things could be sharply demarcated from other things, there would be no prima facie right to their protection. However, in practice, he will say, it is difficult to avoid protecting all of these things if we are to protect the expression of thought that has a clear prima facie right to be protected. The lines are difficult to draw. How shall we distinguish between a deliberate attempt to mislead and a confused or misinformed effort to state facts for the public welfare? Is it safe to entrust such distinctions to administrators, and is there point in trying to make such a distinction in the case of artful people who know how to hide unfavorable evidence? Moreover, there is danger in any suppression of free speech, since there is a strong temptation for those in power to attempt to use it as a means of keeping themselves in power. Some lines, of course, may be drawn. Malicious slander and incitement to acts of violence can be identified, and there is little danger to the public in efforts to suppress them; moreover, failure to suppress them would infringe other highly important prima facie rights. But where there is no specific damage done to specific persons, or where expression of one's thoughts does not directly lead to public injury, there seems to be an obligation to cooperate in securing protection for the expression of a person's thoughts. Thus, although perhaps there would not be a prima facie right for free expression of some thoughts, if they could be taken by themselves, nevertheless in the total context we are obligated to secure and maintain a legal system that protects them all.

The right to property. Ownership consists in the capacity to dispose of something as one wishes. To say, then, that there is a right to own property is to say that there is a right to a capacity to dispose of some material objects as one wishes. Also, to ask about the extent of the prima facie moral right to own is thus to ask about the extent to which one has a prima facie moral right to dispose of objects as one wishes—either which kinds of objects one may own, or what kinds of disposal one may make of them.

Different societies give legal protection to private ownership to different extents. Among the Hopi, for instance, a person has practically unlimited control over his personal property—clothing, cooking utensils, hunting instruments. He can dispose of these as he wishes during his lifetime, and at death he can designate at least which one among several eligible persons is to receive them. But among the Hopi, private ownership of real property is much more limited. A Hopi cannot sell a piece of land at all. Nor can he will it. A man may have a right to the use of a piece of land during his lifetime, but at his death (with certain exceptions) this right passes to the children of his sisters, or to other blood relatives of his mother. Even the fact that a man makes something does not necessarily confer unlimited right to the disposal of it. If a man constructs a house, for instance, ownership is vested immediately in his wife (on whose land it will have been built); a man could be divorced the day after the house was completed and he would still have no title to it. In the United States aside from Indian reservations, however, there is a somewhat different legal right to private ownership. One may dispose of one's possessions somewhat more freely than may a Hopi. There are still limitations, however. There are taxes. There are rules about inheritance: a man must leave something to his widow, and in some states his home goes to his widow quite independently of any provisions in his will. There are zoning laws: a person may not be permitted to make his house into two apartments, installing a second kitchen; or he may not be permitted to build a permanent structure within fifteen feet of the limits of his property; and so on. One may not do anything that is a serious annoyance to one's neighbors: one can "own" a saxophone, but not in a sense that confers a right to play it on one's front lawn at 3 A.M.

In asking about the extent to which ownership is a moral right, we must, as in the case of free speech, inquire why it is thought there is a right at all. What is the reasoning? John Locke wrote as follows:

> Every man has a "property" in his own "person." This nobody has any right to but himself. The "labour" of his body and the "work" of his hands, we may say, are properly his. Whatsoever, then, he removes out of the state that Nature hath provided and left it in, he hath mixed his labour with it, and joined to it something that is his own, and thereby makes it his property. It being by him removed from the common state Nature placed it in, it hath by this labour something annexed to it that excludes the common right of other men. For this "labour" being the unquestionable property of the labourer, no man but he can have a right to what that is once joined to, at least where there is enough, and as good left in common for others.[15]

Karl Marx had somewhat similar views. He believed that the value of any object is determined by the amount of labor that went into its production, and that it is robbery if a worker does not have ownership of such proportion of a collection of objects as represents the proportion of their value for which his labor is responsible.

Locke's reasoning is not convincing. Of course, he went much too far, in supposing he had proved an *absolute* right to the disposal of that to which one had joined one's labor, at least if there was plenty for all, whereas, in fact we do not even have an absolute right to use our own labor as we please—for we have obligations toward others that may claim our labor when we may wish to use it for some other purpose. But does he even establish a prima facie right to the disposal of material objects? Well, perhaps, when there is "as good left in common for others"; but this condition is hardly met anywhere today. Nor is it possible to estimate, in modern productive enterprises, with what one has "mixed one's labor" or to what extent. Thus, there is little to which we could today claim even a prima facie right, even if we accepted his reasoning.

The justification for a right of private ownership that seems convincing today is utilitarian. There are many benefits in private ownership of material objects. First, people wish to have free disposal of material objects, and they enjoy it. Second, ownership is stimulating in many ways: Consider the values inherent in a teen-ager's acquiring and rebuilding a $50 car, in a homeowner's gardening, in the activities of a collector of rocks or paintings. Again, people will improve the condition of objects they own, and usually only these. Persons who rent their homes will know that tenants seldom improve rented property. Some exclusive right to the disposal of some material objects is justified on many counts.

---

[15] *Two Treatises of Civil Government*, Bk. II, chap. 5.

But *how far* should people have exclusive disposal of the physical things they own? And does the prima facie right to private ownership extend to objects of every sort—to objects or land used primarily not for personal enjoyment but for production?

We shall not attempt to answer these questions. The answer to them depends in part on the answer to questions we have already discussed: about economic justice. It seems clear that considerations of utility are of primary importance for them. Thus, the basis for a claim that there is a prima facie right of private ownership of the means of production will be something like the claim that ownership with a minimum of regulation is a prerequisite of efficient use, or that it is a prerequisite of adequate incentive, or that it is required if there is to be an open-market economy at all.

FURTHER READING

A. C. Ewing, *The Individual, the State, and World Government* (New York: The Macmillan Company, 1947), chap. 2.

——, "The Rights of the Individual," *Revue Internationale de Philosophie*, No. 6 (August, 1948).

D. D. Raphael, *Moral Judgment* (London: George Allen & Unwin, Ltd., 1955), pp. 46–56.

E. F. Carritt, *Ethical and Political Thinking* (Oxford: Clarendon Press, 1947), chaps. 6, 15.

W. D. Ross, *The Right and the Good* (Oxford: Clarendon Press, 1930), pp. 48–56.

A. I. Melden and W. K. Frankena, "Human Rights" (symposium), American Philosophical Association (Eastern Div.), I (1952), 167–207.

H. L. A. Hart, S. M. Brown, Jr., and W. K. Frankena, symposium on rights, *Philosophical Review*, LXIV (1955), 175–232.

R. Blake, "On Natural Rights," *Ethics*, XXXVI (1925), 86–96. A utilitarian theory.

L. Garvin, *A Modern Introduction to Ethics* (New York: Houghton Mifflin Company, 1953), chap. 17.

J. Maritain, *Man and the State* (Chicago: University of Chicago Press, 1951), chap. 4.

Thomas Hobbes, *Leviathan*, chaps. 13–15, 17–19.

John Locke, *Two Treatises of Civil Government*, Bk. II, chaps. 2, 7–9.

J. S. Mill, *Liberty*, chaps. 1, 2.

T. H. Green, *Lectures on the Principles of Political Obligation* (London: Longmans, Green & Co., 1950), pp. 142–59.

18

Moral Assessments of Actions and Persons

So far we have discussed two important types of moral judgment in detail: judgments about what is desirable, and judgments about what is obligatory. (We do not count judgments about human rights as a third, because of their close relation to judgments about obligations.) Now we come to a third type of judgment that has hardly been mentioned: judgments in assessment of past actions and persons. "That was a reprehensible thing to do" and "That was a very fine thing to have done" are examples. It is sometimes supposed that the key concepts ("morally reprehensible" and "morally admirable") of such judgments can be defined in terms of the ethical concepts already analyzed. But we shall see that this supposition is incorrect.

These judgments require examination like that given the types of judgment already discussed. The central concepts must be described and their relations to the other main ethical concepts marked, and we must sketch, as far as we can. the broad, basic normative principles in which these concepts occur.

1. THE LANGUAGE OF MORAL ASSESSMENTS

The anthropologist Raymond Firth remarks in commentary on the ways of peoples everywhere, "Commendation or criticism is continually being formed on the way in which a man behaves at work, his treatment of his colleagues, the way a woman keeps her home, the way she acts in a shop queue, how they spend their income, how they bring up their children, how they let their dog react to the neighbor's cat."[1]

Let us analyze a homely example of such criticism, a letter published in a college newspaper, complaining about the conduct of some of its author's fellow undergraduates, who did not respect the conventions of the lunch queues:

[1] *The Elements of Social Organization* (London: Watts & Co., 1951), p. 184.

455

To the Editor:
There are some people attending this College who lack a conscience. Cutting into the meal line with no other intent than to satisfy the sooner *his* desire for food is a flagrant example of the bare egoism of some students. Just what right does a person have to take a place at the head of the lunch line when other people are legitimately joining the line at its tail and waiting patiently their turn? It is nothing but unfair, discourteous, and wrong.

Actually, most people who do cut into meal lines for purely selfish reasons do so sheepishly and with silly, guilty grins. And we are supposed to forgive them because their heart is really in the right place, or they "mean well," etc. Meanwhile, we must wait longer to get into the dining room.

This letter illustrates a number of features typically present in judgments about wrongdoing. (1) The writer believes that the agents are obligated to do something different from what they do. (2) He has views about their motives. The ignoring of obligations to others is not redeemed by any worthy motive. The transgressors simply wish to gratify their desires immediately. (3) He has an unfavorable opinion of the offending individuals as persons: they "lack a conscience" and show "bare egoism." (4) He offers an over-all evaluation of such deeds, as "unfair, discourteous, and wrong." (5) The whole letter serves to express his own attitude, one of indignation; and its content provides the justification for his attitude.

The offense in this case was minor, but our evaluation of a Hitler or an ordinary murderer is apt to contain the same types of element: judgment that an act was objectively wrong and that the agent knew this quite well himself; the assignment of motives; forming a judgment of the agent as a person; over-all evaluation of the deed; the expression of an attitude toward the agent and an implication that this attitude is justified. Moreover, in the normal case of wrongdoing, all of these related judgments will be true.

When we are not writing letters for publication, but merely conversing, we ordinarily do not trouble to *say* all these things. What we say depends on what our hearer is presumed to know. If the hearer knows nothing of the event, we describe to him the situation and what was done; he can be counted upon to make the inferences about motives, about character, and the evaluations. If the hearer is himself a witness of the event, we may content ourselves with expressing our indignation by any one of the several judgments the author of our letter made: such as, "He *knew* what the situation was," or "What an egoist!" and so on. On some occasions, however, we must present more details—when the occasion is extraordinary, when the act may have been wrong but the agent blameless. For instance, we may say: "He certainly didn't pay his debt, but that is no reflection on him; he tried, but just couldn't get the money." Or, we may say, "Yes he paid me in full; but it's no credit to him, since the only reason he paid was that his employer put pressure on him."

Now, what is there here that requires the attention of the philosopher?

(1) We have already discussed the meaning of judgments of obligation (or of wrong); we need not go into this again. (2) The judgment that a person's motive was "desire to eat," or that he was selfishly unconcerned about the desires of others, seems clear enough. But is it? Actually the concept of a "motive" is, in common discourse, an obscure one, and needs clarification. (3) The judgments about defects of character, for example, that a person "lacks a conscience" or is an "egoist" again may seem clear enough. But are they? What is the meaning of "character"? What is a "defect of character"? What is it to "lack a conscience" or to fail in "conscientiousness"? (4) The over-all evaluation of the deed (or of the agent) is even more puzzling. In what sense is a person's deed "wrong," "morally culpable," "reprehensible," "inexcusable," "morally blame-worthy," "immoral," "morally bad," "disgusting," or "shocking"? (It is not suggested that these words are synonyms; but they are closely related.) Presumably, an understanding of the meaning of these terms will shed light on the question of what it is for an attitude of indignation to be "justified."

In the present chapter, we shall discuss all these concepts. However, it is convenient to do so by concentrating on one issue: the fourth one, the over-all evaluations of deeds themselves. What we shall do is explain the meaning of two central terms of over-all evaluation that are typical of the group: "reprehensible" and "morally admirable"; and then later (and more briefly) we shall outline some broad general principles stating when an action is reprehensible or morally admirable. The completion of this job will require discussion of the other concepts of interest to us.

Concentration on these two terms will have the effect of focusing our attention on the moral assessment of actions as distinct from the assessment of persons. We shall have relatively little to say about the second of these two topics, beyond an analysis of the concept of "character." In large part, however, our characterizations of persons, for example, in letters of recommendation, take the form of descriptions of their dominant character traits rather than summary, over-all appraisals (like "He's a fine person"). Insofar as this is true, of course, the analysis of "character trait" provides an elucidation of the central concept.

2. THE MEANING OF "REPREHENSIBLE" AND "MORALLY ADMIRABLE"

What is the meaning of our two central terms? We shall discuss only one of them in detail ("reprehensible") and merely suggest a definition of the other ("morally admirable") at the end. We can largely ignore the second, because the meanings of the two terms are closely parallel and the reasoning that supports our explanation of the one can be used, with obvious modifications, to support a parallel explanation of the other.

These words have all the general features of the ethical terms we have been examining—features that incline some people to offer naturalist or supernaturalist definitions of them, and others to be nonnaturalists or noncognitivists. We may also assume that the conclusions of Chapter 10 about the meaning and confirmability of ethical terms apply to these words. But there is a question whether these words are definable, like "have a right to," in terms of moral words we have already analyzed. If they are, we shall be saved much work, for we have already discussed the question of what are the true ethical principles in which the other major concepts appear. We must look into this. Our conclusion, unfortunately, must be that these terms are *not* definable in this way. Let us consider four proposals.

1. "Reprehensible" might be thought to be a mere synonym of "undesirable." But this is not so. Many things are undesirable that are not reprehensible. For instance, some features of the design of our car may be undesirable—say, the fact that the rear-vision mirror is useless if the back seat is occupied, But it is hardly reprehensible. The same is true even if we confine ourselves to talking about actions. We may think it very undesirable for the Secretary of State to have made a certain statement about foreign policy, but we may not think his action reprehensible—if we think he merely showed poor judgment.

2. Nor can we define "reprehensible" in terms of "moral obligation," at least in any simple way. Clearly it does not follow, from the fact that a person failed to do what it was his objective obligation to do, that his action was reprehensible; he may have failed to do what he ought only because he lacked information he could not get. Nor does it follow, from the fact that a person failed to do what it was his subjective obligation to do, that his action was reprehensible; he may have failed to do what he ought because of an excusable mistake of moral principle, as we suggested on p. 359. "Was reprehensible," then, does not mean "failed to do his duty."

3. But there is a more complex, and much more plausible, type of proposal. Might "X is reprehensible" not mean "It is *desirable* for someone to punish the agent of X, at least by verbal censure, on account of X"? But even this proposal cannot be made to work. True, it usually is desirable for a person to be punished, if and only if he has done something reprehensible. But always? Suppose someone did something reprehensible, and now is in an unstable state of mind, and censure or punishment would result in his committing suicide. Can I not say he did something reprehensible, without saying it is desirable to punish him now, or ever? Moreover, there are some actions it is desirable to punish (for example, minor traffic violations) that may not be reprehensible. It is clear, then, that it is one thing for a deed to be reprehensible; it is another for an act of punishing or censuring the agent to be in order.

4. The reader may feel that the foregoing proposal can easily be refined

so as to meet our objections. He may, therefore, propose that it be repaired as follows. "X is reprehensible," he may suggest, means "It is *normally desirable* (or perhaps, *obligatory* or *permissible*) for someone to punish the agent of an act *like* X, at least by verbal censure, on account of his act." This definition is better, but it is not quite satisfactory, for several reasons. First, it is possible to judge that someone has acted reprehensibly, but *doubt* whether some kind of punishment is normally desirable for acts of the sort in question. (Suppose a person thinks punishment seldom does any good.) Second, there are whole classes of acts it is desirable to punish (minor traffic violations—overparking, and so forth) that we hardly think are reprehensible—and our definition requires us to say that *all* of them are so. Third, it seems that this definition leads us to hold that when we say that one act is *more* reprehensible than another, as we often do, we must mean that deeds like it should, in the normal case, be punished more severely. But this again is dubious. For instance, as Jeremy Bentham pointed out, how severely an offense should be punished is partly dependent on the ease of detection of a crime; if a crime is detected with difficulty, the penalty should be made severe in order to balance the unlikelihood of its being applied at all. But do such considerations affect the degree of reprehensibleness of an act?

Various other suggestions have been made, to the effect that "is reprehensible" means the same as some other phrase in which one of the other central moral terms appears. However, they are less plausible than some we have suggested.[2] We conclude, then, that it is impossible to construe the meaning of "reprehensible" in this way.

If we want a definition of "reprehensible," then, it seems we must look for something after the pattern of the definitions we have proposed for "desirable" and "morally obligatory"—a quasi-naturalist definition, or else a noncognitive analysis of the sort sketched at the conclusion of Chapter 10. There must, of course, be some difference from these other definitions, otherwise "reprehensible" would be simply a synonym of the other ethical words. That there will be *one* difference is obvious—a difference in the "corresponding attitude." That is, just as "X is desirable" means "*Desiring* X is objectively justified" (in the sense of the long phrase on p. 265, "satisfies all the conditions . . . for the endorsement of such attitudes"), so "is reprehensible" can be construed to mean that some attitude or feeling, but a *different* one, is objectively justified. *Which* attitude or feeling? Of course, the attitude or feeling to which we appeal in order to correct, fill out, or criticize our statements about something being reprehensible— remorse or guilt feelings in case the action is our own, and unfavorable

---

[2] The writer has discussed some of the other proposals in "Blameworthiness and Obligation," in A. I. Melden (ed.), *Essays in Moral Philosophy* (Seattle: University of Washington Press, 1958).

feelings like indignation, and perhaps disgust or contempt, in the case of the acts of others.[3]

As a first approximation we might say, then, something like this: "X is reprehensible" means "It is objectively justified for some persons, including the agent, to have some unfavorable attitude to the agent on account of X." This proposal is too simple, however, for it permits us to say that a purely intellectual mistake may be morally reprehensible. It is not easy to remove this difficulty. The most convincing proposal that does it is the following one, which shall adopt. "X is reprehensible," then, may be defined as "Y did X, and X would not have occurred had not the character of Y been in some respect less desirable than average; and on this account it is objectively justified [in the sense of the long phrase, "satisfies . . . attitudes," on p. 265] for Y to feel guilt or remorse, and for others to have unfavorable attitudes such as anger or contempt or disgust toward Y." The definition is distressingly complex. Moreover, it contains the puzzling term "character," which we shall discuss at a later point; and it differs from the other "quasi-naturalist" definitions in containing another ethical word ("desirable"). However, nothing simpler seems to be satisfactory; and the more we reflect on the matter, the more we shall be convinced that the concept of the "reprehensible" is a complex one.[4]

The term "morally admirable" can be explained in a parallel way. "X is morally admirable" means "Y did X, and X would not have occurred had not the character of y been in some respect more desirable than average; and on this account it is objectively justified for Y to feel satisfaction or take pride in his action, and for others to have favorable attitudes such as respect or admiration toward Y."

According to these definitions, a person may do something reprehensible even if, over all, he has a fine character; reprehensible action only requires that one's character fall short in one respect. Conversely, a person may do something admirable even if, over all, his character is far from impressive; an admirable deed requires only that one's character stand out in one respect. These implications correspond, it seems, with what we think.

---

[3] These attitudes are closely related to the ones that are "objectively justified" if someone is morally obligated. See p. 360. But there are differences. Judgments of reprehensibility are properly tested by appeal only to attitudes that are *fully* informed on *all* relevant facts, whereas judgments that someone else is objectively obligated are properly tested by appeal only to attitudes *not* informed about what the agent *thinks* the facts are or *thinks* he ought to do.

[4] The definition of "X is more reprehensible than Y" works out like this: "W did X, and Z did Y, and X would not have occurred had not W's character been in some respect less desirable than average, and this relevant feature of W's character is less desirable than any feature of Z's character responsible for Y; and on this account it is objectively justified for W to feel remorse or guilt more severe than it is justified for Z to feel, and it is objectively justified for other persons to have more severe attitudes such as anger toward W than toward Z."

We shall avoid dealing with this definition in the future!

3. WHAT MAKES ACTIONS, THOUGHTS, OR FEELINGS REPREHENSIBLE?

According to our explanation of the meaning of "reprehensible" and "admirable," the central terms of moral assessments are very similar to other ethical words we have discussed. Therefore, in view of previous discussions, we need not take up the question of how judgments of moral assessment can be confirmed, or the sense in which they can be confirmed. We are ready, then, to consider normative questions, questions about what things *are* morally admirable or reprehensible, and why. In the course of doing this, we shall elucidate some common-sense aspects that play an important part in our assessments of actions and person.

The first problem we must examine is: What *types* of thing is it that makes actions, thoughts, or feelings reprehensible or admirable? What *types* of thing do we have to know about an event, in order to be in a position to decide whether the person's action, thought, or feeling was admirable or reprehensible? There are three major answers to this question.

Before examining these, however, we should say something about a query that is possibly in the reader's mind. "What makes you think," he may be asking, "that thoughts or feelings *are* reprehensible or admirable? Actions are properly said to be reprehensible. Or it is reprehensible *of a person* to *do* a certain thing. But the suggestion that mere thoughts or feelings can be reprehensible—or admirable—I do not find convincing."

We need not quarrel with such readers on this point, for it is not critical for any of the discussion that follows. Nevertheless, we do not agree with them. Certainly it has often been thought by many that it is reprehensible to have certain thoughts. At some points the New Testament states that it is just as reprehensible to have thoughts of performing various acts as it would be to perform the acts themselves. This suggestion is doubtless extreme. Still, if someone is dependent on our thinking through a problem carefully, isn't it reprehensible if we merely sit and daydream? Remember, to have a certain thought is something over which we have control as much as we have over doing something with our bodies. The case of feelings is perhaps more doubtful. Still, suppose a person *enjoys* witnessing the suffering of another. Should we not think less of him for it—think it justified to take a slightly unfavorable attitude toward him on that account?

Let us turn to answering our question: What types of thing make actions (and so on) reprehensible or admirable? There are three main proposals: consequences, intentions, and motives.

1. *Consequences.* Suppose a small boy bats a baseball through our window. Was his action reprehensible? It is agreed that the fact that the window is broken does not settle this; we need more information. Was it an accident, or did he *aim* to hit the window? Or was he negligent, in participating in a ball game on a site where the window might well be the victim of an ill-aimed fly-ball? Obviously, no one would take a condemning

attitude toward the boy unless his deed were either negligent or intentional. So, clearly, the consequences of an act are not the *only* factor relevant to whether an action is reprehensible. But are they *relevant at all?* This question is more difficult. The law makes distinction between murder and merely attempted murder. However, it is difficult to believe that, no matter how justified for its own purposes may be the distinction made by the law, an attempted murder is less morally reprehensible than a successful one (provided, of course, the attempt was a serious one, failing only because of unforeseeable accident). The man who aims and misses has acted, as far as *he* is concerned (aside from marksmanship) exactly as the one who aims and strikes. So, on the one hand, we must recognize that an accident is really an accident, no matter how serious the damage, and no one is properly blamed; and on the other hand, we must recognize that an attempt to harm is an attempt to *harm*, even if it fails on account of contingencies beyond the control of the agent. The relevance of consequences, for *moral* assessments, is only what they show about what the agent intended to do, or was willing to do, or was motivated to do or not motivated to avoid.

2. *Intentions.* It has sometimes been thought that we can assess the morality of an action if we know only about the intentions of its agent. This is a much more plausible proposal. Intentions, of course, are relevant. In fact, if a person does something (for example, drops an expensive dish belonging to his hostess) unintentionally, his act is not reprehensible (except perhaps on grounds of carelessness), whereas it might be highly reprehensible if he had done it intentionally.

But what do we mean by speaking of the "intentions" of an agent? His "intentions" in performing an act are best defined as the *total* set of his beliefs about the consequences, certain or likely, of what he does with his body or his mind—not, by any means, *just* his expectations about the consequences *on account of which he does the act.* If a bank teller embezzles $20,000 to purchase his wife an expensive coat for her birthday, we do not know facts about his deed of the utmost importance for assessing it, if all we know is that he expected, by what he did, to surprise his wife happily on her birthday. No, anyone who thinks that the morality of a deed can be assessed by knowing the intentions of the agent must mean to include more than this in what he counts as "intentions." He includes the other expectations of the agent—expectations of effects that perhaps did not interest him, but which he was willing to accept for the sake of those that did. A man who blows up an airplane in order to collect $50,000 insurance on his mother intends, as this word is here used, not only to collect the insurance but to cause the death of all the occupants of the plane.

Obviously, a person's intentions in this sense are highly relevant for the moral appraisal of his deed. But, if we know about his intentions, we do not yet know everything we need to know. This can most easily be made clear by an example. Suppose I have promised to take my son to the circus.

Subsequent to the promise, I deliberate about whether to keep my promise and tentatively decide not to do so. But, on learning that another philosopher is going, and that he and I can sit together and discuss philosophy during the circus, I decide to keep my promise after all. My intention, in taking my son to the circus, then, includes causing him enjoyment, keeping my promise to him, and talking philosophy with my friend. Therefore, it would seem, my deed must be laudable or at least not questionable. Not so, however. If it is really true that I am *motivated* solely, or almost solely, by the chance to talk philosophy, and but for this would not have taken my son to the circus even though I promised to, my action may very well be reprehensible—on account of what did and didn't *motivate* it. Thus, the moral quality of an action is not a function solely of the intentions of the agent.

3. *Motives.* A third theory has held that whether an action is reprehensible or morally admirable is a matter of the agent's motivation in performing it. This thesis is an important one, and at least very near the truth.

What do we mean by speaking of an agent's "motivation"? Suppose an agent is deliberating between two courses of action, A and B. Each of these involves initiating certain bodily movements; and the agent in deliberating thinks of these as leading, certainly or probably, to various further consequences. Some of the expected consequences of the two courses of action will be the same; but others will be different. So, as he deliberates, he will think of A as leading to certain consequences (say F, G, and H) to which B will not lead, and as not leading to certain consequences (say, L, M, and N) to which B will lead. Now, the thought that A will lead to certain consequences (say F) and *not* to some others (say L) may attract him toward A; the fact that A will lead to certain other consequences (say G) and not to others (say M) may attract him to B; and certain others (say, H and N) of the consequences may not move him either way. Now, let us use the term "an agent's motivation in making a certain choice" in such a way that *complete* information about his motivation will include (*a*) his beliefs about all the things that will be different if he chooses one alternative rather than the other, (*b*) an indication, for each one of these differences, whether the fact it will be a consequence of one action but not of the other is an attractive feature in one direction or the other, or not at all, and (*c*) information about how strong the attraction, in one direction or the other, is in every case. Such information about a person's motivation could be represented by a diagram, on which the names of all the differences in the expected consequences of the two actions appeared, and on which, connected with each name, there was an arrow, pointing toward A or B (depending on the direction in which the consideration moves the agent), and the *length* of the arrow indicated the *strength* of the attraction. If we had such a diagram before us, we could then state what factors among the expected consequences of *A* moved the agent toward *A*, what factors among the probable consequences of *B* also moved him toward *A* (because he wanted to avoid them). We could also say things like this: "If he had been as interested in factor *L* as most people, then he would have chosen *B* instead of A—if other things remained the same."

Sometimes, when we speak of a person's "motives," we refer to something about his action that is much narrower than the kind of picture of a person's motivation we have just suggested. Sometimes we have in mind only the *very strongly moving* facts about the alternatives. But, if we are to say, with plausibility, that the morality of an action is a function solely of the agent's motivation, we have to understand by "motivation" the sort of thing we have suggested—because sometimes an action is reprehensible because the agent was *not* motivated at all by some consequence that should have motivated him. Consider, for instance, the bank teller, referred to above, who was *not* motivated by the thought that other people would have to make up for the losses that he caused. Sometimes, again, an action is admirable or reprehensible because of the *strength* of the motivation, in the total circumstances. For example, why did Jesus praise the giving of the "widow's mite"? Not because the widow wished to give—almost everyone likes to give. It was the strength of her concern for others, which was shown to be greater than what must have been a very strong desire for food and other necessaries of life for herself and her children—things a person in her circumstances must go without if she made her gift. It was this that made it admirable. The same is true for cases in which we judge a person leniently because we think he was strongly tempted, for when a person was strongly tempted, we are free to think that his desire to do what he ought to do may well have been strong, as strong as or stronger than that of most men.[5]

Can we say, then, that the admirableness or reprehensibleness of an action is a function solely of a person's motivation in this broad sense? If we know about the motivation of a deed in this sense, do we know all we have to know in order to assess it morally?

We are at least very close to what we need to know. However, there is some ground for doubt. Should we criticize a deed because it *did not occur* to the agent that it would have certain consequences—although it would have occurred to a person with better character? Again, sometimes we object to a person's conduct because his action is arrogant, or intolerant, or unreasonable. Are such qualities matters of motivation, even in our broad sense? Could we infer that a person was acting arrogantly or intol-

---

[5] In 1947, a Baltimore man received a sentence of only a year for the murder of his wife. According to the Dec. 4 issue of *The New York Times*, the judge remarked: "He put up with an incredible amount of abuse. For four months he was able to tolerate the situation. Then suddenly, he strangled his wife to shut off her torrent of verbal abuse. The jury brought in the most lenient verdict possible and recommended mercy."

erantly or unreasonably, if we had a complete picture of his motivation? If we are cautious, we shall say that whether an action is reprehensible or morally admirable is a matter very largely, but perhaps not wholly of the agent's motivation.

But to say this is to talk only about *actions*. Can we say the same about thoughts or feelings? We have said that these may be reprehensible or morally admirable. If so, what must we know in their case, in order to make an accurate assessment? Well, to *harbor* a thought is to act, and hence there is no reason why a train of thought, insofar as it is consciously controlled, is unlike any other action. Our conclusions about the morality of actions are properly extended to cover this. But how do we assess the unexpected intrusion of a thought into our minds? Or the occurrence of a feeling? To a large extent we hardly control these consciously at all. In their case, let us content ourselves with a mere suggestion: that these, too, manifest the desires or interests of the person, and that it is these interests and their strength, as manifested in the thoughts or feelings, that are the basis for our assessments.

To have said all this does not take us very far. We have reached some conclusions about the *kind* of thing we have to know in order to assess an action (and so on) morally. But to say this is not yet to tell us what we most want to know: Exactly when, on account of what kind of motivation, is an action (and so on) reprehensible or admirable? This question we must postpone to the end of our discussion.

4. CHARACTER AND CONSCIENTIOUSNESS

Two further notions play an important role in our moral assessments: character and conscientiousness. The first is of particular interest if we are right in our suggestion that it is involved in the concept of the reprehensible or the morally admirable. The second, again, is of great interest because various philosophers have thought that actions are reprehensible if and only if they show deficiency in conscientiousness (interest in doing one's duty), and that they are morally admirable only if they show conscientiousness of a high degree.

Character. A person's "character" may be defined as "all his traits of character." Therefore the central job is to explain the phrase "trait of character," or "character trait."

In speaking of a "trait of character" we have in mind the usage by which we say that either honesty or dishonesty is a trait of character, whereas intelligence or energy is not. Thus, we are using "trait of character" in such a way that bad traits (dishonesty) as well as good ones can be traits of character.[6] At the same time, we are using it in a sufficiently narrow

---

[6] We do not always speak in this way. When we say that somebody is a "man of character," what we mean is that he is a man with markedly *good* traits of character (in our sense). We are not using "character" in this sense.

sense that intelligence does not count as a trait of character. Our usage, probably, is by far the most natural one. If someone asks us to write him about the "character" of a prospective employee, he is not asking us to write about his intelligence or his energy level; and he is asking us to tell about both good and bad traits of character.

What, then, can we say about the meaning of "trait of character"? The first thing is that a trait of character is a special kind of *trait of personality,* in the sense in which "trait of personality" is used by psychologists. But what is a "trait of personality"? First of all, it is a response-tendency of a person in the broad sense in which being soluble in water may be said to be a response-tendency of a piece of sugar. It is a response-tendency of a person in such a sense that to say that something has a certain response-tendency is to say that, if it is in certain specified circumstances, it will or will probably or very frequently behave in a certain way. For instance, being irritable is a response-tendency of a person: To say of a man that he is irritable is to say that if he is placed in a certain typical situation (the description of which may be complex), then, at least very often, he will get angry. Or again, being energetic is a response-tendency of a person: To say of a person that he is energetic is to say that in some conditions, for example, after hours of work of a kind to tire out most people, he is still active and ready to do more things. To say that something is a "trait of personality," then, is in part to say that it is a response-tendency of a person in this sense. But what specific kinds of response-tendencies of a person will count as traits of personality? Psychologists do not regard the disposition to have knee-reflexes as a "trait of personality." A trait of personality is concerned somehow with the person *as a whole.* Being energetic, then, even though to be so may be a purely physical characteristic, is counted as a trait of personality; a specific skill like capacity to play the piano is not counted as a trait. Nor is a specific affection for a particular person counted as such. A trait is, at least normally, something we can describe by a sentence beginning with "He is" followed by an adjective such as "humble" or "cruel" or "absent-minded" or "affable." A trait of personality must also be a *relatively enduring* response-tendency of the whole person; thus, homesickness does not count as a trait of personality, although the lack of independence from which perhaps it springs is so classified.

A trait of character, we have said, is a special kind of trait of personality. But what kind? The first thing to notice is that people do identify certain traits, and not others, as traits of character. Among examples of traits of character are virtues such as courage, self-control, generosity, and fairness. In contrast, there are other traits of personality that would be universally denied to be traits of character: intelligence, energy, and a sense of humor. Most people are probably uncertain how to classify certain other traits of personality: for example, caution, excitability, orderliness, self-confidence, shyness, tact, and so on.

Are there any properties that distinguish the traits of personality generally agreed to be traits of character, from those generally agreed not to be? Yes, there are two properties that all character traits have. Many or most noncharacter traits of personality have neither of them, at least to any marked degree; and no noncharacter trait appears to have them both.

The first is that traits of character are either social assets or social liabilities, usually important ones. That a man is reliable and responsible—that he can be counted on to fulfill his commitments or role, irrespective of impulses or inconveniences or distractions—is an important and favorable fact about him, from the point of view of society and interpersonal relations. That he is generous, in the broad sense—interested in others and glad of their welfare and success, not perpetually concerned about putting himself forward—is an important and favorable fact about him, one that helps make life with him tolerable and pleasant. That he is courageous will mean that support can be expected of him when large issues are at stake and the personal risks considerable. And so on for the other qualities that we ordinarily count as good traits of character; the "virtues" are assets for living, usually important ones. The "vices," on the other hand—such as dishonesty, selfishness, cowardice—are always liabilities for living, usually serious ones.[7]

There is a second feature that traits we classify as traits of character have in common. The having of them, or at least behavior as if we had any one of them, is within our voluntary control at least in the sense that we could have behaved as if we had them if our desires or interests had been what they really should be.[8] Can we act honestly if we wish? Of course: all we need do is pay our debts, refrain from deceit, and so on. Can we act generously if we wish? We can pay regard to the welfare of others; we can make gifts. Most noncharacter traits are different. We cannot act intelligently on order. We cannot become gay or effervescent just because we want to; we can try, and to some extent we can succeed, but if we are not naturally gay, we shall need histrionic skill in order to act as if we were.

---

[7] We can define "virtue" as a "desirable trait of character" and "vice" as an "undesirable trait of character."

[8] In most cases such behavior is "within our voluntary control" in a stronger sense than that "we could have . . . if our desires had been different," as the remainder of this paragraph makes clear. Not in all, however. Consider unselfishness. Can we now, if we wish, behave in all the ways typical of unselfishness, even if we are not unselfish? No: for instance, we cannot produce on order the ideas that would occur to a really unselfish person, or the feelings which a really unselfish person would have. What is the difference, then, between unselfishness and intelligence? The answer is that unselfishness is more within our "voluntary control" in the sense that *most* behavior characteristic of unselfishness is open to us even as we are, and that *all* of it would be possible for us if our *interests* were different.

It is this feature of traits of character that makes it possible for us to feel strong indignation, contempt, and disgust toward a person on account of behavior that shows a defect of character. It is true that there are traits of personality (not character) that make us dislike people; perhaps we dislike a person who is always glum and cheerless. But attitudes like indignation and contempt are at least less sharp and stinging when we think a person could not have acted differently no matter how hard he tried, no matter how different his interests.

Noncharacter traits never have both these features. Energy, for instance, is an important feature of personality; but it may be expended in useless activities or antisocial channels, and it is not within our control. A sense of humor is, to be sure, an asset for living; but it is hardly an important one, and whether we have it is not a matter we can control.

Can we say, then, that what we *mean* by "trait of character" is "trait of personality that is either an asset or a liability for social living, and is within our control to a high degree"? Certainly not in the sense of *overt* meaning (p. 163); in the sense of "same meaning" explained in Chapter 7, perhaps we do. What we can be most sure of, however, is that the things we *call* traits of character have these properties; and that traits of personality that we do not ordinarily call traits of character do not have them both.

Is a person's *motivation* in any way related to his traits of character? This is an important question, for we suggested, a few pages back, that whether an action is reprehensible or morally admirable depends largely if not entirely on its motivation. The connection is close. We cannot say that every kind of motivation is an expression of character (desire for food or drink, for instance, is not), but many kinds of motivation are. In fact, *any* kind of motivation on account of which an action can be accounted reprehensible or morally admirable is of this kind. For instance, suppose a deed is reprehensible because it failed to be motivated by regard for the welfare of other persons—say, some selfish act that injured others. But the disposition to ignore the welfare of others—a readiness not to be motivated by thought of injury to them—is precisely a trait of character: one we call "selfishness." Or consider, again, the case of the widow's mite. We praise her act because she was motivated to give, by the thought of the plight of others, money that she needed badly herself. Her doing so showed something about her—concern for others—which again is precisely a trait of character: generosity or sympathy. In general, if we pick out that defect in a person's motivation that we regard as the reason why his action is properly called reprehensible, we shall find that the disposition to be so motivated is something we recognize as a trait of character.

It is for this reason that it is plausible to suggest, in our definition of "reprehensible," that something can be reprehensible only if it would not have occurred but for a defect of character.

Conscientiousness. Many people have thought that conscientiousness is central among traits of character. Some think, in fact, that conscientiousness is just all that there is to good character. Others think that the conscientiousness shown in an act is the only thing that affects whether the act is admirable or reprehensible in a "distinctively moral sense." In order to assess these views, it is necessary to get clear what conscientiousness is.

It may be helpful first to consider what we mean by "conscience." We often speak of having a "bad conscience" about something and of "consulting our conscience." What does such talk mean? When a person has a bad conscience about something, he cannot now justify to himself (by whatever means he uses) what he did; he can find no fully satisfactory excuse for it; when he reflects on the matter he feels guilty or remorseful ("conscience-smitten") about it. Again, when a person "consults his conscience," what he does is reflect about the courses of action open to him and their compatibility with valid moral principles; perhaps he reconsiders what are the valid principles relevant to the issue. Or, he may consider whether he feels obligated to do one thing rather than another, and whether he will probably feel remorse afterwards if he does do it. There is another pair of phrases. One is: "He has *no* conscience." What this means is that the person in question is not given to appraising his past conduct morally or caring about whether contemplated conduct is morally acceptable, that he feels no guilt or shame when he thinks of his misconduct and does not allow moral considerations to affect his plans. Conversely, we sometimes say of someone, "He has a conscience." We assert thereby the opposite state of affairs.

Webster defines "conscientious" as meaning "governed by, or conformed to, a strict regard to the dictates of conscience, or by the known or supposed rules of right and wrong." A conscientious person, then, is one strongly motivated to avoid doing anything he thinks wrong, and who is willing to make considerable sacrifice to do what he thinks is right. He is also one who is scrupulously careful to be sure that his conduct *is* right; he is constantly on the alert about the moral justifiability of what he does or plans to do. By implication, then, he is a person who stands ready to behave in ways obviously required by moral principle: he will do his fair share, will be respectful of the rights of others, and so on.

Let us keep to the core meaning of "conscientious," as strong motivation to do one's duty. Let us ask ourselves what is the relation of conscientiousness in this sense to the other virtues, like unselfishness, kindness, generosity, thrift, prudence, self-control, honesty, and truthfulness. Since language contains all these many different terms, there is prima facie reason for thinking there are corresponding differences between these concepts, and that conscientiousness is not the only virtue, or lack of it the only vice. But then exactly what is the difference between it and the other virtues? (1) The other virtues are tendencies to act in rather more specific ways.

For instance, honesty is essentially scrupulous regard for moral principles in certain areas, particularly property relations, and unwillingness to deceive in order to gain advantage. Conscientiousness is broader and less definite; it is scrupulousness about conforming to moral principle in general. (2) A person having one of the more specific traits is a person who is disposed to act in a certain way *from habit,* that is, without necessarily reflecting on whether a certain sort of action is morally required. A generous person, for instance, "instinctively" inclines to certain forms of behavior, without noticing that moral principle requires him to do so. Being conscientious is not a settled "habit" of behaving in some specific way.

These differences between conscientiousness and the other virtues explain why conscientiousness is *not* the whole of good character, for we approve of being moved to generous, sympathetic acts independently of the thought of duty, and we think there is something lacking in a person who does not have a direct impulse to do certain things in response to the plight of other human beings but does them only because he thinks he ought to. Why should we feel this way? Possibly one reason is that a man can be conscientious and still act wrongly. He may be unintelligent and come to strange conclusions about what is his duty; or he may be imperceptive, not responsive to the welfare of others, particularly in its subtler aspects. On the other hand, if he has the other virtues, he is much less likely to come to mistaken conclusions about his duty, and he will not be imperceptive. Clearly, to be courteous, generous, kind, modest, reasonable, sympathetic, tolerant, truthful, and uncomplaining—to be any of these is in some particular way to have developed a sensitivity and responsiveness to some aspect of human beings or human relations, or something worthwhile, that can be counted upon to make one's judgments about one's obligations more sensitive and reliable.

In saying this we should not forget, however, that conscientiousness is supremely important. If a person had all the other virtues but failed in conscientiousness, it would be unfortunate, indeed, for the very thing that we think distinctively good about some of the virtues other than conscientiousness is also a defect. Take generosity. We suggested that we value an immediate responsiveness to the plight of others, unmediated by any feeling of obligation. But such generosity can be misplaced: impulsive generosity may lead to action in conflict with the best interests, or the long-range interests, not only of the donor but the recipient of benefactions. Generosity needs to be directed by knowledge of the facts, by intelligent application of sound moral principles. Impulsive generosity may suffer from defects of thoughtlessness.

Conscientiousness, then, is highly important but not the whole of good character. It might still be held, however, that behavior is never reprehensible (or admirable) "in the specifically moral sense" except as it manifests defect (or perfection) of conscientiousness. However, to hold this is a mistake. We must concede that serious faults of behavior are rare, when there is no deficiency of conscientiousness. Nevertheless, a conscientious man may be blind to the problems of others; he may be insensitive and mistaken on some moral principles. Hence, he may, for instance, make harsh demands of uprightness and not spare his condemnation when others fail; he may fail in modesty or in tolerance; and so on. And such behavior is reprehensible in the "specifically moral sense."

In consequence, we cannot define "reprehensible," as some have thought we can, by saying that reprehensible behavior is behavior that is due to defect in conscientiousness. Behavior can fail morally in other ways.

5. EXCUSES

We shall get a clearer view of moral assessments if we examine what it is to offer an "excuse" for one's behavior, and what kinds of excuse are cogent in moral contexts. The topic is an intriguing one on its own account, but it is of special interest to us, because a survey of moral "defenses" supports our explanation of what it is to be reprehensible.

An excuse is a statement, claim, or plea, used to mitigate some true charge that tends to discredit a person in some way. Excuses are by no means solely, or even mostly, used in contexts of accusations of immoral action. For instance, a fielder drops an important fly-ball; his doing so naturally leads to inferences about clumsiness or indifference. He excuses himself with the claim that the sun blinded him. A bridge collapses; its doing so naturally leads to inferences about the reliability and competence of the person or company responsible for its design and construction. Then, reputation-saving excuses are offered. In moral contexts, someone may say to me, "You lied!" I may then try to show some fact that exculpates me of, or at least mitigates the degree of, the charge of reprehensibility implied by the accusation. All these are excuses.[9]

One is not offering an excuse by a straightforward denial of a charge that tends to discredit, or by showing that what one did was objectively right or best. The term "excuse" implies the admission of the truth of some charge of wrong, inept, untoward behavior, but the denial of its force. Thus, if a boy offers an "excuse" for missing a day at school, he is not saying he did not miss it; if he says he was not absent, he is not excusing himself but protesting the charge. Or, a man, accused of having lied, is not excusing himself but protesting the charge if he asserts that what he said is true; and it is best to say he was not excusing himself but justifying his act, if he

---

[9] As we shall see later, one may, instead of offering an excuse for an action, make some point that *aggravates* it.
Something else we may do is show that some action deserves less admiration than one might suppose on the basis of information simply about what was done. We might call this "debunking."

argues that what he did was objectively right or best in the total circumstances.

What are excuses aimed to do? Generally they are personal defenses; they fend off unfavorable inferences about a person on the basis of his acts. But excuses in moral contexts are also appropriate replies to the charge, "What you did was reprehensible!" While admitting discrepancy between behavior and the standard or ideal, they shield the agent from the charge of having acted reprehensibly.

Because excuses, in moral contexts, shield from the charge of reprehensible conduct, it will be of interest, as evidence for or against our definition of "reprehensible," to see what kinds of statement function as excuses. As defenses against the charge of acting reprehensibly, their content tells us, presumably, about the substance of the charge. In fact, the types of excuses recognized as acceptable in moral contexts support our definition, for, as we shall see, the point of all but one of them is that, on account of the special circumstances cited in the excuse statement, more favorable judgments about the character of the accused are possible than would normally be justified, in view of the act it is admitted he performed. Excuse statements answer the charge of reprehensibility, usually, by claiming that in the total situation inferences about character are not necessarily unfavorable at all, or at least not as unfavorable as the charge of reprehensibility implies. Such a defense is what we might expect if, as we have suggested, to charge reprehensibility is in part to charge defect of character.[10]

Let us now survey some important types of excuse. (*a*) One kind of excuse is to claim that one acted under compulsion. This is an effective excuse because if stronger hands directed mine, I can say I did not even *do* the deed; or at any rate I can show that however fine my character might have been, I still must have done what I did. Hence, the event cannot lead to discrediting inferences about my character. (*b*) A second kind of effective excuse is that the criticized event was an accident. Such a claim is effective because if I show that no one could have foreseen the result or prevented it, people are prevented from saying the event would not have happened if only my character had been better. (*c*) Again, I may excuse myself by showing it was impossible for me to have done anything other than that for doing which I am criticized. For instance, I may be criticized for failing to pay a debt of $1,000. I shall then (perhaps) try to excuse myself by claiming that, despite every effort to get the money, it could not be ob-

---

10 An alternate interpretation of the facts is possible. One might say that the charge, "That was reprehensible," *implies* (but does not logically entail) the assertion, "Something in your character is below standard"—because it is generally thought to be the case that people do reprehensible things only when there is something wrong with their characters. In this case, the types of excuse do not necessarily show what is *meant* by "reprehensible" but only what is implied by it. It seems simpler, however, to interpret the facts as we do. In any case, this alternative interpretation would not apply to the last type of excuse to be described below.

tained. This excuse is effective because, if I cannot get the money, then the event would have been the same whatever my character, and because the fact that I made every effort to get the money shows my character not to be defective—whatever the whole incident may still prove about my skill in management. (*d*) I may plead that, when I performed a certain act, I was not in conscious control of my body at all. I may show that I was hypnotized, or sleepwalking, or under the influence of drugs, or paralyzed by fright. This excuse is a cogent one because, if I had no voluntary control over my body, my actions cannot be traced to defects of character. (*e*) I may excuse myself for having done something by stating that I *thought* it was right in the circumstances (even if now I agree it wasn't). This plea, again, is a defense of character—an attempt to show that, far from having done what I did because I did not hesitate to do that sort of thing, I was acting from a conviction that to do this was my duty. In this case, however, the excuse opens up other questions. There are some things no decent person will believe to be right (we think), and if we must defend our act by saying we believed what no decent person would believe, we may have condemned ourselves more than excused ourselves. (*f*) Another excuse is to point out that no other person, however fine, would have refrained from doing what I did. For instance, I may have been tortured into giving information to the enemy; and I may say that no one could withstand the torture to which I was subjected. If this claim is convincing, it is obvious why the excuse is successful—if our definition is correct that, to be reprehensible, an action must manifest some trait of character less desirable than the average. (*g*) A very similar type of excuse is pointing out that I was acting under the compulsion of a threat. This kind of "compulsion" is different from sheer physical compulsion. I did the deed, but I argue that the alternative posed was such that either it was right for me to do as I did, or else that anyone else, including persons with fine character, would have done the same. Again, it is obvious why the excuse, if convincing, is successful. But, of course, for it to be convincing, I really do have to show that persons of fine character would have acted as I did.

Other excuses are different from the foregoing, in that they do not exculpate completely, but only reduce the charge. (*a*) Suppose a cat frequently spoils my sleep, and at length I fire at him with a rifle, missing him but killing a passer-by. My first reaction will be to explain that I fired at the cat, with no thought that any human being might be nearby. It is still true, if my claim is accepted, that I fired in a city and that a man who took reasonable precautions would not have done so. I still have to admit, then, to thoughtlessness of human life; but the excuse is successful in its aim, which was to clear me of a much more serious moral charge (and of course the legal charge) of firing with a deliberate intent to kill. (*b*) Suppose, in a fit of temper, I make a cutting remark, or an accusation I had promised not to make. I can defend myself on the ground that my action was impulsive, provoked, not deliberate. This excuses me to some extent. It saves me from the charge of being the kind of person who can be expected to do these things in normal circumstances. I am still left charged, of course, with being the kind of person who will do such things when angry.

The foregoing are not the only kinds of excuses. There are others (not exculpating) that do not defend one's character. For instance, a lawyer may offer as an excuse for a theft that the defendant came from a poor family, left school at the age of twelve, had always lived on the streets, that his father had deserted the family at the time he was born, that his mother had to be away working all day to keep the children in food, and so on. Such excuses are effective. They make people less ready to charge a man with being reprehensible. Why? Perhaps because they show that the culprit, *at core*, is no worse than others, and that his deed is not representative of what he would have done if he had been favored by better opportunities. Or, perhaps what is being urged is that the person has already suffered at the hands of society, that he has not been equally dealt with. In either case, compassion is aroused. In other words, without defending the agent's present character, the showing tends to reduce the severity of the unfavorable attitudes of other persons. We should expect such excuses against charges of reprehensible conduct, if our definition of "reprehensible" is correct.

Sometimes excuse arguments are applied in reverse. One either shows that an excuse that is usually available is not available in the case at hand or that there are not mitigating but rather aggravating circumstances. An example of this is provided by the following excerpt from the remarks of a judge (*The New York Times*, March 25, 1952), which prefaced the imposition of a stiff sentence for misconduct in office. The reasoning is a use, in reverse, largely of the type of excuse last described.

> The record in this case presents a man who has had all the benefits of our free institutions. He had everything to inspire in him honesty, integrity, and good citizenship. He received a good education. He held a high office by virtue of appointment by the President of the United States. He had a good income, a comfortable home, a loyal wife, a family that any man should be proud of, and a host of friends. What moved a man so situated. . . ? He has used a public office of great public trust, not to strengthen and preserve our institutions in this time of stress and strain, but to weaken them by bringing suspicion on honest Governmental employees. . . . By his greed, his grasping for money, the defendant has contributed to just that. Nor did he shrink from perjury or subornation of perjury. If the defendant feels even now the slightest remorse for his wrongdoing, I have seen no evidence of it.

6. NORMATIVE PRINCIPLES FOR MORAL ASSESSMENTS

Thus far we have not formulated any general normative principle that states specifically which things are reprehensible or morally admirable—principles of the form: "An action is reprehensible (morally admirable) if and only if it has the nonethical properties *PQR*." Indeed, our statements have been mostly negative. Let us review them. First, we have held that an act is reprehensible (morally admirable) only if it would not have occurred had not its agent had a character in some respect less (in the case of "admirable," more) desirable than average. According to our proposal, this is true by definition. This statement, however, relates "reprehensible" only to the *ethical* property of manifesting an *undesirable* trait of character. Second, we have suggested that actions, thoughts, and feelings may be reprehensible, and have pointed out that what makes them so is not their consequences, nor even the agent's intentions (although these are relevant), but largely if not entirely their total motivation. However, we also mentioned some possible exceptions worth consideration. Third, we asserted that conscientiousness is the motive, or trait of character, of most importance for the moral assessment of a deed, but it is not the only one. Finally, we have listed several types of excuse generally accepted as valid; and we have suggested that they support the contention embodied in our definition, that an act is reprehensible (morally admirable) only if it would not have occurred had the agent not had a character in some respect less (more) desirable than average.

None of these statements is of the desired form: that "*x* is reprehensible if and only if *x* has the nonethical properties *PQR*." Can we hope to get such general principles? We must recall that we did not reach such generalizations in the case of "desirable" and "morally obligatory." For instance, in the case of "desirable," all we felt entitled to claim is that certain things *make a difference*, favorably or unfavorably, to the intrinsic desirability of a complex whole, that some things, like enjoyment and knowledge (with possible exceptions), enhance the intrinsic worth of something, whereas pain diminishes it.

It seems we must accept the same sort of limitation to our knowledge about reprehensibility and moral admirableness. But just what can we do, then, beyond offering the generalizations we have already stated? There are several things we can do.

First, we could simply list various individual features of motivation or traits of character, such as intolerance or lack of interest in the welfare of other people. Then, we could say that the presence of one of these properties *always* is a favorable or unfavorable factor, or makes something more or less reprehensible (and so on) than it otherwise would have been. This we could do, but we prefer not to attempt such a catalog, even a partial one, with one exception to be mentioned.

There is something more general we can do. We can assert that the presence or absence of any one of a large and specific *class* of motives or traits of character will make something more admirable or less reprehensible, and that the presence of any one of another large and specific class of motives or traits of character will make something less admirable and more reprehensible. We shall, however, have to specify this class by reference to an *ethical* property; but since the property in question happens to be one about which we have some ideas by now, our suggestion will be helpful. What is this general principle?

Let us recall the concept of "prima facie obligation." W. D. Ross, we remember, urged that we are prima facie obligated to promote the welfare of others, keep our promises, and so forth. Our generalization, then, is this: If, in a given community, it is prima facie obligatory to do a certain thing in certain situations, then any motivation or manifestation of a trait of character that shows *indifference* or *unwillingness* to do this sort of thing in this type of situation, below the average for the community, is an unfavorable factor; and any motivation that shows concern to perform actions of this sort, above the average for the community (but not such as to interfere with the performance of other prima facie obligations), is a favorable factor. For instance, indifference to the welfare of other people, or to keeping one's promises, or to speaking the truth, or to repairing injuries wrongfully done to others, are in our community (we suggest) unfavorable factors; whereas an unusual concern about these principles, a willingness to make sacrifices for them (but not to the point of interfering with other obligations) are favorable ones.

Why should we urge this generalization as correct? In the first place, we must simply ask ourselves what things we think are prima facie obligatory in our society, and then ask ourselves if it is not true that any action that manifests a low degree of interest in meeting a prima facie obligation is properly judged more reprehensible than it otherwise would have been. Is it not properly judged reprehensible in the absence of redeeming features (and the reverse for "admirable")? Take the keeping of promises as an example of a prima facie obligation. Obviously, if in a given situation a person's action manifests an inclination to take his pledged word lightly, we tend to regard the action unfavorably, even if we happen to think that what is done is right. In order for us not to view the action as reprehensible over-all, in this case, there must be "redeeming" features—say, a marked show of generosity. There is a second reason. If our proposal has been correct about how we "test" our ethical principles, then there could scarcely fail to be a connection of this sort, for we have suggested that we test obligation statements by appeal to whether we *feel obligated*—an experience that tends to turn into guilt or remorse if the obligation impulse is not obeyed—and by appeal to whether we are inclined to *demand* that others do a certain thing—an experience that tends to become indignation if they do not act accordingly. In other words, to feel obligated to do something and to feel remorseful for having failed to do it are two sides of the same coin; and to demand that others do something and to be indignant if they fail, are two aspects of one phenomenon.[11] It is no surprise that judgments of obligation and of reprehensibility are so closely related that some philosophers have urged that we often "test" our judgments of obligation by asking ourselves if we should properly feel remorseful if we did not do a certain thing.

To say this is not, of course, specifically to identify the types of motivation that are favorable or unfavorable factors; but one's theory about prima facie obligations, if we are correct, commits one to specific generalizations on this point. For instance, if one is a rule-utilitarian, one will hold that there is a prima facie obligation to obey the lowest-order prescriptions in the set of "ideal prescriptions"—ones like "If you have made a promise to do a certain thing, except on the basis of misrepresentations . . . , then do what you promised!" Then, if one's behavior manifests motivation to follow this prescription of a strength below the average for the community, it will be more reprehensible than it otherwise would have been.

One might ask whether any general statement can be made that tells us when we may pass from information that a given action has an unfavorable feature of this sort, to the conclusion that it is reprehensible. The answer seems to be parallel to the relation between prima facie obligation and over-all obligation. For one thing, the only things relevant to an assessment of a particular act or mental occurrence are the reprehensible-making and admirable-making features of that *act* or occurrence. One's character in general is irrelevant. And we can say about a particular act that has *only* unfavorable features that it is reprehensible; and about an act that has only favorable qualities that it is admirable; and about one that has qualities of the two contrary kinds that its over-all quality depends on the "balance" of the qualities of the two contrary kinds.[12]

It would be mistaken, however, to think that the *only* morally favorable and unfavorable qualities of an action or mental occurrence are its manifestation of a concern, or lack of concern, for prima facie obligations. There is one exception to this of major proportion: the interest in doing one's duty in general—conscientiousness. We have said that a person's conscientiousness is by no means the only thing about his motivation that is relevant to whether his deed is admirable or reprehensible. But that it is *one* factor, and a highly important one, there can be no doubt. Moreover, of

---

[11] There are complications that we are here ignoring; for instance, that the appeal of an objective judgment of obligation is to the demand we make on others when we ignore their moral convictions about the case, and their factual beliefs about the case. The appeal, for testing a judgment of reprehensibility, is to an attitude we have when we do not ignore these things.

[12] But we must recall all that we said (p. 393) about how quantitative terminology can mislead, and how in the end to decide whether there is a "balance" is simply to decide whether after all, in the total situation, the action is reprehensible or admirable —by the standard method for deciding such issues.

course, it is not a concern to do any specific kind of thing but to do everything that is objectively our over-all duty.

Like the other more specific morally favorable and unfavorable factors, concern for duty *is* only one factor. It may be present in high degree, yet the action may be reprehensible over-all because of other factors.

But there are still other factors of this sort. If we look at the vocabulary of virtues and vices, we find that more things are regarded as defects or excellences of character than just interest in doing what our prima facie obligations call for. Take being courageous, thrifty, quarrelsome, uncomplaining, self-controlled, impartial, fair-minded, cooperative, modest, unenvious, and persistent. All of these qualities are related to prima facie obligations; having them makes us better, or worse, at fulfilling these obligations. Yet most if not all of them cannot be construed as mere dispositions to fulfill (or not to fulfill) one of these obligations.

Is there no more general statement we can make about these? The following generalization is worth consideration: that the manifestation in conduct of *any* trait of character, the presence or absence of which *normally* promotes or hinders the fulfillment of obligations of some kind, will be either a favorable or an unfavorable factor with respect to that action—and that whether it is favorable or unfavorable depends on whether the trait in question normally promotes or hinders the fulfillment of obligations.

FURTHER READINGS

A. C. Ewing, *Ethics* (London: English Universities Press, 1953), chap. 8.
————, *The Definition of Good* (New York: The Macmillan Company, 1947), pp. 153 ff.
————, "Responsibility toward Oneself and Others," *Revue Internationale de Philosophie*, No. 39 (1957), pp. 51–68.
H. D. Lewis, J. W. Harvey, and G. A. Paul, "The Problem of Guilt," (symposium), The Aristotelian Society, Supplementary volume XXI (1947), 175–218.
P. Nowell-Smith, *Ethics* (Baltimore: Penguin Books, Inc., 1954), chaps. 17–20.
W. D. Ross, "The Nature of a Morally Good Action," *Proceedings*, The Aristotelian Society, 1928–29, pp. 257–74.
————, *The Right and the Good* (Oxford: Clarendon Press, 1930), chap. 7.
M. Mandelbaum, *The Phenomenology of Moral Experience* (Glencoe, Ill.: Free Press, 1955), chaps. 3–4.
E. L. Beardsley, "Moral Worth and Moral Credit," *Philosophical Review*, LXVI (1957), 304–28.
R. B. Brandt, "Blameworthiness and Obligation," in A. I. Melden (ed.), *Essays in Moral Philosophy* (Seattle: University of Washington Press, 1958).
J. O. Urmson, "Saints and Heroes," in A. I. Melden (ed.), *Essays in Moral Philosophy*.
C. D. Broad, "The Doctrine of Consequences in Ethics," *Ethics*, XXIV (1913), 293–320.

W. Hardie, "Naturalistic Ethics," *Proceedings of the British Academy*, XXXIII, 1947.

H. Farmer, "The Notion of Desert Good and Bad," *Hibbert Journal*, XLI (1942–43), 347–53.

L. Garvin, *A Modern Introduction to Ethics* (New York: Houghton Mifflin Company, 1953), pp. 241–44.

G. E. Moore, *Ethics* (Oxford: Oxford University Press, 1949), pp. 116 ff.

C. L. Stevenson, *Ethics and Language* (New Haven: Yale University Press, 1944), pp. 301–10.

John Dewey and J. H. Tufts, *Ethics* (New York: Henry Holt & Company, Inc., 1938), pp. 336–42.

John Dewey, *Human Nature and Conduct* (New York: Carlton House, 1922), pp. 316–20.

D. Braybrooke, "Stevenson, Voltaire, and the Case of Admiral Byng," *Journal of Philosophy*, LIII (1956), 787–95.

S. Moser, "Utilitarian Theories of Punishment and Moral Judgments," *Philosophical Studies*, VIII (1957), 15–19.

C. A. Campbell, *Scepticism and Reconstruction* (London: G. Allen & Unwin, Ltd., 1931), chap. 7.

J. Austin, "A Plea for Excuses," *Proceedings*, The Aristotelian Society (1956–57), pp. 1–30.

C. D. Broad, "Analysis of Some Ethical Concepts," *Philosophy*, III (1928), 285–300.

———, "Conscience and Conscientious Action," *Philosophy*, XV (1940), 115–30.

W. H. F. Barnes, W. D. Falk, A. Duncan-Jones, "Intention, Motive, and Responsibility," (symposium), The Aristotelian Society, Supplementary volume XIX (1945), 230–88.

R. S. Peters, D. J. McCracken, J. O. Urmson, "Motives and Causes," (symposium), The Aristotelian Society, Supplementary volume XXVI (1952), 139–94.

19

Retributive Justice and Criminal Law

The ethical foundations of the institution and principles of criminal justice require examination just as do the ethical foundations of systems of economic distribution. In fact, the two problems are so similar that it is helpful to view either one in the light of conclusions reached about the other. It is no accident that the two are spoken of as problems of "justice," for the institution of criminal justice is essentially a mode of allocating welfare (or "illfare," if we prefer). Also, just as an economic return can be regarded as a reward for past services, the punishment of criminals can be regarded as punishment for past disservices. Moreover, just as a major reason for differences in economic reward is to provide motivation for promoting the public welfare by industrious effort, so a major reason for a system of punishment for criminals is to give motivation for not harming the public by crime. The two topics, then, are very similar; but they are also sufficiently different to require separate discussion.

What is meant by an "examination of the ethical foundations of the institution and principles of criminal justice"? The job of such an examination is *not* to provide a moral blessing for the status quo, for the system of criminal justice as it actually is in the United States, or in the Commonwealth of Pennsylvania. (It would be impossible to do this for all states of the U.S.A. together, or for all the Western nations, for the legal systems of different political units differ in important particulars.) Rather, it is to identify the more important valid ethical principles that are relevant to the institution of criminal justice and to furnish a model of their use in criticism or justification of important features of this institution.

The broad questions to be kept in the forefront of discussion are the following: (1) What justifies anyone in inflicting pain or loss on an individual on account of his past acts? (2) Is there a valid general principle about the punishments proper for various acts? (Possibly there should be no close connection between offense and penalty; perhaps punishment

480

should be suited to the individual needs of the criminal, and not to his crime.) (3) What kinds of defense should excuse from punishment? An answer to these questions would comprise prescriptions for the broad outlines of an ideal system of criminal justice.

One may wonder how the problem, as outlined, is related to the more general problem of the "just" and the "unjust."

In our discussion of "distributive justice," we decided that "to act unjustly" means the same as "to treat unequally, in some matter that involves the distribution of things that are good or bad, except as the inequality is required by moral considerations (principles) with substantial weight in the circumstances." If this definition of "act unjustly" is correct, then there are two distinct ways in which there can be injustice in the treatment of criminals. First, criminals are *punished* whereas noncriminals are not. Punishment, however, is *unequal* treatment, in a matter that involves distribution of things good or bad. Therefore, if punishment is to be just, it must be shown that the unequal treatment is required by moral principles of weight. Thus, one thing that must be done in order to show that the practice of punishing criminals is not unjust, is to show that there are moral principles that require it. But second, the *procedures of applying* the principles directing unequal treatment for criminals may themselves operate unequally. One man gets a "fair" trial and another does not. There can be inequality in the chances given people to escape the application of legal sanctions in their case. Part of treating people "justly," then, is providing legal devices so that everyone has an equal hearing: scrupulous adherence to the rules of evidence, opportunity for appeal to higher courts for remedy of deviation from standard rules in the lower courts, and so on. We shall not here consider details about how legal institutions should be devised in order to secure equal application of the law; that is a specialized inquiry that departs too far from the main problems of ethical principle. It is a part of "justice," however. Indeed, we may view "criminal justice" as having two main aspects: just laws for the punishment of offenders and procedures insuring just application of these laws by the courts and other judicial machinery.

The existence of just laws directing certain punishments for certain offenses, then, is not the whole of justice for the criminal, but we shall concentrate on identifying such laws.

Another question that may be raised is whether it is not artificial to confine our problem, as we have been doing so far, to the treatment of criminals by the legal system. Are there not other punishments, and will not the principles that justify one also justify them all? Many people believe that there is and ought to be divine punishment for the wicked in an afterlife. Children are punished by their parents for going swimming in disobedience to orders or for refusing to eat an egg for breakfast. A sergeant may punish a private with K.P. duty, if he appears for inspection with his shoes inadequately cleaned. The teacher may punish a pupil by making him stay after school, for having thrown chalk around the classroom. Do not all these cases of punishment raise the same fundamental issues?

Yes, they do. An adequate theory of punishment for improper conduct will explain or justify all these various kinds of punishment, insofar as they can be justified. It is misleading to confine ourselves to the complex case of legal systems. Indeed, if we look at primitive societies, we see that there is no sharp break between less formal systems of punishment and the elaborate systems of criminal justice used in the more advanced societies today. In their case, we may wish to speak of a "system" of criminal justice, although these societies have neither formal courts of law nor judges, and only a minimum in the way of prescribed rules of procedure against wrongdoers. So, we must consider what moral principles justify the "unequal treatment" of punishment[1] generally. Nevertheless, it is proper to give emphasis to the special problems of the legal institution of criminal justice, on account of its importance.

1. THE PRINCIPLES OF CRIMINAL LAW

In order to get before us concretely the ideas and practices of which we wish to discover the "ethical foundations," let us review the main concepts and principles of criminal law. Unfortunately there is controversy among judges and professors of law about what these concepts and principles are, and about whether they should be changed; our brief survey must necessarily ignore such differences of opinion and other subtleties, in large part.

The central feature of the system of criminal justice in the United States is the existence of laws, statutory or common, requiring that persons be caused pain or loss by the state if a judicial process has found them guilty of a crime. It is difficult to explain in general what constitutes a crime, but we can, for a start, say that criminal action always includes overt behavior which causes or threatens a "public harm," that is, some effects considered to be harmful to the community as a whole. The law provides different penalties for different offenses, the more severe ones attaching to those crimes considered in some sense more serious. For most offenses the law does not specify an exact penalty for a particular type of offense, but only a range of permitted penalties; the judge must then select some penalty within the permitted range which strikes him as appropriate, everything considered. The executive department of the government, however, has the power to reduce a sentence or pardon a criminal altogether for any reasons which strike it as proper; but it does not have the power to increase the penalty set by the judge. Various boards established by the

[1] Webster defines "punishment" as "any pain, suffering, or loss inflicted on or suffered by a person because of a crime or evildoing."

executive department may pardon or parole, or make recommendations for such actions. Theoretically juries decide only a factual question: whether the accused acted in a way defined by the law as criminal; but practically they often refuse to convict, when they regard the penalty prescribed by law for a certain offense as markedly out of line with the moral merits of the case. In some instances juries may make recommendations about the severity of sentences.

In order to get a deeper understanding of what it is to commit a certain crime, it is helpful to draw an analogy between legal and moral concepts. Let us recall the relations between prima facie obligation, over-all obligation, and blameworthiness. In general we incline to think that, for instance, if a person has promised to do something, he has a prima facie obligation to do that thing. Sometimes, however, he will not have an over-all obligation to do this, on account of the weight of conflicting obligations, such as obligation to avoid serious injury to other persons, or to give important assistance in case of need. A prima facie obligation to keep a promise, then, does not imply an over-all obligation to keep it. Moreover, failure to keep a promise, even if one is over-all obligated to keep it, does not necessarily imply moral blameworthiness. This is obvious if we are talking of *objective* obligation, for a person can be objectively obligated to do something when he does not know that he is; a man of perfect character may fail to perform his objective obligations. But it is true even of subjective obligation—for instance, if a man because of confused moral thinking believes he is obligated to do what he is subjectively obligated not to do (p. 365).

Corresponding roughly to objective prima facie obligations are the law's prohibitions of certain kinds of conduct. The law aims to prevent certain kinds of overt behavior, and sometimes the law states, in a preamble preceding clauses prescribing punishment, what kind of conduct it is aiming to prevent. For instance, it may say that "No company shall sell, . . . or offer for sale . . . any security of its own issue until it shall have . . . secured . . . a permit authorizing it so to do." (California Corporate Securities Act, Cal. Stats. 1917, p. 673.) But the law recognizes that conduct of the sort it aims to prevent in general may sometimes be justified; and therefore it permits, as defense against a criminal charge, a showing that the accused's action was justified (that in the special circumstances the agent did what the law does not really want to prevent). For instance, the law forbids killing another person; but it is prepared to accept the defense that the killing was in self-defense. Roughly, a defense of justification is analogous to a showing, in morals, that although one had a prima facie obligation not to do so-and-so, in the total circumstances doing this was the right thing. Moreover, just as infraction of overall obligation does not imply blameworthiness in morals, so the commission of some act the law intends to prevent is not necessarily criminally culpable, even if it cannot be justified in the foregoing sense. Just as there may be excuses in morals for doing what one ought not, so there are excuses in law. It is useful to distinguish three kinds of excuses in law: (a) excuses which completely exculpate, wholly free from taint of crime, (b) excuses which mitigate in the sense of reducing the crime to one of the types which the law regards as less serious (e.g., reducing from murder in the first degree to involuntary manslaughter), and (c) considerations which are properly viewed by the judge as calling for the selection of a lower penalty from among those permitted by law.

We can now see more clearly what it is to have committed some specific crime, for instance, murder in the first degree. It is (1) to have behaved in some overt way which the law aims to prevent, here to have caused the death of someone, (2) to be unable to show a legally acceptable justification of one's act, and (3) to be unable to offer an excuse of the above types (a) or (b). In a carefully written penal code, the crime of murder in the first degree will be carefully described so that one will not have committed it unless all these conditions are satisfied. To commit a certain crime, then, is to behave in a certain way, and be unable to offer one of these defenses.

It will illuminate the relation between legal liability to punishment and moral excuses and blameworthiness, to review the major types of defense. We begin with the major *justifications*. (1) An act, otherwise subject to punishment, is not a crime if done in reasonable self-defense against unlawful attack, by a soldier in execution of lawful orders, in order to prevent treason or a felony (at least one done with violence), or in the service of public welfare (as destruction of property in order to prevent flood damage or to bring a forest fire under control). (2) An act, otherwise subject to punishment, is not a crime if performed because someone threatened the agent with loss of life or personal injury, in such circumstances as would intimidate a person of ordinary firmness. This justification, however, is ordinarily not accepted for homicide. (3) One may perform a forbidden act with impunity if, in case one does not, the result one causes and worse will in all probability happen anyway. For instance, one judge has indicated that a seaman is not liable for putting persons out of an overcrowded lifeboat in a storm if otherwise the boat would sink, provided the selection of the unfortunates is made in a reasonable manner. (For a contrary opinion, see *Regina* vs. *Dudley and Stephens*.) This is one sense in which "necessity knows no law."

Let us now survey the *excuses which exculpate*. (4) A person is usually exculpated if he causes a harm the law seeks to prevent, by accident, for instance, if he causes the death of someone, but unforeseeably, despite all reasonable precautions. However, such accidental harm is sometimes punished; in many situations in which the defendant is committing an unlawful act when the accident happens, he is treated as if he intended to cause the accident. (5) A man is exculpated if because of an innocent mistake in belief about facts he performs an unlawful act which would have been lawful had the facts been as he thought they were. For instance, it is lawful to shoot a person who has broken into one's house at night for the purpose of theft; and if a person shoots his wife or servant on account of a genuine and innocent supposition that the person fired at is a burglar, he is exonerated.[2] (6) If a person is physically compelled to perform an unlawful act, e.g., if the hands of a stronger person held and guided his dagger, he is thought not to have performed that act at all, and will not be prosecuted. (7) The law excuses a man for doing what it is impossible not to do. It may forbid a car standing in a certain place, but if a car stands there because traffic is jammed and the car cannot be moved, the act is not subject to punishment. (8) A person under seven years of age cannot commit a crime; and he is not guilty of a crime if under fourteen unless malicious intent is established—although he may be subject to treatment under rules for juveniles. (9) A person is excused if he performed an otherwise unlawful act while walking in his sleep. Insanity is also an excuse if the defendant's mental disease or defect is such that he did "not know the nature and quality of the act he was doing; or, if he did know it, that he did not know he was doing what was wrong." (*The Queen* v. *M'Naghten*.)[3] (10) Theoretically a person is excused from guilt if he performs an unlawful act because of involuntary intoxication—even though in practice courts are often reluctant to admit that intoxication is "involuntary."

There are also *mitigating* excuses, which reduce the seriousness of the crime. (11) In the case of homicide, a showing that the act was done impulsively often affects the degree of guilt. Premeditation is commonly necessary for first degree murder. If one kills in the heat of passion, without forethought, he is guilty only of second degree murder. Furthermore, if such heat of passion is brought about by legally recognized provocation—such as finding one's wife in the act of adultery—the defendant may be guilty only of manslaughter. (12) Voluntary intoxication may reduce the degree of crime, but it will not exculpate, on the ground that intoxication is itself an immoral act which cannot be used as a shield for wrong conduct.

Finally, judges regularly take into account various considerations as grounds for reducing the severity of a sentence: such as severe temptation, neurotic constitution, previous lack of opportunities in life, evidence indicating that the culprit is not a menace to society, the convicted person's state of health, probable serious affects of a harsh sentence on his family. Judges sometimes make a sentence *more* severe when they think the outrage of the

---

[2] The supposition must be "innocent" in the sense that it is one a "reasonable" man might make in the circumstances. A person who supposes something negligently is not excused, except in some types of case.

[3] The question of what should constitute legal insanity is the most vigorously discussed issue in criminal law today. For an important alternative view (in *Durham* v. *United States*) and discussion, see L. Hall and S. Glueck, *Cases on Criminal Law and its Enforcement* (St. Paul, Minn.: West Publishing Co., 1958), pp. 298–325.

community requires it—if the law would be brought disrespect by a mild sentence.

The excuses (nos. four to twelve) are of interest because they give practical content to the "mental element" or "guilty mind" (*mens rea*) which the law holds must be present in order for a person to be guilty of a crime on account of his overt behavior. In view of these excuses, is there any general statement possible about the identity of this mental element? There are several things we can say. (1) It must have been possible for the accused to have behaved, as a result of different decisions or volitions, in a way that was lawful (a requirement of excuses nos. six and seven). (2) The agent must have been aware to some degree that the events which the law proscribes would flow from his bodily behavior—or at any rate that they might, that his behavior was *risking* such consequences. (3) The agent must have been aware that it is wrong to produce such consequences, *or* that it is unlawful, *or* at least that society generally regards the production of such consequences as wrong. In general, all these three conditions are required. There are two major exceptions: the so-called "public welfare" or "strict liability" offenses, where *intent* in the sense of (2) is not required at all; and the rule which imputes intent to commit offenses which in fact were accidental, to persons engaged in committing some other wrong intentionally. These exceptions are regarded by many as simply illogical elements in the law, which are without justification.

These conditions required for legal guilt are not exactly identical with those required for moral reprehensibility, the latter requiring that an act show *defect of character*. Moral guilt usually goes with legal guilt, but not necessarily. In practice, imputation of legal guilt is likely to be even more closely conformed to imputation of moral guilt than theory allows; for an unlawful act which is clearly consistent with moral character may not be prosecuted, or if prosecuted the jury may refuse to bring in a verdict of guilty.

How nearly is there a parallel between degree of moral reprehensibility of an act and seriousness of the act as a crime? We must expect some divergencies. The law, for instance, cannot concern itself with minor matters. Again, the law must be drawn in terms of relatively precise general rules, so that its administration does not place an intolerable burden of discretion on the officials charged with its application. Further, the law must be so phrased that available evidence can answer questions about its applicability; it is unfortunate if application of the law must turn on decisions about fact which are necessarily speculative.

At some points moral reprehensibility is more severe than the law. The law condemns only for overt behavior (including attempts) which is in some way publicly undesirable; it never condemns a man for his motives alone, or for his thoughts or feelings. Again, there are morally indefensible injuries of others persons (for instance, refusal to repay borrowed money) which, although they are actionable in civil suits, are not crimes and not punishable in criminal law. Again, there are many minor offenses that are morally wrong but legally are not prohibited. Further, the law automatically excuses offenses in persons under a certain age; moral judgments are more flexible and individual.

At other points, however, the law is more severe. (1) For instance, it is an axiom of the law that "ignorance of the law excuses nobody." And, we can add, it is no excuse to believe that it is morally right to do what the law forbids. Now, to some extent the same principles obtain in moral judgments: we would think it odd if anyone tried to excuse murder or rape on the ground that he did not believe the act to be wrong. Nevertheless, within a certain range, absence of belief that an act is wrong (or positive belief that it is a duty) serves as an excuse in morals; we hardly condemn a Mormon for practising polygamy, and we partly if not wholly excuse a Christian Scientist who refuses to take an ill child to the hospital. The law, however, does not regard the absence of belief that an act was unlawful as an excuse. Part of the reason for this is that the law in major part is enforcing moral rules that are well known and that are respected as right by the vast majority. (This class of cases, however, does not include many regulations that a moral person could hardly be expected to observe as a part of moral behavior, for example, peculiar traffic regulations in a small town. It is not clear that there is any moral justification for the law's refusing to accept ignorance as an excuse, in these cases where law fails to coincide with morals and where a man of character could hardly be expected to know the law.) There is also reason for not permitting conscientious objection to the law as an excuse: the law cannot permit a man to set up his own conscience as the law of the land, since if it did law enforcement could probably not proceed at all, or at least only under great handicaps. So, both the Mormon and the Christian Scientist may go to jail on serious charges.

An even more striking difference (2) between law and moral judgment is the existence of "strict liability." There is a class of infractions of law that are *not excused by demonstrable lack of intent;* any infraction of these laws is liable to punishment even if it was unforeseeable, inadvertent, and practically impossible to prevent. Thus, a butcher who sells diseased meat innocently and without any negligence, and even on the advice of experts about the quality of his meat, may incur a prison sentence. In general, a highly conscientious and law-abiding man might, through no moral fault whatever, infringe one of these laws and be subject to serious penalty. Moral condemnation certainly does not follow the law at this point.

Finally (3) some excuses that exculpate in morals only mitigate in law. In morals, whenever the circumstances are such that a man of character might be expected to do what the defendant did, he is exonerated. This is not so in law. Suppose a person imbibes a cocktail for the first time, not knowing that one drink will affect him so much that he will thoughtlessly accept another, and then be drunk. Suppose as a result of the first drink (and the second), he becomes drunk. Suppose further that this man has no reason to think that, even if he became drunk, he would be belligerent —beyond the vague awareness that some people do become belligerent when drunk. And suppose that, after becoming drunk, this person actually attacks a man and kills him. In law this can be a very serious offense; but in morals it is difficult to believe that the act is not blameless, as far as the homicide is concerned. The man *will* be morally to blame if, knowing what he did, he permits himself to become drunk again. But his drunken action was not rationally foreseeable. (It is a different matter if a man drinks, knowing that he is going to drive a car immediately after doing so.) Similarly, the rule that homicide is automatically manslaughter if the agent was committing a misdemeanor, or murder in the first degree if he was committing a felony, is by no means followed by moral judgment; perhaps in most cases the assumption of intent is reasonable, but it is not necessarily so in all cases.[4]

It is often said that the law takes no account of *motives*, but only of the *intent* to perform a specific act. We have already noted that in practice this is not quite true. But we should also notice that, if we have a clear idea of what a *motive* is (namely, that for a person to have a certain motive is for him to be inclined or disinclined to perform a certain act by his belief that doing so will have a certain property or consequence), we can construe "intent" and *mens rea* as facts about a person's motives. Clearly, if a person intentionally performs a prohibited act, he thereby shows that he was *not motivated sufficiently* to avoid that act, and this fact is as much a fact about his motives as any other. What is true is that the law takes this fact about one's motives as very decisive for the legal culpability of one's act. But other motives also play an important role. One can, if one likes, construe justifying exculpations as based on a consideration of motives: for instance, one might say that the law recognizes the fact that the motive of saving oneself or one's children from death, or saving many from the destruction of a forest fire, is a good and sufficient justification for performing an unlawful act. Moreover, a showing of good motives or strong temptations may, although not exculpating from legal liability, result in a suspended or very light sentence (and, of course, may induce a jury not to convict at all—witness cases in which juries have refused to convict persons who practiced euthanasia under circumstances approved by the jury but against the law).

One might inquire whether any examination of the "ethical foundations" of the law can show that we are obligated to support and maintain the law

---

[4] For a full discussion of some of these moral difficulties in legal practice, see Jerome Hall, *General Principles of Criminal Law* (Indianapolis: Bobbs-Merrill Co., Inc., 1947), chaps. 10, 11, and 13.

at those points where it diverges from judgments of moral culpability. The answer is that it can, on matters where the law is less severe than morals (except for some of the artificial distinctions between crimes and torts—damages actionable in civil suits). It can because there is no alternative for law which is not excessively expensive and burdensome, or which would not introduce objectionably speculative elements into legal procedure. But, on some matters where the law is more severe than moral judgment, it cannot be shown that we ought to support the maintenance of present legal principles. It is quite true that (except for matters like traffic regulations where legal restrictions do not correspond with accepted judgments of moral obligation) it is impossible to accept ignorance of the law, or conscientious disagreement with the law, as an excuse. The law cannot cease to protect what it sets out to protect because some do not agree or are unaware. But the other practices of the law that morals cannot follow appear to be morally unjustified, and there is no obligation to defend them; on the contrary, there is an obligation to do what one can to get them changed. It is sometimes thought that a utilitarian foundation of the law can justify these discrepancies as necessary evils in the service of the public good. However, this is not true: it is only utilitarian theory applied on the basis of false factual premises that has such consequences, and it has not been shown that we maximize net expectable utility by continuing with these legal practices.

2. THE UTILITARIAN THEORY OF CRIMINAL JUSTICE

Historically there has been a cleavage of opinion about the kind of general ethical principles required for coherence with our concrete justified beliefs about criminal justice (those concrete beliefs that are compatible with our "qualified" attitudes)—a cleavage already found in the parallel problem of economic justice. Many writers have thought that a utilitarian principle is adequate. Others have thought that some nonutilitarian principle, or more than one, is necessary. Most of the latter writers (formalists) have espoused some form of *retributive* principle—that is, a principle roughly to the effect that a wrongdoer should be punished approximately in correspondence with either the moral reprehensibility of his offense or with the magnitude of his breach or of the public harm he commits. However, as we shall see, there are other types of formalist theory.

It is convenient to begin with the utilitarian theory. Since we have tentatively concluded that an "extended" rule-utilitarianism is the most tenable form of theory, we shall have this particular type of theory in mind. For present purposes, however, it would make no difference, except at two or three points where we shall make note of the fact, if we confined our attention to a straight rule-utilitarian principle. There is no harm in thinking of the matter in this way. We can ignore the distinction between hedonistic and pluralistic forms for the present topic.

The essence of the rule-utilitarian theory, we recall, is that our actions, whether legislative or otherwise, should be guided by a set of prescriptions, the conscientious following of which by all would have maximum net expectable utility. As a result, the utilitarian is not, just as such, committed to any particular view about how anti-social behavior should be treated by society—or even to the view that society should do anything at all about immoral conduct. It is only the utilitarian principle *combined* with statements about the kind of laws and practices which will maximize expectable utility that has such consequences. Therefore, utilitarians are free to differ from one another about the character of an ideal system of criminal justice; some utilitarians think that the system prevalent in Great Britain and the United States essentially corresponds to the ideal, but others think that the only system that can be justified is markedly different from the actual systems in these Western countries. We shall concentrate our discussion, however, on the more traditional line of utilitarian thought which holds that roughly the actual system of criminal law, say in the United States, is morally justifiable, and we shall follow roughly the classic exposition of the reasoning given by Jeremy Bentham[5]—but modifying this freely when we feel amendment is called for. At the end of the chapter we shall look briefly at a different view.

Traditional utilitarian thinking about criminal justice has found the rationale of the practice, in the United States, for example, in three main facts. (Those who disagree think the first two of these "facts" happen not to be the case.) (1) People who are tempted to misbehave, to trample on the rights of others, to sacrifice public welfare for personal gain, can usually be deterred from misconduct by fear of punishment, such as death, imprisonment, or fine. (2) Imprisonment or fine will teach malefactors a lesson; their characters may be improved, and at any rate a personal experience of punishment will make them less likely to misbehave again. (3) Imprisonment will certainly have the result of physically preventing past malefactors from misbehaving, during the period of their incarceration.

In view of these suppositions, traditional utilitarian thinking has concluded that having laws forbidding certain kinds of behavior on pain of punishment, and having machinery for the fair enforcement of these laws, is justified by the fact that it maximizes expectable utility. Misconduct is not to be punished just for its own sake; malefactors must be punished for their past acts, according to law, as a way of maximizing expectable utility.

The utilitarian principle, of course, has implications for decisions about the severity of punishment to be administered. Punishment is itself an evil,

---

[5] In *Principles of Morals and Legislation.*

and hence should be avoided where this is consistent with the public good. Punishment should have precisely such a degree of severity (not more or less) that the probably disutility of greater severity just balances the probable gain in utility (less crime because of the more serious threat). The cost, in other words, should be counted along with the value of what is bought; and we should buy protection up to the point where the cost is greater than the protection is worth. How severe will such punishment be? Jeremy Bentham had many sensible things to say about this. Punishment, he said, must be severe enough so that it is to no one's advantage to commit an offense even if he receives the punishment; a fine of $10 for bank robbery would give no security at all. Further, since many criminals will be undetected, we must make the penalty heavy enough in comparison with the prospective gain from crime, that a prospective criminal will consider the risk hardly worth it, even considering that it is not certain he will be punished at all. Again, the more serious offenses should carry the heavier penalties, not only because the greater disutility justifies the use of heavier penalties in order to prevent them, but also because criminals should be motivated to commit a less serious rather than a more serious offense. Bentham thought the prescribed penalties should allow for some variation at the discretion of the judge, so that the actual suffering caused should roughly be the same in all cases; thus, a heavier fine will be imposed on a rich man than on a poor man.

Bentham also argued that the goal of maximum utility requires that certain facts should *excuse* from culpability, for the reason that punishment in such cases "must be inefficacious." He listed as such (1) the fact that the relevant law was passed only after the act of the accused, (2) that the law had not been made public, (3) that the criminal was an infant, insane, or was intoxicated, (4) that the crime was done under physical compulsion, (5) that the agent was ignorant of the probable consequences of his act or was acting on the basis of an innocent misapprehension of the facts, such that the act the agent thought he was performing was a lawful one, and (6) that the motivation to commit the offense was so strong that no threat of law could prevent the crime. Bentham also thought that punishment should be remitted if the crime was a collective one and the number of the guilty so large that great suffering would be caused by its imposition, or if the offender held an important post and his services were important for the public, or if the public or foreign powers would be offended by the punishment; but we shall ignore this part of his view.

Bentham's account of the logic of legal "defenses" needs amendment. What he should have argued is that *not* punishing in certain types of cases (cases where such defenses as those just indicated can be offered) reduces the amount of suffering imposed by law and the insecurity of everybody, and that failure to impose punishment in these types of case will cause only a negligible increase in the incidence of crime.

How satisfactory is this theory of criminal justice? Does it have any implications that are far from being acceptable when compared with concrete justified convictions about what practices are morally right?[6]

Many criminologists, as we shall see at the end of this chapter, would argue that Bentham was mistaken in his facts: The deterrence value of threat of punishment, they say, is much less than he imagined, and criminals are seldom reformed by spending time in prison. If these contentions are correct, then the ideal rules for society's treatment of malefactors are very different from what Bentham thought, and from what actual practice is today in the United States. To say all this, however, is not to show that the utilitarian *principle* is incorrect, for in view of these facts presumably the attitudes of a "qualified" person would not be favorable to criminal justice as practiced today. Utilitarian theory might still be correct, but its implications would be different from what Bentham thought—and they might coincide with justified ethical judgments. We shall return to this.

The whole utilitarian approach, however, has been criticized on the ground that it ought not in consistency to approve of *any* excuses from criminal liability.[7] Or at least, it should do so only after careful empirical inquiries. It is not obvious, it is argued, that we increase net expectable utility by permitting such defenses. At the least, the utilitarian is committed to defend the concept of "strict liability." Why? Because we could get a more strongly deterrent effect if everyone knew that *all behavior* of a certain sort would be punished, irrespective of mistaken supposals of fact, compulsion, and so on. The critics admit that knowledge that all behavior of a certain sort will be punished will hardly deter from crime the insane, persons acting under compulsion, persons acting under erroneous beliefs about facts, and others, but, as Professor Hart points out, it does not follow from this that general knowledge that certain acts will always be punished will not be salutary.

The utilitarian, however, has a solid defense against charges of this sort. We must bear in mind (as the critics do not) that the utilitarian principle, *taken by itself, implies nothing whatever* about whether a system of law should excuse persons on the basis of certain defenses. What the

---

[6] Act-utilitarians face some special problems. For instance, if I am an act-utilitarian and serve on a jury, I shall work to get a verdict that will do the most good, irrespective of the charges of the judge, and of any oath I may have taken to give a reasonable answer to certain questions on the basis of the evidence presented—unless I think my doing so will have indirect effects on the institution of the jury, public confidence in it, and so on. This is certainly not what we think a juror should do. Of course, neither a juror nor a judge can escape his prima facie obligation to do what good he can; this obligation is present in some form in every theory. The act-utilitarian, however, makes this the whole of one's responsibility.

[7] See H. L. A. Hart, "Legal Responsibility and Excuses," in Sidney Hook (ed.), *Determinism and Freedom* (New York: New York University Press, 1958), pp. 81–104; and David Braybrooke, "Professor Stevenson, Voltaire, and the Case of Admiral Byng," *Journal of Philosophy*, LIII (1956), 787–96.

utilitarian does say is that, when we *combine* the principle of utilitarianism with *true* propositions about a certain thing or situation, then we shall come out with true statements about obligations. The utilitarian is certainly not committed to saying that one will derive true propositions about obligations if one starts with *false* propositions about fact or about what will maximize welfare, or with *no* such propositions at all. Therefore the criticism sometimes made (for example, by Hart), that utilitarian theory does not render it "obviously" or "necessarily" the case that the recognized excuses from criminal liability should be accepted as excusing from punishment, is beside the point. Moreover, in fact the utilitarian can properly claim that we do have excellent reason for believing that the general public would be no better motivated to avoid criminal offenses than it now is, if the insane and others were also punished along with intentional wrongdoers. Indeed, he may reasonably claim that the example of punishment of these individuals could only have a hardening effect—like public executions. Furthermore, the utilitarian can point out that abolition of the standard exculpating excuses would lead to serious insecurity. Imagine the pleasure of driving an automobile if one knew one could be executed for running down a child whom it was absolutely impossible to avoid striking! One certainly does not maximize expectable utility by eliminating the traditional excuses. In general, then, the utilitarian theory is not threatened by its implications about exculpating excuses.

It might also be objected against utilitarianism that it cannot recognize the validity of *mitigating* excuses (which presumably have the support of "qualified" attitudes). Would not consequences be better if the distinction between premeditated and impulsive acts were abolished? The utilitarian can reply that people who commit impulsive crimes, in the heat of anger, do not give thought to legal penalties; they would not be deterred by a stricter law. Moreover, such a person is unlikely to repeat his crime, so that a mild sentence saves an essentially good man for society.[8] Something can also be said in support of the practice of judges in giving a milder sentence when a person's temptation is severe: at least the *extended* rule-utilitarian can say, in defense of the practice of punishing less severely the crime of a man who has had few opportunities in life, that a judge ought to do what he can to repair inequalities in life, and that a mild sentence to a man who has had few opportunities is one way of doing this. There are, then, utilitarian supports for recognizing the mitigating excuses.

Sometimes it is objected to utilitarianism that it must view imprisonment for crime as morally no different from quarantine. This, it is said, shows that the utilitarian theory must be mistaken, since actually there is a vast

---

[8] The utilitarian must admit that the same thing is true for many deliberate murders; and probably he should also admit that some people who commit a crime in the heat of anger would have found time to think had they known that a grave penalty awaited them.

moral difference between being quarantined and being imprisoned for crime. *Why* is it supposed utilitarian theory must view imprisonment as a kind of quarantine? The answer is that utilitarianism looks to the future; the treatment it prescribes for individuals is treatment with an eye to maximizing net expectable utility. The leper is quarantined because otherwise he will expose others to disease. The criminal is imprisoned because otherwise he, or others who are not deterred by the threat of punishment, will expose the public to crime. Both the convicted criminal and the leper are making contributions to the public good. So, quarantine and imprisonment are essentially personal sacrifices for the public welfare, if we think of punishment as the utilitarian does. But in fact, the argument goes on, we feel there is a vast difference. The public is obligated to do what is possible to make the leper comfortable, to make his necessary sacrifice as easy for him and his family as possible. But we feel no obligation to make imprisonment as comfortable as possible.

Again the utilitarian has a reply. He can say that people cannot help contracting leprosy, but they can avoid committing crimes—and the very discomforts and harshness of prison life are deterring factors. If prison life were made attractive, there might be more criminals—not to mention the indolent who would commit a crime in order to enjoy the benefits of public support. Furthermore, the utilitarian can say, why should we feel that we "ought to make it up to" a quarantined leper? At least partly because it is useful to encourage willingness to make such sacrifices. But we do not at all wish to encourage the criminal to make his "sacrifice"; rather, we wish him not to commit his crimes. There is all the difference between the kind of treatment justified on utilitarian grounds for a person who may have to make a sacrifice for the public welfare through no fault of his own, and for a person who is required to make a sacrifice because he has selfishly and deliberately trampled on the rights of others, in clear view of the fact that if he is apprehended society must make an example of him. There are all sorts of utilitarian reasons for being kindly to persons of the former type, and stern with people of the latter type.

Another popular objection to the utilitarian theory is that the utilitarian must approve of prosecutors or judges occasionally withholding evidence known to them, for the sake of convicting an innocent man, if the public welfare really is served by so doing. Critics of the theory would not deny that there *can* be circumstances where the dangers are so severe that such action is called for; they only say that utilitarianism calls for it all too frequently. Is this criticism justified? Clearly, the utilitarian is not committed to advocating that a provision should be written into the *law* so as to permit punishment of persons for crimes they did not commit if to do so would serve the public good. Any such provision would be a shattering blow to public confidence and security. The question is only whether there should be an informal moral rule to the same effect, for the guidance of judges and prosecutors. Will the rule-utilitarian necessarily be committed to far too sweeping a moral rule on this point? We must recall that he is not in the position of the act-utilitarian, who must say that an innocent man must be punished if in *his particular case* the public welfare would be served by his punishment. The rule-utilitarian rather asserts only that an innocent man should be punished if he falls within a class of cases such that net expectable utility is maximized if *all* members of the class are punished, taking into account the possible disastrous effects on public confidence if it is generally known that judges and prosecutors are guided by such a rule. Moreover, the "extended" rule-utilitarian has a further reason for not punishing an innocent man unless he has had more than his equal share of the good things of life already; namely, that there is an obligation to promote equality of welfare, whereas severe punishment is heaping "illfare" on one individual person. When we take these considerations into account, it is *not* obvious that the rule-utilitarian (or the "extended" rule-utilitarian) is committed to action that we are justifiably convinced is immoral.[9]

In recent years, some philosophers have sought to rescue the utilitarian from his supposed difficulty of being committed to advocate the punishment of innocent men, by a verbal point. Their argument is that it is *logically* guaranteed that only a guilty man may be *punished*. "Punishment," it is said, like "reward" and "forgive," has a backward reference; we properly speak of "punishing *for* . . . ," and if we inflict suffering on someone for the sake of utility and irrespective of guilt for some offense, it is a misuse of the word "punishment" to speak of such a person as being punished.[10] It is not clear, however, that anything is accomplished by this verbal move. If these writers are correct, then it is self-contradictory to say "innocent men may be punished for the sake of the public good," and no one can say that utilitarian theory commits one to uttering such a self-contradiction. But it may still be that utilitarian theory commits one to advocating that prosecutors suppress evidence on certain occasions, that judges aid in conducting unfair trials and pronounce sentences out of line with custom for a particular type of case in times of public danger, and, in short, that innocent men be *locked up* or *executed*—only not *"punished"*—for the sake of the public welfare. So, if there is a difficulty here at all for the utilitarian theory, the verbal maneuver of these philosophers seems not to remove it.

[9] In any case, a tenable theory of punishment must approve of punishing persons who are *morally* blameless. Suppose someone commits treason for moral reasons. We may have to say that his deed is not reprehensible at all, and might even (considering the risk he took for his principles) be morally admirable. Yet we think such persons must be punished no matter what their motives; people cannot be permitted to take the law into their own hands.

[10] For some discussion of the grammar of "punish," see A. M. Quinton, "On Punishment," *Analysis*, XIV (1954), 133–42; and K. Baier, "Is Punishment Retributive?" *Analysis*, XVI (1955), 25–32.

Everything considered, the utilitarian theory seems to be in much less dire distress, in respect of its implications for criminal justice, than has sometimes been supposed. It does not seem possible to show that in any important way its implications are clearly in conflict with our valid convictions about what is right. The worst that can be said is that utilitarian theory does not in a clear-cut way definitely require us to espouse some practices we are inclined to espouse. But to this the utilitarian may make two replies. First, that there is reason to think our ordinary convictions about punishment for crime ought to be thoroughly re-examined in important respects. We shall briefly examine later some proposals currently receiving the strong support of criminologists. Second, the utilitarian may reply that if we consider our convictions about the punishments we should administer *as a parent*—and this is the point where our moral opinions are least likely to be affected by the sheer weight of tradition—we shall find that we think according to the principles of rule-utilitarianism. Parents do regard their punishment of their children as justified only in view of the future good of the child, and in order to make life in the home tolerable and in order to distribute jobs and sacrifices equally.

3. THE RETRIBUTIVE THEORY OF CRIMINAL JUSTICE

If utilitarian ethical principles are regarded as not enough, then the basic system of "axioms" may be enlarged or modified by further principles of a nonutilitarian sort. A formalist system of principles of course may, like Ross' system, contain utilitarian elements, for example, a principle asserting that there is a prima facie obligation to do what good we can.

Any system of basic principles that contains nonutilitarian principles relevant to the treatment of criminals may be called a "retributive" theory of criminal justice. However, it seems better to reserve the term "retributive theory" for a theory that asserts that it is a basic principle of ethics roughly that pain or loss should be caused to persons who have done wrong, with a severity corresponding with the moral gravity of their deed—and of course the "gravity" of the deed not being defined to accord exactly with the utilitarian theory about how severely wrongdoers should be made to suffer.[11] In saying that such a principle is a "basic" principle of ethics, proponents of the retributive theory deny the possibility of deriving this principle from any principle directing to do good, that is, from any kind of utilitarian principle.

Let us now examine some formalist theories, beginning with what may

[11] Notice that we do not need to use the word "punish" at all in stating the retributive theory. This is fatal to the contention of some recent writers that the "retributive" theory—which they interpret as asserting, "Only the guilty should be punished"—is true by definition. See the explanation of this proposal on p. 495.

In fact, the traditional retributive theory has far more to it than merely the claim that only the guilty should be punished.

be viewed as the traditional retributive theory. In order to get a concrete account before us, let us look at a statement by Immanuel Kant. He writes:

> Juridical punishment . . . can be inflicted on a criminal, never *just* as instrumental to the achievement of some other good for the criminal himself or for the civil society, but *only* because he has committed a crime; for a man may never be used just as a means to the ends of another person or mixed up with the objects of Real Right—against which his innate personality protects him, even if he is condemned to lose his civil personality. He must first be found culpable, before there is any thought of turning his punishment to advantage either for himself or society. Penal law is a *categorical* imperative, and woe to him who crawls through the serpentine maze of utilitarian theory in order to find an excuse, in some advantage to someone, for releasing the criminal from punishment or any degree of it, in line with the pharasaical proverb "It is better that one man die than that a whole people perish"; for if justice perishes, there is no more value in man living on the earth. . . . What mode and degree of punishment, then, is the principle and standard of public justice? Nothing but the *principle of equality*. . . . Thus, whatever undeserved evil you inflict on another person, you inflict on yourself. If you insult another, you insult yourself; if you steal from another, you steal from yourself; if you strike another, you strike yourself; if you kill another, you kill yourself. Only the rule of retribution (*lex talionis*)—only, of course, before the bar of justice, not in your own private judgment—can determine the quality and quantity of punishment. . . . Now it appears that differences of rank and class do not permit the exact retribution of like with like; but even if retribution is not possible according to the exact letter, it is still always valid in respect of effect, taking into account the feelings of the superior party. . . . So, for example, a fine for slander has little proportion to the insult, since any one who is well off can then permit himself the luxury of such behavior at his own pleasure; yet the violation of the honor of one person can be the equivalent of damage to the pride of another party, if the court condemns the offender not only to retract and apologize, but to submit to some meaner ordeal such as kissing the hand of the injured person. . . . [But] if a person has committed murder, he must die. There is no likeness or proportion between life, however painful, and death; and therefore there is no equality between the crime of murder and the retaliation of it but what is judicially accomplished by the execution of the criminal. . . . Even if a civil society decided, with the agreement of all, to dissolve (for instance, if an island society decided to break up and scatter into all parts of the world), the last murderer in the prison must first be brought to justice, in order that everyone be meted out desert for his deeds, and in order that the guilt of blood may not taint people who have failed to carry through the punishment—because such a people would have to be regarded as parties to a public violation of justice. . . . The equalization of punishment with offense is possible only through the rule of retribution . . . as is manifest from the fact that only then is sentence pronounced proportionate to internal wickedness. . . .[12]

The essence of Kant's point is that the utilitarian theory of punishment makes the false claim that man or society has the right to use another man

[12] *Gesammelte Werke* (Cassirer edition, Berlin, 1922), VII, 138–40; see translation by W. Hastie of I. Kant, *The Philosophy of Law* (Edinburgh: T. and T. Clark, 1887), pp. 194 ff.

as a means to the welfare of others, as if he were a physical thing. (The reverse of this is the equally false claim, he thinks, that a man need not be punished if that suits the needs of society, irrespective of the quality of his wrongdoing.) A man may be punished *only* if he has done something wrong (and hence it is immoral to punish an innocent man); and if he has done something wrong he *must* be punished. Kant does not hold merely that there is a prima facie obligation on society to punish one who has infringed the rights of others; it is an absolute over-all obligation—punishment must absolutely be meted out or society itself is guilty of wrong. Moreover, a person should be punished to the extent of his injury of his victim. Kant suggests in the last sentence that this amount of punishment corresponds with the moral turpitude of the criminal in that offense (presumably because, at least in the ordinary case, a man may be supposed to have intended to do what he does, so that what he does reflects the state of his character.)[13]

More recent writers have stated much the same theory in a somewhat sharper form. Mr. C. W. K. Mundle, for instance, has stated it as follows:

> The theory to be discussed involves three elements, two ethical claims and a verbal recommendation:
> *Claim* 1, that the fact that a person has committed a moral offense provides a sufficient reason for his being made to suffer;
> *Claim* 2 (or "the principle of proportion"), that if (or when) people are made to suffer for their offences, the suffering imposed ought to be proportionate to the moral gravity of their offences;
> and *the verbal recommendation* that "punishment" should be applied only to cases in which a person is made to suffer because (for the reason that) he deserves it on account of a moral offence.[14]

The traditional retributive principle is perhaps best stated today in a way suggested by Ross' formalist system, somewhat as follows: "It is prima facie obligatory for society to cause pain or loss to every person who commits a morally objectionable act to an extent corresponding with the

---

[13] A survey of historical opinions on the *lex talionis* is to be found in S. Pufendorf, *De Jure Naturae et Gentium* (Oxford: Clarendon Press, 1934), Bk. 8, chap. 3, pp. 1214 ff.

[14] "Punishment and Desert," *Philosophical Quarterly*, IV (1954), 216–28. Mundle himself, however, thinks it possible to justify punishment satisfactorily on utilitarian lines (p. 228).

A similar theory is advocated by Professor Jerome Hall (*op. cit.*), under the name of "the just theory" of punishment. He writes (p. 132): "A major postulate of the theory of just punishment is that punishment should be rationally related to moral culpability. In the greatest part of the criminal law, the gravity of the harm committed is a valid measure of moral culpability inasmuch as the harm intended is substantially the same as the harm committed."

We should notice that this theory is a theory explaining why laws threatening punishment for offenses should be passed and enforced, not merely a theory why the state should carry out its threat to punish once the law has been adopted.

moral gravity of his offense."[15] We can assume that other considerations, such as the obligation to avoid general insecurity, will require that punishment be imposed only for infractions of properly publicized laws, by specially authorized persons, and after a trial according to procedures selected in order to guarantee a fair application of the law.

The foregoing principle remains ambiguous, however, until we decide how to interpret the terms "morally objectionable" and "moral gravity of his offense." Two possible interpretations are more convincing than any others. (1) The terms may be taken to refer to moral reprehensibility in the sense of the preceding chapter, to an act's showing defect of character, and unfavorable attitudes toward the agent being justified on account of it. (2) Or they may be taken to refer to deliberate failure to conform conduct to *subjective* obligation—"moral gravity" being construed as the degree of subjective obligation, everything considered, not to do what the agent did. Let us call (1) the "moral reprehensibility" version, and (2) the *lex talionis* version. Kant's theory is closer to the *lex talionis* version, but is different from it, since the degree of subjective obligation not to perform an act is not necessarily a matter simply of the amount of harm done to other person. The two versions are not so very different, but they do have different implications.[16]

Whichever way we take it, the principle as stated differs in two further respects from the principle apparently supported by Kant. First, it only asserts that there is a prima facie obligation to punish, whereas Kant supposed there is an absolute obligation. As such, the principle does not tell us that we ought ever really to punish, in the total circumstances. In a developed formalist theory, there would be rules giving more information on this point. Second, the principle as stated agrees with Kant in proposing that the more serious offense should be punished *more* severely, but it does not tell us *how* severely any action should be punished.

The content of such a retributive principle—whichever interpretation we adopt—could be incorporated within the framework of an "extended" rule-utilitarianism, by making a further "extension." That is, one could assert that it is *intrinsically desirable* that people be punished for their morally objectionable deeds, to a degree proportionate to the gravity of the deed. Punishment, then, would be an impersonal intrinsic good, along with

[15] In order to avoid saying that society as such has a "moral obligation," this statement must be understood as a statement about the obligations of the individuals constituting society, of the type suggested for the parallel formulation of the prima facie obligation corresponding to a prima facie right (p. 438).

[16] A *"lex talionis"* theory might be so defined that no distinction ought to be made between manslaughter and murder, since the damage to another person is the same in either case. This is perhaps Kant's view. What a person guilty of manslaughter does deliberately, however, is simply *risk* another person's life. The *lex talionis* principle as stated allows for this, since the subjective obligation not to take a risk of this sort is presumably less than the obligation not to do what will certainly cause death.

equality of welfare. A theory approximately of this sort, but within the framework of act-utilitarianism (strictly, universal impersonal pluralism), was asserted by G. E. Moore, who wrote :

> It is in this way that the theory of vindictive punishment may be vindicated. The infliction of pain on a person whose state of mind is bad may, if the pain be not too intense, create a state of things that is better *on the whole* than if the evil state of mind had existed unpunished.[17]

Should we accept the retributive principle as a basic "axiom" about moral obligation (or else the assertion that it is intrinsically better for offenders to be punished than to go unpunished)? Various considerations suggest that we should answer this question *negatively*.

(1) Our ethical theory is *simpler* without this principle, and therefore it should be rejected unless it enables us to deduce, as theorems (when we combine it with true factual premises), ethical principles which are valid, and which cannot be deduced without it. But since our discussion of the rule-utilitarian theory of punishment has not disclosed any major objection to that theory—any concrete judgments coherent with our "qualified" attitudes which are inconsistent with the rule-utilitarian theory, or which do not follow from this theory (with the "extension" involving the intrinsic worth of equality of welfare)—there is no reason to complicate our theory by adding a retributive principle.

(2) We shall see that some people today question the whole practice of assigning "penalties to fit the crime." They think treatment of the criminal should be criminal-centered, not crime-centered. If their point is well-taken, the retributive principle is not true.

(3) The retributive principle, in whichever form we take it, asserts in effect that a principal aim of the law is to punish either moral guilt or intentional deviation from subjective obligation. But if so, then it ought to punish merely *attempted* crimes as severely as successful crimes. Moral reprehensibility, as we have seen, is equal in the two cases; and since an attempt is a case of setting oneself to commit a crime, it is as much a deliberate deviation from subjective obligation as the successful commission of a crime. Assuming that this implication is incorrect, clearly the retributive principle alone will not do as a principle guiding legislative practice.

(4) The "moral reprehensibility" form of the theory is open to serious objection. According to it, laws should be so framed that no one will be punished, no matter what he does, if he is morally blameless. This is objectionable. It is of great importance that the law be able to set up standards of conduct, and require all to conform, whether or not they are convinced of the desirability of the standards. The law must be in a position to demand certain conduct from individuals, say in the Defense Department, whose conscientious deliberations might lead them to betray secrets essential to

[17] *Principia Ethica* (Cambridge, Eng.: Cambridge University Press, 1904), p. 214.

the national defense. Again, the law must be in a position to ban some practice like polygamy, irrespective of the value judgments of any persons. Therefore we must again say that the retributive principle cannot be the only principle guiding the framing of law and judicial practice.

(5) The *lex talionis* version of the theory has its special difficulties. For instance, it is inconsistent with recognition of a difference between first degree murder, second degree murder, and manslaughter on account of provocation, since the degree of subjective obligation is equal in all these cases. Furthermore, the theory is inconsistent with holding that various circumstances are good reasons for imposing a relatively mild penalty, which in practice are regarded as good reasons and which we must agree morally are valid reasons. Thus we must conclude, again, that the retributive principle cannot be the only principle behind justified legal procedures, and one must question ever more forcibly what good reason there can be for saying that a retributive principle must be included in any satisfactory ethical theory.

We shall explore some further difficulties of the theory when we examine the implications of the view that all human behavior is causally determined, in the following chapter.

4. A SECOND FORMALIST THEORY

An interesting nonutilitarian alternative to the traditional retributive theory has been proposed by W. D. Ross. The essential idea of his theory is stated thus:

> Rights of any human being are correlative to duties incumbent on the owner of rights, or, to put it otherwise, to rights owned by those against whom he has rights; and the main element in any one's right to life or liberty or property is extinguished by his failure to respect the corresponding rights in others. There is thus a distinction in kind which we all in fact recognize, but which utilitarianism cannot admit, between the punishment of a person who has invaded the rights of others and the infliction of pain or restraint on one who has not. The state ought, in its effort to maintain the rights of innocent persons, to take what steps are necessary to prevent violations of these rights; and the offender, by violating the life or liberty or property of another, has lost his own right to have his life, liberty, or property respected, so that the state has no *prima facie* duty to spare him, as it has a *prima facie* duty to spare the innocent. It is morally at liberty to injure him as he has injured others . . . exactly as consideration both of the good of the community and of his own good requires.[18]

Ross' view differs from the retributive principle, as stated, in several ways. (What he says is not quite consistent; that side of his view is here emphasized which permits his theory to be classified as an interesting and novel one.) First, the commission of a moral offense does not establish a

[18] *The Right and the Good* (Oxford: Clarendon Press, 1930), pp. 60–61.

prima facie obligation to punish to a degree corresponding with the gravity of the offense, but a *permission* to punish up to a limit corresponding with the gravity of the offense. Second, the extent to which society should avail itself of its right to punish is determined solely by considerations of promoting the public good, of protecting rights. Third, the state's right to punish the malefactor arises from the fact that the malefactor's rights *not* to be injured in respect of life, liberty, or property go only as far as he respects the rights of others. The culprit, Ross says, "has lost his *prima facie* rights of life, liberty, or property, only in so far as these rested on an explicit or implicit undertaking to respect the corresponding rights in others, and in so far as he has failed to respect those rights."[19]

Ross himself appears to think (like Kant) of the "moral gravity" of an offense as fixed by the actual injury done someone. His theory is made more plausible, however, if we think of it as construing "moral gravity" either in the moral reprehensibility, or in the *lex talionis* sense, as these have already been defined.

Ross' theory is closer to utilitarianism than is the retributive theory, on account of its second point: the proposal that considerations of public welfare are the sole determinant of how far society should avail itself (by passing laws to that effect) of its right to punish malefactors. But it is not a utilitarian theory because the right to punish is not established by appeal to utility.

Is this "permissive" type of retributive theory subject to the same objections as the standard retributive theory described above? First, if there are no objections to a straight form of extended rule-utilitarianism, we still do not *need* the theory; it is a cumbersome complication. Second, if we interpret it in the "moral reprehensibility" form, the fourth objection to the standard theory is a decisive objection to it. Where there is no moral blame, this theory implies (in this form) that there is no right to punish. Third, Ross' theory is at least *less* open to the second and third objections we raised to the traditional theory, since on his view the moral gravity of an offense only determines a right to punish. Everything considered, Ross' theory, especially in the *lex talionis* form, seems slightly superior to the traditional retributive theory as we have stated it (and much superior to Kant's formulation); but there is no reason for adopting it in preference to the simpler rule-utilitarian theory (with the "extension" already argued for).

There are still other theories about why punishment by the state is

---

[19] *Ibid.*, p. 62.

Ross also thinks it is intrinsically desirable for happiness to be distributed in accord with moral goodness, and that we have an obligation to produce this good like other goods; but he thinks that punishment of crimes by the state is not a likely way to achieve it. It is impracticable and outside the legitimate business of the state for it to concern itself with achieving this good. Moral goodness, Ross thinks, is in any case a function of character as a whole, and not of particular actions.

justified. Perhaps the most important of these is the proposal that criminals have in some sense *consented* to the operation of a system of criminal justice, and therefore have consented to the application of this system to them. This theory is dubious on several counts. First, it may be questioned whether they have consented, explicitly or in any other manner. Second, even if they have, it does not follow that what is done to them is right. People often consent to things, for example, contracts, when the arrangement consented to is unfair to them. The theory might be amended to say, not that they *have* consented, but that they *would* consent if they were rational and knew what they really wanted. But in this form the theory is open to a third objection, for it may be asked: *Why* must they consent if they are rational? Because the system is right and fair? If the system's being right and fair is to be the reason for their rational assent, then it seems that in order to show that they will consent if they are rational, we must first show that the system is right and fair. We cannot first prove that the system is right and fair by showing that they will assent if they are rational. If so, then the main question whether the system *is* right and fair is still to be answered. Alternatively, it may be replied that the reason why they must consent is that a criminal must see that his *own self-interest* is best served by a system of law and order, that he would not wish to live outside such a system. Hence, if he is reasonable, he must consent to his own punishment as implied by the system of law and order which is a fundamental precondition of his own personal welfare. But is it convincing to argue that a criminal must recognize that his own personal welfare is best served by a particular system of law and order which requires that he himself be destroyed? This is highly dubious.[20]

5. UTILITARIANISM AND REFORM

Some thinkers today believe that criminal justice in Great Britain and the United States is in need of substantial revision. If we agree with their proposals, we have even less reason for favoring the retributive principle; but we must also question the traditional utilitarian emphasis on deterrence as the primary function of the institution of criminal justice.

Their proposal, roughly, is that we should extend, to all criminal justice, the practices of juvenile courts and institutions for the reform of juvenile offenders. Here, retributive concepts have been largely discarded at least in theory, and psychiatric treatment and programs for the prevention of crime by means of slum clearance, the organization of boys' clubs, and so forth, have replaced even deterrence as guiding ideas for social action. The extension of these practices to criminal justice as a whole would

[20] See T. H. Green, *Lectures on Political Obligation* (London: Longmans, Green & Co., 1950), pp. 186–87; G. W. F. Hegel, *The Philosophy of Right* (Oxford: Clarendon Press, 1942), pp. 69–71; Bernard Bosanquet, *The Philosophical Theory of the State* (London: Macmillan & Co., Ltd., 1930); S. Pufendorf, *op. cit.*, II, p. 1168.

work somewhat as follows: First, the present court procedure would be used to determine whether an offense has actually been committed. Such procedure would necessarily include ordinary rules about the admission of evidence, trial by jury, and the exculpating justifications and excuses for offenses (such as wrong suppositions about the facts). Second, if an accused were adjudged guilty, decisions about his treatment would then be in the hands of the experts, who would determine what treatment was called for and when the individual was ready for return to normal social living. The trial court might, of course, set some maximum period during which such experts would have a right to control the treatment of the criminal. What the experts would do would be decided by the criminal's condition; it would be criminal-centered treatment, not crime-centered treatment.

One might object to this proposal that it overlooks the necessity of disagreeable penalties for crime, in order to deter prospective criminals effectively. But it is doubtful whether threats of punishment have as much deterrent value as is often supposed. Threats of punishment will have little effect on morons, or on persons to whom normal living offers few prospects of an interesting existence.[21] Moreover, persons from better economic or social circumstances will be deterred sufficiently by the prospect of conviction in a public trial and being at the disposal of a board for a period of years.

Such proposals have their difficulties. For instance, would the police be as safe as they are, if criminals knew that killing a policeman would be no more serious in its consequences than the crime for which the policeman was trying to arrest them? However, there is much factual evidence for answering such questions, since systems of criminal justice along such lines are already in operation in some parts of the world, in particular among the Scandinavian countries. In fact, in some states the actual practice is closer to the projected system than one might expect from books on legal theory.

Another objection that many would raise is that psychiatry and criminology have not yet advanced far enough for such weighty decisions about the treatment of criminals to be placed in their hands. The treatment of criminals might vary drastically depending on the particular theoretical predilections of a given theorist, or on his personal likes and dislikes. One can probably say as much, or more, however, about the differences between judges, in their policies for picking a particular sentence within the range permitted by law.

---

[21] It is said that picking pockets was once a capital offense in England, and hangings were public, in order to get the maximum deterrent effect. But hangings in public had to be abolished, because such crimes as picking pockets were so frequent during the spectacle! See N. F. Cantor, *Crime, Criminals, and Criminal Justice* (New York: Henry Holt & Company, Inc., 1932).

An institution of criminal justice operating on such basic principles would come closer to our views about how parents should treat their children, or teachers their students, than the more traditional practices of criminal justice today.

We should repeat that this view about the ideal form for an institution of criminal justice is not in conflict with utilitarianism; in fact it is utilitarian in outlook. The motivation behind advocating it is the thought that such a system would do more good. It differs from the kind of institution traditionally advocated by utilitarians like Bentham only in making different factual assumptions, primarily about the deterrence value of threat of imprisonment, and the actual effect of imprisonment on the attitudes of the criminal.

FURTHER READING

J. Bentham, *The Principles of Morals and Legislation*, chaps. 12–15.

H. Rashdall, *Theory of Good and Evil* (Oxford: Clarendon Press, 1924), vol. I, chap. 9. Another utilitarian view.

G. E. Moore, *Principia Ethica* (Cambridge, Eng.: Cambridge University Press, 1929), pp. 214–21.

J. Rawls, "Two Concepts of Rules," *Philosophical Review*, LXIV (1935), 3–32.

F. C. Sharp, *Good Will and Ill Will* (Chicago: University of Chicago Press, 1950), pp. 216–25. Summary of an empirical study of opinions about punishment.

E. F. Carritt, *Ethical and Political Thinking* (Oxford: Clarendon Press, 1947), pp. 70–76, 99–101.

———, *Theory of Morals* (Oxford: Oxford University Press, 1928), chap. 12. A view very similar to that of W. D. Ross.

W. D. Ross, "The Ethics of Punishment," *Philosophy*, IV (1925), 205–11.

———, *The Right and the Good* (Oxford: Clarendon Press, 1930), pp. 56–64.

D. D. Raphael, *Moral Judgment* (London: George Allen & Unwin, Ltd., 1955), pp. 67–77. Rather similar to W. D. Ross.

A. C. Ewing, *The Morality of Punishment* (London: Kegan Paul, Trench, Trubner & Co., Ltd., 1929), chaps. 1–5.

———, "Punishment as a Moral Agency," *Mind*, XXXVI (1942–43), 292–305.

Jerome Hall, *General Principles of Criminal Law* (Indianapolis: Bobbs-Merrill Co., Inc., 1947). An excellent treatise by a professor of law.

W. G. Maclagan, "Punishment and Retribution," *Philosophy*, XIV (1939).

J. D. Mabbott, "Punishment," *Mind*, XLVIII (1939), 152–67.

———, "Freewill and Punishment," in H. D. Lewis (ed.), *Contemporary British Philosophy* (London: George Allen & Unwin, Ltd., 1956).

C. W. K. Mundle, "Punishment and Desert," *Philosophical Quarterly*, IV (1954), 216–28.

A. M. Quinton, "On Punishment," *Analysis*, XIV (1954), 133–42. Linguistic suggestions.

K. Baier, "Is Punishment Retributive?" *Analysis*, XVI (1955), 25–32.

L. Hall and S. Glueck, *Cases on Criminal Law and its Enforcement* (St. Paul: West Publishing Co., 1958).

J. Michael and H. Wechsler, *Criminal Law and its Administration* (Brooklyn: Foundation Press, 1940).

20

Ethics and Determinism

Since early times moral philosophers have been puzzled by the implications of the thesis—the theory of "determinism"—roughly, that all events in the world occur in accordance with an orderly pattern of natural laws. This thesis carries the implication that human conduct and character development are as much lawful events as is the motion of a projectile.[1] Many philosophers have supposed that quite radical conclusions for ethics are required by this implication: that people do not have any moral obligations, that human actions are never either morally reprehensible or admirable, that punishment (except for utilitarian reasons) is never justified, that a good character has no intrinsic worth, and that feelings like remorse and indignation are always inappropriate. Philosophers who think that such serious consequences are demanded by the theory are divided in their inferences: some, believing that the thesis of determinism is true, accept these conclusions in their ethical theory; others, holding that we *know* these conclusions to be mistaken, infer that determinism must be false, and try to formulate a plausible form of determinism. There are thus two separate questions raised by the thesis of determinism. First, *if* determinism about human conduct is true, what kind of normative ethics is called for? Second, *is* determinism a true theory about human conduct? We may include in this second question, as being properly a part of it, the question of whether there is any formulable alternative that does not have equally radical implications for normative ethics.

1. DETERMINISM AND ITS GROUNDS

Let us begin by trying to understand clearly what the central thesis of determinism is, and what are the reasons for believing it.

[1] Notice, however, that we could be determinists about human conduct (think it follows natural laws) *without* accepting the thesis of determinism in its general form. It is determinism about human conduct that is important for ethics, and the moralist need not concern himself with the question whether other events or natural processes follow natural law, except to the extent that evidence about whether they do is some reason for accepting determinism as a thesis about human conduct.

It is difficult to give a precise definition of "determinism," but we shall say that determinism is the view that *any event could be predicted if all the laws of nature were known, and enough were known about previous states of nature to permit use of the laws for prediction.* This definition does not commit a determinist to asserting that we know exactly what information about a state of affairs is needed for prediction.[2]

It may rightly be objected to this definition that we cannot explain exactly what we mean by a "natural law." Nevertheless, it is rather foolish to think there is no problem of determinism because of difficulties in stating precisely what we mean by a "natural law." We know well enough what we mean, to understand that we want to classify the general statements of physics as natural laws but not "All the coins that are in my pocket now are pennies." There are many things we can say about what a natural law must be, that distinguish natural laws from other universal statements, even true ones, that are not natural laws. And if so, this definition of "determinism" is reasonably clear, even if at present we cannot give a complete account of its concepts in terms that will satisfy everybody.

A determinist can illustrate his view about human conduct by an example. Suppose we are going to fire a projectile and wish to predict where it will strike. How shall we proceed? Well, there is a well-established mathematical equation that relates certain variable factors about the motion of projectiles. If we fill in values for some of the variables in this equation, we fix the values of the ones in which we are interested—in this case the instant and place at which the projectile will strike the earth's surface. Thus, if we know the position, the angle of elevation, and the direction of the gun at the instant of discharge, the muzzle velocity, and the force of gravity acting on the projectile after discharge, we can predict where it will strike. The more accurate our information about these things, the more accurately we can predict; by making our information more accurate, we can make our prediction as accurate as we please. (Of course, in real life we also have to allow for air density, wind velocity, the shape of the shell, and other factors.)

The thesis of determinism, as applied to human conduct, is that, in principle, prediction is possible, just as it is in the case of the projectile. In order to make the prediction, we need to know the laws of human behavior. We also need certain information about prior states of affairs—perhaps a vast amount of it. Moreover, the laws of psychology may not be quantitative like physical laws; they may rather be like a telephone book—given the

---

[2] We do not need to know *everything* about some state of nature, in order to apply a law for prediction. For instance, if we want to use the laws of physics in order to predict where a naval shell will strike, we need to know its muzzle velocity, its weight, the angle of elevation, the density of the atmosphere, and other properties, but not the color or content of the shell, the identity of the person who supervises firing it, and so on. We also need to know that there will not be interference from other causal chains; for instance, we need to know it will not collide with a meteor in midair.

information we look in the book and find out what the behavior will be—and not as simple and comprehensive as a different equation. Still, the determinist thinks there are laws. He thinks, further, that in principle we could make our predictions as accurate as we please, if we knew the laws, by getting our information about prior states of affairs correspondingly precise.

If a person is a determinist about human facts and behavior in this sense, he is committed to saying that whatever a person does—indeed whatever *change* of any sort occurs in him at any time—is predictable, provided we know the relevant laws and are given information about the kind of person he is (what he knows and expects, his ideals, motives, habits, and so forth), and about the kind of environment in which he is behaving. Moreover, the kind of person he is now could itself have been predicted from information about the kind of person he was at a still earlier moment, and about the environment in which he was behaving; and so on back. Thus, a determinist about human conduct thinks that, theoretically, if we started with a living being at the moment of its conception in the womb, and knew its properties, and if we knew every situation within which it behaves through its life history, and knew all the laws of nature, we should in principle be able to predict what kind of person this individual would be at every stage, and what he would do and think at every moment.

Henceforth we shall assume that this is what determinism comes to. Why should we (or should we?) believe that it is true, either as a general theory, or just as a thesis about human conduct? Various philosophers have supposed its truth is simply self-evident. In 1907, a very careful moral philosopher, Hastings Rashdall, wrote: .

> Pure chance is as irrational and unthinkable an idea as Fate. . . . Without entering in detail into the idea of Causality, we may say that all accounts of that category agree in this—that everything *which has a beginning* must be accounted for and explained as the necessary outcome of something already in existence before that beginning. . . . In that sense the law of Universal Causality—quite a different thing from the mechanical uniformity of Nature—does present itself to my mind as an absolute necessity of thought.[3]

Many other writers, for example, W. D. Ross and C. D. Broad, in substance agree with this.

Most philosophers today, however, hesitate to make statements about nature when there is no better evidence than that something seems "self-evident." Determinists today, therefore, support their view by an appeal to the history of science. They point to the steady growth of our knowledge of natural laws, and the gradual dwindling of areas in which phenomena are not known to be lawful. They conclude that it is a reasonable extrapolation from the history of science to suppose that all events are lawful. They

[3] *The Theory of Good and Evil* (2nd ed.; Oxford: Oxford University Press, 1924), vol. II, p. 337.

would concede that relatively few laws have as yet been discovered in psychology, but think that in view of the complexity of the human mind this fact is no reason for supposing psychological processes are not lawful processes. Such reasoning is not implausible.

In recent years, however, a difficulty for such extrapolations from the history of science has arisen. Physicists have apparently found a theoretical limit to the predictability of individual events in nature. According to the Heisenberg principle, the behavior of individual particles can be predicted only with a limited degree of accuracy—one that no refinements of observations can improve. There are differences of opinion among physicists about the interpretation of this fact. Some say that the Heisenberg principle is only a reflection of the fact that we must make observations with physical instruments that necessarily interact with and alter the process being observed, to a degree that cannot be known exactly. They think it reasonable to suppose that all processes in nature are orderly and describable in terms of simple principles—that there are laws in nature that apply to the behavior of individual particles, although we do not and cannot know what they are. If there were a being who knew these laws and who could know, without the use of instruments, the position and velocity (and other properties) of particles, he could predict accurately the behavior of small particles on the basis of these laws. *We* cannot, in principle; still, determinism is true, because it could be done by a being who had the relevant information. Other physicists believe that it is sheer speculation to suggest that there are laws governing the behavior of individual particles, although we are in theory incompetent to ascertain these laws. They say that we have a right to assert only what we can confirm empirically. What we can confirm is statistical laws, not laws that permit accurate prediction of the behavior of individual particles. We know, further, that in principle better laws are impossible for us. So, they say, it is unjustified, and a misrepresentation of the results of science, to say that the behavior of small particles is determined. What we are justified in saying is that the behavior of these particles is random to some extent. Whatever the proper solution of this controversy, we must agree that any easy inference to determinism in general, as an extrapolation of the history of science, would be questioned today by many scientists.

One may wonder if these discoveries in physics do not rule out determinism for human conduct, if they rule out—as the latter group of physicists maintains—claims that individual micro-events follow causal laws. In support of this, it may be said that possibly single-particle events sometimes play a key role in a brain process, acting as catalysts for larger processes—particularly since there is reason to believe that the dark-adapted eye is sensitive to light radiation of the order of a single quantum. Thus, if single-particle physical events are unpredictable, and if it is objectionable to say that they follow natural laws, and if they are crucial for brain processes (for example, whether a certain fact occurs to me at a given time might make a big difference to a process of thought), then must we not say that we are on sound ground if we say that mental processes are unpredictable, that they do not follow natural laws? Such inferences may be questioned, for it is not inconsistent with the evidence to suppose that the brain events connected at least with *decisions* are always quite large-scale, involving great numbers of particles. If so, then we are no more debarred, by the facts of quantum mechanics, from thinking that decisions and other mental processes are predictable and lawful, than we are from believing, in view of quantum mechanics, that a pan of water will boil if put over a hot flame. The behavior of the individual particles in a pan of water is unpredictable in theory; but it is not unpredictable that the water will boil. Similarly, the behavior of the particles in the brain is unpredictable in theory —according to these physicists—but this does not preclude the possibility that decisions are in theory predictable. Unpredictability of the micro-events does not imply unpredictability of molar events.

One might say that any inferences to determinism from the general course of the history of science are very tenuous. But such inferences are not the only reason for believing that the *conduct of human beings* is lawful or predictable. There is a vast mass of knowledge about bodily processes and their laws. On the psychological level, much less behavior is as yet understood or predictable, but the literature of experimental psychology is already vast, and the summarizing handbooks are very thick and becoming thicker. In the field of perception in particular, there are many generalizations that can be given the status of laws. In other areas, for example, those of social psychology and the theory of personality, much less is well established, but only an audacious man would affirm that no laws will ever be discovered in these areas.

Evidently there is much in modern science, then, to support the determinist's view of human conduct; but the determinist's view is only an extrapolation from the past successes of science, and it *may* be wrong. Moreover, one cannot deny that quantum mechanics weakens the determinist's case.

Some critics of determinism have taken the offensive, asserting that we can know by simple introspection that we can take either one of two courses of action between which we are deliberating. They say that therefore we know that determinism, with its claim that one's decision is in principle predictable, must be mistaken. But something is wrong with any such argument. Surely no simple inspection of any event can tell us whether it could have been predicted, whether its occurrence is an instance of some causal law. To say that an event was not determined is to say that it was not preceded by some other event, such that every event just like that preceding event is followed by an event just like the one we say is not determined. And the mere inspection of an event cannot tell us this about it; whether an event is a member of a pattern of events, one of which can be predicted when we know about the others, is not an observable aspect of it.

Should we say, then, that there is a stalemate as far as the scientific evidence for determinism is concerned? Perhaps we could say this, although the writer must confess to a strong leaning toward the thesis of determinism, for human conduct. But even if one thinks there is a stalemate, there is good reason for exploring the question of whether the thesis of determinism has important implications—especially shattering implications—for ethics. The reason for this is that the clear alternative to determinism—indeterminism—definitely does have important and shattering implications for ethics, certainly if determinism does. So, we had better explore carefully whether determinism really has the important implications many philosophers have thought it has.

Why do we say that indeterminism has implications for ethics as shattering as those of determinism (if these really are shattering), indeed worse? Let us look at this.

First, it is convenient to speak of a particular event or action as being "determined" if it is an instance of a causal law, so that in theory anyone who knew all natural laws and knew enough about the preceding state of affairs to apply the relevant laws to them, could have predicted this action or event.

Now, philosophers who have been eager to deny determinism have done so because they thought (whether with good reason, we shall decide shortly) that a person is not open to moral criticism or censure for his action, if he *could not* have done anything other than he did—in a sense of "could not" such that his action's being determined implies he *could not* have done anything other in this sense. Indeed, they have gone on to say that if all of a man's behavior and his character development are determined, so that in this sense he "cannot" do anything but what he does (his actions and character were predictable before he was born), it is foolish to say that he is obligated to do anything but what he does.

But are matters mended if one is an indeterminist? At first it seems so, for the determinist can say, "His actions are not determined, and therefore he could have done his duty." But in what sense "could" he, if indeterminism is true? Only in the sense that in the circumstances he *might* have done his duty and he might not; it is impossible that anyone could have predicted which he would do; it is a matter of chance that he did what he did. But does this tell us that a man "could" do his duty in the sense required for moral criticism? Is it fair to say that a person's act is reprehensible for the reason that, at a key instant, a *chance* particle-event in his brain took place, that could as well not have taken place, and which was in principle unpredictable? Well, *if* it is improper to condemn a person for behavior that is a product of his past, it seems no less improper to condemn him for behavior that is a product of his past plus *chance!* Indeterminism, in the sense of a theory insisting that human behavior is unpredictable, unlawful, and random to a certain extent, does not make clear how it is justifiable to condemn people for their behavior—if we assume this is unjustifiable if their behavior is determined.

There is a further reason why indeterminism has serious consequences for ethics. At an earlier stage (p. 460) we suggested that part of what it means to say an act is reprehensible is that "it would not have occurred had not the character of the agent been in some respect less desirable than average." But, if we accept indeterminism, can we ever say that acts have this relation to character? The indeterminist says we cannot draw inferences, from the present character (traits of character) of the agent, to what he will do in the situation; there is not a lawful connection between what he is as a person before he acts, and how he acts. But, if so, then conversely we cannot draw inferences from a person's act to defects of his character. Then we cannot say that the act would not have occurred had his character not been defective. Hence, we cannot say his act was reprehensible! Indeterminism appears to be fatal to the rationality of moral assessments.

These difficulties in the indeterminist's position have been widely recognized, and as a result some philosophers have speculated about the possibility of a middle ground, something that is neither determinism nor indeterminism.[4] A. C. Ewing, for instance, has recently suggested that we should agree with the determinist that "all our actions and states of mind follow from our character, plus our environment," but hold that "our character itself is not completely determined by what went before." He goes on:

> A man could then be blamed because his acts displayed a bad character, and he could not excuse himself by saying that the character was due to somebody else. . . . We can look on a man's character as a set of laws determining his actions. On the ordinary determinist view these laws would be deducible from more general psychological and physical laws as applied to the particular circumstances determining the origin and development of the individual man in question; on the view suggested they would not be thus deducible but must be regarded as ultimate facts about the individual, a sort of causal law peculiar to himself. They would be affected but not completely determined by what went before, so that each individual would be a genuine new beginning. . . . New laws not completely derivable from others would come into force with the birth of every new human being. . . . However the laws would merely have being in a hypothetical sense till actually realized, so we had better think of them as not all created at birth, but as continually coming into being when occasions arise to which they have application. . . . In the case of a converted sinner the laws which determine his behaviour after his conversion would to a large extent have

---

[4] See, for instance, A. C. Ewing, "Indeterminism," *Review of Metaphysics*, V (1951), 199–222; and C. D. Broad, *Determinism, Indeterminism, and Libertarianism*, reprinted in his *Ethics and the History of Philosophy* (London: Routledge & Kegan Paul, Ltd., 1952), pp. 195–217.

no application at all to his earlier life, although they would have some connection with those that did. We could thus think not only of a man's birth, but of other parts in his life as real beginnings. . . . The laws could never be known in advance of the acts to which they applied, because they are not deducible from any other laws, and therefore the prediction could never be effected at all.

Ewing concedes a critic might object that his view is not very different from determinism, since "it does not leave it possible for us ever to have acted differently, our character and circumstances being what they are." One might therefore say, he suggests, that "no advantage is gained by supposing one's character to be undetermined, since this still leaves us dependent on a character which we did not ourselves make." Ewing replies to this that he is "inclined to think that the objection depends on making too sharp a separation between character and acts, as if the former were something apart from the acts which compelled them instead of a law exemplified only in the acts themselves." This particular proposal, although ingenious, is not very satisfying. It will not satisfy those impressed by the advances of psychology, because it asserts that there are not universally valid laws descriptive of human conduct. But neither is it apt to satisfy those who are repelled by determinism, because they think it has serious implications for ethics. According to Ewing's view, it is still true that a man's actions could not have been otherwise than they were—in any sense in which ordinary determinism implies this—given his character and environment, any more than for ordinary determinism.

Everything considered, our conclusion about determinism must be as follows: (1) The truth of its thesis is far from demonstrated, but the advances of empirical knowledge, especially in psychology, give it support; and (2) the known alternatives are no better than determinism, and indeed worse, as far as ethics is concerned. In the circumstances, one reasonable thing to do is examine carefully whether, after all, determinism really is incompatible with conclusions we have already reached about ethics. Perhaps some moral philosophers have been disturbed by determinism without good reason.

2. WHAT DETERMINISM IS NOT

Determinism is sometimes thought to be a much more revolutionary theory than it is, because it is thought to imply some propositions it does not imply at all. If we are to assess its implications for ethics carefully, we must distinguish it from some different but related theses.

1. It is sometimes thought that determinism implies that some things are bound to happen no matter what anybody does—like Oedipus' slaying of his father, and his incestuous marriage with his mother. A student who thinks in this way may think that it is ordained either that he will pass his

final examination, or that he won't—so it will make no difference whether he studies the material or not. But determinism does not imply any such fatalistic view. It does not at all imply that reflection, planning, and human action make no difference to what happens. All it implies is that in principle one can predict how people will reflect, what they will plan and do. We can in theory predict certain events in nature because we can in theory predict the human events that will lead to them.

2. Determinism erases none of the ordinary distinctions between free and coerced action. It may be thought to do so, since the thesis that all behavior is "determined" by character and circumstances sounds rather like saying that character and circumstances "make" us do whatever we do; and this again sounds as if we are not "free" to do anything else, and are coerced. Again, when determinists say (a bit misleadingly) that natural laws determine our behavior, they may seem to be saying something very similar to what we are saying if we assert that civil laws "require" us to behave in certain ways; and this again suggests that all our actions are coerced or compelled.

It may not strike the reader as a natural mistake to pass from the thesis that behavior is determined to the thesis that it is compelled, or coerced. Very likely he is not tempted to draw such inferences. It has been supposed, however, that the thinking of some philosophers has moved precisely in this way; in fact it has been asserted that the whole controversy about determinism has its source in the confusion of "determined" with "coerced" or "compelled."[5]

However this may be, it is clear that to say that all behavior is determined is not at all to say that it is unfree in the sense of coerced. To see that this is so, we need only examine what we mean when we say someone did something freely, without coercion. If, for instance, a man's wife reminds him that he married her "of his own free will," what is she saying? She is denying that he was hypnotized, that anybody guided his hand when he signed the marriage documents, that anyone held a shotgun at his back or held dire threats of any kind over him when he said "Yes." He was not physically forced, nor was he coerced by threats. On the contrary, she is saying that, after full consideration of the alternatives, he did what he thought he wanted most to do.

Determinism does not deny that people often make "free" choices in this sense. What determinism asserts is that free choices are determined—that they could have been predicted.

3. We have noticed that the determinist may say that nobody ever "can" do anything other than what he does. But we must be very careful to notice that the word "can" is here used (unless the determinist is saying what is

[5] See University of California Associates, *Knowledge and Society* (New York: Appleton-Century-Crofts, Inc., 1938), pp. 154–55; Moritz Schlick, *Problems of Ethics* (Englewood Cliffs, N.J.: Prentice-Hall, Inc., 1939), pp. 144–50.

false) in a sense utterly different from that in which it is used when we say "No human being *can* leap over the Empire State Building," or when a losing pitcher in a World's Series contest remarks, "I just *couldn't* get the ball over the plate," or when a student remarks, " I *can't* follow the elliptical reasoning of that physics textbook." What do these statements mean? Perhaps the first one means: "No matter how carefully anybody trained, and no matter how hard he tried, he would still not succeed if he tried to leap the Empire State Building." Perhaps the latter statements mean, "I did try as hard as I could, and I didn't succeed; and even if my life had depended on it, so that I was trying as hard as I possibly could try, I still shouldn't have done better." Let us suggest, then, that the *ordinary* meaning of "He couldn't have done [or, it was impossible for him to have done] anything, on a certain occasion, other than he did" is something like this: "Even if his desire to do something different had been at maximal strength, and he had tried as hard as he possibly could, he would not, on that occasion, have succeeded in doing anything other than he did." We might say, when somebody couldn't have done something in this sense, that it was *physically* (or psychologically) *impossible* for him to do it.[6]

Whether it is physically possible, in this sense, for a man to do something is very important for whether he is morally obligated to do it. We don't believe a man is morally obligated to do anything that he could not have succeeded in doing no matter how hard he tried, no matter how strongly he was motivated. Nor do we say that a man is reprehensible for having failed to do something that he would not have succeeded in doing, no matter how strong his character. So, *if* it were true that it is impossible in this sense for a man ever to do anything but what in fact he does, we would have to say that he is not obligated to do anything other than in fact he does, nor reprehensible for having done what he did, no matter what it was.

But, of course, determinism does not at all imply that a person *cannot* do anything other than what he does in *this* sense of "can." To say of an act, as determinism says one must, that it is an instance of some causal law and in theory could have been predicted, is very far indeed from saying that it would not have been different if the agent had tried, as hard as he could, to do something else. If a pitcher loses an important ball game by throwing wildly, a determinist will say that his behavior was theoretically predicatable. But the determinist may well believe that he "could" have pitched more effectively if he had tried. To show that it was impossible, in the ordinary sense, for him to have pitched better, requires special investigation; evidence is needed that he did not fail merely because he did not try. Simi-

---

[6] This is not the only sense of "impossible for" or "couldn't have done." Take, for instance: "It is impossible for that car to go over 100 miles per hour." And also, "It is impossible for me to come tonight" may simply mean "My previous commitments are such that it is my moral duty not to come tonight." For an interesting discussion of many complications, see J. L. Austin, "Ifs and Cans," *Proceedings of the British Academy,* XLII (1956), 109–32.

larly, if we are determinists we need not excuse a person for a theft, since in the ordinary sense he could have helped it; whereas we shall excuse a kleptomaniac.[7] There is a sense of "couldn't have done otherwise" in which we can still wonder whether a person could have done otherwise, even if we believe his action was determined. The determinist thesis permits us to say that often, if only a person had been motivated more strongly and had tried harder to do something else, he would have succeeded in doing something other than in fact he did—and hence it permits us to say that often he *could* (in the ordinary sense) have done something other than he was causally determined to do.

The determinist's thesis, then, does not imply that it is physically or psychologically impossible for people to do anything other than what in fact they do.

4. The determinist may quite well agree with philosophers who say that the experience of doing what one conceives to be one's duty in the face of contrary personal preferences is a unique kind of experience, not exactly like the rather similar experiences of muscular effort or concentration. He need not hold it is unique; he may find it quite like the experience of foregoing a tempting dessert in order to follow a physician's orders about reducing the waistline (which one would hardly call a conflict between duty and inclination). But he *may* say it is unique. It can perfectly well be a lawful kind of experience even if it is unique in quality.

5. It has been supposed that the determinist is an epiphenomenalist, that is, one who says that mental events and decisions have no influence on behavior. This is a mistake. To say that all behavior is determined is not to say that it is wholly caused by physical antecedents; a determinist may consistently hold that a mental occurrence is often part of the cause of some behavior of our brains, or sometimes even the whole cause. In fact, a determinist can quite well be an idealist, holding that there are no concrete particular things at all in the world except experiences.

3. DETERMINISM AND MORAL OBLIGATION: DOES "OUGHT" IMPLY "CAN"?

We are now ready to examine the question of whether the thesis of determinism has disturbing implications for ethics. Let us begin with its implications as to when, or whether, we are morally obligated. Some philosophers have thought that, if determinism is true, we are never obligated to do anything which in fact we do not do.

Persons who think that determinism has such implications sometimes

---

[7] For a discussion of the difference between the ordinary senses of "can" and "impossible" and the sense in which the determinist says that people cannot do anything other than what they do, see F. Raab, "Free Will and the Ambiguity of 'Could,'" *Philosophical Review*, LXIV (1953), 60–77.

take, as a premise, an assumption about the meaning of "morally obligatory" that we have not yet discussed. This assumption is that "is morally
obligated to do *x*" *means* in part (or *entails*) "*can* do *x* in a sense that is
incompatible with not-*x* being determined." If this assumption is correct,
it is *logically impossible* for a person to be obligated to do what he does
not do, if his actions are determined.

This is a shattering doctrine if it is true. But is it?

It is clear that the assumption, as stated, is incorrect, for we do *say* that
people are "morally obligated" to keep *all their promises,* although we
know that *some* promises *cannot* be kept. So, unless we are contradicting
ourselves when we say that people ought to keep all their promises, we
must be using "morally ought," sometimes, in a sense that does not *entail*
"can." It might be replied, of course, that when we say this we are speaking elliptically, and that what we mean is, "People are morally obligated
to keep their promises *if they can.*" But this is not what we *say.* And in
any case, if we were right in claiming earlier (Chapter 14) that "morally
obligated" is used in two senses, one sense that of "prima facie obligated,"
then we must admit that "morally obligated" is sometimes used in such a
sense that it does not imply "can," in any simple sense. Clearly, in the prima
facie sense it is sensible to say, "I am obligated to go to the concert as I
promised, but I am also obligated to stay home and care for my sick wife;
and I can't do *both.*" Indeed, if our argument was sound at an earlier point
(p. 365), there is an over-all sense of "moral obligation" that does not imply "can"—that is, the subjective sense.

The most that can be claimed, then, is that there are *some* senses in which
"morally obligated" is used, such that to say a person is morally obligated
to do something, in one of those senses, is in part to say that he can do it.

But even if it is true that "X is morally obligated to do *y*" sometimes
means in part "It is physically and psychologically possible for X to do *y*,"[8]
we can by no means infer from this that it entails "It is possible for X to do *y*
in a sense that is incompatible with not-*y* being determined." To be physi-

---

[8] We have not included this in the definition of "morally obligated" in Chapter 14.
But we can still say that " 'ought' *implies* 'can' " when "ought" is used in certain senses.
What could we mean by this? Well, suppose all or almost all hearers say that somebody
ought (in certain senses) only when they believe he can; and suppose all or almost all
hearers will, on this account, take it that a speaker believes someone can if he says he
ought. Then there is an ordinary sense of "imply" in which we can say that, unless a
speaker explicitly repudiates the ordinary inferences when he uses "ought," he has
implied that someone can by saying that he ought.

There is still another sense in which we can say that "ought" implies "can," even if
we do not think that "ought" means "can," in part. Suppose we think it *true and well
established* that somebody ought to do something only if he can. In this case, we shall
feel free to infer, from the premise "he ought," that he also can. Then again we might
say that "ought" implies "can."

One might ask why we do not include "can" in the definition of "moral obligation"
in the objective sense. The reason is that to do so would bring complications, and there
is no advantage, or conclusive ground in linguistic practice, for doing so.

cally and psychologically possible is entirely different from being undetermined.

In fact, we have excellent reason to think that "X is morally obligated to do *y*" does *not* entail "It is not determined that X do not-*y*." Why? Because there are many people who believe determinism is true (and therefore believe that actions are always determined), who continue to make judgments about what a person's objective duty is, knowing full well either that the person did *not* do what they think it was his duty to do, or else believing he will not do it. I may perfectly well say, "The real obligation of people is to cooperate in seeing that no one is discriminated against for reasons of race or religion," knowing full well that many people will do no such thing. The fact that we continue to say such things is conclusive reason for declining to hold that "X is not determined to do not-*y*" is *part of the meaning of* "X is morally obligated to do *y*" (in the objective sense), for reasons explained in Chapter 7.

It is a mistake, then, to think that "X is morally obligated to do *y*" *means*, in part, "X can do *y* in a sense incompatible with not-*y* being determined."

A person might, however, agree to this, and still say that *in fact* a person is morally obligated to do something only if he can do it in a sense incompatible with asserting that his doing something else is determined. Is this a defensible view?

Well, we agree that it is not morally obligatory, in the objective sense, for a person to do what is not physically and psychologically possible for him to do. But we are not committed by this to accepting the foregoing proposal. How then can we assess the tenability of the suggestion? The answer is that we can do so in the very same way in which we decide whether any moral principle is true, for instance whether we are always obligated to keep our promises. It is a question whether the principle "A person is objectively morally obligated over all to do *A* only if it is not determined that he will do not-*A*" can be incorporated into a consistent set of principles that are coherent with our "qualified" attitudes (feelings of obligation, demands on others). In other words, we must decide it very largely by inquiring whether in fact, even if we believed in the truth of determinism and had any other knowledge it is possible to have, we would in our normal and impartial moments continue to feel obligated to do things that in fact later we do not do.

Would we, or would we not, continue to feel obligated and to make demands on others? To this question it seems plausible to answer: "Of course we would." If we know our own weaknesses, we often wonder whether, when the time comes to do a certain thing, we shall really have the moral strength to do it; but this reflection does not make us feel the less obligated to do it. Or, do we feel less like demanding that a bully cease beating a timid child because we reflect that his doing so is in principle predictable? Not at all. We can also add this supporting point: It is a good thing that people do feel so obligated and that they do continue to make demands on others, for the fact that they do feel this way is an important means by which society gets along as well as it does.

The following objection might be raised: "A person who had all relevant knowledge would *not* feel obligated to refrain from doing what he is in fact going to do. Suppose you are going to murder someone. Then, if you had all relevant knowledge, you would *know* you were going to do it. But if you knew you were going to do it, you would accept the fact, and not be disturbed by it or have a feeling of obligation to refrain from it. So, in general, if determinism is true, and people had all relevant knowledge, nobody would ever feel obligated to do anything he is not going to do."

One answer to this argument is that it is *impossible* for a person to know that *he* is going to do something. So the supposition of the foregoing argument is false: that "if you had all relevant knowledge, you would know you were going to do it." *Why* is such knowledge impossible? Because, if you "knew" you were going to do something, you could always use this "knowledge" to avoid doing it; and if so, you don't really "know" it after all. Suppose, for instance, I am a kleptomaniac and have a passion for removing stockings from the counters of Macy's. Suppose, further, I "know" that I am going to steal some stockings during a visit to Macy's on Thursday. Very well; then I can plan to go to Washington on Thursday. Or if I am to be in New York, I can take my watchful wife with me and I can inform her of my "knowledge" so that she will see to it that I never go near Macy's. Or I can go to my psychiatrist, and if necessary he can have me locked up on Thursday. There are all sorts of things I can do to prevent my taking stockings from Macy's on Thursday, if I "know" I am going to do this. (To say this is not to say it is impossible for *others* to know what I am going to do.) It is impossible for a person to know what *he* is going to do in the future.

If we are right in thinking that our feeling obligated and our making demands on others are not modified by the beliefs that people are going to do a certain thing, and that determinism is true, then we are *not* justified in saying that a person is morally obligated to do something, in the objective sense, only if he *can* do it in a sense incompatible with asserting that he is determined to do something else. If so, the sting is gone from determinism, as far as judgments about moral obligation are concerned, for it is baseless to say what some philosophers have said—that if determinism is true, we are never obligated to do anything which in fact we do not do.

4. DETERMINISM AND THE THEORY OF PUNISHMENT

The truth of determinism has also been thought to have grave implications for the theory of punishment. For instance, many people have thought it indefensible for God to punish the wicked by sending them to hell, if he created them in such a way that they would sin, and he knew they would sin before they were born.

It makes a vast difference to the tenability of such views whether or not a utilitarian theory of punishment is satisfactory. It is generally agreed that the utilitarian justification of punishment for wrongdoing is unaffected by the truth of determinism.[9] Why? We have seen that the utilitarian justifies punishment by its effects: primarily the deterrence of prospective criminals but also possible rehabilitating effects of punishment on the criminal, and so on. He argues that because the system of punishment has these effects, it secures a net gain in utility despite its cost both to the criminal and to the public. Now, the truth of determinism would not make the gain of crime reduction any less worth the cost. In fact, the utilitarian insists on the influence of prior events on conduct. His whole reason for punishment assumes that the prior prospect of being punished will motivate persons to refrain from crime. Moreover, he may (although he need not) justify punishment in part by appeal to its rehabilitating effects; and if he does, he is assuming that character can be molded by natural causes.

It has sometimes been argued that, far from utilitarianism and determinism being inconsistent, one must accept the thesis of determinism in order to use the utilitarian justification of punishment consistently. The reason given is that if the thesis of determinism is not true, the utilitarian has no ground for thinking that punishment will have the effects on conduct that he appeals to in order to justify the punishment. But this argument goes too far. Indeterminists do not deny that punishment will have substantial effects in the way of deterrence and rehabilitation; they claim only that there is a limit to the predictability of behavior, such that it is always causally possible, in cases of conflict between inclination and duty, for a person to decide to do what he thinks he ought to do. This the utilitarian need not deny. It is enough for his justification of punishment that punishment (or threat of it) has a "substantial" influence on behavior.

So much for the utilitarian theory of punishment. Let us examine now the retributive theory. Is it consistent with determinism? Since we have already argued that the retributive theory is not a satisfactory theory of punishment in either of its forms, we shall be brief. There are two lines of reasoning worth our attention.

1. The critic of the retributive theory may argue, to a defender of the theory who accepts determinism, as follows: "Your thesis is that people should be punished for their deeds even if it does no good, for no other reason than that they have done something that is either subjectively wrong

---

[9] It may be that no utilitarian justification can be given for divine punishment after death. If so, the truth of determinism may be an objection to divine punishment after death, but not to punishment now by society.

or reprehensible. But this is not consistent for you if you are a determinist. First, surely you will agree that it is not fitting to punish a person *for no other reason*, for conduct of which *he* is not the *ultimate* cause, and for which others or accidents of circumstance are the cause—not his own perverse and willful nature. But second, if you do agree with my first point, as a determinist you are in a difficulty, for as a determinist you must agree that human personality is wholly caused, and that therefore everyone is wholly the effect of circumstances beyond his control. There is no 'perverse nature' for which prior events, human or nonhuman, are not the ultimate causes. No one chooses to be the person he is; indeed, perhaps it makes no sense to say he did so choose. If then we are to exempt from punishment (except for utilitarian reasons) all that conduct of which the wrongdoer himself is not the ultimate cause, we must exempt *all* of a person's misconduct from punishment."

The second stage of the critic's argument is coercive, if determinism is true. The weight of the first part of the argument, then, is crucial. Must one say that retributive punishment is unfitting unless the wrongdoer is himself the *ultimate* cause of his deed? In fact, some writers who feel attracted by the retributive theory do *not* accept this proposal. They are prepared to defend the view that conduct which manifests bad character or which is an intentional deviation from duty ought to be punished irrespective of utilitarian considerations, and that it is quite irrelevant how a bad man came to be bad.[10]

Is there anything the critic can do to force the defender of the retributive theory to accept the first part of his argument? One thing he can do is this. He can say: "Surely you will agree that current practice is proper in treating leniently criminals who have never had a chance, who have come from broken and poverty-stricken homes, and so on. But if you do so, you must be doing so *because* you think that the criminal is not the *ultimate* cause of what he did, that others or circumstances beyond his control have made him what he is. And if this is true, then it is *inconsistent* of you to treat other offenses harshly, in view of the fact that their agents too were not the ultimate causes of their actions; they did what they did because of the original constitution of which their parents were the cause, or else because of the environment in which they had developed."

This argument is not a demonstration. It is an invitation to the defender of the retributive theory to reconsider whether, in view of the truth of determinism, his "qualified" attitudes really do demand the punishment of some wrongdoing, but not that of those who "never had a chance." The point is not without its force.

2. The second argument runs as follows: "You will of course agree that

[10] See, for instance, C. D. Broad, *Five Types of Ethical Theory* (New York: Harcourt, Brace & Company, 1934), pp. 204–05.

wrongdoers should not be punished if at the time of their offense they were not sane: did not know the nature of the act they were committing, or did not know that it was wrong (M'Naghten's Rule). But you will probably go somewhat further: you will say a person should not be punished just as retribution for his offense, if at the time he was emotionally unbalanced—say, as the result of a brain tumor—even if he were sane by M'Naghten's Rule. But then where will you draw a line? *Every* serious antisocial act is a consequence of some emotional imbalance, some emotional immaturity. Therefore, in consistency you must excuse them all."

The critic may then buttress his argument with an example. On February 2, 1945, *The New York Times* printed a psychiatric report about a youth, sixteen years of age, who had strangled a four-year-old apparently without a motive. A staff of psychiatrists had concluded that the boy was "insane and suffering from a brain disorder." (An encephalogram showed abnormal brain waves, suggesting brain damage.) The testifying psychiatrist stated that the boy was in "a very pathological emotional status" particularly in respect to "lack of remorse." He had told the police that, when he tied up his victim, the little boy had "made a gurgling sound. . . . I got goose pimples all over and I had a thrill." The psychiatrist commented: "He was impressed by a scene that had something to do with dying. He said he wanted that experience directly. He wanted to hear just what motions or sounds a dying person would make. He then recounted to us in detail what he did to this boy. . . . His indifference—lack of remorse and callousness—with relation to the crime was rather shocking." He was committed to an institution for mental treatment.

This youth was not suffering from an extreme form of insanity. He was not ignorant of the consequences of what he was doing. If asked at the time, he would probably have conceded freely that his act was wrong. Hence, it is not clear that he was legally insane by the test of M'Naghten's Rule, unless applied very broadly. What we can say is that his thoughts about his action and its consequences did not have their ordinary emotional repercussions, and doubtless his ethical thinking was very primitive.

The defender of the retributive theory must decide whether "qualified" attitudes would demand the punishment of persons in the mental condition of this youth. *If* he decides that such persons should *not* be punished (except perhaps for utilitarian reasons), his critic may then argue that anybody who commits a crime can be regarded as no different from this youth, and claim that all should be excused. In order to make this point vivid, he might introduce a further example.

His second example is that of a kidnapping murder, planned well in advance in all details, by a man and woman who had enjoyed numerous advantages in life, but who had run out of money. They were executed for their offense, and *The New York Times* expressed its editorial indignation in October, 1953, as follows:

. . . This crime is so heinous, so contrary to all human feeling that no punishment the civilized laws of this land allow seems quite adequate.

Is there more than a difference of degree between these cases? The critic of the retributive theory will admit that these individuals were more normal: there were no reports of abnormal brain waves in their case; they showed some remorse before they died; they committed their crime for less trivial reasons. Their characters were better, but like the youth they were emotionally unequipped for social living. The meaning of the suffering of the child and its parents did not get through to them, or else it aroused no normal emotional reverberations. If we excuse the one, should we not excuse the other?

Like the preceding "argument," this reasoning is less a demonstration than an invitation to the defender of the retributive theory to consider whether there is any formulable principle that is coherent with his "qualified" attitudes. The retributionist may find a principle that satisfies him. He may be ready to follow the M'Naghten Rule, exempting only the cognitively disoriented from punishment. If this Rule does not satisfy him, he may find another formula that does. Can he find one that comports with his "qualified" attitudes? We must leave the matter with this question.[11]

The utilitarian, of course, has good reason for treating these two cases differently. The kidnapping murder, he can say, must be punished. If it were not, the inaction would be a standing invitation to unscrupulous people to make money by kidnapping. But sending the boy-murderer to an institution for treatment, and keeping him there until he can safely be freed, instead of executing him, will have no comparable ill effect; normal people simply are not interested in committing his kind of crime.

5. DETERMINISM AND THE MORAL ASSESSMENT OF DEEDS

One may draw a more radical inference from the truth of determinism than the critic of the retributive theory draws. One may argue that it is inconsistent with the truth of determinism to say that acts are ever *morally reprehensible,* or *admirable,* at all. If this is true, then the retributive theory, at least in the "moral reprehensibility" (as distinct from the *lex talionis*) form, is undermined; since it bids us to punish with a severity

[11] For a recent discussion that is similar to the foregoing two arguments, see John Hospers, "What Means This Freedom?" in Sidney Hook (ed.), *Determinism and Freedom* (New York: New York University Press, 1958), and "Free-Will and Psychoanalysis" in W. Sellars and J. Hospers (eds.), *Readings in Ethical Theory* (New York: Appleton-Century-Crofts, Inc., 1952).
One might ask why the foregoing argument is construed as an argument from the fact of determinism. The reason is that it turns on viewing behavior, unbalanced and normal alike, as the result of the engagement or stimulation of a personality structure— itself the result of natural development and interactions—by an environmental situation. It does not recognize any undetermined, especially responsible acts in normal people.

corresponding to "moral gravity," it follows that we are not to punish if it is shown that the moral gravity is always nonexistent.

What exactly does this more radical assertion come to? If our analysis of the nature and grounds of ethical judgments has been correct, it is the assertion that, *in view of the fact of determinism*, it is not "objectively justified" for a person to feel remorse or guilt, or for others to feel anger or contempt or disgust toward him, on account of his having done something that showed a trait of character less desirable than average. Much the same is true for moral admiration. The Qualified Attitude Method will not sanction, it is suggested, such attitudes, in view of the fact of determinism. More particularly, such attitudes will not persist in the mind of an impartial normal person, if he has vividly and clearly in mind the fact that all actions are determined.

Some philosophers assert precisely this. One recent essay, for example, suggests that a clear-headed determinist cannot keep up a feeling of "moral superiority"; he will think that he is merely lucky and that the criminal is merely unlucky; he will view the situation of the criminal as "unfortunate but 'not really his fault' . . . and say he's more to be pitied than censured." Reflections on determinism, it is said, "may prevent us (unless we are compulsive blamers) from indulging in righteous indignation and committing the sin of spiritual pride, thanking God that we are not as this publican here."[12] Anyone who comes to this conclusion, of course, must discard "reprehensible" and "morally admirable" (both, not just the former) from his vocabulary, or at least stop using them in the sense in which they are ordinarily used today.

Is it true that "qualified attitudes" would not include these moral attitudes, if determinism is true (and hence if a fully informed person were clearly aware that it is)? We must look into this. We may begin by noting that there are some attitudes we may have toward a person that are not affected by the truth of determinism, or by information about how he came to be the way he is. Some attitudes are concerned solely with what their object is now. If we like a person because he has a sense of humor, this attitude is not undermined by the information that he inherited it from his mother. And surely there are other attitudes, directed at people on account of their traits of character, which are the same in this respect. If a man has deep defects of character, I shall not sponsor him as a husband for my daughter, irrespective of information that he has them because of rejection by his mother. Is the same true of the attitudes most important for our problem: pride, admiration, remorse, and indignation? We must examine these, and determine how they are affected by belief that people do what they do as the result of a long chain of causes.

Let us consider these in pairs: pride-admiration, and remorse-indignation.

[12] John Hospers, *op. cit.*, pp. 121–127.

We do this because the members of each pair are very similar except for the fact that in one case the attitude is directed toward the self, in the other case toward another person, with corresponding reverberations. We shall see more clearly in what sense this is true as we go on.

Pride-admiration. When do we feel the swellings of pride? There seem to be two conditions. First, we feel them only about something that is related to us roughly in such a way that recognition of its qualities is likely to increase respect or admiration for us, because we have produced it or are members of it or have some other association with it. The relation may be very tenuous, since a student may take pride in his college football team, when he is not even on the squad. Second, the thing in which we take pride must qualify as excellent or superior in some way. Thus, one may take pride in having won a tennis match—or in having held one's temper, or managed to be generous, where others would not have.[13]

Admiration, in contrast, is an attitude we take toward someone else when he has done something worthwhile that is rare and difficult. We may admire a person for a fine game of tennis, or for behaving in a way that is desirable but difficult, such as showing no envy when most people would be envious.

What difference does it make to these attitudes, if we reflect, agreeing with determinism, on the fact that our actions and personalities have causes? Well, it is natural to feel more pride in something we have done ourselves, for instance, a garden we have cultivated with our own hands as compared with one cultivated by the gardener under our direction. But do we take no pride in our own water-color because our mother paints well, and we suspect our talent comes from her? Or should we refuse admiration to J. S. Mill because we think he inherited his genius from his father, and owed much to the careful education he was given? Such reactions would be absurd; nor do we have them. Moreover, if such reactions were reasonable, then, since according to determinism every finite person is a product of causes beyond himself, only God could be a proper object of admiration.

Remorse-indignation. "Remorse" is used vaguely, and applies to several different emotions or attitudes. For instance, it is probably applied to distress caused by awareness of the criticism of others. But the term is also used to cover anger or indignation directed at oneself, as when I say "I hate myself" for what I did, and it is this phenomenon we shall be denoting by the term. Both "remorse" and "indignation" are reserved for moral contexts. Remorse differs from being provoked with oneself, and indignation differs from anger, in that each term implies that the source of one's attitudes is inexcusable wrongdoing.

Under what conditions do we have these experiences? Any answer

[13] There is a third condition, in order for reflection on such facts to produce swellings of pride—that the fact is sufficiently novel not to be taken for granted, or to be an "old story."

to this question must be (like the foregoing discussion of admiration and pride) somewhat speculative, but it seems we can reasonably say two things. First, we have them only if we suppose that the person who is their object (ourselves in the case of remorse) did or attempted to do injury to somebody or something we care about. Second, we have them only if we assume that he did so because of some deficiency of character.

Is there a third condition? Do these attitudes fail to occur, or do they disappear, if we come to believe that the actions or character of the person toward whom these feelings are directed had prior causes? To some extent they do: at least certain judgments about the causal origin of actions and attitudes seem to reduce the strength of our attitudes toward the agent. For instance, if we are angry at ourselves for some self-centered act, the experience may become less poignant if we reflect that probably our self-centeredness is the result of long periods of sickness as a child, when we were a center for family concern. Such thoughts seem to make us less bitterly remorseful, more sadly receptive of ourselves. But the attitude is not wholly dissolved by such reflections, if the thing that has been injured is something highly prized.

Somewhat the same is true of indignation. Information about the causes of the behavior of others tends to soften our anger toward them. But something of it seems to remain—at least contempt tinged with anger. Take, for instance, the German who, we learn, heartily assisted in torturing and murdering Jews during the war, with no excuse. We may form theories as to how he got that way: his father, the old Prussian household, the tradition of race-hatred. And these reflections mellow our indignation, as Spinoza insisted long ago. Nevertheless, we shall not be able to embrace him with warmth when we next see him—any more than we can stifle our admiration for Anne Frank by assuring ourselves that it is only by bad luck that we are not all of us made of stuff as stern as she.[14]

If our analyis of the conditions of these attitudes is correct, then there are some "moral" attitudes toward people on account of their behavior, some favorable and some unfavorable, which do not wholly dissolve when we reflect on the causal origin of the behavior that arouses them, and which we may with some reason suppose to be objectively justified even if determinism is true. If so, then "reprehensible" and "morally admirable," as applied to deeds, have application.

If the reader is inclined to think it proper, in view of modern knowledge of the dynamics of the human mind, to restrain both indignation and admiration, it may be well to point out that it is a good thing that most people

---

[14] We need not suggest that our attitudes toward a person must be all-or-nothing, that if we feel indignation or contempt for a person on account of a deed, we cannot feel differently toward him when we reflect on other sides of his nature. People are complex.

indulge such attitudes without such inhibition. If no one did, the informal means of social control which is the effect of moral judgment would be destroyed. Imagine how impossible little Jimmy would become, if nobody ever genuinely got angry with him for his self-centered behavior! If we were forbidden to feel pride in our occasional achievements or remorse at our shortcomings, if we knew others—insofar as they were well informed —would feel no indignation at our failings and no admiration for our sacrifices, in all probabality we would gradually become less admirable than we now are. Certainly the utilitarian will urge, as Henry Sidgwick did, that we encourage these attitudes (intelligently directed, of course) and their expression in behavior, on account of the desirability of the consequences.

FURTHER READING

G. E. Moore, *Ethics* (Oxford: Oxford University Press, 1949), chap. 6.

P. Nowell-Smith, "Free Will and Moral Responsibility," *Mind*, LVII (1946), 45–61.

———, *Ethics* (Baltimore: Penguin Books, Inc., 1954), chaps. 19–20.

R. E. Hobart, "Free Will as Involving Determinism," *Mind*, XLIII (1934), 1–27.

Sidney Hook (ed.), *Determinism and Freedom* (New York: New York University Press, 1958).

C. L. Stevenson, *Ethics and Language* (New Haven: Yale University Press, 1944), chap. 14.

M. Schlick, *Problems of Ethics* (Englewood Cliffs, N.J.: Prentice-Hall, Inc., 1939), chap. 7.

University of California Associates, *Knowledge and Society* (New York: Appleton-Century-Crofts, Inc., 1938), chap. 6.

W. D. Ross, *Foundations of Ethics* (Oxford: Clarendon Press, 1939), chap. 10.

C. D. Broad, *Five Types of Ethical Theory* (New York: Harcourt, Brace & Company, 1934), pp. 192–208.

———, *Determinism, Indeterminism, and Libertarianism*, reprinted in *Ethics and the History of Philosophy* (London: Routledge & Kegan Paul Ltd., 1952).

L. Wood, "The Free Will Controversy," *Philosophy*, XVI (1941), 386–97. A summary.

F. Raab, "Free Will and the Ambiguity of 'Could,' " *Philosophical Review*, LXIV (1955), 60–77.

W. Hardie, "My Own Free Will," *Philosophy*, XXXII (1957), 21–38.

E. F. Carritt, *Ethical and Political Thinking* (Oxford: Clarendon Press, 1947), chap. 12. A defense of indeterminism.

C. A. Campbell, "Is 'Free-Will' a Pseudo Problem?" *Mind*, LX (1951), 441–65.

———, "The Psychology of Effort of the Will," *Proceedings*, The Aristotelian Society, 1939–40. An indeterminist.

H. Sidgwick, *The Methods of Ethics* (London: Macmillan & Co., Ltd., 1922), pp. 56–66. An influential statement of indeterminism.

A. C. Ewing, "Indeterminism," *Review of Metaphysics*, V (1951), 199–222.

———, "Can We Act against our Strongest Desire?" *Monist*, XLIV, 126–43.

———, *Fundamental Questions of Philosophy* (New York: The Macmillan Company, 1951), chap. 9.

S. Hampshire, W. G. Maclagan, and R. M. Hare, "The Freedom of the Will" (symposium), The Aristotelian Society, Supplementary volume XXV (1951), 161–216.

J. Austin, "Ifs and Cans," *Proceedings of the British Academy,* XLII (1956), 109–32.

A. Montefiore, " 'Ought' and 'Can,' " *Philosophical Quarterly,* VIII (1958), 24–40.

D. Kading, "Does 'Ought' Imply 'Can'?" *Philosophical Studies,* V (1954), 11–15.

W. K. Frankena, "Obligation and Ability," in M. Black (ed.), *Philosophical Analysis* (Ithaca: Cornell University Press, 1950).

Index